## Highlights from our research activities: Connect® French and McGraw-Hill LearnSmart®

- Over the last several years, we've brought together over 250 language professors from around the country to symposia and small-group forums in order to brainstorm new ideas and workshop solutions to the discipline's biggest challenges. The result is our new platform **Connect French**!

- Over 1,600 students, professors, and graduate teaching assistants beta-tested the **LearnSmart** platform for World Languages. The results were astounding: 91% of students said that **LearnSmart** led to success in their course and 97% said they would use **LearnSmart** in the future.

Special thanks to the instructors and students at **Boston College, College of Charleston, Florida Atlantic University, Boca Raton, Kennesaw State University, Portland State University, Texas State University, San Marcos, University of Minnesota, Twin Cities, and University of Rhode Island, Kingston,** for piloting **LearnSmart** for French during the Fall 2013 semester.

## Key findings from the *Vis-à-vis* pre-revision reviews

We surveyed more than 100 introductory French instructors to find out how we could address the specific needs of the *Vis-à-vis* users. This is what we discovered:

- Reduced class hours and the demand for more hybrid and online courses limit the opportunities for meaningful instructor-student interaction in the target language. Instructors and students wanted more opportunities for oral communication, pronunciation practice, in and outside the classroom.

- Student engagement is a crucial factor in student success.

- More effective technology resources are needed to address the new course formats.

# with more opportunities to listen, speak, record, and practice!

## LEARNSMART®

Developed specifically for *Vis-à-vis*, **LearnSmart** for French is an intelligent learning system that uses a series of adaptive questions to pinpoint the unique knowledge gaps of each individual student. **LearnSmart** then provides them with an individualized learning path so that students spend less time in areas they already know and more time in areas they don't. The result is that students retain more knowledge, learn faster, study more efficiently, and come to French class better prepared to participate.

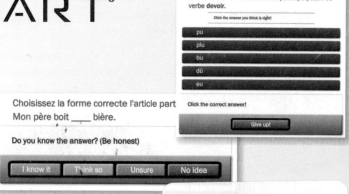

### *Grammaire interactive* tutorials

The **Grammaire interactive** tutorials work hand-in-hand with **LearnSmart** to provide students with the latest digital tools to improve their course outcomes. These tutorials, taught by an animated French instructor, are now available to students in **Connect French** as an alternative resource for reviewing and practicing core concepts. The practice quizzes that follow test students' mastery of the material.

# What's New in the Sixth Edition?

- **Powerful digital tools: Connect® French** is McGraw-Hill's digital platform, which houses the eBook, the Workbook / Laboratory Manual activities, integrated audio and video, peer-editing writing tools, and voice tools, all of which vastly improve the quality of students' out-of-class work.

- **McGraw-Hill LearnSmart®** is the only super-adaptive learning tool on the market that is proven to significantly improve students' learning and course outcomes. As students work on each chapter's grammar and vocabulary modules, **LearnSmart** identifies the areas that students are struggling with most and provides them with the practice they need to master them. **LearnSmart** gives each student a unique learning experience tailored just for them. The **LearnSmart** mobile app allows students to study anytime and anywhere!

- **Contemporary language:** The **64 mini-dialogues** that introduce the grammar points in context have been completely rewritten and now feature the blog characters from the video and **Le blog de…** readings. The line art has been replaced by beautiful photos and the dialogues are presented in appealing, student-friendly formats: text messages, Blackboard IM video messages, and Facebook instant messages, in addition to face-to-face conversations. As in prior editions, the activity following each dialogue prompts students to use the structure in context before they delve into the explanation.

- **More pronunciation practice:** In response to reviewer feedback, the sixth edition offers a more robust treatment of pronunciation. These contextualized activities, which focus on the recognition and production of key sounds in French, build on the **Prononcez bien!** explanations that appear in the margins of each chapter. Both the explanations and the activities have been recorded and may be accessed and assigned in **Connect**.

- **Updated culture:** The **Reportage** readings between **Leçons 2** and **3** have been updated in **Chapitres 6, 9, 10,** and **11** to reflect the interests of today's students. The **Lecture** section of **Leçon 4** has also been revised. Among the five completely new readings in **Chapitres 1, 3, 9, 11,** and **13** are two literary texts, an article on Vélib' and Autolib', and a text with practical information on shopping in France.

# Vis-à-vis

## Beginning French

### SIXTH EDITION

**Evelyne Amon**

**Judith A. Muyskens**
*Nebraska Wesleyan University*

**Alice C. Omaggio Hadley**
*Professor Emerita, University of Illinois,
Urbana-Champaign*

*With contributions by:*

Viviane Ruellot

Nicole Dicop-Hineline

Amanda LaFleur

McGraw Hill Education

VIS-À-VIS: BEGINNING FRENCH, SIXTH EDITION

Published by McGraw-Hill Education, 2 Penn Plaza, New York, NY 10121. Copyright
© 2015 by McGraw-Hill Education. All rights reserved. Printed in the United States of
America. Previous editions © 2011, 2008, and 2004. No part of this publication may be
reproduced or distributed in any form or by any means, or stored in a database or
retrieval system, without the prior written consent of McGraw-Hill Education, including,
but not limited to, in any network or other electronic storage or transmission, or
broadcast for distance learning.

Some ancillaries, including electronic and print components, may not be available to
customers outside the United States.

This book is printed on acid-free paper.

1 2 3 4 5 6 7 8 9 0 DOW/DOW 1 0 9 8 7 6 5 4

ISBN 978–0–07–338647–8
MHID 0–07–338647–2

ISBN 978–1–259–13702–0 (Annotated Instructor's Edition)
MHID 1–259–13702–3

Senior Vice President, Products & Markets: *Kurt L. Strand*
Vice President, General Manager, Products & Markets: *Michael Ryan*
Vice President, Content Production & Technology Services: *Kimberly Meriwether David*
Managing Director: *Katie Stevens*
Senior Brand Manager: *Katherine K. Crouch*
Senior Director of Development: *Scott Tinetti*
Managing Development Editor: *Susan Blatty*
Director of Digital Content: *Janet Banhidi*
Digital Product Analyst: *Sarah Carey*
Digital Development Editor: *Laura Ciporen*
Senior Market Development Manager: *Helen Greenlea*
Executive Marketing Manager: *Craig Gill*
Senior Faculty Development Manager: *Jorge Arbujas*
Editorial Coordinators: *Leslie Briggs / Caitlin Bahrey*
Director, Content Production: *Terri Schiesl*
Content Project Manager: *Kelly A. Heinrichs*
Buyer: *Susan K. Culbertson*
Designer: *Matthew Backhaus*
Cover Image: *Stock Connection Blue/Alamy*
Content Licensing Specialist: *Brenda Rolwes*
Compositor: *Aptara®, Inc.*
Typeface: *10/12 New Aster*
Printer: *R. R. Donnelley*

All credits appearing on page or at the end of the book are considered to be an
extension of the copyright page.

**Library of Congress Cataloging-in-Publication Data**

Amon, Evelyne.
  Vis-à-vis: beginning French / Evelyne Amon, Judy Muyskens, Nebraska Wesleyan
University; Alice Omaggio Hadley, Professor Emerita, University of Illinois, Urbana-
Champaign; Viviane Ruellot, Western Michigan University.—Sixth Edition.
      pages cm.
  Includes index.
  ISBN 978–0–07–338647–8—ISBN 0–07–338647–2 (hard copy : alk. paper)—ISBN
978–1–259–13702–0 (Annotated Instructor's Edition—ISBN 1–259–13702–3 (hard copy:
alk. paper) 1. French language—Textbooks for foreign speakers—English. I. Muyskens,
Judith A. II. Hadley, Alice Omaggio, 1947– III. Ruellot, Viviane. IV. Title.
  PC2129.E5A48 2014
  448.2′421–dc23                    2013035280

The Internet addresses listed in the text were accurate at the time of publication. The
inclusion of a website does not indicate an endorsement by the authors or McGraw-Hill
Education, and McGraw-Hill Education does not guarantee the accuracy of the
information presented at these sites.

www.mhhe.com

# Contents

L'Arc de Triomphe, à Paris, en France

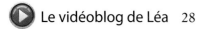

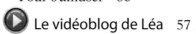

v

# APPENDIXES

# LEXIQUES

# CREDIT

# INDEX

# About the Authors

**Evelyne Amon** studied at the Université de Paris-Sorbonne. She holds a DEA in modern literature, a Master in French as a second language, and a CAPES in modern literature. She has taught French language and literature at the secondary and college levels, and for many years has led a training seminar in Switzerland for professors on advances in methodology and pedagogy. She has conducted several training sessions in teaching French as a second language for teachers at the French Institute Alliance Française (FIAF) in New York. As an author, she has written many reference volumes, textbooks, and academic studies for French publishers such as Larousse, Hatier, Magnard, Nathan, and Bordas. She is the author of the McGraw-Hill French reader *C'est la vie!* and has written for successive editions of *Vis-à-vis*.

**Judith A. Muyskens,** Ph.D., Ohio State University, is Provost and Professor of French at Nebraska Wesleyan University in Lincoln, Nebraska. She continues to visit French-speaking countries and teach French language courses when time allows, especially first- and second-year language classes. For many years, she taught courses in methodology and French language and culture and supervised teaching assistants at the University of Cincinnati. She has contributed to various professional publications, including the *Modern Language Journal*, *Foreign Language Annals*, and the ACTFL Foreign Language Education Series. She is a coauthor of several other French textbooks, including *Rendez-vous: An Invitation to French* and *À vous d'écrire*.

**Alice C. Omaggio Hadley,** Ph.D., Ohio State University, is a Professor Emerita of French at the University of Illinois at Urbana-Champaign. Before she retired in 2005, she was Director of Basic Language Instruction in French for 25 years, supervising teaching assistants and teaching courses in methodology. She is the author of a language teaching methods text, *Teaching Language in Context*. She has also written articles for various journals and contributed to other professional publications, has been a coauthor of several other French textbooks, and has given numerous workshops for teachers across the country.

# Preface

**Vis-à-vis** engages students with its unique integration of contemporary culture and communicative building blocks, providing the tools they need to build a solid foundation in introductory French. The hallmarks of *Vis-à-vis* are well known:

- an easy-to-navigate chapter structure with four lessons in which vocabulary, grammar, and culture work together as integrated units;
- an abundance of practice activities that range from form-focused to communicative;
- a balanced approach to the four skills;
- diverse coverage of the Francophone world that includes an outstanding video program featuring bloggers and cultural footage from eight different Francophone regions.

These features support the core goals of the introductory French course—communicative and cultural competence—and lay the groundwork for student success.

## McGraw-Hill Connect® French and McGraw-Hill LearnSmart®

In its sixth edition, **Vis-à-vis** continues to evolve to meet the changing needs of instructors and students by responding to feedback from the users themselves. Employing a wide array of research tools, we identified a number of areas for potential innovation; the new program builds upon the success of the fifth edition with an expanded emphasis on contemporary language, pronunciation, culture, and technology to create a truly communicative, interactive experience. On the digital side, this new edition offers **Connect French** and **LearnSmart,** with their unparalleled adaptive and digital learning resources. These powerful tools, now an integral part of the sixth edition, complement and support the goals of the *Vis-à-vis* program and address the needs of the evolving introductory French course.

## How do Connect French and LearnSmart Support the Goals of the *Vis-à-vis* Program?

### Communicative Competence

One of the major challenges of any introductory language course is to give each student ample exposure to the language and sufficient opportunity for speaking practice to inspire them to communicate with confidence. In **Connect French,** students have full access to the digitally enhanced e-Book, the online *Workbook / Laboratory Manual* activities, **LearnSmart**, and all of the accompanying audio and video resources, giving them the ability to interact with the materials as often as they wish.

Each chapter of the *Vis-à-vis* program contains the following exciting enhancements to promote communicative practice and competence:

- **Interactive vocabulary presentations** (**Paroles**) with audio allow students to listen, record, and practice the new vocabulary at home.

- **Interactive textbook and workbook activities for vocabulary and grammar in Connect French,** many of which are auto-graded, give students the opportunity to complete their assignments and come to class better prepared to participate in paired and group activities.

- **Blackboard Instant Messaging** provides the necessary tools for students to work in pairs online or to practice speaking together before coming to class.

- The **Voice Board** feature allows individuals to record their own voice as many times as they wish before they post their recording to which other students may respond.

- New **Prononcez bien!** activities with a recording feature provide students with opportunities for discrete-word and contextualized practice that gives them more confidence in their speaking abilities.

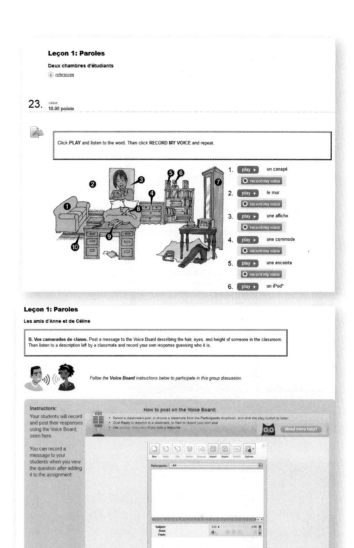

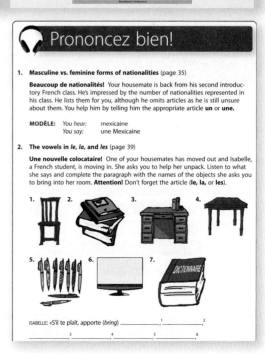

> *I am particularly interested in the inclusion of more pronunciation practice and pronunciation activities. This is what the existing textbooks are usually lacking. The accompanying recording of the explanations and the activities will be very helpful both to students and their instructors.*
> —Andrzej Dziedzic, *University of Wisconsin*

LÉA: Il pleut! Où es-tu?

HECTOR: Je suis dans mon bus. **Je vais arriver** dans dix minutes.

LÉA: J'ai froid! **Je vais** dans un café.

HECTOR: Quel café?

LÉA: À l'angle du boulevard Beaumarchais et de la rue Saint-Gilles.

HECTOR: D'accord. Ensuite,* **nous allons** «Chez Denise» manger des pâtisseries!

LÉA: Et après, **on va** «Chez Clément» manger une soupe à l'oignon!

HECTOR: Tu es folle! **On va être** malades!

le
la
l'
les

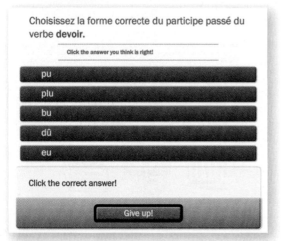

Choisissez la forme correcte du participe passé du verbe **devoir.**

Click the answer you think is right!

pu

plu

bu

dû

eu

Click the correct answer!

Give up!

- **Four new, lively mini-dialogues** featuring the blog characters have been recorded to provide students with a spirited introduction to the new grammatical structures in context.

- Seventeen **Grammaire interactive** tutorials, each with a brief practice quiz, focus on structures that students typically struggle with, such as the partitive, and the **passé composé** vs. the **imparfait.** These tutorials, accessible only in **Connect French**, give students an alternative means of learning, reviewing, and checking their comprehension of selected grammar points.

In addition to the **Connect French** chapter resources, **LearnSmart** modules for vocabulary and grammar have been developed specifically for **Vis-à-vis.** This powerful adaptive system helps students pinpoint their weaknesses and provides them with an individualized study program based on their results. Audio prompts for vocabulary and grammar help students strengthen both their listening and writing skills. All students, no matter their previous language experience, can benefit from using **LearnSmart,** which includes built-in reporting and a competitive scoreboard to increase student engagement. Our research has shown that students using **LearnSmart** have significantly improved their learning and course outcomes.

By using these powerful digital tools, students have myriad opportunities to build their communicative skills. By assigning **Connect French** and **LearnSmart,** instructors save valuable class time for interactive practice.

## Cultural Competence

The program's meaningful and extensive exploration of the rich culture of France and the Francophone world is fully supported in **Connect French** through audio and video resources and interactive activities.

- Every four chapters, *Vis-à-vis* introduces a focus on a new French or Francophone character and region. The personal online journal entries in **Le blog de...**, the related **Reportage**, and the **Bienvenue...** readings that precede Chapter 1 and follow Chapters 4, 8, 12, and 16, expose students to contemporary language and the vast diversity of life and culture in France, Belgium, Tunisia, and Martinique. In **Connect French**, instructors may assign the readings and new auto-graded comprehension activities that prepare students for class discussion.

- **Le vidéoblog de...** and the stunning **Bienvenue** video segments give students a window into the sights and sounds of eight different French-speaking regions/countries: France, Belgium, Switzerland, Quebec, Louisiana, Tunisia, Senegal, Martinique, and Tahiti. Each video is accompanied by comprehension and cross-cultural comparison activities that encourage students to make connections between their culture and those of the French-speaking world. The new video activities in **Connect** break the segments into manageable "chunks" that keep students focused on specific information and help improve their listening skills.

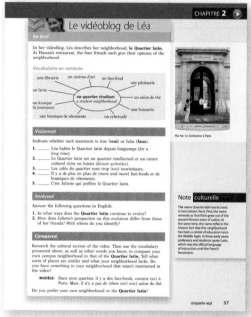

- The **Avant de lire** and **Compréhension** activities that accompany the **Lecture** in the **Perspectives** section (**Leçon 4**) of every chapter may now be done online.

The **Connect French** platform gives students the opportunity to interact with the cultural materials as often as they wish and engage them more fully in their language learning.

As we see the modern French classroom changing, we are looking at teaching and learning in a different light. Our research shows that French instructors seek digital tools to extend learning outside of the classroom in more effective ways. The cutting-edge functionality of **Connect French** and **LearnSmart** enables instructors to achieve their course goals using new online presentation activities, improved homework tools, and a better reporting feature. Together, **Connect French and LearnSmart** create a dynamic learning environment that presents communicative practice and rich cultural content as it motivates students to succeed regardless of the delivery platform. We invite you to experience the new *Vis-à-vis* program to see how our partnership with today's instructors and students has allowed us to identify and address some of the most common needs in today's French classrooms. Discover the power of *Vis-à-vis'* proven approach enhanced by **LearnSmart** and our new digital platform **Connect French**.

> *❝ Vis-à-vis is an exciting, beginning French program that addresses the needs of the 21st century student. There is a rich mixture of language, culture, and technology that will stimulate the reluctant learner. ❞*
> —Dr. Debra Boyd, *North Carolina Central University, Durham*

## Program Supplements

**Connect French:** Used in conjunction with *Vis-à-vis: Beginning French,* **Connect French** provides digital solutions for schools with face-to-face, hybrid, or 100% online modes. In addition to the interactive e-Book, complete *Workbook / Laboratory Manual*, grammar tutorials, and audio and video resources described on the preceding pages, some of the key administrative capabilities of **Connect French** include:

* the ability to customize syllabi and assignments to fit the needs of individual programs;
* an integrated gradebook with powerful reporting features;
* the ability to assign **LearnSmart** modules and monitor student progress;
* access to all instructor's resources, including the *Digital Transparencies, Instructor's Manual, Connect French User's Guide*, pre-made exams, and a customizable testing program with audio for the online delivery of assessments;
* access to **Tegrity,** McGraw-Hill's proprietary video capture software that allows instructors to post short videos, tutorials, and lessons for student access outside of class.

**MH Campus and Blackboard:** Integration of **MH Campus** and **Blackboard** simplifies and streamlines your course administration by integrating with your campus's Learning Management System. With features such as single sign-on for students and instructors, gradebook synchronization, and easy access to all of McGraw-Hill's language content (even from other market-leading titles not currently adopted for your course), teaching an introductory language course has never been simpler.

**Annotated Instructor's Edition:** The *Instructor's Edition* of the text includes a wide variety of suggestions for presenting each section of the book, ideas for recycling vocabulary, helpful cultural notes, suggested expansion activities, and useful follow-up activities. Answers to the text-book activities are provided in the *Instructor's Manual*.

**Workbook / Laboratory Manual:** This print supplement provides more conventional, drill-like practice of the **Paroles** and **Structures** sections presented in the textbook using a variety of written and audio activities. In addition, each chapter includes **Le blog de...** and a **Pause-culture** section that expands upon the cultural themes of the chapter. The **Perspectives** section provides additional pronunciation practice, a capstone listening activity (**À l'écoute**), and two writing activities: **Par écrit**, a guided writing activity, and **Journal intime,** a free-writing activity. For students using the print version, the audio files are posted at **Connect French.**

The *Vis-à-vis* **Video Program,** which contains **Le vidéoblog de...** and the **Bienvenue...** video segments, is available in **Connect French** and on DVD.

# Acknowledgments

The authors wish to acknowledge the team at McGraw-Hill for their continuing support and enthusiasm: Katie Stevens, Scott Tinetti, Janet Banhidi, Katie Crouch, Susan Blatty, Kelly Heinrichs, Brenda Rolwes, Judy Mason, Sue Culbertson, Helen Greenlea, Craig Gill, Jorge Arbujas, Caitlin Bahrey and Leslie Briggs. We would also like to acknowledge our native reader, Nicole Dicop-Hineline, our copyeditor, Peggy Potter, our permissions editor, Veronica Oliva, and our proofreader, Sylvie Waskiewicz. Special thanks as well to the **Connect French** and **LearnSmart** teams for their dedication and creativity in the development of our new digital tools; **Connect French:** Sarah Hill, Laura Ciporen, Jon Fulk, Jason Kooiker, and Justin Swettlen; **LearnSmart:** Bruce Anderson, Abigail Alexander, Géraldine Blattner, Caroline Dequen-McKenzie, Jon Fulk, Lori McMann, Anne-Sabine Nicolas, Françoise Santore, Sandya Shanker, Alicia Soueid, Justin Swettlen, and Valérie Thiers-Thiam.

The authors and the publisher would like to express their gratitude to the following instructors across the country whose valuable suggestions contributed to the preparation of this new edition. The appearance of their names in these lists does not necessarily constitute their endorsement of the text or its methodology.

## LearnSmart® Beta Testers

**Boston College**
Sarah Bilodeau

**College of Charleston**
Shawn Morrison

**Florida Atlantic, Boca Raton**
Géraldine Blattner
Robyn Ezersky
Laurine Ferreira
Sophie Ledeme
Rosemary Rahill
Stephanie Sense

**Kennesaw State University**
Luc Guglielmi

**Portland State University**
Stéphanie Roulon

**Texas State University, San Marcos**
Sabrina Hyde
Moira Di Mauro-Jackson, PhD

**University of Minnesota, Twin Cities**
Adam T. Grant

**University of Rhode Island, Kingston**
Joann Hammadou Sullivan

## Reviewers

**Baruch College, CUNY**
Ali Nematollahy

**Boise State University**
Jason Herbeck

**Borough of Manhattan Community College, CUNY**
Peter Consenstein
Valérie Thiers-Thiam

**Broward College**
Trent Hoy
Celia M. Roberts
Shirley E. Santry

**Cabrillo College**
Bette G. Hirsch, PhD
Robyn Marshall

**Canisius College**
Eileen Angelini

**Central Michigan University**
Amy J. Ransom
Daniela Teodorescu

**City College of New York, CUNY**
Maxime Blanchard

**Clemson University**
Amy Sawyer

**College of Charleston**
Shawn Morrison, PhD

**County College of Morris**
Lakshmi Kattepur
Gene Sisti

**Dakota College at Bottineau**
Linda Grover

**Drury University**
Catherine Blunk, PhD

**Eastern Illinois University**
Kathryn M. Bulver, PhD

**Eastman School of Music, University of Rochester**
Valérie Couderc

**Furman University**
William Allen

**Gordon College**
Damon DiMauro

**Grand Valley State University**
Dan Golembeski

**Hostos Community College**
Philip Wander

**Houston Community College**
Maurice Abboud
David Long, PhD

**Howard Community College**
Heidi Goldenman
Agnès Archambault
Honigmann

**Illinois Wesleyan University**
Lisa Brittingham

**Kalamazoo Valley Community College**
Jonnie Wilhite

**Keene State College**
Brian Donovan
Julia Dutton

**Kennedy-King College, City Colleges of Chicago**
Sonia Elgado-Tall, PhD

**Kennesaw State University**
Luc D. Guglielmi, PhD

**Lee University**
James D. Wilkins

**Lewis & Clark College**
Claudia Nadine

**Liberty University**
Sharon B. Hähnlen, PhD

**Lone Star College–CyFair**
Georges Detiveaux

**Louisiana College**
Cecile Barnhart

**Loyola University Chicago**
Lisa Erceg

**Luther College**
Laurie Zaring

**Manchester University**
Janina Traxler

**Mercy College**
Alan G. Hartman
Jeanne Marie O'Regan

**Mercyhurst University**
Douglas Boudreau

**Missouri Western State University**
Susie Hennessy, PhD

**Montana State University**
Ada Giusti

**Morgan State University**
Helen Harrison

**Morris College**
Catherine Kapi

**Mt. San Jacinto College**
Jennifer S. Doucet

**New Mexico State University**
Claude Fouillade

**New Paltz, SUNY**
Mercedes Rooney

**Norco College, Riverside Community College District**
Dominique Hitchcock, PhD

**North Carolina Central University**
Debra Boyd, PhD

**North Georgia College & State University**
Elizabeth Combier, PhD

**North Lake College**
Cathy Briggs

**Northern Essex Community College**
Denise Minnard Campoli

**Oakton Community College**
Marguerite Solari, PhD

**Ohio University**
Signe Denbow

**Oklahoma State University**
Frédérique Knottnerus

**Onondaga Community College**
Mary-Ellen Faughnan-Kenien, PhD
Elizabeth O'Hara

**Pace University**
Rosemarie Cristina

**Pasadena City College**
Michèle Pedrini, PhD
Charlene Potter

**Portland State University**
Annabelle Dolidon
Jennifer R. Perlmutter
Stéphanie Roulon

**Rutgers University**
Myriam Alami

**Saint Martin's University**
Kathleen McKain

**Samford University**
M. D. Ledgerwood, PhD

**San Diego State University**
Edith Benkov

**San José State University**
Jean-Luc Desalvo

**Shasta College**
Eileen Smith

**Southeastern Louisiana University**
Aileen Mootoo

**Southwestern University**
Glenda Warren Carl

**St. Catherine University**
Jerome Tarmann

**St. Cloud State University**
María Gloria Melgarejo, PhD

**Stephen F. Austin State University**
Joyce Carlton Johnston

**Stetson University**
Richard Ferland

**Stony Brook University, SUNY**
Madeline Turan

**SUNY Fredonia**
Kate Douglass
Edward Kolodziej

**Texas A&M University**
Cheryl Schaile

**Union County College**
Pamela Mansfield

**University of Alabama**
Isabelle Drewelow

**University of Arkansas**
Kathleen Comfort, PhD

**University of California, Berkeley**
Leslie Martin, PhD

**University of California, Riverside**
Kelle Truby

**University of Cincinnati**
Irene Ivantcheva-Merjanska, PhD
Aline Skrzeszewski

**University of Denver**
Terri Woellners

**University of Hawaii at Manoa**
Joan Marie Debrah

**University of Louisville**
Bonnie Fonseca-Greber

**University of Maryland**
Catherine Savell

**University of Massachusetts, Lowell**
Carole Salmon

**University of Missouri–Saint Louis**
Anne-Sophie Blank
Sandra Trapani

**University of Nebraska at Omaha**
Patrice J. Proulx, PhD

**University of New Mexico**
Marina Peters-Newell

**University of North Carolina, Wilmington**
Caroline Hudson

**University of North Georgia**
Elizabeth Combier, PhD
D. Brian Mann, PhD
Amye Sukapdjo

**University of Texas at Arlington**
Antoinette Sol, PhD

**University of Wisconsin**
Andrzej Dziedzic, PhD

**Ursinus College**
Frances Novack

**Utah State University**
Sarah Gordon, PhD

**Utica College**
Marie-Noëlle Little, PhD

**Valdosta State University**
Ellen Lorraine Friedrich, PhD
Ofélia Nikolova, PhD

**Wake Forest University**
Elizabeth Barron, PhD

**Westminster College**
Ingrid Ilinca
Leslie Kealhofer, PhD

**Wichita State University**
Gail Burkett

**William Jewell College**
Michael Foster, PhD

**Williams College**
Brian Martin
Leyla Rouhi

**Worcester State University**
Judith Jeon-Chapman

# Vis-à-vis

# Bienvenue à **Vis-à-vis**

Welcome to *Vis-à-vis* and to **la francophonie,** the French-speaking world. In the **blog** sections between **Leçons 2** and **3** in each chapter, you will read the blogs created by four Parisians with different Francophone backgrounds—Léa, Hassan, Juliette, and Hector. You will also have the opportunity to read the commentaries of other French speakers on their blogs and to watch the videoblogs that they have posted on their sites. The *cartes d'identité** and short biographies of these four *blogueurs* are presented below.

## Les blogueurs

**Chapitres 1–4** feature the blog of Léa Bouchard. **Léa Bouchard,** 19 (dix-neuf) ans,[3] étudiante en 1ère (première) année[4] de Lettres à la faculté de Paris IV Sorbonne. Elle réside avec sa famille, dans un appartement du 6e arrondissement. Sa personnalité: romantique, immature, gracieuse.

**Chapitres 5–8** feature the blog of Hassan Zem. **Hassan Zem,** 28 (vingt-huit) ans, jeune patron[6] d'un restaurant marocain du Quartier latin à Paris. Il occupe un loft du quartier Oberkampf, avec son copain,[7] Abdel. Sa personnalité: charmeur, délicat, généreux.

[1]sixième (arrondissement) = *6th district of Paris*   [2]un mètre soixante-cinq = *5 feet 5 inches*   [3]*years old*
[4]1ère... = *1st year*   [5]un mètre soixante-dix-neuf = *5 feet 10½ inches*   [6]*owner*   [7]*friend*

---

*The **carte d'identité** is an official national identity card. In addition to the photograph and signature of the cardholder **(titulaire),** it includes such information as date of birth **(né[e] le...),** gender **(sexe),** and height **(taille).** The card is not obligatory for French citizens, but it is free, and is the preferred card for identification purposes.

**Chapitres 9–12** feature the blog of Juliette Graf.
**Juliette Graf,** 22 (vingt-deux) ans, étudiante en Master Multimédia Interactif à l'Université de Paris I Panthéon-Sorbonne. Elle occupe une petite chambre au Quartier latin.
Sa personnalité: raisonnée, méthodique, active.

**Chapitres 13–16** feature the blog of Hector Clément.
**Hector Clément,** 25 (vingt-cinq) ans, danseur professionnel. Il réside dans un appartement des Halles, avec des camarades.
Sa personnalité: original, susceptible, talentueux.

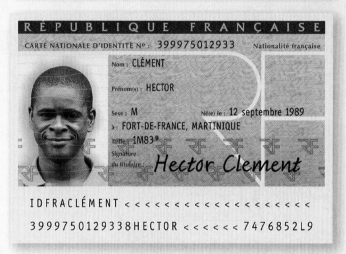

## Les commentateurs

The following people offer their commentaries on the blogs.

**Alexis Lafontaine,** 19 (dix-neuf) ans, étudiant en 1<sup>ère</sup> année d'économie, de sociologie et de géographie. Il est de Montréal. Il réside à Versailles avec son chien,[10] Trésor.
Sa personnalité: intellectuel, moraliste, solitaire.

**Trésor,** 3 (trois) ans, chien d'Alexis Lafontaine. Il adore son maître.
Sa personnalité: intelligent, optimiste, indépendant.

**Mamadou Bassène,** 28 (vingt-huit) ans, journaliste sportif, correspondant du journal[11] sénégalais «Le Soleil». Il est de Dakar. Il réside à Paris, dans le Marais.
Sa personnalité: plein d'humour, relax, charmeur.

**Charlotte Cousin,** 30 (trente) ans, est traductrice[12] à l'OMS (Organisation Mondiale de la Santé.)[13] Elle réside à Genève. Elle est mariée; elle a[14] un enfant.
Sa personnalité: raisonnable, compliquée, anxieuse.

**Poema Dauphin,** 22 (vingt-deux) ans, étudiante en maîtrise de Protection de la nature à l'université de Paris XII. Elle est de Tahiti. Elle loge dans une résidence universitaire de Paris, à la Cité internationale du 14<sup>e</sup> (quatorzième) arrondissement.
Sa personnalité: idéaliste, généreuse, rêveuse.[15]

[8]un mètre soixante-dix = *5 feet 7 inches*  [9]*un mètre quatre-vingt-trois* = *6 feet*  [10]*dog*  [11]*newspaper*  [12]*translator*  [13]*OMS... WHO (World Health Organization)*  [14]*has*  [15]*dreamy*

*Les... Francophone countries*

More than 220 million people in the world speak French, either as their native language or as a second language used in the workplace. French-speaking regions are found throughout the world.

By following the blogs and videoblogs of Léa, Hassan, Juliette, and Hector in *Vis-à-vis*, you will learn more about the customs, traditions, lifestyles, and everyday routines that define France and many Francophone regions.

**Pays:** France (République française)
**Nom des habitants:** Français
**Capitale:** Paris
**Langue officielle:** français
**Unité monétaire:** euro
**Fête nationale:** 14 (quatorze) juillet

**Pays:** Canada
**Nom des habitants:** Canadiens
**Capitale:** Ottawa
**Langues officielles:** anglais, français
**Unité monétaire:** dollar canadien
**Fête nationale:** 1er (premier) juillet

**Province (Canada):** le Québec
**Capitale:** Québec
**Langue:** 80 % (quatre-vingts pour cent) des habitants de la province de Québec parlent (*speak*) français.
**Fête nationale:** 24 (vingt-quatre) juin

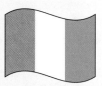

**Pays:** Côte d'Ivoire (République de Côte d'Ivoire)
**Nom des habitants:** Ivoiriens
**Capitale:** Yamoussoukro
**Langue officielle:** français
**Unité monétaire:** franc CFA
**Fête nationale:** 7 (sept) août

**Pays:** Sénégal (République du Sénégal)
**Nom des habitants:** Sénégalais
**Capitale:** Dakar
**Langue officielle:** français
**Unité monétaire:** franc CFA
**Fête nationale:** 4 (quatre) avril

**Pays:** Belgique (Royaume de Belgique)
**Nom des habitants:** Belges
**Capitale:** Bruxelles
**Langues officielles:** français, allemand (*German*), flamand (*Flemish*)
**Unité monétaire:** euro
**Fête nationale:** 21 (vingt et un) juillet

**Pays:** Suisse (Confédération suisse)
**Nom des habitants:** Suisses
**Capitale:** Berne (siège [*seat*] administratif), Lausanne (siège judiciaire)
**Langues officielles:** allemand, français, italien
**Unité monétaire:** franc suisse
**Fête nationale:** 1er (premier) août

**Département d'outre-mer (France):** Martinique
**Nom des habitants:** Martiniquais
**Capitale (chef-lieu et préfecture):** Fort-de-France
**Langue officielle:** français
**Unité monétaire:** euro
**Fête nationale:** 14 (quatorze) juillet

# Bienvenue en France

## Un coup d'œil° sur Paris, en France

*Un... A glance*

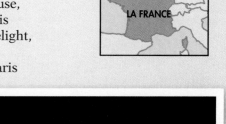

LA FRANCE

Paris, the City of Light, intrigues, astonishes, provokes, overwhelms . . . and gets under your skin. For centuries, the city has served as a muse, inspiring artists, writers, and musicians alike with its beauty. Paris is the apex of architectural beauty, artistic expression, and culinary delight, and it knows it. As stately as the **Arc de Triomphe,** as disarmingly quaint as the lace-curtained bistros found in each neighborhood, Paris seduces newcomers to enjoy unhurried exploration of its picture-perfect streets.

It is a city of vast, noble perspectives and intimate, medieval streets, of formal **espaces verts** (green open spaces) and quiet squares. This combination of the pompous and the private is one of the secrets of its perennial pull. Another is its size: Paris is relatively small as capitals go, with distances between many of its major sights and museums invariably walkable. Paris is an open history book: a stroll through its streets will take you from the Middle Ages right up to the 21st century.

## PORTRAIT **Astérix**

Astérix, the iconic French comic strip character, is a boisterous little Gaul* who lives in a small French village that is holding out against the might of the Roman Empire. Protected by the village druid Panoramix's magic potion, which gives him superhuman strength, Astérix takes the lead in the villagers' perilous attempts to conquer the invading Romans. He is a clever and level-headed warrior who knows when brain is better than brawn. The French see him as a symbol of themselves in his ability to outwit others.

**The Eiffel Tower at night**

*an inhabitant of the ancient region of Gaul, a province of the Roman Empire including territory corresponding to modern France, Belgium, and northern Italy

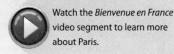

Watch the *Bienvenue en France* video segment to learn more about Paris.

# Une nouvelle° aventure

*new*

**Les dossiers de Léa**

Léa

> Mes photos
> Au café avec Juliette
> Vidéo de Juliette pour mon blog
> Bonjour ou au revoir?

Au café avec Juliette—Les Patios devant la Sorbonne

# Dans ce chapitre...

## OBJECTIFS COMMUNICATIFS

- greeting people
- spelling
- giving numerical information
- introducing yourself
- identifying people, places, and things
- expressing the date
- learning to pronounce the alphabet and selected vowel sounds in French

## PAROLES (Leçons 1 et 2)

- Les bonnes manières
- L'alphabet français
- Les accents
- Les mots apparentés
- Les nombres de 0 à 60
- Les jours et les mois

## STRUCTURES (Leçon 3)

- Dans la salle de classe
- Les articles indéfinis et le genre des noms

## CULTURE

- Le blog de Léa: *Un jour exceptionnel**
- Reportage: *Bisous!*
- Lecture: *Publicité* (Leçon 4)

Vidéo de Juliette pour mon blog

Bonjour ou au revoir?

www.mhconnectfrench.com

*In **Chapitres 1–4** of *Vis-à-vis*, you will read Léa Bouchard's blog about her life in Paris and the commentaries of other Francophone characters about her blog. See **Bienvenue à Vis-à-vis** and **Les pays francophones** (on the preceding pages) for more information on this special feature of *Vis-à-vis*.

# Leçon 1

## Les bonnes manières°

*Les... Good manners*

In the French-speaking world, different greetings reflect the differing degrees of familiarity between people. Formality is the general rule; informal expressions are reserved for family, friends of long standing, and close associates and peers (for example, fellow students). All formal greetings are followed by a title: **Bonjour, madame.**

—Bonjour, mademoiselle.
—Bonjour, madame.

—Bonsoir, monsieur.
—Bonsoir, madame.

—Je m'appelle Lucas Martin. Et vous, comment vous appelez-vous?
—Je m'appelle Juliette Dupont.

—Comment allez-vous?
—Très bien, merci. Et vous?
—Pas mal, merci.

—Salut, ça va?
—Oui, ça va bien. (Ça va mal.) Et toi, comment vas-tu?
—Comme ci comme ça. (Ça peut aller.) (Moyen.)

—Comment? Je ne comprends pas. Répétez, s'il vous plaît.
—C'est Lise Bernard.
—Ah oui, je comprends.

—Oh, pardon! Excusez-moi, mademoiselle.

—Merci (beaucoup).
—De rien.

—Au revoir!
—À bientôt!

 *Allez-y!*

**A. Répondez, s'il vous plaît.** Respond in French.

**1.** Je m'appelle Arthur Lenôtre. Et vous, comment vous appelez-vous? **2.** Bonsoir! **3.** Comment allez-vous? **4.** Merci. **5.** Ça va? **6.** Au revoir! **7.** Bonjour.

**B. Soutenu ou familier?** (*Formal or informal?*) Decide if each situation shown is formal or informal, then provide an appropriate expression for it.

**1.**

**2.**

**3.**

**4.**

**5.**

**6.**

> ### Le parler jeune
>
> | | |
> |---|---|
> | **à plus (A+)** | à plus tard; à bientôt |
> | **ça va super** | ça va très bien |
> | **c'est la cata** | ça va très mal |
> | **tchao** | au revoir |
>
> —Salut! —**À plus!**
>
> —Comment ça va? —**Ça va super!**
>
> Mon mél (*email*) est bloqué: **c'est la cata!**
>
> —Allez **tchao!** —À bientôt!

**C. Le bon choix.** (*The right choice.*) Indicate if the following expressions are used in a formal or informal context. What cues tell you whether it is formal or informal?

**1.** Comment vous appelez-vous?
**2.** Et toi?
**3.** Répète, s'il te plaît.
**4.** Comment vas-tu?
**5.** Comment t'appelles-tu?
**6.** Bonjour, monsieur!
**7.** Et vous?
**8.** Salut!
**9.** Répétez, s'il vous plaît.
**10.** Comment allez-vous?

# L'alphabet français

| | | | | | | | |
|---|---|---|---|---|---|---|---|
| **a** | a | **h** | hache | **o** | o | **v** | vé |
| **b** | bé | **i** | i | **p** | pé | **w** | double vé |
| **c** | cé | **j** | ji | **q** | ku | **x** | iks |
| **d** | dé | **k** | ka | **r** | erre | **y** | i grec |
| **e** | e | **l** | elle | **s** | esse | **z** | zède |
| **f** | effe | **m** | emme | **t** | té | | |
| **g** | gé | **n** | enne | **u** | u | | |

---

### L'alphabet phonétique

| | | | |
|---|---|---|---|
| [a] | **à, la** | [b] | **bonjour** |
| [ɑ] | **pâté** | [k] | **comme, quatre, kilo** |
| [ə] | **je, fenêtre** | [ʃ] | **chaise** |
| [e] | **répétez, aller** | [d] | **dimanche** |
| [ɛ] | **très, mademoiselle, fenêtre** | [f] | **fenêtre** |
| [i] | **il, stylo** | [g] | **garçon** |
| [o] | **stylo, bientôt, bureau** | [ɲ] | **espagnol** |
| [ɔ] | **porte** | [ʒ] | **je, biologie** |
| [u] | **vous** | [l] | **la** |
| [y] | **tu** | [m] | **mademoiselle** |
| [ø] | **deux** | [n] | **neuf** |
| [œ] | **sœur, neuf** | [ŋ] | **parking** |
| [ã] | **comment, écran** | [p] | **pardon** |
| [ɛ̃] | **bien, cinq** | [R] | **répétez** |
| [ɔ̃] | **bonjour** | [s] | **six, cinq, français, classe** |
| [œ̃] | **un** | [t] | **table** |
| [j] | **bien, moyen, juillet** | [v] | **vendredi, wagon** |
| [ɥ] | **huit** | [z] | **chaise, douze** |
| [w]\* | **oui, week-end** | | |

---

\*The spelling **-oi-** as in "bons**oi**r" is pronounced [wɑ].

# Les accents

Accents or diacritical marks sometimes change the pronunciation of a letter and sometimes distinguish between two words otherwise spelled the same. A French word written without its diacritical marks is misspelled.

| | | |
|---|---|---|
| é | e | **accent aigu** |
| à | a | **accent grave** |
| ô | o | **accent circonflexe** |
| ï | i | **tréma** |
| ç | c | **cédille** |

 *Allez-y!*

**A.** **À vous!** Spell your name in French. Then spell the name of a city, and see if your classmates can figure out which one it is.

**B. Inscription.** Several students are signing up to live in the campus international house. Spell their names and cities for the resident assistant.

1. DUPONT Isabelle    Paris
2. EL AYYADI Allal    Rabat
3. GOUTAL Ariane    Papeete
4. GUEYE Jérôme    Dakar
5. HUBERT Sarah    Lille
6. PASTEUR Loïc    Montréal

# Les mots apparentés°

Les... *Cognates*

French and English have many cognates, or **mots apparentés:** words spelled similarly with similar meanings. Their pronunciation often differs dramatically in the two languages.

Here are a few patterns to help you recognize cognates.

| FRANÇAIS | ANGLAIS | |
|---|---|---|
| **-ant** | *-ing* | amus**ant** → amus**ing** |
| **ét-** | *st-* | **ét**at → **st**ate |
| **-ie, -é** | *-y* | cit**é** → cit**y** |
| **-eux, -euse** | *-ous* | séri**eux** → seri**ous** |
| **-ique** | *-ic, -ical* | prat**ique** → prac**tical** |
| **-iste** | *-ist, -istic* | material**iste** → material**istic** |
| **-ment** | *-ly* | rapide**ment** → rapid**ly** |
| **-re** | *-er* | ord**re** → ord**er** |

Be aware that there are also many apparent cognates, called **faux amis** (*false friends*). Here are a few examples along with the correct terms (**mots justes**).

| FAUX AMIS | | MOTS JUSTES | |
|---|---|---|---|
| collège | *secondary school* | université | *college, university* |
| librairie | *bookstore* | bibliothèque | *library* |
| rester | *to stay, remain* | se reposer | *to rest* |

 *Allez-y!*

**A. Répétez, s'il vous plaît!** Pronounce these French cognates as your instructor does.

1. attitude
2. police
3. balle
4. bracelet
5. passion
6. conclusion
7. injustice
8. hôpital
9. champagne
10. parfum
11. magazine
12. présentation

**B. Les mots apparentés.** Figure out the English equivalents for the first five words. Then try to figure out the French equivalents for the last five words.

MODÈLES: étranger → *stranger*
            *generally* → généralement

1. logique
2. centre
3. étude
4. liberté
5. courageuse
6. *imperialistic*
7. *strange*
8. *tender*
9. *logically*
10. *historic*

# Leçon 2

## Les nombres de 0 à 60°

*Les... Numbers from 0 to 60*

| | | | | | | | |
|---|---|---|---|---|---|---|---|
| 0 | zéro | 6 | six | 11 | onze | 16 | seize |
| 1 | un | 7 | sept | 12 | douze | 17 | dix-sept |
| 2 | deux | 8 | huit | 13 | treize | 18 | dix-huit |
| 3 | trois | 9 | neuf | 14 | quatorze | 19 | dix-neuf |
| 4 | quatre | 10 | dix | 15 | quinze | 20 | vingt |
| 5 | cinq | | | | | | |

| | | | | | |
|---|---|---|---|---|---|
| 21 | vingt et un | 26 | vingt-six | 40 | quarante |
| 22 | vingt-deux | 27 | vingt-sept | 50 | cinquante |
| 23 | vingt-trois | 28 | vingt-huit | 60 | soixante |
| 24 | vingt-quatre | 29 | vingt-neuf | | |
| 25 | vingt-cinq | 30 | trente | | |

### Un peu plus...°

*Un... A little more*

**Combien de drapeaux y a-t-il?**
*(How many flags are there?)* The French flag has great symbolic value for the nation. It appeared during the French Revolution in 1789 to replace the blue and white flag of the monarchy, the **fleur de lys.** The **tricolore,** as the flag is sometimes called, combines white with blue and red (the colors of Paris). The three colors are often associated with the principles upon which the French republic was founded: **liberté, égalité, fraternité.** The French flag is increasingly displayed alongside the flag of the European Union, blue with a circle of twelve gold stars. The number 12 is a traditional symbol of perfection, completeness, and unity. The circle formation represents solidarity and harmony. What does your national flag symbolize?

▶ *Le tricolore et le drapeau de l'Union européenne*

 *Allez-y!*

**A. Problèmes de mathématiques.** Alternating with a partner, do the following math problems.

**VOCABULAIRE UTILE**

| + plus, et | − moins | × fois | = font |
|---|---|---|---|

Combien font 3 plus 10?  *How much is 3 + 10?*

**MODÈLE:** 6 + 2 →

É1*: Combien font six plus (et) deux?
É2:  Six plus (et) deux font huit.

1. 8 + 2
2. 5 + 9
3. 4 + 1
4. 3 + 8
5. 43 − 16
6. 60 − 37

7. 56 − 21
8. 49 − 27
9. 2 × 10
10. 3 × 20
11. 6 × 5
12. 7 × 3

**B. Les numéros de téléphone.** In French, telephone numbers are said in groups of five two-digit numbers. Look at Marine's contact list and, alternating with a partner, read aloud some of her most frequently called numbers.

**MODÈLE:** É1: Simon Beaujour?
É2: 02.40.29.07.39

## MES AMIS

| nom | prénom | adresse | tél. |
|---|---|---|---|
| Duclos | Maxime | 60, bd. de l'égalité | 02.41.48.05.52 |
| Bercegol | Valentine | 98, avenue Patton | 02.41.46.42.60 |
| de Bailleux | Bénédicte | 83, rue des Renardières | 02.41.57.13.44 |
| Koehulein | Alice | 7, rue de Verneuil | 02.41.35.21.08 |
| Beaujour | Simon | 12, rue du Temple | 02.40.29.07.39 |

---

*É1 and É2 stand for **Étudiant(e) 1** and **Étudiant(e) 2** (*Student 1* and *Student 2*). These abbreviations are used in partner/pair activities throughout *Vis-à-vis*.

# Quel jour sommes-nous?°

Quel... *What day is it?*

## La semaine° de Claire

*week*

| | |
|---|---|
| lundi | examen de biologie |
| mardi | examen de chimie |
| mercredi | dentiste |
| jeudi | tennis avec° Augustin |
| vendredi | laboratoire |
| samedi | théâtre avec Augustin |
| dimanche | en famille |

°*with*

In French, the days of the week are not capitalized. The week begins with Monday.

—Quel jour sommes-nous (aujourd'hui)? / Quel jour est-ce (aujourd'hui)?    *What day is it (today)?*

—Nous sommes mardi. / C'est mardi.    *It's Tuesday.*

 **Allez-y!**

**La semaine de Claire.** Look over Claire's calendar. Then, alternating with a partner, tell what day of the week it is.

**MODÈLE:** Claire est au (*is at the*) laboratoire. →
    É1: Claire est au laboratoire. Quel jour est-ce? (Quel jour sommes-nous?)
    É2: C'est vendredi. (Nous sommes vendredi.)

1. Claire va (*goes*) au théâtre avec Augustin.
2. Claire est chez (*at*) le dentiste.
3. Claire a (*has*) un cours de biologie.
4. Claire est en famille.
5. Claire joue au (*is playing*) tennis avec Augustin.
6. Claire a un examen de chimie.

# Quelle est la date d'aujourd'hui?

**LES MOIS** (*m.*)

| | | | |
|---|---|---|---|
| décembre | mars | juin | septembre |
| janvier | avril | juillet | octobre |
| février | mai | août | novembre |

In French, the day is usually followed by the month: **Nous sommes le 21 mars** (abbreviated as 21.3). The word **le** (*the*) usually precedes the day of the month.

Dates in French are expressed with cardinal numbers (**le 21 mars**), with the exception of the first of the month: **le 1ᵉʳ (premier) janvier.**

 **Allez-y!**

**A. Fêtes** (*Holidays*) **américaines.** What months do you associate with the following holidays?

1.  2.  3.

4.  5.  6.

7.  8.

**B. Le voyageur bien informé.** It can be useful to know the holidays of the countries you visit. Look at the following lists and compare the three countries. Note that the dates of some holidays vary from country to country and from year to year.

| SUISSE | | ÉTATS-UNIS | | FRANCE | |
|---|---|---|---|---|---|
| 1<sup>er</sup> janv. | Nouvel An | 1<sup>er</sup> janv. | Nouvel An | 1<sup>er</sup> janv. | Nouvel An |
| 2 janv. | Fête légale | 20 févr. | Anniversaire de Washington | 27 mars | Lundi de Pâques |
| 24 mars | Vendredi saint | | | 1<sup>er</sup> mai | Fête du Travail |
| 26 mars | Pâques | 24 mars | Vendredi saint | 4 mai | Ascension |
| 27 mars | Lundi de Pâques | 29 mai | Jour du Souvenir | 8 mai | Armistice |
| 4 mai | Ascension | 4 juill. | Fête de l'Indépendance | 15 mai | Lundi de Pentecôte |
| 15 mai | Lundi de Pentecôte | | | 14 juill. | Fête nationale (Prise de la Bastille) |
| 1<sup>er</sup> août | Fête nationale | 5 sept. | Fête du Travail | | |
| 25 déc. | Noël | 11 nov. | Fête des Anciens Combattants | 15 août | Assomption |
| 26 déc. | Lendemain de Noël | | | 1<sup>er</sup> nov. | Toussaint |
| | | 23 nov. | Action de Grâce | 11 nov. | Jour du Souvenir |
| | | 25 déc. | Noël | 25 déc. | Noël |

1. Quelles fêtes aux États-Unis ne sont pas célébrées en France? en Suisse? Donnez (*Give*) la date de ces (*these*) fêtes.
2. Y a-t-il plus de (*more*) fêtes religieuses en France et en Suisse qu'aux (*than in the*) États-Unis? Nommez-les (*Name them*) et donnez leur date.
3. Donnez les dates des fêtes nationales dans les trois pays.
4. Quel est votre jour de fête préféré? Pourquoi? (*Why?*)

Le 14 juillet, la fête nationale, à Paris

**C. La fête des patrons.** (*Saint's day.*) In France, each day of the year is associated with a particular saint. Look over the list of names and dates on the following page. Choose six of them and, with a partner, ask and answer questions about name days.

**MODÈLE:** É1: Quand est (*When is*) la fête de Jules?
É2: Le vingt-trois mai. Et la fête de Gilbert?

# fêtes à souhaiter°

## a

| | | |
|---|---|---|
| ADOLPHE | 30 | juin |
| ADRIEN | 8 | sept |
| AGNES | 21 | janv |
| AIME | 13 | sept |
| AIMEE | 20 | fév |
| ALAIN | 9 | sept |
| ALBAN | 22 | juin |
| ALBERT | 15 | nov |
| ALEXANDRE | 22 | avril |
| ALEXIS | 17 | fév |
| ALFRED | 15 | août |
| ALICE | 16 | déc |
| ALINE | 20 | oct |
| ALPHONSE | 1 | août |
| AMAND | 6 | fév |
| ANATOLE | 3 | fév |
| ANDRE | 30 | nov |
| ANGE | 5 | mai |
| ANGELE | 27 | janv |
| ANNE | 26 | juil |
| ANSELME | 21 | avril |
| ANTOINE | 17 | janv |
| ANTOINETTE | 28 | fév |
| ANTONIN | 2 | mai |
| ARISTIDE | 31 | août |
| ARLETTE | 17 | juil |
| ARMAND | 8 | juin |
| ARMEL | 16 | août |
| ARNAUD | 10 | fév |
| ARTHUR | 15 | nov |
| AURORE | 13 | déc |

## b

| | | |
|---|---|---|
| BAUDOUIN | 17 | oct |
| BEATRICE | 13 | fév |
| BENJAMIN | 31 | mars |
| BENOIT | 11 | juil |
| BERNADETTE | 18 | fév |
| BERNARD | 20 | août |
| BERTHE | 4 | juil |
| BERTRAND | 6 | sept |
| BRIGITTE | 23 | juil |

## c

| | | |
|---|---|---|
| CAMILLE | 14 | juil |
| CARINE | 7 | nov |
| CAROLE | 17 | juil |
| CATHERINE | 25 | nov |
| CECILE | 22 | nov |
| CELINE | 21 | oct |
| CHANTAL | 12 | déc |
| CHARLES | 2 | mars |
| CHRISTEL (LE) | 24 | juil |
| CHRISTIAN | 12 | nov |
| CHRISTINE | 24 | juil |
| CHRISTOPHE | 21 | août |
| CLAIRE | 11 | août |
| CLAUDE | 6 | juin |
| CLEMENCE | 21 | mars |
| CLEMENT | 23 | nov |
| CLOTILDE | 4 | juin |
| COLETTE | 6 | mars |
| CORINNE | 18 | mai |
| CYRILLE | 18 | mars |

## d

| | | |
|---|---|---|
| DANIEL | 11 | déc |
| DAVID | 29 | déc |
| DELPHINE | 26 | nov |
| DENIS | 9 | oct |
| DENISE | 15 | mai |
| DIDIER | 23 | mai |
| DOMINIQUE | 8 | août |

## e

| | | |
|---|---|---|
| EDITH | 13 | sept |
| EDMOND | 20 | nov |
| EDOUARD | 5 | janv |
| ELIANE | 4 | juil |
| ELIE | 20 | juil |
| ELISABETH | 17 | nov |
| ELISE | 17 | nov |
| ELOI | 1 | déc |
| EMILE | 22 | mai |
| EMILIENNE | 5 | janv |
| EMMANUEL | 25 | déc |
| ERIC | 18 | mai |
| ERNEST | 7 | nov |
| ESTELLE | 11 | mai |
| ETIENNE | 26 | déc |
| EUGENE | 13 | juil |
| EVA | 6 | sept |
| EVELYNE | 27 | déc |

## f

| | | |
|---|---|---|
| FABIEN | 20 | janv |
| FABRICE | 22 | août |
| FELIX | 12 | fév |
| FERDINAND | 30 | mai |
| FERNAND | 27 | juin |
| FRANÇOIS | 4 | oct |
| FRANÇOISE | 12 | déc |
| FREDERIC | 18 | juil |

## g

| | | |
|---|---|---|
| GABRIEL (LE) | 29 | sept |
| GAEL | 17 | déc |
| GAETAN | 7 | août |
| GASTON | 6 | fév |
| GAUTIER | 9 | avril |
| GENEVIEVE | 3 | janv |
| GEOFFROY | 8 | nov |
| GEORGES | 23 | avril |
| GERALD | 5 | déc |
| GERARD | 3 | oct |
| GERAUD | 13 | oct |
| GERMAIN | 31 | juil |
| GERMAINE | 15 | juin |
| GERVAIS | 19 | juin |
| GHISLAIN | 10 | oct |
| GILBERT | 7 | juin |
| GILBERTE | 11 | août |
| GILLES | 1 | sept |
| GINETTE | 3 | janv |
| GISELE | 7 | mai |
| GODEFROY | 8 | nov |
| GONTRAN | 28 | mars |
| GREGOIRE | 3 | sept |
| GUILLAUME | 10 | janv |
| GUSTAVE | 7 | oct |
| GUY | 12 | juin |

## h

| | | |
|---|---|---|
| HELENE | 18 | août |
| HENRI | 13 | juil |
| HERVE | 17 | juin |
| HONORE | 16 | mai |
| HORTENSE | 5 | oct |
| HUBERT | 3 | nov |
| HUGUES | 1 | avril |

## i

| | | |
|---|---|---|
| IRENE | 5 | avril |
| ISABELLE | 22 | fév |

## j

| | | |
|---|---|---|
| JACINTHE | 30 | janv |
| JACQUELINE | 8 | fév |
| JACQUES | 25 | juil |
| JEAN | 24 | juin |
| JEANNE | 30 | mai |
| JEROME | 30 | sept |
| JOACHIM | 26 | juil |
| JOEL | 13 | juil |
| JOHANNE | 30 | mai |
| JOSEPH | 19 | mars |
| JOSETTE | 19 | mars |
| JOSSELIN | 13 | déc |
| JULES | 12 | avril |
| JULIEN | 2 | août |
| JULIENNE | 16 | fév |
| JULIETTE | 30 | juil |
| JUSTE | 14 | oct |

## k

| | | |
|---|---|---|
| KARINE | 7 | nov |

## l

| | | |
|---|---|---|
| LAETITIA | 18 | août |
| LAURENT | 10 | août |
| LEA | 22 | mars |
| LEON | 10 | nov |
| LILIANE | 4 | juil |
| LINE | 20 | oct |
| LIONEL | 10 | nov |
| LISE | 17 | nov |
| LOIC | 25 | août |
| LOUIS | 25 | août |
| LOUISE | 15 | mars |
| LUC | 18 | oct |
| LUCIE | 13 | déc |
| LUCIEN | 8 | janv |
| LUDOVIC | 25 | août |

## m

| | | |
|---|---|---|
| MADELEINE | 22 | juil |
| MARC | 25 | avril |
| MARCEL | 16 | janv |
| MARCELLE | 31 | janv |
| MARIANNE | 9 | juil |
| MARIANNICK | 15 | août |
| MARIE | 15 | août |
| MARIE-THERESE | 7 | juin |
| MARTHE | 29 | juil |
| MARTIAL | 30 | juin |
| MARTINE | 30 | janv |
| MARYVONNE | 15 | août |
| MATHILDE | 14 | mars |
| MATTHIAS | 14 | mai |
| MATTHIEU | 21 | sept |
| MAURICE | 22 | sept |
| MICHEL | 29 | sept |
| MICHELINE | 19 | juin |
| MIREILLE | 15 | août |
| MONIQUE | 27 | août |
| MURIEL | 15 | août |

## n

| | | |
|---|---|---|
| NATHALIE | 27 | juil |
| NELLY | 18 | août |
| NICOLAS | 6 | déc |
| NICOLE | 6 | mars |
| NOEL | 25 | déc |

## o

| | | |
|---|---|---|
| ODETTE | 20 | avril |
| ODILE | 14 | déc |
| OLIVIER | 12 | juil |

## p

| | | |
|---|---|---|
| PASCAL | 17 | mai |
| PATRICE | 17 | mars |
| PAUL | 29 | juin |
| PAULE | 26 | janv |
| PHILIPPE | 3 | mai |
| PIERRE | 29 | juin |
| PIERRETTE | 31 | mai |

## r

| | | |
|---|---|---|
| RAOUL | 7 | juil |
| RAPHAEL | 29 | sept |
| RAYMOND | 7 | janv |
| REGINE | 7 | sept |
| REGIS | 16 | juin |
| REMI | 15 | janv |
| RENAUD | 17 | sept |
| RENE (E) | 19 | oct |
| RICHARD | 3 | avril |
| ROBERT | 30 | avril |
| RODOLPHE | 21 | juin |
| ROGER | 30 | déc |
| ROLAND | 15 | sept |
| ROLANDE | 13 | mai |
| ROMAIN | 28 | fév |
| RONALD | 17 | sept |
| ROSELINE | 17 | janv |
| ROSINE | 11 | mars |

## s

| | | |
|---|---|---|
| SABINE | 29 | août |
| SAMUEL | 20 | août |
| SANDRINE | 2 | avril |
| SEBASTIEN | 20 | janv |
| SERGE | 7 | oct |
| SIMON | 28 | oct |
| SOLANGE | 10 | mai |
| SOPHIE | 25 | mai |
| STANISLAS | 11 | avril |
| STEPHANE | 26 | déc |
| SUZANNE | 11 | août |
| SYLVAIN | 4 | mai |
| SYLVESTRE | 31 | déc |
| SYLVIE | 5 | nov |

## t

| | | |
|---|---|---|
| TANGUY | 19 | nov |
| THERESE | 1 | oct |
| THIBAUT | 8 | juil |
| THIERRY | 1 | juil |
| THOMAS | 3 | juil |

## v

| | | |
|---|---|---|
| VALENTIN | 14 | fév |
| VALENTINE | 25 | juil |
| VALERIE | 28 | avril |
| VERONIQUE | 4 | fév |
| VICTOR | 21 | juil |
| VINCENT de Paul | 27 | sept |
| VIRGINIE | 7 | janv |
| VIVIANE | 2 | déc |

## w

| | | |
|---|---|---|
| WALTER | 9 | avril |
| WILFRIED | 12 | oct |

## x

| | | |
|---|---|---|
| XAVIER | 3 | déc |

## y

| | | |
|---|---|---|
| YOLANDE | 11 | juin |
| YVES | 19 | mai |
| YVETTE | 13 | janv |
| YVON | 19 | mai |

°fêtes… *celebrating saints' days*

# Le blog de Léa

## Un jour exceptionnel°

*jour... special day*

**vendredi 13 mai**

Bonjour! Ça va?

Je m'appelle Léa. Je suis[1] étudiante. Et voilà, je crée un blog avec mes amis[2]! C'est pour communiquer, exprimer[3] des idées, des sentiments, des secrets… Aujourd'hui, c'est le vendredi 13! Un jour exceptionnel. Un jour de chance:[4] Mon blog sera[5] un succès. C'est sûr!

Au revoir, à bientôt
Léa la blogueuse[6]

Vidéo de Juliette pour mon blog

. . . . . . . . . . . . . . . . . . . . . . . . . . . . . . . . . . . . . . . . . . . .

**COMMENTAIRES**

**Alexis**
Léa, le vendredi 13, c'est de la pure superstition!

**Mamadou**
Léa, créer un blog un vendredi 13, c'est risqué! Le vendredi 13, c'est une combinaison fatale. ATTENTION.

**Poema**
Le vendredi 13: c'est le jour du Super Loto.[7]

Welcome to **Le blog de Léa.** Here, at the center of each chapter of *Vis-à-vis,* you will find:

- The blogs of four Parisians with different Francophone backgrounds. **Chapitres 1–4** feature **Le blog de Léa,** a 19-year-old student at the Sorbonne who lives in the **Quartier latin.** The blogs are followed by commentaries of other Francophone characters.
- The **Reportage** presents up-to-date information related to the chapter theme that depicts life in France, Quebec, North and West Africa, French-speaking Europe, or the Antilles.
- **À vous** offers comprehension questions and personalized questions to accompany the **Reportage.**
- **Parlons-en!** (*Let's talk about it!*) gives students the opportunity to do pair and group work using information from the reading and preceding sections.

[1]Je... *I am*   [2]avec... *with my friends*   [3]*express*   [4]jour... *lucky day*   [5]*will be*   [6]*person who has a blog*   [7]jour... *day of the French lottery drawing with a large cash prize*

## Bisous!

**"Bonjour! Ça va?"** With these words, Arielle greets her friend Luc and kisses him on the cheek. This is how French friends typically greet each other.

In France, to say "hello" or "good-bye," you give two, three, or sometimes four kisses, depending on the region in which you find yourself. The **bisou** is a kiss on the cheek. The term **bisou** has an affectionate connotation: You give a **bisou** to children, friends, and family in greeting.

In Belgium, a single kiss suffices, but three are necessary to celebrate joyful occasions.

In Quebec, the custom differs. Maria, who was born in Montreal, explains, "Like Americans, Canadians are warm and charming, but they often maintain a physical distance when greeting newcomers. Close friends and family members, however, share a **bisou.**"

Bonjour ou au revoir? Baiser amical (*friendly kiss*) ou baiser d'amoureux (*lovers'*)? En France, en Belgique, au Canada, au Maroc ou au Sénégal? C'est difficile à dire (*to say*). Que pensez-vous? (*What do you think?*)

In Muslim countries, people typically do not touch but exchange friendly greetings such as **As-salaam'alaykum** (*Peace*) or **Que la paix de Dieu soit avec vous** (*God's peace be with you*).

Remember: You don't give a **bisou** to a person you are meeting for the first time. You politely say **bonjour** and shake his/her hand.

**À vous!**

1. In your culture, what do you do when you meet someone for the first time? How do you greet friends and family members?
2. What greeting customs from other cultures do you know?

**Parlons-en!**

Work with a classmate to decide how you would greet the following French speakers in the situations listed below. Be sure to use the appropriate expressions and gestures. Use the information from the **Reportage** and from **Les bonnes manières,** page 8 to guide you.

1. Marie (20 years old) meets her mother at the supermarket in Montreal.
2. Aïcha (15 years old) meets her piano teacher, Madame Clément (40 years old), in the street in Poitiers.
3. Monsieur Kedadou, director of the French department at the Sorbonne, greets Isabelle, a first-year student, in the hall outside of class.
4. Jeanne, who lives in Brussels, greets her best friend, Victoire, who has just arrived to pick her up to go to the movies.

# Leçon 3

STRUCTURES

## Dans la salle de classe°

Dans... *In the classroom*

3. un tableau
4. un écran
6. une porte
7. une fenêtre
10. une télévision
11. un lecteur de DVD
12. un ordinateur
13. une souris
8. un étudiant
9. un crayon
5. un professeur
14. une table
15. un stylo
16. une étudiante
17. un livre
19. un portable
18. un cahier
1. une chaise
2. un bureau

|||| **Allez-y!**

**A. Qu'est-ce que c'est?** (*What is it?*) **Qui est-ce?** (*Who is it?*) Alternating with a classmate, identify the people and objects in the illustration above.

> **MODÈLE:** É1: Le numéro un, qu'est-ce que c'est?
> É2: C'est une (*It's a*) chaise.
> É1: Le numéro cinq, qui est-ce?
> É2: C'est un professeur.

**B. Combien?** (*How many?*) Taking turns with a classmate, ask and answer questions about the number of people and objects there are in the illustration. Use the expression **Il y a.**

> **MODÈLE:** étudiants →
> É1: Il y a combien d'étudiants?
> É2: Il y a quatre étudiants.

## Mots clés

### Using *il y a*

The expression **il y a** (*there is, there are*) is used to state the existence of something or to specify the quantity.

**Il y a** un cours de français.
*There is a French class.*

**Il y a** quatre étudiants dans la classe.
*There are four students in the classroom.*

# Les articles indéfinis et le genre des noms

*Identifying People, Places, and Things*

## Étudier ou communiquer?

*Léa contacte Mamadou sur sa page Facebook (Messagerie instantanée).*

 LÉA: Salut Mamadou! J'ai **un** blog et toi, tu as **une** page Facebook!

 MAMADOU: Oui! J'ai aussi **un** compte Twitter et **un** smartphone. Pour communiquer.

 LÉA: Moi, j'ai **une** tablette, **des** cahiers et **des** livres. Pour étudier!

Vrai ou faux?

| **Léa étudie avec...** | **Mamadou communique avec...** |
|---|---|
| **1.** un blog | **1.** un blog |
| **2.** une page Facebook | **2.** une page Facebook |
| **3.** un compte Twitter | **3.** un compte Twitter |
| **4.** un smartphone | **4.** un smartphone |
| **5.** une tablette | **5.** une tablette |
| **6.** des cahiers | **6.** des cahiers |
| **7.** des livres | **7.** des livres |

## Singular Forms of Indefinite Articles

In French, all nouns (**noms**) are either masculine (**masculin**) or feminine (**féminin**), as are the articles that precede them.

The following chart shows the forms of the singular indefinite article in French, corresponding to *a* (*an*) in English.

| MASCULINE | | FEMININE | |
|---|---|---|---|
| **un** ami | *a friend (m.)* | **une** amie | *a friend (f.)* |
| **un** accent | *an accent* | **une** action | *an action* |

 **Prononcez bien!**

**The sounds in *un* and *une***

Note the pronunciation difference between **un** and **une**: un is made of only one sound (the nasal vowel [œ̃]), while **une** has two sounds (the vowel [y] as in **tu,** and the consonant [n]).

Let the air go through both your mouth and your nose when you pronounce **un;** *don't* pronounce the letter *n.*

[œ̃]: **un, lundi, commun**

Let the air go through your mouth only when pronouncing the vowel sound [y] in **une,** and *do* pronounce the *n.*

[y]: **une, lune, brune**

**Un** is used for masculine nouns and **une** for feminine nouns. **Un** and **une** can also mean *one,* depending on the context.

| | |
|---|---|
| Voilà **un** café. | *There's a café.* |
| Il y a **une** étudiante. | *There is one student.* |

## The Gender of Nouns

Because the gender (**le genre**) of a noun is not always predictable, it is best to learn it along with the noun; for example, learn **un livre** rather than just **livre.** Here are a few general guidelines to help you determine gender; you will become more familiar with nouns in all of these categories as you work through the chapters of *Vis-à-vis.*

**1.** Nouns that refer to males are usually masculine; nouns that refer to females are usually feminine.

| | |
|---|---|
| **un** homme | *a man* |
| **une** femme | *a woman* |

**2.** Sometimes the ending of a noun is a clue to its gender.

| MASCULINE | | FEMININE | |
|---|---|---|---|
| **-eau** | un bur**eau** | **-ence** | une différ**ence** |
| **-isme** | un pr**isme** | **-ion** | une réact**ion** |
| **-ment** | un monu**ment** | **-ie** | une librair**ie** |
| | | **-ure** | une lect**ure** |
| | | **-té** | une universi**té** |

**3.** Nouns borrowed from other languages are usually masculine.

un coca-cola, un couscous, un baklava

**4.** The names of languages are masculine. They are not capitalized.

| | |
|---|---|
| Elle parle un français impeccable! | *She speaks perfect French!* |

**5.** Some nouns that refer to people can be changed from masculine to feminine by adding **e** to the noun ending.

| un ami | *a friend (m.)* | une ami**e** | *a friend (f.)* |
|---|---|---|---|
| un étudiant | *a student (m.)* | une étudiant**e** | *a student (f.)* |
| un Français | *a French man (m.)* | une Français**e** | *a French woman (f.)* |

**Note:** Final **t, n, d,** and **s** are silent in the masculine form. When followed by **-e** in the feminine form, they are pronounced.

**6.** Many nouns that end in **-e** have only one singular form, used to refer to both males and females. Sometimes the gender is indicated by the article.

| **un** touriste | *a tourist (male)* |
|---|---|
| **une** touriste | *a tourist (female)* |

Sometimes even the article is the same for both masculine and feminine.

| **un** professeur | *a professor (male or female)* |
|---|---|
| **un** médecin | *a doctor (male or female)* |
| **une** personne | *a person (male or female)* |
| **une** vedette | *a movie star (male or female)* |

[Allez-y! A]

**Note:** The information between brackets refers you to an exercise for that grammar point. In this case, **Allez-y!**, Activity A below, will allow you to practice this point.

## Plural Forms of Indefinite Articles

| SINGULAR | PLURAL |
|---|---|
| **un** touriste | **des** touristes |
| **une** touriste | |

The plural form (**le pluriel**) of the indefinite articles is always **des**.* Usually, an **s** is added to the noun:

un ami → **des** ami**s**        *a friend; some friends, friends*
une question → **des** question**s**        *a question; some questions, questions*

[Allez-y! B-C]

> **Grammaire interactive**
>
> For more on indefinite articles and the gender and number of nouns, watch the corresponding Grammar Tutorial and take a brief practice quiz at **Connect French.**
>
> **connect** |FRENCH
>
> **www.mhconnectfrench.com**

**A. Qu'est-ce que c'est?** (*What is it?*) Working with a partner, identify the following items and people.

MODÈLE: →  É1: Qu'est-ce que c'est?
          É2: C'est une table.

1.     2.     3.     4.

5.     6.     7.     8.

**B. Dans une salle de classe.** Give the plural.

MODÈLE:  un stylo → Voilà (*Here are*) des stylos.

1. une table          3. une chaise          5. une porte
2. un écran           4. un ordinateur       6. un cahier

---

*In French, the final **s** of the article is usually silent, except when followed by a vowel or vowel sound: **des étudiants; des hommes.** In these cases, the **s** is pronounced like the letter **z.** This linking is called **liaison.**

**C. C'est trop!** (*It's too much!*) Give the singular.

**MODÈLE:** Des jours? → Non, un jour!

1. Des livres?
2. Des problèmes (*m.*)?
3. Des chaises?
4. Des ordinateurs?
5. Des tables?
6. Des mois?

## Prononcez bien!

1. **The vowels in *ci*, *les*, and *mai*** (page 15)

   A. **Au café.** While waiting to meet your French friends at a Parisian café, you hear the following conversation between a man and a woman sitting at the next table. Listen to their conversation and check the vowel in the right column that corresponds to the bold one in the left column.

   |  | [i]: **ci** | [e]: **les** | [ɛ]: **mai** |
   |---|---|---|---|
   | 1. Bonjour, je m'app**e**lle Éloïse. | ☐ | ☐ | ☒ |
   | 2. Moi, c'est Ér**i**c. Comment ça va? | ☒ | ☐ | ☐ |
   | 3. Ça peut all**er**. (*The server brings the bill.*) | | | |
   | 4. Ça fait tr**ei**ze euros, s'il vous plaît. | ☐ | ☐ | ☐ |
   | 5. Voi**ci**. À plus tard, Éloïse. | ☐ | ☐ | ☐ |
   | 6. À bientôt, Ér**i**c. | ☐ | ☐ | ☐ |

   B. **L'alphabet français.** Your housemate is also an international student who has just started taking French. You help him learn the French alphabet sounds by writing in one column the letters that are pronounced with a sound like the one in **les** and in the other, those that contain a sound like the one in **mai**.

   **Lettres:** z, p, v, r, d, s, g, l, t, c, m, f, b, n

   | [e]: **les** | [ɛ]: **mai** |
   |---|---|
   |  |  |

2. **The sounds in *un* and *une*** (page 21)

   **À l'aéroport.** You and your friend are flying to Italy for the weekend. As you wait to board your plane, your friend tries to guess the occupation of the other passengers. Listen to what he says and decide whether he's referring in each case to a man or a woman.

   |  | m. | f. |
   |---|---|---|
   | 1. | ☐ | ☐ |
   | 2. | ☐ | ☐ |
   | 3. | ☐ | ☐ |
   | 4. | ☐ | ☐ |
   | 5. | ☐ | ☐ |
   | 6. | ☐ | ☐ |

 Lecture°

*Reading*

## Avant de lire°

Avant... *Before reading*

**Recognizing cognates.** French is a Romance language—that is, it is derived from Latin. English was also heavily influenced by Latin, with the result that the two languages share vocabulary items similar in form and meaning. As you already know (see **Leçon 1**), these words are called cognates (**mots apparentés**). Here are two additional patterns:

| FRANÇAIS | ANGLAIS | | |
|---|---|---|---|
| **-eur** | *-or, -er* | vend**eur** | *vendor, seller* |
| **-é** | *-ed* | rembours**é** | *reimbursed* |

Over the centuries, the French and English languages have borrowed heavily from each other. Although French has absorbed many words from English, some people view these **anglicismes** as threats to the integrity of the language and culture. Words such as **champagne** and **cologne** were borrowed directly from French. Can you think of any others?

The ad on the following page is from the French website **La boutique de l'étudiant.fr.** Just like students everywhere, French students use books or the Internet to make decisions about which school to choose, how to study, or how to prepare for and do well on difficult exams.

**Abonnez-vous en ligne** means *subscribe online*. What do you think the expression **Profitez d'offres exceptionnelles** means?

Now read the ad through. Then go back and underline all the words you recognize as cognates, and circle the words you don't understand.

> **ABONNEZ-VOUS**
en ligne à l'Etudiant.

> **PROFITEZ**
d'offres exceptionnelles.

> **ACCÉDEZ**
à votre espace client.

> **DÉCOUVREZ**
toutes nos offres
numériques.

*nos engagements* **boutique.letudiant.fr**

Satisfait ou
remboursé

Livraison
en 3 à 7 jours

Paiement 100%
sécurisé

Un service client
à votre écoute

### Compréhension

**Quel mot?** (*Which word?*) Now that you have read the ad, find the word in the text that means:

1. discover
2. studies
3. universities of the future
4. art school
5. to earn points on the «bac» (*French high school exit exam*)
6. guide to higher education
7. make a difference

 Écriture°

*Writing*

The writing activities **Par écrit** and **Journal intime** can be found in the Workbook/Laboratory Manual to accompany *Vis-à-vis*.

# Pour s'amuser

~~~~~~~~~~~~~~~~~~~~~~~~~~~~~~~~~~~~~~~~~~~~~~~~~~

### Les mots cachés°

*Les... Word search*

In this grid, find the following words: **avril, bisou, femme, homme, mardi, salut, semaine, soir.**

```
c e d a m a r d i f o d
v s e m a i n e e d i g
b i s o u u s o i r e d
u x a v r i l p o r t i
m a d a m s a l u t m j
f e m m e o h o m m e g
```

# Le vidéoblog de Léa

## En bref

In this scene, we first meet Léa and learn about her three friends Hassan, Juliette, and Hector. In her videoblog, Léa describes how French speakers typically greet each other and say good-bye.

On fait la bise pour dire (*say*) «au revoir».

## Vocabulaire en contexte

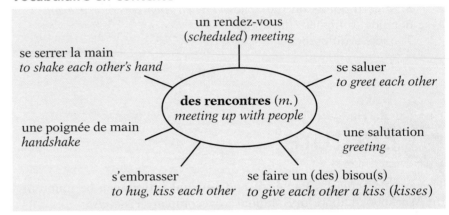

un rendez-vous
(*scheduled*) *meeting*

se serrer la main
*to shake each other's hand*

se saluer
*to greet each other*

**des rencontres** (*m.*)
*meeting up with people*

une poignée de main
*handshake*

une salutation
*greeting*

s'embrasser
*to hug, kiss each other*

se faire un (des) bisou(s)
*to give each other a kiss (kisses)*

## Visionnez!

Choose the correct response.

|  | Léa | Juliette | Hassan | Hector |
|---|---|---|---|---|
| 1. Qui a (*Who has*) rendez-vous chez le dentiste? | ☐ | ☐ | ☐ | ☐ |
| 2. Qui étudie le multimédia? | ☐ | ☐ | ☐ | ☐ |
| 3. Qui a 28 ans? | ☐ | ☐ | ☐ | ☐ |
| 4. Qui aime (*likes*) la danse? | ☐ | ☐ | ☐ | ☐ |
| 5. Qui a créé (*created*) un vidéoblog? | ☐ | ☐ | ☐ | ☐ |

## Analysez!

Answer the following questions in English.

1. How do greetings differ in France?
2. What do you think the social consequences are of *not* greeting someone in a culturally appropriate way? What impressions can that leave?

## Comparez!

Compare appropriate greetings and gestures in your culture to those of a French-speaking culture for the following people: two young female friends, two young male friends, a young male meeting a young female for the first time, a young male or female meeting an older adult male or female for the first time. What conclusions can you draw?

## Note culturelle

Juliette is working on her degree, *le Master Multimédia Interactif,* at the *Université Paris I Panthéon-Sorbonne.* This two-year specialization in computer science and multimedia was introduced into the curriculum in 2000. It allows students who have obtained *la licence* after three years of study to further specialize in their chosen field.

# Vocabulaire

### Les bonnes manières

**À bientôt.** See you soon.
**Au revoir.** Good-bye.
**Bonjour.** Hello. Good day.
**Bonsoir.** Good evening.
**Ça peut aller.** All right.
   Pretty well.
**Ça va?** How's it going?
**Ça va bien.** Fine. (Things are
   going well.)
**Ça va mal.** Things are going
   badly.
**Comme ci comme ça.** So so.
**Comment?** What?; How?
**Comment allez-vous? /
   Comment vas-tu?** How are
   you?
**Comment vous appelez-vous? /
   Comment t'appelles-tu?**
   What's your name?
**De rien.** Not at all. Don't mention
   it. You're welcome.
**Et vous? / Et toi?** And you?
**Excusez-moi. / Excuse-
   moi.** Excuse me.
**Je m'appelle...** My name is . . .
**Je ne comprends pas.** I don't
   understand.
**madame** Mrs. (ma'am)
**mademoiselle** Miss
**Merci (beaucoup).** Thank you
   (very much).
**monsieur** Mr. (sir)
**Moyen.** All right.
**Pardon.** Pardon (me).
**Pas mal.** Not bad(ly).
**Répétez. / Répète.** Repeat.
**Salut!** Hi!
**S'il vous plaît. / S'il te
   plaît.** Please.
**Très bien.** Very well (good).

### Les nombres de 0 à 60

**un, deux, trois, quatre, cinq, six,
   sept, huit, neuf, dix, onze,
   douze, treize, quatorze,
   quinze, seize, dix-sept, dix-
   huit, dix-neuf, vingt, vingt et
   un, vingt-deux,** etc., **trente,
   quarante, cinquante, soixante**

### Dans la salle de classe

**un bureau** a desk
**un cahier** a notebook
**une chaise** a chair
**un crayon** a pencil
**un écran** a screen
**un étudiant** a (male) student
**une étudiante** a (female) student
**une fenêtre** a window
**un lecteur de DVD** a DVD player
**un livre** a book
**un ordinateur** a computer
**un portable** a laptop
**une porte** a door
**un professeur** a professor,
   instructor (male or female)
**une salle de classe** a classroom
**un smartphone** a smartphone
**une souris** a mouse
**un stylo** a pen
**une table** a table
**une tablette** a tablet computer,
   an iPad
**un tableau** a (chalk)board
**une télévision** a television

### Les jours de la semaine

**Quel jour sommes-nous /
   est-ce?** What day is it?

**Nous sommes / C'est... lundi,
   mardi, mercredi, jeudi,
   vendredi, samedi,
   dimanche.** It's . . . Monday,
   Tuesday, Wednesday, Thursday,
   Friday, Saturday, Sunday.

### Les mois (*m.*)

**janvier** January
**février** February
**mars** March
**avril** April
**mai** May
**juin** June
**juillet** July
**août** August
**septembre** September
**octobre** October
**novembre** November
**décembre** December

### Mots et expressions divers

**aujourd'hui** today
**beaucoup** very much, a lot
**bien** well
**c'est un/une...** it's a (an) . . .
**combien de** how many
**et** and
**une femme** a woman
**un homme** a man
**il y a** there is/are
**mal** badly
**non** no
**oui** yes
**quel/quelle** what; which
**Quelle est la date?** What is the
   date?
**Qu'est-ce que c'est?** What is it?
**Qui est-ce?** Who is it?

# Nous, les étudiants

Léa

Les dossiers de Léa

➤ Mes photos
  ➤ Ma fac
  ➤ Le restaurant d'Hassan
  ➤ Un café du Quartier latin

Ma fac: la Sorbonne à Paris

## Dans ce chapitre...

### OBJECTIFS COMMUNICATIFS
- ➤ identifying people, places, and things
- ➤ talking about academic subjects
- ➤ talking about nationalities
- ➤ expressing actions
- ➤ expressing disagreement
- ➤ learning to distinguish between and pronounce selected sounds in French

Le restaurant d'Hassan

### PAROLES (Leçon 1)
- ➤ Les lieux
- ➤ Les matières
- ➤ Les pays et les nationalités
- ➤ Les distractions

### STRUCTURES (Leçons 2 et 3)
- ➤ Les articles définis
- ➤ Les verbes réguliers en **-er**
- ➤ Le verb **être**
- ➤ La négation **ne... pas**

Un café du Quartier latin

### CULTURE
- ➤ Le blog de Léa: *Salut tout le monde!*
- ➤ Reportage: *Quartier latin: le quartier général des étudiants*
- ➤ Lecture: *Étudier le français... à Québec, bien sûr!* (Leçon 4)

www.mhconnectfrench.com

# Leçon 1

## Les lieux°

Les… (*m.*) *Places*

Voici l'amphithéâtre (l'amphi).

Voici la cité universitaire
(la cité-U).

Voici le restaurant universitaire
(le resto-U).

Voici la bibliothèque.

**AUTRES MOTS UTILES**

| | |
|---|---|
| **le bureau** | office |
| **l'école** (*f.*) | school |
| **le gymnase** | gymnasium |
| **le laboratoire de langues** | language lab |
| **la librairie** | bookstore |
| **la salle de classe** | classroom |

### *Allez-y!*

**A. Une visite.** Associate the following nouns with their location.

**MODÈLES:** un examen de français → l'amphithéâtre
un coca → le restaurant universitaire

1. un dictionnaire
2. une tablette
3. un casque (*headset*)
4. un livre
5. une télévision
6. un cours de français
7. un sandwich
8. une encyclopédie

**B. C'est bizarre? C'est normal?** Give your opinion!

**MODÈLE:** Un match de football dans le restaurant universitaire... →
Un match de football dans le restaurant universitaire, c'est
bizarre!

1. Un cours de français dans l'amphithéâtre...
2. Une tablette dans la bibliothèque...
3. Un examen dans la cité universitaire...
4. Un café dans l'amphithéâtre...
5. Un dictionnaire dans la bibliothèque...
6. Un magazine dans la librairie...
7. Un smartphone dans la salle de classe

# Les matières°

Les... (*f.*) *Academic subjects*

À la faculté des lettres et sciences humaines, on étudie (*one studies*)...

**la littérature**
**la linguistique**
**les langues** (*f.*) **étrangères**
(*foreign languages*)
**l'allemand** (*m.*)
**l'anglais** (*m.*)
**le chinois**
**l'espagnol** (*m.*)
**l'italien** (*m.*)
**le japonais**
**l'histoire** (*f.*)
**la géographie**
**la philosophie**
**la psychologie**
**la sociologie**

À la faculté des sciences, on étudie…

**les mathématiques (les maths)** (*f.*)
**l'informatique** (*computer science*)
**la physique**
**la chimie** (*chemistry*)
**les sciences** (*f.*) **naturelles**
(**la géologie** et
**la biologie**)

AUTRES MOTS UTILES

**le commerce**   business
**le cours**   class
**le droit**   law
**l'économie** (*f.*)   economics
**le génie**   engineering

 *Allez-y!*

A. **Les études et les professions.** Imagine what subjects are necessary for the following professions.

MODÈLE:   un(e) diplomate  →  On étudie les langues étrangères.

1. un(e) psychologue
2. un(e) chimiste
3. un professeur de physique
4. un professeur d'histoire
5. un(e) ingénieur

B. **Mes** (*My*) **cours à l'université.** Look back over the lists of **matières,** then tell about yourself by completing the following sentences.

1. J'étudie (*I study*)…
2. J'aime étudier (*I like to study*)…
3. Je n'aime pas (*don't like*) étudier…
4. J'aimerais bien (*would like*) étudier…

C. **Et vos camarades?** Find out what three classmates are studying this term.

MODÈLE:   É1: Moi (*Me*), j'étudie le français, l'histoire et l'informatique. Et toi?
É2: Moi aussi (*too*), j'étudie le français, et j'étudie la philosophie et la chimie.

# Les pays et les nationalités°

*Les... Countries and nationalities*

la France

l'Allemagne

l'Espagne

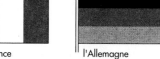
les États-Unis

**LES PAYS** (*m.*)

l'Algérie
l'Allemagne
l'Angleterre
la Belgique
le Canada
la Chine
la Côte d'Ivoire
l'Espagne
les États-Unis
la France
l'Italie
le Japon
le Liban
le Maroc
le Mexique
le Québec*
la République
  Démocratique
  du Congo
la Russie
le Sénégal
la Suisse
la Tunisie
le Vietnam

**LES NATIONALITÉS** (*f.*)

| PERSONNES | ADJECTIFS |
|---|---|
| l'Algérien, l'Algérienne | algérien, algérienne |
| l'Allemand, l'Allemande | allemand, allemande |
| l'Anglais, l'Anglaise | anglais, anglaise |
| le/la Belge | belge |
| le Canadien, la Canadienne | canadien, canadienne |
| le Chinois, la Chinoise | chinois, chinoise |
| l'Ivoirien, l'Ivoirienne | ivoirien, ivoirienne |
| l'Espagnol, l'Espagnole | espagnol, espagnole |
| l'Américain, l'Américaine | américain, américaine |
| le Français, la Française | français, française |
| l'Italien, l'Italienne | italien, italienne |
| le Japonais, la Japonaise | japonais, japonaise |
| le Libanais, la Libanaise | libanais, libanaise |
| le Marocain, la Marocaine | marocain, marocaine |
| le Mexicain, la Mexicaine | mexicain, mexicaine |
| le Québécois, la Québécoise | québécois, québécoise |
| le Congolais, la Congolaise | congolais, congolaise |
| | |
| le/la Russe | russe |
| le Sénégalais, la Sénégalaise | sénégalais, sénégalaise |
| le/la Suisse | suisse |
| le Tunisien, la Tunisienne | tunisien, tunisienne |
| le Vietnamien, la Vietnamienne | vietnamien, vietnamienne |

> 🎧 **Prononcez bien!**
>
> **Masculine vs. feminine forms of nationalities**
>
> Adding **-e** to the masculine forms of most nouns and adjectives of nationality makes them feminine. The final consonant is then pronounced.
>
> **allema<u>nde</u>, angla<u>ise</u>, chino<u>ise</u>, libana<u>ise</u>**
>
> The addition of **-e** to masculine forms ending with the letter *n* denasalizes the vowel [ɛ̃]. It becomes [ɛ], and the *n* is pronounced.
>
> **améric<u>ain</u>** [ɛ̃] → **améric<u>aine</u>** [ɛn]
> **maroc<u>ain</u>** → **maroc<u>aine</u>**
> **mexic<u>ain</u>** → **mexic<u>aine</u>**
>
> Note that when [ɛ̃] is spelled **-ien** in the masculine form, an extra *n* is added in the feminine form.
>
> **algérien** → **algérie<u>nn</u>e**
> **canadien** → **canadie<u>nn</u>e**
> **tunisien** → **tunisie<u>nn</u>e**

The adjective of nationality is identical to the noun except that it is not capitalized. Example: un Anglais; un étudiant anglais.

l'Angleterre

le Mexique

la Chine

la Tunisie

*In 2006, the Canadian House of Commons recognized "that the Québécois (*people of Quebec*) form a nation within a united Canada."

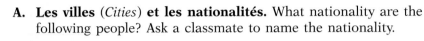

### Allez-y!

**A. Les villes** (*Cities*) **et les nationalités.** What nationality are the following people? Ask a classmate to name the nationality.

la Tunisie

Karim / Tunis

Djamila / Tunis

**MODÈLES:**   É1: Karim habite à (*lives in*) Tunis.
   É2: Ah! Il est (*He is*) tunisien, n'est-ce pas?

   É1: Djamila habite à Tunis.
   É2: Ah! Elle est (*She is*) tunisienne, n'est-ce pas?

## Mots clés

**The preposition *à* + *ville***

**À** indicates location or movement. Used before the name of a city, it means you are in the city or going to the city.

J'habite **à** Genève.
*I live in Geneva.*

Vous allez **à** Montréal.
*You are going to Montreal.*

**1.** Gino / Rome

l'Italie

**2.** Kai / Kyoto

le Japon

**3.** M^me Roberge / Montréal

le Canada

**4.** Éva / Beyrouth

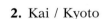

le Liban

**5.** Léopold / Dakar

le Sénégal

**6.** Aurélie / Bruxelles

la Belgique

**7.** Salima / Casablanca

le Maroc

**8.** Zoé / Genève

la Suisse

**B. Les nationalités et les langues.** Working with a partner, give the nationality and probable language(s) of the people from Activity A.

MODÈLES:  Karim → É1: Karim?
  É2: Karim est tunisien. Il parle (*He speaks*) arabe et français.

  Djamila → É2: Djamila?
  É1: Djamila est tunisienne. Elle parle (*She speaks*) arabe et français.

**Langues:** allemand, anglais, arabe, flamand, français, italien, japonais

# Les distractions°

Les... (*f.*) *Entertainment*

Julien    Fatima    Rémi    Anne-Laure    Marc    Thu    Sophie    Allal

| LA MUSIQUE | LE SPORT | LE CINÉMA |
|---|---|---|
| le jazz | le basket-ball | les films (*m.*) d'amour |
| la musique classique | le football | les films d'aventures |
| le rap | le football américain | les films d'horreur |
| le rock | le jogging | les films de science-fiction |
| la world music | le ski | |
| | le tennis | |

 *Allez-y!*

**Préférences.** What do these people like?

MODÈLE:  Rémi → Rémi aime le rock.

1. Et Thu?    3. Et Julien?    5. Et Allal?    7. Et Marc?
2. Et Sophie?    4. Et Anne-Laure?    6. Et Fatima?    8. Et vous?

# Leçon 2

STRUCTURES

## Les articles définis

*Identifying People, Places, and Things*

### Le journaliste et l'étudiante

*Léa contacte Mamadou sur sa page Facebook (Messagerie instantanée).*

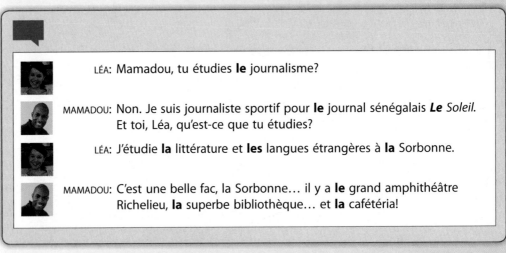

LÉA: Mamadou, tu étudies **le** journalisme?

MAMADOU: Non. Je suis journaliste sportif pour **le** journal sénégalais *Le Soleil*. Et toi, Léa, qu'est-ce que tu étudies?

LÉA: J'étudie **la** littérature et **les** langues étrangères à **la** Sorbonne.

MAMADOU: C'est une belle fac, la Sorbonne… il y a **le** grand amphithéâtre Richelieu, **la** superbe bibliothèque… et **la** cafétéria!

Complétez les phrases selon le dialogue.

1. Mamadou est spécialisé dans _____ journalisme sportif.
2. Léa étudie _____ littérature et _____ langues étrangères à _____ fac de _____ Sorbonne.
3. Mamadou apprécie _____ grand amphi Richelieu, _____ bibliothèque et _____ cafétéria de _____ Sorbonne.

## Singular Forms of Definite Articles

Here are the forms of the singular definite article (**le singulier de l'article défini**) in French, corresponding to *the* in English.

| MASCULINE | | FEMININE | | MASCULINE OR FEMININE BEGINNING WITH A VOWEL OR MUTE **h***| |
|---|---|---|---|---|---|
| **le** livre | *the book* | **la** femme | *the woman* | **l'**ami | *the friend* (m.) |
| **le** cours | *the course* | **la** table | *the table* | **l'**amie | *the friend* (f.) |
| | | | | **l'**homme | *the man* (m.) |
| | | | | **l'**histoire | *the story* (f.) |

*In French, **h** is either *mute* (**muet**, *nonaspirate*) or *aspirate* (**aspiré**). In **l'homme,** the **h** is called *mute*, which simply means that the word **homme** "elides" with a preceding article (**le** + **homme** = **l'homme**). Most **h**'s in French are of this type. However, some **h**'s are aspirate, which means there is no elision; **le héros** (*the hero*) is an example of this. However, in neither case is the **h** pronounced.

**1.** The definite article in French is used to indicate a specific noun.

    Voici **le** resto-U.          *Here's the university restaurant.*

**2.** In French, the definite article is also used with nouns employed in a general sense.

    J'aime **le** café.          *I like coffee.*
    C'est **la** vie!            *That's life!*

[Allez-y! A]

## Plural Form of Definite Articles

|  | SINGULAR | PLURAL |
|---|---|---|
| *Masculine* | **le** touriste | **les** touristes |
| *Feminine* | **la** touriste | |
| *Before a vowel* | **l'**artiste | **les** artistes |

**1.** The plural form (**le pluriel**) of the definite article is always **les.***

    le livre, **les** livres         *the book, the books*
    la femme, **les** femmes      *the woman, the women*
    l'examen, **les** examens     *the exam, the exams*

**2.** Note that in English, the article is omitted with nouns used in a general sense. In French, the definite articles **le, la, l',** and **les** are used.

    J'aime **le** ski.          *I like skiing.*
    **Les** Français aiment **le** vin.    *(Generally speaking) French people like wine.*

## Plural of Nouns

**1.** Most French nouns are made plural by adding an **s** to the singular, as seen in the preceding examples. Here are some other common patterns.

- **-s, -x, -z** → no change

    le cour**s** → les cour**s**     *the course, the courses*
    un choi**x** → des choi**x**     *a choice, some choices*
    le ne**z** → les ne**z**        *the nose, the noses*

---

> ### 🎧 Prononcez bien!
>
> **The vowels in *le, la,* and *les***
>
> Be sure to clearly distinguish between the vowels in **le** (d**e**, **je**, f**e**nêtre), **la** (ç**a**, m**a**dame, ordin**a**teur), and **les** (**et**, c**a**hier, répét**ez**). Tighten the muscles in your mouth and do the following:
>
> Close your mouth and round your lips for **le.**
>
>     [ə]: **le cours**
>
> Open your mouth wide and stretch your lips in a semi-smile for **la.**
>
>     [a]: **la table**
>
> Close your mouth and stretch your lips in a wide smile for **les.**
>
>     [e]: **les cahiers**

---

*As with the indefinite article **des,** there is a **liaison** with a vowel or a vowel sound: **les étudiants, les hommes.**

- **-eau, -ieu** $\rightarrow$ **-eaux, -ieux**

| | |
|---|---|
| le tabl**eau** $\rightarrow$ les tabl**eaux** | *the board, the boards* |
| le bur**eau** $\rightarrow$ les bur**eaux** | *the desk, the desks* |
| le l**ieu** $\rightarrow$ les l**ieux** | *the place, the places* |

- **-al, -ail** $\rightarrow$ **-aux**

| | |
|---|---|
| un hôpit**al** $\rightarrow$ des hôpit**aux** | *a hospital, hospitals* |
| le trav**ail** $\rightarrow$ les trav**aux** | *the work, tasks* |

2. Note that the masculine form is used in French to refer to a group that includes at least one male.

un étudian**t** et sept étudian**tes** $\rightarrow$ des étudian**ts**
un Français et une Français**e** $\rightarrow$ des Français

[Allez-y! B-C]

## Allez-y!

**A. Pensez-y!** (*Think about it!*) Figure out the gender of the following words. Then add the definite article.

**MODÈLE:** femme $\rightarrow$ féminin; la femme

| | | | |
|---|---|---|---|
| **1.** appartement | **4.** tableau | **7.** université | **10.** tourisme |
| **2.** division | **5.** coca-cola | **8.** aventure | **11.** science |
| **3.** italien | **6.** biologie | **9.** personne | **12.** homme |

**B. Suivons le guide!** (*Let's follow the tour guide!*) Show your guests around campus, using the plural of these expressions.

**MODÈLE:** la salle de classe $\rightarrow$ Voilà les salles de classe.

| | |
|---|---|
| **1.** la bibliothèque | **4.** l'étudiant |
| **2.** l'amphi(théâtre) | **5.** le laboratoire de langues |
| **3.** le professeur | **6.** le bureau |

**C. À l'université.** Create sentences using the following words. Then create a different sentence by changing the number and the place.

**MODÈLE:** étudiante / salle de classe $\rightarrow$
Il y a une étudiante dans la salle de classe.
Il y a des étudiantes dans la librairie.
*ou* Il y a des étudiantes dans les salles d'ordinateurs.

| | |
|---|---|
| **1.** tableau / salle de classe | **5.** ordinateur / salle d'ordinateurs |
| **2.** une réunion (*meeting*) / amphithéâtre | **6.** Américaine / restaurant |
| **3.** télévision / laboratoire | **7.** dictionnaire / bibliothèque |
| **4.** cahier / bureau | **8.** écran / salle de classe |

*Le parler jeune*

| | |
|---|---|
| **la fac** | la faculté |
| **une nana** | une fille |
| **un mec, un gars** | un garçon |
| **potasser** | étudier, réviser |
| **un pote** | un ami |

La **fac** de droit est située rue d'Assas.

Voici Virginie. C'est une **nana** sympa!

Ce **mec**, il travaille chez Virgin.

Allô? Non, pas ce soir, je **potasse** mes maths!

Mon **pote** Jules déteste les maths.

# Les verbes réguliers en -er

*Expressing Actions*

## Les étudiants de la Sorbonne

*Mamadou téléphone à Léa.*

MAMADOU: **Tu aimes mieux** la littérature ou les langues étrangères?

LÉA: **J'adore** la littérature et les langues étrangères! Actuellement,* **j'étudie** le russe. Et dans ma classe, nous **commençons** le chinois au deuxième semestre.

MAMADOU: **Vous commencez** le chinois! Bravo! Les étudiants de la Sorbonne sont ambitieux…

LÉA: Et courageux! **Nous travaillons** beaucoup. Mais **nous aimons** aussi les distractions…

*Currently

Des livres pour étudier

Trouvez (*Find*) la forme correcte du verbe dans le dialogue.

1. Tu ———— la littérature ou les langues?
2. J' ———— la littérature.
3. J' ———— le russe.
4. Nous ———— le chinois.
5. Vous ———— le chinois!
6. Nous ———— beaucoup.
7. Nous ———— les distractions.

## Subject Pronouns and *parler*

The subject of a sentence indicates who or what performs the action of the sentence: ***L'étudiant* visite l'université.** A pronoun (**un pronom**) is a word used in place of a noun (**un nom**): ***Il* visite l'université.**

| SUBJECT PRONOUNS AND **parler** (*to speak*) | | | |
|---|---|---|---|
| **SINGULAR** | | **PLURAL** | |
| je parle *I speak* | | nous parlons *we speak* | |
| tu parles *you speak* | | vous parlez *you speak* | |
| il parle *he, it (m.) speaks* | | ils parlent *they (m., m. + f.) speak* | |
| elle parle *she, it (f.) speaks* | | elles parlent *they (f.) speak* | |
| on parle *one speaks* | | | |

1. **Je.** Note that **je** is not capitalized unless it starts a sentence. When a verb begins with a vowel sound, **je** becomes **j'.**

En hiver, **j'aime** faire du ski.  *In winter, I like to go skiing.*

2. **Tu** and **vous.** There are two ways to say *you* in French: **Tu** is used when speaking to a friend, fellow student, relative, child, or pet; **vous** is used when speaking to a person you don't know well or when addressing an older person, someone in authority, or anyone with whom you wish to maintain a certain formality. The plural of both **tu** and **vous** is **vous.** The context will indicate whether **vous** refers to one person or to more than one.

| | |
|---|---|
| Emma, **tu** parles espagnol? | *Emma, do you speak Spanish?* |
| Madame, où habitez-**vous**? | *Ma'am, where do you live?* |
| **Vous** parlez bien français, madame. | *You speak French well, ma'am.* |
| Pardon, messieurs (mesdames, mesdemoiselles), est-ce que **vous** parlez anglais? | *Excuse me, gentlemen (ladies), do you speak English?* |

3. **Il** and **elle.** As you know, all nouns—people and objects—have gender in French. **Il** is the pronoun that refers to a masculine person or object, and **elle** refers to a feminine person or object.

| | |
|---|---|
| Paul travaille. **Il** travaille à la bibliothèque. | *Paul works. He works at the library.* |
| L'ordinateur est cher, mais **il** est aussi utile. | *The computer is expensive, but it is useful as well.* |
| Agathe? **Elle** travaille au café. | *Agathe? She works at the café.* |
| La bibliothèque? **Elle** est ouverte le samedi. | *The library? It is open on Saturdays.* |

The plural counterparts **ils** and **elles** are used in the same way as the singular forms. **Ils** corresponds to masculine plural nouns and to a group that includes at least one masculine noun; **elles** corresponds to feminine plural nouns.

| | |
|---|---|
| Luc et Diane? **Ils** sont toujours ensemble. | *Luc and Diane? They are always together.* |

4. **On.** In English, the words *people, we, one,* or *they* are often used to convey the idea of an indefinite subject. In French, the indefinite pronoun **on** is used, always with the third-person singular of the verb.

| | |
|---|---|
| Ici **on** parle français. | *One speaks French here.* *People (They, We) speak French here.* |

**On** is also used frequently in informal French instead of **nous.**

Nous parlons français. → **On** parle français.

[Allez-y! A]

## Present Tense of -er Verbs

Most French verbs have infinitives ending in **-er: parler** (*to speak*), **aimer** (*to like; to love*). To form the present tense of these verbs, drop the final **-er** and add the endings shown in the chart.*

| PRESENT TENSE OF **aimer** (*to like; to love*) | |
| --- | --- |
| j' aim**e** | nous aim**ons** |
| tu aim**es** | vous aim**ez** |
| il/elle/on aim**e** | ils/elles aim**ent** |

**1.** Note that the present tense (**le présent**) in French has several equivalents in English.

Je **parle** français.
> *I speak French.*
> *I am speaking French.*
> *I do speak French.*

**2.** Other verbs conjugated like **parler** and **aimer** include:

| | | | |
| --- | --- | --- | --- |
| **adorer** | *to love; to adore* | **fumer** | *to smoke* |
| **aimer mieux** | *to prefer* (*to like better*) | **habiter** | *to live* |
| | | **manger**‡ | *to eat* |
| **chercher** | *to look for* | **penser** | *to think* |
| **commencer**† | *to begin* | **porter** | *to wear* |
| **danser** | *to dance* | **regarder** | *to watch; to look at* |
| **demander** | *to ask for* | **rêver** | *to dream* |
| **détester** | *to detest; to hate* | **skier** | *to ski* |
| | | **travailler** | *to work* |
| **donner** | *to give* | **trouver** | *to find* |
| **écouter** | *to listen to* | **visiter** | *to visit* (*a place*) |
| **étudier** | *to study* | | |

Vous **cherchez** le resto-U? — *Are you looking for the cafeteria?*

Nous **étudions** l'informatique. — *We're studying computer science.*

**3.** Some verbs, such as **adorer, aimer (mieux),** and **détester,** can be followed by an infinitive.

J'**aime écouter** la radio. — *I like listening to the radio.*
Je **déteste regarder** la télévision. — *I hate watching television.*

[Allez-y! B-C-D-E]

> ### Grammaire interactive
>
> For more on the present tense of **-er** verbs, watch the corresponding Grammar Tutorial and take a brief practice quiz at **Connect French.**
>
>
>
> |FRENCH
>
> **www.mhconnectfrench.com**

---

*As you know, final **s** is usually not pronounced in French. Final **z** of the second-person plural and the **-ent** of the third-person plural verb forms are also silent.
†The **nous** form of **commencer** is **commençons**. The **cédille** is added to retain the soft **s** sound.
‡The **nous** form of **manger** is **mangeons**. The **e** is kept to retain the soft **g** sound.

## Allez-y!

A. **Dialogue en classe.** Complete the following dialogue with subject pronouns or forms of **parler.**

> LE PROFESSEUR: Tout le monde (*Everybody*), _____¹ parlez français?
> LA CLASSE: Oui, nous _____² français.
> LE PROFESSEUR: Ici, en classe, on _____³ français?
> JIM: Oui, ici _____⁴ parle français.
> GILDAS: Marc et Marie, vous _____⁵ chinois?
> MARC ET MARIE: Oui, _____⁶ parlons chinois.
> CHARLOTTE: Jim, tu _____⁷ allemand?
> JIM: Oui, _____⁸ parle allemand.
> CÉCILE: Paul parle italien?
> JAMEL: Oui, _____⁹ parle italien.

B. *Tu ou vous?* A student guide is asking questions of various people at the Sorbonne. Complete the questions, using the appropriate pronoun (**tu** or **vous**) and the correct form of the verb in parentheses.

1. Madame, _____ _____ (habiter) près de (*near*) l'université?
2. Romain, _____ _____ (chercher) la faculté des sciences?
3. Paul et Lucie, _____ _____ (visiter) le Quartier latin?
4. Monsieur, _____ _____ (trouver) ce que (*what*) _____ _____ (chercher)?
5. Richard, _____ _____ (demander) des renseignements (*information*) sur la cité universitaire?

Étudiants au jardin du Luxembourg

**C. Portraits.** State the preferences of the following people.

> **MODÈLE:** Mon (*My*) cousin… → Mon cousin aime bien le football, mais (*but*) il aime mieux le basket. Il adore le rock et il déteste le travail!

| | | |
|---|---|---|
| Je… | aimer bien | le tennis |
| Mon (Ma) camarade… | aimer mieux | le jogging |
| Mes parents… | adorer | le cinéma |
| Les étudiants… | détester | la littérature |
| Le professeur… | | les maths |
| | | la physique |

**D. Une interview.** Interview your instructor.

> **MODÈLE:** aimer mieux danser ou (*or*) skier → Vous aimez mieux danser ou skier?

1. aimer mieux la télévision ou le cinéma
2. aimer ou détester regarder la télévision
3. aimer mieux le rock ou la musique classique
4. aimer mieux la musique ou le sport
5. aimer mieux les livres ou les magazines

**E. Curiosité.** Find out how your classmate spends his/her free time by asking whether . . .

> **MODÈLE:** il/elle écoute de temps en temps la radio →
> É1: Tu écoutes de temps en temps la radio?
> É2: Oui, j'écoute quelquefois la radio. Et toi?
> É1: Moi, je n'écoute pas la radio.

1. il/elle regarde souvent ou rarement la télévision le week-end
2. il/elle aime le cinéma, en général
3. il/elle mange quelquefois au restaurant
4. il/elle adore ou déteste le sport
5. il/elle skie bien
6. il/elle danse souvent le week-end

Now say which response you find original or strange.

> **MODÈLE:** Sonia déteste le cinéma. C'est bizarre!

## Mots clés

**To express how often you do something**

The following adverbs usually follow the verb.

| | |
|---|---|
| **toujours** | *always* |
| **souvent** | *often* |
| **quelquefois** | *sometimes* |
| **rarement** | *rarely* |

**D'habitude** (*Usually*), **en général** (*generally*), and **de temps en temps** (*from time to time*) are adverbs that are most often placed at the beginning of a sentence.

Je regarde **souvent** la télévision.

Annie et moi, nous étudions **quelquefois** à la bibliothèque.

**En général,** j'étudie le week-end.

# Le blog de Léa

## Salut tout le monde!

mardi 17 mai

*Bonjour! Guten Tag! Hello! Salaam! Buon giorno! Nǐ hǎo! Buenos días! Shalom!* Salut tout le monde!

J'ai[1] une amie belge: c'est Juliette. J'ai un ami martiniquais: il s'appelle Hector. Et j'ai un copain marocain, Hassan. Il a un restaurant au Quartier latin, proche de ma fac.[2] Mais je cherche aussi des amis chinois, japonais, mexicains, allemands, américains… des amis de tous les pays.[3] À Paris, c'est possible, non?

Léa

Moi, devant le restaurant d'Hassan

### COMMENTAIRES

**Alexis**
Bonjour Léa!
Mon chien et moi,[4] nous sommes[5] québécois. Nous parlons français. Nous sommes très sympathiques.[6]

**Poema**
Léa, bonjour!
Je m'appelle Poema. Je ne suis pas[7] chinoise, je ne suis pas américaine… Je suis tahitienne. Je suis isolée[8] à Paris et je cherche des amis français.

**Mamadou**
Salut Léa!
J'ai[9] une amie française: c'est toi. Mais tu as des copines[10]… Tu me les présentes[11]? Juliette, par exemple… À bientôt, j'espère[12]!

---

[1]*I have* [2]*proche… close to the university* (la Sorbonne) [3]*de… from all over the world* [4]*Mon… My dog and I* [5]*nous… we are* [6]*nice*
[7]*Je… I'm not* [8]*lonely* [9]*I have* [10]*girlfriends* [11]*Tu… Will you introduce them to me?* [12]*I hope*

## Quartier latin: le quartier général des étudiants

À la terrasse du café de la Sorbonne, Éva, d'origine russe, discute avec ses trois amis: Bruno, un étudiant lyonnais, Maren, une jeune Allemande qui étudie le droit social à Paris, et Ahmed, un jeune Marocain en doctorat de cinéma. Cette scène est typique du Quartier latin, zone cosmopolite, sorte de campus international au centre de Paris.

Avec ses librairies et ses bibliothèques, le Quartier latin est l'univers de la culture. Les grands lycées (Louis-le-Grand, Henri IV) et les universités comme[1] la célèbre Sorbonne fondée en 1257[2] par Robert de Sorbon continuent à former[3] les élites intellectuelles.

**Un café du Quartier latin.** Une population jeune, internationale, active et cultivée habite au Quartier latin. C'est le quartier des amitiés éternelles, des idées géniales et des discussions passionnées sur la politique, l'art et la vie. C'est le symbole de la vie étudiante.

Dans les boutiques du boulevard Saint-Michel, les vêtements[4] remplacent les livres. Mais les petites rues adjacentes ont encore[5] beaucoup de charme: petits restaurants délicieux, cinémas comme le fameux Champollion, boutiques exotiques, bistros et bars animés, cybercafés.

Le jardin du Luxembourg est le parc du quartier. Dans ses allées[6] romantiques, les étudiants discutent, méditent, se relaxent avant ou après un examen. Au Quartier latin, tout est conçu[7] pour le travail et pour le bonheur[8] des étudiants.

[1]*such as*  [2]mille deux cent cinquante-sept  [3]*educate*  [4]*clothes*  [5]*ont… still have*  [6]*footpaths*  [7]*conceived*  [8]*happiness*

**À vous!**

1. Désirez-vous visiter le Quartier latin? Pourquoi? Imaginez votre itinéraire.
2. Le Quartier latin est-il différent d'un campus à l'américaine? Développez votre réponse.
3. Quels détails vous intéressent sur cette photo du Quartier latin?

**Parlons-en!**

1. Trouvez un plan du Quartier latin sur Internet. Imprimez-le. (*Print it.*)
2. Par groupes de trois étudiants, observez le plan.
3. Situez le boulevard Saint-Michel, la Sorbonne, le lycée Henri IV, le jardin du Luxembourg.
4. À partir du (*Starting from the*) métro Saint-Michel (sur la photo), créez un itinéraire pour visiter le Quartier latin.
5. Présentez votre itinéraire à la classe. Utilisez le verbe *visiter*:

**On visite la Sorbonne, le jardin du Luxembourg…**

# Leçon 3

**STRUCTURES**

## Le verbe *être*

*Identifying People and Things*

### Les amis de Léa

*Appel (Call) vidéo entre Mamadou et Léa.*

MAMADOU: Salut Léa! Tu parles de tes amis sur ton blog. **Ils sont** sympas?

LÉA: **Mes amis sont** intelligents, amusants et originaux. Juliette et moi, **nous sommes** particulièrement proches.*

MAMADOU: Hector, qui **est-ce?**

LÉA: Hector, **c'est** un danseur professionnel.

MAMADOU: Et Hassan, **c'est** qui?

LÉA: **C'est** un ami adorable!

MAMADOU: Moi aussi, **je suis** adorable! Et toi aussi, **tu es** adorable!

▼ AUDIO & VIDEO

MESSAGE          VIDEO ●

*close

Vrai ou faux?

1. Les amis de Léa sont amusants.
2. Léa et Juliette sont vraiment (*really*) proches.
3. Hector est l'ami de Mamadou.
4. Hassan est l'ami de Léa.
5. Hassan est danseur.

## Forms of *être*

| PRESENT TENSE OF **être** (*to be*) | | | |
|---|---|---|---|
| je | **suis** | nous | **sommes** |
| tu | **es** | vous | **êtes** |
| il/elle/on | **est** | ils/elles | **sont** |

## Uses of *être*

**1.** The uses of **être** closely parallel those of *to be*.

| | |
|---|---|
| Fabrice **est** intelligent. | *Fabrice is intelligent.* |
| Est-ce que Clarisse **est** organisée? | *Is Clarisse organized?* |
| Fabrice et Clarisse **sont** à la bibliothèque. | *Fabrice and Clarisse are at the library.* |

**2.** In identifying someone's nationality, religion, or profession, no article is used following **être.**

| | |
|---|---|
| Je **suis anglais.** | *I am English.* |
| Je **suis catholique;** mon ami **est musulman.** | *I'm (a) Catholic; my friend is (a) Muslim.* |
| —Vous **êtes professeur?** | *Are you a teacher?* |
| —Non, je **suis étudiant.** | *No, I am a student.* |

## *C'est* versus *il/elle est*

**1.** The indefinite pronoun **ce (c')** is an invariable third-person pronoun. **Ce** has various English equivalents: *this, that, these, those, he, she, they,* and *it.*

**2.** The expression **c'est** (plural, **ce sont**) is used before modified nouns (always with an article) and proper names; it usually answers the questions **Qui est-ce?** and **Qu'est-ce que c'est?**

| | |
|---|---|
| —Qui est-ce? | *Who is it?* |
| —C'est Maxime. C'est un étudiant belge. | *It's Maxime. He is a Belgian student.* |
| —Ce sont des Français? | *Are they French?* |
| —Non, ce sont des Italiens. | *No, they're Italian.* |
| —Qu'est-ce que c'est? | *What is that?* |
| —C'est un ordinateur. | *That's (It's) a computer.* |
| —Et ça, qu'est-ce que c'est? | *And that, what is it?* |
| —Oh ça, c'est une souris. | *Oh, that's a mouse.* |

**3.** **C'est** can also be followed by an adjective, to refer to a general situation or to describe something that is understood in the context of the conversation.

| | |
|---|---|
| Le français? C'est facile! | *French? It's easy!* |
| J'adore la France. C'est magnifique! | *I love France. It's great!* |

*(continued)*

## Prononcez bien!

**The vowels in *et* and *est***

Be sure to pronounce a single and brief sound in both **et** and **est**, as opposed to the combination of sounds in the English letter *a*. Close your mouth and stretch your lips for [e] in **et** more than for [ɛ] in **est**. The sound [e] is usually found at the end of a syllable or word, whereas [ɛ] tends to appear before a pronounced consonant.*

[e]: **t<u>é</u>lé, all<u>er</u>, n<u>ez</u>, <u>et</u>**

[ɛ]: **mat<u>iè</u>res, <u>ê</u>tre, <u>ai</u>me, s<u>ei</u>ze, m<u>e</u>rci**

*some exceptions: **mai, est, très**

4. **Il/Elle est** (and **Ils/Elles sont**) are generally used to describe someone or something already mentioned in the conversation. They are usually followed by an adjective, a prepositional phrase, and occasionally by an unmodified noun (without an article).

—La librairie?　　　　　　　　*The bookstore?*
—Elle est dans la rue Mouffetard.　*It's on Mouffetard Street.*

—Voici Karim. Il est étudiant en biologie.　　　　*Here's Karim. He's a biology student.*
—Il est français?　　　　　　*Is he French?*
—Oui, il est français, d'origine algérienne.　*Yes, he's French, of Algerian descent.*

 *Allez-y!*

A. **Un examen.** Complete the following dialogue between Fabrice and Clarisse using the correct forms of the verb **être.**

FABRICE: Ces livres _____¹ difficiles!
CLARISSE: Pas pour toi, tu _____² un génie!
FABRICE: Oui, mais le professeur _____³ très exigeant (*demanding*).
CLARISSE: Et il dit (*says*) toujours: «Vous _____⁴ une étudiante intelligente, mademoiselle.»
FABRICE: Nous _____⁵ peut-être (*maybe*) intelligents, mais moi, je ne _____⁶ pas prêt pour l'examen!

**Qui est-ce?** Identify each person described here, based on the dialogue.

1. C'est une personne très exigeante. C'est _____.
2. C'est une étudiante intelligente. C'est _____.
3. Il n'est pas prêt pour l'examen. C'est _____.

B. **Deux étudiants africains à Paris.** Tell about these young people by completing the descriptions with **c', il,** or **elle.**

Voici Fatima. _____¹ est marocaine. _____² est étudiante en philosophie. _____³ est une personne sociable et dynamique. Son petit ami (*boyfriend*) s'appelle Barthélémy. _____⁴ est sénégalais. _____⁵ est un jeune homme enthousiaste. _____⁶ est aussi un peu timide. _____⁷ est un étudiant sérieux.

C. **La France et les Français.** Taking turns with a classmate, ask and answer questions using **c'est** and **ce n'est pas** (*it's not*).

MODÈLE: le sport préféré des Français:
le jogging, le football →
É1: Le sport préféré des Français, c'est le jogging ou le football?
É2: Ce n'est pas le jogging, c'est le football!

1. un symbole de la France: la rose, la fleur de lys
2. un président français: Sartre, Hollande
3. un cadeau (*present*) des Français aux Américains: la Maison-Blanche (*White House*), la Statue de la Liberté
4. une ville avec beaucoup de Français: La Nouvelle-Orléans, St. Louis
5. un génie français: Mᵐᵉ Curie, Albert Einstein
6. parler français: difficile, facile

**D. Et vous, comment êtes-vous?** Tell a little about yourself.

Je m'appelle _____.
Je suis un(e) _____. (femme / homme)
Je suis _____. (étudiant[e] / professeur)
Je suis _____. (nationalité)
J'habite à _____. (ville)
Je suis l'ami(e) de _____.
J'aime _____.

Now describe one of your classmates using the same guidelines.

Il/Elle s'appelle…

# La négation *ne… pas*

*Expressing Disagreement*

## Le Festival du film d'horreur

*Juliette téléphone à Léa.*

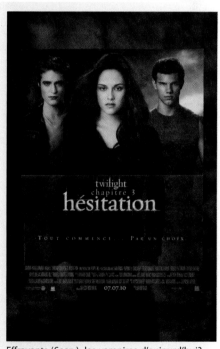

JULIETTE: Allô, Léa, Il y a un festival du film d'horreur au Champollion. Ce soir, c'est *Dracula*.
LÉA: **Je n'aime pas** les films d'horreur.
JULIETTE: **Tu n'aimes pas** les films d'horreur? **Ce n'est pas** possible!
LÉA: C'est possible! Parce que **je n'aime pas** la violence.
JULIETTE: Mais *Dracula*, **ce n'est pas** un film violent! Il y a de l'humour…
LÉA: **Je n'apprécie pas** cette sorte d'humour.
JULIETTE: Qu'est-ce que tu aimes alors?
LÉA: J'adore les films d'amour…
JULIETTE: **Tu n'es pas** originale!

Effrayants (*Scary*), les vampires d'aujourd'hui?

Vrai ou faux?

1. Léa aime les films d'horreur.
2. *Dracula* est un film d'amour.
3. Léa apprécie l'humour du film *Dracula*.
4. Léa n'est pas originale.

1. To make a sentence negative in French, **ne** is placed before a conjugated verb and **pas** after it.

Je **parle** chinois. → Je **ne parle pas** chinois.
Elles **regardent** souvent la télévision. → Elles **ne regardent pas** souvent la télévision.

**Grammaire interactive**

For more on subject pronouns, the verb **être,** and negation, watch the corresponding Grammar Tutorial and take a brief practice quiz at **Connect French.**

www.mhconnectfrench.com

**2. Ne** becomes **n'** before a vowel or a mute **h.**

> Elle aime les films vampire. → Elle **n'a**ime pas les films vampire.
> Nous habitons ici. → Nous **n'h**abitons pas ici.

**3.** If a verb is followed by an infinitive, **ne** and **pas** surround the conjugated verb.

> Il aime étudier. → Il **n'aime pas** étudier.

**4.** In informal conversation, the **e** in **ne** is usually not pronounced; some people do not say the **ne** at all.

> Je **ne** pense **pas** (*I don't think so*).
> Je n∉ pense **pas.** → J∉ (n∉) pense **pas.**

 *Allez-y!*

**A. Portrait de Victor.** Here is some information about Victor.

Victor habite à la cité universitaire et, en général, il étudie à la bibliothèque. Après (*After*) les cours, il parle avec ses (*his*) amis au café. Le soir (*In the evening*), il écoute la radio: il aime beaucoup le jazz! Il adore le sport, il skie très bien et le week-end, il regarde les matchs de football à la télévision.

Clarisse is quite different from Victor. Tell what Clarisse doesn't like and doesn't do. Replace **il** with **elle** in the paragraph and make all the verbs negative. **Clarisse...**

**B. Interview à deux.** Find out about a classmate by asking about the following activities, habits, and preferences. Answer your partner's questions, too.

> **MODÈLE:** travailler →
> É1: Tu travailles?
> É2: Non, je ne travaille pas. (Oui, je travaille.) Et toi?

**1.** parler italien; russe; espagnol; anglais
**2.** habiter quelle ville; Paris; New York; Abidjan; Cincinnati; la cité-U
**3.** étudier la psychologie; la littérature; l'informatique; la biologie; le commerce; les langues étrangères
**4.** aimer les examens; les films de science-fiction; les films d'amour; le rap; la musique country
**5.** aimer le sport; le football américain; le football; le basket-ball; le hockey
**6.** détester les maths; l'histoire; la politique; la science; la pyschologie
**7.** surfer le Web; écouter la radio; parler avec des amis; manger au restaurant; manger au resto-U; skier; danser

**Résumez!** Now summarize for the class five things you found out about your partner.

**C. Et vous?** Tell about yourself by completing the sentences.

**1.** J'aime _____, mais (*but*) je n'aime pas _____.
**2.** J'adore _____, mais je déteste _____.
**3.** J'écoute _____, mais je n'écoute pas _____.
**4.** J'aime _____, mais j'aime mieux _____.
**5.** Je n'étudie pas _____. J'étudie _____.

Prononcez bien!

1. **Masculine vs. feminine forms of nationalities** (page 35)

   **Beaucoup de nationalités!** Your housemate is back from his second introductory French class. He's impressed by the number of nationalities represented in his class. He lists them for you, although he omits articles as he is still unsure about them. You help him by telling him the appropriate article **un** or **une.**

   **MODÈLE:** *You hear:* mexicaine
   *You say:* une Mexicaine

2. **The vowels in *le, la,* and *les*** (page 39)

   **Une nouvelle colocataire!** One of your housemates has moved out and Isabelle, a French student, is moving in. She asks you to help her unpack. Listen to what she says and complete the paragraph with the names of the objects she asks you to bring into her room. **Attention!** Don't forget the article (**le, la,** or **les**).

   **1.**  **2.**  **3.**  **4.**

   **5.**  **6.**  **7.**

   ISABELLE: «S'il te plaît, apporte (*bring*) _____,[1] _____,[2]

   _____,[3] _____,[4] _____,[5] _____,[6]

   et _____.[7] Merci!»

3. **The vowels in *et* and *est*** (page 50)

   **Où étudier?** You are a new student at the university. See what Isabelle has to say about good places to study. Read the following paragraph aloud. Your partner will indicate whether the bold letters correspond to [e] as in **et** or to [ɛ] as in **est**.

   En gén**é**ral,[1, 2] j'**ai**me[3] **é**tudi**er**[4, 5] à la biblioth**è**que.[6] Il y a beaucoup de caf**és**[7] dans le quarti**er**[8] univ**er**sitaire,[9, 10] m**ai**s[11] p**er**sonn**e**llement,[12, 13] je d**é**teste[14, 15] y (*there*) **é**tudier[16]: il y a trop de bruit (*too much noise*).

   | | [e] | [ɛ] | | [e] | [ɛ] | | [e] | [ɛ] | | [e] | [ɛ] |
   |---|---|---|---|---|---|---|---|---|---|---|---|
   | **1.** | ☐ | ☐ | **5.** | ☐ | ☐ | **9.** | ☐ | ☐ | **13.** | ☐ | ☐ |
   | **2.** | ☐ | ☐ | **6.** | ☐ | ☐ | **10.** | ☐ | ☐ | **14.** | ☐ | ☐ |
   | **3.** | ☐ | ☐ | **7.** | ☐ | ☐ | **11.** | ☐ | ☐ | **15.** | ☐ | ☐ |
   | **4.** | ☐ | ☐ | **8.** | ☐ | ☐ | **12.** | ☐ | ☐ | **16.** | ☐ | ☐ |

# Leçon 4

 ## Lecture

### Avant de lire

**Predicting from context.**   When reading a text in your native language, you constantly—though perhaps unconsciously—make use of contextual information. This information gives you an immediate, overall orientation; it also allows you to figure out the meaning of unfamiliar words. Here are some ways to use contextual information when reading French texts. You will practice these techniques in the reading that follows.

1. Orient yourself using graphic elements: logos, illustrations, headings, and large or heavy type.

   • First, scan the brochure that follows and identify the institution being publicized and its location. Look at the photo. How would you describe the setting? (Is it modern? traditional? cosmopolitan?)
   • Next, quickly read through the first paragraph, underlining the cognates (**mots apparentés**) that you find. How well did your description match the text?

2. Use cognates to help you deduce the meaning of unfamiliar terms.

   • Read the following phrase from the brochure and try to figure out the meaning of the word **logement:**

      **logement** dans des familles francophones ou dans les résidences universitaires

   Were you able to infer that **logement** means *lodging*?

3. Watch for near cognates.

   • In the following phrases, your developing linguistic intuition should tell you that the words in boldface cannot be translated by the English form that most closely resembles them. Can you find an alternative to them that is close in meaning?

      **plus de** soixante ans d'expérience
      **formation** solide des enseignants (*teachers*)
      activités de **bénévolat** en milieu (*setting*) francophone

4. Also be aware of false cognates.

   • What do you think are the false cognates in the following phrases?

      équipe de moniteurs
      stages de travaux pratiques en milieu de travail

5. Now that you have had the chance to refine your ability to recognize cognates, near cognates, and false cognates, scan the bulleted lists beneath each heading in the text and give a suitable English equivalent for them. Although you may not determine the precise meaning of those headings, you should be able to come close.

**À propos de la lecture...**
This reading is taken from a brochure published by the **Université Laval** in Quebec City. There are many schools and colleges that offer French immersion programs throughout France and the French-speaking world.

## Étudier le français... à QUÉBEC, bien sûr!

Plaque tournante de la francophonie, Québec vous offre le meilleur de deux mondes, le charme européen au cœur de la modernité nord-américaine.

Un séjour linguistique à Québec vous assure une immersion totale dans une ville francophone aux dimensions humaines (632 000 habitants), où vous vous sentirez en toute sécurité.

## et à l'Université LAVAL évidemment!

### QUALITÉ DES COURS
- plus de soixante-quinze ans d'expérience
- formation solide des enseignants
- matériel pédagogique «sur mesure»

### SOUTIEN PÉDAGOGIQUE
- conseillers pédagogiques
- enseignement complémentaire «individualisé» pour les étudiants qui éprouvent des difficultés (trimestres d'automne et d'hiver)
- laboratoires de langues et laboratoires informatiques
- enseignement assisté par ordinateur

### ENCADREMENT
- équipe de moniteurs
- activités socio-culturelles et sportives
- excursions
- stages de travaux pratiques en milieu de travail (trimestres d'automne et d'hiver)
- activités de bénévolat en milieu francophone (trimestres d'automne et d'hiver)

## Cours à tous les niveaux pendant toute l'année

### Programme spécial de français pour non-francophones

Les étudiants peuvent s'inscrire à l'une ou l'autre des sessions suivantes:

| ÉTÉ | mai-juin | (5 sem. – 7 crédits) |
| | juillet-août | (5 sem. – 7 crédits) |
| AUTOMNE | septembre-décembre | (15 sem. – 16 crédits) |
| HIVER | janvier-avril | (15 sem. – 16 crédits) |

Lors des trimestres d'automne et d'hiver les étudiants du niveau supérieur suivent leurs cours dans le cadre des programmes réguliers de français langue seconde (certificat, diplôme, baccalauréat).

### PRIX ABORDABLE
- tous les étudiants de ces programmes de français paient les frais de scolarité des étudiants québécois
- coût de la vie peu élevé
- logement dans des familles francophones ou dans les résidences universitaires

### Pour obtenir plus de renseignements sur
- les cours
- l'admission
- le logement
- le visa d'étudiant
- les assurances maladie
- les activités socio-culturelles
- etc.

### demandez notre brochure en écrivant à:
École des langues vivantes
Pavillon Charles-De Koninck (2301)
Université Laval
Québec (Québec) G1V 0A6 Canada
Téléphone: (418) 656-2321
Télécopieur: (418) 656-7018
Courriel: elul@elul.ulaval.ca
http://www.elul.ulaval.ca/lecole

*Compréhension*

**À l'Université Laval.** Are the following statements true (**vrai**) or false (**faux**)? Underline the words in the brochure on the preceding page that support your answers, and correct any false statements to make them true.

1. V  F  The **Université Laval** has just begun to offer French courses for foreign students.
2. V  F  Individualized instruction is offered for those who need help.
3. V  F  Students may rent apartments in town.
4. V  F  The university offers both classroom and extracurricular activities.
5. V  F  Some courses are given in English.

 Écriture

The writing activities **Par écrit** and **Journal intime** can be found in the Workbook/Laboratory Manual to accompany *Vis-à-vis*.

# Pour s'amuser

Un prof de philo présente un sujet de discussion: «Prouvez que cette chaise n'existe pas.»

Immédiatement, la classe cherche des idées. Les étudiants proposent des arguments, développent des raisonnements compliqués...

Seule Mélanie est silencieuse. Soudain, elle demande: «Quelle chaise?»

 # Le vidéoblog de Léa

## En bref

In her videoblog, Léa describes her neighborhood, **le Quartier latin.** At Hassan's restaurant, the four friends each give their opinion of the neighborhood.

## Vocabulaire en contexte

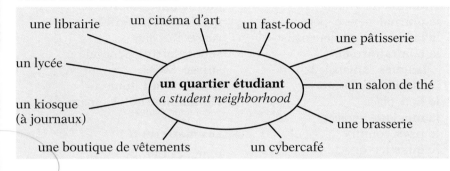

une librairie · un cinéma d'art · un fast-food · une pâtisserie · un lycée · **un quartier étudiant** *a student neighborhood* · un salon de thé · un kiosque (à journaux) · une brasserie · une boutique de vêtements · un cybercafé

Ma fac: la Sorbonne à Paris

## Visionnez!

Indicate whether each statement is true (**vrai**) or false (**faux**).

1. _____ Léa habite le Quartier latin depuis longtemps (*for a long time*).
2. _____ Le Quartier latin est un quartier intellectuel et un centre culturel riche en loisirs (*leisure activities*).
3. _____ Les cafés du quartier sont trop (*too*) touristiques.
4. _____ Il y a de plus en plus de (*more and more*) fast-foods et de boutiques de vêtements.
5. _____ C'est Juliette qui préfère le Quartier latin.

## Analysez!

Answer the following questions in English.

1. In what ways does the **Quartier latin** continue to evolve?
2. How does Juliette's perspective on this evolution differ from those of her friends? With whom do you identify?

## Comparez!

Rewatch the cultural section of the video. Then use the vocabulary presented above, as well as other words you know, to compare your own campus neighborhood to that of the **Quartier latin.** Tell what sorts of places are similar and what your neighborhood lacks. Do you have something in your neighborhood that wasn't mentioned in the video?

> **MODÈLE:** Dans mon quartier, il y a des fast-foods, comme (*as*) à Paris. Mais, il n'y a pas de (*there isn't any*) salon de thé.

Do you prefer your own neighborhood or the **Quartier latin**?

## Note culturelle

The name *Quartier latin* has its roots in two historic facts. First, the name reminds us that Paris grew out of the ancient Roman town of *Lutèce*. At the same time, the name reflects the historic fact that this neighborhood has been a center of education since the Middle Ages. In those early years, professors and students spoke Latin, which was the official language of instruction until the French Revolution.

# Vocabulaire

## Verbes

**adorer** to love; to adore
**aimer** to like; to love
  **aimer mieux** to prefer (like better)
**chercher** to look for
**commencer** to begin
**danser** to dance
**demander** to ask for
**détester** to detest
**donner** to give
**écouter** to listen to
**être** to be
**étudier** to study
**fumer** to smoke
**habiter** to live
**manger** to eat
**parler** to speak
**regarder** to look at; to watch
**rêver** to dream
**skier** to ski
**travailler** to work
**trouver** to find
**visiter** to visit (*a place*)

## Substantifs

**l'ami(e)** (*m., f.*) friend
**l'amphithéâtre** (*m.*) lecture hall
**la bibliothèque** library
**le bureau** office; desk
**le café** café; cup of coffee
**le cinéma** movies; movie theater
**la cité universitaire (la cité-U)** residence halls
**le cours** course
**le dictionnaire** dictionary
**l'école** (*f.*) school
**l'examen** (*m.*) test, exam

**la faculté** division (*academic*)
**la femme** woman
**le film** film
**le gymnase** gymnasium
**l'homme** (*m.*) man
**le journal** newspaper
**le/la journaliste** journalist
**le laboratoire de langues** language lab
**la librairie** bookstore
**le lieu** place
**la musique** music
**le pays** country
**le quartier** quarter, neighborhood
**la radio** radio
**le restaurant** restaurant
**le restaurant universitaire (le resto-U)** university cafeteria
**le sport** sport; sports
**le travail** work
**l'université** (*f.*) university
**la vie** life
**la ville** city
**la visite** visit

À REVOIR: **le cahier, l'étudiant(e), le livre, le professeur, la salle de classe**

## Les nationalités (f.)*

**algérien(ne)** Algerian
**allemand(e)** German
**américain(e)** American
**anglais(e)** English
**belge** Belgian
**canadien(ne)** Canadian
**chinois(e)** Chinese
**espagnol(e)** Spanish

**français(e)** French
**italien(ne)** Italian
**japonais(e)** Japanese
**libanais(e)** Lebanese
**marocain(e)** Moroccan
**mexicain(e)** Mexican
**russe** Russian
**sénégalais(e)** Senegalese
**suisse** Swiss
**tunisien(ne)** Tunisian
**vietnamien(ne)** Vietnamese

## Les matières (f.)

**l'allemand** (*m.*) German
**l'anglais** (*m.*) English
**la biologie** biology
**la chimie** chemistry
**le chinois** Chinese
**le commerce** business
**le droit** law
**l'économie** (*f.*) economics
**l'espagnol** (*m.*) Spanish
**le flamand** Flemish
**le génie** engineering
**la géographie** geography
**la géologie** geology
**l'histoire** (*f.*) history
**l'informatique** (*f.*) computer science
**l'italien** (*m.*) Italian
**le japonais** Japanese
**les langues** (*f.*) **étrangères** foreign languages
**la linguistique** linguistics
**la littérature** literature
**les mathématiques (les maths)** (*f.*) mathematics
**la philosophie** philosophy

---

*These nationalities are capitalized when used as a noun (*e.g.,* **une Algérienne, des Français,** etc.)

**la physique** physics
**la psychologie** psychology
**les sciences** (*f.*)
   **naturelles** natural sciences
**la sociologie** sociology

**Mots et expressions divers**

**à** at; in
**après** after
**aussi** also

**avec** with
**d'accord** okay; agreed
**dans** in
**de** of, from
**de temps en temps** from time
   to time
**en** in
**en général** generally
**ici** here
**maintenant** now
**mais** but

**moi** me
**ou** or
**pour** for, in order to
**quelquefois** sometimes
**rarement** rarely
**souvent** often
**toujours** always
**voici** here is/are
**voilà** there is/are

# Elles ont l'air chic!°

*Elles... They look stylish!*

Léa

**Les dossiers de Léa**

➤ Mes photos
  ➤ Le nouveau chic parisien
  ➤ Mes bonnes adresses
  ➤ Le marché aux puces

Le nouveau chic parisien

# Dans ce chapitre...

## OBJECTIFS COMMUNICATIFS

➤ describing people, places, and things

➤ talking about personalities, clothing, and colors

➤ expressing possession and sensations

➤ mentioning specific places or people

➤ getting information

➤ learning to distinguish between and pronounce selected sounds in French

Mes bonnes adresses

## PAROLES (Leçon 1)

➤ Les adjectifs de personnalité

➤ Les vêtements et les couleurs

➤ Les descriptions physiques et mentales

## STRUCTURES (Leçons 2 et 3)

➤ Le verbe **avoir**

➤ Les adjectifs qualificatifs

➤ Les questions à réponse affirmative ou négative

➤ Les prepositions **à** et **de**

Le marché aux puces

## CULTURE

➤ Le blog de Léa: *En jupe ou en pantalon?*

➤ Reportage: *Dis-moi où tu t'habilles*

➤ Lecture: *Paris-Shopping: quelques recommandations* (Leçon 4)

Mc Graw Hill Education **connect** |FRENCH
www.mhconnectfrench.com

# Leçon 1

## Quatre personnalités différentes

Hadrien est un jeune homme **enthousiaste, idéaliste** et **sincère.** Il est **sensible** (*sensitive*) mais **travailleur** (*hard-working*).

Béatrice est une jeune femme **sociable, sympathique** (*nice, likeable*) et **dynamique.** Elle n'est pas **égoïste** (*selfish*).

Nathalie est une jeune femme **calme, réaliste** et **raisonnable.** Elle est rarement **triste** (*sad*). Ses études sont assez **difficiles.**

Olivier est un jeune homme **individualiste, excentrique** et **drôle** (*funny*). Il n'est pas **paresseux** (*lazy*).

## Allez-y!

**A. Qualités.** Tell about these people by paraphrasing each statement.

**MODÈLE:** Béatrice aime parler avec des amis. →
C'est une jeune femme sociable.

1. Hadrien parle avec sincérité.
2. Nathalie n'aime pas l'extravagance.
3. Olivier est amusant.
4. Béatrice aime l'action.
5. Hadrien parle avec enthousiasme.
6. Olivier n'est pas conformiste.
7. Nathalie regarde la vie avec réalisme.
8. Olivier aime l'excentricité.
9. Nathalie n'est pas nerveuse.

**B. Question de personnalité.** What are these different people like? Describe them using at least three adjectives.

**Autres adjectifs possibles:** antipathique, calme, conformiste, hypocrite, matérialiste, modeste, optimiste, pauvre (*poor*), pessimiste, riche, solitaire

**MODÈLE:** votre meilleur ami / meilleure amie (*f.*) (*your best friend*) →
Il/Elle est calme, sincère...

1. votre meilleur ami / meilleure amie
2. votre père (*father*)
3. votre mère (*mother*)
4. votre camarade de chambre (*roommate*)
5. votre professeur de français
6. le président américain
7. Lady Gaga
8. LeBron James
9. Bradley Cooper
10. Angelina Jolie

**Et vous?** Now describe yourself. Begin your sentence with **Je suis...** , **mais je ne suis pas...**

**C. Interview.** Ask a classmate the following questions. Use **très, assez, peu,** or **un peu** when appropriate.

**MODÈLE:** sociable ou solitaire →
É1: Es-tu sociable ou solitaire?
É2: Moi, je suis assez sociable. Et toi?

1. sincère ou hypocrite
2. excentrique ou conformiste
3. triste ou drôle
4. sympathique ou antipathique
5. calme ou dynamique
6. réaliste ou idéaliste
7. raisonnable ou inflexible
8. optimiste ou pessimiste

Now summarize by stating a few characteristics of your classmate, along with their opposites.

---

### Mots clés

**How to qualify your description**

When you first learn a foreign language, you inevitably exaggerate a little because you do not yet have the tools to convey nuances. The following adverbs may be useful.

| | |
|---|---|
| **très** | *very* |
| **assez** | *somewhat* |
| **peu** | *hardly* |
| **un peu** | *a little* |

Jeanne est **très** calme mais Jacques est **un peu** nerveux.

Mon chien (*dog*) est **peu** intelligent mais il est **assez** drôle.

# Les vêtements et les couleurs

un imperméable
un jean
un blouson
un chemisier
un manteau
un tailleur
une veste
un veston
une cravate
une chemise
un costume
une jupe
un chapeau
un sac à dos
une robe
un sac à main
des chaussures (f.)
une chaussette
des bottes (f.)
un pull-over
des tennis (m.)
un maillot de bain
un tee-shirt
des sandales (f.)
un pantalon
un short

jaune   orange   rouge   rose   violette   bleu   vert

marron   noir   gris   blanche

M. Beaujour **porte** (*is wearing*) **un costume gris** et **une cravate orange.**

## Allez-y!

**A. Qu'est-ce qu'ils portent?** Describe what these people are wearing.

**Bruno**　　　　**M^me Dupuy**　　　　**Aurélie**　　　　**M. Martin**

1. Bruno porte une casquette, _____.
2. M^me Dupuy porte _____.
3. Aurélie porte un béret, _____.
4. M. Martin porte _____.

**B. Un vêtement pour chaque (*each*) occasion.** Describe in as much detail as possible what you wear when you go to these places.

1. à un match de football américain
2. à un concert de rock
3. à une soirée
4. à une interview
5. à l'université
6. à la plage (*beach*)

**C. De quelle couleur?** Ask a classmate to state the colors of the following things.

**MODÈLE:** le drapeau (*flag*) américain →
　　　　É1: De quelle couleur est le drapeau américain?
　　　　É2: Le drapeau américain est rouge, blanc et bleu.

1. le drapeau français
2. le ciel (*sky*)
3. un éléphant
4. le charbon (*coal*)
5. le lait (*milk*)
6. un tigre
7. un zèbre
8. le jade

# Les amis d'Anne et de Céline

Lise est grande, belle et dynamique. Elle a (*has*) les yeux verts et les cheveux blonds. (Elle est blonde.)

Léo a les cheveux noirs. Il est beau et charmant. Il est de taille moyenne (*medium height*).

Laure est aussi de taille moyenne. Elle a les yeux marron et les cheveux courts et roux. (Elle est rousse [*redheaded*].)

Jacques est très sportif. Il est grand, il a les cheveux longs et châtains* (*light brown*).

Thu est très petite et intelligente. Elle a les cheveux noirs et raides (*straight*).

## Allez-y!

**A. Erreur!** Correct any statements that are wrong.

> **MODÈLE:** Léo a les cheveux châtains. → Non, il a les cheveux noirs.

**1.** Jacques a les cheveux courts. **2.** Laure a les cheveux longs et châtains. **3.** Thu a les cheveux noirs. **4.** Laure a les yeux noirs. **5.** Lise a les cheveux roux. **6.** Léo est très grand. **7.** Lise est de taille moyenne. **8.** Thu est petite. **9.** Léo et Lise sont petits. **10.** Laure est blonde et Lise est rousse.

**B. Vos camarades de classe.** Describe the hair, eyes, and height of someone in the classroom. Your classmates will guess who it is.

> **MODÈLE:** Il/Elle a les cheveux longs et noirs, il/elle a les yeux marron et il/elle est de taille moyenne.

**C. Personnalités célèbres.** What color hair do the following people have?

> **MODÈLE:** Steve Martin → Steve Martin? Il a les cheveux blancs.

**1.** Reese Witherspoon     **3.** Ron Weasley, l'ami de Harry Potter
**2.** Michelle Obama     **4.** Brad Pitt

———
*literally, *chestnut;* invariable in gender

## Le verbe *avoir*

*Expressing Possession and Sensations*

### Deux cents amis!

*Mamadou contacte Léa sur sa page Facebook (Messagerie instantanée).*

 MAMADOU: **Tu as** beaucoup d'amis, Léa!

 LÉA: Oui, beacoup. **J'ai de la chance!** Et toi?

 MAMADOU: **J'ai** des amis journalistes. Mais **j'ai envie de** rencontrer d'autres personnes. Toi, par exemple! **Tu as l'air** intéressante. **Ton amie Juliette** aussi **a l'air** sympa.

 LÉA: **Tu as** déjà deux cents amis sur ta page Facebook! **Tu n'as pas besoin** de nous!

 MAMADOU: Oui, mais **j'ai** peu d'amies françaises.

 LÉA: Ce soir, **nous avons rendez-vous** au cinéma, Juliette et moi. **Tu as envie** de nous rejoindre?

 MAMADOU: Oh! **Je n'ai pas de chance\*!** Ce soir, c'est impossible parce que **j'ai** du travail.

*\*Je... I'm not lucky!*

Vrai ou faux?

1. Léa a beaucoup d'amis.
2. Mamadou a des amis étudiants.
3. Mamadou a deux cents amis sur sa page Facebook.
4. Mamadou a beaucoup d'amies françaises.
5. Léa a rendez-vous avec Juliette.
6. Mamadou n'a pas de chance.

## Forms of *avoir*

The verb **avoir** is irregular in form.

| PRESENT TENSE OF **avoir** (*to have*) | |
|---|---|
| j' **ai** | nous **avons** |
| tu **as** | vous **avez** |
| il/elle/on **a** | ils/elles **ont** |

—**J'ai** un studio agréable.
—**Avez**-vous une camarade de chambre sympathique?
—Oui, elle **a** beaucoup de patience.

*I have a nice studio apartment.*
*Do you have a nice roommate?*

*Yes, she has lots of patience.*

To ask someone his/her age, use **Quel âge *avez*-vous?** or **Quel âge *as*-tu?**

[Allez-y! A, E]

## Expressions with *avoir*

The verb **avoir** is used in many common idioms.

Elle **a chaud.**
Il **a froid.**

Elles **ont faim.**
Ils **ont soif.**

Loïc, tu **as tort.** Magalie, tu **as raison.**

Frédéric **a l'air** content. Il **a de la chance.**

L'immeuble **a l'air** moderne.

Théo **a sommeil.**

Ingrid **a besoin d'**une lampe.

**Avez-vous envie de** danser?

Il **a rendez-vous** avec le professeur.

Il **a peur du** chien.

La petite fille **a honte.**

Isabelle **a quatre ans.**

Note that with **avoir besoin de, avoir envie de,** and **avoir peur de,** the preposition **de** is used before an infinitive or a noun.

[Allez-y! B-C-D]

### ▌▌▌▌ *Allez-y!*

**A. Vive la musique!** You and your friends are planning a musical evening. Say what each person has to contribute to the occasion.

**MODÈLE:** Isaac / une trompette → Isaac a une trompette.

1. Yasmine et Marc / un iPod®*
2. vous / une guitare
3. tu / une clarinette
4. je / un violon
5. nous / un piano
6. Isabelle / une flûte

———
*iPod is a registered trademark of Apple Inc.

**B. Quel âge ont-ils?** Working with a partner, ask and answer questions about the age of the following people. Make educated guesses!

> **MODÈLE:** É1: Quel âge a-t-il?
> É2: Il a deux ou trois ans.

**1.**      **2.**      **3.**      **4.**

**C. Dans quel contexte?** For each situation, use an expression with **avoir**.

> **MODÈLE:** Pour moi, un coca-cola, s'il vous plaît. → J'ai soif.

1. Je porte un pull et un manteau.
2. Il est minuit (*midnight*).
3. J'ouvre (*open*) la fenêtre.
4. Je mange une quiche.
5. Paris est la capitale de la France.
6. Des amis français m'invitent (*invite me*) à Paris.

**D. Désirs et devoirs** (*duties*). What do you and the people you know *want* to do? What do you *have* to do? Use **avoir envie / besoin de** to tell about these people. **Verbes utiles:** danser, écouter, étudier, parler, rêver, skier, travailler, voyager

> **MODÈLE:** je →
> J'ai envie de jouer au tennis, mais j'ai besoin d'étudier!

1. je
2. mon meilleur ami / ma meilleure amie
3. mes parents
4. le professeur de français
5. mon/ma camarade de chambre

**E. Conversation.** Ask a classmate the following questions.

1. Tu as peur de quoi (*what*)?
2. Tu as quoi dans ta chambre?
3. Tu as besoin de quoi pour préparer ton cours de français?
4. Tu as envie de quoi quand tu as faim? quand tu as soif?
5. Tu as envie de quoi maintenant?

**Résumez!** Now tell the other students the most surprising or unusual fact you learned about your classmate.

> **MODÈLE:** Éric a trois dictionnaires dans sa chambre!

---

 **Prononcez bien!**

**The pronunciation of final consonants**

In French, consonant letters ending words are generally not pronounced.*

> **restauran~t~, il~s~ dan~sent~, cour~s~, asse~z~, beaucou~p~, alleman~d~**

Final **-c, -r, -f,** and **-l,** however, are pronounced.

> **ave~c~, bonjour, neuf, ma~l~**

Exceptions to this rule include the **c** in blan~c~ as well as the **r** in the infinitive of **-er** verbs and in words ending in **-er** and **-ier.**

> **alle~r~, adore~r~, quartie~r~, cahie~r~**

*unless they precede a word starting with a vowel (See **Prononcez bien!** on liaison, p. 261)

---

**Géant. J'ai envie** *

---

*slogan for a French supermarket

# Les adjectifs qualificatifs

*Describing People, Places, and Things*

## Des professeurs excellents!

*Léa téléphone à Juliette.*

LÉA: Salut Juliette! Tu es contente de ton cours de gym? C'est **difficile?**

JULIETTE: Ce n'est pas **facile** quand on commence, mais je suis **persévérante** et la prof est **excellente!**

LÉA: Elle est **patiente?** C'est **important.** La patience, c'est une qualité **essentielle.**

JULIETTE: Elle est toujours **calme.** Elle observe nos mouvements et elle donne des explications très **précises.** Je suis vraiment **contente!** Et toi, ton cours de tennis?

LÉA: On a un **nouveau** prof.

JULIETTE: Il est comment?

LÉA: Il est **grand, beau, charmant...**

JULIETTE: Et **sportif!**

Répondez aux questions.

1. Qui est excellente, patiente et calme?
2. Qui est grand, beau et charmant?
3. Qui est persévérante?
4. La gym, c'est difficile ou c'est facile?
5. Qui donne des explications très précises: le professeur de gym ou le professeur de tennis?

## Position of Descriptive Adjectives

Descriptive adjectives (**les adjectifs qualificatifs**) give information about people, places, and things. In French, they usually follow the nouns they modify. They may also follow the verb **être.**

C'est un professeur **intéressant.**

*He's/She's an interesting teacher (professor).*

Le professeur pose des questions **faciles.**

*The teacher (professor) asks easy questions.*

J'aime les personnes **sincères** et **individualistes.**

*I like sincere and individualistic people.*

Gabrielle est **sportive.**

*Gabrielle is athletic.*

A few common adjectives that generally precede the nouns they modify are presented in **Chapitre 4, Leçon 3.**

## Agreement of Adjectives

In French, adjectives agree in gender (masculine or feminine) and number (singular or plural) with the nouns they modify. Most adjectives follow the pattern illustrated in the following table.

| | MASCULINE | FEMININE |
|---|---|---|
| *Singular* | un étudiant intelligent | une étudiante intelligent**e** |
| *Plural* | des étudiants intelligent**s** | des étudiantes intelligent**es** |

**1.** Most feminine adjectives are formed by adding an **e** to the masculine form. Exception: adjectives whose masculine form ends in an unaccented **-e**.

> Hugo est **persévérant.** → Sylvie est **persévérante.**
> Paul est **triste.** → Claire est **triste.**

Remember that final **d, s,** and **t,** usually silent in French, are pronounced when **e** is added.

**2.** **C'est** can be used to describe a general truth or to refer back to something that has already been mentioned. The adjective that follows **c'est** is always in the masculine singular form.

> Le français? C'est **facile!**
> L'amour (*love*), c'est **essentiel.**

**3.** Most plural adjectives of either gender are formed by adding an **s** to the singular form. Exception: adjectives whose singular form ends in **-s** or **-x.**

> Elle est **charmante.** → Elles sont **charmantes.**
> L'étudiant est **sénégalais.** → Les étudiants sont **sénégalais.**
> Marc est **courageux.** → Marc et Loïc sont **courageux.**

**4.** If a plural subject refers to one or more masculine items or people, the plural adjective is masculine.

> Sylvie et Inès sont **françaises.**
> Sylvie et Adam sont **français.**

### Prononcez bien!

**The nasal vowels in** *blond,* ***grand,*** **and** *bain*

To pronounce these sounds, let the air coming from your lungs go through both your mouth and nose. Close your mouth and round your lips to say [ɔ̃] as in **blond;** pronounce [ɑ̃] with an open mouth and lips more relaxed in **grand;** for [ɛ̃] in **bain,** your mouth is more open than for [ɔ̃] in **blond,** but less than for [ɑ̃] in **grand,** and your lips are stretched in a smile.

> [ɔ̃]: **b**on**j**our, **c**ombien
>
> [ɑ̃]: **c**omm**ent,** quar**a**nte, sept**em**bre
>
> [ɛ̃]: **b**ientôt, **v**ingt, améric**ain,** f**aim**

Les magazines.

Accrochants.[1]

Captivants.

Enrichissants.

[1]Catchy.

## Descriptive Adjectives with Irregular Forms

| PATTERN | | SINGULAR | | PLURAL | |
|---|---|---|---|---|---|
| MASC. | FEM. | MASC. | FEM. | MASC. | FEM. |
| -eux<br>-eur } → | -euse | heureux (*happy*)<br>travailleur | heureuse<br>travailleuse | heureux<br>travailleurs | heureuses<br>travailleuses |
| -er → | -ère | cher (*expensive*) | chère | chers | chères |
| -if → | -ive | sportif | sportive | sportifs | sportives |
| -il → | -ille | gentil (*nice, pleasant*) | gentille | gentils | gentilles |
| -el → | -elle | intellectuel | intellectuelle | intellectuels | intellectuelles |
| -ien → | -ienne | parisien | parisienne | parisiens | parisiennes |

Other adjectives that follow these patterns include **courageux / courageuse, paresseux / paresseuse, sérieux / sérieuse, fier / fière** (*proud*), **naïf / naïve** (*naive*), and **canadien / canadienne.** The feminine forms of **beau** (*handsome, beautiful*) and **nouveau** (*new*) are **belle** and **nouvelle.** The adjective **chic** (*stylish*) is invariable in gender and number.

## Adjectives of Color

**1.** Most adjectives of color have both masculine and feminine forms.

> un chemisier **blanc / bleu / gris / noir / vert / violet**
> une chemise **blanche / bleue / grise / noire / verte / violette**

**2. Jaune, rouge,** and **rose** are invariable in gender.

> un pantalon **jaune** / une robe **jaune**

**3. Marron** and **orange** are invariable in gender and number.

> une robe **marron / orange**        des robes **marron / orange**

 *Allez-y!*

**A. Dans la salle de classe.** Arthur has a wonderful class. Describe it, choosing the appropriate expressions from the second column.

**1.** Le professeur est...          **a.** bleue et blanche.
**2.** Les étudiants sont...          **b.** confortables et nombreuses.
**3.** La salle de classe est...      **c.** intelligent et dynamique.
**4.** Les chaises sont...            **d.** sociables et amusants.

**B. Des âmes sœurs.** (*Soulmates.*) Patrice and Patricia are alike in every respect. Describe them, taking turns with a partner.

> **MODÈLE:** français →
> > É1: Patrice est français. Et Patricia?
> > É2: Patricia est française.

| | | |
|---|---|---|
| **1.** optimiste | **5.** sérieux | **9.** sportif |
| **2.** intelligent | **6.** parisien | **10.** courageux |
| **3.** charmant | **7.** naïf | **11.** travailleur |
| **4.** fier | **8.** gentil | **12.** intellectuel |

**C. À mon avis.** (*In my opinion.*) Complete these sentences according to your own opinions.

1. L'homme idéal est _____. Il a une voiture _____ (couleur).
2. La femme idéale est _____. Elle a les yeux _____ (couleur).
3. Le/La camarade de classe idéal(e) est _____.
4. Le professeur idéal est _____.
5. Le chauffeur de taxi idéal est _____.

**D. Un mél.** Here is the email that Max dreads receiving from his girlfriend. Transform it into the more positive one that is actually on the way by changing the adjectives and some verbs.

> Angers, le 7 janvier
>
> Max,
>
> Je te déteste. Tu es stupide et antipathique. Tous les jours (*Every day*) tu es nerveux, tu ne rêves pas parce que tu es peu idéaliste, et tu es même (*even*) souvent hypocrite. En plus (*Furthermore*) je trouve que tu es paresseux.
>
> Je ne veux pas te revoir. (*I don't want to see you again.*)
>
> Adieu.
>
> Catherine

> **MODÈLE:** Max, je t'adore…

**Un peu plus…**

**Café culture in France.**

Cafés in France are important parts of each neighborhood. Many French people go to their favorite café in the morning for a coffee and a croissant, at lunch for a sandwich, or for a drink before dinner, an **apéro** (**apéritif).** There are **tabacs** in many cafés where one can purchase tobacco, stamps, bus tickets, and other items. Cafés in France are also important places to socialize, where people gather and hold lively conversations. Cafés are also welcoming if you prefer just to sit and relax with a delicious **cappuccino.** Is café culture important in your community? Where do people usually go to socialize?

◄ Qu'est-ce qu'elle dit? (*What is she saying?*)

# Le blog de Léa

## En jupe ou en pantalon?

**lundi 23 mai**

Samedi soir, il y a une soirée[1] chez mon copain[2] Hector.
J'ai envie d'être très belle, très «jeune femme[3]». Mais hélas,
j'ai toujours l'air d'avoir 15 ans!

J'ai besoin d'acheter[4] des vêtements originaux et à petit prix.[5]
Et aussi des chaussures! Et un sac! La solution, c'est peut-être[6]
d'acheter du vintage au marché aux puces[7]?

Je suis petite, brune; j'ai les yeux marron. Vous avez des idées?

Léa

Tu as de bonnes adresses?

### COMMENTAIRES

**Alexis**

Léa,

Pour être[8] originale, tu portes un tee-shirt vert, une veste
rose, un jean. Sur le jean, tu mets un short rouge.

**Trésor (chien d'Alexis)**

Idiot!

**Charlotte**

C'est difficile de sélectionner des vêtements pour une soirée. Moi, je suggère une
petite robe noire, très courte avec des tennis blanches. Simple, classique, chic.

**Mamadou**

En jupe, en pantalon, en maillot de bain, en short, je suis sûr que tu es charmante!

---

[1]*party*  [2]*friend*  [3]*jeune… young woman*  [4]*to buy*  [5]*à… cheap*  [6]*maybe*  [7]*marché… flea market*  [8]*Pour… To be*

## Dis-moi où tu t'habilles!°

*Tell me where you buy your clothes!*

À Paris, est-ce qu'on a besoin d'être riche pour avoir l'air chic? Non! Ce paradoxe a une explication: le fameux chic français n'est pas dans ce qu'[1]on achète mais dans l'art d'assembler les vêtements et les accessoires.

Les étudiants connaissent[2] ce principe essentiel de l'élégance. Et ils font[3] des miracles avec des petits budgets. Mais où trouvent-ils leurs vêtements? D'abord, dans les boutiques pour jeunes comme H&M. Il y a aussi le marché aux puces. Fabien explique: «J'adore la fripe—les vieux vêtements—ils sont originaux.»

Mais que faire si on[4] aime le luxe?

Il y a deux solutions. Anne, par exemple, s'habille dans les «stocks»,[5] magasins où s'accumulent les excès de production de vêtements. Cette semaine, elle a acheté une jupe de la collection Zara pour quinze euros! Gaëlle, qui est BCBG,[6] a une autre solution. Elle va dans un «dépôt-vente» de son quartier où elle achète des vêtements déjà portés mais presque neufs[7]: «Souvent j'ai de la chance, déclare-t-elle. La semaine dernière,[8] pour soixante-neuf euros, j'ai trouvé[9] un foulard[10] Hermès!»

[1]ce... *what*  [2]*understand*  [3]*create*  [4]*que... what do you do if you*
[5]*outlet stores*  [6]*preppy*  [7]presque... *almost new*  [8]*last*
[9]ai... *found*  [10]*scarf*

**Le marché aux puces de la Porte de Clignancourt.** C'est une véritable caverne d'Ali-Baba: les amateurs visitent le marché de préférence le samedi matin. Ils cherchent, ils explorent, ils achètent. Ils ont raison! Avec un peu de chance et beaucoup d'efforts, ils trouvent des trésors parmi (*among*) des montagnes de vêtements.

**À vous!** Dans quels magasins trouvez-vous vos vêtements? Êtes-vous plutôt comme Fabien, comme Anne ou comme Gaëlle? Expliquez vos préférences.

**Parlons-en!** Cet été, vous participez à un programme universitaire d'été, à Nice, sur la Côte d'Azur. Vous achetez des vêtements pour ce voyage. Vous avez un budget de $300.

1. Travaillez en groupes de trois ou quatre. Préparez deux listes: une pour les filles (*girls*), une pour les garçons (*boys*).
2. Dans chaque liste, proposez les vêtements nécessaires: tee-shirt, short, chemise, chemisier, pantalon, jupe, etc. Précisez le nom des magasins (*stores*) où vous achetez ces vêtements et donnez les prix.
3. Comparez la liste de votre groupe aux listes des autres. Quel groupe a la liste la plus (*the most*) adaptée à un programme universitaire d'été? la plus économique? la plus classique? la plus extravagante?
4. Quelle est la liste idéale? Votez!

STRUCTURES

# Leçon 3

## Les questions à réponse affirmative ou négative

*Getting Information*

### Une robe noire ou une robe grise?

*Appel vidéo entre Juliette et Léa.*

JULIETTE: Finalement, **est-ce que tu portes** une jupe pour la soirée d'Hector?

LÉA: Non, je porte un jean avec un chemisier blanc. **Est-ce** assez chic?

JULIETTE: Oui! Un chemisier blanc, c'est très chic! Mais le jean… **tu ne penses pas que** c'est un peu commun?

LÉA: Commun? Certainement pas! C'est simple et élégant. Et toi, **tu portes** une robe?

JULIETTE: Oui, mais j'hésite entre une robe noire et une robe grise. C'est un choix impossible! (Elle rit.*)

▼ AUDIO & VIDEO

MESSAGE    VIDEO ●

*Elle… *She laughs*

Voici les réponses. Trouvez les questions dans le dialogue.

1. Non, je porte un jean avec un chemisier blanc.
2. Oui! Un chemisier blanc, c'est très chic!
3. Oui, mais j'hésite entre une robe noire et une robe grise.

In French, there are several ways to ask a question requiring a *yes* or *no* answer.

## Questions Without Change in Word Order

1. You can raise the pitch of your voice at the end of a sentence.

—Vous ne parlez pas anglais?      *You don't speak English?*
—Si, un peu.*                      *Yes, a little.*

---

*Note that **si,** not **oui,** is used to answer *yes* to a negative question.

2. When confirmation is expected, add the tag **n'est-ce pas** to the end of the sentence.

> Il aime la musique, **n'est-ce pas?**  *He likes music, doesn't he?*
> Nous ne mangeons pas au  *We don't eat at the cafeteria,*
>    resto-U, **n'est-ce pas?**    *do we?*

3. Another way is to precede a statement with **Est-ce que (Est-ce qu'** before a vowel sound).

> **Est-ce que** Nathan étudie  *Does Nathan study Spanish?*
>    l'espagnol?
> **Est-ce qu'**elles écoutent la radio?  *Are they listening to the radio?*

[Allez-y! A-B with **Mots clés**]

## Questions with Change in Word Order

Questions can also be formed by inverting the subject and the verb. This question formation is more common in written French.

1. When a pronoun is the subject of the sentence, the pronoun and verb are inverted and hyphenated.

| PRONOUN SUBJECT |
| --- |
| *Statement:*      Il est touriste. |
| *Question:*      **Est-il** touriste? |

> **Es-tu** étudiante en philosophie?  *Are you studying philosophy?*
> **Aiment-ils** les discussions  *Do they like animated*
>    animées?    *discussions?*

The final **t** of third-person plural verb forms is pronounced when followed by **ils** or **elles: aiment-elles.** When third-person singular verbs end with a vowel, **-t-** is inserted between the verb and the pronoun.

> Elle aim**e** les jupes. →  **Aime-t-elle** les jupes?
> Il port**e** un veston. →  **Porte-t-il** un veston?

**Je** is seldom inverted. **Est-ce-que** is used instead: **Est-ce que je suis élégant?**

2. When a noun is the subject of the sentence, the noun subject is retained; the third-person pronoun corresponding to the subject follows the verb and is attached to it by a hyphen.

| NOUN SUBJECT |
| --- |
| *Statement:*      Paul est touriste. |
| *Question:*      **Paul est-il** touriste? |

> **Marc est-il** étudiant?  *Is Marc a student?*
> **Delphine travaille-t-elle** beaucoup?  *Does Delphine work a lot?*
> **Les amis arrivent-ils** ce soir?  *Are our friends arriving tonight?*

[Allez-y! C-D]

## Allez-y!

**A. C'est difficile à croire!** You find it hard to believe what Manon is telling you. Express your surprise by turning each statement into a question. (Your intonation should express your disbelief!)

MODÈLE: Jade est de Paris. → Jade est de Paris?

1. Pascal est aussi de Paris.
2. Jade et Pascal sont belges.
3. Louis est le camarade de Pascal.
4. C'est un garçon drôle.
5. Il n'habite pas à Paris.
6. Sandra est canadienne.

**B. Des personnalités compatibles.** With a partner, play the roles of two people whose personalities are perfectly matched. Use the expressions from **Mots clés** as in the model.

MODÈLE: calme →
É1: Est-ce que tu es calme?
É2: Oui, je suis calme. Et toi?    Non, je ne suis pas calme. Et toi?
↓              *or*        ↓
É1: Moi aussi, je suis calme.    Moi non plus, je ne suis pas calme.

1. sympathique
2. sportif / sportive
3. curieux / curieuse
4. sérieux / sérieuse
5. patient(e)
6. travailleur / travailleuse

### Mots clés

**The expressions *moi aussi, moi non plus***

If you agree with someone's comment, your answer will be either **moi aussi** (*me too*) or **moi non plus** (*me neither*).

—Je suis fatigué!
**—Moi aussi!**

—Mais je n'ai pas faim!
**—Moi non plus!**

**C. Étudiants à la Sorbonne.** You are writing an article on student life in Paris. Verify the information you have jotted down by expressing your statements as questions.

MODÈLE: Stéphane étudie à la Sorbonne. →
Est-ce que Stéphane étudie à la Sorbonne?

1. Il est belge.
2. Vous admirez Stéphane.
3. Stéphane et Carole sont étudiants en philosophie.
4. Ils sont sympathiques.
5. Carole habite à la cité-U.

**D. Portrait d'un professeur.** Ask your instructor about his or her personality, tastes, and clothing. Use inversion in your questions. **Verbes suggérés:** aimer, danser, écouter, être, parler, regarder, skier

MODÈLES: Êtes-vous pessimiste?
Aimez-vous les cravates orange?

Now see if your classmates were listening. Ask a classmate three questions about your instructor.

MODÈLE: Est-ce que le professeur est pessimiste?

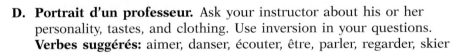

# Les prépositions *à* et *de*

*Mentioning Specific Places or People*

## Tennis, poker ou restaurant?

*Léa contacte Hector sur sa page Facebook (Messagerie instantanée).*

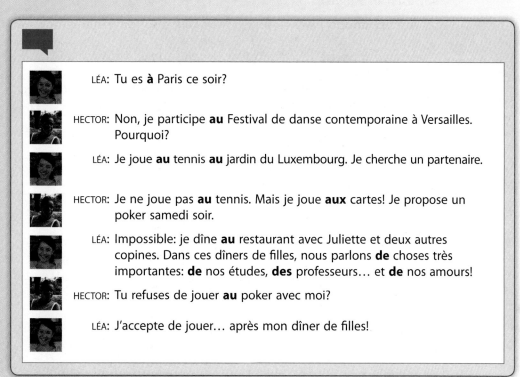

LÉA: Tu es **à** Paris ce soir?

HECTOR: Non, je participe **au** Festival de danse contemporaine à Versailles. Pourquoi?

LÉA: Je joue **au** tennis **au** jardin du Luxembourg. Je cherche un partenaire.

HECTOR: Je ne joue pas **au** tennis. Mais je joue **aux** cartes! Je propose un poker samedi soir.

LÉA: Impossible: je dîne **au** restaurant avec Juliette et deux autres copines. Dans ces dîners de filles, nous parlons **de** choses très importantes: **de** nos études, **des** professeurs… et **de** nos amours!

HECTOR: Tu refuses de jouer **au** poker avec moi?

LÉA: J'accepte de jouer… après mon dîner de filles!

Complétez les phrases.

**Hector**

1. Hector est _____ Versailles.
2. Il participe _____ Festival de danse.
3. Il ne joue pas _____ tennis.
4. Il joue _____ cartes.
5. Il joue _____ poker.

**Léa**

6. Léa est _____ Paris.
7. Elle joue _____ jardin du Luxembourg.
8. Elle dîne _____ restaurant avec des copines.
9. Elles parlent _____ choses importantes.

Prepositions (**les prépositions**) give information about the relationship between two words. Examples in English are *at, before, for, in, of, to, under, without.* In French, the prepositions **à** and **de** sometimes contract with articles.

## The Preposition *à*

1. **À** indicates location or destination. It has several English equivalents.

| | |
|---|---|
| Arnaud habite **à** Paris. | *Arnaud lives in Paris.* |
| Il étudie **à** la bibliothèque. | *He studies at (in) the library.* |
| Il arrive **à** Bruxelles demain. | *He's coming to Brussels tomorrow.* |

2. With verbs such as **donner, montrer, parler,** and **téléphoner, à** introduces the indirect object (usually a person) even when *to* is not used in English.

| | |
|---|---|
| Arnaud **donne** un livre **à** son copain. | *Arnaud gives his friend a book.* |
| Arnaud **montre** une photo **à** Delphine. | *Arnaud shows Delphine a photo.* |
| Il **parle à** un professeur. | *He's speaking to a professor.* |
| Il **téléphone à** un ami. | *He's calling a friend.* |

The preposition *to* is not always used in English, but **à** must be used in French with these verbs.

## The Preposition *de*

1. **De** indicates where something or someone comes from.

| | |
|---|---|
| Medhi est **de** Casablanca. | *Medhi is from Casablanca.* |
| Il arrive **de** la bibliothèque. | *He is coming from the library.* |

2. **De** also indicates possession (expressed by *'s* or *of* in English) and the concept of belonging to, being a part of.

| | |
|---|---|
| Voici la librairie **de** Madame Vernier. | *Here is Madame Vernier's bookstore.* |
| J'aime mieux la librairie **de** l'université. | *I prefer the university bookstore (the bookstore of the university).* |

3. When used with **parler, de** means *about*.

| | |
|---|---|
| Nous parlons **de** la littérature contemporaine. | *We're talking about contemporary literature.* |

## The Prepositions *à* and *de* with the Definite Articles *le* and *les*

| | |
|---|---|
| **à + le = au** | Arnaud arrive **au** cinéma. |
| **à + les = aux** | Arnaud arrive **aux** cours. |
| **à + la = à la** | Arnaud arrive **à la** librairie. |
| **à + l' = à l'** | Arnaud arrive **à l'**université. |
| | |
| **de + le = du** | Arnaud arrive **du** cinéma. |
| **de + les = des** | Arnaud arrive **des** cours. |
| **de + la = de la** | Arnaud arrive **de la** librairie. |
| **de + l' = de l'** | Arnaud arrive **de l'**université. |

## The Verb *jouer* with the Prepositions *à* and *de*

When **jouer** is followed by the preposition **à,** it means to play a team sport or a game. When it is followed by **de,** it means to play a musical instrument.

Naïma
**joue au tennis.**

Philippe
**joue du piano.**

 *Allez-y!*

**A. Où est-ce qu'on va?** (*Where do we go?*) Answer, taking turns with a partner. **Suggestions:** l'Alliance (*Institute*) française, l'amphithéâtre, la bibliothèque, le café, le cinéma, le concert, les courts de tennis, le Quartier latin, le restaurant universitaire, la salle de sport

MODÈLE: pour écouter une symphonie →
É1: Où est-ce qu'on va pour écouter une symphonie?
É2: On va au concert.

**1.** pour regarder un film  **2.** pour jouer au tennis  **3.** pour jouer au volley-ball  **4.** pour écouter le professeur  **5.** pour apprendre (*learn*) le français  **6.** pour étudier  **7.** pour manger  **8.** pour visiter la Sorbonne  **9.** pour parler avec des amis

**B. Camille, une personne très active.** Adapt the following sentences, using the words in parentheses.

**1.** Camille téléphone *à Sophie.* (le professeur / les amies / Gabriel / le restaurant)
**2.** Elle parle *de la littérature africaine.* (le rap / la politique française / les livres de Marguerite Duras / le cours de japonais)
**3.** Camille arrive *de la librairie.* (le resto-U / New York / la bibliothèque / les courts de tennis)
**4.** Elle aime jouer *au football.* (le piano / les cartes / le basket-ball / la guitare)

**C. Les passe-temps.** Complete the following sentences with **jouer à** or **de.** Match the players with the sports or instruments they play.

**MODÈLE:** Aaron Rodgers → Aaron Rodgers joue au football américain.

1. Wynton Marsalis
2. Serena Williams
3. Carlos Santana
4. Alicia Keys
5. Kevin Durant
6. Phil Mickelson
7. David Beckham
8. Miguel Cabrera
9. Yo-Yo Ma
10. Hikaru Nakamura

a. le violoncelle
b. le golf
c. les échecs (*chess*)
d. la trompette
e. le piano
f. le basket-ball
g. le base-ball
h. la guitare
i. le foot
j. le tennis

**D. Trouvez quelqu'un qui...** Find someone in the classroom who does each of the following activities. On a separate piece of paper, note down his/her name next to the activity. See who can complete the list the fastest.

**MODÈLE:** Est-ce que tu joues au tennis?
Oui, je joue au tennis. (*ou* Non, je ne joue pas au tennis.)

aimer le laboratoire de langues
aimer les films français
jouer au base-ball
jouer au bridge
jouer au poker
jouer au tennis

jouer au volley
jouer aux cartes
jouer de la clarinette
jouer de la guitare
manger à la cafétéria aujourd'hui
?

LE MONDE DE YAYO

© Yayo/Cartoonists & Writers Syndicate http://cartoonweb.com

Qu'est-ce que vous pensez de cette illustration?

## Prononcez bien!

1.  **The vowels in *bleu* and *couleur*** (page 64)

    **A.  Nathalie et Olivier.** Isabelle talks about two of your mutual friends. Listen to her and indicate whether she's referring to Nathalie or to Olivier.

    **B.  Trouvez l'intrus.** You and Isabelle are playing *Odd Man Out*. Read each series of words aloud and your partner will say the word that doesn't belong.

      **1.** deux, peu, fleur, bleu, cheveux
      **2.** sœur, deux, couleur, œuf, peur
      **3.** yeux, jeudi, danseuse, peu, jeune

2.  **The pronunciation of final consonants** (page 69)

    **Stéphane.** Isabelle is talking about Stéphane. You know you've met him but you can't remember much about him. First, read her description of Stéphane and indicate whether the final consonants in bold are pronounced or not. Then, read the paragraph aloud.

    Rappelle-toi (*Remember*)! Stéphane est étudian**t** en alleman**d**. Il est gran**d**, sporti**f** et intellectue**l**. Il travaille dans un restauran**t** du quartie**r** le vendredi soi**r**. Il porte souven**t** un pantalo**n** gri**s**, un tee-shirt ver**t** et un sa**c** blan**c**. D'accor**d**? Tu vois (*see*) maintenan**t**?

3.  **The nasal vowels in *blond*, *grand,* and *bain*** (page 71)

    **A.  Le jeu des voyelles nasales.** Your French instructor has invented a game to help you practice the French nasal vowels. You will hear three sets of seven words, each containing one of the three sounds listed below. Write the words you hear from each set in the correct category.

      **1.** [ɔ̃] as in **blond**
      **2.** [ɑ̃] as in **grand**
      **3.** [ɛ̃] as in **bain**

    **B.  Les soldes.** You and your housemates took advantage of the department store sales to update your wardrobes. With your partner, take turns reading the list of what you all bought, making sure to distinguish between the sounds [ɔ̃] as in **blond**, [ɑ̃] as **grand,** and [ɛ̃] as in **bain.**

Nous av**on**s acheté c**in**q blous**on**s bl**an**cs, qu**in**ze p**an**tal**on**s marr**on**, trois m**an**teaux or**an**ge, v**in**gt s**an**dales et deux gr**an**ds sacs à m**ain**!

Est-ce que la jeune femme va acheter ce chemisier?

PERSPECTIVES

 Lecture

## *Avant de lire*

**Gaining confidence in your reading skills.** You have already practiced two strategies that facilitate comprehension of a written text: recognizing cognates (**Chapitre 1**) and predicting the content using the context (**Chapitre 2**). These strategies *do* work. The more you practice them, the more confidence you will gain, enabling you to read texts in French with greater ease and enjoyment. Here is some additional advice:

- *Read and reread.* Read the text once to get the general sense. Then read it a second time, using the techniques you already know to fill in the gaps.
- *Don't fret over every word.* Break the habit of reading for word-for-word translation. Concentrate on getting the meaning of larger "chunks" of text—phrases and entire sentences.
- *Use the dictionary as a last resort.* After using all of your reading strategies, try to decide whether the meaning of an unfamiliar word is truly crucial for your comprehension of the general meaning. If it is, consult a dictionary. The dictionary is an important tool, but it should be used with moderation.

**Parlons de la mode.** Paris is one of the great centers of the fashion industry, and French fashion terms have been incorporated extensively into English. For this reason, in fashion advertising in English, it is not unusual to see French words used unaltered. Do you know the meanings of the following words?

| | | |
|---|---|---|
| parfum | boutique | haute couture |
| couturier | mode | prêt-à-porter |

**Des mots apparentés!** The following sentences are excerpted from the reading selection. Guess the meaning of the cognates in italics.

1. Mais c'est dans le Marais que les jeunes *créateurs* sont rassemblés. Dans des boutiques très *originales*, ils *proposent* des vêtements et des *accessoires innovants*, parfois vraiment *excentriques*. Les garçons et les filles (*boys and girls*) *adorent!*
2. Pour les étrangers (*foreigners*) *en visite* à Paris, acheter des vêtements et des chaussures est une *expérience intéressante* et même une *aventure!* Mais attention: la *politesse* avant tout!
3. *Bravo!* Vous êtes *éduqué(e)*, aimable, *respectueux/respectueuse*: dans un magasin, vous êtes *sûr(e)* d'obtenir (*to obtain*) une *assistance immédiate*.

# Paris-shopping: quelques recommandations

*Paris est la ville des jolies boutiques de mode. Pour les filles, pour les garçons, pour les jeunes, pour les adultes, pour les seniors, il y a le choix. On trouve tout, à tous les prix.[1]*

## Les Champs-Élysées et le Marais

Les beaux quartiers privilégient les marques[2] prestigieuses (et chères!): Louis Vuitton, Christian Dior, Hermès ou Chanel. Sur les Champs-Élysées, rue François 1er, rue Montaigne et rue Saint-Honoré, les magasins chic exposent les trésors fabuleux du prêt-à-porter de luxe: foulards, sacs, chemises, cravates et costumes.

Mais c'est dans le Marais que les jeunes créateurs sont rassemblés. Dans des boutiques très originales, ils proposent des vêtements et des accessoires innovants, parfois vraiment excentriques. Les garçons et les filles adorent, par exemple, les sacs de la boutique Matières à réflexion fabriqués avec du vieux cuir[3] recyclé.

Le prêt-à-porter de luxe

## Expédition shopping

Pour les étrangers en visite à Paris, acheter des vêtements et des chaussures est une expérience intéressante et même une aventure! Mais attention: la politesse avant tout! Voici donc quelques recommandations pour vos expéditions-shopping:

* Pour être bien reçu(e)[4] dans les boutiques de mode, respectez les bonnes manières: Un «bonjour» est indispensable quand vous poussez la porte!
* Puis quand on vous demande: «Est-ce que je peux vous aider?[5]», vous répondez: «Non, merci; je regarde». Ou bien vous posez une question: «S'il vous plaît, quel est le prix des chaussures noires exposées dans la vitrine?[6]»
* Enfin, quand la vendeuse vous présente les fameuses chaussures, surtout n'oubliez pas de dire «merci»!

Bravo! Vous êtes éduqué(e), aimable, respectueux/respectueuse: dans un magasin, vous êtes sûr(e) d'obtenir une assistance immédiate! Et un sourire![7]

Des créations originales

---

[1]*à... at all (different) prices*  [2]*brands*  [3]*leather*  [4]*received, welcomed*  [5]*Est-ce que... May I help you?*
[6]*shop window*  [7]*smile*

### Compréhension

1. Où est-ce qu'on trouve les magasins et boutiques de luxe à Paris? Quelles sortes de vêtements est-ce qu'on y trouve?
2. Dans quel quartier est-ce qu'on trouve des vêtements et des accessoires originaux appréciés des jeunes?
3. À votre avis, quelle est l'expression la plus utile à connaître pour une expédition shopping agréable à Paris?

 Écriture

The writing activities **Par écrit** and **Journal intime** can be found in the Workbook/Laboratory Manual to accompany *Vis-à-vis*.

## Pour s'amuser

### Mots en désordre°

Mots... *Word scramble*

The letters of these words have been scrambled. Find the original words. (Hint: They all have to do with clothing and colors.)

o r e s

n a j e

l a n b c

p e u j

l e i l a t u r

n a l p o n t a

m e c h e s i

# Le vidéoblog de Léa

## En bref

In this episode, Léa and Hassan meet at a café, where they talk about clothing. In her videoblog, Léa describes the various places one can buy clothing in Paris; Hassan talks about how people dress in Morocco.

### Vocabulaire en contexte

une bonne adresse
*good/favorite place to shop*

dépenser de l'argent
*to spend money*

être en solde
*to be on sale*

le luxe
*luxury*

**la mode**
*fashion*

le marché aux puces
*flea market*

la haute couture
*high fashion, designer clothing*

un (petit, gros) budget vêtements
*(small, large) clothing budget*

On fait (*does*) du shopping au Maroc.

## Visionnez!

|  | Léa | Hassan | Les deux |
|---|---|---|---|
| **1.** Qui ne dépense pas beaucoup d'argent pour ses vêtements? | ☐ | ☐ | ☐ |
| **2.** Qui a une liste de bonnes adresses? | ☐ | ☐ | ☐ |
| **3.** Qui porte presque (*almost*) toujours un jean? | ☐ | ☐ | ☐ |
| **4.** Qui est quelquefois sportif, quelquefois élégant? | ☐ | ☐ | ☐ |
| **5.** Qui aime les vêtements chic? | ☐ | ☐ | ☐ |

## Analysez!

Voici une liste de vêtements marocains traditionnels mentionnés par Hassan: **des babouches, une djellaba, un fez / un tarbouch, un foulard** (*scarf*). Qui porte chaque (*each*) vêtement—un homme, une femme ou les deux? Ces vêtements ont-ils des équivalents occidentaux (*Western*)?

> **MODÈLE:** Un homme porte un fez. Un fez est une sorte de chapeau.

## Comparez!

Make a list of the **bonnes adresses** in your area. Which stores are good for a small clothing budget, which are good for a large one, and which articles of clothing in particular are these stores known for? How do these stores compare to those described in the video?

> **MODÈLE:** Si vous avez un petit budget vêtements, le magasin Marshall's est super: on y trouve (*finds there*)...

## Note culturelle

French families are spending a much smaller percentage of their income on clothing than they used to (5.6% today compared to 11% in 1960). Clothing is now less of a social symbol. It is a way of expressing one's identity. France is still known as the land of luxury products, however, and the new tendencies determined by *haute couture* collections are still carefully dissected on news broadcasts every season. Some of the most famous *couturiers* are Dior, Chanel, Givenchy, Ungaro, Gaultier, Lacroix, to name only a few.

## Vocabulaire

### Verbes

**arriver** to arrive
**avoir** to have
**jouer** to play
    **jouer à** to play (*a sport or game*)
    **jouer de** to play (*a musical instrument*)
**montrer** to show
**porter** to wear; to carry
**téléphoner à** to telephone

À REVOIR: **regarder, travailler**

### Expressions avec *avoir*

**avoir (20) ans** to be (20) years old
**avoir besoin de** to need (to)
**avoir chaud** to be warm
**avoir de la chance** to be lucky
**avoir envie de** to want (to), feel like (*doing s.th.*)
**avoir faim** to be hungry
**avoir froid** to be cold
**avoir honte** to be ashamed
**avoir l'air** (+ *adj.*); **avoir l'air de** (+ *inf.*) (+ *noun*) to seem, look, appear
**avoir peur (de)** to be afraid (of, to)
**avoir raison** to be right
**avoir rendez-vous avec** to have a meeting (date) with
**avoir soif** to be thirsty
**avoir sommeil** to be sleepy
**avoir tort** to be wrong

### Substantifs

**le/la camarade de chambre** roommate
**les cartes** (*f.*) cards
**les cheveux** (*m. pl.*) hair
**les échecs** (*m. pl.*) chess
**la fille** girl
**le garçon** boy

**la jeune femme** young woman
**le jeune homme** young man
**le magasin** store
**la personne** person
**la soirée** party
**les yeux** (*m.*) eyes

À REVOIR: **l'ami(e), la bibliothèque, l'université**

### Adjectifs

**antipathique** unpleasant
**beau / belle** beautiful
**blond(e)** blond
**châtain** (*inv. in gender*) chestnut brown
**cher / chère** expensive
**chic** (*inv.*) stylish
**court(e)** short
**drôle** funny, odd
**égoïste** selfish
**facile** easy
**fatigué(e)** tired
**fier / fière** proud
**gentil(le)** nice, pleasant
**grand(e)** tall, big
**heureux / heureuse** happy; fortunate
**hypocrite** hypocritical
**nouveau / nouvelle** new
**paresseux / paresseuse** lazy
**pauvre** poor
**petit(e)** small, short
**prêt(e)** ready
**raide** straight
**roux / rousse** redheaded
**sensible** sensitive
**sportif / sportive** *describes someone who likes physical exercise and sports*
**sympa(thique)** nice, likeable
**travailleur / travailleuse** hardworking
**triste** sad

À REVOIR: **espagnol(e), français(e), italien(ne)**

### Adjectifs apparentés

**amusant(e), blond(e), calme, charmant(e), conformiste, content(e), courageux / courageuse, curieux / curieuse, (dés)agréable, différent(e), difficile, dynamique, élégant(e), enthousiaste, essentiel(le), excellent(e), excentrique, extraordinaire, idéal(e), idéaliste, (im)patient(e), important(e), individualiste, inflexible, intellectuel(le), intelligent(e), intéressant(e), long(ue), modeste, naïf / naïve, nerveux / nerveuse, optimiste, ordinaire, parisien(ne), patient(e), persévérant(e), pessimiste, précis(e), raisonnable, réaliste, riche, sérieux / sérieuse, sincère, snob, sociable, solitaire**

### Les vêtements

**le béret** beret
**le blouson** windbreaker
**les bottes** (*f.*) boots
**la casquette** baseball cap
**le chapeau** hat
**les chaussettes** (*f.*) socks
**les chaussures** (*f.*) shoes
**la chemise** shirt
**le chemisier** blouse
**le costume** (*man's*) suit
**la cravate** tie
**l'imperméable** (*m.*) raincoat
**le jean** jeans
**la jupe** skirt
**le maillot de bain** swimsuit

**le manteau** coat
**le pantalon** pants
**le pull-over** sweater
**la robe** dress
**le sac à dos** backpack
**le sac à main** handbag
**les sandales** (*f.*) sandals
**le short** shorts
**le tailleur** woman's suit
**le tee-shirt** T-shirt
**les tennis** (*m.*) tennis shoes
**la veste** sports coat, blazer
**le veston** suit jacket

**Les couleurs**

**blanc / blanche** white
**bleu(e)** blue
**gris(e)** gray
**jaune** yellow
**marron** (*inv.*) brown
**noir(e)** black
**orange** (*inv.*) orange
**rose** pink
**rouge** red
**vert(e)** green
**violet(te)** violet

**Mots et expressions divers**

**assez** somewhat
**de taille moyenne** of medium
 height
**moi aussi** me too
**moi non plus** me neither
**n'est-ce pas?** isn't it so?
**peu** not very; hardly
**un peu** a little
**Quel âge avez-vous
 (as-tu)?** How old are you?

# CHAPITRE **4**

# À la maison°

À... *At home*

**Les dossiers de Léa**

Léa

➤ 📁 Mes photos
  ➤ 📁 Des appartements de luxe
  ➤ 📁 Un petit «chez moi»
  ➤ 📁 De vieilles maisons à Montréal

Des appartements de luxe dans le septième arrondissement

# Dans ce chapitre...

## OBJECTIFS COMMUNICATIFS

- ➤ locating people and objects
- ➤ expressing the absence of something
- ➤ getting information
- ➤ expressing actions
- ➤ describing people, places, and things
- ➤ learning to distinguish between and pronounce selected sounds in French

Un petit «chez moi»: une chambre de bonne

## PAROLES (Leçon 1)

- ➤ Les prépositions de lieu
- ➤ L'ameublement

## STRUCTURES (Leçons 2 et 3)

- ➤ Les articles indéfinis après **ne... pas**
- ➤ Les mots interrogatifs
- ➤ Les verbes en **-ir**
- ➤ La place de l'adjectif qualificatif

De vieilles maisons à Montréal

## CULTURE

- ➤ Le blog de Léa: *Chez moi*
- ➤ Reportage: *Montréal: vivre en français*
- ➤ Lecture: *La colocation* (Leçon 4)

connect
|FRENCH
www.mhconnectfrench.com

# Leçon 1

## Clarisse, Justin et la voiture°

*car*

Justin est **dans** le parc, **entre** le banc (*bench*) et l'arbre (*tree*).

Clarisse est **dans** sa voiture, **loin du** parc.

Maintenant, elle est **en face de** l'université, **près du** parc.

Justin est **devant** la voiture.

Clarisse est **à côté de** la voiture. Justin est **sur** la voiture.

---

### Prononcez bien!

**The vowels in *sous* and *sur***

The difference between these two vowels lies in tongue position: in the back of your mouth for [u] in **sous,** and all the way to the front, pressing against your lower teeth, with tensely rounded and protruding lips, for [y] in **sur.**

> [u]: **j<u>ou</u>e, c<u>ou</u>rt, bl<u>ou</u>son**

> [y]: **j<u>u</u>pe, c<u>u</u>re, sal<u>u</u>t**

To help you produce the sound [y], pronounce the sound [i] in **dit,** and progressively round your lips, making sure your tongue does not shift to the back of your mouth: **du.**

> **dit → du**

> **vie → vue**

> **lit → lu**

---

Justin pousse la voiture. Il est **derrière** la voiture.

Clarisse est **sous** la voiture. Justin est **à gauche de** la voiture. Les outils (*tools*) sont **par terre, à droite de** la voiture.

| LES PRÉPOSITIONS DE LIEU | |
|---|---|
| **dans** | *in* |
| **entre** | *between* |
| **chez** | *at the home of; at the office of* |
| **à côté de** | *next to, beside* |
| **en face de** | *across from, opposite* |
| **devant ≠ derrière** | *in front of ≠ behind* |
| **sur ≠ sous** | *on ≠ under* |
| **à gauche de ≠ à droite de** | *to the left of ≠ to the right of* |
| **près de ≠ loin de** | *near ≠ far from* |
| **par** | *by; through* |
| **par terre** | *on the ground* |

 *Allez-y!*

A. **Vrai ou faux?** The following statements correspond (by number) to the drawings on the previous page. Correct any statements that are wrong.

   1. Justin est assis (*seated*) sur le banc.
   2. Clarisse est à côté du parc.
   3. Elle est près de l'université.
   4. Justin est derrière la voiture.
   5. Clarisse est à gauche de la voiture.
   6. Justin est en face de la voiture.
   7. Clarisse est sur la voiture.

B. **Désordre.** Justin has a problem with clutter! Describe his room, using **les prépositions de lieu.**

   **MODÈLE:** Il y a deux livres sous la chaise.

# Deux chambres d'étudiants

La chambre de Céline est en désordre. Elle loue un appartement dans un immeuble moderne.

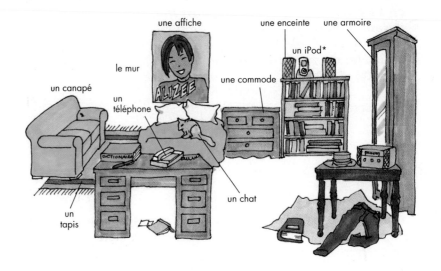

La chambre d'Anne est en ordre. Elle habite dans une maison.

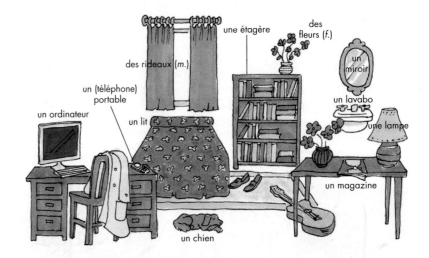

**AUTRES MOTS UTILES**

| | |
|---|---|
| **une chambre de bonne** | a maid's room; a garret |
| **un meuble** | a piece of furniture |
| **un réveil** | an alarm clock |
| **une station d'accueil** | a docking station (iPod, cellphone) |
| **un studio** | a studio (one-room apartment) |

---

*iPod is a trademark of Apple, Inc.

# ||||| *Allez-y!*

**A. Deux chambres.** Taking turns with a partner, ask and answer questions about the two rooms. Start with **Qu'est-ce qu'il y a...** (*What is there . . .* ).

> **MODÈLE:** derrière l'étagère d'Anne? →
> É1: Qu'est-ce qu'il y a derrière l'étagère d'Anne?
> É2: Il y a un mur.

1. sur le bureau de Céline? d'Anne?
2. à côté du lit de Céline? d'Anne?
3. sous la table de Céline? d'Anne?
4. sur le lit de Céline?
5. sur l'étagère de Céline? d'Anne?
6. devant le lit d'Anne?
7. à côté du téléphone de Céline?
8. sur le mur de Céline? d'Anne?
9. par terre dans la chambre de Céline? d'Anne?
10. sur la table d'Anne?
11. à côté de l'étagère d'Anne?
12. sur le tapis de Céline? d'Anne?

**B. L'intrus.** Three items are similar and one is different in each of the following series. Find the items that are out of place.

1. lit / commode / armoire / fleur
2. iPod / affiche / guitare / enceintes
3. lavabo / livre / magazine / étagère
4. miroir / affiche / rideaux / magazine

**C. Préférences.** What might you find in the room of a person with the following interests?

> **MODÈLE:** les arts →
> Sur le mur, il y a des affiches; il y a des livres d'art dans l'étagère et à côté du lit,...

1. étudier
2. écouter de la musique
3. parler à des amis
4. le sport
5. la mode
6. le cinéma

Décrivez (*Describe*) cette chambre d'étudiant à la cité-U.

# Leçon 2

## Les articles indéfinis après *ne... pas*

*Expressing the Absence of Something*

### Un logement pour une copine

*Léa téléphone à Juliette.*

LÉA: Salut Juliette! Est-ce que tu as un canapé dans ton nouveau studio?

JULIETTE: Léa, **je n'ai pas de** studio, mais simplement une chambre de bonne! Et **je n'ai pas de** canapé: c'est minuscule, chez moi! J'ai un lit, une chaise, une commode et un bureau. C'est tout!

LÉA: Ah... c'est ennuyeux... C'est pour une copine italienne. Elle est à Paris pour deux jours et **elle n'a pas de** logement.

JULIETTE: Elle a certainement de l'argent pour un petit hôtel au Quartier latin... Elle a de la famille... des amis...

LÉA: Non. **Elle n'a pas d'**argent... **pas de** famille à Paris... et **pas d'**amis, excepté moi.

JULIETTE: Et moi, **je n'ai pas de** place.

Une chambre de bonne sous les toits (*rooftops*)

Complétez les phrases selon le dialogue.

1. Juliette n'a pas... (*trois choses*)
2. L'amie italienne n'a pas... (*quatre choses*)

1. In negative sentences, the indefinite article (**un, une, des**) becomes **de (d')** after **pas.**

Il a une amie.

Elle porte une casquette.

Il y a des voitures dans la rue.

Il n'a pas d'amie.

Elle ne porte pas
de casquette.

Il n'y a pas de
voitures dans la rue.

—Est-ce qu'il y a **un livre** sur
la table?

*Is there a book on the table?*

—Non, il n'y a **pas de livre**
sur la table.

*No, there is no book on the table.*

—Est-ce qu'il y a **des fleurs**
sur la table?

*Are there any flowers on the
table?*

—Non, il n'y a **pas de fleurs**
sur la table.

*No, there aren't any flowers on
the table.*

[Allez-y! A]

**2.** In negative sentences with **être,** however, the indefinite article does
not change.

> —**C'est un livre?**
> —**Non, ce n'est pas un livre.**

**3.** The definite article (**le, la, les**) does not change in a negative
sentence.

> —Elle a **la** voiture aujourd'hui?
> —Non, elle n'a pas **la** voiture.

[Allez-y! B]

## ||||| *Allez-y!*

**A. Chambre à louer.** (*Room for rent.*) The room Jacob is inquiring
about is very sparsely furnished. Play the roles of Jacob and his
prospective landlord or landlady, following the example.

**MODÈLE:** une télé →
    É1: Est-ce qu'il y a une télé dans la chambre?
    É2: Non, il n'y a pas de télé.

**1.** un lavabo      **4.** des étagères
**2.** une armoire      **5.** une commode
**3.** des tapis      **6.** un lit

**B.** **Une interview.** Interview a classmate. Pay close attention to the articles.

> **MODÈLES:** avoir un ordinateur →
>> É1: Tu as un ordinateur?
>> É2: Non, je n'ai pas d'ordinateur. *or* Oui, j'ai un ordinateur.
>
> aimer les ordinateurs →
>> É1: Tu aimes les ordinateurs?
>> É2: Non, je n'aime pas les ordinateurs. *or* Oui, j'aime les ordinateurs.

1. étudier le russe (l'italien, l'allemand)
2. avoir une chambre (un appartement, une maison)
3. travailler le soir (*in the evening*) (le samedi, le dimanche)
4. avoir des albums de Beyoncé (des albums de musique classique, des albums de jazz)
5. aimer les chats (les chiens)
6. ?

**Résumez!** Now summarize what you have learned about your classmate for the rest of the class: **Il/Elle a... , mais il/elle n'a pas de (d')...**

# Les mots interrogatifs

*Getting Information*

## Studio à louer

*Appel vidéo entre Hassan et Léa.*

| | |
|---|---|
| HASSAN: | **Commen**t vas-tu, Léa? |
| LÉA: | Très bien... Je révise. J'ai un examen de littérature. |
| HASSAN: | **Quand?** Demain? |
| LÉA: | Non, jeudi. **Pourquoi**[1]**?** |
| HASSAN: | Parce que[2] je visite un appartement tout à l'heure. Tu m'accompagnes? |
| LÉA: | Mais, c'est nouveau! Tu déménages? **Où?** Dans **combien de** temps? |
| HASSAN: | Dans quelques[3] jours, peut-être. Il y a un studio à louer, juste en face de mon restaurant. C'est une opportunité! |
| LÉA: | **Qui** est le propriétaire? |
| HASSAN: | C'est un client! Un jeune homme charmant... |
| LÉA: | Vraiment? Alors, j'arrive! |

[1]*Why?*  [2]*Parce... Because*  [3]*several*

Trouvez les mots interrogatifs qui correspondent aux réponses ci-dessous.

1. Très bien.
2. Jeudi.
3. Parce que je visite un appartement.
4. En face de mon restaurant.
5. Dans quelques jours, peut-être.
6. Un client.

# Information Questions with Interrogative Words

Information questions ask for new information or facts. They often begin with interrogative expressions. Here are some of the most common interrogative adverbs in French.

| | | | |
|---|---|---|---|
| **où** | *where* | **pourquoi** | *why* |
| **quand** | *when* | **combien de** | *how much,* |
| **comment** | *how* | | *how many* |

Information questions can be formed with **est-ce que** or with a change in word order. (You may wish to review the presentation of yes/no questions in **Chapitre 3, Leçon 3.**) The interrogative word is usually placed at the beginning of the question.

**1.** These are information questions with **est-ce que.**

> **Où**
> **Quand**
> **Comment** } **est-ce que** Samuel joue du banjo?
> **Pourquoi**

> **Combien de** fois par semaine (*times a week*) **est-ce que** Samuel joue?

**2.** These are information questions with a change in word order.

PRONOUN SUBJECT

> **Où**
> **Quand**
> **Comment** } étudie-t-il la musique?
> **Pourquoi**

> **Combien d'**instruments a-t-il?

NOUN SUBJECT

> **Où**
> **Quand**
> **Comment** } Samuel étudie-t-il la musique?
> **Pourquoi**

> **Combien d'**instruments Samuel a-t-il?

**3.** These are information questions consisting of a noun subject and verb only. With **où, quand, comment,** and **combien de,** it is possible to ask information questions using only a noun subject and the verb, with no pronoun.

> **Où**
> **Quand** } étudie Samuel?
> **Comment**
> **Combien d'**instruments a Samuel?

However, the pronoun is almost always required with **pourquoi.**

> **Pourquoi** Samuel étudie-t-**il?**

[Allez-y! A-B-F]

## Prononcez bien!

**The pronunciation of *quand***

Unlike English, in which *qu* is often pronounced [kw], in French, **qu** is generally pronounced [k], as in **que.**

> [k]: **que, quand, quatre, Québec, physique**

Only when **qu** precedes *oi* is it pronounced [kw]: **pourquoi.**

In liaison, the **d** of **quand** is pronounced [t].

> [t]: **quand est-ce que, quand on parle**

## Information Questions with Interrogative Pronouns

Some of the most common French interrogative pronouns (**les pronoms interrogatifs**) are **qui**, **qu'est-ce que**, and **que**. **Que** becomes **qu'** before a vowel or mute **h**. **Qui** is invariable.

1. **Qui** (*who, whom*) is used to ask about a person or people.

| | |
|---|---|
| **Qui** étudie le français? | *Who studies French?* |
| **Qui** regardez-vous? | |
| **Qui** est-ce que vous regardez? | *Whom are you looking at?* |
| **À qui** Samuel parle-t-il? | |
| **À qui** est-ce que Samuel parle? | *Whom is Samuel speaking to?* |

 *est-ce que ou inversion*

2. **Qu'est-ce que** and **que** (*what*) refer to things or ideas. **Que** requires inversion.

| | |
|---|---|
| **Qu'est-ce que** vous étudiez? | |
| **Qu'**étudiez-vous? | *What are you studying?* |
| **Que** pense-t-il de la chambre? | *What does he think of the room?* |

[Allez-y! C-D-E-F]

## ||||| *Allez-y!*

**A. De l'argent.** Monsieur Harpagon is sometimes stingy. Respond to these statements as he would, using **pourquoi.**

**MODÈLE:** J'ai besoin d'un manteau. →
Pourquoi avez-vous besoin d'un manteau?

1. Nous avons besoin d'une étagère.
2. Ariane a besoin d'un dictionnaire d'anglais.
3. Paul a besoin d'une voiture.
4. J'ai besoin d'un nouveau tapis.

**B. Une chambre d'étudiant.** Complete the conversation with the appropriate interrogative expressions. **Suggestions:** comment, où, pourquoi, quand, combien de...

**MODÈLE:** SABINE: Comment est la chambre?
JULIEN: La chambre est *très agréable.*

SABINE: _____? *Où*
JULIEN: La chambre est *sur la rue Napoléon.*
SABINE: _____? *quand*
JULIEN: J'emménage (*I move in*) *jeudi.*
SABINE: _____? *Comment*
JULIEN: La chambre est *petite mais confortable.*

SABINE: _____? *combien de*
JULIEN: Il y a *deux* chaises et *une* table.
SABINE: _____? *Où*
JULIEN: La lampe est *à côté de la station d'accueil.*
SABINE: _____? *pourquoi*
JULIEN: J'ai un iPod *parce que j'adore la musique.*
SABINE: _____? *quand*
JULIEN: J'écoute de la musique *quand j'étudie.*

> ## Mots clés
>
> ### Giving reasons
>
> To answer the question **pourquoi?**, use **parce que** (**parce qu'** before a vowel sound). *because*
>
> Je travaille **parce que** j'ai besoin d'argent.

**C.** **Une visite chez Camille et Lola.** Ask a question in response to each statement about Camille and Lola's new apartment. Use **qu'est-ce que** or **que.**

> **MODÈLE:** Nous visitons le logement de Camille et Lola. →
> Qu'est-ce que vous visitez? (*ou* Que visitez-vous?)

1. Nous admirons l'ordre de la chambre de Camille.
2. Il y a un miroir sur le mur.
3. Je regarde les affiches de Camille.
4. Je trouve des magazines intéressants.
5. Habib n'aime pas les rideaux à fleurs.
6. Nous aimons bien la vue et le balcon.
7. Ah non, la porte est ouverte! Tout le monde cherche le chat de Camille.

**D.** **Les étudiants et le logement.** *housing* With a little help from her friends, Brigitte finds a new room. Create a question, using **qui** or **à qui,** that corresponds to each item of information.

> **MODÈLE:** *Brigitte* cherche un logement. →
> Qui cherche un logement?

1. *M^{me} Boucher* a une petite chambre à louer dans une maison.
2. Vanessa et Richard parlent de M^{me} Boucher à *Brigitte.*
3. Brigitte téléphone à *M^{me} Boucher.*   4. M^{me} Boucher montre la chambre à *Brigitte.*   5. *Brigitte* loue la chambre de M^{me} Boucher.

**E.** **Voici les réponses.** Invent questions for these answers.

> **MODÈLE:** Dans la chambre de Claire. →
> Où est-ce qu'il y a des affiches de cinéma?
> Où sont les livres de Cécile?

1. C'est un magazine français.
2. À l'université.
3. Parce que je n'ai pas envie d'étudier.
4. Vingt-quatre étudiants.
5. À Laure.
6. Djamila.
7. Très bien.
8. Parce que j'ai faim.
9. Maintenant.

**F.** **Êtes-vous curieux/curieuse?** Why is it always the instructor who asks questions? It's your turn to question him/her. Be formal; use inversion.

> **MODÈLES:** D'où êtes-vous?
> Pourquoi aimez-vous le français?

# Le blog de Léa

## Chez moi

Un petit «chez moi»: une chambre de bonne

**mercredi 25 mai**

Chers amis du blog, j'ai un problème.

J'ai 19 ans et j'habite encore avec maman et papa. Ils trouvent ça normal. Pas moi.

Habiter un petit «chez moi», c'est mon rêve.[1] Juste un studio ou une simple chambre de bonne avec un lit, une armoire et une douche. Comme Juliette.

Voilà mon idéal: une petite chambre sous les toits,[2] à côté de la fac.

Mais ce n'est pas facile de trouver un logement à Paris, spécialement au Quartier latin. Je cherche, je regarde les petites annonces[3]… Rien.[4]

Quand est-ce que je vais trouver?

Hassan me conseille la colocation[5]: il a peut-être raison…

Léa

· · · · · · · · · · · · · · · · · · · · · · · · · · · · · · · · · · · · · · · · · · · · · · · ·

### COMMENTAIRES

**Alexis**

Salut Léa!

Au Québec, comme aux États-Unis, les étudiants n'habitent pas chez leurs parents. Ils ont une chambre à l'université. Déménage[6]! Tu es une adulte, après tout.

**Mamadou**

Moi aussi, Léa, pour étudier en France, j'ai déménagé à Paris. Ma famille habite toujours au Sénégal.

**Charlotte**

Pourquoi déménager? On est bien chez ses parents…

**Poema**

Ton copain[7] Hassan n'a pas tort: la colocation, c'est une solution intéressante. Propose à tes parents! D'ailleurs,[8] à côté de chez moi, il y a une chambre à louer. Elle a l'air pas mal. C'est une colocation. Regarde l'annonce sur Internet: «Étudiante d'origine québécoise cherche colocataire. Propose jolie chambre de 12 m² [9] dans bel appartement. Immeuble avec concierge. Au 5e étage[10] sans ascenseur.[11] 500 euros/mois, charges comprises.[12]»

---

[1]*dream* [2]*sous… on the top floor (lit. under the roof)* [3]*petites… classified advertisements* [4]*Nothing* [5]*me… is advising me to get a roommate* [6]*Move out!* [7]*buddy* [8]*Moreover* [9]12 *mètres carrés = 12 square meters = approx. 129 sq. ft.* [10]*cinquième… = 6th floor (of an American building)* [11]*sans… without elevator* [12]*included*

## Montréal: vivre en français

Parler français, dans une ambiance française, mais sur le continent américain, est-ce que c'est possible? Bien sûr!

Il y a près de chez vous un territoire francophone. C'est la province de Québec, au Canada. Dans cette région, le français est la langue officielle des administrations, du travail, du commerce et des communications.

Combien de membres représente cette communauté? Huit millions de personnes. Très actives et passionnément francophiles, elles désirent protéger leur héritage culturel francophone.

Étudiante américaine, Deborah étudie le français à l'université de Montréal pour devenir professeur. Tous les jours, elle lit[1] *Le journal de Montréal* ou *La presse*. À la télévision, elle regarde des programmes français proposés par le Réseau de l'Information[2] (RDI).

**Montréal est la ville des contrastes:** Les demeures (*residences*) anciennes du Vieux-Montréal et d'autres quartiers montréalais s'opposent aux grands immeubles ultra modernes d'autres secteurs de la ville.

Elle aime se promener[3] dans les rues tranquilles de la vieille ville. «J'ai l'impression d'être en Europe», dit-elle. On comprend[4] pourquoi: Montréal a été fondé[5] par les Français en 1642.[6] Ses origines sont évidentes dans son architecture, dans les noms des rues, dans le Vieux-Port. Mais surtout,[7] à Montréal, on attache une importance essentielle à la beauté de l'environnement et à la qualité de vie. Exactement comme à Paris, à Rome ou à Madrid.

[1]*reads*  [2]*Réseau... Information Network*  [3]*se... to walk*  [4]*understands*  [5]*a... was founded*  [6]mille six cent quarante-deux  [7]*especially*

1. Regardez la carte à la fin du livre. Où est la province de Québec? la ville de Montréal?
2. Pourquoi est-ce qu'on parle français à Montréal?
3. Pourquoi Deborah aime-t-elle particulièrement Montréal?
4. Sur la photo, quels détails suggèrent que Montréal est une ville francophone?

Travaillez à deux. Répondez, tour à tour, à ces deux questions que vous pose votre camarade:

Comment s'appelle la ville où tu es né(e) (*born*)? Où est-elle située? Utilisez les prépositions de lieu données dans votre manuel (page 93). Suivez le modèle.

**MODÈLE:**  Je suis né(e) à La Nouvelle-Orléans. La ville est située sur le Mississippi. La Nouvelle-Orléans n'est pas loin du Golfe du Mexique.

# Leçon 3

## Les verbes en *-ir*

*Expressing Actions*

### Du camping à Londres?

*Léa et Juliette discutent au café.*

JULIETTE: **Tu réfléchis à** nos vacances?

LÉA: Oui! J'ai envie de faire du ski d'été dans les Alpes. Ou bien de visiter Londres. **Tu choisis!**

JULIETTE: Léa, **on finit** toujours par aller où tu désires! Alors, tu décides!

LÉA: Bon: c'est Londres!

JULIETTE: Ça va. J'aime bien l'Angleterre. Si **nous réussissons** à trouver un petit hôtel pas cher, c'est d'accord.

LÉA: Non. L'hôtel, c'est impersonnel. **Je réfléchis à** une autre solution de logement.

JULIETTE: Le camping, par exemple? (Elle rit.)

Complétez les phrases par les verbes en **-ir** qui figurent dans le dialogue.

**1.** Tu _____ à nos vacances?

**2.** Tu _____ les Alpes ou Londres?

**3.** Comme toujours, on _____ par aller où tu désires!

**4.** Nous _____ à trouver un petit hôtel.

**5.** Je _____ à une solution.

Londres, une des destinations préférées des jeunes français

Although the infinitives of the largest group of French verbs end in **-er,** those of a second group end in **-ir.** To form the present tense of these verbs, drop the final **-ir** and add the endings shown in the chart.

| PRESENT TENSE OF **finir** (*to finish*) | | | |
|---|---|---|---|
| je | fin**is** | nous | fin**issons** |
| tu | fin**is** | vous | fin**issez** |
| il/elle/on | fin**it** | ils/elles | fin**issent** |

The **-is** and **-it** endings of the singular forms have silent final consonants. The double **s** of the plural forms is pronounced.

**1.** Other verbs conjugated like **finir** include:

| | |
|---|---|
| **agir** | *to act* |
| **choisir** | *to choose* |
| **réfléchir (à)** | *to reflect (upon), to consider* |
| **réussir (à)** | *to succeed (in)* |

| | |
|---|---|
| J'**agis** toujours avec logique. | *I always act logically.* |
| Nous **choisissons** des affiches. | *We're choosing some posters.* |

**2.** The verb **réfléchir** requires the preposition **à** before a noun when it is used in the sense of *to consider, to think about,* or *to reflect upon something.*

| | |
|---|---|
| Elles **réfléchissent aux** questions de Paul. | *They are thinking about Paul's questions.* |

**3.** The verb **réussir** requires the preposition **à** before an infinitive or before the noun* in the expression **réussir à un examen** (*to pass an exam*).[†]

| | |
|---|---|
| Je **réussis** souvent **à** trouver les réponses. | *I often succeed in finding the answers.* |
| Marc **réussit** toujours **à** l'examen d'histoire. | *Marc always passes the history exam.* |

**4.** The verb **finir** requires the preposition **de** before an infinitive. When **finir** is followed by **par** + infinitive, it means *to end up (doing).*

| | |
|---|---|
| En général, je **finis d'**étudier à 8 h 30. | *I usually finish studying at 8:30.* |
| On **finit** souvent **par** regarder la télé. | *We often end up watching TV.* |

 *Allez-y!*

**A. À la bibliothèque.** Read the following description of Céline's visit to the library. Then imagine that Céline and Anne are there together and restate the account using **nous.**

Je choisis un livre de référence sur la Révolution française. Je réfléchis au sujet. Je réussis à trouver une revue intéressante sur la Révolution. Je finis très tard.

**B. En cours de littérature.** Complete the sentences with appropriate forms of **agir, choisir, finir, réfléchir,** or **réussir.**

1. Le professeur _____ des textes intéressants.
2. Les étudiants _____ avant de répondre aux questions du professeur.
3. Pierre et Anne _____ toujours leur travail très vite (*fast*).
4. Nous _____ toujours aux examens.
5. Toi, tu _____ souvent sans (*without*) réfléchir.

---

*Note the exception: **réussir sa vie** (*to make a success of one's life*) does not require the preposition **à.**
[†]**Passer un examen** means *to take an exam,* not *to pass* one.

---

**Prononcez bien!**

**The consonant *s***

When the letter **s** begins a word and when it occurs between a vowel and a consonant, pronounce it as [s].

[s]: ré**p**on**s**e

When it is surrounded by two vowels, pronounce it as [z].

[z]: choi**s**ir

To make an [s] sound between two vowels, the spelling is usually **ss.** Remember to write **ss** in conjugations that require it.

[s]: fini**ss**ez, réu**ss**i**ss**ons

Notice that the sound [s] can also be produced by other letters.

[s]: mer**c**i, **ç**a, na**t**ion, soi**x**ante

**C. Choisissez!** What might these people pick out for their new rooms? **Suggestions:** une armoire, des enceintes, des étagères, un iPod, un miroir, un ordinateur

**MODÈLE:** Karim. Il aime la musique. → Il choisit un iPod.

**1.** Ako. Elle étudie l'informatique.   **2.** Fatima et Julie. Elles ont beaucoup de livres.   **3.** Luc. Il est vaniteux (*vain*).   **4.** Antoine et Romain. Ils ont beaucoup de vêtements.   **5.** Chantal. Elle aime écouter la musique très fort (*loud*).

**D. Une conversation.** Use the following cues as a springboard for discussion with a classmate.

**MODÈLE:** réussir / aux examens →
  É1: Est-ce que tu réussis toujours aux examens?
  É2: Oui, bien sûr, je réussis toujours aux examens!
  É1: Ah, tu es intelligent(e)! Moi, je ne réussis pas toujours aux examens.

**1.** agir / souvent / sans réfléchir
**2.** finir / exercices / français
**3.** choisir / cours (difficiles, faciles,… )
**4.** réfléchir / problèmes (politiques, des étudiants,… )
**5.** choisir / camarade de chambre (patient, intellectuel, calme,… )

# La place de l'adjectif qualificatif

*Describing People, Places, and Things*

## Cinquante euros la nuit

*Léa téléphone à Juliette.*

LÉA: Juliette, je suis sur le site Booking.com. Voici une proposition **intéressante:** «Loue **beau** studio dans **joli petit** immeuble **ancien. Bon** quartier de Londres.»
JULIETTE: Tu as des photos?
LÉA: Oui, deux photos. Je regarde… Ah! La vue est horrible: un parking!
JULIETTE: Comment est la salle de bains?
LÉA: Il y a une **petite** douche avec un **vieux** rideau. Les murs sont jaunes!
JULIETTE: Stop! C'est non! Je déteste le jaune!
LÉA: Mais Juliette, ce n'est pas cher! 50 euros la nuit!

Quelles sont les caractéristiques du studio, de l'immeuble et du quartier? Utilisez les adjectifs du dialogue.

**1.** C'est un _____ studio.
**2.** C'est un _____ _____ immeuble ancien.
**3.** C'est un _____ quartier.
**4.** C'est une _____ douche.
**5.** C'est un _____ rideau.

Booking.com

accueil → royaume-uni → londres → appartements : londres
12.569 établissements   1.167 établissements   240 établissements

Rechercher des appartements : Londres

Du                    Au
[ Jour ] [ Mois ]     [ Jour ] [ Mois ]

Je n'ai pas de dates de séjour précises
Personnes [ 2 adultes (1 chambre) ]

**Rechercher**

Plus d'1 milliard de nuitées réservées et chaque jour un peu plus… ❶

Le boom des réservations sur Internet

## Adjectives That Usually Precede the Noun

**1.** Certain short and commonly used adjectives usually precede the nouns they modify.

| REGULAR | IRREGULAR | IDENTICAL IN MASCULINE AND FEMININE |
|---|---|---|
| **grand(e)*** *big, tall; great* <br> **joli(e)** *pretty* <br> **mauvais(e)** *bad* <br> **petit(e)** *small, little* <br> **vrai(e)** *true* | **ancien / ancienne*** *old; former* <br> **beau / belle** *beautiful, handsome* <br> **bon(ne)** *good* <br> **cher / chère*** *dear; expensive* <br> **dernier / dernière** *last* <br> **faux / fausse** *false* <br> **gentil(le)** *nice, kind* <br> **gros(se)** *large; fat, thick* <br> **long(ue)** *long* <br> **nouveau / nouvelle** *new* <br> **premier / première** *first* <br> **vieux / vieille** *old* | **autre** *other* <br> **chaque** *each, every* <br> **jeune** *young* <br> **pauvre*** *poor; unfortunate* |

| | |
|---|---|
| Marise habite une **petite** chambre en cité-U. | *Marise lives in a small room at the university dormitory.* |
| Les **jeunes** étudiants aiment bien le cinéma. | *Young students like to go to the movies.* |
| C'est une **bonne** idée! | *It's a good idea!* |

**2.** The adjectives **beau, nouveau,** and **vieux** are irregular. They have two masculine forms in the singular.

*[handwritten margin note:]*
*Beauty*
*Age*
*Newness*
*Goodness*
*Size*

| SINGULAR | | |
|---|---|---|
| MASCULINE | MASCULINE BEFORE VOWEL OR MUTE **h** | FEMININE |
| un **beau** livre <br> un **nouveau** livre <br> un **vieux** livre | un **bel** appartement <br> un **nouvel** appartement <br> un **vieil** appartement | une **belle** voiture <br> une **nouvelle** voiture <br> une **vieille** voiture |

| PLURAL | |
|---|---|
| MASCULINE | FEMININE |
| de **beaux** appartements <br> de **nouveaux** appartements <br> de **vieux** appartements | de **belles** voitures <br> de **nouvelles** voitures <br> de **vieilles** voitures |

[Allez-y! A]

---

*More information about **grand, ancien, cher,** and **pauvre** can be found on the next page.

## Adjectives Preceding Plural Nouns

When an adjective precedes a noun in the plural form, the plural indefinite article **des** generally becomes **de.**\*

J'ai **des** livres de français. —→ J'ai **de** nouveaux livres de français.
Il y a **des** films à la télé. —→ Il y a **de** vieux films à la télé.

[Allez-y! B-C]

## Adjectives That Can Precede or Follow Nouns They Modify

The adjectives **ancien / ancienne** (*old; former*), **cher / chère** (*dear; expensive*), **grand(e),** and **pauvre** can either precede or follow a noun, but their meaning depends on their position. Generally, the adjective in question has a literal meaning when it follows the noun and a figurative meaning when it precedes the noun.

| LITERAL SENSE | FIGURATIVE SENSE |
|---|---|
| Il a des chaises **anciennes.** *He has antique chairs.* | M. Sellier est l'**ancien** propriétaire. *Mr. Sellier is the former landlord.* |
| C'est un lecteur de DVD très **cher.** *That's a very expensive DVD player.* | Ma **chère** amie... *My dear friend . . .* |
| C'est un homme très **grand.**† *He's a very tall man.* | C'est un très **grand** homme. *He's a great man.* |
| Les étudiants **pauvres** reçoivent une bourse de l'État. *Poor (not rich) students receive a scholarship from the state.* | **Pauvres** étudiants! Il y a un examen demain! *The poor (unfortunate) students! There is an exam tomorrow!* |

## Placement of More Than One Adjective

When more than one adjective modifies a noun, each adjective precedes or follows the noun as if it were used alone.

C'est une **petite** femme **blonde.**
J'ai de **bons** livres **français.**
C'est un **vieil** immeuble **agréable.**

---

\*In informal speech, **des** is often retained before the plural adjective: **Elle a toujours *des belles* plantes.**
†The adjective **grand(e)** is placed *after* the noun to mean *big* or *tall* only in descriptions of people. In descriptions of things and places, **grand(e)** is placed *before* the noun to mean *big, large,* or *tall:* **les grandes fenêtres, un grand appartement, une grande table.**

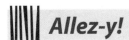 *Allez-y!*

**A. Vous déménagez?** You are moving out of the apartment you share with a friend. Specify which items you are taking with you.

> **MODÈLE:** la table / vieux → J'emporte la vieille table.

*les belles chaises*

1. le lit / petit
2. les tapis / grand
3. l'ordinateur / nouveau
4. le lecteur de DVD / vieux
5. la commode / grand
6. les chaises / beau

**B. David emménage!** David has moved into his new apartment, and he's explaining where everything goes. Give the plural form of the nouns, and make the appropriate agreements.

> **MODÈLE:** Je place <u>un beau vase</u> sur l'étagère. →
> Je place de beaux vases sur l'étagère.

Pour décorer, je mets <u>une vieille affiche</u>[1] sur le mur. Près du lit, il y a <u>une petite lampe</u>[2]. J'ai <u>une nouvelle chaise</u>[3] pour la table de cuisine. À la fenêtre, j'installe <u>un long rideau</u>.[4] Pour me détendre (*relax*), je passe (*play*) <u>un bon album</u>.[5] Pour finir, j'invite <u>un vieux copain</u>[6] (*buddy*).

**C. L'amie de David.** David's friend Julie has joined him to go shopping for things for his new apartment. For each sentence, provide the proper form and placement for the adjectives within parentheses.

> **MODÈLE:** David regrette les _____ excursions _____. (ennuyeux, long) →
> David regrette les longues excursions ennuyeuses.

1. Il cherche une _____ commode _____. (ancien, autre)
2. Julie est une _____ femme _____. (petit, sympathique)
3. Elle porte une _____ robe _____. (beau, blanc)
4. Le petit ami de Julie est un _____ homme _____. (dynamique, jeune)
5. Il aime les _____ voitures _____. (américain, vieux)

**D. Jeu de logique.** Complete the following thoughts logically using **les mots de liaison** found in the **Mots clés.**

1. J'habite dans un beau quartier, _____ c'est un peu cher.
2. Je vais déménager (*I'm going to move*) _____ je trouve un nouvel appartement.
3. J'ai envie d'habiter dans le vieux quartier de la ville _____ en banlieue (*in the suburbs*).
4. Pour le moment, mon amie Jeanne n'a pas d'argent, _____ elle habite chez ses (*her*) parents.
5. C'est une femme calme _____ organisée.
6. Elle commence un nouvel emploi (*job*) le mois prochain (*next*), _____ elle pense emménager avec moi.

**E. Chez moi.** Ask a classmate to describe his/her room. Use questions to get information on placement, color, size, and so on. As he/she gives you the details, draw a plan of the room. Then repeat the exercise, answering his/her questions about your room.

---

**Le parler jeune**

| | |
|---|---|
| un **appart** | un appartement |
| un **coloc** | un colocataire |
| une **piaule** | une chambre |
| un **pieu** / un **plumard** | un lit |
| un **proprio** | un propriétaire |

Mon **appart** est joli mais trop petit!

Ton **coloc** est un ami?

Max loue une **piaule** au Quartier latin.

Le matin, impossible de sortir de mon **pieu**!

Ton **proprio**, il est sympa?

---

## Mots clés

**Using conjunctions**

To make more complex and interesting sentences, use the following words:

| | |
|---|---|
| **et** | *and* |
| **alors** | *so* |
| **ou** | *or* |
| **mais** | *but* |
| **si** | *if* |
| **donc** | *therefore* |

Geneviève est riche **et (mais)** généreuse.

J'habite près de l'université **donc (alors)** j'étudie souvent à la bibliothèque.

# Prononcez bien!

1. **The vowels in *sous* and *sur*** (page 92)

   A. **Questions pour un champion!** You and your roommate Hugo are watching your favorite game show on TV. Hugo is talking about Justine, one of the contestants from the day before. You don't remember her, so Hugo describes her. Listen and complete the paragraph with the words you hear. Each one contains the sound [u] as in **sous** or [y] as in **sur**.

   HUGO: Rappelle-toi! Elle était (*was*) _____,[1] aux cheveux _____,[2] avec une _____,[3] un _____ [4] et des _____ [5] _____,[6] _____ [7] à l'_____,[8] en _____ ;[9] intelligente et _____.[10]

   B. **Le jeu de l'autre mot.** The show starts with a game in which the host says a word containing either [u] as in **sous** or [y] as in **sur** and asks contestants to come up with a similar-sounding word containing the other vowel. Your partner will play the **présentateur/présentatrice** (*host*) and read the following words while you play one of the **candidats** (*contestants*) and give the answers.

   MODÈLE: PRÉSENTATEUR/PRÉSENTATRICE: rousse
              CANDIDAT(E): russe

   1. cure
   2. jus (*juice*)
   3. doux (*soft*)
   4. vue (*view*)
   5. tout (*all*)
   6. nu (*naked*)
   7. pur(e)

2. **The consonant *s*** (page 105)

   A. **Un nouveau joueur.** One of the contestants was eliminated and replaced by a new one, who is now introducing himself. Listen and complete the sentences.

   _____[1]! Je m'appelle _____.[2] Je suis _____ [3] de _____ [4] à l'_____ [5] de la Sorbonne. Mes étudiants aiment bien mes cours. Ils _____ [6] qu'ils sont _____,[7] mais _____ [8] et, parfois, _____.[9] Quand les étudiants font des efforts et qu'ils _____ [10] beaucoup, ils _____ [11] bien au cours.

   B. **Trouvez l'intrus.** After the contestants' introduction, the show resumes with two *Odd Man Out* games. The presenter will read two lists of five words that contain the letter s. Say the word that doesn't belong, based on its sound.

# Leçon 4

 Lecture

### Avant de lire

**Predicting content from titles.** The title of a reading selection often helps you anticipate content by activating your background knowledge about a topic. Brainstorming topics based on a title before you read will make reading easier, because you will already have information in mind that can aid your comprehension.

The text you will read in this section is called "La colocation." What do you already know about renting a room or a house with another person? Make a short list of the advantages and disadvantages. Use the following questionnaire as a guide. Then, as you read, see how many of the items you mentioned appear in the text.

**Acceptable ou inacceptable?** Which of the following situations would you consider acceptable or unacceptable behavior from a housemate?

|  | ACCEPTABLE | INACCEPTABLE |
|---|---|---|
| **1.** Votre colocataire (*housemate*) organise une soirée; vous n'êtes pas invité(e). | ☐ | ☐ |
| **2.** Les amis de votre colocataire arrivent à l'improviste (*unexpectedly*). | ☐ | ☐ |
| **3.** Le petit ami / La petite amie de votre colocataire emménage chez vous. | ☐ | ☐ |
| **4.** Votre colocataire mange vos provisions, mais il/elle aime cuisiner (*to cook*) pour vous. | ☐ | ☐ |
| **5.** Votre colocataire déménage sans donner de préavis (*without notice*). | ☐ | ☐ |

# La colocation

### *En France: un phénomène nouveau et populaire*

Vous êtes jeune, avec un petit budget, et vous cherchez un logement? Bonne chance! Trouver un logement indépendant à Paris et dans les grandes villes est presque[1] impossible! Pourquoi? Parce que les chambres de bonne sous les toits, les studettes[2] et les studios pour étudiants sont rares et chers. Et les candidats très nombreux. Mais il y a une solution: partager[3] un appartement avec des amis.

[1]*almost*   [2]*maids' rooms, typically with shared bathrooms and showers*   [3]*share*

**À propos de la lecture...**
This reading was adapted from *Quo* magazine.

Voici un petit appartement à partager.
Est-ce que vous aimez le décor?
Pourquoi / Pourquoi pas?

## *Une expérience unique*

Vivre ensemble dans un appartement, étudier, partager la même salle de bains, faire les courses, préparer à dîner, c'est amusant, mais ce n'est pas facile. Pour les Français qui sont très indépendants, la colocation, ce phénomène nouveau, demande des efforts et de la patience. Mais quelle expérience enrichissante! Voilà une occasion unique d'apprendre la tolérance et d'établir des amitiés éternelles.

## *Bien vivre en colocation*

Pour une colocation réussie, voici quelques règles de vie commune.

- **Les amis.** N'encouragez pas vos amis à venir à l'improviste, surtout juste avant un examen. Présentez vos amis à votre colocataire.
- **Les soirées.** Écrivez les dates de vos soirées sur un calendrier commun pour éviter[4] de mauvaises surprises. Invitez votre colocataire à vos soirées de temps en temps.
- **Le petit ami / La petite amie.** Si le contrat stipule deux personnes, la colocation n'est pas pour trois ou quatre personnes!
- **La nourriture.**[5] Achetez la nourriture séparément et ne mangez pas les provisions de l'autre.
- **Le ménage.**[6] Il y a des degrés variables de tolérance au désordre. Il est nécessaire de parler de ce sujet avec votre colocataire et de partager le travail.

Et n'oubliez pas[7]: le dialogue et l'humour sont essentiels quand on partage un appartement!

[4]*avoid*   [5]*Food*   [6]*Housework*   [7]*n'... don't forget*

### *Compréhension*

**A. Pourquoi?** Expliquez pourquoi...

1. les étudiants choisissent la colocation plus souvent que les autres groupes.
2. il est difficile pour les Français de vivre en colocation.
3. la colocation est une expérience enrichissante.

**B. Oui ou non?** Indiquez si l'auteur du texte conseille (*recommends*) ou déconseille les comportements suivants.

1. Si le petit ami / la petite amie de votre colocataire emménage chez vous, accueillez-le/la (*welcome him/her*).
2. Désignez une personne pour faire le ménage, une autre pour faire la cuisine.
3. Parlez des problèmes immédiatement.
4. N'invitez pas votre colocataire à vos soirées.
5. La nourriture dans le frigo appartient à (*belongs to*) tout le monde.

### Un peu plus...

**Vincent Van Gogh.**
Van Gogh (1853–1890) was born in the Netherlands but lived and worked most of his life in France. Early in his career, he lived in Paris among a community of artists in Montmartre, a neighborhood in the northern part of the city. He later left Paris for the south of France, where he was particularly inspired by the vivid colors of nature. The colors and bright sunlight of Provence are captured in some of his more well-known paintings of sunflowers, gardens, and his bedroom in Arles. Art critics speak of the intensity of emotion associated with this painting, *Chambre d'Arles*. What makes this work so intense?

◀ Vincent Van Gogh: *Chambre d'Arles*, 1888. (Musée d'Orsay, Paris)

# Écriture

The writing activities **Par écrit** and **Journal intime** can be found in the Workbook/Laboratory Manual to accompany *Vis-à-vis*.

# Pour s'amuser

### Le rébus

Work with a partner and use the lexique to solve the puzzle.

# Le vidéoblog de Léa

Léa visite l'appartement de Sonia

## En bref

In this episode, Léa meets Sonia, a young woman originally from Montreal who lives in Paris and is looking for a roommate to share her apartment. After being shown around the apartment, Léa asks Sonia to describe the architectural landscape of Montreal for her videoblog.

### Vocabulaire en contexte

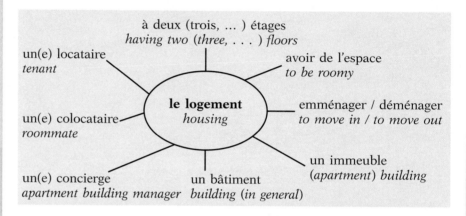

à deux (trois, … ) étages
*having two (three, . . . ) floors*

un(e) locataire
*tenant*

avoir de l'espace
*to be roomy*

**le logement**
*housing*

emménager / déménager
*to move in / to move out*

un(e) colocataire
*roommate*

un immeuble
*(apartment) building*

un(e) concierge
*apartment building manager*

un bâtiment
*building (in general)*

## Visionnez!

For each statement, choose the adjective that best describes Sonia's apartment and neighborhood.

1. Léa trouve que l'appartement de Sonia est petit / grand.
2. Elle pense que le séjour (*living room*) est très sombre / clair.
3. La chambre de Sonia est simple / en désordre.
4. La chambre à louer (*for rent*) est petite / grande.
5. L'appartement est dans un quartier super / désagréable.
6. Les locataires sont vraiment cool / désagréables.

## Analysez!

1. Sonia dit (*says*) que Montréal est une ville «où l'architecture du passé et du présent coexistent». Donnez des exemples.
2. Sonia dit aussi que Montréal est une ville «ouverte». Expliquez.

## Comparez!

Watch Léa's visit to Sonia's apartment again. Is Sonia's apartment similar to student apartments near your campus? Using the vocabulary presented above, as well as other words you know, describe the housing possibilities for students in your area.

> **MODÈLE:** Il y a de petits appartements dans des immeubles à deux étages, et il y a aussi…

# Vocabulaire

## Verbes

**agir** to act
**bavarder** to chat
**choisir** to choose
**déménager** to move out
**emménager** to move in
**finir (de** + *inf.*) to finish (*doing s.th.*)
  **finir par** + *inf.* to end up (*doing s.th.*)
**louer** to rent
**passer un examen** to take an exam
**réfléchir (à)** to think (about)
**réussir (à)** to succeed (in); to pass (*a test*)

## Substantifs

**l'affiche** (*f.*) poster
**l'appartement** (*m.*) apartment
**l'armoire** (*f.*) wardrobe, closet
**le (baladeur) iPod** iPod (player)
**le canapé** sofa
**la chambre** bedroom
  **chambre de bonne** maid's room; garret
**le chat** cat
**le chien** dog
**la commode** chest of drawers
**le couloir** hallway
**la douche** shower
**l'enceinte** (*f.*) speaker
**l'étagère** (*f.*) shelf
**la fleur** flower
**la guitare** guitar
**l'immeuble** (*m.*) apartment building
**la lampe** lamp
**le lavabo** bathroom sink
**le lit** bed
**la location** rent
**le logement** lodging, place of residence
**le magazine** magazine

**la maison** house
**le meuble** piece of furniture
**le miroir** mirror
**le mur** wall
**le réveil** alarm clock
**le rideau** curtain
**la rue** street
**la station d'accueil** docking station (iPod, cell phone)
**la studette** small studio (apartment) with shared bathroom
**le studio** studio (apartment)
**le tapis** rug
**le téléphone** telephone
**le (téléphone) portable** cell phone
**les toilettes** (*f. pl.*) **(les W.-C.)** restroom
**la voiture** car

À REVOIR: **le bureau, la chaise, l'ordinateur, la table, la télé(vision)**

## Adjectifs

**ancien(ne)** old, antique; former
**autre** other
**bon(ne)** good
**chaque** each
**dernier / dernière** last
**faux / fausse** false
**gros(se)** large; fat; thick
**jeune** young
**joli(e)** pretty
**mauvais(e)** bad
**premier / première** first
**vieux / vieil / vieille** old
**vrai(e)** true

À REVOIR: **beau / bel / belle, cher / chère, facile, gentil(le), grand(e), long(ue), nouveau / nouvel / nouvelle, pauvre, petit(e)**

## Prépositions de lieu

**à côté de** beside
**à droite de** on the right of
**à gauche de** on the left of
**chez** at the home of; at the office of
**derrière** behind
**devant** in front of
**en face de** across from
**entre** between
**loin de** far from
**par** by
  **par terre** on the ground
**près de** near
**sous** under
**sur** on

## Mots interrogatifs

**combien (de)** how many, how much
**comment** how, what
**où** where
**pourquoi** why
**qu'est-ce que, que** what
**quand** when
**qui** who, whom

## Mots et expressions divers

**alors** so; then
**donc** then; therefore
**en désordre** disorderly
**en ordre** orderly
**parce que** because
**si** if

# Bienvenue...

LA LOUISIANE

La Nouvelle-Orléans

## Un coup d'œil sur La Nouvelle-Orléans et le pays des Cadiens,° en Louisiane

*Cajuns*

Le célèbre Café du Monde à La Nouvelle-Orléans

Quand on parle de la Louisiane, on pense souvent à La Nouvelle Orléans et au Mardi Gras. Et c'est vrai, il y a des traces françaises dans l'architecture, la cuisine, les noms et les traditions de La Nouvelle Orléans. Mais à l'extérieur de cette grande ville, il y a toute une autre culture francophone à découvrir—le pays des Cadiens. Au sud-ouest de la ville, vous pouvez[1] explorer les bayous et parler français avec les habitants des communautés de nom français, comme LaRose et Belle Rivière. Si vous continuez plus vers le nord-ouest, vous allez traverser le Bassin de l'Atchafalaya, un grand marais[2] entre Bâton Rouge et Lafayette. Si vous avez le temps, allez à Henderson pour faire une visite guidée de l'Atchafalaya en bateau—vous allez peut-être y voir des cocodrils[3]! Si vous avez faim, goûtez du boudin* ou des écrevisses.[4] On mange bien en Louisiane!

Qui sont les Cadiens? Ce sont les descendants des Acadiens, un peuple d'origine française, exilés du Canada par les Anglais en 1755. Alors, beaucoup d'Acadiens s'installent en Louisiane, qui est un territoire francophone. Ce qu'on appelle «cadien» aujourd'hui est vraiment un mélange[5] de cultures. La musique, la cuisine et même la langue cadiennes sont influen-cées par les Créoles, les Espagnols, les Amérindiens[6] et d'autres groupes ethniques en Louisiane. La Louisiane française, c'est un véritable gombo!

[1]*can*  [2]*swamp*  [3]*alligators (Cajun)*  [4]*crawfish*  [5]*mixture*  [6]*Native Americans*

## PORTRAIT Feufollet[†]

Feufollet: un groupe de jeunes musiciens de Louisiane

La musique et la danse cadiennes sont populaires partout dans le monde, surtout là où on parle français. Feufollet est un groupe de jeunes musiciens de Louisiane qui jouent de la musique traditionnelle avec une saveur[1] originale. Ils découvrent la musique cadienne quand ils sont encore à l'école primaire, lors[2] d'un pro-gramme d'immersion française où ils étudient les maths, les sciences et même l'éducation physique en français. Avec leurs parents, ils vont aux Festivals Acadiens et Créoles où ils entendent de la musique traditionnelle. Bientôt ils commencent à jouer et à chanter en français comme leurs ancêtres. Aujourd'hui, ces jeunes adultes jouent leur musique en Louisiane, en France, au Canada—et aux Festivals Acadiens et Créoles! Les musiciens de Feufollet trouvent qu'il est important de comprendre et de parler la langue qu'ils chantent. Ils s'amusent, ils gagnent de l'argent et ils préservent leur héritage.

[1]*flavor*  [2]*during*

***Boudin** is a spicy sausage made of rice, ground pork, onions, and other seasonings. It is sold widely in local grocery stores as a quick snack or meal. The traditional blood sausage that the French call **boudin** also exists in Louisiana, where it is known as **boudin rouge**.
[†]In southwestern Louisiana, the **feu follet** refers to a shining light seen over the swamps at night. Folk tales came up with many different meanings for these lights, such as the souls of babies who had died without being baptized.

# en Amérique du Nord

LE CANADA

## Un coup d'œil sur Québec, au Canada

Est-ce que vous aimez faire du ski[1]? Avez-vous envie de faire du magasinage,[2] ou est-ce que vous préférez visiter les musées? Venez voir la ville de Québec, la capitale de la province de Québec, et l'une des seules[3] villes fortifiées en Amérique du Nord. Les Québécois sont toujours très fiers de leur héritage francophone et, pour environ[4] 80 % des Québécois, le français est leur langue maternelle.

Dans le Vieux-Québec, il y a beaucoup de magasins chic et de bons restaurants. Visitez le musée de la Civilisation, qui propose des expositions sur l'histoire et la culture contemporaine du Québec. Sur la terrasse Dufferin, derrière le château Frontenac, vous pouvez écouter des musiciens québécois pendant l'été[5] ou faire des glissades[6] pendant l'hiver.[7] Chaque février pendant le carnaval de Québec, on célèbre les plaisirs de l'hiver avec des feux d'artifice,[8] de la musique et une grande compétition de sculptures sur neige[9]!

L'hiver dans le Vieux-Québec

[1]faire... *go skiing*  [2]faire... *go shopping (Quebec expression)*
[3]*only*  [4]*approximately*  [5]pendant... *during the summer*
[6]faire... *go tobogganing*  [7]*winter*  [8]feux... *fireworks*
[9]sculptures... *snow sculptures*

### PORTRAIT Samuel de Champlain (c. 1567[1]–1635[2])

Grand géographe et explorateur français, Samuel de Champlain explore, entre 1603[3] et 1633,[4] les régions du fleuve[5] Saint-Laurent, l'Acadie (appelée[6] aujourd'hui la Nouvelle-Écosse et le Nouveau-Brunswick) et le Québec. Champlain devient[7] l'ami des Amérindiens Hurons et des Algonquins, qui lui font découvrir[8] leur pays. Il fonde la ville de Québec en 1608.[9]

[1]mille cinq cent soixante-sept  [2]mille six cent trente-cinq  [3]mille six cent trois  [4]mille six cent trente-trois
[5]*river*  [6]*called*  [7]*becomes*  [8]qui... *who help him discover*  [9]mille six cent huit

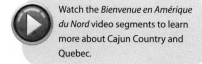 Watch the *Bienvenue en Amérique du Nord* video segments to learn more about Cajun Country and Quebec.

# De génération en génération

Les dossiers d'Hassan

Hassan

➤ Mes photos
➤ Un mariage à Rennes
➤ Abdel, Carole et moi
➤ Une famille marocaine

Un mariage à Rennes dans une salle élégante

# Dans ce chapitre...

## OBJECTIFS COMMUNICATIFS

- ➤ talking about family and relatives
- ➤ identifying rooms in a house
- ➤ talking about weather
- ➤ expressing possession
- ➤ talking about plans and destinations
- ➤ expressing what you are doing and making
- ➤ expressing actions
- ➤ learning to distinguish between and pronounce selected sounds in French

Abdel, Carole et moi dans mon restaurant

## PAROLES (Leçon 1)

- ➤ La famille
- ➤ La maison
- ➤ Les saisons et le temps

Une famille marocaine

## STRUCTURES (Leçons 2 et 3)

- ➤ Les adjectifs possessifs
- ➤ Le verbe **aller** et le futur proche
- ➤ Le verbe **faire**
- ➤ Les verbes en **-re**

## CULTURE

- ➤ Le blog d'Hassan: *Un mariage franco-marocain*\*
- ➤ Reportage: *La famille au Maroc: une valeur sûre*
- ➤ Lecture: *Giverny: le petit paradis de Monet* (Leçon 4)

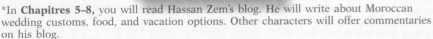

www.mhconnectfrench.com

\*In **Chapitres 5–8,** you will read Hassan Zem's blog. He will write about Moroccan wedding customs, food, and vacation options. Other characters will offer commentaries on his blog.

# Leçon 1

## Trois générations d'une famille

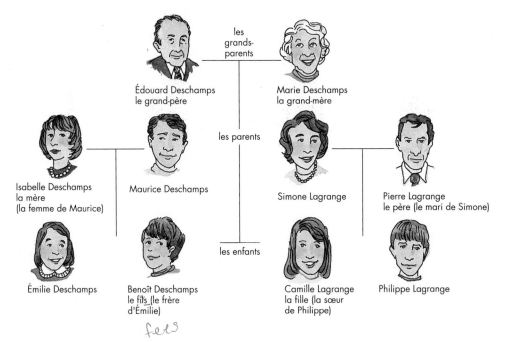

les grands-parents

Édouard Deschamps
le grand-père

Marie Deschamps
la grand-mère

les parents

Isabelle Deschamps
la mère
(la femme de Maurice)

Maurice Deschamps

Simone Lagrange

Pierre Lagrange
le père (le mari de Simone)

les enfants

Émilie Deschamps

Benoît Deschamps
le fils (le frère
d'Émilie)

Camille Lagrange
la fille (la sœur
de Philippe)

Philippe Lagrange

**AUTRES MOTS UTILES**

**le petit-enfant**  grandchild
**la petite-fille**  granddaughter
**le petit-fils**  grandson

**le parent**  parent (*or* relative)
**les arrière-grands-parents** (*m. pl.*)
    great-grandparents

**le cousin, la cousine**  cousin
**le neveu**  nephew
**la nièce**  niece
**l'oncle** (*m.*)  uncle
**la tante**  aunt

**célibataire**  single
**divorcé(e)**  divorced
**marié(e)**  married
**pacsé(e)**  joined legally by a PACS*

**le beau-frère**  brother-in-law
**la belle-sœur**  sister-in-law
**le demi-frère**  half brother (*or* stepbrother)
**la demi-sœur**  half sister (*or* stepsister)
**le beau-père**  father-in-law (*or* stepfather)
**la belle-mère**  mother-in-law (*or* stepmother)
**le gendre**  son-in-law
**la bru**  daughter-in-law

---

*The **Pacte civil de solidarité** is a type of civil union voted into French law in 1999 by the National Assembly. Two adults (same sex or not) may enter into a **PACS** by registering with the court clerk. Same sex marriage became legal in France on May 18, 2013.

 *Allez-y!*

A. **La famille Deschamps.** Étudiez l'arbre généalogique (*family tree*) de la famille Deschamps et répondez aux questions.

1. Comment s'appelle la femme d'Édouard?
2. Comment s'appelle le mari d'Isabelle?
3. Comment s'appelle la tante d'Émilie et de Benoît? Et l'oncle?
4. Combien d'enfants ont les Lagrange? Combien de filles et de fils?
5. Comment s'appelle le frère d'Émilie?
6. Combien de cousins ont Émilie et Benoît? Combien de cousines?
7. Comment s'appelle la grand-mère de Philippe? Et le grand-père?
8. Combien de petits-enfants ont Édouard et Marie? Combien de petites-filles? Combien de petits-fils?
9. Comment s'appelle la sœur de Philippe?
10. Comment s'appellent les parents de Maurice et de Simone?

B. **Qui sont-ils?** Complétez les définitions suivantes.

1. Le frère de mon père est mon _____.
2. La fille de ma tante est ma _____.
3. Le père de ma mère est mon _____.
4. La femme de mon grand-père est ma _____.

Maintenant définissez les personnes suivantes .

5. une nièce               8. un grand-père
6. des arrière-grands-parents     9. une belle-sœur
7. une tante               10. un demi-frère

C. **Une famille américaine.** Posez (*Ask*) les questions suivantes à votre camarade.

1. As-tu des frères, des sœurs, des demi-frères ou des demi-sœurs? Combien? Comment s'appellent-ils/elles? (Ils/Elles s'appellent... )
2. As-tu des grands-parents? Combien? Habitent-ils chez toi, dans une maison ou dans un appartement?
3. As-tu des cousins ou des cousines? Combien? Habitent-ils/elles près ou loin de la famille?
4. Combien d'enfants (de fils ou de filles) désires-tu avoir? Combien d'enfants est-ce qu'il y a dans une famille idéale?

D. **Une famille française.** Avec un(e) camarade, décrivez la famille sur la photo. Donnez le nombre de personnes, et devinez (*guess*) qui sont les personnes et quel âge elles ont. Puis imaginez leur (*their*) profession, leurs goûts (*tastes*), leur personnalité. Donnez le plus de détails (*as many details as*) possibles.

C'est une affaire de famille. Qui voyez-vous?

# Chez les Chabrier

MAISON À LOUER: 3 pièces (*f.*)
+ cuisine, salle de bains

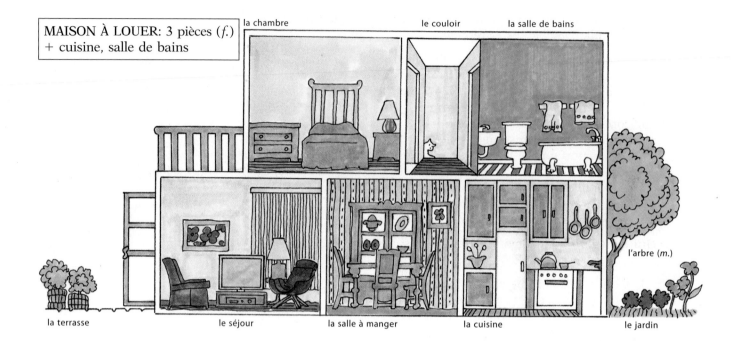

AUTRES MOTS UTILES

| | |
|---|---|
| **le bureau** | study, office |
| **la clé** | key |
| **l'escalier** (*m.*) | stairway |
| **le rez-de-chaussée** | ground floor |
| **le premier (deuxième) étage** | second (third) floor (*in North America*) |
| **le sous-sol** | basement |

 *Allez-y!*

A. **Les pièces de la maison.** Trouvez les pièces d'après (*according to*) les définitions suivantes.

MODÈLE: C'est un lieu qui donne sur (*that overlooks*) la terrasse. →
C'est le balcon.

1. la pièce où il y a une table pour manger  2. la pièce où il y a une télévision  3. la pièce où il y a un lavabo  4. la pièce où on prépare le dîner  5. un lieu de passage  6. la pièce où il y a un lit

B. **Dans quelle pièce?** Regardez encore une fois la maison des Chabrier. Où est-ce qu'on fait (*does*) les choses suivantes? Commencez vos phrases avec **On...**

1. regarder la télé: sur le balcon / dans le séjour
2. planter des fleurs: dans le jardin / dans la chambre
3. jouer avec le chat: dans la salle de bains / dans le couloir
4. manger: dans le couloir / dans la salle à manger
5. préparer un café: dans la cuisine / sur le balcon

# Quel temps fait-il? Les saisons et le temps°

*Quel… How's the weather?*
*Seasons and weather*

Au **printemps,** chez les Belges…
Le temps est nuageux. *cloudy*
Il fait frais. *fresh*
*chilly*
*cool*

En **été,** chez les Martiniquais…
Il fait beau. *nice/sunny*
Il fait du soleil. (Il fait soleil.)
Il fait chaud. *hot*

En **automne,** chez les Bretons…
Il pleut. *rain*
Il fait mauvais. *bad*
Le temps est orageux. *stormy*

En **hiver,** chez les Québécois…
Il neige. *snow*
Il fait froid. *cold*
Il fait du vent. (Il y a du vent.) *windy*

- To ask about the weather:

  Quel temps fait-il?

- To tell about the season:

  Nous sommes au printemps (en été, en automne, en hiver).

 **Prononcez·bien!**

**The pronunciation of *premier***

The **-er** in **premier** and **dernier** (*last*) has two different pronunciations: [e], as in **et,** when it ends a sentence or is followed by a word starting with a consonant, and [ɛʀ], as in **mère,** when it precedes a word beginning with a vowel sound.

[e]: **le premier jour, le dernier mois**

[ɛʀ]: **le premier étage, le dernier été, le premier homme**

 *Allez-y!*

**A. Parlons du temps.** Répondez aux questions suivantes.

1. En quelle saison est Pâques (*Easter*)?
2. Quel temps fait-il en hiver en Alaska?
3. Est-ce qu'il fait beau l'hiver à Seattle?
4. En quelle saison est le Jour d'action de grâce (*Thanksgiving Day*)?
5. C'est le mois de mai. Quel temps fait-il chez vous?

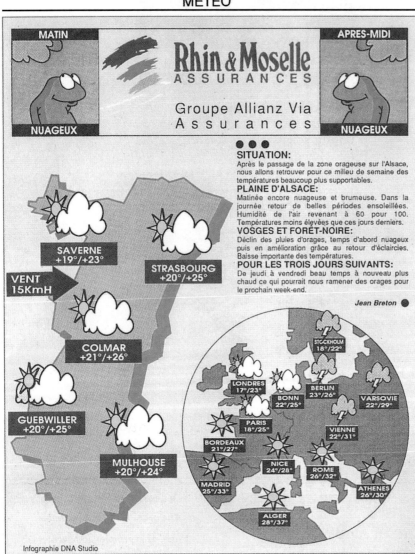

**B. Les prévisions de la météo.** (*Weather forecast.*) Regardez le temps prévu pour l'Alsace et l'Europe et répondez aux questions suivantes.

1. Quel temps fait-il en Alsace?
   a. Il neige.
   b. Le temps est nuageux.
   c. Il pleut.
2. Quel temps fait-il à Berlin?
   a. Il fait (du) soleil.
   b. Le temps est orageux.
   c. Il fait beau.
3. Quel temps fait-il à Alger?
   a. Il fait mauvais.
   b. Il fait froid.
   c. Il fait (du) soleil.

**C. Le temps et les goûts.** Qu'est-ce que vous aimez porter quand... ?

1. il fait très chaud
2. il fait froid et qu'il neige
3. il fait beau et frais
4. il pleut

# Leçon 2

## Les adjectifs possessifs

*Expressing Possession*

### Vacances d'été

*Mamadou contacte Léa sur sa page Facebook (Messagerie instantanée).*

 MAMADOU: Léa, quels sont **tes** projets pour l'été?

 LÉA: **Mon** programme de juillet est très agréable: un petit voyage à Londres avec **mon** amie Juliette, et deux semaines à la montagne avec **ma** sœur et **son** mari, **mes** parents, **leur** chien… et **mon** chat!

 MAMADOU: Il a de la chance, **ton** chat! Et en août?

 LÉA: **Ma** sœur, **mes** cousins, **mon** chat et moi sommes chez **nos** grands-parents dans **notre** maison de famille en Normandie. C'est une tradition.

 MAMADOU: Quand est-ce que **vos** vacances finissent?

 LÉA: Le 31 août. Nous retournons tous à Paris!

 MAMADOU: Avec **ton** chat?

 LÉA: Avec **mon** chat!

Vrai ou faux?

1. Léa voyage en juillet avec son amie Juliette.
2. Juliette va (*is going*) à la montagne avec sa sœur, ses parents et leur chien.
3. En août, Léa et sa sœur vont (*are going*) chez leurs grands-parents.
4. Leurs cousins aussi vont être chez leurs grands-parents.
5. Léa retourne à Paris sans (*without*) son chat.

One way to indicate possession in French is to use the preposition **de: la maison *de* Claudine.** Another way is to use the possessive adjectives presented on the next page.

| | SINGULAR | | PLURAL |
| | MASCULINE | FEMININE | MASCULINE AND FEMININE |
|---|---|---|---|
| *my* | **mon** père | **ma** mère | **mes** parents |
| *your (informal)* | **ton** père | **ta** mère | **tes** parents |
| *his, her, its, one's* | **son** père | **sa** mère | **ses** parents |
| *our* | **notre** père | **notre** mère | **nos** parents |
| *your (formal and plural)* | **votre** père | **votre** mère | **vos** parents |
| *their* | **leur** père | **leur** mère | **leurs** parents |

1. In French, possessive adjectives agree in gender and number with the nouns they modify.

> **Mon frère** et **ma sœur** aiment le sport.
>
> Voilà **notre maison.**
>
> Habitez-vous avec **votre sœur** et **vos parents?**
>
> Ils skient avec **leurs cousins** et **leur oncle.**

> *My brother and my sister like sports.*
>
> *There's our house.*
>
> *Do you live with your sister and your parents?*
>
> *They're skiing with their cousins and their uncle.*

2. The forms **mon, ton,** and **son** are also used before feminine nouns that begin with a vowel or mute **h.**

> affiche (*f.*) ⟶ **mon affiche**
> amie (*f.*) ⟶ **ton amie**
> histoire (*f.*) ⟶ **son histoire**

3. Pay particular attention to the use of **son, sa, ses** (*his, her*). Whereas English has two possessives, corresponding to the gender of the possessor (*his, her*), French has three, corresponding to the gender and number of the noun possessed (**son, sa, ses**).

> SINGULAR NOUNS:
> Masculine    Il / Elle } aime **son** chien.
>
> Feminine    Il / Elle } aime **sa** maison.
>
> PLURAL NOUNS:    Il / Elle } aime **ses** oncles et **ses** tantes.

**Prononcez bien!**

**The vowels in *notre* and *nos***

Clearly distinguish between the vowel [ɔ] in the singular form **notre/votre** and the vowel [o] in the plural form **nos/vos** of the possessive adjective.

Open your mouth and keep your tongue in a central position for **notre/votre;** close your mouth further, shift your tongue to the front of your mouth, and let your lips protrude for **nos/vos.**

The sound [ɔ] is generally spelled **o: div**o**rcé, s**o**l, al**o**rs.**

The sound [o] is also often spelled **o** when it is the last pronounced sound in the syllable: **lavab**o**, j**o**li.**

Other spellings for the sound [o] include **bient**ô**t, ch**au**d,** and **b**eau**.**

In the preceding examples, **son, sa,** and **ses** can all mean *his* or *her*. Usually, their meaning will be clear in context. Look at the following examples.

Carine habite une grande maison. **Son** jardin est magnifique.

Pierre a deux enfants: **sa** fille a 5 ans et **son** fils a 3 ans. **Ses** enfants sont jeunes.

*Carine lives in a big house. Her garden is magnificent.*

*Pierre has two children: His daughter is 5 years old and his son is 3 years old. His children are young.*

### Grammaire interactive

For more on possessive adjectives, watch the corresponding Grammar Tutorial and take a brief practice quiz at **Connect French.**

**connect**
|FRENCH

www.mhconnectfrench.com

*Allez-y!*

**A. Le vide-grenier.** (*Garage sale.*) À la fin du semestre, les étudiants organisent un vide-grenier. Formulez des questions et répondez.

> **MODÈLES:** la lampe de Nicolas? (oui) →
> É1: Est-ce que c'est la lampe de Nicolas?
> É2: Oui, c'est sa lampe.
>
> les lampes de Nicolas (non) →
> É1: Est-ce que ce sont les lampes de Nicolas?
> É2: Non, ce ne sont pas ses lampes.

**1.** la chaise de Pierre? (oui)
**2.** la commode de Léa? (non)
**3.** les affiches de Jean? (non)
**4.** le piano de Pierre et de Sophie? (oui)
**5.** les meubles d'Annick? (non)
**6.** les bureaux des parents? (oui)
**7.** l'ordinateur de Fatima? (oui)
**8.** l'étagère de Fabrice? (non)

**B. Casse-tête familial.** (*Family puzzle.*) Posez rapidement les questions suivantes à un(e) camarade.

> **MODÈLE:** Qui est le fils de ton oncle? → C'est mon cousin.

**1.** Qui est la mère de ton père?
**2.** Qui est la fille de ta tante?
**3.** Qui est la femme de ton oncle?
**4.** Qui est le père de ton père?
**5.** Qui est le frère de ta mère?
**6.** Qui est la sœur de ta mère?
**7.** Qui sont les femmes de tes frères?
**8.** Qui sont les enfants de tes sœurs?

**Le parler jeune**

| | |
|---|---|
| un copain/mec | un petit ami |
| une copine/meuf | une petite amie |
| sortir avec | avoir comme copain ou copine |
| un(e) frangin(e) | un frère / une sœur |
| un(e) gosse | un(e) enfant |

J'ai un nouveau **copain.**

Il parle des heures au téléphone avec sa **meuf.**

Mathilde **sort** avec le frère de sa meilleure amie.

J'ai une **frangine** et deux **frangins.**

Dans ma famille, on était trois **gosses.**

**C. La fête des voisins.** Les gens du quartier organisent un barbecue à l'occasion de la fête des voisins. Complétez les dialogues suivants avec les adjectifs possessifs. Étudiez bien le contexte avant de (*before*) choisir l'adjectif.

1. É1: Paul et Florence adorent les animaux.
   É2: Oui, ils ont un chien et deux chats: _leur_ chien s'appelle Marius et _leurs_ chats Minou et Félix.

2. É1: Tiens, voilà Pierre. Avec qui est-il?
   É2: Il est avec _ses_ parents et _son_ amie Laure.
   É1: Et _sa_ sœur n'est pas là?
   É2: Non, elle est en vacances au Maroc.

3. É1: Salut, Alain!
   É2: Salut, Pierre. Dis, la jolie fille aux cheveux blonds, c'est _ta_ cousine belge?
   É1: Oui. Viens. (*Come.*) Alain, je te présente _ma_ cousine Sylvie.
   É2: Enchanté, mademoiselle.

4. É1: Pardon, vous êtes Monsieur et Madame Legrand, n'est-ce pas?
   É2: Oui.
   É1: Je suis Monsieur Smith, le professeur d'anglais de _vos_ enfants.
   É2: Oh, mais ce ne sont pas _mes_ enfants, ce sont les fils de mon frère Laurent. Voici _son_ fils.

5. É1: Tu as de la chance, tu as une famille super! _Tes_ parents sont très sympas! Est-ce que _votre_ grand-père habite avec vous?
   É2: Non, mais il est souvent à la maison.
   É1: _Mon_ grand-père, malheureusement (*unfortunately*), habite très loin.

**D. Interview.** Posez les questions suivantes à un(e) camarade de classe.

1. Quel membre de ta famille (un cousin, une cousine, un neveu, et cetera) est-ce que tu admires particulièrement? Pourquoi?
2. Comment s'appelle-t-il/elle?
3. Où est-ce qu'il/elle habite? Avec qui? Comment est sa maison?
4. Quel est son sport préféré? sa musique favorite?

Maintenant faites le portrait du parent proche (*close relative*) préféré de votre camarade.

# Le verbe *aller* et le futur proche

*Talking About Plans and Destinations*

## Un bon programme

*Léa et Hector échangent des textos (SMS).*

LÉA: Il pleut! Où es-tu?

HECTOR: Je suis dans mon bus. **Je vais arriver** dans dix minutes.

LÉA: J'ai froid! **Je vais** dans un café.

HECTOR: Quel café?

LÉA: À l'angle du boulevard Beaumarchais et de la rue Saint-Gilles.

HECTOR: D'accord. Ensuite,* **nous allons** «Chez Denise» manger des pâtisseries!

LÉA: Et après, **on va** «Chez Clément» manger une soupe à l'oignon!

HECTOR: Tu es folle! **On va être** malades!

*Then

Vrai ou faux?

1. Hector va arriver dans dix minutes.
2. Léa va dans un café.
3. Hector et Léa vont «Chez Denise» pour manger une soupe à l'oignon.
4. Hector et Léa vont «Chez Clément» pour manger des pâtisseries.
5. Hector et Léa vont être malades.

## Forms of *aller*

The verb **aller** is irregular in form.

| PRESENT TENSE OF **aller** (*to go*) | | | |
|---|---|---|---|
| je | **vais** | nous | **allons** |
| tu | **vas** | vous | **allez** |
| il/elle/on | **va** | ils/elles | **vont** |

**Allez-vous** à Grenoble pour vos vacances? — *Are you going to Grenoble for your vacation?*

Comment est-ce qu'**on va** à Grenoble? — *How do you go to (get to) Grenoble?*

You have already used **aller** in several expressions.

Comment **allez-vous**? — *How are you?*
Salut, ça **va**? — *Hi, how's it going?*
Ça **va** bien / mal. — *Fine. / Badly.*

[Allez-y! A]

### Mots clés

**Exprimer le futur proche**

| | |
|---|---|
| tout à l'heure | *in a while* |
| tout de suite | *immediately* |
| bientôt | *soon* |
| demain | *tomorrow* |
| la semaine prochaine | *next week* |
| l'année prochaine | *next year* |
| dans quatre jours | *in four days* |
| ce week-end | *this weekend* |
| ce matin | *this morning* |
| cet après-midi | *this afternoon* |
| ce soir | *this evening* |

## *Aller* + Infinitive

In French, **aller** + infinitive is used to express an event that will occur in the near future. English also uses *to go* + infinitive to express actions or events that are going to happen soon. In French, this construction is called **le futur proche.**

Paul **va louer** un appartement. — *Paul is going to rent an apartment.*
**Allez**-vous **visiter** la France cet été? — *Are you going to visit France this summer?*

## *Ne... pas* and the *futur proche*

When the **futur proche** is used in the negative, **ne** precedes the form of **aller,** and **pas** follows.

Sylvie **ne** va **pas** étudier ce week-end. — *Sylvie is not going to study this weekend.*

[Allez-y! B-C-D]

### Grammaire interactive

For more on the verb **aller,** the **futur proche,** and the preposition **à** and its contractions, watch the corresponding Grammar Tutorial and take a brief practice quiz at **Connect French.**

www.mhconnectfrench.com

 ***Allez-y!***

**A. Où est-ce qu'on va?** La solution est simple!

> **MODÈLE:** J'ai envie de regarder un film. →
> Alors, je vais au cinéma!

1. Nous avons faim.      dans le séjour
2. Il a envie de parler français.      à la bibliothèque
3. Elles ont besoin d'étudier.      dans la cuisine
4. J'ai soif.      à Paris
5. Tu as sommeil.      dans la salle à manger
6. Vous avez envie de regarder la télévision.      dans la chambre
     au cinéma

**B. Des projets.** (*Plans.*) Qu'est-ce qu'on va faire (*to do*)?

> **MODÈLE:** tu / regarder / émission (*show*) préférée / soir →
> Tu vas regarder ton émission préférée ce soir.

1. je / finir / travail / semaine prochaine
2. nous / écouter / du jazz
3. vous / jouer / guitare
4. Frédéric / trouver / livre de français / bientôt
5. je / choisir / film préféré
6. les garçons / aller au cinéma / voiture / cet après-midi
7. tu / aller / concert / avec / amis

**C. À vous la parole!** Répondez aux questions suivantes.

1. Avec qui allez-vous prendre le petit déjeuner (*eat breakfast*) demain?
2. Qu'est-ce que vous allez faire demain après-midi?
3. Est-ce que vous allez faire du sport ce soir?
4. Quand allez-vous retourner à la maison ce soir?
5. Quand est-ce que vous allez passer votre prochain test de français?
6. La semaine prochaine, allez-vous aller au cinéma?
7. L'année prochaine, allez-vous continuer à étudier le français?

**D. Quels sont vos projets pour le week-end?** Interviewez un(e) camarade de classe. Rapportez à la classe les projets de votre camarade. Utilisez **peut-être** (*maybe*) si vous n'êtes pas certain(e).

**Suggestions:** rester (*stay*) à la maison, écouter la radio (de la musique), préparer un dîner (des leçons), regarder un film (la télévision), travailler à la bibliothèque (dans le jardin), aller au restaurant (au cinéma), parler avec des amis, finir un livre intéressant, et cetera.

> **MODÈLE:** aller au cinéma →
> É1: Vas-tu aller au cinéma?
> É2: Oui, je vais peut-être aller au cinéma. (*ou* Non, je ne vais pas aller au cinéma.) Et toi?

### Un peu plus...

**La famille.**
La photo date des années 50 (*the 1950s*): à cette époque (*at that time*), on se marie et ensuite, on a des enfants. Aujourd'hui, le mariage n'est plus le seul moyen (*only means*) acceptable de former une famille. En France, 56,6 % des enfants sont nés (*born*) de parents non-mariés. Et chez vous?

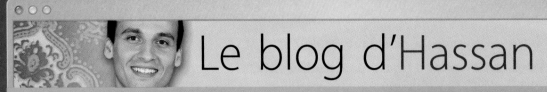

# Le blog d'Hassan

## Un mariage franco-marocain

jeudi 2 juin

Salut! Vous entrez dans le blog d'Hassan. Pour le moment j'écris,[1] mais bientôt je vais aussi faire des films vidéos comme un vrai pro des nouvelles technologies!

J'ai une grande nouvelle[2]: Mon copain Abdel va se marier.[3] Il est amoureux! Sa chérie s'appelle Carole. Elle est française.

Ça va être un mariage franco-marocain, un mariage interculturel.

Mais va-t-il être célébré en France ou au Maroc? Je ne sais pas: les fiancés n'ont pas encore pris leur décision.[4]

En tout cas, on va bien manger, c'est sûr! Et pourtant,[5] ce n'est pas moi qui vais préparer le repas de noces[6]…

On prévoit[7] au moins 110 invitations pour les parents, les grands-parents, les oncles et les tantes, les cousins et les cousines des deux côtés.[8] Et aussi les amis!

Hassan

Abdel, Carole et moi dans mon restaurant

. . . . . . . . . . . . . . . . . . . . . . . . . . . . . . . . . . . . . . . . . . . . . . . . . . . . . . . . . . . . . . . . .

### COMMENTAIRES

**Mamadou**

Salut, Hassan
Chez nous, en Afrique, la famille c'est synonyme de bonheur et de puissance.[9]
Si Abdel est comme un frère pour toi, tu vas bientôt avoir de nouveaux neveux et nouvelles nièces! Tu vas devenir tonton[10] adoptif! Tu es content?

**Alexis**

Tu es célibataire, Hassan? Veinard[11]! Le mariage, c'est une horrible invention humaine!

**Poema**

Tu es cynique, Alexis! Moi, je veux me marier,[12] je veux un mari et des enfants.
En Polynésie, la famille c'est une bénédiction.

**Charlotte**

Tu as raison, Poema. Le mariage, c'est l'équilibre! Ici, à Genève, j'ai une petite fille adorable et un mari très présent, et je suis heureuse.

---

[1]*I am writing* [2]grande… *big news* [3]va… *is getting married* [4]n'ont… *have not yet decided* [5]*however* [6]repas… *wedding meal* [7]On… *We are planning* [8]*sides* [9]bonheur… *happiness and strength* [10]*uncle* (fam.) [11]*Lucky you!* [12]veux… *want to get married*

## La famille au Maroc: une valeur sûre

Le Maroc change: en 2003, le Roi[1] Mohammed VI modernise le code de la famille. Le nouveau code introduit un principe révolutionnaire dans une société traditionnelle: l'égalité entre l'homme et la femme. Comme la Tunisie et le Liban, deux autres pays francophones, le Maroc choisit donc le progrès.

Une famille marocaine

Dans le couple d'aujourd'hui, l'homme et la femme ont des droits[2] et des obligations réciproques. Dans la société marocaine traditionnelle, au contraire, la femme devait[3] obéir à son mari et la polygamie était autorisée. Maintenant aussi, la femme a le droit de demander le divorce et, dans ce cas, elle a, en priorité, la garde[4] des enfants.

«C'est à travers une multitude de petits faits significatifs que l'on peut apprécier l'évolution de la société marocaine, explique Dounia, jeune mère et femme active. L'âge légal du mariage pour les femmes est de 18 ans au lieu de[5] 15 ans. La politique s'ouvre[6] aux femmes: le Maroc a des ambassadrices, et le Roi accepte d'avoir des conseillères. Dans les entreprises, les femmes ont accès à des postes de responsables.» Et Dounia ajoute: «Nous avons maintenant l'élection d'une Miss Maroc! Tout cela était inconcevable pour nos parents.»

Elle continue: «Mais attention! Le modèle européen n'est pas applicable chez nous. Le Maroc a des traditions qui fondent sa culture. Nous ne voulons pas y renoncer.[7] Par exemple, pour une Française ou une Américaine, servir son mari, c'est de la soumission. Pour une femme marocaine, c'est un moyen[8] d'établir son influence.»

Le mariage est toujours fortement valorisé[9] au Maroc. Plus de 90[10] pour cent des Marocains pensent qu'il est préférable aux hommes et aux femmes de se marier et d'avoir des enfants. Et la solidarité familiale reste fondamentale: pour les Marocains, les parents âgés doivent être pris en charge[11] par les enfants et non pas par l'État.

[1]*King* [2]*rights* [3]*had to* [4]*care* [5]au... *instead of* [6]*is opening up* [7]y... *reject them* [8]*means* [9]fortement... *highly valued*
[10]quatre-vingt-dix [11]doivent... *should be cared for*

À vous!

1. Que fait le Roi du Maroc en 2003 pour améliorer (*to improve*) la condition et le statut (*status*) de la femme marocaine?
2. Quels sont les nouveaux droits de la femme marocaine?
3. Expliquez: «Le modèle européen n'est pas applicable chez nous. Le Maroc a des traditions qui fondent sa culture.»
4. Comment s'exprime (*is expressed*) la solidarité familiale au Maroc? Et dans votre culture? Comment les Marocains traitent-ils leurs parents âgés? Et les Américains?

Parlons-en!

1. Dans quels domaines l'égalité entre les hommes et les femmes est-elle effective dans la société américaine? Parlez des études, du travail, du couple, du ménage et de la cuisine.
2. Comparez les droits de la femme marocaine et de la femme américaine. Qui est la plus émancipée—la femme marocaine ou la femme américaine? Expliquez. Qui valorise le plus le mariage? les enfants? les responsabilités professionnelles?

# Leçon 3

STRUCTURES

# Le verbe *faire*

*Expressing What You Are Doing or Making*

## Je fais tout!

*Hector téléphone à Hassan.*

HECTOR: Salut Hassan: ton restaurant, ça va?
HASSAN: Non. C'est terrible! Mon chef de cuisine est absent. **Je fais** tout!
HECTOR: **Tu fais** le service?
HASSAN: **Je fais** les courses, **je fais** la cuisine, **je fais** le service.
HECTOR: Moi aussi, **je fais** beaucoup de choses!
HASSAN: Toi, **tu fais** de la danse: c'est différent, c'est de l'art…
HECTOR: Mais avec mes colocataires, nous aussi, **nous faisons** tout à la maison: **nous faisons** le marché, la lessive, le ménage… Et ça, ce n'est pas de l'art!

Répondez aux questions.

1. Qu'est-ce qu'Hassan fait au restaurant?
2. Qui fait de la danse?
3. Qu'est-ce qu'Hector et ses colocataires font dans la maison?

Faire la lessive à la laverie automatique, ça, ce n'est pas de l'art!

## Forms of *faire*

The verb **faire** is irregular in form.

| PRESENT TENSE OF **faire** (*to do; to make*) | | | |
|---|---|---|---|
| je | **fais** | nous | **faisons** |
| tu | **fais** | vous | **faites** *(fette)* |
| il/elle/on | **fait** | ils/elles | **font** |

Note the difference in pronunciation of **fais / fait, faites,** and **faisons.**

**Je fais** mon lit.      *I make my bed.*
**Nous faisons** le café.      *We're making coffee.*
**Faites** la vaisselle.      *Do the dishes.*

## Expressions with *faire*

The verb **faire** is used in many idiomatic expressions.

| | |
|---|---|
| **faire attention (à)** | *to pay attention (to); to watch out (for)* |
| **faire la connaissance (de)** | *to meet (for the first time), make the acquaintance (of)* |
| **faire les courses** | *to do errands* |
| **faire la cuisine** | *to cook* |
| **faire ses devoirs** | *to do one's homework* |
| **faire la lessive** | *to do the laundry* |
| **faire le marché** | *to do the shopping; to go to the market* |
| **faire le ménage** | *to do the housework* |
| **faire une promenade** | *to take a walk* |
| **faire la queue** | *to stand in line* |
| **faire un tour (en voiture)** | *to take a walk (a ride)* |
| **faire la vaisselle** | *to do the dishes* |
| **faire un voyage** | *to take a trip* |

Le matin je **fais le marché**, et le soir je **fais mes devoirs**.

*In the morning I do the shopping, and in the evening I do my homework.*

1. **Faire** is also used to talk about individual sports: **faire du sport, faire du jogging, de la voile** (*sailing*), **du ski, de l'aérobic.**

2. As seen in **Leçon 1, il fait** is also used to describe the weather.

**Il fait** tellement beau! *It's so nice outside!*

 *Allez-y!*

**A. Faisons connaissance!** À une petite soirée à l'université, les gens se rencontrent (*meet each other*). Suivez le modèle.

**MODÈLE:** je / le professeur d'italien →
Je fais la connaissance du professeur d'italien.

1. tu / la sœur de Louise
2. nous / un cousin
3. Élodie / une étudiante sympathique
4. les Levêque / les parents de Clara
5. je / la femme du professeur
6. vous / la nièce de M. de La Tour

**B. Activités du week-end.** Qui fait les activités suivantes? Faites des phrases logiques avec les éléments des deux colonnes.

1. Tu... D
2. Pierre... F
3. Anne et Laure... E
4. Mon frère et moi, nous... A
5. Benoît et toi, vous... C
6. Non, moi le dimanche, je... B

a. faisons du jogging dans le parc.
b. ne fais pas le ménage.
c. faites vos devoirs de français.
d. fais la cuisine pour tes amis.
e. font des courses en ville.
f. fait du sport avec ses copains.

**C. D'habitude, qu'est-ce que vous faites?** Avec un(e) camarade de classe, faites une liste de vos activités habituelles. Utilisez les expressions suivantes: **le matin, le midi, le soir; le lundi (matin), le mardi,** et cetera; **le week-end, une fois par semaine** (*once a week*), **tous les jours** (*every day*).

> **MODÈLE:** É1: D'habitude, qu'est-ce que tu fais le soir?
> É2: Je fais du jogging tous les soirs.

**D. Mimes.** Formez deux groupes. Choisissez une expression avec **faire** en le tirant par hasard d'un chapeau. Faites deviner cette expression par les membres de votre groupe. Si votre équipe (*team*) devine la réponse, elle a un point. L'équipe qui a le plus de points gagne (*wins*).

# Les verbes en -*re*

*Expressing Actions*

## J'arrive!

*Juliette téléphone à Léa.*

> JULIETTE: Allô, allô! **Tu entends?**
> LÉA: **J'entends** mal; je suis dans le métro, à Opéra.
> JULIETTE: **Tu descends** à quelle station?
> LÉA: **Je descends** à Bastille.
> JULIETTE: Je suis avec Hector. **Nous attendons** devant le cinéma UGC. Nous faisons la queue. Le film commence à 20 h.
> LÉA: J'arrive! **Vous m'attendez,** hein!

Vrai ou faux?

1. Juliette demande à Léa si elle entend.
2. Léa entend mal.
3. Léa descend à Opéra.
4. Juliette et Hector attendent Léa au café.
5. Léa demande à ses amis d'attendre.

A third group of French verbs has infinitives that end in **-re.**

| PRESENT TENSE OF **vendre** (*to sell*) | | | |
|---|---|---|---|
| je | vend**s** | nous | vend**ons** |
| tu | vend**s** | vous | vend**ez** |
| il/elle/on | vend | ils/elles | vend**ent** |

**1.** Other verbs conjugated like **vendre** include the following.

| | | | |
|---|---|---|---|
| **attendre** | *to wait (for)* | **rendre** | *to give back, return* |
| **descendre** | *to go down; to get off* | **rendre visite à** | *to visit (someone)* |
| **entendre** | *to hear* | | |
| **perdre** | *to lose; to waste* | **répondre à** | *to answer* |

**Elle attend** le dessert.
**Nous descendons de** l'autobus.
**Le commerçant rend** la
monnaie à la cliente.
**Je réponds à** sa question.

*She's waiting for dessert.*
*We're getting off the bus.*
*The storekeeper gives change*
*back to the customer.*
*I'm answering his/her question.*

**2.** The expression **rendre visite à** means to visit a *person* or *people*. The verb **visiter** is used only with places or things.

> **Je rends visite à** mon ami.
> **Les touristes visitent** les monuments de Paris.

 *Allez-y!*

A. **Ah bon?** Le samedi, on fait ce qu'on n'a pas le temps de faire pendant la semaine. Tristan est très occupé et il n'est pas le seul. Suivez le modèle et faites attention aux adjectifs possessifs.

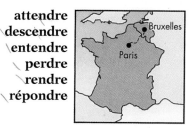

> **MODÈLE:** vendre des DVD sur eBay (moi) →
> É1: Tristan vend des DVD sur eBay.
> É2: Ah bon? Moi aussi je vends des DVD sur eBay!

1. rendre ses livres à la bibliothèque (nous)
2. attendre le bus pour aller faire des courses (mon frère)
3. descendre au sous-sol (vous)
4. perdre trop de temps à lire ses méls (toi)
5. entendre à la radio une publicité pour un concert (mes copains)
6. répondre à beaucoup de coups de téléphone (*phone calls*) (moi)

B. **Un week-end à Paris.** Complétez l'histoire avec les verbes à droite.

Alain et Marie-Lise habitent à Bruxelles. Aujourd'hui ils descendent¹ à Paris en train. Ils vont rendre² visite à leur cousine Pauline. Les trois cousins ont toujours beaucoup de projets et ne perdent³ pas une minute quand ils sont ensemble (*together*). Alain et Marie-Lise aiment beaucoup Pauline parce qu'elle répond⁴ toujours à leurs méls. Pauline aime aussi ses cousins, et elle attend⁵ leur arrivée avec impatience. Elle entend⁶ enfin la sonnette (*doorbell*)!

> attendre
> descendre
> entendre
> perdre
> rendre
> répondre

C. **Perdez-vous souvent patience?** Interviewez un(e) camarade de classe. Il/Elle utilise **souvent, pas souvent** ou **toujours** dans sa réponse.

> **MODÈLE:** É1: Tu attends l'autobus, mais il n'arrive pas.
> Est-ce que tu perds patience?
> É2: Oui, je perds souvent patience.

**1.** Tu attends un coup de téléphone. La personne ne téléphone pas. **2.** Un ami / Une amie ne répond pas à tes textos. **3.** Tu perds les clés de ta voiture ou de ton appartement. **4.** Tu as rendez-vous avec un ami / une amie. Tu attends longtemps (*for a long time*), mais il/elle n'arrive pas.

 **Prononcez bien!**

**The consonant *r***

When you pronounce a French **r**, the back of your tongue almost touches the back of your palate. Force air out, as when you pronounce an **h**, and maintain that very narrow passage between the back of your tongue and the back of your palate. You will get that rattling sound characteristic of the French **r**.

[R]: pa**r**ent, pou**r**, a**rr**iver, **r**hume

The **r** occurring at the end of a word is usually pronounced, with the exception of the following:

- infinitive verbs ending in **-er: aller, donner, parler**
- professions ending in **-er: boucher, plombier**

Prononcez bien!

1. **The pronunciation of *premier*** (page 123)

   **Journal intime.** Vous rangez (*clean*) votre chambre et retrouvez le journal intime que vous avez commencé à votre arrivée en France. Avec un(e) camarade, lisez les phrases suivantes à voix haute (*aloud*) en faisant attention à la prononciation de «premier».

   > *Cher journal,*
   >
   > 1. Aujourd'hui, c'est le ***premier*** août.
   > 2. Je suis très content(e) parce que j'emménage dans mon ***premier*** appartement avec Hugo.
   > 3. Hugo, c'est mon ***premier*** ami français!
   > 4. Je vais avoir mon ***premier*** bureau.
   > 5. Je vais acheter mon ***premier*** ordinateur.
   > 6. Et je vais avoir mon ***premier*** lit aussi. C'est super!

2. **The vowels in *notre* and *nos*** (page 126)

   **Week-end chez les parents d'Hugo.** Vous passez le week-end avec Hugo chez ses parents. Sa mère pose des questions sur votre vie aux États-Unis. Complétez les phrases avec **notre, nos** ou **votre, vos**. Ensuite, jouez la scène avec un(e) camarade de classe.

   LA MÈRE: Comment est _____¹ maison aux États-Unis? Est-ce que _____² cuisine est grande, comme celle-ci (*like this one*)?

   VOUS: _____³ maison est grande et jolie, mais la cuisine est plus petite.

   LA MÈRE: Est-ce que vous habitez chez _____⁴ parents?

   VOUS: Oui, et nous avons deux chiens aussi. Ils adorent jouer dans le jardin de _____⁵ voisins!

3. **The consonant *r*** (page 137)

   **A. La famille d'Hugo.** Vous continuez votre conversation avec la mère d'Hugo. Jouez le rôle de la mère et lisez sa description de la famille à voix haute. Faites attention à la prononciation du *r*.

   > Les grands-parents paternels d'Hugo sont morts (*dead*). Moi, j'ai encore (*still*) mon père, Gérard—il a 80 ans!—et ma mère, Catherine. J'ai aussi quatre frères et trois sœurs. En tout (*Altogether*), Hugo a quatorze cousins et cousines! J'ai invité (*invited*) Christophe et Karine, les cousins les plus proches (*closest*) d'Hugo, à manger avec nous ce soir.

   **B. Devinettes.** En attendant l'arrivée des cousins d'Hugo, vous jouez aux devinettes (*riddles*) avec lui (*him*). Trouvez les pièces de la maison qui correspondent aux définitions que lit Hugo (votre camarade de classe).

   **MODÈLE:** É1: C'est la pièce où il y a un ordinateur et des livres pour travailler.
   É2: C'est le bureau!

   1. C'est la pièce où il y a un lit.
   2. C'est la pièce où il y a un canapé, des fauteuils et une télévision.
   3. C'est la partie de la maison où il y a le séjour, la salle à manger et la cuisine.
   4. C'est l'espace (*area*) où il y a des arbres et des roses.
   5. C'est l'espace où il y a des chaises longues et où on prend le petit déjeuner (*breakfast*) en été.

Lecture

### Avant de lire

**Identifying a pronoun's referent.** As you know, a pronoun may "stand in" for a noun. By using a pronoun to replace a noun, an author can avoid repeating the noun, which would result in unnatural sounding language. To illustrate this, reformulate the following sentence from the text by replacing the pronoun **il** with the noun it refers to:

> C'est en 1883[1] que l'artiste s'installe avec sa famille à Giverny, en Normandie, à 75[2] kilomètres de Paris. Il va y habiter pendant 43 ans. Il adore Giverny. Il transforme sa propriété en un jardin riche en symétries, en perspectives et en couleurs.

• Without the pronoun, the text sounds repetitive and awkward.

A pronoun may also refer to a person or group that can be identified by context. For example, this text begins:

> Nous sommes à Giverny, chez le peintre Claude Monet...

You can infer that the subject **nous** includes the reader as well as the author; the use of this inclusive **nous** creates a bond between the reader and the author, inviting the reader to "come along for the ride."

Recall too that French does not have a single pronoun that corresponds to "it"; a third-person pronoun such as **il, elle,** or **ce** plays this role. In the sentence below, which **il** refers to Monet and which is an impersonal pronoun?

> Monet aime observer la nature quand il fait beau, quand il pleut, quand il fait du vent, et analyser la lumière du matin, de l'après-midi, du soir. C'est à Giverny qu'il trouve son inspiration et qu'il définit son art.

As you read the text, be sure that you are able to identify the referent for each pronoun to ensure accurate comprehension.

[1]mille huit cent quatre-vingt-trois   [2]soixante-quinze

# Giverny: le petit paradis de Monet

«Mon cœur[1] est à Giverny, toujours et toujours... »
Claude Monet

Le pont japonais à Giverny

## Une destination touristique

Nous sommes à Giverny, chez le peintre Claude Monet (1840[2]–1926[3]). Chaque année, 500 000[4] visiteurs découvrent avec émotion ce petit paradis. Dans la maison, toutes les pièces semblent encore habitées: la salle à manger, les salons et les chambres. Devant la maison rose qui a aussi charmé les amis de Monet (les peintres Cézanne, Renoir et Matisse, et l'écrivain Zola), les visiteurs découvrent le Clos normand,[5] un immense jardin symétrique planté de fleurs et d'arbres et, plus loin, le Jardin d'eau[6] avec son célèbre[7] pont japonais.

## Une inspiration pour le père de l'impressionnisme

C'est en 1883[8] que l'artiste s'installe[9] avec sa famille à Giverny, en Normandie, à 75[10] kilomètres de Paris. Il va y habiter pendant 43 ans. Il adore Giverny. Il transforme sa propriété en un jardin riche en symétries, en perspectives et en couleurs, et arrange les fleurs dans un désordre apparent. Le résultat est une véritable œuvre d'art.[11]

Monet aime observer la nature quand il fait beau, quand il pleut, quand il fait du vent, et analyser la lumière[12] du matin, de l'après-midi, du soir. C'est à Giverny qu'il trouve son inspiration et qu'il définit son art. Cet endroit magnifique inspire à l'artiste des œuvres célèbres comme *Le Champ d'iris jaunes à Giverny* (1887[13]), le *Printemps, Giverny* (1890[14]) et les *Nymphéas*, une série de 250[15] tableaux qui évoquent les nénuphars[16] du bassin.

«Je veux réussir à traduire ce que je ressens[17]» explique-t-il. Ses peintures ne reproduisent pas les objets mais une impression ou une émotion. C'est un nouveau mouvement de peinture. Monet est bien le père de l'impressionnisme.

[1]*heart* [2]*mille huit cent quarante* [3]*mille neuf cent vingt-six* [4]*cinq cent mille* [5]*Clos... field in the Norman style* [6]*water* [7]*famous* [8]*mille huit cent quatre-vingt-trois* [9]*settles* [10]*soixante-quinze* [11]*œuvre... work of art* [12]*light* [13]*mille huit cent quatre-vingt-sept* [14]*mille huit cent quatre-vingt-dix* [15]*deux cent cinquante* [16]*water lilies* [17]*réussir... to succeed in translating what I feel*

### Compréhension

**Une brochure publicitaire.** Create a travel brochure for Monet's garden in Giverny by filling in the blanks with the appropriate expressions from the text.

Un petit paradis terrestre? Ça existe à quelques _____[1] de Paris! Découvrez Giverny où le peintre _____[2] a trouvé son inspiration. Son œuvre ne reproduit pas les objets, mais _____[3] ou _____[4] —c'est le principe de l'impressionnisme.

    La maison a l'air toujours _____,[5] marquée par la présence des amis illustres de Monet, parmi eux (*among them*), l'écrivain _____.[6]

    Devant la maison de Monet, on trouve un immense jardin symétrique qui s'appelle «_____».[7] En traversant le célèbre Pont japonais, on arrive au fameux _____[8] qui a donné naissance à une série de 250 _____[9] appelés «_____».[10]

    Giverny, c'est la nature, la lumière, les couleurs, les nuances. Venez découvrir ce lieu privilégié!

Claude Monet: *Nymphéas*, 1916–1919. (Musée Marmottan Monet, Paris)

# Écriture

The writing activities **Par écrit** and **Journal intime** can be found in the Workbook/Laboratory Manual to accompany *Vis-à-vis*.

# *Pour s'amuser*

Un homme raconte ses vacances à son collègue.

—La première semaine, on a eu (*we had*) mauvais temps: la pluie, la neige, le vent, le froid…
—Et la deuxième semaine? …
—Une catastrophe!
—Vraiment? Pourquoi?
—Mes beaux-parents sont arrivés…

# Le vidéoblog d'Hassan

## En bref

Dans cet épisode, Hassan est dans son restaurant avec son copain Abdel et Carole, la fiancée d'Abdel. Abdel et Carole mentionnent des endroits (lieux) possibles pour leur cérémonie et leur réception de mariage.

## Vocabulaire en contexte

Indiquez vos préférences pour une cérémonie et une réception idéale de mariage.

**Les invités**
- ☐ **seulement** (*only*) moi et mon fiancé / ma fiancée
- ☐ seulement les deux familles
- ☐ seulement de très bons amis
- ☐ les deux familles et de bons amis
- ☐ **tout le monde** (*everyone*)!

**Les lieux**
- ☐ sur une **péniche** (*river barge*)
- ☐ au 56ᵉ étage d'une **tour** (*tower*)
- ☐ sur la terrasse d'un musée ou d'un institut
- ☐ dans un hôtel de grand **luxe** (*luxury*)
- ☐ dans une église (*church*), une mosquée, une synagogue

Une péniche pour la réception de mariage

## Visionnez!

Choisissez la bonne réponse.

1. Pour Carole, le détail le plus (*most*) important est _____.
   **a.** le nombre d'invités **b.** le lieu **c.** le mois de l'année
2. Pour Carole, une réception de mariage sur une péniche _____.
   **a.** **coûte** (*costs*) trop cher **b.** est très romantique **c.** est une mauvaise idée
3. La tour Montparnasse et l'Institut du **monde** (*world*) arabe offrent de belles vues _____.
   **a.** quand il fait beau **b.** seulement le soir **c.** seulement en été
4. On fête un mariage au Maroc _____.
   **a.** à la plage (*beach*) **b.** chez les parents du marié **c.** dans un **ryad** (*Moroccan villa*)

## Analysez!

Répondez aux questions.

1. De quels lieux à Paris parlent-ils dans la vidéo? Quel est l'avantage et/ou l'inconvénient de chaque (*each*) lieu? Quel lieu préférez-vous?
2. Abdel et Carole forment-ils un couple «traditionnel»? Pourquoi?

## Comparez!

Faites la description d'une cérémonie ou d'une réception de mariage typique dans votre culture. Regardez encore une fois (*once more*) la partie culturelle de la vidéo: les lieux de mariage en France ressemblent-ils aux lieux de mariage aux États-Unis? Expliquez.

## Note culturelle

Un ryad (ou riad) est une belle maison bourgeoise, d'architecture traditionnelle mauresque[1] construite autour d'un patio, généralement avec une fontaine. Les ryads, qui servent souvent aujourd'hui de Maisons d'hôtes,[2] sont souvent luxueux, avec plusieurs salons et chambres, et un décor typiquement marocain.

[1]*Moorish* [2]*Maisons… small hotels*

## Vocabulaire

### Verbes

**aller** to go
  **aller** + *inf.* to be going (to do something)
  **aller mal** to feel bad (ill)
**attendre** to wait (for)
**descendre** to go down; to get off
**entendre** to hear
**faire** to do; to make
**perdre** to lose; to waste
**préparer** to prepare
**rendre** to give back; to return; to hand in
  **rendre visite à** to visit (*someone*)
**répondre à** to answer
**rester** to stay, remain
**vendre** to sell

À REVOIR: **étudier, habiter, jouer (à) (de), manger**

### Substantifs

**l'arbre** (*m.*) tree
**l'autobus** (*m.*) (city) bus
**le bruit** noise
**la clé** key
**la famille** family
**la météo** weather forecast
**les projets** (*m. pl.*) plans
**le temps** time; weather
**les vacances** (*f. pl.*) vacation

À REVOIR: **l'affiche** (*f.*), **le chien, la commode, le couloir, le lavabo, le lit, le logement**

### Adjectifs

**célibataire** single (*person*)
**divorcé(e)** divorced
**marié(e)** married
**pacsé(e)** joined legally by a **PACS**
**préféré(e)** favorite, preferred

### La famille

**les arrière-grands-parents** great-grandparents
**le beau-frère** brother-in-law
**le beau-père** father-in-law; stepfather
**la belle-mère** mother-in-law; stepmother
**la belle-sœur** sister-in-law
**la bru** daughter-in-law
**le cousin** cousin (*male*)
**la cousine** cousin (*female*)
**le demi-frère** half brother; stepbrother
**la demi-sœur** half sister; stepsister
**l'enfant** (*m., f.*) child
**la femme** wife
**la fille** daughter
**le fils** son
**le frère** brother
**le gendre** son-in-law
**la grand-mère** grandmother
**le grand-parent (les grands-parents)** grandparent(s)
**le grand-père** grandfather
**le mari** husband
**la mère** mother
**le neveu** nephew
**la nièce** niece
**l'oncle** (*m.*) uncle
**le parent** parent; relative
**le père** father
**la petite-fille** granddaughter
**le petit-enfant** grandchild
**le petit-fils** grandson
**la sœur** sister
**la tante** aunt

### La maison

**le balcon** balcony
**le bureau** office
**la chambre** bedroom

**la cuisine** kitchen
**l'escalier** (*m.*) stairway
**le jardin** garden
**la pièce** room
**le premier/deuxième étage** second/third floor
**le rez-de-chaussée** ground (first) floor
**la salle à manger** dining room
**la salle de bains** bathroom
**le séjour** living room
**le sous-sol** basement
**la terrasse** terrace

### Expressions avec *faire*

**faire attention (à)** to pay attention (to); to watch out (for)
**faire la connaissance (de)** to meet (*for the first time*), make the acquaintance (of)
**faire les courses** to do errands
**faire la cuisine** to cook
**faire ses devoirs** to do one's homework
**faire la lessive** to do the laundry
**faire le marché** to do the shopping, go to the market
**faire le ménage** to do the housework
**faire une promenade** to take a walk
**faire la queue** to stand in line
**faire du sport** to play/do sports
  **faire de l'aérobic** to do aerobics; **... du jogging** to run, jog; **... du ski** to ski; **... du vélo** to go cycling; **... de la voile** to go sailing
**faire un tour (en voiture)** to take a walk (ride)
**faire la vaisselle** to do the dishes
**faire un voyage** to take a trip

## Le temps

**Quel temps fait-il?** How's the weather?
**Il fait beau.** It's nice (out).
**Il fait chaud.** It's hot.
**Il fait (du) soleil.** It's sunny.
**Il fait du vent. (Il y a du vent.)** It's windy.
**Il fait frais.** It's cool.
**Il fait froid.** It's cold.
**Il fait mauvais.** It's bad (out).
**Il neige.** It's snowing.
**Il pleut.** It's raining.
**Le temps est nuageux.** It's cloudy.
**Le temps est orageux.** It's stormy.

## Les saisons

**Au printemps** (*m.*)… In spring …
**En automne** (*m.*)… In fall …
**En été** (*m.*)… In summer …
**En hiver** (*m.*)… In winter …

## Mots et expressions divers

**l'année prochaine** next year
**après** after; afterward
**bientôt** soon
**ce week-end** this weekend
**cet après-midi / ce matin / ce soir** this afternoon / morning / evening
**chez** at the home (establishment) of
**dans quatre jours** in four days (from now)
**demain** tomorrow
**d'habitude** usually
**une fois par semaine** once a week
**le lundi / le vendredi soir** on Mondays / on Friday evenings
**peut-être** maybe
**la semaine prochaine** next week
**tous les jours** every day
**tout à l'heure** in a while
**tout de suite** immediately
**le week-end** on weekends

CHAPITRE **6**

# À table!°

*À... Let's eat!*

Les dossiers d'Hassan

Hassan

➤ Mes photos
  ➤ Une belle salade niçoise
  ➤ Leçon 1—une salade marocaine
  ➤ Mangez, bougez!°

*Mangez... Eat, move!*

Une belle salade niçoise avec de la laitue, du thon, des olives noires, des œufs durs, des tomates et des anchois

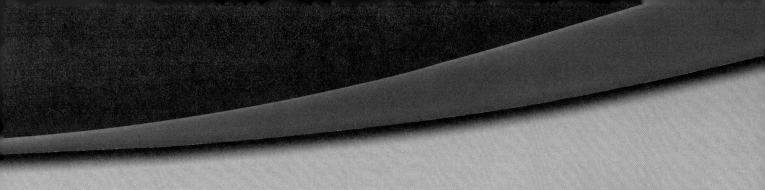

## Dans ce chapitre...

### OBJECTIFS COMMUNICATIFS
- ➤ talking about food and drink
- ➤ expressing quantity
- ➤ giving commands
- ➤ telling time
- ➤ learning to distinguish between and pronounce selected sounds in French

### PAROLES (Leçon 1)
- ➤ Les repas, la nourriture et les boissons
- ➤ Le verbe **préférer**
- ➤ Le couvert à table

### STRUCTURES (Leçons 2 et 3)
- ➤ Les verbes **prendre** et **boire**
- ➤ Les articles partitifs
- ➤ L'impératif
- ➤ L'heure

### CULTURE
- ➤ Le blog d'Hassan: *Miam-miam!*
- ➤ Reportage: *Mangez, bougez!*
- ➤ Lecture: *Saveurs du monde francophone* (Leçon 4)

Leçon 1—une salade marocaine de carottes râpées à l'orange

Sandwich et fruits pour les gens pressés

www.mhconnectfrench.com

# Leçon 1

## Les repas de la journée*

Voilà des aliments (*m.*) populaires en France.

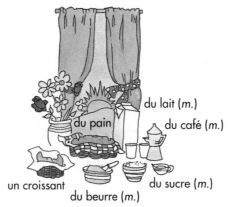

du lait (*m.*)
du pain
du café (*m.*)
un croissant
du beurre (*m.*)
du sucre (*m.*)

**Le matin: le petit déjeuner**

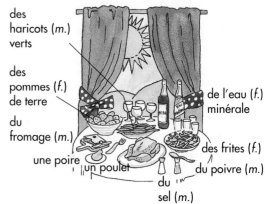

des haricots (*m.*) verts
des pommes (*f.*) de terre
du fromage (*m.*)
une poire
un poulet
de l'eau (*f.*) minérale
des frites (*f.*)
du poivre (*m.*)
du sel (*m.*)

**Le midi: le déjeuner**

du chocolat (*m.*)
du thé (*m.*)
des serviettes (*f.*)
des gâteaux (*m.*) au chocolat
une tarte aux pommes

**L'après-midi: le goûter**†

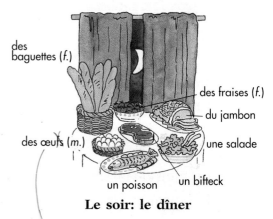

des baguettes (*f.*)
des fraises (*f.*)
du jambon
des œufs (*m.*)
une salade
un poisson
un bifteck

**Le soir: le dîner**

*singular pronounce "f"*

---

***La journée** (*The day*) is used instead of **le jour** to emphasize the notion of an entire day, as in the expression **Quelle journée!** (*What a day!*) or **Bonne journée!** (*Have a nice day!*).
†**Le goûter** is an afternoon snack: **des petits pains au chocolat pour les enfants; du thé ou du café et des gâteaux pour les adultes.**

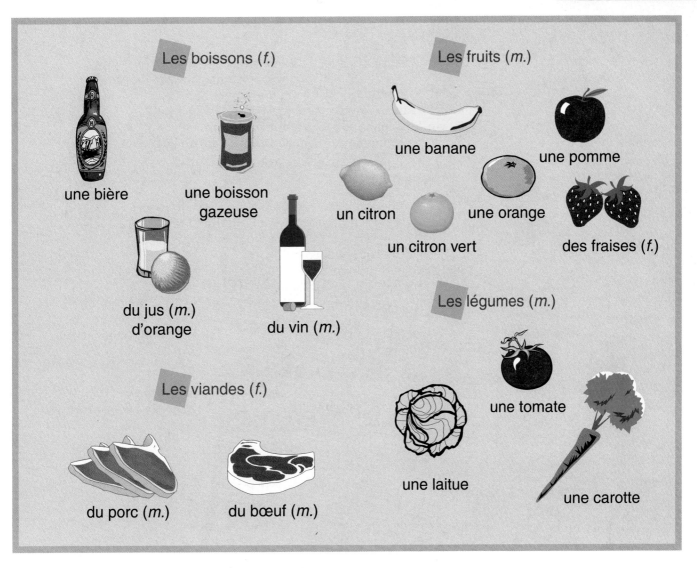

Les boissons (*f.*)

une bière

une boisson
gazeuse

du jus (*m.*)
d'orange

du vin (*m.*)

Les fruits (*m.*)

une banane

une pomme

un citron

une orange

un citron vert

des fraises (*f.*)

Les légumes (*m.*)

une tomate

une laitue

une carotte

Les viandes (*f.*)

du porc (*m.*)

du bœuf (*m.*)

**AUTRES MOTS UTILES**

| | | | |
|---|---|---|---|
| **les brocolis** (*m.*) | broccoli | **le poivron** | bell pepper |
| **le champagne** | champagne | **le plat** | dish (of food) |
| **le champignon** | mushroom | **les produits** | fresh products |
| **la crème** | cream | (*m.*) **frais** | |
| **le dessert** | dessert | **déjeuner** | to eat lunch |
| **l'oignon** (*m.*) | onion | **dîner** | to eat dinner |

*[handwritten notes:]*
la dinde  turkey
l'agneau  lamb
pâtes  pasta
des crevettes  shrimp

|||| *Allez-y!*

**A. Catégories.** Ajoutez (*Add*) d'autres aliments dans les catégories
mentionnées.

**MODÈLE:** La mousse au chocolat est *un dessert.*→
Le gâteau, la tarte aux pommes et les fraises sont aussi
des desserts.

1. La bière est *une boisson.*
2. La pomme de terre est *un légume.*
3. Le porc est *une viande.*
4. La banane est *un fruit.*

**B. L'intrus.** Dans les groupes suivants, trouvez le mot qui ne va pas avec les autres. Expliquez votre choix.

1. café / fraise / bière / thé / lait
2. haricots verts / salade / carotte / œuf / pomme de terre
3. bifteck / porc / pain / jambon / poulet
4. sel / gâteau / poivre / sucre / beurre
5. vin / banane / pomme / orange / melon
6. tarte aux pommes / fromage / chocolat / thé / gâteau au chocolat

**C. Les habitudes alimentaires.** Posez les questions suivantes à un(e) camarade de classe.

1. D'habitude, est-ce que tu prends un petit déjeuner? Si oui, qu'est-ce que tu manges? Sinon, pourquoi pas?
2. Quelle boisson préfères-tu prendre le matin?
3. Où déjeunes-tu et avec qui?
4. Est-ce que tu prends un goûter quelquefois pendant la journée? Si oui, qu'est-ce que tu manges?
5. Pour le dîner, tu aimes cuisiner? Si oui, qu'est-ce que tu aimes préparer?
6. Est-ce que tu préfères manger à la maison ou aller manger au restaurant?

# Le verbe *préférer*

Elle préfère le chocolat blanc.

| PRESENT TENSE OF **préférer** (*to prefer*) | | |
|---|---|---|
| je **préfère** | nous | préférons |
| tu **préfères** | vous | préférez |
| il/elle/on **préfère** | ils/elles | **préfèrent** |

Although the endings are regular, the verb **préférer** is irregular. For the forms of **je, tu, il/elle/on,** and **ils/elles,** the second **é** from the stem (**préfér-**) changes to **è** (je **préfère**). The **nous** and **vous** forms are regular. Verbs conjugated like **préférer** include **répéter, espérer** (*to hope*), **célébrer,** and **considérer.**

 *Allez-y!*

**A. Fiche** (*Form*) **gastronomique.** Demandez à un(e) camarade de classe quelles sont ses préférences, et complétez la fiche. Utilisez **quel** (*m.*) ou **quelle** (*f.*) et le verbe **préférer.**

**MODÈLE:** É1: Quelle boisson préfères-tu?
　　　　　 É2: Je préfère le/la...

boisson: _____

viande: _____

légume: _____

fruit: _____

dessert: _____

repas: _____

plat: _____

Maintenant, avec vos camarades de classe, examinez les différentes fiches et déterminez quels sont les plats et les boissons préférés de la classe.

**B. Question de préférence.** Avec un(e) camarade, répondez aux questions suivantes.

1. Quel repas est-ce que tu préfères? Pourquoi?
2. Est-ce que, selon toi (*in your opinion*), tu es bon cuisinier / bonne cuisinière (*cook*)?
3. Dans quel restaurant est-ce que tu espères aller prochainement (*next*)?
4. Chez toi, quelles fêtes est-ce qu'on célèbre? Qu'est-ce que vous préparez pour célébrer cette/ces (*this/those*) fête(s)?

# À table

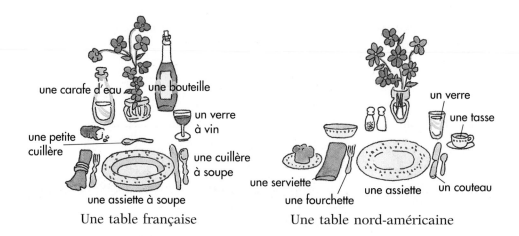

Une table française      Une table nord-américaine

**AUTRES MOTS UTILES**

| | |
|---|---|
| **un bol** | bowl-shaped cup (*for* **café au lait**) |
| **une nappe** | tablecloth |
| **la soupe** | soup |

 *Allez-y!*

**A. L'objet nécessaire.** Quels objets utilisez-vous?

    **MODÈLE:** le café au lait →
          J'utilise un bol pour le café au lait.

| | | |
|---|---|---|
| **1.** le vin | **5.** le thé | **7.** l'eau |
| **2.** la viande | **6.** la mousse au | **8.** le café express |
| **3.** la soupe |     chocolat | |
| **4.** la salade | | |

**B. L'art de la table.** Mettre le couvert (*Setting the table*) est souvent un art. Regardez la photo tirée du magazine *Gault Millau* et répondez aux questions.

**1.** Décrivez ce qu'il y a sur la table. Est-ce une table pour un repas simple ou élégant? Quel est l'objet en papier à gauche?

**2.** À votre avis, pourquoi est-ce qu'il y a quatre verres?

**3.** Et chez vous, qu'est-ce qu'on place sur la table au petit déjeuner, au déjeuner, au dîner, pour un repas spécial?

© Gault Millau

Une table élégante

# Leçon 2

## Les verbes *prendre* et *boire*

*Talking About Food and Drink*

### Petit déjeuner entre amis

*Hassan et Abdel échangent des textos (SMS).*

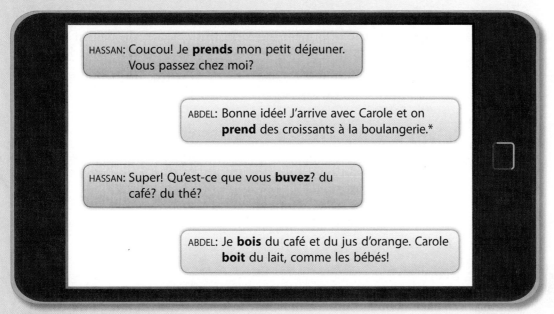

HASSAN: Coucou! Je **prends** mon petit déjeuner. Vous passez chez moi?

ABDEL: Bonne idée! J'arrive avec Carole et on **prend** des croissants à la boulangerie.*

HASSAN: Super! Qu'est-ce que vous **buvez**? du café? du thé?

ABDEL: Je **bois** du café et du jus d'orange. Carole **boit** du lait, comme les bébés!

*bakery

Répondez aux questions.

1. Quel repas prend Hassan?
2. Qu'est-ce qu'Abdel et Carole prennent à la boulangerie?
3. Qu'est-ce qu'Abdel boit?
4. Pourquoi est-ce qu'Abdel compare Carole à un bébé?
5. Qu'est-ce que vous buvez le matin?

## *Prendre* and Similar Verbs

The verb **prendre** is irregular in its plural forms.

| PRESENT TENSE OF **prendre** (*to take*) | | | |
|---|---|---|---|
| je | **prends** | nous | **prenons** |
| tu | **prends** | vous | **prenez** |
| il/elle/on | **prend** | ils/elles | **prennent** |

**1.** Verbs conjugated like **prendre** include **apprendre** (*to learn*) and **comprendre** (*to understand; to include*).

| | |
|---|---|
| —Qu'est-ce que vous **prenez?** | *What are you having?* |
| —Je **prends** la salade verte. | *I'm having the green salad.* |
| Il **apprend** l'espagnol. | *He's learning (how to speak) Spanish.* |
| Est-ce que tu **comprends** l'allemand? | *Do you understand German?* |
| Le menu à 20 euros **comprend** une entrée, un plat et un dessert. | *The meal for 20 euros includes an appetizer, the main course, and a dessert.* |

**2.** When an infinitive follows **apprendre,** the preposition **à** must be used.

| | |
|---|---|
| **Apprenez**-vous **à** skier? | *Are you learning (how) to ski?* |

**Apprendre** can also mean *to teach.* In this case, the person taught is preceded by **à.** If the thing taught is a verb, it is also preceded by **à.**

| | |
|---|---|
| J'**apprends** le russe à Lola. | *I'm teaching Lola Russian.* |
| J'**apprends** à Lola à parler russe. | *I'm teaching Lola to speak Russian.* |

**3.** Some common expressions with **prendre** include:

| | |
|---|---|
| **prendre du temps** | *to take (a long) time* |
| **prendre son temps** | *to take one's time* |
| **prendre un repas** | *to eat a meal* |
| **prendre le petit déjeuner** | *to have breakfast* |
| **prendre un verre** | *to have a drink (usually alcoholic)* |

## Boire

Offrir un verre aux amis, c'est sympa! Qu'est-ce qu'on boit ici? Qu'est-ce qu'on mange?

The verb **boire** is also irregular in form.

| PRESENT TENSE OF **boire** (*to drink*) | | | |
|---|---|---|---|
| je | **bois** | nous | **buvons** |
| tu | **bois** | vous | **buvez** |
| il/elle/on | **boit** | ils/elles | **boivent** |

| | |
|---|---|
| Tu **bois** de l'eau minérale. | *You're drinking mineral water.* |
| Nous **buvons** de la bière. | *We're drinking beer.* |

## Allez-y!

**A. Des étudiants modèles?** Lisez les phrases, puis faites les substitutions suivantes: (1) tu, (2) mon meilleur ami / ma meilleure amie, (3) mon/ma camarade et moi, (4) je, (5) mes copains.

**1.** Vous apprenez le français.   **2.** Vous comprenez presque (*almost*) toujours le professeur.   **3.** Pour préparer les examens, vous prenez des livres à la bibliothèque.   **4.** Pour faire votre travail, vous prenez votre temps.   **5.** Mais malheureusement (*unfortunately*), vous buvez trop de (*too much*) café.

**B. Qu'est-ce qu'on boit?** Choisissez la boisson qui convient à chaque situation.

**Boissons:** de la bière, du café, du champagne, de l'eau, du jus d'orange, du jus de pomme, du lait chaud, de la limonade, du thé, du vin

**MODÈLE:** Nous sommes le 31 décembre. (Loïc) →
Il boit du champagne.

**1.** Il fait très chaud. (vous)   **2.** Il fait froid. (Christian)   **3.** Il est minuit (*midnight*). (tu)   **4.** Il est huit heures du matin (*8 AM*). (je)
**5.** Nous sommes au café. (nous)   **6.** Emma et Inès sont au restaurant. (elles)

**C. Conversations au café.** Vous êtes au café. Qu'est-ce que les gens disent? Complétez les conversations avec les verbes **prendre, apprendre** et **comprendre**.

**1.**   FANNY: Est-ce que tu _____ un café?
     AZIZ: Non, je _____ une bouteille d'eau minérale.
**2.**   LÉA: Est-ce que tu _____ l'anglais?
  FRANCO: Oui, et j' _____ aussi l'anglais à mes enfants. Et vous deux, qu'est-ce que vous _____ comme (*as*) langue étrangère?
  CLÉMENT: Nous, nous _____ le japonais.
**3.**   CLAUDE: Est-ce que vous _____ toujours le professeur de philosophie?
  DAVID: Non, mais les autres (*others*) _____ tout!

**D. Mission impossible?** Posez une question avec **Est-ce que tu...** pour trouver un(e) camarade de classe qui (*who*)...

**1.** ne prend pas de petit déjeuner   **2.** prend en général des crêpes (*pancakes*) au petit déjeuner   **3.** boit cinq tasses de café ou plus par jour   **4.** boit un verre de lait à chaque repas   **5.** apprend un nouveau sport ce semestre   **6.** comprend le sens de la vie (*meaning of life*)

# Les articles partitifs

*Expressing Quantity*

## Pas de gâteau pour le dessert!

*Hassan téléphone à Carole.*

HASSAN: Salut, Carole! Alors, le dîner que tu prépares pour les parents d'Abdel, il est prêt[1]?

CAROLE: Non… mais mon menu est prêt: **du** poulet avec des pommes de terre. **De la** salade verte. Et pour finir, **du** fromage et des fruits. J'adore les repas simples!

HASSAN: C'est un menu quotidien[2] trop banal pour une grande occasion. Pourquoi pas une belle salade niçoise avec **de la** laitue, des œufs, **du** thon,[3] des oignons? Et ensuite,[4] un bœuf aux carottes avec **de l'**huile[5] d'olive? Ce n'est pas compliqué…

CAROLE: Et pour le dessert, un gâteau?

HASSAN: **Pas de** gâteau: **De la** mousse au chocolat! Avec **du** citron: c'est original, et… très très facile!

Délicieuse, la mousse au chocolat!

[1]*ready* [2]*daily* [3]*tuna* [4]*next* [5]*oil*

Trouvez, dans le dialogue, la phrase disant que…

1. Carole compose un menu avec de la viande, des légumes et des fruits.
2. Carole n'aime pas les repas compliqués.
3. Dans la salade niçoise, il y a plusieurs (*several*) ingrédients.
4. Hassan n'est pas favorable au gâteau pour le dessert.
5. La mousse au chocolat, c'est facile à préparer.

## Forms of Partitive Articles

In addition to the definite and indefinite articles, there is a third article in French, called the partitive (**le partitif**). It has three forms: **du** (*m.*), **de la** (*f.*), and **de l'** (before a vowel or mute **h**). It agrees in gender and number with the noun it precedes.

| | |
|---|---|
| Prenez-vous **du** jambon? | *Are you having (some) ham?* |
| **de la** salade? | *(some) salad?* |
| **de l'**eau minérale? | *(some) mineral water?* |

## Partitive versus Indefinite Articles

1. The partitive article is used to indicate part of a quantity that is measurable but not countable. This idea is sometimes expressed in English by *some* or *any;* usually, however, *some* is only implied.

Examples of noncountable nouns (also called *mass nouns*) include **beurre, chocolat, eau, glace, lait, pain, sucre, viande, vin, argent,** and **temps.**

| | |
|---|---|
| Avez-vous **du** thé? | *Do you have tea?* |
| Je voudrais **du** sucre. | *I would like (some) sugar.* |
| Mangez-vous **du** poisson? | *Do you eat fish?* |

2. When something is countable or is considered as a whole, the indefinite article is used instead.

| | |
|---|---|
| Après le dîner, je prends **un** thé. | *After dinner, I have (a cup of) tea.* |
| Je voudrais **un** sucre dans mon café. | *I would like one (cube of) sugar in my coffee.* |
| Je mange **un** poisson par semaine. | *I eat a (whole) fish every week.* |

## Partitive versus Definite Articles

1. The partitive article is used with verbs such as **acheter,*** **boire, manger,** and **prendre,** because they usually involve consuming or buying a *portion* of something. However, after verbs of preference such as **adorer, aimer, aimer mieux, détester,** and **préférer,** the definite article is used, because these verbs generally express a reaction to an entire category.

| | |
|---|---|
| Beaucoup de Français mangent **du** fromage à la fin du repas, mais moi, je déteste **le** fromage. | *Many French people eat cheese at the end of the meal, but I hate cheese.* |

2. The partitive is also used with abstract qualities attributed to people, whereas the definite article is used to talk about these qualities in general.

| | |
|---|---|
| Elle a **du** courage. | *She has (some) courage.* |
| Elle déteste **l'**hypocrisie. | *She hates hypocrisy.* |

## Partitives in Negative Sentences

1. In negative sentences, partitive articles become **de (d'),** except after **être.** This is also true with the plural indefinite article **des.**

| | | |
|---|---|---|
| Je bois **du** lait. | → | Je ne bois **pas de** lait. |
| Elle mange **de la** soupe. | → | Elle ne mange **pas de** soupe. |
| Tu prends **de l'**eau. | → | Tu ne prends **pas d'**eau. |
| BUT: C'est **du** vin espagnol. | → | Ce n'est pas **du** vin espagnol. |
| Vous mangez **des** carottes. | → | Vous ne mangez **pas de** carottes. |
| BUT: Ce sont **des** poires. | → | Ce ne sont **pas des** poires. |

---

*Acheter** means *to buy*. It will be presented in *Chapitre 8*. Meanwhile, see Appendix B for the conjugation of **acheter.**

**2.** The expression **ne… plus** (*no more, no longer, not any more*) surrounds the conjugated verb, like **ne… pas.**

Nils et Zoé? Ils **ne** mangent **plus** de viande.
Je suis désolé, mais nous **n'**avons **plus** de vin.

*Nils and Zoé? They don't eat meat anymore.*
*I'm sorry, but we have no more wine.*

[Allez-y! A]

## Partitives with Expressions of Quantity

Partitive articles also become **de** (**d'**) after expressions of quantity.

Elle commande **du vin.**

**Combien de verres** est-ce qu'elle commande?

Elle commande **un peu de vin.**

Elle commande **beaucoup de vin.**

Elle commande **un verre de vin.**

Elle a **assez de vin.**

Elle boit **trop de vin.**

Dans son verre, il y a **peu de vin.**

[Allez-y! B-C]

 ***Allez-y!***

**A. À table!** Qu'est-ce que vous prenez, en général, à chaque repas? Qu'est-ce que vous ne prenez pas? Pensez-y!

**Possibilités:** du bacon, un bifteck, du café au lait, des croissants, des frites, du fromage, un fruit, un hamburger, de la pizza, du poulet, des spaghettis…

MODÈLE: Au petit déjeuner… →
Au petit déjeuner, je prends du jus d'orange, mais je ne prends pas de café au lait.

**1.** Au petit déjeuner… **2.** Au déjeuner… **3.** Au dîner…

**B. Dîner d'anniversaire** (*birthday*). Avec un(e) camarade, vous préparez un dîner surprise pour fêter l'anniversaire d'un ami / d'une amie. Mais avez-vous tous (*all*) les ingrédients nécessaires?

> **MODÈLE:** carottes (assez) / (ne... pas) tomates →
> É1: Est-ce que tu as des carottes?
> É2: Oui, j'ai assez de carottes, mais je n'ai pas de tomates.

1. eau minérale (3 bouteilles) / (ne... plus) jus d'orange
2. café (un peu) / (ne... plus) thé
3. fraises (beaucoup) / (ne... pas) melon
4. chocolat (trop) / (ne... pas) œufs
5. viande (assez) / (ne... pas) légumes
6. sucre (un bol) / (ne... plus) sel

**C. La réponse est simple!** Trouvez des solutions aux problèmes suivants. Utilisez les verbes **boire, apprendre, comprendre** et **prendre** et des expressions avec **prendre**.

> **MODÈLE:** Je désire parler avec un ami. → Je prends un verre au café avec un ami.

1. J'ai faim.  2. J'ai soif.  3. Je désire bien parler français.
4. Je désire étudier les mathématiques.  5. Je n'aime pas le vin.
6. Je ne suis pas pressé(e) (*in a hurry*).

**D. Dis-moi ce que tu manges!** Regardez les résultats d'une enquête sur les habitudes alimentaires des Français et répondez aux questions suivantes.

1. Est-ce que les Français dépensent (*spend*) plus pour acheter des boissons alcoolisées ou non alcoolisées (sans compter le lait)?
2. Nommez deux catégories de produits frais que les Français aiment consommer.
3. Quels sont les produits que les Français végétariens ne consomment pas?
4. Dans la liste, nommez deux catégories de produits que l'on (*that one*) achète généralement au marché en plein air (*open-air*).
5. À votre avis, quelles sont les différences entre les habitudes alimentaires des Français et des Nord-Américains?

### Le parler jeune

| | |
|---|---|
| **la bouffe** | la nourriture, le repas |
| **un casse-dalle** | un sandwich |
| **un kawa** | un café |
| **une patate** | une pomme de terre |
| **le pinard** | le vin |

Ce soir, on a décidé de faire une petite **bouffe** à la maison.

À midi, je mange un **casse-dalle** au café du coin.

Un petit **kawa** après le dessert?

Un steak avec des **patates** frites: c'est le bonheur!

Je te sers un peu de **pinard**?

## Ce que les Français consomment (en % du total des dépenses alimentaires)

**18,2** Produits laitiers et œufs
Source : Secodip-Ania

**15,8** Viandes/ volailles

**7,5** Charcuterie/traiteur/ plats cuisinés

**2,6** Conserves

**5,7** Surgelés/ glaces

**1,4** Pâtes/ féculents/ farines

Pain **0,7**

Produits de la mer (poissons, crustacés...) **3,5**

**1,4** Corps gras (huile, margarine...)

Condiments/ potages/ épices **2**

**9,9** Confiserie/ biscuits/ petits déjeuners

**2,4** Café/ thé/ infusions

**9,6** Boissons alcoolisées

**5,3** Boissons non alcoolisées

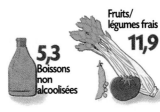
Fruits/ légumes frais **11,9**

Aliments pour animaux **2,1**

# Le blog d'Hassan

## Miam-miam!°

*Miam… Yum yum!*

Leçon 1—une salade marocaine de carottes râpées à l'orange

**vendredi 5 juin**

Salut les ennemis de la cuisine!

Vous adorez les bons petits plats mais vous détestez cuisiner? C'est parfait! Je vais créer un blog culinaire pour vous: un blog avec plein de recettes[1] délicieuses à accomplir en 10 minutes maximum. Les explications vont être simples, avec des photos et des petits films vidéo.

Je vais proposer des recettes marocaines diététiques, réalisées[2] avec des produits du marché: du poisson, du poulet, de la viande de bœuf, des légumes, des fruits. Dans ces plats, je vais utiliser des épices pour donner du goût[3]: du cumin, du safran, de l'harissa.[4]

Mon copain Hector est mon premier «client»! Il est danseur et il doit absolument avoir une alimentation équilibrée.[5] Je vais lui apprendre à cuisiner. Regardez la vidéo: c'est notre première leçon. Hector prépare une salade marocaine de carottes râpées[6] à l'orange! C'est un étudiant très sérieux. Je suis content de lui.

Bon appétit les amis,
Hassan

· · · · · · · · · · · · · · · · · · · · · · · · · · · · · · · · · · · · · · · · · · · · · · · · · · · · · · · · · · · · ·

## COMMENTAIRES

**Mamadou**

Dans la cuisine africaine, on utilise beaucoup d'épices. C'est le secret du goût.

**Charlotte**

Hassan, j'attends ton blog! La cuisine, ça prend trop de temps. Préparer un bon dîner en 10 minutes, c'est le top[7]!

**Poema**

Personnellement, je suis au régime.[8] Bravo pour les recettes diététiques marocaines! Je vais craquer[9] pour ton blog!

**Alexis**

Tu vas nous faire mourir[10] avec tes recettes minceur[11]! Moi, je mange et je bois de tout: «Bonne cuisine et bon vin, c'est le paradis sur terre[12]». C'est une parole du roi[13] Henri IV…

**Trésor**

Tu vas aussi inventer des recettes pour les chiens? Moi, j'adore les os[14] avec de la sauce!

---

[1]plein… *lots of recipes*  [2]*prepared, made*  [3]épices… *spices to give flavor*  [4]*North African spice made from ground or pureed peppers*  [5]alimentation… *well-balanced diet*  [6]*grated*  [7]*best*  [8]au… *on a diet*  [9]Je… *I'll be unable to resist*  [10]nous… *kill us*  [11]*slimming*  [12]*earth*  [13]parole… *saying of King*  [14]*bones*

## Mangez, bougez!

«Encore un peu de fromage avec un bon petit verre de vin pour finir le repas? Et pour le dessert, du gâteau au chocolat?»

En France, la nourriture est une cause nationale; manger est un plaisir,[1] et même une passion. Un anniversaire, une promotion, une fête,[2] tout est prétexte à faire un bon repas en famille ou avec des amis.

Mais bien manger signifie souvent trop manger. Et ce n'est pas bon pour la santé[3]! Alors, comment faire? Avec son programme officiel «Manger-Bouger», l'Institut national de prévention et d'éducation pour la santé propose une solution: manger oui, mais à condition de consommer des produits frais, d'équilibrer[4] ses repas et d'avoir des activités physiques.

Sandwich et fruits pour les gens pressés

Les Français sont d'accord, comme Zoé, une étudiante en médecine qui nous parle de ses habitudes alimentaires[5]: «Pour le petit déjeuner, je prends des céréales, je mange beaucoup de pain avec du beurre et de la confiture, je bois du jus d'orange. Pour le déjeuner, je n'ai pas beaucoup de temps, alors, une pomme ou une banane me suffisent. Dans la journée, je bois du thé et je mange du chocolat... trop de chocolat! Le soir, je prépare un vrai dîner: je mange des pâtes ou du riz, parce que c'est facile à préparer, des légumes et des fruits parce que c'est bon pour la santé. Je cuisine peu de viande et de poisson parce que c'est cher! Je précise aussi que je suis très sportive: je marche[6] beaucoup; je fais de la gym et du tennis une fois par semaine. Je sais[7] que mes repas ne sont pas toujours équilibrés, mais j'apprends à manger correctement... C'est important!»

Luc, étudiant en Droit, est très sérieux: il boit du lait le matin et de l'eau à tous les repas; il adore les légumes; il achète du poisson deux fois par semaine, de la viande tous les lundis et il fait du sport chaque jour. «Vous pensez que je suis trop raisonnable? Mais non! Quand je suis avec mes copains, mon menu change: je bois de la bière—jamais[8] trop de bière—et je mange des frites, mon plat préféré! Et le lendemain,[9] je fais un footing[10]... ».

Vous voyez, les habitudes alimentaires des Français ne sont pas encore parfaites. Mais le programme «Manger-Bouger» fait réfléchir et progresser. Même[11] les enfants apprennent à sélectionner leurs aliments et à cuisiner. Et pour l'activité physique, pas de problème: ils sont toujours en mouvement... parce que ce sont sont des enfants!

[1]*pleasure* [2]*holiday* [3]*health* [4]*balance* [5]*habitudes... eating habits* [6]*walk* [7]*know* [8]*never* [9]*the next day* [10]*fais... go for a run* [11]*Even*

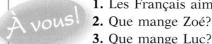
*À vous!*

1. Les Français aiment bien manger. Et les Américains? Expliquez.
2. Que mange Zoé?
3. Que mange Luc? Est-il raisonnable quand il mange avec ses copains? Commentez son attitude.
4. Et vous, quels sont vos plats préférés?
5. Présentez le programme «Manger-Bouger». Selon vous, est-ce qu'il est difficile à appliquer? Expliquez.

*Parlons-en!*

1. Travaillez en groupes de trois. Composez un petit déjeuner, un déjeuner ou un dîner équilibré pour le programme «Manger-Bouger». Associez des activités physiques à vos menus.
2. Présentez votre menu et votre programme d'activités physiques à la classe. Répondez aux commentaires et aux suggestions de vos camarades. Qui a le programme le plus réussi (*successful*)? Votez!

# Leçon 3

## L'imperatif

*Giving Commands*

### Deux baguettes et du sel!

*Abdel et Carole échangent des textos (SMS).*

CAROLE: **Sois**[1] gentil, **apporte**[2] deux baguettes pour ce soir.

ABDEL: Je prends un gâteau pour le dessert?

CAROLE: Non. **Achète**[3] du sel.

ABDEL: Du sel pour le dessert?

CAROLE: Idiot! Du sel pour mon bœuf aux carottes. **Ne perds pas** de temps. Tes parents arrivent dans 20 minutes!

ABDEL: **Fais** attention: mes parents sont toujours en avance…

CAROLE: **Dépêche-toi,**[4] dépêche-toi!

Trouvez la phrase où…

1. Carole demande gentiment (*politely*) à Abdel d'apporter deux baguettes.
2. Carole demande à Abdel d'acheter du sel.
3. Abdel explique que ses parents vont bientôt arriver.
4. Carole ordonne à Abdel de se dépêcher.

[1]*Be* [2]*bring* [3]*Buy* [4]*Hurry up*

The imperative is the command form of a verb. It is used to express an order, a piece of advice, or a suggestion. There are three forms in French. As in English, subject pronouns are not used with the imperative.

| | | |
|---|---|---|
| (tu) | **Arrête** de parler! | *Stop talking!* |
| (nous) | **Allons** au restaurant! | *Let's go to the restaurant!* |
| (vous) | **Passez** une bonne journée! | *Have a nice day!* |

1. Verbs ending in **-er:** The imperatives are the same as the corresponding present-tense forms, except that the **tu** form does not end in **-s.**

| INFINITIVE | **tu** | **nous** | **vous** |
|---|---|---|---|
| regarder | **Regarde!** | **Regardons!** | **Regardez!** |
| entrer | **Entre!** | **Entrons!** | **Entrez!** |

| | |
|---|---|
| **Écoute!** | *Listen!* ~~drops~~ |
| **Regardez!** Un restaurant russe. | *Look! A Russian restaurant.* |
| **Entrons!** | *Let's go in!* |

The imperative forms of the irregular verb **aller** follow the pattern of regular **-er** imperatives: **va, allons, allez.**

2. Verbs ending in **-re** and **-ir:** The imperative forms are identical to their corresponding present-tense forms. This is true even of most irregular **-re** and **-ir** verbs.

| INFINITIVE | **tu** | **nous** | **vous** |
|---|---|---|---|
| attendre | **Attends!** | **Attendons!** | **Attendez!** |
| finir | **Finis!** | **Finissons!** | **Finissez!** |
| faire | **Fais... !** | **Faisons... !** | **Faites... !** |

| | |
|---|---|
| **Attends! Finis** ton verre! | *Wait! Finish your drink!* |
| **Faites** attention! | *Pay attention! (Watch out!)* |

3. The verbs **avoir** and **être** have irregular command forms.

| INFINITIVE | **tu** | **nous** | **vous** |
|---|---|---|---|
| avoir | **Aie... !** | **Ayons... !** | **Ayez... !** |
| être | **Sois... !** | **Soyons... !** | **Soyez... !** |

| | |
|---|---|
| **Sois** gentil, Michel. | *Be nice, Michel.* |
| **Ayez** de la patience. | *Have patience.* |

4. In negative commands, **ne** comes before the verb and **pas** follows it.

| | |
|---|---|
| **Ne prends pas** de sucre! | *Don't have any sugar!* |
| **Ne buvons pas** trop de café. | *Let's not drink too much coffee.* |
| **N'attendez pas** le dessert. | *Don't wait for dessert.* |

*(continued)*

**5.** When using these command forms, you should be aware that they are not the most polite way of expressing your wishes. Later on you will learn about indirect commands or requests with the conditional, which are much more polite. With the imperative, the use of **s'il vous plaît** and **s'il te plaît** will make your requests more polite.

> **Aie** de la patience, **s'il te plaît.**     *Please have patience.*
> **Ne fumez pas, s'il vous plaît.**     *Please don't smoke.*

 ***Allez-y!***

**A. Les bonnes manières.** Vous êtes à table avec un enfant. Dites-lui ce qu'il faut (= il est nécessaire de) faire ou ne pas faire.

> **MODÈLE:** ne pas jouer avec ton couteau ⟶
> Ne joue pas avec ton couteau!

**1.** attendre ton frère    **2.** prendre ta serviette    **3.** finir ta soupe
**4.** manger tes carottes    **5.** regarder ton assiette    **6.** être sage (*good* [*lit., wise*])    **7.** ne pas manger de sucre    **8.** boire ton verre de lait
**9.** ne pas demander de dessert

**B. Un job d'été.** Vous travaillez comme serveur/serveuse dans un café. Voici les recommandations de la patronne (*owner*).

> **MODÈLE:** faire attention aux clients ⟶ Faites attention aux clients.

**1.** être aimable    **2.** avoir de la patience    **3.** écouter les clients
**4.** répondre aux questions    **5.** ne pas perdre de temps    **6.** rendre correctement la monnaie (*change*)

Maintenant vous parlez avec un autre serveur / une autre serveuse de ce qu'il faut faire au travail. Répétez les recommandations de la patronne.

> **MODÈLE:** faire attention aux clients ⟶ Faisons attention aux clients!

 **C. Le robot.** Vous avez un robot qui travaille pour vous. La classe choisit un étudiant / une étudiante pour jouer le rôle du robot. Donnez cinq ordres en français au robot. Il/Elle est obligé(e) d'obéir. Utilisez «s'il te plaît».

> **MODÈLE:** Va au tableau, s'il te plaît!

# L'heure

*Telling Time*

## Quelle heure est-il?

Il est **sept heures.** Quel repas est-ce que Vincent prend?

Il est **dix heures et demie.*** Où est Vincent?

Il est **midi.** Quel repas est-ce qu'il prend?

Il est **deux heures et quart.** Où est Vincent?

Il est **quatre heures moins le quart.** Qu'est-ce qu'il fait?

Il est **huit heures vingt.** Il dîne en famille?

Il est **minuit moins vingt.** Est-ce qu'il étudie encore?

Il est **minuit,** et Vincent dort (*is sleeping*).

**1.** To ask the time:

    **Excusez-moi, quelle heure est-il?**    *Excuse me, what time is it?*

**2.** To ask at what time something happens:

    —**À quelle heure** commence le    *At what time does the*
      film?                              *movie start?*
    —**À** deux heures et demie.     *At 2:30.*

**3.** To tell the time:

    **Il est** une **heure.**         *It is 1:00.*
    **Il est** deux **heures.**     *It is 2:00.*
    **Il est** presque **midi / minuit.**    *It's almost noon / midnight.*

**4.** To make a distinction between A.M. and P.M.:

    Il est neuf heures **du matin.**    *It's 9 A.M. (in the morning).*
    Il est quatre heures **de**      *It's 4 P.M. (in the afternoon).*
      **l'après-midi.**
    Il est onze heures **du soir.**    *It's 11 P.M. (in the evening, at night).*

---

*To tell the time on the half hour, **et demie** is used after the feminine noun **heure(s)** and **et demi** is used after the masculine nouns **midi** and **minuit.**

   Il est trois heures **et demie.**    *It's 3:30 (half past three).*
   Il est midi **et demi.**       *It's 12:30 (half past noon).*

> ### 🎧 Prononcez bien!
>
> **Liaison with *heures***
>
> Note the pronunciation of the last letter in the following numbers when they are followed by the word **heures.**
>
> [z]: Il est **deux** heures.
>      Il est **trois** heures.
>      Il est **six** heures.
>      Il est **dix** heures.
> [v]: Il est **neuf** heures.

The 24-hour clock is used for official announcements (e.g., TV or transportation schedules), to make appointments, and to avoid ambiguity. For time expressed in figures, **h** (**heures**) is used (without a colon).

|  | OFFICIAL 24-HOUR | 12-HOUR |
|---|---|---|
| 9 h 15 | neuf heures quinze | neuf heures **et quart** (du matin) |
| 15 h 30 | quinze heures trente | trois heures **et demie** (de l'après-midi) |
| 18 h 45 | dix-huit heures quarante-cinq | sept heures **moins le quart** (du soir) |
| 20 h 50 | vingt heures cinquante | neuf heures **moins dix** (du soir) |

## Mots clés

**Exprimer le temps de façon générale**

Il est **tard.**
*It's late.*

Il est **tôt.**
*It's early.*

Jamal prend son repas **de bonne heure.**
*Jamal eats early.*

Gabriel est **en retard** aujourd'hui.
*Gabriel is late today.*

D'habitude, il est **en avance.**
*Usually, he's early.*

Camille est toujours **à l'heure.**
*Camille is always on time.*

## ▎▎▎▎ *Allez-y!*

**A. Quelle heure est-il?** Donnez l'heure selon les deux systèmes.

1.
2.
3.
4.

5.
6.
7.
8.

9.
10.
11.
12.

**B. Quelle heure est-il pour vous?** Qu'est-ce que vous faites?

1.
2.
3.
4.

**C. Les bars et restaurants de Carcassonne.** Imaginez que vous êtes à Carcassonne et que vous consultez la liste des restaurants et cafés de la ville. Voici des informations sur quatre établissements et leurs horaires (*schedules*).

1. À quelle heure préférez-vous prendre votre petit déjeuner? Où pouvez-vous (*can you*) aller? Est-il possible de prendre votre repas à sept heures et demie dans ce restaurant? à huit heures et demie?
2. Samedi, vous voulez (*want*) surfer sur Internet pendant votre déjeuner à midi. Est-ce que le QC est ouvert (*open*)? À quelle heure décidez-vous d'aller au QG?
3. Où allez-vous pour manger une spécialité méditerranéenne? À quelle heure s'arrête le service du déjeuner? À quelle heure commence le service du dîner?
4. Est-il possible de dîner à l'Auberge des Chênes le lundi? Pourquoi? Est-il possible de déjeuner dans ce restaurant le lundi? À quelle heure?
5. Quel restaurant reste ouvert après minuit? Jusqu'à (*Until*) quelle heure?

# LES BARS ET RESTAURANTS DE CARCASSONNE

## L'Auberge des Chênes
Formule midi 15€ en semaine - Menus 22€ à 42€ - Carte
Fermé° lundi soir et samedi midi
1 Rte de Limoux - Tél. 04 68 25 40 11

*Closed*

## L'ESCALIER
## Pizzas - TEX-MEX
Spécialités méditerranéennes
De 12h à 14h et de 19h à minuit.
La pizzeria qui fait disjoncter
le Guide du Routard
**22, bd Omer Sarraut 11000 CARCASSONNE**
**Tél. 04 68 25 65 66**

## Cyber Café le QG

Mail - Connexion internet - Jeux en réseau

Restauration rapide à toutes heures - Boissons chaudes/froides

Ouvert° du lundi au vendredi 8h-19h - Samedi 13h-19h fermé le dimanche
**80 allée d'Iéna - Tél. 0811 094 015**

*Open*

## Le Colonial Lounge
**Restaurant - Bar d'ambiance**
Vous invite à l'évasion tous les jours de 11h à 16h
et de 19h à 2h du mat' - Formule à partir de 10€50 et sa carte
**Au bord du canal, face à la gare - 3, avenue Maréchal Foch**
Tél. 04 68 72 48 43 - mail.lecoloniallounge@aol.com

# Prononcez bien!

1. **La voyelle dans *du* et *de*** (page 157)

   A. **Au supermarché.** Vous êtes au supermarché, mais vous n'avez pas votre liste avec vous. Vous téléphonez à votre colocataire. Elle vous dit (*tells you*) les choses que vous avez et que vous n'avez pas. La communication est mauvaise et vous avez des difficultés à entendre si elle dit « il y a **du** ____ » ou « il n'y a pas **de** ____ »? Faites attention à la prononciation des voyelles **u** et **e** dans les articles pour choisir la bonne réponse.

   | | | |
   |---|---|---|
   | 1. **a.** Il y a du lait. | **b.** Il n'y a pas de lait. |
   | 2. **a.** Il y a du thé. | **b.** Il n'y a pas de thé. |
   | 3. **a.** Il y a du chocolat. | **b.** Il n'y a pas de chocolat. |
   | 4. **a.** Il y a du sucre. | **b.** Il n'y a pas de sucre. |
   | 5. **a.** Il y a du jambon. | **b.** Il n'y a pas de jambon. |
   | 6. **a.** Il y a du poisson. | **b.** Il n'y a pas de poisson. |

   B. **Au restaurant.** Vous êtes au restaurant avec votre ami(e) et un serveur passe avec un plat qui a l'air délicieux (la photo de ce plat est à la page 146). Votre ami(e) vous demande s'il y a les ingrédients suivants dans ce plat: **beurre, café, céleri, fromage, pain, poivre, poulet, raisin, sel, tomates, thon, vin.**

   **MODÈLE:**  É1: Est-ce qu'il y a du café?
   É2: Non, il n'y a pas de café.

2. **Liaison with *heures*** (page 165)

   A. **Un week-end entre amis!** Les amis de votre colocataire, qui n'habitent pas tous en France, viennent (*are coming*) passer le week-end avec vous. Votre colocataire parle de la durée de voyage de ses amis. Cochez les temps mentionnés.

   | | | | |
   |---|---|---|---|
   | **1.** Christophe | **a.** 2 h | **b.** 12 h |
   | **2.** Zoé | **a.** 3 h | **b.** 13 h |
   | **3.** Éric et Isabelle | **a.** 6 h | **b.** 16 h |
   | **4.** Marc | **a.** 3 h | **b.** 13 h |
   | **5.** Simon | **a.** 6 h | **b.** 16 h |
   | **6.** Carine | **a.** 2 h | **b.** 12 h |

   B. **Horaires des arrivées.** Les amis de votre colocataire (votre camarade de classe) vont arriver en train à des heures différentes. Vous téléphonez à votre colocataire pour demander leurs heures d'arrivée. Posez les questions 1 à 3 à votre colocataire selon le modèle. Ensuite, changez de rôle pour les questions 4 à 6. Faites bien attention à la liaison avec le mot **heures.**

   **MODÈLE:**  Christophe (8 h 45)
   É1: À quelle heure arrive Christophe?
   É2: Il arrive à 8 h 45.

   | | | |
   |---|---|---|
   | **1.** Zoé (9 h 55) | **3.** Isabelle (2 h 10) | **5.** Simon (6 h 30) |
   | **2.** Éric (2 h 05) | **4.** Marc (3 h 29) | **6.** Carine (6 h 45) |

Lecture

### Avant de lire

**Scanning (Part 1).** You are planning a dinner party featuring dishes from a number of French-speaking countries. One of your guests doesn't eat fish; another is allergic to dairy products. As you look for recipes, you rapidly *scan* the list of ingredients, rejecting those that contain salmon and/or cream, for example. Scanning allows you to read more efficiently. Instead of reading line by line, you can skip much of a text and still find the information you need.

Scan the recipes in this section. Would you be able to prepare both of them for the guests described here?

**Le vocabulaire culinaire.** In recipes, instructions are often given in the infinitive form, which can be translated by an imperative in English.

| | |
|---|---|
| Râper finement les carottes. | *Finely grate the carrots.* |
| Couper en morceaux un kilo de poissons. | *Cut up a kilo of fish into pieces.* |

In addition, many cooking instructions include the verbs **faire** and **laisser.** Read the following examples carefully.

| | |
|---|---|
| Faire bouillir… | *Boil . . .* |
| Laisser mijoter… | *Let simmer . . .* |

Can you guess the meaning of the expression **laisser cuire**? (Note that the verb **cuire** is related to the noun **cuisine**).

**Voyons voir…** Parcourez rapidement (*Scan*) les recettes à la page suivante et décidez si les affirmations sont vraies ou fausses.

1. V F La salade marocaine est sucrée.
2. V F On sert la soupe avec du riz.
3. V F La soupe se cuit (*cooks*) assez rapidement.
4. V F Il y a du jus d'orange dans la salade.
5. V F La soupe contient beaucoup de matières grasses (*fat*).

# *Saveurs du monde francophone*

## Salade marocaine de carottes râpées à l'orange

### Ingrédients

500 g de carottes

1 pincée de cannelle[1]

1 cuillerée à soupe de
   sucre en poudre

1 cuillerée à soupe d'eau
   de fleur d'oranger

1 verre de jus d'orange

le jus d'un citron

2 oranges

### Préparation

Râper finement les
carottes. Les arroser du
mélange cannelle, jus de
citron, sucre, eau de
fleur d'oranger, jus
d'orange. Mélanger.
Disposer sur assiettes et
décorer de tranches[2]
d'oranges pelées à vif.[3]

Servir frais.

## *Blaff de poissons martiniquais*°

Blaff... *Fish poached
in broth, Fish soup*

### Ingrédients

1 kilo de poissons variés

1 citron vert

1 citron

2 oignons

1 gousse d'ail[4]

1 clou de girofle[5]

1 pincée de thym

2 cuillerées à soupe de
   persil finement haché[6]

3 cives[7] hachées

un morceau de piment[8]

du sel et du poivre

### Préparation

Préparer le court-
bouillon: Faire bouillir
longuement dans une
casserole[9] d'eau le
girofle, le thym, le
persil, et les oignons
préalablement[10] coupés en
rondelles,[11] les cives hachées,
le sel, le poivre, et le piment.
Couper en morceaux[12] un
kilo de poissons, les frotter[13]
de citron vert et les plonger
dans le court-bouillon.

Laisser cuire de 10 à 15
minutes. Ajouter[14] le jus
d'un citron et la gousse d'ail
écrasée.[15] Laissez mijoter
pendant quelques minutes.

Servir les poissons dans ce
bouillon très parfumé.[16]

[1]*pincée... pinch of cinammon*  [2]*slices*  [3]*pelées... peeled with the zest removed*  [4]*gousse... clove of garlic*
[5]*clove*  [6]*chopped*  [7]*chives*  [8]*hot pepper*  [9]*pot*  [10]*ahead of time*  [11]*round slices*  [12]*pieces*  [13]*rub*  [14]*Add*
[15]*crushed*  [16]*flavorful*

## Compréhension

**Quel verbe, quel ingrédient?** Choisissez l'ingrédient de la colonne de droite qui suit logiquement le verbe dans la colonne de gauche. **Attention:** Parfois il y a plus d'une réponse possible.

1. Écraser _____.
2. Hacher _____.
3. Faire bouillir _____.
4. Peler _____.
5. Râper _____.
6. Couper _____.

a. l'eau
b. les oranges
c. les carottes
d. les oignons
e. la gousse d'ail
f. les cives

# Écriture

The writing activities **Par écrit** and **Journal intime** can be found in the Workbook/Laboratory Manual to accompany *Vis-à-vis.*

# Pour s'amuser

«Le vin est la partie intellectuelle d'un repas. Les viandes et les légumes n'en sont que la partie matérielle.»

—Alexandre Dumas

Selon vous, est-ce que le vin est une boisson «intellectuelle»? Expliquez.

# Le vidéoblog d'Hassan

## En bref

Dans cet épisode, Léa et Juliette regardent le vidéoblog d'Hassan. Le jeune homme donne une petite leçon de cuisine à Hector. Les deux amis préparent une salade marocaine traditionnelle: des carottes râpées à l'orange. Ensuite, Hector parle de la cuisine martiniquaise.

## Vocabulaire en contexte

Mesurez *votre* talent en cuisine et décrivez *votre* repas typique.

**Votre talent en cuisine**
- ☐ Moi, je suis un excellent cuisinier / une excellente cuisinère!
- ☐ **Je sais** (*I know how*) préparer de bons **plats.**
- ☐ Il y a un ou deux plats que je sais préparer.
- ☐ Je suis incapable de faire un sandwich!

**Votre repas typique**
- ☐ un repas **diététique** composé de produits frais
- ☐ un repas équilibré traditionnel
- ☐ un repas lourd et gras (*heavy and greasy*)
- ☐ un repas fast-food

Une brochette de poisson à la martiniquaise

## Visionnez!

Regardez la vidéo et trouvez l'équivalent des mots en caractères gras.

1. _____ Hassan **râpe** les carottes.
2. _____ Hector **coupe** les oranges en tranches fines (*thin slices*).
3. _____ Hector **verse** le jus de citron sur les carottes.
4. _____ Hassan **ajoute** du sucre et de l'eau de fleur d'oranger.
5. _____ Hassan **met** un peu de cannelle sur la salade.
6. _____ Hassan **mélange** les ingrédients.

**a.** *cuts*
**b.** *adds*
**c.** *pours*
**d.** *grates*
**e.** *mixes*
**f.** *puts*

## Analysez!

Répondez aux questions.

1. Le climat a une influence sur la cuisine d'un pays. Existe-t-il d'autres influences? Donnez des exemples.
2. Trouvez-vous la cuisine martiniquaise appétissante? Pourquoi (pas)?

## Comparez!

Qu'est-ce qui influence la cuisine de votre région? Quels sont les plats et les ingrédients typiques? Regardez encore une fois la partie culturelle de la vidéo: préférez-vous la cuisine de votre région ou la cuisine martiniquaise? Expliquez.

## Note culturelle

Au Maroc, pays à l'hospitalité légendaire, le thé à la menthe[1] vous est proposé à toute heure. Préparé dans une théière[2] de métal, on vous le présente bien chaud et très sucré. On le verse[3] très haut[4] dans un petit verre. Refuser un thé à la menthe est impoli. C'est parfois[5] considéré comme une offense.

[1]*mint* [2]*teapot* [3]*pours* [4]*high* [5]*sometimes*

# Vocabulaire

## Verbes

**apporter** *to bring*
**apprendre** to learn
**boire** to drink
**célébrer** to celebrate
**commander** to order (*in a restaurant*)
**comprendre** to understand; to include
**considérer** to consider
**déjeuner** to eat lunch
**dîner** to dine, eat dinner
**espérer** to hope
**passer** to pass, spend (*time*)
**préférer** to prefer
**prendre** to take; to have (to eat; to order)
  **prendre le petit déjeuner** to have breakfast
  **prendre du temps** to take (a long) time
  **prendre son temps** to take one's time
  **prendre un repas** to eat a meal
  **prendre un verre** to have a drink (*usually alcoholic*)

À REVOIR: **aimer mieux, préparer**

## Substantifs

**l'après-midi** (*m.*) afternoon
**la cuisine** cooking; kitchen
**le déjeuner** lunch
**le dîner** dinner
**le goûter** afternoon snack
**la journée** (whole) day
**le matin** morning
**le midi** noon
**le plat** dish (*of food*)
**le petit déjeuner** breakfast
**le produit** product
**le repas** meal
**le soir** evening

## Les provisions

**l'aliment** (*m.*) food
**le beurre** butter
**la bière** beer
**le bifteck** steak
**le bœuf** beef
**la boisson gazeuse** soft drink

**le champignon** mushroom
**le citron** lemon
**le citron vert** lime
**la crème** cream
**l'eau** (*f.*) **(minérale)** (mineral) water
**la fraise** strawberry
**les frites** (*f. pl.*) French fries
**le fromage** cheese
**le gâteau** cake
**les haricots*** (*m. pl.*) **verts** green beans
**le jambon** ham
**le jus (d'orange)** (orange) juice
**le lait** milk
**le légume** vegetable
**la nourriture** food
**l'œuf** (*m.*) egg
**l'oignon** (*m.*) onion
**le pain** bread
**la poire** pear
**le poisson** fish
**le poivre** pepper
**le poivron** bell pepper
**la pomme de terre** potato
**le poulet** chicken
**les produits** (*m.*) **frais** fresh products
**le sel** salt
**le sucre** sugar
**la tarte** pie
**le thé** tea
**la viande** meat
**le vin** wine

## À table

**l'assiette** (*f.*) plate
**le bol** wide cup
**la bouteille** bottle
**le couteau** knife
**la cuillère (à soupe)** (soup) spoon
**la fourchette** fork
**la glace** ice cream
**la nappe** tablecloth
**la serviette** napkin
**la tasse** cup
**le verre** glass

## Substantifs apparentés

**la baguette, la banane, les brocolis** (*m. pl.*)**, la carafe, la carotte, le champagne, le chocolat, le croissant, le dessert, le fruit, la laitue, l'orange** (*f. pl.*)**, le porc, la salade, la soupe, la tomate**

## Adjectif

**frais/fraîche** fresh

## L'heure

**Quelle heure est-il?** What time is it?
**Il est... heure(s).** It is . . . o'clock.
  **... et demi(e)** half past (the hour)
  **... et quart** quarter past (the hour)
  **... moins le quart** quarter to (the hour)
  **... du matin** in the morning
  **... de l'après-midi** in the afternoon
  **... du soir** in the evening, at night
**Il est midi.** It's noon.
**Il est minuit.** It's midnight.
**À quelle heure... ?** At what time . . . ?

## Les expressions de quantité

**assez de** enough of
**beaucoup de** a lot of
**peu de** little of
**trop de** too much of, too many of
**un peu de** a little of

## Mots et expressions divers

**à l'heure** on time
**de bonne heure** early
**Dépêche-toi!** *Hurry up!*
**en avance** early
**en retard** late
**je voudrais** I would like
**ne... plus** no more, no longer, not any more
**plusieurs** several
**presque** almost
**Sois gentil!** *Be nice!*
**tard** late
**tôt** early
**vers** around, about (*with time expressions*)

---

*The initial **h** is aspirate here, which means there is no elision with the article **les**.

# Les plaisirs de la cuisine

Les dossiers d'Hassan

Hassan

➤ 📁 Mes photos
  ➤ 📁 Un beau marché en plein air
  ➤ 📁 Faire le marché
  ➤ 📁 Un tajine marocain

Un beau marché en plein air

## Dans ce chapitre...

### OBJECTIFS COMMUNICATIFS

- ➤ asking about choices
- ➤ pointing out people and things
- ➤ expressing desire, ability, necessity, and obligation
- ➤ talking about past events
- ➤ learning to distinguish between and pronounce selected sounds in French

Faire le marché, c'est un plaisir!

### PAROLES (Leçon 1)

- ➤ Les magasins d'alimentation
- ➤ Au restaurant
- ➤ Les nombres supérieurs à 60

### STRUCTURES (Leçons 2 et 3)

- ➤ L'adjectif interrogatif **quel**
- ➤ Les adjectifs démonstratifs
- ➤ Les verbes **vouloir, pouvoir** et **devoir**
- ➤ Le passé composé avec l'auxiliaire **avoir**

Un tajine marocain

### CULTURE

- ➤ Le blog d'Hassan: *Marché ou cybermarché?*
- ➤ Reportage: *Comment voyager dans son assiette?*
- ➤ Lecture: *Les grandes occasions* (Leçon 4)

**connect** |FRENCH

www.mhconnectfrench.com

# Leçon 1

## Les magasins (*m.*) d'alimentation

M^me Barbet va d'abord (*first*) à la boulangerie, puis (*then*) à la poissonnerie, et ensuite (*then*) à la boucherie.

 **Prononcez bien!**

**The semivowel in *ail***

Pronounce the semivowel [j] the same way you pronounce the first letter of the English word *you*, with the sides of your tongue pressing against the sides of your palate. Below are the most common spellings of the sound [j].

[j]: **b**i**en, yeux, ma**ill**ot***

The **-il** at the end of a word is also pronounced [j].

[j]: **a**il**, trava**il**, somme**il**, vie**il

One exception to this rule is **gentil,** where the **-il** is pronounced [i].

***mille, ville, villa, village, tranquille** are exceptions to this rule and the **-ill** is pronounced [il].

### AUTRES MOTS UTILES

| | | | |
|---|---|---|---|
| **de l'ail** (*m.*) | garlic | **de l'huile** (*f.*) | oil |
| **une boîte (de conserve)** | a can (of food) | **des pâtes** | pasta |
| | | **un saucisson** | a salami |
| **des crevettes** (*f.*) | shrimp | **du saumon** | salmon |
| **un homard**† | a lobster | | |

---

*There are also separate stores; **la boulangerie,** where one buys bread, **la pâtisserie,** where one buys pastries, **la boucherie,** where one buys beef and poultry, and **la charcuterie** where one buys pork products.
†The **h** in **homard** is aspirate, which means that there is no "elision" with the article **le** (i.e., **le homard**). Note how this is different from **l'huître,** which has a mute **h.** In both cases, the **h** is silent.

 *Allez-y!*

**Les magasins du quartier.** Où est-ce qu'on va pour acheter les produits suivants?

> **MODÈLE:** des éclairs au chocolat →
> Pour acheter des éclairs au chocolat, on va à la boulangerie-pâtisserie.

1. des saucisses et un rôti de veau
2. des huîtres et des crabes
3. des sardines à l'huile
4. des côtes de porc
5. de la sole et du saumon
6. du pâté de campagne et du filet de bœuf
7. de l'ail et des boîtes de conserve
8. un pain de campagne

# Au restaurant

---

### Restaurant La Guirlande de Julie
Ouvert de 12 h 00 à 14 h 30 et de 19 h 00 à 22 h 30.
Fermé le lundi.

#### Pour commencer

| | |
|---|---|
| Kir[1] | 9 euros |
| Coupe[2] de champagne | 15 euros |
| Américano | 8 euros |

#### Nos formules[3]

*(excepté le soir, le samedi, le dimanche et les jours fériés)*

| | |
|---|---|
| Plat du marché | 14 euros |
| Entrée, plat du marché | 18 euros |

ou

| | |
|---|---|
| Plat du marché, dessert | 18 euros |
| Entrée, plat du marché, dessert | 20 euros |

#### Les entrées

| | |
|---|---|
| Fromage de chèvre au basilic et à l'huile d'olive | 7 euros |
| Escargots de Bourgogne | 9 euros |
| Terrine de gibier,[4] petite salade «selon saison» | 9 euros |
| Foie gras de canard[5] maison | 15 euros |

#### Les plats

| | |
|---|---|
| Notre spécialité «Pot-au-feu[6] royal» | 16 euros |
| Confit de canard, pommes bûcheronnes, champignons | 17 euros |
| Rognons de veau[7] bordelais et petits oignons | 15 euros |
| Saumon braisé en croûte d'herbes, tagliatelle de légumes | 18 euros |

#### Nos fromages

| | |
|---|---|
| Petit chèvre frais mariné à l'huile vierge | 7 euros |
| Assiette de fromages | 7 euros |

#### Les desserts

| | |
|---|---|
| Tarte aux pommes, glace à la cannelle | 8 euros |
| Crème brûlée à la vanille de Bourbon | 8 euros |
| Glaces et sorbets, parfums au choix | 8 euros |

*Prix nets, service compris*

---

[1]*White wine with blackcurrant liqueur* [2]*Goblet* [3]*Special of the day generally including* un plat *and* une entrée *or* un dessert. [4]*Terrine… Game paté* [5]*duck* [6]*Stew* [7]*Rognons… Veal kidneys*

**AUTRES MOTS UTILES**

| | |
|---|---|
| l'addition (*f.*) | check |
| l'argent (*m.*) | money |
| autre chose | something else |
| la carte | menu |
| compris(e) | included |
| l'entrée (*f.*) | first course |
| les escargots (*m.*) | snails |
| goûter | to taste |
| le menu | fixed-price meal (*usually including* **une entrée, un plat,** *and* **du fromage** *or* **un dessert**) |
| la mousse au chocolat | chocolate mousse |
| le plat | course (*of a meal*); dish (*type of food*) |
| le plat principal | main course |
| le pourboire | tip |
| le prix | price |
| quelque chose | something |
| le serveur / la serveuse | waiter / waitress |

 *Allez-y!*

**A. La Guirlande de Julie.** Mettez le dialogue dans le bon ordre. Numérotez les phrases de 1 à 10.

**LE SERVEUR**

__3__ Vous désirez quelque chose à boire?

__9__ (*plus tard*) Vous désirez autre chose?

__5__ Une eau minérale. Vous désirez une entrée?

__1__ Bonjour, madame. Avez-vous choisi? (*Have you decided?*)

__7__ Très bien, madame. (*plus tard*) Prenez-vous du fromage, un dessert?

**LA CLIENTE**

__4__ Une eau minérale, s'il vous plaît.

__2__ Oui, j'ai fait mon choix (*choice*).

__6__ Oui, comme entrée, je vais prendre le foie gras de canard, et ensuite, le pot-au-feu.

__8__ Euh, je vais prendre une crème brûlée à la vanille, s'il vous plaît.

__10__ Non, merci. Apportez-moi (*Bring me*) l'addition, s'il vous plaît.

**B. Au restaurant.** Avec un(e) camarade, regardez la carte de La Guirlande de Julie. Jouez les rôles du serveur / de la serveuse et du client / de la cliente. Notez ce que le client / la cliente commande.

**MODÈLE:** LE SERVEUR / LA SERVEUSE: Qu'est-ce que vous prenez comme entrée? (plat principal, boisson… )

LE CLIENT / LA CLIENTE: Je prends le/la*…

---

*The definite article, rather than the partitive, is often used when one orders a dish from a menu.

# Les nombres supérieurs à 60

| | | | | | |
|---|---|---|---|---|---|
| 60 | soixante | 72 | soixante-douze | 90 | quatre-vingt-dix |
| 61 | soixante **et** un | 73 | soixante-treize | 91 | quatre-vingt-onze |
| 62 | soixante-deux | 80 | quatre-vingt**s** | 92 | quatre-vingt-douze |
| 63 | soixante-trois | 81 | quatre-vingt-un | 93 | quatre-vingt-treize |
| 70 | soixante-dix | 82 | quatre-vingt-deux | 100 | cent |
| 71 | soixante **et** onze | 83 | quatre-vingt-trois | | |

• Note that **quatre-vingts** takes an **-s,** but that numbers based on it do not: **quatre-vingt-un,** and so on.

| | | | | |
|---|---|---|---|---|
| 101 | cent un | 600 | six cents | |
| 102 | cent deux | 700 | sept cents | |
| 200 | deux cents | 800 | huit cents | |
| 201 | deux cent un | 900 | neuf cents | |
| 300 | trois cents | 999 | neuf cent quatre-vingt-dix-neuf | |
| 400 | quatre cents | 1 000 | mille | |
| 500 | cinq cents | 999 999 | ? | |

• Note that the **-s** of **cents** is dropped if it is followed by any other number: **deux cent un, sept cent trente-cinq.**
• Like **cent, mille** (*one thousand*) is expressed without an article. **Mille** is invariable and thus never ends in **-s: mille quatre, sept mille, neuf mille neuf cent quatre-vingt-dix-neuf.**

Préférez-vous les légumes, les fruits de mer ou la viande?

Radis (France): 2,89 €/kg

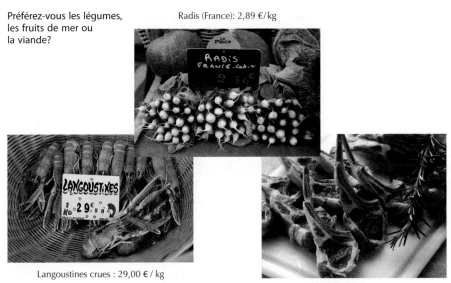

Langoustines crues : 29,00 € / kg

Côtes d'agneau : 19,06 € / kg

- French currency is **l'euro** (*m.*)(€); it is divided into **centimes.** The most common way of writing prices in **euros** is: 48,50 €, **(quarante-huit euros cinquante).**
- The nouns **million** and **milliard** (*billion*) take **-s** in the plural. When introducing a noun, they are followed by **de (d').**

Ce château a coûté sept **millions d'**euros.

*This chateau cost seven million euros.*

*Allez-y!*

**A. Problèmes de mathématiques.** Inventez six problèmes, puis demandez à un(e) camarade de les résoudre (*solve them*).

**Vocabulaire utile:** + (plus, et), − (moins), × (fois), ÷ (divisé par), = (font, égalent)

**MODÈLES:**  37 + 42 →
> É1: Trente-sept plus (et) quarante-deux?
> É2: Trente-sept plus (et) quarante-deux font (égalent) soixante-dix-neuf.

10 × 10 000 →
> É1: Dix fois dix mille?
> É2: Dix fois dix mille font (égalent) cent mille.

**B. La cuisine diététique.** Votre partenaire et vous avez un restaurant français qui sert de la cuisine diététique. Créez un menu à moins de (*fewer than*) 1 000 calories. Le menu doit (*must*) avoir…

un hors-d'œuvre ou une entrée
un plat principal
des légumes
un fromage ou un dessert

| VALEUR CALORIQUE DE QUELQUES ALIMENTS **(pour 100 grammes)** | | | | | | | |
|---|---|---|---|---|---|---|---|
| **TRÈS CALORIQUES** | | **CALORIQUES** | | **PEU CALORIQUES** | | **TRÈS PEU CALORIQUES** | |
| Saucisson | 559 | Brie | 271 | Banane | 97 | Poire | 61 |
| Chocolat | 500 | Pain | 259 | Crevettes | 96 | Pomme | 61 |
| Pâté de foie gras | 454 | Côte d'agneau | 256 | Pommes de terre | 89 | Carotte | 43 |
| Biscuits secs | 410 | Filet de porc | 172 | Lait | 67 | Fraise | 40 |
| Macaronis, pâtes | 351 | Œufs | 162 | Artichaut | 64 | Orange | 40 |
| Riz | 340 | Poulet | 147 | | | Champignons | 31 |
| Camembert | 312 | Canard | 135 | | | Tomates | 22 |

**C. Les promotions du mois.** Ce soir, vous faites des courses. Vous allez dans un magasin spécialisé en produits surgelés (*frozen*). Vous achetez un plat principal, des légumes et un dessert. Qu'est-ce que vous allez choisir?

## CHEZ PICARD SURGELÉS

Tarte aux pommes : *le kg 7.84 €*, 5,20 € la pièce de 680 g

**Côtes d'agneau**
(pièces de 60 g environ)
le sac de 1 kg .................15,80

**Gigot d'agneau prêt à découper**
(pièce de 1,4 à 1,8 kg) le kg ...............12,60

**4 steaks hachés**
(100 g) Picard, *le kg 9,45 €*,
la boîte de 400 g .................5,90

**10 steaks hachés**
(100 g) Picard,
la boîte de 1 kg .................10,20

**Crevettes crues**
(10-20 au kg) élevées à
Madagascar, *le kg 37,50 €*,
l'étui de 800 g .................32,00

**Magret de canard**
(pièce de 300-400 g)
le kg .................18,40

**2 cuisses de poulet rôties**
avec partie de dos,
*le kg 11,40 €*, le sac de 400 g ...............6,60

**Poulet à la mexicaine**
hauts de cuisses marinés,
cuits (5 pièces) *le kg 13,62 €*,
le sac de 400 g .................6,95

**Petits pois doux extra-fins et jeunes carottes**
*le kg 2,84 €*, le sac de 450 g.................4,30

**Petits pois doux à la française**
(avec laitue en tablettes
et petits oignons blancs)
le sac de 1 kg.................5,70

**Carottes jeunes entières extra-fines**
le sac de 1 kg.................5,10

**Carottes en rondelles**
le sac de 1 kg.................4,90

**20 crêpes au jambon-fromage**
la boîte de 1 kg .................7,20

**2 crêpes savoyardes**
reblochon, pommes de terre,
lardons, oignons,
*le kg 13,36 €*, la boîte de 250 g.........4,40

**4 crêpes campagnardes**
champignons, jambon, lard
fumé, *le kg 10,56 €*,
la boîte de 460 g.................5,90

**Framboises brisées**
Chili, le sac de 1 kg .................8,20

**Framboises entières**
Chili, le sac de 1 kg .................6,90

**2 mousses au chocolat**
Picard, *le kg 15,70 €*,
la boîte de 170 g .................5,10

**2 Petits Plaisirs au chocolat**
recette Lenôtre, Brossard,
*le kg 33,38 €*, la boîte de 130 g .........5,50

**2 Tiramisù**
crème au mascarpone,
génoise imbibée de café,
saupoudrage cacao, Picard,
*le kg 19,25 €*, la boîte de 200 g .........4,80

Composez votre menu.

Maintenant calculez le prix de ce que vous allez acheter.

|  | **PRIX** |
|---|---|
| Plat principal | _____ |
| Légumes | _____ |
| Dessert | _____ |
| Total | _____ |

Enfin, donnez votre menu et les résultats de vos calculs à la classe. Qui compose le menu le plus cher (*most expensive*), le plus original?

# Leçon 2

## L'adjectif interrogatif *quel*

*Asking About Choices*

### Tout le monde° au restaurant!

*Everybody*

*Hector téléphone à Hassan.*

HECTOR: Allô, Hassan? J'organise une petite fête.[1]

HASSAN: Super! **Quel** jour? Pour **quelle** occasion?

HECTOR: Pour le 14 juillet: la fête[2] nationale! On dîne et ensuite, on va danser avec des amis.

HASSAN: **Quels** amis?

HECTOR: J'invite Juliette… Léa… son copain Mamadou… Abdel et sa fiancée…

HASSAN: Tu cuisines?

HECTOR: Non. J'invite tout le monde au restaurant!

HASSAN: C'est une bonne idée. Dans **quel** restaurant?

HECTOR: Dans TON restaurant!

[1]*party, celebration*  [2]*holiday*

Paris en fête

Trouvez dans le dialogue, la question qui correspond à ces réponses en utilisant la forme correcte de **quel.** Faites des phrases complètes.

1. *Pour le 14 juillet*, Hector organise une petite fête.
2. *Pour la fête nationale*, Hector propose de dîner et ensuite d'aller danser avec des amis.
3. Hector invite *Juliette, Léa, son copain Mamadou, Abdel et sa fiancée.*
4. Hector invite tout le monde *dans le restaurant d'Hassan.*

### Forms of *quel*

**Quel (quelle, quels, quelles)** means *which* or *what*. It agrees in gender and number with the noun it modifies. You are already familiar with **quel** in expressions such as **Quelle heure est-il?** and **Quel temps fait-il?** It is used to obtain more precise information about a noun already mentioned or implied. Questions with **quel** can be formed either with inversion or with **est-ce que.**

| | |
|---|---|
| **Quel** fromage voulez-vous goûter? | Which (What) cheese would you like to try? |
| À **quelle** heure est-ce que vous dînez? | (At) what time do you eat dinner? |

| | |
|---|---|
| Dans **quels** restaurants aimez-vous manger? | *In what (which) restaurants do you like to eat?* |
| **Quelles** boissons préférez-vous? | *What (Which) beverages do you prefer?* |

**Quel** is also used in exclamations.

| | |
|---|---|
| **Quel** plat exemplaire! | *What an exemplary dish!* |
| **Quelle** horreur! | *How awful!* |

[Allez-y! A-B]

## Quel with *être*

**Quel** can also stand alone before **être** followed by the noun it modifies.

| | |
|---|---|
| **Quel est** le prix de ce champagne? | *What's the price of this champagne?* |
| **Quelle est** la différence entre le Perrier et l'Évian? | *What's the difference between Perrier and Évian?* |

 *Allez-y!*

**A. Qui vient dîner?** M^me Guilloux veut organiser un dîner demain soir. Son mari l'interroge (*asks her questions*). Complétez leur dialogue avec **qu'est-ce que, quel(le)** ou **qui**.

M. GUILLOUX: _qui_^1 vas-tu inviter?

M^ME GUILLOUX: Maxime, Isabelle et Laurence.

M. GUILLOUX: Et _quest_^2 tu vas préparer?

M^ME GUILLOUX: Un rôti de bœuf avec des pommes de terre sautées.

M. GUILLOUX: Oh là là, _____^3 chance (*luck*)! Mais _qui_^4 va faire les courses?

M^ME GUILLOUX: Toi, bien sûr.

M. GUILLOUX: Bien voyons! _____^5 vin est-ce que je dois acheter?

M^ME GUILLOUX: Je ne sais pas. _____^6 tu préfères?

M. GUILLOUX: Un vin rouge. Un bordeaux, par exemple.

M^ME GUILLOUX: Très bien. _____^7 heure est-il?

M. GUILLOUX: 18 h 30.

M^ME GUILLOUX: Déjà! _____^8 tu attends? Dépêche-toi (*Hurry up*), les magasins vont bientôt fermer.

**B. Une conversation à table.** Parlez avec vos camarades de leurs goûts. Utilisez l'adjectif interrogatif **quel** et variez la forme de vos questions.

**MODÈLE:** sport → Quel sport est-ce que tu préfères?
*ou* Quel sport préfères-tu?

1. boisson
2. légume
3. viande
4. repas
5. distractions
6. chansons (*f.*)
7. boîte (*f.*) de nuit (*nightclub*)
8. émission (*f.*) de télévision (*TV program*)
9. livres
10. magazines
11. couleur
12. matières
13. vêtements
14. films

Le parler jeune

| | |
|---|---|
| **avoir la dalle** | avoir faim |
| **le resto** | le restaurant |
| **se taper la cloche** | faire un bon repas |
| **le troquet** | le café; le bar |

J'ai pas mangé depuis ce matin: j'**ai la dalle**!

On va dîner au **resto**, après le cinéma?

Dimanche, on s'est **tapé la cloche** en famille.

On prend un café au **troquet** du coin?

# Les adjectifs démonstratifs

*Pointing Out People and Things*

## À table!

*Hassan, Hector, Juliette, Léa, Mamadou, Abdel discutent au restaurant d'Hassan.*

LÉA: **Cette** salade marocaine, c'est un délice!

JULIETTE: Et **ces** brochettes grillées! Une merveille!

MAMADOU: Parlons aussi de **ce** filet de bœuf: il est exquis!

ABDEL: Moi, c'est **ce** gâteau au caramel que je trouve super. Donne-nous la recette,* Hassan!

HECTOR: Nous sommes tous d'accord: **ce** dîner est exceptionnel!

HASSAN: Quel triomphe, mes amis! Mais **ces** compliments sont un peu exagérés…

HECTOR: Pas du tout! Ne sois pas modeste!

LÉA: Hassan, tu vas avoir un bon pourboire! (*Elle rit.*)

Qu'est-ce qu'ils disent? Trouvez les phrases du dialogue qui répondent aux questions suivantes.

*Donne... *Give us the recipe*

Qu'est-ce qui est…

1. un délice?
2. une merveille?
3. exquis?
4. super?
5. exceptionnel?
6. exagéré?

Bon appétit!

## Forms of Demonstrative Adjectives

Demonstrative adjectives (*this / that, these / those*) are used to specify a particular person, object, or idea. They agree in gender and number with the nouns they modify.

|  | SINGULAR | PLURAL |
|---|---|---|
| *Masculine* | **ce** magasin | **ces** magasins |
|  | **cet** escargot | **ces** escargots |
|  | **cet** homme | **ces** hommes |
| *Feminine* | **cette** épicerie | **ces** épiceries |

Note that **ce** becomes **cet** before masculine nouns beginning with a vowel or mute **h.**

[Allez-y! A-B]

## Use of *-ci* and *-là*

In English, *this / these* and *that / those* indicate the relative distance to the speaker. In French, the suffix **-ci** is added to indicate closeness, and **-là**, to indicate greater distance.

—Prenez-vous **ce** gâteau-**ci?**   *Are you having this cake (here)?*
—Non, je préfère **cet** éclair-**là.**   *No, I prefer that éclair (over there).*

[Allez-y! C]

## *Allez-y!*

**A.** **Au supermarché.** Qu'est-ce que vous achetez?

   **MODÈLE:** une bouteille d'huile → J'achète cette bouteille d'huile.

   **1.** une boîte de sardines  **2.** un camembert  **3.** des tomates  **4.** une bouteille de vin  **5.** quatre poires  **6.** une bouteille d'eau minérale  **7.** des pommes de terre  **8.** un éclair au café  **9.** un artichaut

**B.** **Exercice de contradiction.** Vous allez faire un pique-nique. Vous faites des courses avec un(e) camarade, mais vous n'êtes pas d'accord! Jouez les rôles.

   **MODÈLE:** pain / baguette →
       É1: On prend ce pain?
       É2: Non, je préfère cette baguette.

   **1.** saucisson / tranche (*f.*)        **6.** pommes / bananes
       (*slice*) de jambon           **7.** tarte / éclair
   **2.** pâté / poulet froid          **8.** gâteau / glace
   **3.** filet de bœuf / rôti de veau     **9.** jus de fruits / bouteille de vin
   **4.** haricots verts / oignons      **10.** boîte de sardines / morceau
   **5.** pizza (*f.*) / sandwich           (*m.*) (*piece*) de fromage

**C.** **Chez le traiteur.** (*At the delicatessen.*) Jouez les rôles du client / de la cliente et du traiteur.

   **MODÈLE:** poulet →
       LE CLIENT / LA CLIENTE: Donnez-moi un poulet, s'il
                   vous plaît.
           LE TRAITEUR: Quel poulet? Ce poulet-ci ou ce
                   poulet-là?
       LE CLIENT / LA CLIENTE: Ce poulet-ci. Et donnez-moi
                   aussi un peu de ce fromage.
           LE TRAITEUR: Tout de suite, monsieur / madame.

   **1.** salade
   **2.** rôti
   **3.** légumes
   **4.** pâté
   **5.** pizza
   **6.** saucisses

# Le blog d'Hassan

## Marché ou cybermarché?

dimanche 7 juin

Salut tout le monde!

Dimanche prochain, Juliette et moi on va faire les courses au marché de la place Monge. Ensuite, avec nos potes,[1] on va préparer le déjeuner chez moi. Hector et Léa vont acheter une tarte pour le dessert, Juliette va préparer les légumes et moi le poisson! Ça va être marrant[2]!

Juliette aime bien le marché, mais elle préfère les cybermarchés. Un seul clic et tout apparaît[3] sur l'écran: la charcuterie, l'épicerie, la poissonnerie et la pâtisserie. La livraison[4] est souvent gratuite.[5]
Je dois dire que c'est pas mal…

Mais moi, je préfère le marché: c'est animé; je peux sentir[6] l'odeur des produits frais; je peux toucher, peser,[7] sélectionner et quelquefois goûter! C'est vraiment agréable!

Et vous? Vous faites vos courses en ligne ou au marché?

Hassan

Faire le marché, c'est un plaisir!

. . . . . . . . . . . . . . . . . . . . . . . . . . . . . . . . . . . . . . . . . . . . . . . . .

### COMMENTAIRES

**Alexis**

Moi aussi, je commande sur Internet, c'est tellement[8] facile! Tu cliques sur un rôti de bœuf, et il est dans ton assiette!

**Trésor**

Alexis, je déteste le cybermarché: la bouffe, ce n'est pas virtuel! C'est réel!

**Mamadou**

Chez moi, au Sénégal, tous les matins, ma mère fait son marché. Le marché africain, c'est l'odeur du poivre et des épices associé au parfum des mangues et des poissons frais.

**Charlotte**

Tu sais Hassan, pour une mère de famille, le supermarché c'est la solution idéale. À Genève, je fais les courses le samedi matin et je suis tranquille pour huit jours. Et il y a toujours des promotions!

**Poema**

Les marchés de Papeete sentent le tiare—c'est la fleur emblème de Tahiti—l'ananas[9] et la vanille.

[1]*buddies*  [2]*lots of fun*  [3]*appears*  [4]*delivery*  [5]*free*  [6]*je… I can smell*  [7]*weigh*  [8]*so*  [9]*pineapple*

## Comment voyager dans son assiette?

Chaque nation dans le monde a une spécialité culinaire. Le plat national, c'est un peu le drapeau d'un pays, sa culture, son âme.[1]

Un tajine marocain

Pour connaître les saveurs[2] des tables francophones, faisons un voyage culinaire…

Nous voilà d'abord en Suisse. Quel est le plat national ici? La fondue! Arrêtons-nous maintenant en Belgique. Que mange-t-on dans les petits restaurants populaires de Bruxelles? Des moules-frites[3]! Faisons une petite excursion en France. C'est étrange: au pays de la gastronomie, le plat du jour idéal, c'est tout simplement un steak-frites accompagné d'un petit vin rouge!

Maintenant, nous voyageons au Québec. Ici «la poutine» est sur tous les menus de restaurants. Inventé dans les années 1950, ce plat est préparé avec des frites, du fromage et de la sauce brune.[4] C'est parfait pour un pays froid!

Enfin, nous visitons l'Afrique. Au Cameroun, on adore le «n'dolé», une préparation d'épinards,[5] de crevettes, de poisson ou de viande mélangés à des arachides.[6] En Algérie, le couscous, à base de semoule,[7] est sur toutes les tables. On peut le préparer de mille et une façons.[8] C'est la même chose pour «le tajine», le plat national du Maroc. Ce ragoût[9] de viande, de volaille,[10] de poisson et de légumes est délicieux pour la bouche et beau pour les yeux. Regardez la photo!

Tous ces plats traditionnels des pays francophones vous invitent au voyage. Partez! L'aventure commence dans votre assiette.

[1]*soul*  [2]*flavors*  [3]*mussels with French fries*  [4]sauce… *gravy*  [5]*spinach*  [6]*peanuts*  [7]*semolina*  [8]*ways*  [9]*stew*  [10]*poultry*

 À vous!

1. Qu'est-ce qu'un «plat national»?
2. Quel est le plat national de chaque pays francophone mentionné dans ce reportage? Quels autres plats de ces pays connaissez-vous? Si possible, citez aussi les plats nationaux d'autres pays francophones.
3. Quand vous voyagez, aimez-vous goûter des aliments ou des plats nouveaux? Racontez une de vos découvertes culinaires dans un pays étranger ou dans un restaurant étranger de votre ville.
4. Quel est le plat national de votre pays? Comment est-il préparé?
5. Quels ingrédients y a-t-il dans le tajine sur la photo? Avez-vous envie de le goûter? Expliquez.

Parlons-en!

Travaillez en petits groupes et répondez aux questions suivantes. Qui est le plus aventurier / la plus aventurière du groupe?

1. En France, on mange des grenouilles, des escargots, du lapin (*rabbit*) et du cheval. Vous acceptez de manger ces plats? Pourquoi?
2. Combien d'étudiants dans votre groupe accepte cette aventure culinaire? Comptez!
3. Quels plats français les étudiants moins aventuriers aimeraient-ils essayer (*to try*)? Pour quelle raison?
4. Quels plats extraordinaires avez-vous déjà essayés? C'était bon?

# Leçon 3

## Les verbes *vouloir, pouvoir* et *devoir*

*Expressing Desire, Ability, and Obligation*

### Les vins de Napa Valley

*Hector et Hassan échangent des textos (SMS).*

HASSAN: **Tu veux** goûter un vin américain?

HECTOR: Un vin américain?

HASSAN: Oui, américain: **Je dois** écrire[1] un blog sur les vins de la Napa Valley.

HECTOR: Pourquoi pas? J'arrive! Où es-tu?

HASSAN: Au Quartier latin, dans un bar à vin.

HECTOR: **Nous pouvons** boire gratuitement[2]?

HASSAN: Non, **nous devons** payer. Mais je t'invite!

[1]*to write*  [2]*for free*

Vrai ou faux? Corrigez les phrases fausses.

1. Hassan propose à Hector de goûter des vins français.
2. Il doit écrire un blog sur les vins de la Napa Valley.
3. Hector accepte de goûter ces vins avec Hassan.
4. Ils doivent payer pour boire.
5. Hassan veut inviter Hector.

## Forms of *vouloir, pouvoir,* and *devoir*

The verbs **vouloir** (*to want*), **pouvoir** (*to be able to*), and **devoir** (*to have to; to be obliged to; to owe*) are all irregular in form.

| vouloir | | pouvoir | | devoir | |
|---|---|---|---|---|---|
| je | **veux** | je | **peux** | je | **dois** |
| tu | **veux** | tu | **peux** | tu | **dois** |
| il/elle/on | **veut** | il/elle/on | **peut** | il/elle/on | **doit** |
| nous | **voulons** | nous | **pouvons** | nous | **devons** |
| vous | **voulez** | vous | **pouvez** | vous | **devez** |
| ils/elles | **veulent** | ils/elles | **peuvent** | ils/elles | **doivent** |

## Uses of *vouloir, devoir,* and *pouvoir*

**1. Vouloir** can be followed by a noun or an infinitive.

| Je **veux** un café. | *I want a cup of coffee.* |
|---|---|
| Je **veux** commander un café. | *I want to order a cup of coffee.* |

**Vouloir bien** means *to be willing to, be glad (to do something)*. **Vouloir dire** expresses *to mean*.

| Il **veut bien** goûter les escargots. | *He's willing to taste the snails.* |
|---|---|
| Qu'est-ce que ce mot **veut dire**? | *What does this word mean?* |

**2. Devoir,** followed by an infinitive, expresses necessity, obligation, or probability.

| Je suis désolé, mais nous **devons** partir. | *I'm sorry, but we must leave.* |
|---|---|
| Marc est absent; il **doit** être malade. | *Marc is absent; he must be sick.* |

🎧 **Prononcez bien!**

**The vowels in *veux* and *veulent***

Make sure to distinguish between the two vowel sounds [ø] and [œ] as you pronounce the singular and plural forms of **vouloir** and **pouvoir.** Remember to round your lips for both sounds.

For the [ø] in **veux, veut, peux,** and **peut,** close your mouth and keep your tongue in the front of your mouth.

[ø]: **Je v<u>eu</u>x** du fromage.

For the [œ] in **veulent** and **peuvent,** open your mouth a bit wider and slightly shift your tongue to the middle of your mouth.

[œ]: Ils **p<u>eu</u>vent** dormir.

When not followed by an infinitive, **devoir** means *to owe*.

—Combien d'argent est-ce que
tu **dois** à tes amis?

*How much money do you
owe to your friends?*

—Je **dois** 10 euros à Jacques et
20 euros à François.

*I owe Jacques 10 euros
and François 20 euros.*

**3. Pouvoir** is usually followed by an infinitive.

Vous **pouvez** arriver à 15 h?

*Can you arrive at 3:00 P.M.?*

 *Allez-y!*

**A. Une soirée compliquée.** Composez un dialogue entre Noémie et Simon.

NOÉMIE: je / avoir / faim / et / je / vouloir / manger / maintenant
SIMON: tu / vouloir / faire / cuisine?
NOÉMIE: non… / est-ce que / nous / pouvoir / aller / restaurant?
SIMON: oui, je / vouloir / bien
NOÉMIE: où / est-ce que / nous / pouvoir / aller?
SIMON: on / pouvoir / manger / couscous / Chez Bébert
NOÉMIE: nous / devoir / inviter / Carole
SIMON: tu / pouvoir / inviter / Jean-Pierre / aussi
NOÉMIE: ce / soir / ils / devoir / être / cité universitaire?
SIMON: oui, ils / devoir / préparer / un / examen
nous / pouvoir / parler / de / ce / examen / restaurant

**B. Le Ritz.** Pour fêter son anniversaire (*To celebrate his birthday*), Stéphane invite ses amis américains Ben et Jessica au restaurant «le Ritz». Complétez leur dialogue avec les verbes **pouvoir**, **devoir** et **vouloir** à la forme appropriée. Quelquefois plusieurs réponses sont possibles.

BEN: Qu'est-ce qu'on _____[1] prendre?
STÉPHANE: Comme entrée, vous _____[2] prendre le pâté de lapin, il est excellent. Et comme plat de résistance…
JESSICA: Pardon, que _____[3] dire «plat de résistance»?
STÉPHANE: Bon, c'est le plat principal du repas. Vous _____[4] absolument essayer (*try*) la truite (*trout*) aux amandes, c'est la spécialité de la maison. Comme dessert si vous _____[5], vous _____[6] prendre une charlotte aux framboises.
JESSICA: Ça _____[7] être très nourrissant (*rich, fattening*) tout ça, non?
STÉPHANE: Un peu, mais ce n'est pas tous les jours mon anniversaire. Tu _____[8] oublier ton régime pour aujourd'hui.

**C. Vos impressions.** Complétez les phrases suivantes à la forme affirmative ou à la forme négative, selon votre opinion personnelle. Utilisez **devoir**, **pouvoir** ou **vouloir** + infinitif dans chaque phrase.

MODÈLE: Les étudiants \_\_\_\_\_. → Les étudiants ne doivent pas étudier jusqu'à (*until*) minuit tous les soirs.

**1.** Le professeur \_\_\_\_\_. **2.** Les parents \_\_\_\_\_. **3.** Mes camarades \_\_\_\_\_. **4.** Les hommes \_\_\_\_\_. **5.** Les femmes \_\_\_\_\_. **6.** Je \_\_\_\_\_.

## Mots clés

**Demander poliment et remercier**

**Je voudrais** (presented in **Chapitre 6**) and **je pourrais** (*I could*) are conditional forms of **vouloir** and **pouvoir**, respectively. They are used to make a request sound more polite.

Je veux l'addition.
*I want the check.*

Je **voudrais** l'addition.
*I would like the check.*

Est-ce que je peux avoir de l'eau?
*Can I have some water?*

Est-ce que je **pourrais** avoir de l'eau?
*Could I have some water?*

Don't forget to add **s'il vous plaît** to your request and to say **merci**.

The appropriate answers for **merci** are:

**De rien.** (*more familiar*)
**Il n'y a pas de quoi.**
**Je vous en prie,** madame.* (*formal*)

*In polite conversation in French, **monsieur, madame,** and **mademoiselle** are used much more often than *ma'am* or *sir* in English.

**D. Soyons polis!** Avec un(e) partenaire, demandez et remerciez selon le modèle.

**MODÈLE:** vouloir / tasse / café
 É1: Je voudrais une tasse de café, s'il vous plaît.
 É2: Voilà, madame / monsieur.
 É1: Merci, monsieur / madame.
 É2: Il n'y a pas de quoi.

**1.** pouvoir avoir / carafe / eau?  **3.** pouvoir avoir / bouteille / vin?
**2.** vouloir / morceau / fromage  **4.** vouloir / kilo / poulet

# Le passé composé avec l'auxiliaire *avoir*

*Talking About the Past*

## Le vin: un sujet très sérieux!

*Hector contacte Léa sur la page Facebook d'Hector (Messagerie instantanée).*

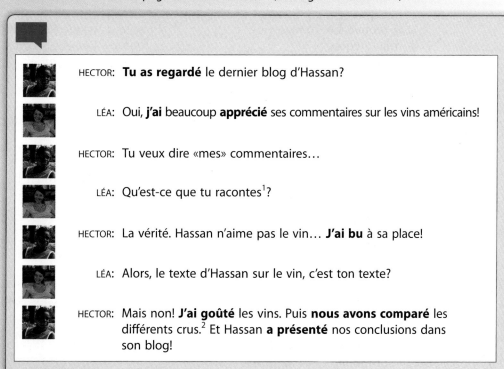

HECTOR: **Tu as regardé** le dernier blog d'Hassan?

LÉA: Oui, **j'ai** beaucoup **apprécié** ses commentaires sur les vins américains!

HECTOR: Tu veux dire «mes» commentaires…

LÉA: Qu'est-ce que tu racontes[1]?

HECTOR: La vérité. Hassan n'aime pas le vin… **J'ai bu** à sa place!

LÉA: Alors, le texte d'Hassan sur le vin, c'est ton texte?

HECTOR: Mais non! **J'ai goûté** les vins. Puis **nous avons comparé** les différents crus.[2] Et Hassan **a présenté** nos conclusions dans son blog!

[1]Qu'est-ce que… *What are you talking about?*  [2]*vintages*

Répondez aux questions. Faites des phrases complètes.

**1.** Qui a regardé le blog d'Hassan?
**2.** Qui a apprécié ses commentaires?
**3.** Qui a goûté les vins?
**4.** Qui a présenté les conclusions dans son blog?

The **passé composé** is a compound past tense. It relates events that began and ended at some point in the past. The **passé composé** of most verbs consists of the present tense of the auxiliary verb (**le verbe auxiliaire**) **avoir** plus the past participle (**le participe passé**) of the verb in question.

| PASSÉ COMPOSÉ OF **dîner** (*to dine, eat dinner*) | | | |
|---|---|---|---|
| j' | **ai dîné** | nous | **avons dîné** |
| tu | **as dîné** | vous | **avez dîné** |
| il/elle/on | **a dîné** | ils/elles | **ont dîné** |

The **passé composé** has several equivalents in English. For example, **j'ai dîné** can mean *I dined (ate dinner), I have dined (have eaten dinner), I did dine (did eat dinner)*, according to the context.

## Regular Past Participles

The following chart illustrates the formation of regular past participles.

| | | |
|---|---|---|
| Verbs ending in **-er:** | **-er → -é** | trouver → trouvé |
| Verbs ending in **-ir:** | **-ir → -i** | choisir → choisi |
| Verbs ending in **-re:** | **-re → -u** | perdre → perdu |

| | |
|---|---|
| **J'ai trouvé** une pâtisserie magnifique. | *I found a wonderful pastry shop.* |
| Tu **as choisi** une tarte aux pommes? | *Have you chosen an apple pie?* |
| Non, nous **avons perdu** l'adresse de la pâtisserie. | *No, we lost the address of the pastry shop.* |

## Irregular Past Participles

Most irregular verbs have irregular past participles, and they must be memorized. However, there are some predictable patterns.

**1.** The past participle of many verbs in **-oir** ends in **-u.**

| | |
|---|---|
| avoir → **eu** | pouvoir → **pu** |
| devoir → **dû** | vouloir → **voulu** |
| pleuvoir (*to rain*) → **plu** | |

| | |
|---|---|
| Hier, il **a plu** toute la journée. | *Yesterday, it rained all day long.* |

**2.** The past participle of some verbs in **-re** ends in **-is.**

| | |
|---|---|
| apprendre → **appris** | prendre → **pris** |
| comprendre → **compris** | |

| | |
|---|---|
| **J'ai pris** l'autobus à la boulangerie. | *I took the bus to the bakery.* |

**3.** Other important irregular past participles include:

| | |
|---|---|
| boire → **bu** | faire → **fait** |
| être → **été** | |

| | |
|---|---|
| Elle **a fait** le marché. | *She did the shopping.* |

[Allez-y! A-B]

## Negative and Interrogative Sentences in the *passé composé*

**1.** In negative sentences, **ne... pas** surrounds the auxiliary verb (**avoir**).

| | |
|---|---|
| Nous **n'avons pas** préparé les hors-d'œuvre. | *We have not prepared the hors-d'œuvres.* |
| Vous **n'avez pas** pris de dessert? | *Didn't you have a dessert?* |

**2.** In questions with inversion, only the auxiliary verb and the subject are inverted.

| | |
|---|---|
| **As-tu oublié** le dessert? | *Did you forget dessert?* |

[Allez-y! C-D]

 *Allez-y!*

**A. Un voyage.** Qu'est-ce que ces personnes ont fait dans le sud de la France? Faites des phrases complètes au passé composé.

**MODÈLE:** nous / choisir / huîtres
→ Nous avons choisi des huîtres.

1. vous / goûter / crevettes
2. Sylvie / finir / bouteille de vin
3. toi et moi, nous / boire / coca-cola / café
4. Thibaut / perdre / porte-monnaie (*wallet*)
5. Julie et Martin / visiter / pâtisserie magnifique
6. Morgane et toi, vous / apprendre / à parler avec l'accent marseillais
7. je / faire / de la planche à voile (*windsurfing*)

**B. Une carte postale.** Complétez la carte postale de Marie. Choisissez le verbe approprié et conjuguez-le au passé composé.

| commencer | être | passer | rendre |
|---|---|---|---|
| décider | faire | préparer | visiter |

Chère Eva,

J' _____[1] mes vacances d'hiver une semaine avant Noël avec Yasmine. Nous _____[2] deux semaines à la montagne en Suisse.

Nous _____[3] de rester à Zermatt. Nous _____[4] du ski et du shopping. Nous _____[5] une fondue délicieuse. Au retour, nous _____[6] visite à des amis à Genève et nous _____[7] le Palais des Nations de l'ONU. Notre séjour et les repas en Suisse _____[8] inoubliables. Je t'embrasse, *Marie*

Le Mont Cervin et le village de Zermatt, en Suisse

C. **À Orange.** Tristan pose des questions à ses cousins Zoé et Thibaud, qui (*who*) ont visité la ville historique d'Orange, près d'Avignon. Jouez les rôles avec deux camarades.

**MODÈLE:** trouver un restaurant pas cher à Orange →
TRISTAN: Avez-vous trouvé un restaurant pas cher à Orange?
THIBAUD: Non, nous n'avons pas trouvé de restaurant pas cher à Orange.

1. prendre le petit déjeuner près de l'amphithéâtre romain
2. faire une promenade dans la vieille ville
3. contempler la vieille fontaine
4. étudier les inscriptions romaines
5. apprendre l'histoire de France
6. chercher des fruits à l'épicerie
7. envoyer (*to send*) une description de la ville à vos parents

## Mots clés

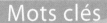

**Exprimer le passé**

**avant-hier**
*the day before yesterday*

**hier, hier matin, hier soir**
*yesterday, yesterday morning, last night*

le mois / l'hiver **dernier (passé)**
*last month, last winter*

la semaine / l'année **dernière (passée)**
*last week, last year*

**toute la matinée / la journée / la soirée\* / la nuit**
*all morning, all day, all evening, all night*

\*Use **matinée, journée,** and **soirée** rather than **matin, jour,** and **soir** if you wish to express a duration. They are often used with **toute.**

L'amphithéâtre à Orange, près d'Avignon, en France. Combien de personnes peuvent s'y asseoir (*sit there*)?

D. **Interview.** Posez des questions à un(e) camarade sur ses activités passées. Essayez d'utiliser les expressions des **Mots clés.** Voici des suggestions:

**Le matin:** boire du café, faire du sport, faire le marché, prendre le petit déjeuner, regarder la télévision, …

**L'après-midi / Le soir:** étudier une leçon, inviter des amis, jouer aux cartes, pique-niquer, skier, …

**La semaine / L'année dernière:** dîner au restaurant, finir une dissertation, rendre visite à des amis, travailler dans un magasin, voyager en Europe, …

**MODÈLE:** É1: Est-ce que tu as fait du sport hier matin?
É2: Oui, j'ai fait du jogging jusqu'à onze heures.
(Non, je n'ai pas fait… ) Et toi?

Puis racontez à la classe ce que votre camarade a fait.

Prononcez bien!

1. **The semivowel in *ail*** (page 176)

A. **Dîner d'anniversaire.** Hugo et son ami Yann discutent du dîner d'anniversaire de leur ami Rémi. Avec votre camarade, lisez leur conversation à voix haute en faisant bien attention à la prononciation des mots français *en italique*.

HUGO: Je suis arrivé en *premier* et j'ai garé (*parked*) ma voiture devant celle (*the one*) de Rémi.

YANN: Moi, je suis arrivé en *dernier* et j'ai garé ma moto *derrière* sa voiture!

HUGO: Au dîner, j'ai mangé à côté d'une *fille* qui s'appelle *Camille*.

YANN: Ah oui, elle a de beaux *yeux* bleus.

B. **Dîner d'anniversaire (suite).** Hugo et Yann parlent de leur repas. Avec votre camarade, lisez leur conversation à voix haute et complétez les phrases à l'aide des images.

HUGO: Qu'est-ce que tu as pris: du poisson ou de la _____¹ ?

YANN: Du poisson, avec une demi- _____² de vin blanc. Et toi, qu'est-ce que tu as bu?

HUGO: Oh, juste une _____³ .

YANN: C'est tout?! Tu n'es pas dans ton _____⁴ (*aren't feeling well*) ce matin?

HUGO: Si, mais j'ai encore sommeil.

2. **The vowels in *veux* and *veulent*** (page 189)

A. **Un nouveau joueur.** La famille d'Hugo va bientôt déménager. Écoutez les phrases et décidez si Hugo parle de ses parents ou de son petit frère.

| | Les parents | Le petit frère |
|---|---|---|
| **1.** vendre la maison | ☐ | ☐ |
| **2.** habiter dans un grand appartement en ville | ☐ | ☐ |
| **3.** vendre le lit et l'armoire de la chambre d'amis | ☐ | ☐ |
| **4.** visiter des appartements dès (*as early as*) le week-end prochain | ☐ | ☐ |
| **5.** une grande chambre | ☐ | ☐ |

B. **Un dîner.** Vos colocataires et vous organisez un dîner chez vous. Chaque invité va apporter quelque chose (*something*). Avec votre camarade, lisez les phrases à voix haute et complétez-les avec la forme appropriée du verbe entre parenthèses.

1. Annette _____ (vouloir) apporter l'entrée.
2. Éric et Christine _____ (pouvoir) se charger (*be in charge of*) du plat principal.
3. Isabelle, tu _____ (pouvoir) faire le dessert?
4. Christophe et Karine _____ (vouloir) apporter du pain.
5. Moi, je _____ (pouvoir) m'occuper (*take care of*) de la salade.

##  Lecture

### *Avant de lire*

**Using titles and visuals.** You have already used a number of strategies to help you guess the content of a text before you start reading. In many cases, visuals such as photos, graphs, and diagrams also allow you to anticipate the major themes of the text. Look at the title, the photos, and the photo captions in the following reading selection: What kinds of information do you think you might find in this passage? After you have read through the text, decide whether the title describes the content adequately. If not, suggest a title that is more descriptive. How well do the photos correspond to the text? What other ideas in the text would you like to see illustrated?

**Ça se fête!** Quelles sont les plus grandes occasions de l'année pour vous: votre anniversaire, Noël, le nouvel an? Comment célébrez-vous ces occasions? Faites une liste des plats que vous mangez.

**À propos de la lecture...** Les auteurs de *Vis-à-vis* ont écrit ce texte.

Une galette des Rois

# Les grandes occasions

En France, les jours de fête sont l'occasion de se réunir[1] en famille ou entre amis. À chaque fête, on mange des plats typiques qui varient parfois[2] selon les régions. Voici les fêtes les plus gourmandes[3] du calendrier français.

### *La fête des Rois\**

Pour la fête des Rois, le 6 janvier, on achète chez le pâtissier une galette. C'est un gâteau qui contient une fève.[4] La personne qui trouve la fève dans son morceau de gâteau est le roi (ou la reine),[5] et cette personne choisit sa reine (ou son roi). La famille ou les amis boivent à leur santé.[6]

### *Pâques[7]*

Pâques est, bien sûr, la fête du chocolat. C'est aussi un jour où l'on se retrouve ensemble, en famille à l'église et à table. On

[1]se... *get together*  [2]*sometimes*  [3]les plus... *où l'on mange bien*  [4]*bean*  [5]roi... *king (or queen)*
[6]*health*  [7]*Easter*

---

\*This Christian holiday, Epiphany, also called Twelfth Night, commemorates Christ's appearance to the Gentiles (represented by the Three Kings).

fait un grand repas, et au dessert, grands et petits mangent des œufs, des cloches,[8] des poules ou des poissons en chocolat remplis[9] de bonbons.

## Noël

Noël est peut-être la fête des fêtes. Le Réveillon[10] de Noël est un grand dîner que l'on prend le plus souvent après la messe[11] de minuit. Au menu: huîtres, foie gras, dinde aux marrons[12] et beaucoup de champagne! Au dessert, on mange une bûche[13] de Noël, un gâteau roulé au chocolat en forme de bûche. Les enfants, bien sûr, attendent avec impatience l'arrivée du Père Noël.

[8]bells  [9]filled  [10]Le… Midnight supper  [11]cérémonie catholique  [12]dinde… turkey with chestnuts  [13]log

Une bûche de Noël pour le Réveillon

### Compréhension

Match the following quotations with the relevant paragraphs in "Les grandes occasions."

1. «C'est ma fête préférée parce que j'adore les œufs en chocolat.»
2. «Je suis le roi!»
3. «Nous attendons toujours avec impatience l'arrivée de la bûche.»

# Écriture

The writing activities **Par écrit** and **Journal intime** can be found in the Workbook/Laboratory Manual to accompany *Vis-à-vis*.

# Pour s'amuser

Un monsieur très avare dit à ses enfants:

—Si vous êtes gentils ce soir, je vous montrerai la photo de quelqu'un qui mange une glace.

# Le vidéoblog d'Hassan

## En bref

Dans cet épisode, Juliette et Hassan sont au marché. Ils cherchent des ingrédients pour le dîner qu'ils vont préparer pour Léa et Hector. Dans son vidéoblog, Hassan décrit ses marchés préférés à Paris et au Maroc et Hector décrit les marchés à la Martinique.

## Vocabulaire en contexte

Imaginez que vous faites votre marché en France. Quels produits dans la liste désirez-vous avoir pour votre propre (*own*) dîner ce soir?

**Provisions possibles**

- ☐ des **fruits de mer** (*seafood*)
- ☐ du saumon frais
- ☐ des **huîtres** (*oysters*)
- ☐ des fruits/légumes bio (*organic*)
- ☐ du fromage **de chèvre** (*goat*)
- ☐ du pain **de campagne**
- ☐ des **épices/piments** (*spices/ hot peppers*)
- ☐ des fleurs
- ☐ tout (*everything*)

Un marchand d'olives à Marrakech, au Maroc

## Visionnez!

Qu'est-ce que les quatre amis vont manger ce soir? Écoutez bien et faites le menu.

**Entrée**
_____

**Pain**
_____

**Dessert**
_____

**Plat principal**
_____
_____
_____

**Fromages**
_____
_____
_____

**Boisson**
_____

## Note culturelle

Le souk[1] est un élément fondamental de la vie marocaine. Il joue un rôle social et économique: 40 000 artisans et 5 000 commerçants travaillent dans les souks de Marrakech et aussi des milliers[2] de porteurs, guides, marchands ambulants, et cetera. Vous pouvez tout acheter: du téléphone portable aux babouches faites main.[3] Noter qu'en français, le mot «souk» désigne aussi un lieu en désordre («C'est un vrai souk, ici!»).

[1]marché marocain  [2]*thousands*
[3]babouches... *handmade slippers*

## Analysez!

Répondez aux questions.

1. Quelles différences y a-t-il entre les marchés de France et les marchés d'autres pays francophones?
2. Qu'est-ce qu'un marché offre à sa clientèle qu'un *supermarché* n'offre pas?

## Comparez!

Où allez-vous normalement «faire votre marché»? Y a-t-il un marché semblable (*similar*) aux marchés parisiens dans votre région? Regardez encore une fois la partie culturelle de la vidéo: où préférez-vous faire votre marché? Expliquez.

# Vocabulaire

## Verbes

**apporter** to bring; to carry
**coûter** to cost
**devoir** to have to, be obliged to; to owe
**goûter** to taste
**laisser** to leave (behind)
**pleuvoir** to rain
**pouvoir** to be able to, can
**vouloir** to want
   **vouloir bien** to be willing; to agree
   **vouloir dire** to mean

À REVOIR: **apprendre, avoir, boire, choisir, commander, comprendre, dîner, être, faire, perdre, prendre, préparer, trouver, vendre**

## Substantifs

**l'addition** (*f.*) bill, check (*in a restaurant*)
**l'ail** (*m.*) garlic
**l'argent** (*m.*) money
**la boîte (de conserve)** can (*of food*)
**la carte** menu
**le centime** 1/100th of a euro
**les conserves** (*f. pl.*) canned goods
**le copain/la copine** (boy)friend/(girl)friend
**la côte** chop
**la chose** thing
**les crevettes** (*f.*) shrimp
**l'éclair** (*m.*) eclair (*pastry*)
**l'entrée** (*f.*) first course
**l'escargot** (*m.*) snail
**l'euro** (*m.*) euro (*European Union currency*)
**la fête** holiday; party; celebration
**le filet** fillet (*beef, fish, etc.*)
**le homard** lobster

**l'huile** (*f.*) **(d'olive)** (olive) oil
**l'huître** (*f.*) oyster
**le kilo(gramme)** kilo(gram)
**le magasin** store, shop
**la matinée** morning
**le menu** fixed (price) menu
**le morceau** piece
**la mousse au chocolat** chocolate mousse
**la nuit** night
**le pain de campagne** country-style wheat bread
**le pâté de campagne** (country-style) pâté
**les pâtes** (*f.*) pasta
**le plat** course (*meal*)
   **plat principal** main dish
**le pourboire** tip
**le prix** price
**le régime** diet
**le rôti** roast
**les sardines (à l'huile)** (*f.*) sardines (in oil)
**la saucisse** sausage
**le saucisson** salami
**le saumon** salmon
**le serveur / la serveuse** waiter / waitress
**la soirée** evening
**la sole** sole (*fish*)
**la tranche** slice
**le veau** veal

À REVOIR: **l'assiette** (*f.*), **le bœuf, la boisson, le crabe, la cuisine, le déjeuner, le dîner, le fromage, la glace, le gâteau, les haricots verts, le matin, le pain, le petit déjeuner, la pomme, la pomme de terre, le porc, le soir, la viande, le vin**

## Les magasins

**la boucherie** butcher shop
**la boulangerie** bakery
**la charcuterie** pork butcher's shop (delicatessen)
**l'épicerie** (*f.*) grocery store
**la pâtisserie** pastry shop; pastry
**la poissonnerie** fish store

## Expressions temporelles

**avant-hier** the day before yesterday
**dernier / dernière** last
**hier** yesterday
   **hier soir** last night
**passé(e)** last
**toute la matinée / la journée / la soirée / la nuit** all morning / day / evening / night

## Mots et expressions divers

**autre chose** something else
**ça** this, that
**ce (cet, cette) / ces** this, that / these, those
**compris(e)** included
**d'abord** first
**ensuite** next, then
**Il n'y a pas de quoi.** You're welcome.
**je pourrais** I could
**Je vous en prie.** You're welcome. (*formal*)
**(et) puis** (and) then, next
**quel(le)(s)** which, what
**tout le monde** everybody

À REVOIR: **je voudrais, de rien**

# CHAPITRE 8

# Vive les vacances!

Les dossiers d'Hassan

Hassan

➤ 📁 Mes photos

   ➤ 📁 Les Contamines dans les Alpes

   ➤ 📁 À La Nouvelle-Orléans

   ➤ 📁 En vacances à Cannes

Un beau jour aux Contamines près de Chamonix dans les Alpes françaises

## Dans ce chapitre...

### OBJECTIFS COMMUNICATIFS
- ➤ talking about vacation, recreational equipment
- ➤ expressing dates and actions
- ➤ talking about the past
- ➤ expressing how long ago something happened
- ➤ expressing location
- ➤ learning to distinguish between and pronounce selected sounds in French

### PAROLES (Leçon 1)
- ➤ Les régions de la France et les loisirs
- ➤ Le verbe **acheter**
- ➤ L'équipement de sport et de voyage
- ➤ L'année

### STRUCTURES (Leçons 2 et 3)
- ➤ Quelques verbes irréguliers en **-ir**
- ➤ Le passé composé avec l'auxiliaire **être**
- ➤ L'expression impersonnelle **il faut**
- ➤ Les prépositions devant les noms de lieu

### CULTURE
- ➤ Le blog d'Hassan: *Partir!*
- ➤ Reportage: *France: le pays des grandes vacances*
- ➤ Lecture: *Des vacances au Maroc* (Leçon 4)

Ça, c'est vraiment La Nouvelle-Orléans!

En vacances à Cannes

www.mhconnectfrench.com

# Leçon 1

**PAROLES**

## En vacances

L'ANGLETERRE

LE NORD

Faire du camping en forêt (*f.*)

LA BRETAGNE

Faire du vélo* sur les routes (*f.*) de campagne (*f.*)

Faire du bateau sur les fleuves (*m.*)

LE MASSIF CENTRAL

Faire du ski en montagne (*f.*)

LES ALPES

Nager dans les lacs (*m.*)

LA CÔTE D'AZUR

Faire de la planche à voile à la mer

Bronzer à la plage

Faire de l'alpinisme en montagne

LES PYRÉNÉES

L'ESPAGNE

LA CORSE

### Prononcez bien!

**The pronunciation of *montagne***

To pronounce the sequence **gn** as [ɲ], blend the sounds [n] and [j] as you do in the English words *onion* and *union*. This sound is most often spelled **gn,** and sometimes **ni.**

[ɲ]: **magnifique, champignon, dernier**

For words ending in **-gne,** make sure you don't pronounce the final **-e.**

[ɲ]: **montagne, campagne**

### AUTRES MOTS UTILES

| | |
|---|---|
| faire... **du cheval, de l'équitation** | to go . . . horseback riding |
| **de la plongée libre** | snorkeling |
| **de la plongée sous-marine** | scuba diving |
| **du ski nautique** | waterskiing |
| **du ski alpin** | downhill skiing |
| **du ski de fond** | cross-country skiing |
| **une randonnée** | for a hike |
| **aller à la pêche** | to go fishing |
| **patiner** | to skate |
| **prendre des vacances** | to take a vacation |
| **un endroit** | a place |

*\***Faire du vélo** is synonymous with **faire de la bicyclette.**

## Allez-y!

**A. Où passer les vacances?** Quels sont les avantages touristiques des endroits suivants?

1. Qu'est-ce qu'on peut faire en montagne?
2. Au bord d'un lac?
3. À la plage?
4. Sur une route de campagne?
5. Sur un fleuve?
6. En forêt?
7. À la mer?

Maintenant expliquez où vous voulez passer vos prochaines vacances et quelles activités on peut faire à cet endroit.

**B. Activités de vacances.** Qu'est-ce qu'ils font?

1. Que fait un nageur / une nageuse? Où est-ce qu'on trouve beaucoup de nageurs?
2. Que fait un campeur / une campeuse? Où est-ce qu'on fait du camping en France? aux États-Unis?
3. Que fait un skieur / une skieuse? Où est-ce qu'on fait du ski en France? aux États-Unis?
4. Que fait un(e) cycliste? Où est-ce qu'on fait du vélo en France? aux États-Unis?
5. Combien de nageurs, de campeurs, de skieurs, de cyclistes est-ce qu'il y a dans la classe? D'habitude, où est-ce qu'ils passent leurs vacances?

# Le verbe *acheter*

The verb **acheter** (*to buy*) is irregular. The **e** from the stem (**achet-**) becomes **è** for the forms of **je, tu, il/elle/on,** and **ils/elles.** The forms of **nous** and **vous** are regular. Note that all the endings are regular.

| PRESENT TENSE OF **acheter** | | | |
|---|---|---|---|
| j' | **achète** | nous | achetons |
| tu | **achètes** | vous | achetez |
| il/elle/on | **achète** | ils/elles | **achètent** |

Faire du shopping en vue des vacances. Va-t-elle faire du bateau ou du vélo en vacances? Qu'est-ce qu'elle achète? Qu'est-ce qu'elle porte?

**Allez-y!**

**Les besoins sont différents.** Ces personnes préparent leurs vacances. Complétez les phrases avec la forme appropriée du verbe **acheter.**

1. Caroline veut aller à la plage. Elle _____ un maillot de bain.
2. Nous voulons passer les vacances de Noël à la Martinique. Nous _____ des shorts et des tee-shirts.
3. Tu veux bien aller à la montagne. Tu _____ un sac à dos.
4. Rock et Marine organisent un voyage à Londres. Ils _____ des imperméables.
5. L'été prochain, vous voulez rendre visite à des amis à Paris. Vous _____ une jupe noire et un pull rouge.

# Au magasin de sports

des skis (*m.*)
des lunettes (*f.*) de soleil
des lunettes de ski
un maillot de bain
un sac de couchage
un anorak
une tente
un parapluie
une serviette de plage
des chaussures (*f.*) de ski
un pantalon de ski
des chaussures (*f.*) de montagne

**AUTRES MOTS UTILES**

| | | | |
|---|---|---|---|
| **un casque** | helmet | **des gants** (*m.*) | gloves |
| **une crème solaire** | suntan lotion | **un sac à dos** | backpack |
| **un écran solaire** | sunblock | **une valise** | suitcase |

 *Allez-y!*

**A. Achats.** (*Purchases.*) Complétez les phrases en vous basant sur le dessin à la page 204.

1. Le jeune homme va acheter des _____. Il va passer ses vacances à Grenoble où il veut _____.
2. La jeune femme veut acheter un _____, une _____ et des _____. Elle va descendre sur la Côte d'Azur (*French Riviera*) où elle va _____ et _____.
3. La jeune fille a envie d'acheter des _____ de ski, des chaussures de _____ et un _____ de ski. Sa famille va passer les vacances dans les Alpes où elle va _____.
4. L'homme va acheter un _____ et une _____. Il va _____ dans le nord de la France ce week-end.

**B. L'intrus.** Dans les groupes suivants, trouvez le mot qui ne va pas avec les autres. Expliquez votre choix.

1. le maillot de bain / les lunettes de soleil / la crème solaire / l'anorak
2. la tente / le maillot de bain / le sac de couchage / le sac à dos
3. les gants de ski / la serviette de plage / les skis / l'anorak
4. les lunettes de soleil / les chaussures de ski / le short / le maillot de bain

**C. Choix de vêtements.** Qu'est-ce qu'on porte pour faire les activités suivantes?

MODÈLE: pour aller à la pêche →
Pour aller à la pêche, on porte un chapeau...

**1.** pour faire du ski nautique  **2.** pour aller à la montagne  **3.** pour faire une promenade dans la forêt  **4.** pour faire du vélo  **5.** pour faire du bateau  **6.** pour faire du ski de fond

Et vous? Décrivez les vêtements que vous portez quand vous faites votre sport favori.

**D. Conseils pratiques.** Vous préparez un voyage en Tunisie. Voici les vêtements qu'on vous recommande.

1. Selon (*According to*) la brochure, quels vêtements sont recommandés pour un voyage en hiver, en été? Donnez des exemples.
2. À votre avis, quel temps fait-il en Tunisie en hiver, en été?

> **Les vêtements**
> *En hiver : quelques pulls, un imperméable et des vêtements de demi-saison.[1]*
> *En été : des vêtements légers[2] en fibres naturelles, maillot de bain, lunettes de soleil, chapeau, chaussures aérées,[3] tenues[4] pratiques pour les excursions. Sans oublier un léger pull pour les soirées et les hôtels climatisés.[5]*
>
> [1]*spring or autumn*  [2]*lightweight*  [3]*well-ventilated*
> [4]*outfits, clothes*  [5]*air-conditioned*

Imaginez maintenant que vous travaillez dans une agence de voyages. Quels vêtements allez-vous conseiller (*to suggest*) à des touristes qui vont en Alaska, au Mexique ou dans le Grand Canyon? Quels autres achats conseillez-vous?

# Des années importantes

La machine à calculer inventée par Blaise Pascal en **1642** (mille six cent quarante-deux).

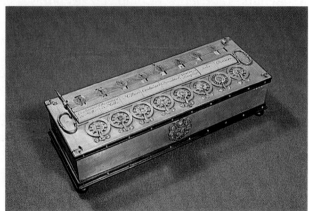

L'Aéro-Montgolfière dénommée « Tour de Calais » 1785.

Le ballon à air chaud inventé par les frères Montgolfier en **1783** (mille sept cent quatre-vingt-trois).

Les procédés de développement des images photographiques inventés par Jacques Daguerre en **1835** (mille huit cent trente-cinq).

- In French, years are expressed with a multiple of **mille** or with **cent**.

| | |
|---|---|
| **mille neuf cents** (*or* **dix-neuf cents**) | *1900* |
| **mille neuf cent quatre-vingt-dix-neuf** | *1999* |
| (*or* **dix-neuf cent quatre-vingt-dix-neuf**) | |
| **deux mille quatorze** | *2014* |

- The preposition **en** is used to express *in* with a year.

| | |
|---|---|
| **en** mille neuf cent vingt-trois | *in 1923* |

- Note the expression **les années 50** (*the* [*nineteen*] *fifties*): **les années cinquante**.

## Allez-y!

**A. Un peu d'histoire.** Êtes-vous bon(ne) en histoire? Avec un(e) camarade, trouvez la date qui correspond à chaque événement historique. Les événements sont présentés par ordre chronologique!

1. Charlemagne est couronné (*crowned*) empereur d'Occident.
2. Guillaume, duc de Normandie, conquiert (*conquers*) l'Angleterre
3. Jeanne d'Arc bat (*beats*) les Anglais à Orléans.
4. Prise de la Bastille.
5. Napoléon est couronné empereur des Français.
6. Gustave Eiffel construit la tour Eiffel.
7. Débarquement (*Landing*) anglo-américain en France.

**a.** 1944
**b.** 1804
**c.** 1889
**d.** 1066
**e.** 1429
**f.** 1789
**g.** l'an 800

**B. L'avenir.** (*The future.*) Quels sont vos projets d'avenir? Posez les questions suivantes à un(e) camarade. Ensuite, présentez à la classe une observation sur l'avenir de votre camarade.

1. En quelle année vas-tu obtenir (*to obtain*) ton diplôme universitaire?
2. En quelle année vas-tu passer des vacances en France?
3. En quelle année vas-tu avoir 65 ans?

# Leçon 2

## Quelques verbes irréguliers en *-ir*

*Expressing Actions*

### Vacances à Versailles

*Alexis contacte Poema sur sa page Facebook (Messagerie instantanée).*

ALEXIS: Poema, **tu pars** cet été?

POEMA: **Je pars** à la Guadeloupe au mois d'août. Et toi?

ALEXIS: Moi, **je reviens** juste de Montréal. Je suis fatigué. **Je dors** toute la journée!

POEMA: **Tu dors**! Tu ne travailles pas?

ALEXIS: Non. Je suis en vacances!

POEMA: **Tu viens** à la Guadeloupe avec moi?

ALEXIS: Merci pour l'invitation, mais Trésor et moi nous restons à Versailles.

POEMA: À Versailles? Mais qu'est-ce qu'on fait à Versailles en été?

ALEXIS: **On dort** le matin, on fait du vélo dans le parc du château l'après-midi, **on sort** le soir.

Vrai ou faux? Corrigez les phrases fausses.

1. Poema part au Canada cet été.
2. Alexis revient de Montréal.
3. Poema est fatiguée. Elle dort toute la journée.
4. Poema demande à Alexis de venir à la Guadeloupe avec elle.
5. Alexis dit: «On sort le matin, on dort le soir».

## *Dormir* and Similar Verbs

The verb **dormir** (*to sleep*) has an irregular conjugation.

| PRESENT TENSE OF **dormir** | | | |
|---|---|---|---|
| je | **dors** | nous | **dormons** |
| tu | **dors** | vous | **dormez** |
| il/elle/on | **dort** | ils/elles | **dorment** |

| | |
|---|---|
| Je **dors** très bien. | *I sleep very well.* |
| **Dormez**-vous à la belle étoile? | *Do you sleep in the open air?* |
| Nous **dormons** jusqu'à 7 h 30. | *We sleep until 7:30.* |

Verbs conjugated like **dormir** include:

**partir** *to leave, depart*
**sentir** *to feel; to sense; to smell*
**servir** *to serve*
**sortir** *to leave; to go out*

| | |
|---|---|
| Je **pars** en vacances. | *I'm leaving on vacation.* |
| Ce plat **sent** bon/mauvais. | *This dish smells good/bad.* |
| Nous **servons** le petit déjeuner à 8 h. | *We serve breakfast at 8:00.* |
| À quelle heure allez-vous **sortir** ce soir? | *What time are you going out tonight?* |

## *Partir* and *sortir*

**Partir** and **sortir** mean *to leave,* but they are used differently.

1. **Partir** is the opposite of **arriver**. It can be used alone or followed by a preposition.

| | |
|---|---|
| Je **pars** demain. | *I'm leaving (departing) tomorrow.* |
| Elle **part** de/pour Cannes. | *She's leaving from/for Cannes.* |

2. **Sortir** is the opposite of **entrer** (*to enter*). It can also be used alone or followed by a preposition.

| | |
|---|---|
| Ils **sortent** du théâtre. | *They're leaving the theater.* |
| Elle **sort** de la caravane. | *She's getting out of the camper.* |
| **Sortons** de l'eau! | *Let's get out of the water!* |

**Sortir** can also mean that one is going out for the evening, or seeing another person regularly.

| | |
|---|---|
| Tu **sors** ce soir? | *Are you going out tonight?* |
| Iris et Édouard **sortent** ensemble. | *Iris and Édouard are going out together.* |

Note: **Quitter** (a regular **-er** verb) means *to leave (go away from) something or someone.* It always requires a direct object, either a place or a person.

| | |
|---|---|
| Je **quitte** Paris. | *I'm leaving Paris.* |
| Elle **quitte** son ami. | *She's leaving her boyfriend.* |

[Allez-y! A-D]

> ### Grammaire interactive
>
> For more on regular **-re** and **-ir** verbs and verbs like **sortir,** watch the corresponding Grammar Tutorial and take a brief practice quiz at **Connect French.**
>
>
> www.mhconnectfrench.com

## *Venir* and the *passé récent*

The verb **venir** (*to come*) is irregular.

| PRESENT TENSE OF **venir** | | | |
|---|---|---|---|
| je | **viens** | nous | venons |
| tu | **viens** | vous | venez |
| il/elle/on | **vient** | ils/elles | **viennent** |

| | |
|---|---|
| Nous **venons** de Saint-Malo. | *We come from Saint-Malo.* |
| **Viens** voir la plage! | *Come see the beach!* |

1. **Venir de** + infinitive means *to have just* (*done something*). This is called **le passé récent.**

| | |
|---|---|
| Je **viens de** nager. | *I've just been swimming.* |
| Mes amis **viennent de** téléphoner. | *My friends have just telephoned.* |

2. Verbs conjugated like **venir** include:

**devenir** *to become*
**obtenir** *to obtain*
**revenir** *to come back*

| | |
|---|---|
| Ils **reviennent** de vacances. | *They're coming back from vacation.* |
| On **devient** expert grâce à l'expérience. | *One becomes an expert with (thanks to) experience.* |

[Allez-y! B-C-D]

 *Allez-y!*

A. **Que faire?** Clara et Philippe, les amis de Romain, désirent sortir ce soir. Romain hésite. Complétez la conversation avec les verbes corrects: **partir, quitter** ou **sortir.**

PHILIPPE: On _____¹ ce soir? Il y a un bon film qui passe au ciné!

ROMAIN: Désolé! Mes cousins sont en vacances chez moi et ils _____² demain matin, alors je vais rester avec eux ce soir.

PHILIPPE: Oh allez! Tu les _____³ pendant deux heures, le temps du film. Ce n'est pas long!

CLARA: Attends. Tes cousins, ils ne _____⁴ pas le samedi soir? Ils ont quel âge?

ROMAIN: Si bien sûr, mais quand vous _____⁵ la maison à 5 h du matin, est-ce que vous _____⁶ tard la veille, vous?

PHILIPPE: Tu _____⁷ en vacances demain, toi, Clara?

CLARA: Ben non...

PHILIPPE: Nous _____⁸ donc ce soir?

CLARA: Ah oui!

PHILIPPE: O.K., on te raconte le film demain, Romain. Bonne soirée avec tes cousins!

**B. Au pays des pharaons.** Loïc et Nathalie sont en vacances en Égypte avec le Club Aquarius. Ils envoient (*send*) une carte postale à leur grand-mère. Complétez la carte avec les verbes de la colonne de droite.

Chère mamie,

Nous _venons_[1] d'arriver en Égypte. Le Club Aquarius, c'est le grand confort. Nous _dormons_[2] dans des chambres immenses et tous les matins on _sert_[3] le petit déjeuner dans la chambre. Demain nous _____[4] pour le temple de Louxor. Nous _____[5] des experts en égyptologie. Nous _____[6] en France dans quatre jours.

À bientôt et grosses bises.

*Loïc et Nathalie*

**devenir** *to become*

~~**dormir**~~

**partir** *to go*

**revenir**

**servir** *to serve*

**venir** *to come*

**C. La curiosité.** Imaginez avec un(e) camarade ce que ces personnes viennent de faire. Donnez trois possibilités pour chaque phrase.

**MODÈLE:** Albert rentre d'Afrique. →
Il vient de visiter le Sénégal. Il vient de passer une semaine au soleil. Il vient de faire un safari.

1. Jennifer part en vacances.
2. Je sors du magasin de sports.
3. Nous revenons de la montagne.
4. Anthony et Yvon reviennent de la campagne.
5. Aïcha rentre du Canada.

**D. Conversation.** Engagez avec un(e) camarade une conversation basée sur les questions suivantes. Ensuite, faites un commentaire sur les habitudes (*habits*) ou les attitudes de votre camarade.

1. Tu pars souvent en voyage? Tu vas où? Tu viens d'acheter des vêtements ou d'autres objects nécessaires pour tes vacances? Qu'est-ce que tu viens d'acheter?
2. Tu sors souvent pendant (*during*) le week-end ou tu restes à la maison? Tu sors souvent pendant la semaine? Qu'est-ce que tu portes quand tu sors?
3. Tu aimes la fin des vacances? Tes ami(e)s sentent une différence quand tu rentres chez toi? Tu es plus calme? nerveux/nerveuse? triste? heureux/heureuse?

Une école de ski à Méribel en Savoie, en France

# Le passé composé avec l'auxiliaire *être*

*Talking About the Past*

## De Londres à Cannes

*Appel vidéo entre Hector et Juliette.*

HECTOR: **Vous êtes arrivées** à Londres?

JULIETTE: En fait, **nous sommes descendues** à Cannes.

HECTOR: À Cannes? Je ne comprends rien. Vous avez changé vos projets? **Vous n'êtes pas parties** en Angleterre?

JULIETTE: **Nous sommes restées** deux jours à Londres. Mais il pleuvait.* Alors, **nous sommes revenues** à Paris et **nous sommes parties** sur la Côte d'Azur.

HECTOR: Vous avez trouvé un petit hôtel?

JULIETTE: Sans problème. C'est facile: **Nous sommes allées** sur TripAdvisor!

*il... *it was raining*

▼ AUDIO & VIDEO

MESSAGE VIDEO ●

Trouvez la question dans le dialogue.

**1.** En fait, nous sommes descendues à Cannes.

**2.** Nous sommes restées deux jours à Londres. Nous sommes revenues à Paris et nous sommes parties sur la Côte d'Azur.

**3.** Sans problème. Nous sommes allées sur TripAdvisor!

Most French verbs form the **passé composé** with **avoir** as the auxiliary verb. A few, however, require **être** as the auxiliary verb. One of these verbs is **aller.**

| PASSÉ COMPOSÉ OF **aller** | |
|---|---|
| je suis all**é(e)** | nous sommes all**é(e)s** |
| tu es all**é(e)** | vous êtes all**é(e)(s)** |
| il/on est all**é*** | ils sont all**és** |
| elle est all**ée** | elles sont all**ées** |

*When **on** clearly represents a plural subject, the past participle agrees with the subject (**on est allés**, **on est allées**). The auxiliary verb will always stay singular.

1. The past participle of verbs conjugated with **être** in the **passé composé** agrees with the subject in gender and number.

| | |
|---|---|
| Marc est all**é** au Japon. | *Marc went to Japan.* |
| Agathe est all**ée** en Côte d'Ivoire. | *Agathe went to Ivory Coast.* |
| Benjamin et Loïc sont all**és** à Chartres. | *Benjamin and Loïc went to Chartres.* |
| Elles sont all**ées** à Hawaï. | *They went to Hawaii.* |

2. The following verbs take **être** in the **passé composé.** Note that most convey motion or a change in state. Irregular past participles are indicated in parentheses.

**aller** *to go*
**arriver** *to arrive*
**descendre** *to go down; to get off*
**devenir (devenu)** *to become*
**entrer** *to enter*
**monter** *to go up; to climb*
**mourir (mort)** *to die*
**naître (né)** *to be born*
**partir** *to leave*

**passer** *to pass*
**rentrer** *to return; to go home*
**rester** *to stay*
**retourner** *to return; to go back*
**revenir (revenu)** *to come back*
**sortir** *to go out*
**tomber** *to fall*
**venir (venu)** *to come*

[Allez-y! A-B-C]

*Dr. (and) mrs. vandertrampp*
*Past être verb.*

**3.** Word order in negative and interrogative sentences in the **passé composé** with **être** is the same as that for the **passé composé** with **avoir.**

Je **ne suis pas** allé au cours.     *I did not go to class.*
**Sont-ils** arrivés à l'heure?     *Did they arrive on time?*

[Allez-y! D-E]

L'année dernière, je suis allée voir le Centre Pompidou à Paris. C'est une usine (*factory*)? une église? un musée?

## Mots clés

**L'expression *il y a***

The expression **il y a** used with a time period means *ago.* It requires a past tense.

Ils sont allés au Mexique **il y a** deux ans.
   *They went to Mexico two years ago.*

### Allez-y!

**A. Des sorties.** Dites où et quand ces personnes sont allées en vacances. Utilisez l'expression **il y a.**

> **MODÈLE:** une semaine / Nora / la Côte d'Azur →
> Il y a une semaine, Nora est allée à la Côte d'Azur.

**1.** un mois / Fabrice / plage
**2.** deux jours / tu / forêt / faire du camping
**3.** six mois / M^me Robert / montagne / faire du ski
**4.** trois jours / nous / campagne
**5.** deux ans / je / Nice

**B. Départ en vacances.** Les Astier, vos voisins, sont partis en vacances ce week-end. Vous racontez maintenant la scène à vos amis. Complétez l'histoire de façon logique et mettez les verbes au passé composé.

Ce matin, mes voisins les Astier _____[1] en vacances.    **aller**
Ils _____[2] à la mer. À 8 h, M. Astier et son fils    **entrer**
_____[3] et _____[4] de la maison plusieurs fois avec des    **partir**
sacs et des valises. M^me Astier _____[5] cinq fois dans    **retourner**
la maison pour aller chercher des objets oubliés.    **sortir**
   Enfin, trois heures plus tard, toute la famille    **descendre**
_____[6] dans la voiture et elle _____[7]. Mais pas de    **monter**
chance, une des valises _____[8] de la galerie (*roof*    **partir**
*rack*). M. Astier _____[9] de la voiture pour la    **repartir**
remettre sur la galerie et ils _____[10]. Moi, je _____[11]    **rester**
chez moi.    **tomber**

**C. Week-end en Suisse.** Valentine et Edgar ont passé le week-end à Genève. Mettez l'histoire au passé composé et faites attention au choix de l'auxiliaire (**avoir** ou **être**).

Edgar vient[1] chercher Valentine pour aller à la gare. Ils montent[2] dans le train. Ils cherchent[3] leur voiture. Le train part[4] quelques minutes plus tard. Il entre[5] en gare de Genève à midi. Edgar et Valentine descendent[6] du train et vont[7] tout de suite à l'hôtel. L'après-midi, ils sortent[8] visiter la ville. Le soir, ils dînent[9] dans un restaurant élégant. Dimanche Valentine va[10] au musée et prend[11] beaucoup de photos de la ville. Edgar reste[12] à l'hôtel. Valentine et Edgar quittent[13] Genève en fin d'après-midi. Ils arrivent[14] à Paris fatigués mais contents de leur week-end.

Qu'est-ce que Valentine a fait qu'Edgar n'a pas fait?

**D. Les voyageurs.** Gaspard, Julien et Arthur ont passé une partie de leurs vacances ensemble (*together*). Ils regardent les photos des vacances et essaient de se souvenir (*try to remember*) des détails. Complétez leur conversation au passé composé.

GASPARD: Tu te souviens quand nous _____[1]?                          **arriver**

JULIEN: Nous _____[2] dans le train à Metz le 19 avril          **monter**
vers 6 h et nous _____[3] à Nice le soir.                              **partir**

GASPARD: Est-ce que Arthur _____[4] voir sa copine               **passer**
de Nice le même (*same*) jour?

JULIEN: Non, il _____[5] chez elle le lendemain                   **aller**
et ils _____[6] pour l'Italie le 21.                                  **partir**

GASPARD: Arthur et toi, vous _____[7] ensemble                    **rentrer**
à la fin des vacances, non?

JULIEN: Oui, et toi tu _____[8] à la plage une                    **rester**
semaine de plus et tu _____[9] en mai.                              **revenir**
C'est vraiment trop injuste!

**E. Souvenirs de vacances.** Décrivez les vacances de l'année passée d'un(e) camarade. D'abord, posez les questions suivantes à votre camarade. Si vous voulez, posez encore d'autres questions. Ensuite, présentez à la classe une description de ses vacances.

1. Quand es-tu parti(e)? Où es-tu allé(e)? Es-tu resté(e) aux États-Unis ou es-tu allé(e) à l'étranger? As-tu visité un endroit exotique?
2. Es-tu allé(e) voir l'endroit où tes parents sont nés? Où es-tu né(e)?
3. Qu'est-ce que tu as fait pendant les vacances? Est-ce que tu as rencontré des gens (*people*) intéressants?
4. Comment es-tu rentré(e): en avion ou en voiture? Es-tu revenu(e) mort(e) de fatigue?
5. Est-ce que tu prépares déjà tes vacances de l'année prochaine?

# Le blog d'Hassan

## Partir!

samedi 13 juin

L'été dernier, j'ai passé des vacances super originales: j'ai fait un échange de logements. Je vous explique: je voulais[1] aller en Louisiane, mais pas comme un simple touriste. Je voulais vivre une expérience authentique. Par Internet, j'ai contacté une famille de La Nouvelle-Orléans qui voulait passer ses vacances à Paris. Et nous avons échangé nos logements: je suis allé chez eux; ils sont venus chez moi.

J'ai découvert La Nouvelle-Orléans, capitale du jazz; j'ai pique-niqué dans le parc Louis Armstrong, j'ai descendu le Mississippi en bateau… Le soir, je rentrais[2] «chez moi» pour cuisiner les spécialités locales. Depuis mon séjour[3] en Louisiane, je suis le champion des haricots rouges avec du riz!

Pendant ce temps, Debby et son mari Scott vivaient[4] dans mon appartement parisien et arrosaient[5] mes plantes!

Maintenant, une amitié est née entre nous.

Et vous? Vous avez déjà pratiqué ce type d'échanges? C'était comment[6]?

Hassan

Ça, c'est vraiment La Nouvelle-Orléans!

. . . . . . . . . . . . . . . . . . . . . . . . . . . . . . . . . . . . . . . . . . . . . . . . . . . . . . .

## COMMENTAIRES

### Alexis

C'était fabuleux: il y a trois ans, j'ai échangé mon appartement de Québec avec un couple de la Réunion. Trésor et moi, nous sommes restés deux semaines chez eux, dans une belle villa avec piscine.[7] On a visité l'île; on a fait de la planche à voile, du ski nautique, de la plongée sous-marine, des randonnées… Eux, ils sont «tombés en amour[8]» pour le Québec!

### Trésor

Moi, j'ai nagé dans l'océan Indien!

### Charlotte

Hassan et Alexis, je pense que vous êtes fous[9]! Des étrangers dorment dans votre lit; ils mangent dans vos assiettes…

### Alexis

Et alors? C'est comme à l'hôtel.

### Poema

Alexis, est-ce que tu as déjà des projets de vacances pour l'année prochaine? Mes parents ont une jolie villa en Polynésie, à Bora-Bora…

[1]*wanted* [2]*returned* [3]*Depuis… Since my stay* [4]*were living* [5]*were watering* [6]*C'était… How was it?* [7]*pool* [8]*tombés… fell in love (expression used in Quebec)* [9]*crazy*

## France: le pays des grandes vacances

Chez les Beaufour, on voyage énormément. M^me Beaufour est professeur et a presque[1] quatre mois de congés[2] payés; M. Beaufour, comme tous les salariés, a au minimum cinq semaines de vacances. «À Noël, explique M^me Beaufour, toute la famille part à la neige. Les vacances de février sont généralement consacrées à[3] un petit voyage en Suisse. Pour Pâques, nous passons toujours une semaine chez ma mère qui possède une maison de campagne à Aix-en-Provence. Enfin, pour les vacances d'été, nous aimons le camping.»

En France, les vacances sont sacrées et intouchables.

À Noël et en février, les Français privilégient[4] la montagne. À Pâques, on choisit souvent des vacances familiales. En été, on va se faire bronzer sur les plages de la Côte d'Azur ou on pratique le «tourisme vert» à la campagne.

Les jours de départ en vacances sont souvent un vrai cauchemar[5] à cause des embouteillages[6]: pour ne pas perdre une seule minute de leurs précieuses vacances, les Français partent tous le même jour, à la même heure, sur les mêmes autoroutes! Alors voici un bon conseil: en hiver et au printemps, évitez[7] de vous trouver sur les routes du soleil ou de la montagne la veille[8] de Noël ou de Pâques. C'est l'enfer[9]! Et en été, ne partez pas le 1^er juillet ou le 1^er août: sur l'autoroute du Sud, les vacanciers restent prisonniers de leurs voitures pendant des heures!

Voilà les vacances! À Cannes, sur la Côte d'Azur, on peut bronzer, nager, faire de la planche à voile ou de la plongée libre et s'amuser.

[1]almost  [2]vacation  [3]consacrées... devoted to  [4]favor  [5]nightmare  [6]à... because of traffic jams  [7]avoid  [8]day before  [9]hell

1. Combien de semaines de vacances ont M. et M^me Beaufour? Leur cas est-il unique en France?
2. À quels moments les Français prennent-ils leurs vacances?
3. Comparez les vacances des Français à celles (*those*) des Américains: quelles différences observez-vous? Préférez-vous le système français ou le système américain? Pourquoi?

- Dans quelle ville, quelle région, quel pays passez-vous vos vacances?
- Pour combien de temps partez-vous en vacances?
- Quelles sont vos activités pendant les vacances?
- Quels pays rêvez-vous de visiter? Pourquoi?

1. Répondez, par écrit, aux questions ci-dessus (*above*). Écrivez chaque réponse sur une fiche (*index card*) différente.
2. Donnez vos fiches au professeur. Il/Elle va les mélanger (*mix them up*) et les redistribuer.
3. Lisez à voix haute la fiche que vous avez reçue (*received*).
4. Avec l'aide de la classe, devinez qui est l'auteur de la fiche.

STRUCTURES

# Leçon 3

## L'expression impersonnelle *il faut*

*Expressing Obligation and Necessity*

### Des vacances aux Antilles

*Poema téléphone à Alexis.*

POEMA: Pour aller à la Guadeloupe, est-ce qu'**il faut**[1] un visa?
ALEXIS: Non! La Guadeloupe, c'est la France! **Il faut présenter** une carte d'identité ou un passeport.
POEMA: Je suis toujours anxieuse quand je voyage! J'ai peur d'oublier quelque chose.[2]
ALEXIS: Poema, sois cool! Aux Antilles, **il faut** simplement des lunettes de soleil, une serviette de plage et une crème solaire. C'est tout!
POEMA: Et pour le soir?
ALEXIS: Pour le soir, **il faut avoir** une jolie robe pour aller danser!

Le bonheur simple à la Guadeloupe

[1]il est nécessaire d'(avoir)   [2]d'oublier... *of forgetting something*

**Répondez aux questions. Utilisez l'expression il faut.**

1. Pour aller à la Guadeloupe, quels documents administratifs faut-il?
2. Pour la plage, qu'est-ce qu'il faut?
3. Et pour le soir, qu'est-ce qu'il faut avoir?

1. The expression **il faut** is the impersonal form of the verb **falloir.** Followed by an infinitive, it is used to express general obligation or a necessity.

| | |
|---|---|
| **Il faut** étudier pour réussir. | *One has to study to do well.* |
| **Il faut** manger pour vivre. | *One has to (It is necessary to) eat to live.* |

In the near future (**le futur proche**), **il faut** + infinitive becomes **il va falloir** + infinitive. In the **passé composé,** it becomes **il a fallu.**

| | |
|---|---|
| Nous avons une réservation pour le train à 8 h: **il va falloir** arriver à l'heure. | *We have a train reservation for 8:00: We will have to be on time.* |
| **Il a fallu** réserver très tôt en avance. | *We had to make our reservation very early.* |

**2.** In the negative, the form **il ne faut pas** (*one must not*) expresses a prohibited action.

> **Il ne faut pas** boire d'eau non-potable.
>
> *You must not (should not) drink untreated water.*

**3. Il faut** can also be followed by nouns referring to objects or to qualities to talk about what is needed. The indefinte or partitive article is usually used before the noun in the construction **il faut** + noun.

> Pour aller à la Guadeloupe, **il faut** un visa?
>
> *To go to Guadeloupe, do you need a visa?*
>
> Pour faire de la soupe à l'oignon, **il faut** des oignons, du consommé de bœuf, du gruyère et du pain.
>
> *To make onion soup, you need onions, beef broth, Swiss cheese, and bread.*
>
> **Il faut** du courage pour manger des escargots!
>
> *One needs courage to eat snails!*

## Allez-y!

**A. Qu'est-ce qu'il faut?** Répondez aux questions avec un(e) camarade et notez vos conclusions. Répondez avec **il faut** + *infinitif* ou *nom*.

> **MODÈLE:** pour passer une soirée à la française? →
> Qu'est-ce qu'il faut pour passer une soirée à la française?
> Il faut des amis. (*ou* Il faut aimer la bonne cuisine. /
> Il faut prendre son temps.)

1. pour passer des vacances parfaites?
2. pour fêter son anniversaire?
3. pour s'amuser (*to have fun*) à une soirée à l'américaine?
4. pour se faire «une bonne bouffe (*a big meal*)»?
5. pour ne pas grossir (*not to gain weight*)?
6. pour être en bonne santé (*health*)?
7. pour bien dormir?

**B. Conversation à trois.** Avec deux autres camarades, vous allez organiser un voyage pour toute la classe. Qu'est-ce que vous voulez faire? Où voulez-vous voyager? Qu'est-ce qu'il faut faire avant de partir? Qu'est-ce qu'il faut acheter? Comment voulez-vous partager le travail? Utilisez les verbes **pouvoir, vouloir** et **devoir** et l'expression **il faut**.

**Expressions utiles:** devoir acheter, devoir apporter, devoir commander, devoir demander, pouvoir acheter, pouvoir choisir, vouloir bien

Après votre conversation, décrivez le voyage à la classe.

---

### Le parler jeune

**avoir la pêche** être en forme, de bonne humeur et plein d'énergie
**se barrer / se casser** partir
**s'éclater / se marrer** s'amuser
**marrant** amusant, intéressant
**quel pied!** exprime le plaisir absolu

Moi, pour **avoir la pêche,** je fais du sport.

La copine de Sébastien n'est pas à la fête, alors il **se casse.**

Les vacances, c'est fait pour **s'éclater.**

C'est **marrant,** la plongée sous-marine, avec tous ces poissons…

Bronzer sur une plage de Tunisie, **quel pied!**

# Les prépositions devant les noms de lieu

*Expressing Location*

## Soyez extravagants!

*Hassan, Abdel et Carole discutent.*

HASSAN: Finalement, vous allez vous marier **à** Paris!

ABDEL: Oui, on va faire un mariage marocain à l'Institut du monde arabe, dans le 5ᵉ arrondissement. Il y a une belle salle au dernier étage, avec une grande terrasse.

CAROLE: Avec ce choix, tout le monde est content: on est à la fois[1] **au** Maroc et **en** France!

ABDEL: Ensuite, on va aller **à** Venise, **en** Italie!

CAROLE: Pour notre voyage de noces[2]!

HASSAN: Venise? Quel conformisme! Pourquoi n'allez-vous pas **à** Tahiti **en** Polynésie française, **à** Zanzibar en Afrique, ou **aux** Seychelles dans l'océan Indien? Soyez extravagants!

CAROLE: Pas question! C'est trop cher! Et puis, j'aime Venise parce que c'est romantique.

ABDEL: … Et moi, j'aime Carole et je veux lui faire plaisir[3]!

Une plage de rêve aux Seychelles

[1]à... *at the same time*  [2]voyage... *honeymoon*  [3]lui... *make her happy*

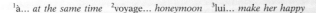

Répondez aux questions.

1. Dans quelle ville le mariage va-t-il être organisé?
2. Dans quel pays est l'Institut du monde arabe?
3. Où les futurs mariés vont-ils faire leur voyage de noces?
4. Quels pays et quelles villes Hassan suggère-t-il?

## Gender of Geographical Nouns

1. In French, most place names that end in **-e** are feminine; most others are masculine. One important exception: **le Mexique.**

2. The names of the continents are feminine: **l'Afrique, l'Amérique du Nord, l'Amérique du Sud, l'Antarctique, l'Asie, l'Europe, l'Océanie** (Australia and the Pacific islands).

**3.** The names of most states in the United States are masculine regardless of their ending: **le Texas, le Tennessee.** There are nine exceptions:

| | |
|---|---|
| la Californie | la Louisiane |
| la Caroline du Nord et du Sud | la Pennsylvanie |
| la Floride | la Virginie |
| la Géorgie | la Virginie-Occidentale |

## Prepositions with Geographical Names

| | TO, AT, IN | | FROM | |
|---|---|---|---|---|
| cities<br>islands | **à** | Suzanne habite **à** Lyon.<br>Ils sont allés **à** Cuba. | **de**<br>**(d')** | Elle vient **de** Montréal.<br>Ils arrivent **d'**Hawaï. |
| continents | **en** | Lidia est née **en** Amérique du Sud. | **de**<br>**(d')** | Je pars **d'**Europe. |
| feminine countries, states, provinces | **en** | Il y a deux ans, vous avez fait un voyage **en** Suisse.<br>Bâton Rouge est **en** Louisiane.<br>Les explorateurs sont arrivés **en** Nouvelle-Écosse. | **de**<br>**(d')** | Jean arrive **de** Floride.<br>Viviane est **de** Colombie-Britannique. |
| masculine countries, states, or provinces starting with a vowel | | On a voyagé **en** Israël.<br>Il est né **en** Alaska.<br>Elle a travaillé **en** Ontario. | | Elle vient **d'**Iran.<br>Ils arrivent **d'**Oregon.<br>Mariane est originaire **d'**Ontario. |
| masculine countries or provinces starting with a consonant | **au** | **Au** Canada, il y a dix provinces. Je voudrais aller **au** Québec.* | **du** | Ils reviennent **du** Brésil.<br>Il va partir **du** Nouveau-Brunswick. |
| all plural countries | **aux** | Il y a dix ans, ils sont arrivés **aux** États-Unis. | **des** | Quand sont-ils partis **des** Pays-Bas? |
| regions<br>masculine states[†] starting with a consonant | **dans le** | Elle va **dans le** Poitou.<br>J'aime l'automne **dans le** Vermont. | **du**<br>**(de l')** | Nous revenons **du** Sud.<br>Elle vient **du** Colorado. |

---

*au Québec refers to the province; à Québec refers to the city
[†]Some exceptions: **au / du** Texas
        **au / du** Nouveau-Mexique
        **dans l'état de / de l'état de** New York / Washington (to distinguish the states from the cities)

### Prononcez bien!

**The vowels in *à*, *au*, and *aux***

Make sure you clearly distinguish between [a] and [o] when you pronounce **à** and **au.** Pronounce brief and tense sounds.

Open your mouth wide to say **à.**

[a]: **à Montréal, à La Nouvelle-Orléans**

Close your mouth and round your lips to say **au** and **aux.**

[o]: **au Sénégal, aux Pays-Bas**

## Allez-y!

**A.** **Jeu géographique.** Voici quelques villes francophones. Dans quels pays se trouvent-elles? (Voir les cartes à la fin du livre.)

**MODÈLE:** Paris est en France.

1. Rabat
2. Montréal
3. Kinshasa
4. Alger
5. Dakar
6. Bruxelles
7. Tunis
8. Abidjan
9. Port-au-Prince
10. Genève

**a.** Haïti
**b.** la Belgique
**c.** la Tunisie
**d.** la République Démocratique du Congo
**e.** le Canada
**f.** la Suisse
**g.** le Maroc
**h.** la Côte d'Ivoire
**i.** l'Algérie
**j.** le Sénégal

**B.** **Retour de vacances.** Un groupe de touristes rentre de vacances. D'après ce qu'ils ont dans leurs valises, dites d'où ils arrivent.

**MODÈLE:** une montre
la Suisse → Ils arrivent de Suisse.

| SOUVENIRS | PAYS |
|---|---|
| 1. du parfum | le Cameroun |
| 2. un caméscope (*video camera*) | la Hollande |
| 3. une bouteille de tequila | l'Italie |
| 4. un masque d'initiation | le Mexique |
| 5. des chaussures en cuir (*leather*) | le Japon |
| 6. un pull en cachemire | l'Écosse |
| 7. des tulipes | le Maroc |
| 8. du café | la Colombie |
| 9. un couscoussier (*couscous maker*) | la Belgique |
| 10. du chocolat | la France |

À Tunis, on trouve de beaux tapis.

**C. Un(e) jeune globe-trotter.** Votre camarade va faire le tour du monde. Vous lui demandez où il/elle va aller.

**Continents:** l'Afrique, l'Amérique du Nord, l'Amérique du Sud, l'Antarctique, l'Asie, l'Europe, l'Océanie

**Pays:** l'Algérie, l'Allemagne, l'Australie, le Brésil, le Canada, la Chine, le Danemark, l'Égypte, les États-Unis, la Finlande, la Grèce, l'Inde, l'Italie, le Japon, le Maroc, le Mexique, la Polynésie française, la Norvège, le Vietnam…

**MODÈLE:** É1: Vas-tu en Asie?
É2: Oui, je vais en Chine (au Japon… ).

**D. Interview.** Posez les questions à un(e) camarade de classe. Ensuite, révélez sa réponse la plus surprenante à la classe.

1. D'où viens-tu? De quelle ville? De quel état? Et tes parents?
2. Où habitent tes parents? Et le reste de ta famille?
3. Dans quels états as-tu voyagé?
4. Est-ce qu'il y a un état que tu préfères? Pourquoi?
5. Dans quel état est-ce qu'il y a de beaux parcs? de beaux lacs? de belles montagnes? de grandes villes? de grands déserts?

## Un peu plus…

**Le Mont-Saint-Michel.**
C'est un monument avec une histoire riche. Située au large des (*off the*) côtes bretonne et normande, la petite île rocheuse héberge (*shelters*) depuis l'an 966 une abbaye bénédictine dédiée à Saint Michel. Haut lieu de spiritualité, les pèlerinages (*pilgrimages*) au Mont-Saint-Michel ont eu lieu tout au long de son histoire. L'abbaye héberge également des documents précieux qui datent du Moyen Âge. Aujourd'hui, le Mont-Saint-Michel accueille des visiteurs du monde entier. Avez-vous déjà visité un monument avec une histoire riche? Expliquez.

◄ *Le Mont-Saint-Michel, en Normandie*

# Prononcez bien!

1. **The pronunciation of *montagne*** (page 202)

   A. **La pêche.** Hugo parle de son activité préférée: la pêche. Choisissez le mot que vous entendez dans chaque phrase.

   |   |   |   |   |
   |---|---|---|---|
   | **1.** ☐ Line | ☐ ligne (*line*) |
   | **2.** ☐ Line | ☐ ligne |
   | **3.** ☐ reine (*queen*) | ☐ règne (*rules* [verb]) |
   | **4.** ☐ reine | ☐ règne |
   | **5.** ☐ panés (*deep-fried*) | ☐ panier (*basket*) |
   | **6.** ☐ panés | ☐ panier |

   B. **La pêche (suite).** Hugo raconte son meilleur souvenir (*best memory*) de pêche. Avec votre camarade, répétez ses mots. Faites bien attention à la prononciation des mots français en italique.

      1. La *dernière* fois (*time*) que j'ai pêché à la *ligne*, c'était pendant le voyage que j'ai *gagné* à la loterie.
      2. Pour ce voyage, je suis allé à *Cologne*, en *Allemagne*. C'était *magnifique*! Je voudrais bien y retourner (*go back there*)!

2. **The vowels in *viens* and *viennent*** (page 210)

   **Un nouveau joueur.** Hugo parle de son frère Simon et de la fiancée de Simon. Décidez si Hugo parle uniquement de Simon, ou de Simon et Lisa.

   |   | Simon | Simon et Lisa |
   |---|---|---|
   | **1.** venir samedi prochain | ☐ | ☐ |
   | **2.** revenir de vacances à Vienne, en Autriche | ☐ | ☐ |
   | **3.** tenir à (*to be eager to*) me présenter sa fiancée | ☐ | ☐ |
   | **4.** devenir de plus en plus amoureux (*more and more in love*) | ☐ | ☐ |

3. **The vowels in *à, au,* and *aux*** (page 221)

   A. **Voyage.** Isabelle parle des vacances qu'elle a passées en Amérique du Nord l'été dernier. Écoutez et complétez le paragraphe avec *à* ou **au.**

   Je suis allée _____¹ Texas, _____² Hawaï, _____³ Nouveau-Mexique, _____⁴ Nevada, _____⁵ New York, _____⁶ Québec et _____⁷ Saskatchewan. C'était (*It was*) super!

   B. **Voyage.** Hugo parle aussi de ses vacances. Il était au Canada. Avec votre camarade, jouez la scène suivante.

   HUGO: Moi, j'étais (*I was*) au Canada l'été dernier.
   ISABELLE: Ah oui? Où ça?
   HUGO: À Saint-Louis-du-Ha! Ha!, au Québec.
   ISABELLE: Saint…? Comment est-ce que ça s'écrit? (*How is it spelled?*)
   HUGO: S A I N T - L O U I S - D U - H A ! H A ! Ce n'est pas loin du lac Témiscouata dans le sud-est du Québec.
   ISABELLE: Ah! Je sais (*know*) comment ça s'écrit! S A I N T - L O U I S - D U - H A ! H A !
   HUGO: Exactement!

 Lecture

### Avant de lire

**Skimming for the gist.** Skimming is a useful way to approach any new text, particularly in a foreign language. You will usually find it easier to understand more difficult passages once you have a general idea of the content. At this point, you need not be concerned with understanding everything when reading authentic French texts. Just try to get the gist, then answer the questions that follow the reading to check your overall comprehension.

In the following article, glance at the title and headings. What kind of information do you think the text contains, and how is the information organized? Next, skim the article to get the impression of the major points. Do not attempt to understand every word. Then, read the sections that may have appeared most difficult when you skimmed the article, and guess the meaning based on the rest of the text.

**Un peu de pratique.** Parcourez rapidement le texte suivant, puis choisissez la ville qui correspond à la description.

1. C'est un centre culturel.
2. C'est le centre politique du Maroc.
3. C'est une ville située près du désert.

# Des vacances au Maroc

Prenez votre appareil photo et vos lunettes de soleil. Nous partons pour le Maroc en Afrique du Nord (au Maghreb*). Le Maroc est connu pour son climat exceptionnel et la variété de ses paysages. Villes impériales, oasis sahariennes, marchés extraordinaires: Oui, le Maroc a beaucoup de charme.

### À voir

#### Sur la côte: Casablanca et Rabat, les deux capitales

La ville de Casablanca est la capitale économique du pays. Au bord de l'océan Atlantique, on trouve la mosquée Hassan II, la troisième plus grande mosquée du monde. Quatre-vingt

**À propos de la lecture...**
Les auteurs de *Vis-à-vis* ont écrit ce texte.

---

*Le Maghreb est l'ensemble des pays du nord-ouest de l'Afrique, situés entre la Méditerranée et le Sahara, l'océan Atlantique et le désert de Libye.

La mosquée Hassan II à Casablanca

kilomètres[1] au nord se trouve la ville de Rabat, une des quatre villes impériales (avec Fès, Marrakech et Meknès) et la capitale administrative et politique du pays. Les anciens quartiers européens aux grandes avenues modernes contrastent avec la médina[2] et ses monuments.

### À l'intérieur: Fès, ville d'artisans

Fès est le centre culturel et spirituel du pays. Sa médina est la plus grande au monde avec plus de 9 000 ruelles[3] et de nombreux souks.[4] Les artisans travaillent, les marchands appellent les clients, il y a beaucoup de monde et beaucoup d'ambiance. Fès a une longue tradition de tannage du cuir,[5] d'art du bronze et de poterie bleue.

### Au sud: Marrakech et Ouarzazate, les portes du désert

Marrakech, surnommée «la ville rouge», est entourée par une muraille[6] rouge et ocre, et une palmeraie[7] de 100 000 arbres. À l'intérieur des remparts, il y a la médina avec ses charmants ryads.[8] Mais Marrakech est surtout célèbre pour sa Place Jemaa El Fna où on peut voir tous les jours des conteurs,[9] des acrobates, des musiciens et même des charmeurs de serpents.

Située aux portes du Sahara et près des montagnes, Ouarzazate attire de nombreux touristes avec son atmosphère sereine, ses kasbahs[10] et ses paysages extraordinaires. C'est aussi un endroit très populaire avec Hollywood: *La Dernière Tentation du Christ*, *Gladiateur*, *Lawrence d'Arabie*, et *La Momie* ont été tournés[11] dans la région.

La Place Jemaa El Fna à Marrakech

## À faire

### Le sport

Au bord de la mer: voile, planche à voile, ski nautique, plongée, pêche, etc.

Dans le désert: planche à sable dans les dunes et excursions à dos de dromadaire.

### Les festivals

Les nombreux festivals, en particulier le Festival des Musiques Sacrées du Monde à Fès, le Festival International du Film à Marrakech et la Fête des Roses dans la Vallée du Dadès.

[1]80 km = *about 50 miles*   [2]vieille ville arabe   [3]*alleys*   [4]marchés   [5]tannage… *tanning leather*   [6]*wall*   [7]*palm grove*   [8]*villas*   [9]*storytellers*   [10]quartier fortifié   [11]*filmed*

## À goûter

Le tajine, c'est le plat national du Maroc. On mange aussi du couscous (le repas traditionnel du vendredi), des pastillas (feuilletés[12] au pigeon) et des pâtisseries à base d'amandes, de noisettes[13] et de dattes. On boit souvent du thé à la menthe. Passez de bonnes vacances!

[12]*flaky pastries*  [13]*hazelnuts*

### Compréhension

**La destination de prédilection.** Des touristes organisent leur itinéraire. Quel endroit mentionné dans le texte intéresserait (*would interest*) les personnes suivantes?

1. M. Os est passionné par le travail des artisans.
2. M^me Langlois fait une enquête sur le système politique marocain.
3. M^me Léonie aime les paysages désertiques.
4. Les enfants de M. Roman adorent le cirque.
5. M^lle Négoce est une femme d'affaires qui veut créer une entreprise.

# Écriture

The writing activities **Par écrit** and **Journal intime** can be found in the Workbook/Laboratory Manual to accompany *Vis-à-vis*.

# Pour s'amuser

Dorothée est en vacances avec sa famille. Sa grand-mère lui téléphone:

—Alors, ces vacances, ça se passe bien?
—Génial!
—Que fais-tu?
—Rien!
—Et ton frère?
—Il m'aide!

# Le vidéoblog d'Hassan

## En bref

Dans cet épisode, Léa et Hassan consultent un site Web qui leur donne des renseignements (*information*) sur des échanges de logement au Québec, au Maroc et à la Martinique. Hassan évoque les activités touristiques à Paris.

## Vocabulaire en contexte

Où aimez-vous vous loger et qu'est-ce que vous aimez faire quand vous êtes en vacances? Indiquez vos préférences.

| **Logement** | **Activités** |
|---|---|
| ☐ une tente et un sac de couchage | ☐ bronzer à la plage |
| ☐ un appartement en ville | ☐ faire des randonnées et du rafting |
| ☐ une villa **au bord de la mer** (*at the seaside*) | ☐ aller dans des musées et des galeries d'art |
| ☐ un chalet à la montagne | ☐ faire de la pêche et de la plongée sous-marine |
| ☐ un hôtel somptueux dans une capitale **étrangère** (*foreign*) | ☐ **flâner** (*stroll*); observer la vie **quotidienne** (*everyday*) des gens |

Le Saute-Moutons brave les rapides de Lachine sur le fleuve Saint-Laurent près de Montréal.

## Note culturelle

Le Saute-Moutons est une des principales attractions de Montréal. Il consiste à embarquer de 40 à 50 de personnes pour une excursion à travers[1] les rapides de Lachine sur le fleuve Saint-Laurent. Le bateau-jet se lance à toute vitesse[2] dans les eaux agitées du fleuve avec parfois des virages[3] à 360 degrés. Manteau de pluie, bottes et gilet de sauvetage[4] sont indispensables pendant l'expédition.

[1]à… *through*  [2]se… *throws itself at top speed*  [3]*turns*  [4]gilet… *lifejacket*

## Visionnez!

Indiquez si les phrases suivantes sont vraies ou fausses.

1. _____ Léa cherche à faire un **échange** de logements.
2. _____ Hassan pense que l'échange de logements est une bonne formule.
3. _____ Le **vacancier** (*vacationer*) à Montréal a apprécié le mélange de sports et de culture.
4. _____ Le vacancier à Marrakech a apprécié les bains de mer.
5. _____ Le vacancier à la Martinique a apprécié la cuisine.

## Analysez!

1. Comment l'environnement—paysage (*landscape*) et climat—influence-t-il les activités de vacances proposées dans chaque pays?
2. Quels sont les avantages et les inconvénients de l'échange de logements?

## Comparez!

Regardez encore une fois les commentaires des trois vacanciers. Puis, proposez, dans un message éléctronique, un échange de logements à une personne qui habite dans un des trois lieux présentés dans la vidéo. Mentionnez les avantages de votre propre (*own*) domicile et de la ville où vous habitez.

# Vocabulaire

## Verbes

**acheter** to buy
**aller à la pêche** to go fishing
**bronzer** to get a suntan
**devenir** to become
**dormir** to sleep
**entrer** to enter
**faire une randonnée** to go hiking
**falloir (il faut)** to be necessary
**monter** to go up; to climb
**mourir** to die
**nager** to swim
**naître** to be born
**obtenir** to obtain, get
**oublier** to forget
**partir (à) (de)** to leave (for) (from)
**passer (par)** to pass (by)
**patiner** to skate
**prendre des vacances** to take a vacation
**quitter** to leave (*someone or someplace*)
**rentrer** to return; to go home
**retourner** to return; to go back
**revenir** to come back to, return (*someplace*)
**sentir** to feel; to sense; to smell
**servir** to serve
**sortir** to leave; to go out
**tomber** to fall
**venir** to come
   **venir de** + *inf.* to have just (*done something*)
**voyager** to travel

À REVOIR: **descendre, porter, pouvoir, rendre visite à, rester**

## Substantifs

**l'alpinisme** (*m.*) mountaineering
**le bateau (à voile)** (sail)boat
**la campagne** country(side)
**le camping** camping
**la carte d'identité** ID card
**le cheval** horse
**l'endroit** (*m.*) place
**l'équitation** (*f.*) horseback riding
**l'état** (*m.*) state
**le fleuve** (large) river
**la forêt** forest
**le lac** lake
**la mer** sea, ocean
**le monde** world
**la montagne** mountain
**le parapluie** umbrella
**le passeport** passport
**la plage** beach
**la planche à voile** windsurfing
**la plongée libre** snorkeling
**la plongée sous-marine** scuba diving
**la randonnée** hike
**la route** road
**le ski alpin** downhill skiing
   **...de fond** cross-country skiing
   **...nautique** waterskiing
**le vélo** bicycle
**le visa** visa

À REVOIR: **la carte postale, le pays, la promenade, les vacances** (*f. pl.*)

## Les vêtements et l'équipement sportifs

**l'anorak** (*m.*) (ski) jacket
**le casque** helmet
**les chaussures** (*f.*) **de ski** ski boots
   **...de montagne** hiking boots
**la crème solaire** suntan lotion
**l'écran** (*m.*) **solaire** sun block
**les gants** (*m.*) gloves
**les lunettes** (*f. pl.*) glasses
   **lunettes de ski** ski goggles
   **lunettes de soleil** sunglasses
**le sac de couchage** sleeping bag
**la serviette de plage** beach towel
**le ski** ski
**la tente** tent
**la valise** suitcase

À REVOIR: **la chaussure, le maillot de bain, la robe**

## Expressions temporelles

**les années (cinquante)** the decade (era) of (the fifties)
**il y a** ago

## Mots et expressions divers

**ensemble** together
**il faut** It is necessary to ...; One must ... / One needs ...
**Il ne faut pas** + *inf.* One must not ...
**même** same; even
**selon** according to

# Bienvenue...

## Un coup d'œil sur Tunis, en Tunisie

À quelques heures d'avion de New York, vous pouvez partir à la découverte de la Tunisie en Afrique du Nord. Le désert du Sahara constitue 40 % du territoire, mais il y a aussi 1298 km[1] de côtes qui bordent la Méditerranée. La ville principale est Tunis, la capitale du pays depuis 1159. Il faut absolument voir la médina, avec ses monuments, ses mosquées et ses souks. N'oubliez pas de négocier les prix si vous faites des achats dans ces petites rues remplies[2] de boutiques de tapis, de parfums, d'objets en cuir,[3] de poteries, et cetera. À l'ouest de la ville, visitez le Musée national du Bardo, un musée archéologique particulièrement riche en mosaïques romaines.

Un peu au nord de Tunis: Carthage et Sidi Bou Saïd. Ancienne puissance[4] maritime, commerciale et militaire, Carthage est détruite[5] puis reconstruite[6] par les Romains. Aujourd'hui, on peut admirer les ruines des villas romaines, de l'amphithéâtre et des thermes.[7] Le village de Sidi Bou Saïd est perché sur une falaise[8] dominant Carthage et le golfe de Tunis. Avec ses jolies maisons peintes en bleu et blanc, ses artistes et ses cafés, c'est un endroit pittoresque qui mérite le détour.

[1]1298 km = *806 miles*  [2]*filled*  [3]*leather*  [4]*power*  [5]*destroyed*  [6]*rebuilt*
[7]*Roman baths*  [8]*cliff*

Le minaret de la mosquée Zitouna à Tunis

## PORTRAIT Albert Memmi, le droit à la différence

Albert Memmi est né en 1920 à Tunis dans une famille juive de langue arabe. Au début du XX[1] siècle, la Tunisie est une colonie française majoritairement musulmane. Il existe des tensions entre les Musulmans et les Juifs, alors de nombreux Juifs tunisiens choisissent de s'assimiler à la culture coloniale française. Albert va donc au lycée français de Tunis. Pendant la Deuxième Guerre mondiale, à cause des lois antisémites du gouvernement de Vichy,* on l'envoie dans un camp de travail forcé. Après avoir retrouvé sa liberté, il poursuit des études de philosophie, devient enseignant et épouse une Française. Il s'installe à Paris après l'indépendance de la Tunisie et prend la nationalité française en 1973.

Ces expériences influencent ses œuvres. Ses deux romans les plus célèbres, *La Statue de sel* (1953) et *Agar* (1955), sont autobiographiques et explorent les thèmes de l'aliénation et des mariages mixtes. Memmi écrit aussi plusieurs livres sur le racisme et le colonialisme en Afrique, et des essais où il analyse les effets négatifs de la colonisation. Lauréat de plusieurs prix littéraires prestigieux, Albert Memmi est l'un des plus grands écrivains tunisiens de langue française.

L'écrivain Albert Memmi

[1]*vingtième*

*The Vichy regime refers to the French government proclaimed by Marshal Philippe Pétain following the military defeat of France. It collaborated with the Germans. Following the liberation of France, General Charles de Gaulle proclaimed a new government recognized by all the allies on October 23, 1944.

# en Afrique francophone

## Un coup d'œil sur Dakar, au Sénégal

Au Sénégal dont[1] elle est la capitale, Dakar est l'une des pointes[2] les plus avancées de l'Afrique de l'Ouest dans l'océan Atlantique. Les Dakarois vous accueillent toujours avec amitié, «teranga». Visitez avec eux le Marché Sandaga, près de la petite gare, et regardez partir les bateaux qui relient[3] Dakar à la Casamance ou à la Gambie voisines. Dans l'arrondissement du Plateau, vous voyez aussi l'Assemblée nationale et le Palais présidentiel.

Là-bas,[4] on voit dans l'océan l'Île de Gorée, ce joyau[5] de l'architecture coloniale avec ses petites rues et l'ombre[6] fraîche des bougainvillées. Mais, cet endroit tranquille cache[7] un passé terrible: le point de départ de la traite négrière[8] dès le XVI[9] siècle. La Maison des Esclaves résonne encore de la tragédie de femmes, enfants, hommes, transportés dans des conditions inhumaines vers les Antilles et les Amériques.

[1]*of which*   [2]*headlands*   [3]*link*   [4]*There*   [5]*jewel*   [6]*shade*   [7]*hides*
[8]traite... *slave trade*   [9]seizième

Voici Dakar sur sa péninsule.

## PORTRAIT Oumou Sy, la tradition et la modernité

Oumou Sy est née à Podor au nord du Sénégal. Autodidacte, elle ne sait ni lire ni écrire,[1] mais elle ouvre son premier atelier[2] de couture à l'âge de 14 ans. Créatrice de mode, costumière, femme d'affaires, activiste, elle habite aujourd'hui à Dakar. Dans ses collections de haute couture et de prêt-à-porter, elle allie les traditions africaines et la mode européenne. Elle travaille aussi dans le monde du spectacle, où elle crée des costumes pour des chanteurs sénégalais tels que[3] Youssou N'Dour et de grands cinéastes[4] africains comme Ousmane Sembène. En plus, c'est une femme engagée dans le développement de son pays: en 1990, elle ouvre une école chargée d'enseigner les arts traditionnels et modernes du costume et, en 1996, avec son mari, elle ouvre Metissacana, le premier cybercafé de l'Afrique de l'Ouest.

[1]ne... *can neither read nor write*   [2]*studio*   [3]*such as*   [4]*filmmakers*

Oumou Sy dans son atelier

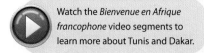

Watch the *Bienvenue en Afrique francophone* video segments to learn more about Tunis and Dakar.

# En route!

Les dossiers de Juliette

- Mes photos
  - En route en Provence
  - Je voyage en première classe
  - Le covoiturage

Juliette

En route parmi les champs de lavande en Provence

# Dans ce chapitre...

## OBJECTIFS COMMUNICATIFS

- ➤ talking about transportation
- ➤ expressing actions
- ➤ expressing how long, how long ago, and since when
- ➤ talking about the past
- ➤ expressing negation
- ➤ learning to distinguish between and pronounce selected sounds in French

Avec mon vélo, je voyage en première classe!

## PAROLES (Leçon 1)

- ➤ À l'aéroport
- ➤ À la gare
- ➤ En route!
- ➤ Les points cardinaux

## STRUCTURES (Leçons 2 et 3)

- ➤ Le verbe **conduire**
- ➤ **Depuis** et **pendant**
- ➤ Les adverbes affirmatifs et négatifs
- ➤ Les pronoms affirmatifs et négatifs

Le covoiturage: un système simple et sympathique

## CULTURE

- ➤ Le blog de Juliette: *La Rolls du vélo*\*
- ➤ Reportage: *Le covoiturage: quelle bonne idée!*
- ➤ Lecture: *Vélib' et Autolib': on innove dans les transports* (Leçon 4)

www.mhconnectfrench.com

\*In **Chapitres 9–12,** Juliette Graf creates a blog and writes about cycling in Paris, the everpresent technologies in Parisian life, the pleasures of living in a city, and her love of art.

# Leçon 1

## À l'aéroport

Air France Vol 512
à destination de New York

un avion — le pilote — le steward — l'hôtesse de l'air

Première classe — Classe affaires — Classe économique — un siège

une passagère

une carte d'embarquement — un passager

||||| *Allez-y!*

**Bienvenue à bord!** Complétez les phrases d'après le dessin.

1. Le _____ est le conducteur (*driver*) de l'avion.
2. L' _____ apporte les repas.
3. Les gens très riches voyagent en _____.
4. Le _____ sert les boissons.
5. On présente une _____ pour monter dans l'avion.
6. Les hommes et les femmes d'affaires voyagent en _____.
7. Les étudiants voyagent en _____.
8. Le départ du _____ 512 est à 13 h 50.

# À la gare

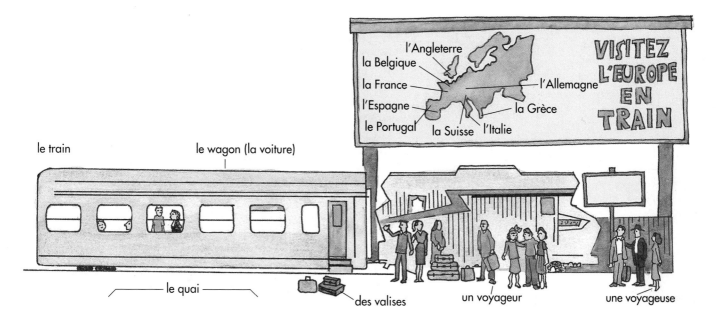

le train      le wagon (la voiture)

l'Angleterre
la Belgique
la France      l'Allemagne
l'Espagne
le Portugal   la Suisse   l'Italie     la Grèce

**VISITEZ L'EUROPE EN TRAIN**

— le quai —      des valises      un voyageur      une voyageuse

### AUTRES MOTS UTILES

| | |
|---|---|
| **un aller-retour** | round trip; round-trip ticket |
| **le billet** | ticket |
| **le compartiment** | compartment |
| **la couchette** | berth |
| **le guichet** | (ticket) window |

 *Allez-y!*

**A. Définitions.** Répondez, s'il vous plaît!

1. Quel moyen de transport est-ce qu'on trouve dans une gare?
2. Comment s'appelle chaque voiture d'un train?
3. Comment s'appellent les personnes qui voyagent?
4. Comment s'appelle la partie du wagon où les voyageurs sont assis (*seated*)?
5. Où est-ce que les voyageurs attendent l'arrivée d'un train?
6. Où est-ce qu'on achète les billets?

**B. Interview.** Demandez à un(e) camarade s'il / si elle a voyagé en train. Est-ce qu'il/elle a mangé dans un wagon-restaurant? Est-ce qu'il/elle a dormi dans un wagon-lit? Quelle ville est-ce qu'il/elle a visitée pendant ce voyage? À qui est-ce qu'il/elle a rendu visite? Ensuite, racontez à la classe le voyage de votre camarade.

**C. Train + Vélo.** Beaucoup de Français prennent leur vélo avec eux quand ils voyagent en train. Lisez la publicité de la SNCF (Société nationale des chemins de fer français), puis indiquez si les phrases suivantes sont vraies ou fausses.

1. _____ Il est facile de se balader en vélo quand on visite des régions de France.
2. _____ Il n'est pas possible de transporter son vélo dans le train quand on sort du territoire français.
3. _____ Pour voyager en train avec son vélo, il n'y a qu'une seule solution: le prendre avec soi à la gare le jour du départ.
4. _____ On peut laisser son vélo dans certaines gares pendant (*while*) qu'on travaille.
5. _____ On peut louer un vélo dans certaines gares.
6. _____ Toutes les gares de SNCF ont un parc à vélos.

# Train + Vélo

**P**artez avec votre bicyclette à la découverte de nouvelles balades en France comme à l'étranger, grâce à l'espace vélo aménagé par la SNCF à bord de nombreux trains Grandes Lignes (Corail et TGV). Vous pouvez également vous évader avec votre vélo en profitant d'un transport simple et rapide offert par les trains régionaux (TER et Transilien).

Et si vous désirez voyager plus léger, nous vous proposons notre service Bagages qui expédiera votre vélo là où vous le souhaitez.

Aller à la gare à vélo...
Une bonne façon de partir travailler tout en gardant la forme ! Pour faciliter vos déplacements quotidiens, la SNCF équipe ses gares de parcs à vélos et vous invite également à profiter des services proposés dans certaines gares par les Points Vélos : gardiennage, atelier de réparation, service de location...

À vous de choisir la formule qui vous correspond le mieux pour enfourcher votre bicyclette ! D'autant que cet exercice, bon pour la forme, l'est aussi pour l'environnement.

Source: SNCF, 2010

# En route!

Virgile conduit (*drives*)
sa **moto** avec prudence.

Agathe **roule** toujours très **vite.**
Elle préfère **l'autoroute**!

Marianne **fait le plein** d'**essence**
(*f.*) à **la station-service.**

Magali et Anne **traversent**
la France **à vélo.**

---

> ## Mots clés
>
> ### Les prépositions devant les moyens de transport
>
> **En** is used with means of transportation that you enter.
>
> > **en** autocar, **en** autobus, **en** avion, **en** bateau, **en** camion, **en** métro, **en** train, **en** voiture, et cetera
>
> **À** is used with means of transportation that you mount or on which you ride. It is also used in the expression **à pied.**
>
> > **à** bicyclette, **à** cheval, **à** moto, **à** vélo, et cetera

## ||||| *Allez-y!*

**A. Moyens de transport.** Comment vous rendez-vous à (*How do you get to*) votre destination dans les situations suivantes? Utilisez les **Mots clés** et les verbes **aller, voyager,** et cetera.

> **MODÈLE:** Vous voulez aller sur l'autre rive (*shore*) du lac. →
> Je voyage en bateau.

1. La classe fait une excursion.
2. Il y a des pistes cyclables (*bicycle paths*) dans votre ville.
3. Vous allez en Europe.
4. Vous voulez faire de l'équitation.
5. Vous aimez l'autoroute.
6. Votre famille déménage.
7. Vous voulez vous rendre vite au centre-ville.
8. Vous passez le week-end sur l'île Catalina.

**B. Interview.** Posez les questions suivantes à un(e) camarade.

1. Comment préfères-tu voyager en vacances? Pourquoi? Est-ce que ça dépend de ta destination?
2. Quels moyens de transport préfères-tu prendre en ville?
3. Nomme des moyens de transport qui correspondent à chacun des adjectifs suivants: **agréable, dangereux, économique, polluant, rapide.**
4. Est-ce qu'il y a des problèmes de transport dans ta ville ou ta région? Si oui, lesquels (*which ones*)?

# Les points cardinaux

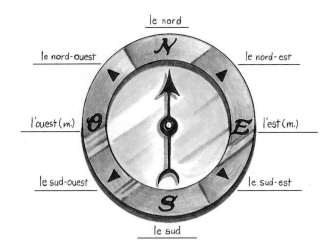

 ***Allez-y!***

**Quelques pays européens et leurs capitales.** Quel pays est situé dans chacune des régions mentionnées ici? Quelle est sa capitale? (Consultez la carte géographique de l'Europe à la fin de ce livre.)

MODÈLE: au sud-est de l'Italie →
La Grèce est située au sud-est de l'Italie. Capitale: Athènes.

| RÉGIONS | CAPITALES |
|---|---|
| 1. au nord-est de l'Espagne | Londres |
| 2. à l'est de la Belgique | Madrid |
| 3. au sud-ouest de la France | Bruxelles |
| 4. à l'ouest de l'Espagne | Berne |
| 5. au nord de la France | Berlin |
| 6. au sud-est de la France | Rome |
| 7. au nord de l'Italie | Lisbonne |
| 8. au nord-est de la France | Paris |

# Leçon 2

## Le verbe *conduire*

*Expressing Actions*

### Comment transporter une table?

*Léa et Hector discutent en voiture.*

LÉA: **Tu conduis** bien, Hector!

HECTOR: Tu es gentille. Juliette trouve que **je conduis** trop vite…

LÉA: Elle dit* aussi que **je conduis** mal!

HECTOR: En réalité, elle déteste la voiture: elle considère que **ça détruit** l'environnement.

LÉA: Elle a raison, mais les voitures polluantes, c'est bientôt fini: **on produit** maintenant des voitures hybrides. **Elles réduisent** les émissions de $CO_2$.

HECTOR: Elles sont écologiques!

LÉA: Voiture… métro… bus… train… Moi, je préfère le vélo comme Juliette.

HECTOR: Oui, mais pour transporter une table, ce n'est pas très pratique, n'est-ce pas, Léa!

*says

La voiture électrique: une réalité dans Paris

Complétez les phrases en utilisant les verbes du dialogue.

**1.** Tu _____ bien.
**2.** Je _____ trop vite.
**3.** Je _____ mal.
**4.** Les voitures polluantes, ça _____ l'environnement.
**5.** On _____ des voitures hybrides.
**6.** Elles _____ la pollution.

| PRESENT TENSE OF **conduire** (*to drive*) | | | |
|---|---|---|---|
| je | condu**is** | nous | condu**isons** |
| tu | condu**is** | vous | condu**isez** |
| il/elle/on | condu**it** | ils/elles | condu**isent** |

| *past participle:* **conduit** |
|---|

All verbs ending in **-uire** are conjugated like **conduire.**

**construire** *to construct*     Nous **construisons** une nouvelle ville.

### 🎧 Prononcez bien!

**The semivowel in *conduire***

French has three semivowels: [j] as in **trava<u>ill</u>er,** [w] as in **<u>voi</u>ture,** and [ɥ] as in **cond<u>ui</u>re.** These three sounds are pronounced very rapidly and are linked to the following vowel. To pronounce the sound [ɥ] in **cond<u>ui</u>re,** start from the [y] in **tu** (with your lips rounded and protruding, and your tongue all the way to the front, pressing against your lower teeth), and immediately pronounce the following vowel.

[ɥ]: **cond<u>ui</u>re, dep<u>ui</u>s, d<u>ue</u>l, s<u>ua</u>ve, b<u>ué</u>e** (*mist*)

| | |
|---|---|
| **détruire** *to destroy* | On **détruit** le vieux pour construire du neuf. |
| **produire** *to produce* | Le soleil **produit** de l'énergie. |
| **réduire** *to reduce* | **Réduisez** votre vitesse dans les zones scolaires. |
| **traduire** *to translate* | **Traduis** cette brochure en espagnol. |

In French, the verb **conduire** is used to express the physical act of driving. It is used with types of cars, ways of driving, and so on.

Sébastien **conduit** une Peugeot.          *Sébastien drives a Peugeot.*
Les jeunes **conduisent**          *Young people drive fast.*
rapidement.

However, the construction **aller en voiture** is used to express *to drive somewhere.*

Ils sont allés en Belgique          *They drove to Belgium.*
en voiture.

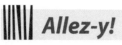

*Allez-y!*

**A.** **Sur la route.** Complétez le texte suivant sur les nouvelles voitures plus écologiques. Utilisez les éléments donnés.

1. ma vieille voiture / produire / trop de pollution
2. les gaz toxiques / détruire / l'environnement
3. nous / conduire / de nouveaux véhicules
4. ils / réduire / le niveau (*level*) de pollution
5. conduire (*impératif, vous*) / avec prudence

**B.** **Interview.** Posez les questions suivantes à un(e) camarade de classe. Ensuite, mentionnez le fait le plus intéressant à la classe.

1. Conduis-tu souvent? Quand tu sors avec des copains, conduisez-vous ou utilisez-vous les transports en commun?
2. Dans ta famille, qui conduit le plus (*the most*) souvent? Qui ne conduit pas?
3. Aimes-tu conduire? Quelle marque de voiture préfères-tu? Pourquoi? Préfères-tu les voitures américaines ou les voitures fabriquées à l'étranger (*abroad*)?
4. Penses-tu que les voitures détruisent la qualité de la vie en ville? Est-ce qu'on construit trop d'autoroutes aux États-Unis?
5. Qu'est-ce que tu penses des motos et des vélos?
6. As-tu déjà traversé les États-Unis en voiture? Si oui, quand et avec qui?

### Le parler jeune

| | |
|---|---|
| **une bagnole** | une voiture |
| **une bécane** | un vélo, une bicyclette, une moto |
| **une meule** | une moto, une mobylette |
| **une valoche** | une valise |

On peut monter à six dans ma **bagnole.**

Ma **bécane,** c'est une japonaise.

Regarde, elle est belle ma **meule,** hein?

Moi, je voyage léger: une seule **valoche!**

# *Depuis* et *pendant*

*Expressing How Long, How Long Ago, and Since When*

## Pendant les embouteillages

*Juliette et Hector discutent en voiture.*

JULIETTE: Tu conduis **depuis combien de temps,** Hector?

HECTOR: Je conduis **depuis sept ans**. J'adore les voitures!

JULIETTE: Pas moi... Je n'ai pas mon permis et je n'ai pas de voiture.

HECTOR: C'est pourtant pratique...

JULIETTE: Vraiment? Et qu'est-ce que tu fais **pendant** les embouteillages[1]? Tu danses?

HECTOR: **Pendant** les embouteillages, je chante[2]!

JULIETTE: Moi, je deviens folle.[3]

HECTOR: Fais comme moi. Chante!

[1]*traffic jams*   [2]*sing*   [3]*crazy*

Les objets indispensables du conducteur

Répondez aux questions en utilisant **depuis** et **pendant**.

**1.** Depuis combien de temps Hector conduit-il?
**2.** Que fait Hector pendant les embouteillages?
**3.** Que fait Juliette pendant les embouteillages?

## *Depuis*

**Depuis** is used with a verb in the present tense to talk about an activity that began in the past and continues in the present time. The most frequent English equivalent is *have been* + -*ing*.

**1.** With a starting point that can be a date (day, month, year) or a noun:

> **Depuis quand... ?** + *present tense*          = Since when . . . ?
> *present tense* + **depuis** + *starting point in the past* = . . . since . . .

| | |
|---|---|
| **Depuis quand** est-ce que tu conduis? | *Since when have you been driving?* |
| Je conduis **depuis** 2011. | *I have been driving since 2011.* |
| Je conduis plus lentement **depuis** mon accident. | *I have been driving more slowly since my accident.* |

**2.** To express a duration:

| | |
|---|---|
| **Depuis combien de temps... ?** + <br> *present tense* | = (For) How long . . . ? |
| *present tense* + **depuis** + *period of time* = . . . for (*duration*) | |

| | |
|---|---|
| **Depuis combien de temps** est-ce que vous prenez l'autobus? | (*For*) *How long have you been taking the bus?* |
| Je prends l'autobus **depuis** six mois. | *I have been taking the bus for six months.* |

[Allez-y! A-B-C]

## Pendant

**1.** **Pendant** expresses the duration of a habitual or repeated action, situation, or event with a definite beginning and end. It is often used with the **passé composé.**

| | |
|---|---|
| **Pendant combien de temps... ?** + <br> *present or past tense* | = (For) How long . . . ? |
| *present or past tense* + **pendant** + *time period* = . . . for (*duration*) | |

| | |
|---|---|
| **Pendant combien de temps** es-tu resté en Belgique? | (*For*) *How long did you stay in Belgium?* |
| Je suis resté en Belgique **pendant** deux semaines. | *I stayed in Belgium for two weeks.* |
| D'habitude, le matin, j'attends l'autobus **pendant** vingt minutes. | *Usually, in the morning, I wait for the bus for twenty minutes.* |

**2.** **Pendant** can also mean *during.*

| | |
|---|---|
| Qu'est-ce que tu as fait **pendant** ce temps? | *What did you do during this time?* |

Reminder: **Il y a** + *time period* = ago

| | |
|---|---|
| J'ai fait mes réservations **il y a** un mois. | *I made my reservations a month ago.* |

[Allez-y! B]

 **Allez-y!**

**A.** **Le temps passe.** Carole (C) et Thomas (T), deux étudiants étrangers à l'université de Lyon, parlent de leur vie en France. Avec un(e) camarade, à tour de rôle, posez les questions et répondez. Utilisez **depuis quand** ou **depuis combien de temps** selon l'indice.

> **MODÈLE:** (C) habiter / Europe (2012) →
> CAROLE: Depuis quand est-ce que tu habites en Europe?
> THOMAS: J'habite en Europe depuis 2012.

1. (T) travailler / Lyon (deux ans)
2. (C) faire / vélo (mon arrivée en France)
3. (T) étudier / cette université (un an)
4. (C) conduire (2010)
5. (T) être mariée (six mois)
6. (C) étudier l'informatique (l'automne dernier)

**B.** **Expressions de temps.** Thomas et Carole continuent leur conversation. Complétez les phrases suivantes en utilisant **depuis, pendant** ou **il y a.**

Thomas a rencontré sa femme Carole _____[1] les vacances. Aujourd'hui, ils sont mariés _____[2] trois ans. Ils aiment partir en voyage ensemble. _____[3] deux mois, Carole a fait un voyage en Tunisie sans Thomas. Elle est restée à Sousse _____ [4] trois semaines et Thomas lui a beaucoup manqué. Cet été, ils veulent aller en Belgique \_\_\_\_\_[5] deux semaines. Et ils veulent partir ensemble! Alors, _____ [6] deux jours, ils ont fait leurs réservations sur Internet. Ça n'a pas été facile. Ils ont comparé les prix. Ils ont cherché _____[7] plus de deux heures! Finalement, ils ont trouvé une formule «couple» pas chère. Et c'est fait: ils partent ensemble!

**C.** **Activités.** Demandez à vos camarades depuis quand ou depuis combien de temps ils/elles font les activités suivantes.

> **MODÈLE:** être étudiant(e) →
> —Depuis combien de temps est-ce que tu es étudiant(e)?
> —Je suis étudiant(e) depuis…

1. étudier le français
2. pratiquer son sport préféré
3. être à l'université
4. avoir son ordinateur
5. habiter à …
6. ?

### Un peu plus…

**En voiture.** Voyager en France est facile. Le système ferroviaire (les chemins de fer) et le système routier (les autoroutes) sont très développés. Les voitures en France sont souvent plus petites qu'en Amérique. Ceci facilite la circulation dans les rues étroites des villes médiévales, et la taille modeste des voitures leur permet de consommer moins d'essence, chose indispensable étant donné (*given*) le prix beaucoup plus élevé (*higher*) de l'essence en France. Il y a deux grandes marques de voiture fabriquées en France: PSA Peugeot Citroën et Renault. Quelle marque de voiture préférez-vous?

◄ *Sur la route, dans les environs de Saint-Rémy-de-Provence*

# Le blog de Juliette

## La Rolls du vélo

vendredi 10 juillet

Salut!

J'espère que vous allez aimer mon blog. Je viens de le créer et j'ai déjà une bonne nouvelle! Depuis longtemps, je rêve d'un vélo! Et voilà! Il est là, mon vélo neuf.[1] C'est un vélo hollandais, la Rolls du vélo: il est solide, élégant, écolo.[2] Regardez la photo!

Moi, j'ai toujours détesté les transports en commun.[3] Mais pendant deux ans—depuis que j'habite Paris—j'ai pris le bus ou le métro. Ces modes de transport ne sont pas très agréables: il y a trop de gens!

Au contraire, Paris à vélo, quel bonheur et quelle liberté! Cet après-midi, j'ai roulé pendant des heures du Quartier latin à La Villette, dans de petites rues, de grandes avenues et sur la piste cyclable du Canal Saint-Martin.

Mais rouler à Paris, c'est vraiment du sport! Ça monte et ça descend constamment! Pour aller à Montmartre, à la Montagne Sainte-Geneviève, à Belleville et Ménilmontant, il faut pédaler dur[4]! Alors, voilà une suggestion: pour faire du vélo à Paris, mangez des vitamines!

Juliette

Avec mon vélo, je voyage en première classe!

. . . . . . . . . . . . . . . . . . . . . . . . . . . . . . . . . . . . . . . . . . . . . . . . . . . . . . . . . . . . . . . . . . . .

## COMMENTAIRES

**Charlotte**
Le vélo, c'est un moyen de transport économique, agréable et excellent pour l'environnement. Mais c'est dangereux, non? Tu roules au milieu des voitures et des gaz toxiques… Tu risques un accident… Il faut porter un casque!

**Poema**
Moi, je suis une fan du Vélib'[5]! C'est pratique, pas cher et vraiment top.

**Mamadou**
Juliette, tu vas aller sur les Champs-Élysées pour l'arrivée du Tour de France le 23 juillet?

**Alexis**
Salut, Juliette
Moi aussi, j'ai un vélo. Des balades dans Paname,[6] ça t'intéresse? J'habite à Versailles, mais je peux mettre mon vélo dans le RER.

**Trésor**
Je veux venir!

[1]*new*  [2]*ecological (fam.)*  [3]transports… *public transportation*  [4]*hard*  [5]*a public bicycle rental program*
[6]*affectionate name for Paris*

## Le covoiturage: quelle bonne idée!

Qu'est-ce que le covoiturage? C'est une solution idéale pour réduire la circulation, contrôler la pollution, préserver les ressources naturelles et rencontrer de nouveaux amis. Le principe est simple: vous possédez une voiture. Quand vous faites un voyage, vous proposez d'emmener des gens avec vous en partageant la dépense.[1] Mais ces gens, vous ne les connaissez pas! Alors, comment faire pour leur communiquer votre itinéraire, vos conditions et votre prix?

Encore une fois, Internet nous donne la solution. Il y a, en France, de nombreux sites spécialisés dans le covoiturage. Le propriétaire d'une voiture publie une annonce sur le site et les personnes intéressées le contactent. C'est simple et sympathique.

Voici un exemple d'annonce:

Le covoiturage: un système simple et sympathique

---

**Paris → Lyon**

Prix: 25 euros/passager
Départ: jeudi 28 février, à 07 h 00.
Flexibilité horaire: +/− 15 minutes
Durée estimée: 4 h 30
Distance estimée: 480 km
Émissions estimées: 100 kg de $CO_2$
Cigarette: non

Animaux: non
Bagages: un petit sac
Lieu de rendez-vous: Métro Saint-Paul (75003)
Lieu de dépose:[2] Lyon, gare de la Part-Dieu.
Détours[3]: OK pour détour de 15 minutes si besoin.
Véhicule: Peugeot 507. Couleur: grise.
Confort: Normal

---

### La réputation du conducteur

Après un voyage, le conducteur est évalué par ses passagers: «Conducteur très agréable, prudent et sympathique» (11 févr. 2013); «Bon voyage, bon chauffeur, bonne compagnie» (22 nov. 2013); «Super voyage!!! Merci beaucoup, Brice!» (13 janvier 2014). Ces évaluations aident les futurs passagers à choisir un conducteur prudent, ponctuel et agréable.

### Dans toute l'Europe

Inauguré aux USA pendant la Deuxième Guerre[4] mondiale, quand l'essence était très chère, le covoiturage triomphe maintenant en Europe. Avec la crise économique, chaque individu cherche à contrôler ses dépenses. Le covoiturage signifie aussi qu'on limite le nombre des voitures: c'est bon pour l'environnement! Enfin, ce système de transport correspond, chez les Français, à un désir de partager et d'être ensemble.

[1]en... *by sharing expenses*   [2]lieu... *drop-off spot*   [3]*Side trips*   [4]*War*

---

**À vous!**

1. Quels sont les avantages et les inconvénients du covoiturage?
2. Comment trouve-t-on les passagers?
3. Comment est-ce que les passagers peuvent évaluer les conducteurs?
4. Faites-vous ou aimeriez-vous faire du covoiturage? Expliquez.

**Parlons-en!**

1. Préparez, avec toute la classe, le texte d'une annonce à publier sur un site Internet de covoiturage.
2. Travaillez à deux. Jouez le rôle du propriétaire (*owner*) de la voiture et d'une personne intéressée par l'annonce. Cette personne pose des questions bizarres et indiscrètes. Par exemple, est-ce vous êtes allergique aux chats? Vous êtes marié(e)? Le dialogue se déroule (*takes place*) au téléphone. Présentez-le devant vos camarades.

# Leçon 3

## Les adverbes affirmatifs et négatifs

*Expressing Negation*

### La pluie sur la tête

*Juliette contacte Charlotte, une amie, sur sa page Facebook (Messagerie instantanée).*

JULIETTE: Charlotte, le vélo ce n'est pas dangereux. Il faut simplement être prudent.

CHARLOTTE: Je **n'**ai **pas encore** adopté cette solution… J'hésite… On est vulnérable à bicyclette. Et je **n'**aime **pas du tout** recevoir la pluie sur la tête!

JULIETTE: Il **ne** pleut **pas toujours** à Genève! Quand il fait beau, le vélo c'est le bonheur*! Tu as **déjà** essayé?

CHARLOTTE: Non, **jamais**… Je prends **souvent** le bus et **parfois** la voiture.

JULIETTE: Et ton mari, comment est-ce qu'il va à son travail?

CHARLOTTE: Mon mari: il marche!

*happiness*

Trouvez, dans le dialogue, les réponses de Charlotte à ces questions.

1. Est-ce que tu as adopté la solution du vélo?
2. Est-ce que tu aimes recevoir la pluie sur la tête?
3. Est-ce qu'il pleut souvent à Genève?
4. Est-ce que tu as déjà essayé le vélo quand il fait beau?
5. Est-ce que tu prends le bus? la voiture?

The adverbs **toujours, souvent,** and **parfois** (*sometimes*) generally
follow the verb in the present tense. The expression **ne (n')... jamais,**
constructed like **ne... pas,** is the negative adverb (**l'adverbe de
négation**) equivalent to *never* in English.

Henri voyage **toujours** en train.* ⎫
Marie voyage **souvent** en train.* ⎬    Je **ne** voyage **jamais** en train.
Hélène voyage **parfois** en train. ⎭    *I never travel by train.*

Other common adverbs follow this pattern.

| AFFIRMATIVE | NEGATIVE |
|---|---|
| **encore** *still* | **ne (n')... plus** *no longer, no more* |
| Le train est **encore** sur le quai. | Le train **n'**est **plus** sur le quai. |
| *The train is still at the platform.* | *The train is no longer at the platform.* |
| **déjà** *already* | **ne (n')... pas encore** *not yet* |
| Nos valises sont **déjà** là? | Nos valises **ne** sont **pas encore** là. |
| *Are our suitcases there already?* | *Our suitcases aren't there yet.* |
| **déjà** *ever* | **ne... jamais** *never* |
| Est-ce que tu es **déjà** allé à Lyon? | Non, je **ne** suis **jamais** allé à Lyon. |
| *Have you ever been to Lyon?* | *No, I have never been to Lyon.* |

**1.** As with **ne (n')... pas,** the indefinite article and the partitive article
become **de (d')** when they follow negative adverbs.

| AFFIRMATIVE | NEGATIVE |
|---|---|
| Je vois **toujours des Américains** dans l'autocar. | Je **ne** vois **jamais de Français** dans l'autocar. |
| *I always see Americans on the tour bus.* | *I never see (any) French people on the tour bus.* |
| Avez-vous **encore des billets** à vendre? | Non, je **n'**ai **plus de billets** à vendre. |
| *Do you still have (some) tickets to sell?* | *No, I have no more (I don't have any more) tickets to sell.* |
| Karen a **déjà des amis** en France. | Vincent **n'**a **pas encore d'amis** aux États-Unis. |
| *Karen already has (some) friends in France.* | *Vincent doesn't have any friends in the United States yet.* |

**2.** Definite articles do not change.

Je ne vois jamais **le** contrôleur (*conductor*) dans ce train.
Anne ne prend plus **l'**autoroute pour aller à Caen.
On ne voit pas encore **le** sommet de la montagne.

**3.** In the **passé composé,** affirmative adverbs are generally placed
between the auxiliary and the past participle.

M. Huet a **toujours / souvent / parfois** pris l'avion.

---

*Sentences whose verbs are modified by **toujours** and **souvent** can also be negated by **ne
(n')... pas**: Henri ne voyage pas toujours en train. Il voyage parfois en avion. Marie
ne voyage pas souvent en train. Elle préfère conduire.

**4. Ne... pas du tout** is used instead of **ne... pas** for emphasis.

Je **n'**aime **pas du tout** les avions!    *I don't like planes at all!*

—As-tu faim?    *Are you hungry?*
—**Pas du tout!**    *Not at all!*

### Allez-y!

**A. Un voyageur nerveux.** Chaque fois qu'il part en vacances, M. Laffont se préoccupe de tout (*worries about everything*). M^me Laffont essaie toujours de le calmer (*calm him down*). Avec un(e) camarade, jouez les rôles de M. et M^me Laffont. Suivez le modèle.

**MODÈLE:**    M. LAFFONT: Tu n'as pas encore trouvé les valises.
      M^ME LAFFONT: Mais si!* J'ai déjà trouvé les valises.

1. Nous ne faisons jamais de voyages agréables.
2. Il n'y a plus de places dans le train.
3. Il n'y a plus de billets en seconde classe.
4. Nous ne sommes pas encore arrivés.
5. Il n'y a jamais de téléphone à la gare.
6. Il n'y a plus de voitures à louer.
7. Tu n'as pas encore trouvé la carte.
8. Nous ne sommes pas encore sur la bonne route (*the right road*).

**B. En voyage.** Dites ce que font ces personnes quand elles sont en voyage. Remplacez **seulement** par **ne... que.**

**MODÈLE:**    Je prends seulement le train. →
      Je ne prends que le train.

1. Martin envoie (*sends*) seulement des cartes postales.
2. Vous achetez seulement des souvenirs drôles.
3. Mes cousins mangent seulement dans les fast-foods.
4. Tu prends seulement une valise.
5. Nous dormons seulement dans des auberges de jeunesse.
6. Sophie regarde seulement les bateaux sur la mer.

**C. Préparatifs de voyage.** Quand vous partez en voyage, faites-vous les choses suivantes? Utilisez **toujours, souvent, parfois** ou **ne... jamais** dans vos réponses.

**MODÈLE:**    arriver à l'aéroport à la dernière minute →
      É1: Est-ce que tu arrives toujours à l'aéroport à la dernière minute?
      É2: Moi non, je n'arrive jamais à l'aéroport à la dernière minute! (J'arrive parfois à l'aéroport à la dernière minute.) Et toi?

1. oublier ton passeport (ton billet, ta carte de crédit... )
2. prendre ton appareil photo (un guide, une carte... )
3. acheter de nouveaux vêtements (de nouvelles chaussures, de nouvelles lunettes de soleil... )
4. tracer un itinéraire (à l'avance, au dernier moment... )
5. faire ta valise au dernier moment (la veille [*the day before*], une semaine avant... )

---

*Remember that **si** rather than **oui** is used to contradict a negative question or statement.

### Mots clés

**La négation *ne... que***

The expression **ne (n')... que (qu')** is used to indicate a limited quantity of something or a limitation of choices. It has the same meaning as **seulement** (*only*).

Je **n'**ai **qu'**un billet.
J'ai **seulement** un billet.
*I have only one ticket.*

Hélène **n'**a fait **que** deux réservations.
Hélène a fait **seulement** deux réservations.
*Hélène made only two reservations.*

**D. Voyages exotiques.** Interviewez vos camarades.

> MODÈLE: camper dans le Sahara
>> VOUS: N'as-tu jamais fait de camping dans le Sahara?
>> VOTRE CAMARADE: Non, je n'ai jamais fait de camping dans le Sahara. (*ou* Si, j'ai fait du camping dans le Sahara [l'été passé, il y a deux ans, et cetera].)

1. faire du bateau sur le Nil
2. voir le Sphinx en Égypte
3. faire une expédition en Antarctique
4. passer tes vacances à Tahiti
5. faire de l'alpinisme dans l'Himalaya
6. voir les chutes Victoria (*Victoria Falls*) en Afrique
7. faire un safari-photos au Cameroun
8. ?

Qui dans votre classe a fait le voyage le plus exotique?

# Les pronoms affirmatifs et négatifs

*Expressing Negation*

**La grève des transports**

*Léa et Juliette échangent des textos (SMS).*

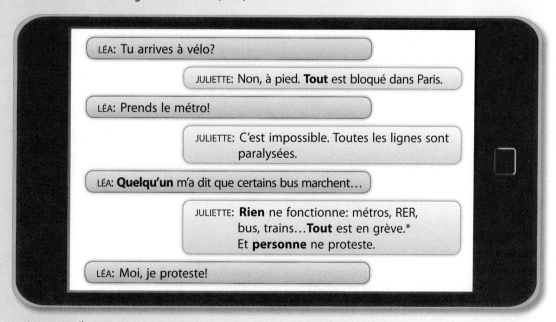

LÉA: Tu arrives à vélo?

JULIETTE: Non, à pied. **Tout** est bloqué dans Paris.

LÉA: Prends le métro!

JULIETTE: C'est impossible. Toutes les lignes sont paralysées.

LÉA: **Quelqu'un** m'a dit que certains bus marchent…

JULIETTE: **Rien** ne fonctionne: métros, RER, bus, trains…**Tout** est en grève.* Et **personne** ne proteste.

LÉA: Moi, je proteste!

*en… *on strike*

Répondez aux questions à l'aide des pronoms indéfinis du dialogue.

1. Qu'est-ce qui est bloqué dans Paris?
2. Qui a dit que certains bus marchent?
3. Qu'est-ce qui fonctionne?
4. Qu'est-ce qui est en grève?
5. Est-ce que les gens protestent?

Just as there are affirmative and negative adverbs (see pages 246–248), there are also affirmative and negative pronouns.

1. **Quelqu'un*** (*Someone*), **quelque chose** (*something*), **tout** (*everything, all*), and **tout le monde** (*everybody*) are indefinite pronouns (**des pronoms indéfinis**). All four can serve as the subject of a sentence, the object of a verb, or the object of a preposition.

**Personne** (*No one, nobody, not anybody*) and **rien** (*nothing, not anything*) are negative indefinite pronouns generally used in a construction with **ne** (**n'**). They can be the subject of a sentence, the object of a verb, or the object of a preposition.

🎧 **Prononcez bien!**

**The consonant sounds [p], [t], and [k]**

In English, these sounds are aspirated, that is, they are pronounced with a very noticeable puff of air. Hold your hand close to your mouth as you pronounce the English words *pat, tap,* and *cat*. When you pronounce the following French words, the puff of air should be considerably lighter: **pâtes, tape** (*v.* type), **quatre.** Holding your breath to minimize aspiration might help you until you feel more comfortable with these sounds. Notice the spellings of each sound.

[p]: **a**ppeler, **p**ersonne, **p**orte

[t]: a**tt**endre, sympa**th**ique, **t**out

[k]: **c**lasse, d'a**cc**ord, psy**ch**ologie, **qu**elqu'un, s**k**ier

| AFFIRMATIVE | NEGATIVE |
|---|---|
| **quelqu'un / tout le monde** | **personne** |
| **Quelqu'un** est monté dans le train. | **Personne** n'est monté dans le train. |
| *Someone got on the train.* | *No one got on the train.* |
| J'ai vu **quelqu'un** sur le quai. | Je **n'**ai vu **personne** sur le quai. |
| *I saw someone on the platform.* | *I didn't see anyone on the platform.* |
| Jacques a parlé avec **quelqu'un**. | Jacques **n'**a parlé avec **personne**. |
| *Jacques spoke with someone.* | *Jacques didn't speak with anyone.* |
| **Tout le monde** est prêt? | **Personne n'**est prêt. |
| *Is everyone ready?* | *No one is ready.* |

| AFFIRMATIVE | NEGATIVE |
|---|---|
| **quelque chose / tout** | **rien** |
| **Quelque chose** est arrivé. | **Rien n'**est arrivé. |
| *Something happened.* | *Nothing happened.* |
| Marie a acheté **quelque chose** de bizarre. | Marie **n'**a **rien** acheté de bizarre. |
| *Marie bought something strange.* | *Marie didn't buy anything strange.* |
| Je pense à **quelque chose** d'intéressant. | Je **ne** pense à **rien** d'intéressant. |
| *I'm thinking of something interesting.* | *I'm not thinking of anything interesting.* |
| **Tout** est possible. | **Rien n'**est impossible. |
| *Everything is possible.* | *Nothing is impossible.* |

2. As the object of a verb in the **passé composé, rien** precedes the past participle, whereas **personne** follows it.

| | |
|---|---|
| Marie **n'**a **rien** acheté au buffet de la gare. | *Marie didn't buy anything at the station restaurant.* |
| Je **n'**ai vu **personne**. | *I didn't see anyone.* |

[Allez-y! A–C]

———

*****Quelqu'un** is invariable in form: It can refer to both males and females.

3. Like **jamais, rien** and **personne** can be used without **ne** to answer a question.

|  |  |
|---|---|
| —Qu'est-ce qu'il y a sur la voie? | *What's on the track?* |
| —**Rien.** | *Nothing.* |
| —Qui est au guichet? | *Who's at the ticket counter?* |
| —**Personne.** | *Nobody.* |

4. You may have noticed that when used with adjectives, the expressions **quelque chose, quelqu'un, ne... rien,** and **ne... personne** are followed by **de (d')** plus the masculine singular form of the adjective.

|  |  |
|---|---|
| J'ai rencontré **quelqu'un d'intéressant** dans le compartiment d'à côté. | *I met someone interesting in the next compartment.* |
| Je **n'**ai parlé à **personne d'important.** | *I didn't speak to anyone important.* |

[Allez-y! B-C]

**Grammaire interactive**

For more on negative words, watch the corresponding Grammar Tutorial and take a brief practice quiz at **Connect French.**

McGraw Hill Education **connect** |FRENCH

www.mhconnectfrench.com

## Allez-y!

**A. À la gare.** Vous avez des ennuis avant de partir en voyage. Transformez les phrases suivantes.

MODÈLE: Tout le monde est prêt! ⟶ Personne n'est prêt!

1. Chloé demande l'heure du départ à quelqu'un.
2. Tout est prêt une heure avant le départ.
3. Quelqu'un a pensé à sortir les valises de la voiture sur le parking.
4. Quelqu'un a acheté les billets avant d'arriver sur le quai.
5. Thomas a quelque chose à porter s'il fait froid.
6. Mehdi a tout emporté pour prendre des photos.

**B. La vie en rose.** Transformez les phrases pessimistes de votre camarade. Suivez le modèle.

MODÈLE: Il n'y a personne à la caisse (*cash register*). ⟶
É1: Il n'y a personne à la caisse.
É2: Mais si! Il y a quelqu'un à la caisse.

1. Il n'y a personne dans ce restaurant.   2. Il n'y a rien de bon sur le menu.   3. Il n'y a rien dans ce magasin de sports.   4. Il n'y a rien de joli ici.   5. Il n'y a personne dans cette agence de voyages.   6. Il n'y a rien d'intéressant dans ces brochures.   7. Il n'y a rien de moderne dans ce quartier.   8. Il n'y a rien d'intéressant dans les rues.

**C. Trouvez quelqu'un...** Circulez dans la classe et trouvez quelqu'un qui a fait les choses suivantes. Avec un(e) camarade, posez les questions et répondez. (Attention à la question qu'il faut poser!)

1. prendre sa voiture pour aller au marché (hier)
2. avoir quelque chose d'important à faire (la semaine dernière)
3. voir quelqu'un d'intéressant (avant de venir en classe)
4. travailler jusqu'à une heure du matin (hier soir)
5. arriver en classe à 8 heures (ce matin)
6. finir tous les devoirs pour demain (déjà)

## 🎧 Prononcez bien!

1. **The semivowel in *conduire*** (page 239)

   A. **Louis.** Louis, le frère de votre colocataire Isabelle, va passer le week-end avec vous. Isabelle parle de lui (*him*). Pour chaque phrase que vous entendez, écrivez le mot qui contient le son [ɥ] comme dans *conduire*.

   1. _____   3. _____   5. _____   7. _____
   2. _____   4. _____   6. _____   8. _____

   B. **Révisions.** Vous révisez le vocabulaire pour votre prochain examen de français en utilisant les images ci-dessous. Avec votre camarade, identifiez à voix haute les choses représentées.

   1.

   4.

   7.

   2.

   5.

   8.

   3.

   6.

2. **The consonant sounds in [p], [t], and [k]** (page 250)

   **Dans l'avion.** Vous allez passer le week-end en Italie. Pendant le vol, vous entendez discuter les passagers devant vous. Avec votre camarade, jouez la scène. Mettez (*Put*) la main tout près de la bouche (*mouth*) pour faire bien attention à la prononciation des sons [p], [t], et [k].

   PASSAGER A: Tu as entendu? Le pilote est une femme. Elle s'appelle Caroline. Je pense qu'elle est québécoise: elle parle avec un accent canadien.
   PASSAGER B: Ah oui, je l'ai vue (*I saw her*). Elle est petite avec les cheveux courts sous sa casquette. Elle porte un tailleur kaki.
   PASSAGER A: Regarde! Les derniers passagers ont embarqué. On va bientôt partir.
   PASSAGER B: Oui. Dans quelques (*a few*) minutes, l'hôtesse de l'air va servir du café aux passagers. Tant mieux (*So much the better*)! Je suis encore un peu fatigué.

## Lecture

### *Avant de lire*

**Using background knowledge and knowledge of text type to predict content.** Before reading a new text, your general knowledge of the subject matter may help you anticipate important details. Sometimes the type or genre of a text can help you predict its content.

The text you will be reading contains information about two relatively new rideshare programs in France.

Look at the information below from the **Vélib'** website page entitled "**Comment ça marche?**" What can you already predict about the rest of the passage? How might **Autolib'** be different from **Vélib'**? Make a list of two things you will probably learn about each service.

### *Utiliser Vélib'*

Prendre un vélo dans une station, le déposer dans une autre. Vélib' est un système de location en libre-service simple à utiliser, disponible 24 heures sur 24 et 7 jours sur 7.

### *Retirer un vélo*

Pour louer un vélo, identifiez-vous sur la borne, accédez au menu et choisissez un vélo parmi ceux proposés sur l'écran.

GAGNEZ DU TEMPS ET ABONNEZ-VOUS À L'ANNÉE!

Grâce à la carte annuelle Vélib' et au passe NAVIGO©, vous pouvez retirer un vélo directement sur le point d'attache.

### *Restituer son vélo*

Une fois votre trajet terminé, accrochez le vélo sur un point d'attache libre dans n'importe quelle station Vélib'.

Attendez quelques instants, un signal sonore et un voyant lumineux vous confirmeront que le vélo a bien été restitué.

■

Now scan the following reading and look for this information. How accurate were your predictions?

PERSPECTIVES

## Vélib' et Autolib': on innove dans les transports

On les voit partout dans Paris: ce sont les Vélib' et les Autolib', ces bicyclettes et ces mini-voitures que chacun peut utiliser librement selon ses besoins, pour un coût[1] très raisonnable. L'idée, c'est de partager des bicyclettes et des voitures pour lutter[2] contre l'excès de trafic et contre la pollution. En adoptant ces moyens de transport, on fait une bonne action écologique et on économise de l'argent: voilà deux arguments irrésistibles!

## Vélib': Des vélos pour tout le monde

Vélib' est un système de location[3] de vélos en libre-service,[4] disponible[5] 24 heures sur 24 et 7 jours sur 7. Depuis 2007, plus de 20 000 vélos attendent leurs clients dans 1 500 stations. On les utilise dans la semaine pour aller au travail ou en cours, et le week-end pour se promener dans les rues de la capitale. Le fonctionnement du service est très simple: on prend un vélo dans une station, on va où on veut aller, et on dépose[6] le vélo dans une autre station.

Le vélo pour tous

## Autolib': Une voiture électrique dans la ville

L'Autolib' obéit au même principe. Depuis 2011, 1 800 mini-voitures électriques disposées dans des centaines[7] de stations proposent une alternative aux Parisiens qui n'aiment pas pédaler. Propre[8] et silencieuse, pratique et facile, l'Autolib' est une voiture sans défaut[9]! La voiture du futur! Elle permet de bouger en ville, d'aller en proche banlieue, de transporter facilement des enfants, des amis... ou des paquets! Et de faire des économies: avec Autolib', pas d'assurance,[10] pas d'entretien,[11] pas de parking!

Des petites voitures pour la ville

## Comment ça marche?

Pour accéder au service Vélib', on doit acheter un abonnement[12] annuel (29 euros) ou un ticket pour une journée, une semaine ou quelques jours. Dans tous les cas, les 30 premières minutes de chaque trajet[13] sont gratuites.[14] Ensuite, chaque demi-heure coûte à peu près un euro. Toutes les informations sur les prix sont données sur le site Vélib' de la Mairie de Paris. Pour Autolib', plusieurs tarifs et abonnements sont proposés sur leur site.

[1]cost  [2]fight  [3]rental  [4]en... self-service  [5]available  [6]drop off  [7]hundreds  [8]Clean  [9]fault  [10]insurance
[11]maintenance  [12]subscription  [13]trip  [14]free

### *Quelques critiques*

Le Vélib' et L'Autolib' sont aujourd'hui bien installés à Paris. Mais tout n'est pas encore parfait: d'abord, pourquoi ces vélos et ces voitures sont-ils gris? Pourquoi pas jaunes, verts ou bleus? Quel dommage! Les Français tellement attachés à l'esthétique détestent cette absence de couleur: «Ces vélos et ces voitures ressemblent à des tanks de la dernière guerre». Voilà ce qu'on entend! Certains utilisateurs reprochent aussi au Vélib' son poids: 22,5 kilos, c'est très lourd quand vous devez monter à Montmartre ou au parc des Buttes Chaumont! Quant aux[15] mini-voitures, elles sont souvent en panne[16] et les délais de réparation sont trop longs. «Simple défaut de jeunesse» répondent les fans!

[15]Quant... *As for* [16]*en... broken down*

---

### *Compréhension*

1. Qu'est-ce que le Vélib'? l'Autolib'?
2. Comment est-ce qu'on accède au service Vélib' ou au service Autolib'?
3. Quels sont les avantages du Vélib' et de l'Autolib'?
4. Que disent les critiques? À votre avis, est-ce que leurs objections sont valables? Expliquez.
5. Dans votre ville ou votre pays, est-ce qu'il y a des systèmes de location équivalents? Comparez-le(s) au système Vélib' et Autolib'.

# Écriture

The writing activities **Par écrit** and **Journal intime** can be found in the Workbook/Laboratory Manual to accompany *Vis-à-vis*.

---

# *Pour s'amuser*

Dans le train, le contrôleur parle à une vieille dame:

—Madame, votre billet est pour Bordeaux. Mais ce train va à Nantes!
—Ça c'est ennuyeux, proteste la voyageuse. Moi je vais à Bordeaux!...
Et le conducteur* se trompe souvent comme ça?

*driver, engineer*

# Le vidéoblog de Juliette

## En bref

Dans cet épisode, Juliette a rendez-vous avec Léa au jardin du Luxembourg; elle y arrive sur son nouveau vélo. Les deux amies veulent regarder l'arrivée du Tour de France—la célèbre course cycliste que Juliette décrit dans son vidéoblog.

## Vocabulaire en contexte

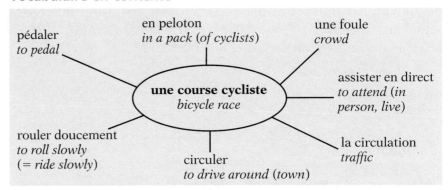

pédaler
*to pedal*

en peloton
*in a pack (of cyclists)*

une foule
*crowd*

**une course cycliste**
*bicycle race*

assister en direct
*to attend (in person, live)*

rouler doucement
*to roll slowly*
(= *ride slowly*)

circuler
*to drive around (town)*

la circulation
*traffic*

## Visionnez!

Indiquez si les phrases sont vraies ou fausses.

1. _____ Juliette va rouler à vélo au lieu d'utiliser (*instead of using*) les transports en commun.
2. _____ Juliette et Léa comptent (*plan on*) regarder l'arrivée du Tour de France ensemble.
3. _____ Juliette préfère regarder l'arrivée du Tour de France à la télé.
4. _____ Le Tour de France passe dans toute la France pendant quatre semaines.
5. _____ Le cycliste victorieux porte un maillot tricolore (bleu, blanc, rouge).

## Analysez!

Répondez aux questions suivantes.

1. L'arrivée à Paris du Tour de France est une grande fête populaire. Donnez des exemples.
2. Comment la ville de Paris se prépare-t-elle pour l'arrivée du Tour de France?

## Comparez!

Quel est l'événement sportif le plus prestigieux dans votre pays? Où et quand a-t-il lieu? Regardez encore une fois la partie culturelle de la vidéo: en France, le Tour de France est une grande fête populaire. Est-ce que c'est aussi le cas pour le grand événement sportif dans votre pays? Expliquez.

L'arrivée à Paris du Tour de France sur les Champs-Élysées

## Note culturelle

En France, le vélo urbain est un phénomène de société. Moyen de transport écologique, le vélo en libre-service triomphe à Paris avec le Vélib', à Lyon avec le Vélo'v, à Dijon avec le Vélodi, à Bordeaux avec V³, à Nice avec le Vélobleu. Toutes les villes de France adoptent ce système qui, pour un prix très bas, met à la disposition des habitants des milliers de vélos, 24 heures sur 24, 7 jours sur 7.

#  Vocabulaire

## Verbes

**conduire** to drive
**construire** to construct
**détruire** to destroy
**faire le plein** to fill it up
  (*gas tank*)
**produire** to produce
**réduire** to reduce
**rouler** to roll; to travel (*in a car,
  on a bike*)
**traduire** to translate
**traverser** to cross

À REVOIR: **partir, voyager**

## Substantifs

**l'aéroport** (*m.*) airport
**un aller-retour** round trip;
  round-trip ticket
**l'arrivée** (*f.*) arrival
**l'auberge** (*f.*) **de jeunesse** youth
  hostel
**l'autocar** (*m.*) interurban bus
**l'autoroute** (*f.*) highway
**l'avion** (*m.*) airplane
**le billet** ticket
**le camion** truck
**la carte d'embarquement**
  boarding pass
**la classe affaires** business class
**la classe économique** tourist
  class
**le coffre** trunk
**le compartiment** compartment
**le conducteur / la
  conductrice** driver
**la consigne (automatique)** coin
  locker
**la couchette** berth
**le départ** departure
**la deuxième classe** second class

**l'ennui** (*m.*) problem, trouble
**l'essence** (*f.*) gasoline
**la gare** train station
**le guichet** (ticket) window
**l'hôtesse** (*f.*) **de l'air** stewardess
**le métro** subway
**la moto(cyclette)** motorcycle
**le moyen de transport** means of
  transportation
**le passager / la passagère**
  passenger
**le pilote** pilot
**la première classe** first class
**le quai** platform (*at the train
  station*)
**le siège** seat
**la station-service** service station
**le steward** steward
**le train** train
**le vol** flight
**le wagon** train car

À REVOIR: **l'endroit** (*m.*)**, l'état**
  (*m.*)**, la fois, le monde, le
  pays, la semaine, la valise,
  la voiture**

## Expressions affirmatives
## et négatives

**déjà** already; ever
**encore** still
**ne... jamais** never
**ne... pas du tout** not at all
**ne... pas encore** not yet
**ne... personne** no one, nobody
**ne... plus** no longer
**ne... que** only
**ne... rien** nothing
**parfois** sometimes
**quelque chose** something
**quelqu'un** someone
**seulement** only

**tout** everything
**tout le monde** everybody,
  everyone

## Les points cardinaux

**l'est** (*m.*) east
**le nord** north
**le nord-est** northeast
**le nord-ouest** northwest
**l'ouest** (*m.*) west
**le sud** south
**le sud-est** southeast
**le sud-ouest** southwest

## Mots et expressions divers

**à** by; on (*bicycle, horseback, foot*)
**à destination de** to, for
**à l'est / l'ouest** to the east / the
  west
**à l'étranger** abroad, in a foreign
  country
**à l'heure** on time
**à pied** on foot
**à velo** by bike
**au nord / sud** to the north / south
**depuis** since, for
  **Depuis combien de temps... ?**
    (For) How long . . . ?
  **Depuis quand... ?** Since
    when . . . ?
  **en** in; by (*train, plane, bus*)
  **pendant** for; during
    **Pendant combien de
      temps... ?** (For) How
      long . . . ?
**si** yes (*response to a negative
  question*)
**vite** quickly

# Comment communiquez-vous?

**Les dossiers de Juliette**

Juliette

➤ 📁 Mes photos
   ➤ 📁 Wi-Fi à la gare du Nord
   ➤ 📁 J'adore mes gadgets!
   ➤ 📁 Vive le SMS!

La gare du Nord à Paris: Partout où on va, on est connecté.

## Dans ce chapitre...

J'adore mes gadgets!

### OBJECTIFS COMMUNICATIFS

- ➤ talking about communication, the media, and modern technology
- ➤ describing the past
- ➤ speaking succinctly
- ➤ expressing observations and beliefs
- ➤ learning to distinguish between and pronounce selected sounds in French

### PAROLES (Leçon 1)

- ➤ Les nouvelles technologies
- ➤ Les médias et la communication
- ➤ Quelques verbes de communication

Vive le SMS!

### STRUCTURES (Leçons 2 et 3)

- ➤ L'imparfait
- ➤ Les pronoms d'objet direct
- ➤ L'accord du participe passé
- ➤ Les verbes **voir, croire** et **recevoir**

### CULTURE

- ➤ Le blog de Juliette: *Ordinateur, mon amour!*
- ➤ Reportage: *Les accros du texto*
- ➤ Lecture: *Rencontres en ligne: rendez-vous avec le bonheur* (Leçon 4)

connect
|FRENCH
www.mhconnectfrench.com

# Leçon 1

## Les nouvelles technologies

Qu'est-ce que vous voulez comme cadeau (*m.*) (*gift*)?

un smartphone

un appareil (photo)
numérique

un caméscope

un iPod, un mp3

le moniteur, l'écran (*m.*)

le clavier — la souris

un ordinateur de bureau,
un micro (micro-ordinateur)

un ordinateur portable
(un portable)

une imprimante

un scanner

une liseuse
un livre numérique

**AUTRES MOTS UTILES**

| | |
|---|---|
| **cliquer sur** | to click on |
| **une connexion ADSL** | DSL connection/line |
| **le courriel, le mél** | e-mail message |
| **le fichier** | file |
| **Internet** (*m.*) **(sur Internet)** | Internet (on the Internet) |
| **le logiciel** | software (program) |
| **le navigateur** | browser |
| **un photocopieur** | photocopy machine |
| **le site** | site |
| **surfer sur le Web** | to surf the web |
| **une tablette** | tablet computer |
| **télécharger** | to download |
| **le traitement de texte** | word processing |
| **le Web** | (World Wide) Web |
| **le Wi-Fi** | Wi-Fi, wireless (connection) |

 **Allez-y!**

**Définitions.** Regardez les illustrations et la liste de vocabulaire et trouvez le mot qui correspond à chaque définition. Faites une phrase avec **C'est un(e)...**

1. C'est un appareil qui vous permet d'imprimer vos fichiers.
2. C'est un appareil qu'on utilise pour faire des films.
3. C'est un appareil qui nous permet d'écouter notre musique préférée.
4. Ce sont deux machines qu'on peut utiliser pour copier une image.
5. C'est un message écrit sur l'ordinateur.
6. Avec ces appareils, on prend des photos.
7. Avec ces appareils, on peut regarder des vidéos sur un écran.
8. On fait cette action si on reçoit (*receives*) un fichier avec un mél.
9. Avec ces appareils, on peut lire un livre numérique.
10. Avec ce service, on surfe très vite (*fast*) sur le Web.

# Les médias et la communication

**1.** Nous écrivons (*write*) et nous envoyons*...

une carte postale — une adresse — un timbre — (La Poste) — une enveloppe — une lettre — un colis — un fax — le courrier — une boîte aux lettres

Où est la dame sur l'illustration? Qu'est-ce qu'il y a, en général, sur une enveloppe? Où se trouve la boîte aux lettres? Que fait-on quand on a besoin d'une copie d'un document tout de suite. Qu'est-ce qu'on envoie souvent pendant les vacances? Si vous envoyez un cadeau à quelqu'un, qu'est-ce que vous envoyez?

---

*The conjugation of **écrire** (*to write*) is presented on page 265. The present-tense conjugation of **envoyer** (*to send*) is **j'envoie, tu envoies, il/elle/on envoie, nous envoyons, vous envoyez, ils/elles envoient.**

**2.** Nous lisons (*read*)*...

**AUTRES MOTS UTILES**

**les petites annonces** (*f.*)        classified ads
**un roman**                           novel

Où est-ce qu'on va pour acheter des journaux? Où se trouvent (*are found*) les petites annonces? Pour quelles raisons est-ce qu'on lit les petites annonces?

**3.** Nous parlons...

**AUTRES MOTS UTILES**

| | |
|---|---|
| **l'annuaire** (*m.*) **électronique** | online telephone directory |
| **appeler**‡ | to call |
| **la boîte vocale** | voice mail |
| **composer le numéro** | to dial the number |
| **consulter l'annuaire électronique** | to look up (a phone number) in the online directory |
| **envoyer un SMS, un texto** | to send a text message |

Comment est-ce qu'on cherche les numéros de téléphone? Qu'est-ce qu'on fait pour appeler un ami? Que dit la personne qui répond? Qu'est-ce qu'on fait si on veut envoyer un message court (*short*)?

---

*The conjugation of **lire** is presented on page 265.
†**Une revue** is generally a monthly publication of a scholarly or informational nature; **un magazine,** on the other hand, contains articles on a wide variety of topics and has many photographs and advertisements.
‡The present-tense conjugation of **appeler** (*to call*) is **j'appelle, tu appelles, il/elle/on appelle, nous appelons, vous appelez, ils/elles appellent. Appeler** takes a direct object: **Il appelle sa petite amie.**

**4.** Nous écoutons et nous regardons...

le journal télévisé,
les informations (*f. pl.*)

une retransmission sportive

un documentaire

une émission de musique

un jeu télévisé

une publicité

**AUTRES MOTS UTILES**

| | |
|---|---|
| **le câble** | cable television |
| **une chaîne** | television channel; network |
| **un DVD (des DVD)** | DVD |
| **une émission de télé réalité** | reality show |
| **un feuilleton** | soap opera |
| **un lecteur de DVD** | DVD player |
| **une série télévisée** | serial drama |
| **une télécommande** | remote control |
| **la télévision satellite** | satellite television |
| **la TNT (télévision numérique terrestre)** | high-definition television |

Aimez-vous les émissions de musique classique? les retransmissions
sportives? les documentaires? les séries humoristiques? Regardez-vous
régulièrement le journal télévisé? Que pensez-vous des publicités?
Préférez-vous regarder un film ou une émission télévisée? Pourquoi?
Utilisez-vous souvent la télécommande?

**Les nouvelles technologies et la communication.** Posez les questions suivantes à un(e) ou plusieurs camarades.

1. Tu as un ordinateur? Est-ce un portable ou un ordinateur de bureau? Est-ce que tu as ton propre (*own*) site Web? Que fais-tu sur le Web? En général, qu'est-ce que tu fais sur ton ordinateur?
2. Est-ce que tu préfères télécharger des films et les regarder chez toi ou aller au cinéma? Explique.
3. Est-ce que tu as un iPod / un mp3? Décris-le.
4. Tu as un caméscope? Si oui, qu'est-ce que tu aimes filmer?
5. Vas-tu souvent à la poste? Pourquoi (pas)?
6. Quels journaux, magazines ou revues achètes-tu régulièrement?
7. Tu as une ligne fixe et un mobile / un téléphone portable ou un smartphone? Quelles technologies de communication sont indispensables pour toi? Explique.
8. Que fais-tu si tu veux contacter une personne qui n'est pas chez elle (*at home*)? Que fais-tu quand elle est chez elle?
9. Préfères-tu la télé ou Internet? Explique.
10. Quelle est ton émission préférée à la télé? Pourquoi?

# Quelques verbes de communication

dire bonjour

lire le journal

écrire un mél / un courriel

mettre une lettre à la boîte

| dire<br>*(to say; to tell)* | lire<br>*(to read)* | écrire<br>*(to write)* | mettre<br>*(to place; to put)* |
|---|---|---|---|
| je **dis** | je **lis** | j' **écris** | je **mets** |
| tu **dis** | tu **lis** | tu **écris** | tu **mets** |
| il/elle/on **dit** | il/elle/on **lit** | il/elle/on **écrit** | il/elle/on **met** |
| nous **disons** | nous **lisons** | nous **écrivons** | nous **mettons** |
| vous **dites** | vous **lisez** | vous **écrivez** | vous **mettez** |
| ils/elles **disent** | ils/elles **lisent** | ils/elles **écrivent** | ils/elles **mettent** |
| *Past participle:* **dit** | **lu** | **écrit** | **mis** |

Another verb conjugated like **écrire** is **décrire** (*to describe*). **Mettre** can also be used to mean *to put on* (*clothing*). **Mettre le couvert** means *to set the table*. **Mettre une lettre (une carte) à la poste** means *to mail a letter (card)*.

 **Allez-y!**

**A. Message aux parents.** Vous racontez à un(e) camarade ce que vous mettez dans le mél que vous écrivez à vos parents. Complétez les phrases avec les verbes **décrire, dire, écrire** et **lire,** au présent. Faites tous les changements nécessaires.

Cet après-midi, je/j' _____[1] un long mél à mes parents. Dans mon mél, je _____[2] mes cours et ma vie à l'université. Je donne aussi beaucoup de détails sur mes camarades et mes professeurs parce que mes parents sont très curieux. Ils sont aussi très compréhensifs (*understanding*) et je leur _____[3] toujours la vérité quand j'ai des problèmes. Avant de l'envoyer, je _____[4] mon message une dernière fois (*last time*).

Racontez la même histoire, mais cette fois remplacez **je** par **mon (ma) camarade de chambre,** puis par **Stéphanie et Albane.** Faites tous les changements nécessaires.

**B. Interview.** Posez les questions suivantes à un(e) camarade, puis inversez les rôles.

1. Est-ce que tu écris souvent des lettres ou des cartes postales? À qui écris-tu? D'habitude, pour donner de tes nouvelles à tes amis, préfères-tu écrire un texto, un mél ou préfères-tu téléphoner ou contacter les gens sur Facebook?
2. Est-ce que tu aimes lire? Lis-tu le journal tous les jours? Si oui, lequel? As-tu déjà cherché un appartement dans les petites annonces? Quel(s) magazine(s) achètes-tu régulièrement? As-tu lu un bon livre récemment? Quel est le titre de ce livre? Préfères-tu lire des livres papier ou des livres numériques? As-tu une liseuse?
3. Est-ce que tu regardes la télévision tous les soirs? Quelles émissions préfères-tu? Que penses-tu de la télévision américaine? À ton avis, y a-t-il trop de publicité à la télévision?

D'après ses réponses, que pouvez-vous dire de votre camarade et de ses goûts?

# Leçon 2

## L'imparfait

*Describing the Past*

### Une enfant de l'Internet

*Appel vidéo entre Charlotte et Juliette.*

CHARLOTTE: Tu aimes la technologie?

JULIETTE: Beaucoup! Je prépare un Master[1] multimédia interactif à la Sorbonne.

CHARLOTTE: **Tu avais** un ordinateur quand **tu étais** petite?

JULIETTE: Moi non, mais mon père **possédait** un Mac.

CHARLOTTE: **Tu naviguais** sur le Web?

JULIETTE: Pas exactement! **Je regardais** des films, **je dessinais,**[2] **je faisais** des puzzles, **j'écoutais** des chansons.[3]

CHARLOTTE: **Tu étais** déjà une enfant de l'Internet!

▼ AUDIO & VIDEO

MESSAGE    VIDEO ●

[1]*2-year professional degree*  [2]*drew*  [3]*songs*

*Vrai ou faux? Corrigez les phrases fausses.*

**Quand Juliette était petite...**

1. elle avait un ordinateur.
2. son père possédait un PC.
3. elle naviguait sur le Web.
4. elle ne faisait rien sur Internet.
5. elle était déjà une enfant de l'Internet.

You are already familiar with one past tense in French: the **passé composé,** used to relate events that began and ended in the past. In contrast, the **imparfait** (*imperfect*) is used to describe continuous, repeated, or habitual past actions or situations.* It is also used in descriptions.

The **imparfait** has several equivalents in English. For example:

$$\textbf{Je parlais.} \quad \begin{cases} \textit{I talked.} \\ \textit{I was talking.} \\ \textit{I used to talk.} \\ \textit{I would talk.} \end{cases}$$

---

*You will learn more about the differences between the **passé composé** and the **imparfait** in **Chapitre 11, Leçon 2.**

## Formation of the *imparfait*

The formation of the **imparfait** is identical for all French verbs except **être.** To find the regular imperfect stem, drop the **-ons** ending from the present-tense **nous** form. Then add the imperfect endings.

nous parlǿn̸s̸    **parl-**      nous vendǿn̸s̸    **vend-**
nous finissǿn̸s̸  **finiss-**    nous avǿn̸s̸      **av-**

| IMPARFAIT OF **parler** | | | |
|---|---|---|---|
| je | parl**ais** | nous | parl**ions** |
| tu | parl**ais** | vous | parl**iez** |
| il/elle/on | parl**ait** | ils/elles | parl**aient** |

J'**allais** au bureau de poste tous les matins.

*I used to go to the post office every morning.*

Mon grand-père **disait** toujours: «L'excès en tout est un défaut.»

*My grandfather always used to say, "Moderation in all things."*

Quand j'**habitais** avec les Huet, je **mettais** souvent la table.

*When I lived with the Huets, I would often set the table.*

1. Verbs with an imperfect stem that ends in **-i** (**étudier: étudi-**) have a double **i** in the first- and second-person plural of the **imparfait: nous étudiions, vous étudiiez.** The **ii** is pronounced as a lengthened *i* sound, to distinguish the **imparfait** from the present-tense forms **nous étudions** and **vous étudiez.**
2. Verbs with stems ending in **-c** or **-g** have a spelling change when the **imparfait** endings start with **a: je mangeais, nous mangions; elle commençait, nous commencions.** In this way, the pronunciation of the stem is preserved.
3. The verb **être** has an irregular stem in the **imparfait: ét-.** The endings, however, are regular.

| IMPARFAIT OF **être** | | | |
|---|---|---|---|
| j' | **étais** | nous | **étions** |
| tu | **étais** | vous | **étiez** |
| il/elle/on | **était** | ils/elles | **étaient** |

Quand tu **étais** petit, tu aimais bien lire les contes de ma mère l'Oye.

*When you were little, you liked to read Mother Goose stories.*

J'**étais** très heureux quand j'habitais à Paris.

*I was very happy when I lived in Paris.*

À Paris, j'allais au bureau de poste tous les jours pour envoyer des cartes postales. Est-ce que vous envoyez des cartes postales quand vous voyagez ou est-ce que vous envoyez des photos et des MMS avec votre smartphone?

## Uses of the *imparfait*

In general, the **imparfait** is used to describe actions or situations that existed for an indefinite period of time in the past. There is usually no mention of the beginning or end of the event. The **imparfait** is used in the following situations.

**1.** In descriptions, to set a scene:

| | |
|---|---|
| C'**était** une nuit tranquille à Paris. Il **pleuvait** et il **faisait** froid. M. Cartier **lisait** le journal. M^me Cartier **regardait** la télévision. | *It was a quiet night in Paris. It was raining and (it was) cold. Mr. Cartier was reading the newspaper. Mrs. Cartier was watching television.* |

**2.** For habitual or repeated actions:

| | |
|---|---|
| Quand j'étais jeune, j'**allais** chez mes grands-parents tous les dimanches. Nous **faisions** de belles promenades. | *When I was young, I went to my grandparents' home every Sunday. We would take (used to take) lovely walks.* |

**3.** To describe feelings and mental states:

| | |
|---|---|
| Cécile **était** très heureuse— elle **avait** envie de chanter. | *Cécile was very happy—she felt like singing.* |

**4.** To tell the time of day, the date, and to express age in the past:

| | |
|---|---|
| C'était un samedi. Il **était** cinq heures et demie du matin. C'était son anniversaire; il **avait** 12 ans. | *It was a Saturday. It was 5:30 A.M. It was his birthday; he was 12 years old.* |

**5.** To describe appearance and physical traits:

| | |
|---|---|
| Le suspect **portait** un jean; il **avait** les cheveux blonds et les yeux verts. | *The suspect was wearing jeans; he had blond hair and green eyes.* |

**6.** To describe an action or situation that was happening when another event (usually in the **passé composé**) interrupted it:

Emmanuel **lisait** le journal quand le téléphone a sonné.

*Emmanuel was reading the paper when the phone rang.*

 *Allez-y!*

**A. Sorties.** L'an dernier, vous sortiez régulièrement avec vos amis. Faites des phrases complètes selon le modèle.

**MODÈLE:** dîner ensemble → Nous dînions ensemble.

**1.** jouer au tennis   **2.** prendre un café   **3.** faire des promenades l'après-midi   **4.** pique-niquer à la campagne   **5.** aller en boîte tous les week-ends   **6.** partir en vacances ensemble

**B. Souvenirs d'enfance.** Qui dans votre famille faisait les choses suivantes quand vous étiez petit(e)?
**Expressions utiles:** mes parents, mon frère / ma sœur, mon meilleur ami / ma meilleure amie et moi

**1.** Qui lisait le journal tous les matins?   **2.** Qui regardait la télévision après le dîner?   **3.** Qui aimait écouter la radio le matin?   **4.** Qui faisait beaucoup de sport?   **5.** Qui étudiait tous les après-midis?

**C. Avant la télévision.** Marc demande à son arrière-grand-mère (*great grandmother*) Isabelle de parler de sa jeunesse (*youth*). Complétez la conversation avec les verbes appropriés à l'imparfait.

MARC: Est-ce que tu _____¹ la télé tous les soirs quand tu _____² jeune?

ISABELLE: Mais non, il n'y _____³ pas de télévision!

MARC: Et alors, qu'est-ce que vous _____⁴ chaque soir?

ISABELLE: D'habitude, nous _____⁵ la radio. Mais moi, j' _____⁶ lire pendant que (*while*) mon frère _____⁷ du piano.

MARC: Dis donc, la vie n' _____⁸ pas très intéressante en ce temps-là.

ISABELLE: Ce n'est pas vrai. En général, nous _____⁹ très heureux. Toute la famille _____¹⁰ du temps ensemble. Tous les dimanches, nous _____¹¹ chez mes grands-parents et après le déjeuner nous _____¹² au cinéma ou au parc. Aujourd'hui, il est difficile de trouver du temps pour partager des activités.

aimer
aller
avoir
déjeuner
écouter
être (×3)
faire
jouer
passer
regarder

**D. Conversation.** Posez les questions suivantes à un(e) camarade. En 2005...

**1.** Quel âge avais-tu?   **2.** Habitais-tu à la campagne, dans une petite ville ou dans une grande ville? Avec qui habitais-tu?   **3.** Comment était ta maison ou ton appartement?   **4.** Étais-tu bon(ne) élève (*pupil*)? Aimais-tu tes instituteurs (*teachers*)?   **5.** Où passais-tu tes vacances?   **6.** Faisais-tu du sport?

Maintenant racontez à la classe ce que votre camarade faisait en 2005.

**E. Mon enfance.** D'abord, posez les questions suivantes (et encore d'autres) à un(e) camarade. Ensuite, trouvez quelque chose que vous avez en commun avec ce (cette) camarade et une chose que vous n'avez pas en commun.

1. Quand tu étais petit(e), est-ce que tu voyais beaucoup de films? Quels films est-ce que tu aimais surtout (*especially*)? Avec qui est-ce que tu allais au cinéma?
2. Qu'est-ce que tu regardais à la télé? Quelles étaient tes émissions préférées? Jusqu'à quelle heure est-ce que tu pouvais regarder la télé?
3. Tu lisais beaucoup? Quels livres est-ce que tu aimais? Quelles bandes dessinées (*comic strips*)? Quand est-ce que tu lisais?

# Les pronoms d'objet direct

*Speaking Succinctly*

## Nos jouets technologiques

*Dans le magasin Apple du Carrousel du Louvre, Juliette et Hector discutent.*

HECTOR: Regarde Juliette, le nouvel iPhone! Tu **le** trouves joli?

JULIETTE: Je **le** trouve pas mal. Mais il n'a rien d'exceptionnel. Je préfère le modèle de Samsung.

HECTOR: Pas moi. Quand tu **le** mets dans ta poche,[1] il est trop grand.

JULIETTE: Qu'est-ce que tu penses[2] de cette tablette? Je **la** trouve futuriste.

HECTOR: Elle est belle mais trop chère... Smartphones, tablettes, ordinateurs: tu **les** achètes et ils sont obsolètes trois mois après.

JULIETTE: Et alors?

HECTOR: Et alors, c'est décourageant.[3]

Le magasin Apple du Carrousel du Louvre à Paris

[1]*pocket* [2]*think* [3]*discouraging*

Trouvez dans le dialogue les mots remplacés par le pronom d'objet direct.

1. Hector le trouve joli.
2. Juliette le trouve pas mal.
3. Quand on le met dans sa poche, il est trop grand.
4. Juliette la trouve futuriste.
5. On les achète et ils sont obsolètes trois mois après.

Direct objects are nouns that receive the action of a verb. They usually answer the question *what?* or *whom?* For example, in the sentence *Malik reads the text message.* The noun *text message* is the direct object of the verb *reads*.

Direct object pronouns (**les pronoms complément d'objet direct**) replace direct object nouns: Malik *reads it.*

| | |
|---|---|
| J'aime bien mon ordinateur. Je **l'**utilise tous les jours. | *I like my computer. I use it every day.* |
| J'ai écrit ce texto hier: Je **l'**ai envoyé tout de suite. | *I wrote this text yesterday. I sent it right away.* |

## Forms and Position of Direct Object Pronouns

| DIRECT OBJECT PRONOUNS | | | |
|---|---|---|---|
| **me (m')** | *me* | **nous** | *us* |
| **te (t')** | *you* | **vous** | *you* |
| **le (l')** | *him, it* | **les** | *them* |
| **la (l')** | *her, it* | | |

1. Usually, French direct object pronouns immediately precede the verb in the present and the imperfect tenses and the auxiliary verb in the **passé composé.**

   Malik lit **le texto.**  
   Malik **le** lit.

   Malik lisait **le texto.**  
   Malik **le** lisait.

   Malik a lu **le texto.**  
   Malik **l'**a lu.

2. Third-person direct object pronouns agree in gender and in number with the nouns they replace.

   | | |
   |---|---|
   | —Est-ce que Robin lisait **le journal**? | *Was Robin reading the newspaper?* |
   | —Oui, il **le** lisait. | *Yes, he was reading it.* |
   | —Vois-tu **ma mère?** | *Do you see my mother?* |
   | —Oui, je **la** vois. | *Yes, I see her.* |
   | —Est-ce que vous postez **ces lettres**? | *Are you mailing these letters?* |
   | —Oui, je **les** poste. | *Yes, I'm mailing them.* |

3. If the verb following the direct object pronoun begins with a vowel sound, the direct object pronouns **me, te, le,** and **la** become **m', t',** and **l'.**

   | | |
   |---|---|
   | J'achète la carte postale. Je **l'**achète. | *I'm buying the postcard. I'm buying it.* |
   | Isabelle **t'**admirait. Elle ne **m'**admirait pas. | *Isabelle used to admire you. She didn't admire me.* |
   | Nous avons lu le journal. Nous **l'**avons lu. | *We read the newspaper. We read it.* |

**Grammaire interactive**

For more on direct object pronouns, watch the corresponding Grammar Tutorial and take a brief practice quiz at **Connect French.**

**|FRENCH**

**www.mhconnectfrench.com**

**4.** If the direct object pronoun is the object of an infinitive, it is placed immediately before the infinitive.

| | |
|---|---|
| Alexandra va **poster la lettre** demain. | *Alexandra is going to mail the letter tomorow.* |
| Alexandra va **la poster** demain. | *Alexandra is going to mail it tomorrow.* |
| Elle allait **la poster.** Elle est allée **la poster.** | *She was going to mail it. She went to mail it.* |

**5.** In a negative sentence, the direct object pronoun always immediately precedes the verb to which it refers.

| | |
|---|---|
| Nous ne regardons pas **la télévision.** Nous ne **la** regardons pas. | *We don't watch TV. We don't watch it.* |
| Je ne vais pas acheter **les billets.** Je ne vais pas **les** acheter. | *I'm not going to buy the tickets. I'm not going to buy them.* |
| Elle n'est pas allée chercher **le journal.** Elle n'est pas allée **le** chercher. | *She did not go to get the newspaper. She did not go to get it.* |

**6.** Direct object pronouns also precede **voici** and **voilà**.

| | |
|---|---|
| **Le** voici! | *Here he (it) is!* |
| **Me** voilà! | *Here I am!* |

## Le parler jeune

| | |
|---|---|
| **une bafouille** | une lettre |
| **les infos** | les informations, les actualités |
| **un ordi** | un ordinateur |
| **la pub** | la publicité |
| **tchatcher** | parler |

Je viens de recevoir une petite **bafouille** d'Anna.

Moi, je regarde les **infos** sur TF1.

Mon **ordi** commence à être fatigué.

J'adore la **pub**!

Magali **tchatche** pendant des heures au téléphone.

## Allez-y!

**A. Eurêka!** Suivez le modèle.

**MODÈLE:** Je cherche le bureau de poste. → Le voilà. (*ou* Le voici.)

1. Où est mon portable?
2. Elle a perdu le numéro de téléphone.
3. Où est le téléphone?
4. Il cherche le kiosque.
5. Il a envie de lire *Le Monde* d'hier.
6. Avez-vous le journal?
7. Où est l'adresse des Thibaudeau?
8. J'ai besoin de la grande enveloppe blanche.
9. Où sont les toilettes?
10. Aïcha et Nathan, où êtes-vous?

**B. De quoi parlent-ils?** Vous êtes dans un café parisien et vous entendez les phrases suivantes. Trouvez dans la colonne de droite l'information qui correspond à chaque pronom.

1. Je vais les poster cet après-midi.
2. Elle le consulte.
3. Je l'écris sur l'enveloppe.
4. Nous venons de la lire.
5. Je les achète à la poste.
6. Je l'ai déjà composé.

a. l'adresse
b. les lettres
c. le numéro
d. l'annuaire électronique
e. la revue
f. les timbres

**C. Projets de voyage.** Luca et Philippe font toujours la même chose. Avec un(e) camarade, parlez de leurs projets selon le modèle.

**MODÈLE:** étudier le français cette année →
É1: Est-ce que Luca va étudier le français cette année?
É2: Oui, et Philippe va l'étudier aussi.

1. apprendre le français très rapidement
2. prendre l'avion pour Paris en juin
3. lire les journaux le matin
4. admirer la vue du haut de la tour Eiffel
5. prendre ses repas dans de bons restaurants
6. regarder les gens sur les Champs-Élysées
7. essayer de lire les romans de Flaubert

Maintenant imaginez que Luca est l'opposé de Philippe.

**MODÈLE:** É1: Est-ce que Luca va étudier le français cette année?
É2: Oui, mais Philippe, il ne va pas l'étudier.

*Le Figaro,* un petit café crème: un après-midi parisien. Lisez-vous un journal? Quel journal? Quand le lisez-vous?

**D. Interview.** Interviewez un(e) camarade de classe sur ses préférences. Votre camarade doit utiliser un pronom complément d'objet direct dans sa réponse.

1. Utilises-tu souvent ton portable / ton mobile?
2. Appelles-tu souvent tes camarades de classe? tes professeurs? tes parents?
3. Est-ce que tes parents t'appellent souvent? tes amis?
4. Regardes-tu souvent la télé?
5. Aimes-tu regarder la publicité?
6. Préfères-tu apprendre les nouvelles dans le journal ou à la radio? à la télé ou sur Internet?
7. Lis-tu les bandes dessinées?
8. Tu utilises souvent Internet pour faire des recherches? pour faire des achats?

# Le blog de Juliette

## Ordinateur, mon amour!

jeudi 18 juin

Salut tout le monde!

Je vous pose une question: «Peut-on vivre aujourd'hui sans ordinateur?»

Ma réponse est NON. Sans mon ordinateur, je suis comme un poisson hors de[1] l'eau. Je meurs[2]!

J'adore mes gadgets!

Avec mon ordinateur, je fais tout: je travaille, j'étudie, je lis, j'écris. Je surfe sur le Web, je lis la presse, je participe à des forums, et, bien sûr, j'écris mon blog! En plus, chaque jour, je reçois[3] et j'envoie des dizaines de courriels, je regarde des films et j'écoute de la musique. Donc, mon ordinateur, c'est mon oxygène.

Pour vous montrer une image exacte de mon univers technologique, je vais vous faire une confession: je vis scotchée[4] à mon smartphone. Je suis la championne des SMS et des textos; j'appelle mes amis cent fois par jour (Léa, 50 fois!).

Chez moi, j'ai une télé, un ordinateur portable avec la Wi-Fi, une imprimante, un appareil photo numérique, un iPod, et, pour Noël, mes parents m'ont offert une tablette! Bon, vous avez compris: je suis une technophile.

Mais j'ai une excuse: la technologie, c'est mon univers! Je prépare un Master multimédia à la Sorbonne.

Juliette

. . . . . . . . . . . . . . . . . . . . . . . . . . . . . . . . . . . . . . . . . . . . . . . . . . . . . . . . . . . . . . . . . . .

COMMENTAIRES

**Poema**

Est-ce qu'il te reste du temps pour rêver et pour ne rien faire?

**Alexis**

Tu massacres la langue française avec des textos? Tu me déçois,[5] Juliette…

**Charlotte**

Nos parents, ils n'avaient pas tous ces gadgets technologiques et ils étaient très heureux! Mais j'apprécie ton blog Juliette, et je le lis régulièrement.

**Mamadou**

Quand j'étais petit, au Sénégal, on avait rarement la télévision; le téléphone était réservé aux riches; on rêvait de posséder un ordinateur. Aujourd'hui, l'Afrique est entrée dans la société de l'information, comme nous tous.

[1]hors… *out(side) of*  [2]*am dying*  [3]*receive*  [4]vis… *live glued (slang)*  [5]me… *disappoint me*

## LES ACCROS° DU TEXTO

°fanatics

Qu'est-ce qu'un accro du texto? C'est un individu, souvent jeune, qui passe son temps à envoyer des textos (SMS), petits textes de 160 caractères maximum. Seul ou en compagnie, en famille, avec des amis, en classe, au travail, à la maison, dans le métro, dans le bus, l'accro du texto vit en intimité avec son téléphone. Il est encouragé par les offres des opérateurs téléphonie mobile[1] (Free, Orange, SFR et Bouygues) qui proposent des formules «textos illimités». Comment résister dans ces conditions?

En France, SMS (*Short Message Service*) est très populaire parmi les utilisateurs des portables.

### Le portable: un inséparable compagnon

Sophie, 17 ans, explique: «J'envoie des messages 24 heures sur 24. Le matin je me lève, j'envoie des messages. Sous la douche, aux WC, pendant que je m'habille, je pianote.[2] Je textote[3] partout, matin, midi, soir, nuit, tout le temps. Oui, je me sens dépendante de mon téléphone, totalement». Sa copine Justine ajoute: «C'est vital pour moi. Dans le bus, dans le train, à la boulangerie, j'échange 12 000 SMS par mois… Non, non, je n'exagère pas; c'est la vérité!»

Caricature? Absolument pas! Car l'accro du texto n'a pas de limites. Il écrit vite et utilise des abréviations. Pour lui, l'orthographe, la ponctuation, la grammaire et les accents ne sont pas importants: «mwa je lach jamè mn port chui akro je lè 24h/24 è 7j/7!!» (Moi, je ne lâche[4] jamais mon portable, je suis accro, je l'ai 24 h sur 24 et 7 jours sur 7); «mon portable c toute ma vie si je lé pa partou ou je vé je meur» (Mon portable, c'est toute ma vie; si je ne l'ai pas partout où je vais, je meurs[5]).

### Des mini-messages tellement pratiques!

On doit reconnaître que, dans la vie de tous les jours, les SMS sont très pratiques. Un bref message et tout est dit: on donne un rendez-vous («K penses-tu du resto VIRGILE, vers 20 h? Confirme SVP!»), on avertit[6] qu'on est en retard («trafic +++; j'arrive dans 10 mn»), on donne son avis («C trop top!»), on envoie des félicitations («Congrats pour ton job!»)… Dans les grandes occasions, ils sont indispensables. Pour le Nouvel An, par exemple, les accros ont échangé, cette année, plus de 500 millions de textos! Et détail important, les SMS transmettent aux amoureux des messages enflammés: «Tu é le soleil ki illumine ma vie» (Tu es le soleil qui illumine ma vie); «Je taiiimeee!!!!! » (je t'aime).

[1]opérateurs… *cellphone service providers*  [2]*type clumsily*  [3]*text (fam.)*  [4]*part with*  [5]*die*  [6]*lets (someone) know*

**À vous!**

1. Décrivez «un accro du texto» typique, selon l'évocation du *Reportage*. Donnez au moins (*at least*) trois caractéristiques.
2. Dans quels endroits est-ce que les accros aiment échanger leurs messages?
3. Quels sont les caractéristiques du langage des SMS?
4. Quels sont les avantages et les inconvénients des textos?

Travaillez en petits groupes et répondez aux questions suivantes.

**Parlons-en!**

1. Qui possède un smartphone?
2. Comment communiquez-vous? Par SMS, MMS, Tweet, mél, téléphone? Avec Facebook, BBIM (Blackboard Messagerie instantanée), Skype?
3. Comparez vos habitudes et expliquez vos préférences.

Qui est l'accro le/la plus fanatique de la classe?

# Leçon 3

## L'accord du participe passé

*Talking About the Past*

### Facile!

*Juliette et Charlotte discutent sur la page Facebook de Juliette.*

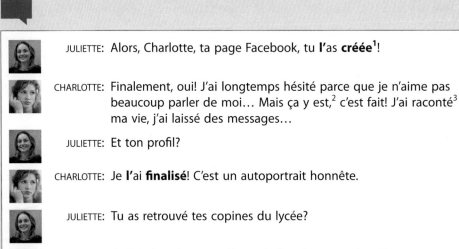

JULIETTE: Alors, Charlotte, ta page Facebook, tu l'as **créée**[1]!

CHARLOTTE: Finalement, oui! J'ai longtemps hésité parce que je n'aime pas beaucoup parler de moi… Mais ça y est,[2] c'est fait! J'ai raconté[3] ma vie, j'ai laissé des messages…

JULIETTE: Et ton profil?

CHARLOTTE: Je l'ai **finalisé**! C'est un autoportrait honnête.

JULIETTE: Tu as retrouvé tes copines du lycée?

CHARLOTTE: Oui! Je **les** ai **retrouvées** et je **les** ai **contactées**. Nous avons échangé des photos.

JULIETTE: Tu **les** as **reconnues**[4] sur les photos?

CHARLOTTE: Je **les** ai toutes **identifiées**. Finalement nous n'avons pas tellement[5] changé… Nous sommes toujours[6] jeunes et belles!

[1]*created*  [2]*ça… there it is*  [3]*told about*  [4]*recognized*  [5]*so much*  [6]*still*

Complétez les réponses aux questions suivantes en utilisant les formes verbales du dialogue.

1. Charlotte a créé sa page Facebook? Oui, …
2. Elle a finalisé son profil? Oui, …
3. Elle a retrouvé ses copines du lycée? Oui, …
4. Elle a contacté ses copines? Oui, …
5. Elle a reconnu et identifié ses copines sur les photos? Oui, …

In the **passé composé,** the past participle is generally used in its basic form. However, when a direct object—noun or pronoun—precedes the auxiliary verb **avoir** plus the past participle, the participle agrees with the preceding direct object in gender and number.

J'ai lu le **journal.**

Je **l'**ai **lu.**

J'ai lu **la revue.**

Je **l'**ai **lue.**

Quels **amis** avez-vous
**appelés?**

J'ai lu les **journaux.**

Je **les** ai **lus.**

J'ai lu les **revues.**

Je **les** ai **lues.**

Quelles **émissions** avez-vous
**regardées?**

 **Allez-y!**

**A. Un nouveau travail.** Vous travaillez comme assistant administratif / assistante administrative. Votre patronne (*boss*) vous pose des questions. Répondez à la forme affirmative ou négative.

**MODÈLE:** Avez-vous regardé *le calendrier* ce matin? →
Oui, je l'ai regardé. (Non, je ne l'ai pas regardé.)

1. Est-ce que vous avez donné *notre numéro de téléphone* à M^me Milaud?
2. Est-ce que vous avez mis *le nouveau nom de la firme* sur les enveloppes?
3. Avez-vous contacté *la responsable de notre Comité de Direction*?
4. Avez-vous fini *le rapport*?
5. Avez-vous appelé *Georges Dupic et Catherine Duriez*?
6. Avez-vous vu *Anne et Clémentine* ce matin?
7. *M'*avez-vous comprise pendant la réunion (*meeting*) hier?

**B. Conversation.** Posez les questions suivantes à un(e) camarade. Il/elle utilise, quand c'est possible, un pronom complément d'objet direct dans ses réponses.

1. Quand tu étais enfant, aimais-tu l'école? les vacances? les voyages? l'aventure? Quelle sorte d'aventure aimais-tu?
2. L'année dernière, as-tu passé tes vacances à la montagne? à l'étranger? en famille?
3. As-tu déjà essayé le camping? l'alpinisme? le bateau? le ski?
4. As-tu lu le dernier numéro de *Time*? de *People*? de *Sports Illustrated*? de *L'Express*?
5. As-tu lu les romans d'Albert Camus? les livres de Saint-Exupéry?
6. Quand as-tu appelé tes grands-parents? tes parents? ton professeur de francais? Pourquoi?

# Les verbes *voir, croire* et *recevoir*

*Expressing Observations and Beliefs*

## Être ou ne pas être matérialiste

*Hassan téléphone à Juliette.*

HASSAN: **Tu crois** qu'Hector* a finalement acheté un iPad?

JULIETTE: Non, **je** ne **crois** pas. Il n'est pas un grand consommateur[1] de technologies.

HASSAN: Pourtant[2] il a un ordinateur. **Il reçoit** et il envoie vingt courriels par jour!

JULIETTE: C'est vrai, mais il est satisfait avec sa vieille machine. **Il** ne **voit** pas l'intérêt de dépenser[3] de l'argent pour une tablette…

HASSAN: Hector est un artiste… Il n'est pas matérialiste…

JULIETTE: **Tu crois** ça? Tu ignores certainement qu'il adore les voitures de luxe!

[1]*consumer*  [2]*Nevertheless*  [3]*spend*

Un peu bling-bling: la voiture préférée d'Hector!

Trouvez, dans le dialogue, les phrases où…

1. Hassan demande si Hector a acheté un iPad.
2. Juliette suggère qu'Hector n'a pas acheté d'iPad.
3. Hassan explique qu'Hector utilise la messagerie de son ordinateur.
4. Juliette explique qu'Hector n'aime pas dépenser de l'argent pour la technologie.
5. Juliette révèle qu'Hector est matérialiste.

The verbs **voir** (*to see*) and **croire** (*to believe*) are irregular.

| voir | | croire | |
|---|---|---|---|
| je **vois** | nous **voyons** | je **crois** | nous **croyons** |
| tu **vois** | vous **voyez** | tu **crois** | vous **croyez** |
| il/elle/on **voit** | ils/elles **voient** | il/elle/on **croit** | ils/elles **croient** |
| *Past participle:* **vu** | | *Past participle:* **cru** | |

*Croire and **voir** must be followed by **que** (*that*) when they introduce another clause.

| | |
|---|---|
| J'**ai vu** Michèle à la plage la semaine passée. | *I saw Michèle at the beach last week.* |
| Est-ce que tu **crois** cette histoire? | *Do you believe this story?* |
| Je **crois** qu'il va faire beau demain. | *I think the weather is going to be fine tomorrow.* |
| Tu **crois?** | *You think so? / Are you sure?* |

**1. Revoir** (*to see again*) is conjugated like **voir.**

| | |
|---|---|
| Je **revois** les Moreau. | *I'm seeing the Moreau family again.* |

**2. Croire à** means *to believe in* a concept or an idea.

| | |
|---|---|
| Nous **croyons à** la chance. | *We believe in luck.* |
| Ils **croient au** Père Noël. | *They believe in Santa Claus.* |

**3. Croire en** means *to believe in* a god or to have confidence in someone.

| | |
|---|---|
| Vous **croyez en** Dieu? | *Do you believe in God?* |

**4. Croire que** means *to think* (*that*), *to believe* (*that*) and is followed by another clause. It is used to express an opinion.

| | |
|---|---|
| Je **crois qu'**Internet est la grande invention du XX$^e$ siècle. | *I think (that) the Internet is the great invention of the 20th century.* |

**Note:** The verb **recevoir** (*to receive; to entertain as guests*) is also irregular. The conjugation is similar to the verb **voir** in the singular forms, but differs in the plural forms.

| recevoir | | | |
|---|---|---|---|
| je | **reçois** | nous | **recevons** |
| tu | **reçois** | vous | **recevez** |
| il/elle/on | **reçoit** | ils/elles | **reçoivent** |
| *Past participle*: **reçu** | | | |

Elle **reçoit** beaucoup de textos tous les jours.

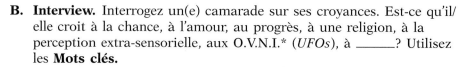

**Allez-y!**

## Mots clés

**Marquer une hésitation ou une pause**

| | |
|---|---|
| **Eh bien,...** | *Well, . . .* |
| **Voyons,...** | *Let's see, . . .* |
| **C'est-à-dire que...** | *That is / I mean . . .* |
| **Euh...** | *Uhmm . . .* |
| **Oui, mais...** | *Yes, but . . .* |

**A. Paris dans le brouillard** (*fog*). Trois étudiants étrangers sont désorientés. Complétez la conversation avec les verbes **croire** et **voir** au présent, sauf quand le passé composé est indiqué.

JULIE: Tu _____¹ où on est?

KANI: Non, je ne _____² pas cette rue sur le plan.

WAN QING: Vous faites confiance à ce vieux plan?

JULIE: Non, nous _____³ ce que nous a dit Anne, le guide.

KANI: Elle a beaucoup d'expérience et je _____⁴ ce qu'elle dit.

WAN QING: Moi, je pense qu'elle _____⁵ à la chance!

JULIE: Très drôle... mais dis, Kani, tu _____⁶ (*passé composé*) le guide quelque part?

KANI: Oui, j' _____⁷ (*passé composé*) Anne, mais il y a environ une heure, au café...

WAN QING: Cette fois, je _____⁸ que nous sommes perdus! Heureusement, j'ai mon portable!

**B. Interview.** Interrogez un(e) camarade sur ses croyances. Est-ce qu'il/elle croit à la chance, à l'amour, au progrès, à une religion, à la perception extra-sensorielle, aux O.V.N.I.* (*UFOs*), à _____? Utilisez les **Mots clés.**

**C. Conversation.** Avec un(e) camarade, parlez d'une ville qu'il/elle a visitée récemment. Qu'est-ce qu'il/elle a vu? Qui est-ce qu'il/elle a rencontré? Qu'est-ce qu'il/elle veut revoir? Qui veut-il/elle revoir? Ensuite, racontez à la classe l'expérience la plus intéressante (*most interesting*) de votre camarade.

De quoi parle-t-elle?

---

*Objets volants non identifiés

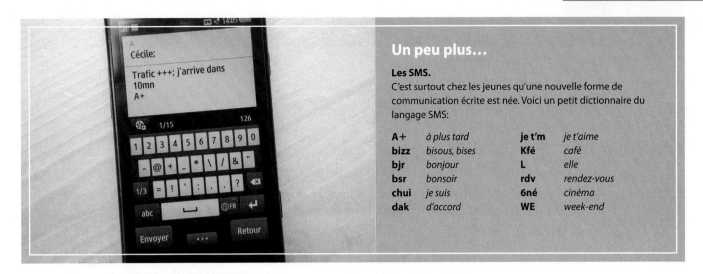

### Un peu plus...

**Les SMS.**

C'est surtout chez les jeunes qu'une nouvelle forme de communication écrite est née. Voici un petit dictionnaire du langage SMS:

| | | | |
|---|---|---|---|
| **A+** | *à plus tard* | **je t'm** | *je t'aime* |
| **bizz** | *bisous, bises* | **Kfé** | *café* |
| **bjr** | *bonjour* | **L** | *elle* |
| **bsr** | *bonsoir* | **rdv** | *rendez-vous* |
| **chui** | *je suis* | **6né** | *cinéma* |
| **dak** | *d'accord* | **WE** | *week-end* |

 # Prononcez bien!

**Final consonants and *liaison*** (page 261)

**L'arrivée de Louis.** En rentrant à la maison après les cours, vous trouvez Hugo seul dans le salon. Avec votre camarade de classe, jouez la scène. Faites bien attention aux liaisons.

VOUS: Isabelle n'est pas là?

HUGO: Non, elle est_allée chercher Louis, son frère. Elle est née le premier_avril et demain c'est son_anniversaire. Pour l'occasion, son frère va passer le week-end avec_elle et lui faire (*give her*) beaucoup de cadeaux.

VOUS: Il voyage en_autobus?

HUGO: Non, en_avion.

VOUS: Quand_est-ce qu'ils_arrivent?

HUGO: Dans deux_heures. C'est_un grand_aéroport et il faut beaucoup de temps pour en (*of it*) sortir!

# Leçon 4

##  Lecture

### Avant de lire

**Identifying a text's logical structure.** Being able to identify words that authors use to sequence their presentation of ideas, express cause and effect, or qualify an observation will facilitate your comprehension of a text's logical structure. For example, words such as **d'abord, en plus, puis, ensuite, enfin,** and **finalement** may be used to develop an argument or support a point of view. To support the point of view that technology has revolutionized communication, an author might write:

D'abord, Internet facilite la communication.
En plus, on peut communiquer plus rapidement.
Finalement, on peut contacter des gens partout dans le monde.

To affirm a preceding idea, words such as **alors, en effet** (*indeed*), and **effectivement** might be used:

Internet est un outil (*tool*) important dans la vie quotidienne. En effet, il a transformé nos goûts et nos habitudes.

**Cependant** (*However, Nevertheless*) and **pourtant** (*yet*) qualify a preceding idea or express a reservation:

Cependant, certains pensent qu'Internet a des effets négatifs.

As you read, pay attention to these important words that express logical development and the relationship between ideas.

---

**À propos de la lecture...**
Les auteurs de *Vis-à-vis* ont écrit ce texte.

## Rencontres en ligne°: rendez-vous avec le bonheur

Rencontres... *Online dating*

Vous rêvez de sortir de votre solitude? Vous êtes timide? Vous n'avez tout simplement pas le temps pour la séduction? Internet peut vous aider! Les sites de rencontre vous ouvrent les portes du bonheur. La plupart[1] sont très sérieux et contrôlent la bonne moralité des membres inscrits.[2] Ils attirent[3] un grand nombre de célibataires—jeunes, adultes et même retraités[4]—à la recherche de l'amour. Plusieurs millions de Français fréquentent chaque jour les sites de rencontre sur Internet.

[1]La... *Most*  [2]*registered*  [3]*attract*  [4]*retired people*

Une histoire d'amour à Paris

## *Pourquoi ce fabuleux succès?*

- D'abord, parce que c'est pratique et facile. Un «clic» et le contact est établi! On choisit un pseudonyme et un mot de passe; on décrit son profil; on définit le partenaire idéal et on peut immédiatement envoyer son premier message. On se présente avec des photos ou une vidéo. C'est déjà une façon[5] de séduire!
- Ensuite, parce que c'est anonyme. Le pseudonyme permet aux candidats de contacter les autres membres en gardant le secret de leur véritable identité.
- En plus, ça favorise le dialogue. Pour séduire, les internautes[6] parlent de leurs sentiments et échangent des idées. Ils écrivent de belles lettres pleines d'humour ou de romantisme.
- Enfin, on augmente ses chances de rencontre. Un seul courrier électronique peut générer plusieurs centaines de réponses, surtout si on décide de mettre une photo avec son profil. C'est vérifié: les candidats qui ont des photos ont beaucoup plus de succès.

## *Et pourtant, il y a des malchanceux...*

Certains n'ont pas de chance sur Internet, comme Marc, un jeune agriculteur[7] de 35 ans. Les jeunes femmes qu'il a rencontrées n'ont pas toléré l'isolement[8] de sa ferme. Elles sont toutes reparties en le laissant seul avec ses vaches[9] et son ordinateur.

Les statistiques confirment ce cas: les rencontres Internet favorisent surtout les citadins.[10] De même, les deux sexes ne sont pas également représentés: sur les sites, on trouve trois hommes pour une femme.

Alors, bonne chance, mesdames!

[5]*way, means*   [6]*Internet users*   [7]*farmer*   [8]*isolation*   [9]*cows*   [10]*city dwellers*

Avez-vous envie de lire ce livre? Pourquoi ou pourquoi pas?

## *Compréhension*

**A. Vocabulaire.** Pour chaque mot, donnez l'équivalent en anglais.

1. en ligne    3. un pseudonyme    5. un(e) internaute
2. un clic    4. un mot de passe

**B. Vrai ou faux?** Si c'est faux, donnez la solution correcte.

1. Il y a peu de sites Web où vous pouvez trouver l'amour en ligne en France.
2. Les sites de rencontre en ligne attirent des gens de tout âge.
3. Le succès des rencontres en ligne est d'abord dû à la facilité de l'usage.
4. D'habitude, les gens qui habitent en ville trouvent plus facilement l'amour sur les sites de rencontre que les gens qui habitent à la campagne.

C. **Opinions.** Lisez la phrase suivante et donnez votre opinion.

Internet est un outil important dans la vie quotidienne [...], cependant certains pensent qu'il a des effets négatifs.

### Internet: un monde vaste!

Voici une liste de quelques autres mots et expressions utiles pour parler des smartphones, des ordinateurs et d'Internet.

| | |
|---|---|
| **appuyer** | *press/push a key* |
| **(re)lier** | *to link* |
| **un abonnement** | *subscription* |
| **une base de données** | *database* |
| **une clé USB** | *flash drive* |
| **un clic** | *click* |
| **un dossier** | *document, file* |
| **un fournisseur d'accès** | *Internet provider* |
| **un graveur de CD/DVD** | *CD/DVD burner* |
| **un identifiant** | *username* |
| **un lien** | *a link* |
| **le matériel** | *hardware* |
| **la mémoire** | *memory* |
| **un MMS** | *multimedia message* |
| **un mot de passe** | *password* |
| **un moteur de recherche** | *search engine* |
| **un opérateur** | *service provider* |
| **une page d'accueil** | *home page* |
| **un port USB** | *USB port* |
| **un répertoire** | *directory* |
| **un réseau** | *network* |
| **le survol** | *browsing* |

 Écriture

The writing activities **Par écrit** and **Journal intime** can be found in the Workbook/Laboratory Manual to accompany *Vis-à-vis*.

## Pour s'amuser

Y a un copain qui m'a dit:

—Prouve-moi que c'est utile ton Internet.

—Okay, je sais pas quoi faire cet été, je fais une recherche sur le mot «vacances». 7 395 sites à visiter. Ça va m'occuper tout l'été.

—Anne Roumanoff, extrait du sketch *Internet*

 # Le vidéoblog de Juliette

## En bref

Dans cet épisode, Juliette et Hector répondent aux questions d'un sondage (*survey*) sur l'utilisation des téléphones portables. Dans son vidéoblog, Juliette continue à parler des nouvelles technologies dans le monde francophone.

### Vocabulaire en contexte

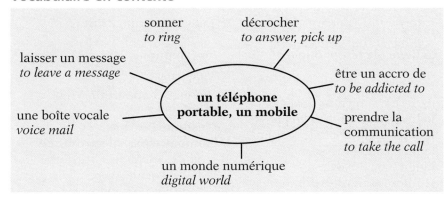

sonner
*to ring*

décrocher
*to answer, pick up*

laisser un message
*to leave a message*

être un accro de
*to be addicted to*

une boîte vocale
*voice mail*

**un téléphone portable, un mobile**

prendre la communication
*to take the call*

un monde numérique
*digital world*

Le mobile: un phénomène universel

## Visionnez!

Indiquez qui fait les activités suivantes: Juliette, Hector ou les deux.

| | Juliette | Hector | les deux |
|---|---|---|---|
| 1. téléphoner à quelqu'un avant le petit déjeuner | ☐ | ☐ | ☐ |
| 2. prendre son mobile dans les toilettes | ☐ | ☐ | ☐ |
| 3. décrocher quand le téléphone sonne dans un restaurant | ☐ | ☐ | ☐ |
| 4. annoncer que le mobile symbolise l'amitié | ☐ | ☐ | ☐ |
| 5. avoir son mobile dans son lit la nuit | ☐ | ☐ | ☐ |

## Analysez!

Répondez aux questions suivantes.

1. Quels éléments, autres que le téléphone portable, font partie de la «culture du multimédia»?
2. Selon la vidéo, nous vivons dans un «monde numérique». Est-ce une bonne chose, selon vous? Pourquoi ou pourquoi pas?

## Comparez!

Est-ce que votre propre culture est aussi une culture du multimédia? Expliquez pourquoi (pas). Êtes-vous, comme Juliette et Hector, «accro» du téléphone portable? Regardez encore une fois la partie culturelle de la vidéo: utilisez-vous les nouvelles technologies plus (*more*) ou moins (*less*) souvent qu'une personne typique de votre pays?

## Note culturelle

En France, il est interdit[1] de téléphoner dans un hôpital ou dans sa voiture si on n'a pas de kit mains-libres.[2] Dans de nombreux lycées, il est interdit de téléphoner en cours ou dans les couloirs, mais l'utilisation du mobile est permis dans les cours de récréation.[3] En avion, Air France interdit l'utilisation du mobile pendant le vol. Dans le train, il est demandé aux voyageurs d'utiliser leur mobile avec discrétion pour ne pas irriter les autres voyageurs.

[1]*prohibited*  [2]*kit... hands-free phone*
[3]*cours... playgrounds*

# Vocabulaire

## Verbes

**appeler** to call
**composer le numéro** to dial the number
**consulter l'annuaire électronique** to look up (a phone number) in the online directory
**croire** to believe
**décrire** to describe
**dépenser** to spend
**dessiner** to draw
**dire** to say
**écrire (à)** to write (to)
**envoyer (à)** to send (to)
**lire** to read
**mettre** to put, place; to put on (clothes)
  **mettre le couvert** to set the table
  **mettre une lettre (une carte) à la poste** to mail a letter (card)
**naviguer** to navigate, to browse
**penser** to think
**poster** to mail
**raconter** to tell (a story)
**recevoir** to receive
**revoir** to see again
**télécharger** to download
**voir** to see

MOTS APPARENTÉS: **cliquer, échanger, payer, posséder, surfer sur le Web**

À REVOIR: **acheter, écouter, entendre, jouer, regarder, rendre**

## Substantifs

**l'appareil** (*m.*) apparatus
**le bureau de tabac** tobacco store
**le cadeau** gift
**la monnaie** coins, change
**la poche** pocket

## Les nouvelles technologies

**l'appareil** (*m.*) **(photo) numérique** digital camera
**le caméscope** digital camcorder

**le clavier** keyboard
**la connexion ADSL** DSL connection/line
**le courriel** e-mail message
**le fichier** file
**l'imprimante** (*f.*) printer
**Internet** (*m.*) Internet
  **sur Internet** on the Internet
**la ligne / le téléphone fixe** landline
**la liseuse** e-reader
**le livre numérique** e-book
**le livre papier** print book
**le logiciel** software (program)
**le mél** e-mail message
**le mp3** mp3 player
**le micro (micro-ordinateur)** desktop computer
**le navigateur** browser
**l'ordinateur** (*m.*) **de bureau** desktop computer
  **l'ordinateur portable** (*fam.* **le portable**) laptop computer
**le traitement de texte** word processing

MOTS APPARENTÉS: **le moniteur, le photocopieur, le scanner, le site, le Web, le Wi-Fi**

À REVOIR: **l'iPod, l'écran** (*m.*), **l'ordinateur** (*m.*), **la souris, la tablette**

## Au bureau de poste

**la boîte aux lettres** mailbox
**le bureau de poste (La Poste)** post office
**le colis** package
**le courrier** mail
**la poste** mail
**le timbre** stamp

MOTS APPARENTÉS: **l'adresse** (*f.*), **la carte postale, l'enveloppe** (*f.*), **le fax, la lettre**

## Au kiosque

**le journal (les journaux)** newspaper; news

**le kiosque** kiosk; newsstand
**les petites annonces** (*f.*) classified ads
**le roman** novel

MOTS APPARENTÉS: **la revue**

À REVOIR: **le magazine**

## Au téléphone

**Allô.** Hello.
**Qui est à l'appareil?** Who's calling?
**C'est moi.** It's me.
**l'annuaire** (*m.*) **électronique** online telephone directory
**la boîte vocale** voice mail
**le mobile** cell phone
**le numéro (de téléphone)** (telephone) number
**le téléphone portable** cell phone
**le texto** text message

MOTS APPARENTÉS: **le smartphone**

À REVOIR: **le SMS, le téléphone**

## À la télévision

**la chaîne** televison channel; network
**l'émission** (*f.*) program; broadcast
  **émission de musique** music program
  **émission de télé réalité** reality show
**le feuilleton** soap opera
**les informations** (*f. pl.*) news
**le jeu télévisé** game show
**le journal télévisé** television news program
**la publicité** commercial; advertisement; advertising
**la retransmission sportive** sports broadcast
**la série** series
  **série télévisée** serial drama
**la télécommande** remote control

**la TNT (télévision numérique terrestre)** high-definition television

MOTS APPARENTÉS: **le câble, le documentaire, la télévision satellite**

À REVOIR: **le DVD (les DVD), le lecteur de DVD, la télé(vision)**

**Autres mots et expressions**

**C'est-à-dire (que)...** That is / I mean . . .
**Eh bien,...** Well, . . .
**Euh...** Uhmm . . .
**là-bas** over there
**Oui, mais...** Yes, but . . .
**surtout** especially

**tous les (jours, après-midi, matins, soirs, et cetera)** every (day, afternoon, morning, evening, etc.)
**tout, toute, tous, toutes** all; every
**toutes les semaines** every week
**Voyons,...** Let's see, . . .

À REVOIR: **d'habitude, en général, souvent**

# Vivre en ville

Les dossiers de Juliette

Juliette

➤ 📁 Mes photos
   ➤ 📁 La Place du Capitole à Toulouse
   ➤ 📁 La campagne à Paris
   ➤ 📁 Le village de Riquewihr, en Alsace

Un restaurant sur la Place du Capitole à Toulouse

# Dans ce chapitre...

## OBJECTIFS COMMUNICATIFS

- ➤ talking about city life
- ➤ describing past events
- ➤ speaking succinctly
- ➤ expressing what and whom you know
- ➤ learning to distinguish between and pronounce selected sounds in French

La campagne à Paris

## PAROLES (Leçon 1)

- ➤ La ville et les directions
- ➤ Les arrondissements de Paris et les nombres ordinaux

## STRUCTURES (Leçons 2 et 3)

- ➤ Le passé composé et l'imparfait
- ➤ Les pronoms d'objet indirect
- ➤ Les verbes **savoir** et **connaître**
- ➤ Les pronoms **y** et **en**

Le village de Riquewihr, en Alsace

## CULTURE

- ➤ Le blog de Juliette: «*Ajoutez deux lettres à Paris: c'est le Paradis.*»
- ➤ Reportage: *Jolis villages de France*
- ➤ Lecture: «Le chat abandonné» (poème de Paul Degray) (Leçon 4)

connect
|FRENCH
www.mhconnectfrench.com

# Leçon 1

## Une petite ville

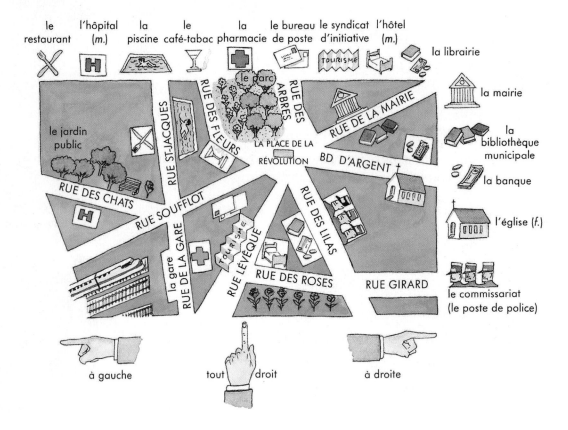

**AUTRES MOTS UTILES**

| | |
|---|---|
| **le bâtiment** | building |
| **le carrefour** | intersection |
| **le chemin** | way; road |
| **le coin** | corner |
| **jusqu'à** | up to, as far as |
| **le marché en plein air** | open-air market |
| **le plan** | map (*of a city*) |
| **se trouver** | to be located (situated) |

—Comment fait-on pour aller de la banque à la pharmacie?
—On **prend** le boulevard d'Argent **à droite** et on va **jusqu'à** la place de la Révolution. On **traverse** la rue des Lilas et on **prend** la rue Lévêque **à gauche**. On **continue tout droit jusqu'au coin** et on **prend** la rue de la Gare **à droite**. La pharmacie est **en face de** la gare.

 *Allez-y!*

**A. Les endroits importants.** Où est-ce qu'on va pour _____?

**MODÈLE:** acheter des livres →
Pour acheter des livres, on va à la librairie.

**1.** retirer de l'argent du distributeur automatique (*ATM*) **2.** acheter de l'aspirine **3.** parler avec le maire (*mayor*) de la ville **4.** obtenir des brochures touristiques **5.** nager **6.** admirer des plantes et des fleurs **7.** assister à (*to attend*) des services religieux catholiques **8.** acheter des timbres **9.** prendre une bière

**B. Où est-ce?** Précisez l'emplacement des endroits suivants selon le plan de la ville à la page précédente.

**MODÈLE:** Où est l'hôtel? →
L'hôtel est en face du syndicat d'initiative dans* la rue Lévêque.

**1.** Où est le jardin public?    **4.** Où est l'église?
**2.** Où est le commissariat?    **5.** Où est la librairie?
**3.** Où est la bibliothèque?    **6.** Où est le syndicat d'initiative?

**C. Trouvez votre chemin.** Regardez le plan de la ville. Imaginez que vous êtes à la gare. Un(e) touriste vous demande où est le bureau de poste; vous lui indiquez le chemin. Jouez les rôles avec un(e) camarade.

**MODÈLE:** LE/LA TOURISTE: Pardon, madame / monsieur, pourriez-vous me dire où est le bureau de poste?
*turn* VOUS: Tournez à gauche. Prenez la rue Soufflot à droite et vous y êtes (*you're there*). → *to take*
LE/LA TOURISTE: Je tourne à gauche, je prends la rue Soufflot à droite et j'y suis.

**1.** le café-tabac **2.** le restaurant **3.** l'hôtel **4.** la banque **5.** le poste de police **6.** le parc **7.** la mairie **8.** la pharmacie **9.** le jardin public **10.** la place de la Révolution **11.** la piscine **12.** le syndicat d'initiative

Maintenant, avec un(e) autre camarade de classe, faites une liste de cinq ou six endroits sur votre campus ou dans votre ville. À tour de rôle, indiquez le chemin pour aller à ces endroits. Votre salle de classe est votre point de départ.

 **Prononcez bien!**

**Nasal vowels**

Remember to let the air go through both your nose and mouth as you pronounce nasal vowels. Pay attention to the openness of your mouth and the shape of your lips.

For [ɔ̃] as in **bon**, close your mouth and round your lips.

[ɔ̃]: **on, révoluti**on**, connexi**on**, feuilleton, voy**ons

For [ɛ̃] as in **chemin**, open your mouth and stretch your lips in a smile.

[ɛ̃]: **timbre, jard**in**, syndicat, Internet, mat**in

For [ɑ̃] as in **plan**, open your mouth and relax your lips.

[ɑ̃]: **banque, bâtim**ent**, prend, argent, en**

---

*One says **dans la rue, sur le boulevard,** and **sur** or **dans l'avenue.**

# Les arrondissements°
# de Paris

*districts*

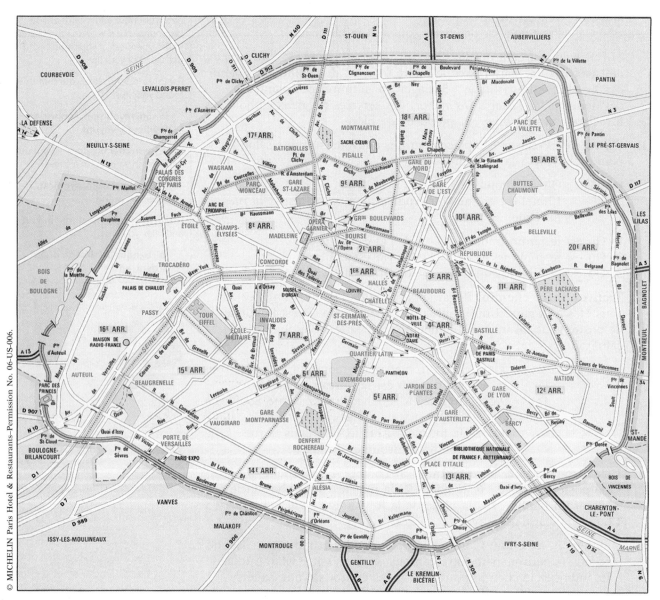

**AUTRES MOTS UTILES**

| | |
|---|---|
| **la banlieue** | suburbs |
| **la carte** | map (*of a region, country*) |
| **le centre-ville** | downtown |
| **la Rive droite / gauche** | Right / Left Bank |

Les vingt arrondissements de Paris:

| | |
|---|---|
| 1ᵉʳ le premier | 11ᵉ le onzième |
| 2ᵉ le deuxième | 12ᵉ le douzième |
| 3ᵉ le troisième | 13ᵉ le treizième |
| 4ᵉ le quatrième | 14ᵉ le quatorzième |
| 5ᵉ le cinquième | 15ᵉ le quinzième |
| 6ᵉ le sixième | 16ᵉ le seizième |
| 7ᵉ le septième | 17ᵉ le dix-septième |
| 8ᵉ le huitième | 18ᵉ le dix-huitième |
| 9ᵉ le neuvième | 19ᵉ le dix-neuvième |
| 10ᵉ le dixième | 20ᵉ le vingtième |

## Les nombres ordinaux

- Ordinal numbers (*first, second,* and so on) are formed by adding **-ième** to cardinal numbers. Note the irregular form **premier / première,** and the spelling of **cinquième** and **neuvième.**
- **Le** and **la** do not elide before **huitième** and **onzième: le huitième.**
- The superscript abbreviation ᵉ indicates that a number should be read as an ordinal: 7 = **sept**; 7ᵉ = **le/la septième.**
- Note the forms **vingt et unième, trente et unième,** and so on.

***Allez-y!***

**A. Les arrondissements de Paris.** Quels arrondissements se trouvent sur la Rive gauche de la Seine? sur la Rive droite? Quel arrondissement est situé au bord du bois de Boulogne? du bois de Vincennes? Où est l'île de la Cité?*

**B. Le plan de Paris.** Avec un(e) partenaire, situez les endroits suivants.

MODÈLE: É1: la tour Eiffel?
　　　　　É2: Euh, voyons… La tour Eiffel se trouve dans le septième arrondissement.

| | | |
|---|---|---|
| **1.** le Panthéon† | **5.** Montmartre‡ | **8.** l'opéra Bastille |
| **2.** Notre-Dame | **6.** Beaubourg§ | **9.** l'arc de Triomphe |
| **3.** la gare de l'Est | **7.** le Sacré-Cœur | |
| **4.** le Louvre | | |

---

*The **île de la Cité** is the historical center of Paris; it is one of the two islands on the Seine in Paris. The other is the **île St-Louis.**
†The **Panthéon** is a building in the **5ᵉ arrondissement** in Paris where several famous people are buried, including Voltaire, Rousseau, Marie Curie, and Louis Braille.
‡**Montmartre** is a lively area in northern Paris where Sacré-Cœur, a basilica, is located. The name **Montmartre** comes from **Mont des Martyrs** because several church officials were killed there long ago.
§**Beaubourg** is an ultramodern museum in Paris, and is also known as the **Centre Pompidou.** It is often surrounded by street artists and contains a wonderful collection of modern art.

STRUCTURES

# Leçon 2

## Le passé composé et l'imparfait

*Describing Past Events*

### Guide touristique à Paris

*Alexis téléphone à Poema.*

ALEXIS: Finalement **tu es partie** à la Guadeloupe?

POEMA: Mais non! **J'ai** tout **annulé**[1]: au dernier moment, **mes parents** m'**ont annoncé** leur arrivée à Paris. Alors **j'ai joué** les guides touristiques!

ALEXIS: Qu'est-ce que **vous avez fait**?

POEMA: Tous les jours la même chose! Le matin, **nous prenions** le petit déjeuner à la terrasse d'un café; ensuite **nous visitions** la capitale. À pied!

ALEXIS: Et le soir?

POEMA: **J'étais** complètement KO[2]! Maintenant qu'**ils sont partis,** j'ai vraiment besoin de vacances!

*repeated past*

Paris: On fait la queue devant le musée d'Orsay.

[1]*cancelled*  [2]*exhausted*

Répondez aux questions selon le dialogue.

**1.** Poema est-elle partie à la Guadeloupe?
**2.** Pourquoi a-t-elle changé ses projets?
**3.** Quel rôle a-t-elle joué avec ses parents?
**4.** Qu'est-ce que Poema et ses parents faisaient, tous les jours, à Paris?
**5.** Le soir, dans quel état était Poema?
**6.** Où sont ses parents maintenant?

When speaking about the past in English, you choose which past tense forms to use in a given context: *I visited Guadeloupe, I did visit Guadeloupe, I was visiting Guadeloupe, I used to visit Guadeloupe,* and so on. Usually only one of these options will convey exactly the meaning you want to express. Similarly in French, the choice between the **passé composé** and the **imparfait** depends on the kind of past action or condition that is being conveyed, and sometimes on the speaker's point of view with respect to the past event.

As you've learned, the **passé composé** is used to indicate a single completed action, something that began and ended in the past, or a sequence of such actions. The **imparfait,** on the other hand, usually indicates an ongoing or habitual action in the past. It does not emphasize the end of that action.

**1.** Compare the following sets of examples.

| | |
|---|---|
| J'**écrivais** des lettres. | *I was writing letters.* |
| J'**ai écrit** des lettres. | *I wrote (have written) letters.* |
| Je **commençais** mon travail. | *I was starting on my assignments.* |
| J'**ai commencé** mon travail. | *I started (have started) my assignments.* |
| Elle **allait** au parc le dimanche.* | *She went (used to go) to the park on Sundays.* |
| Elle **est allée** au parc dimanche. | *She went to the park on Sunday.* |

**2.** The following chart sets out the major differences between these two tenses.

| IMPARFAIT | PASSÉ COMPOSÉ |
|---|---|
| **1.** *Ongoing action with no emphasis on the completion or end of the action* | *Completed action, or a series of completed events or actions* |
| **J'allais** en France. <br> Je **visitais** des monuments. | Je **suis allé(e)** en France. <br> J'**ai visité** des monuments. |
| **2.** *Habitual or repeated action* | *A single event* |
| **J'allais** en France tous les ans. <br> Je **visitais** souvent le château de Versailles. | Je **suis allé(e)** en France l'année dernière. <br> J'**ai visité** Versailles un samedi matin. |
| [Allez-y! A] | |
| **3.** *Description or "background" information; how things were or what was happening when . . .* | *. . . an event or events occurred.* <br> *("foreground" information)* |
| Je **visitais** Beaubourg... | ...quand on **a annoncé** la projection d'un vieux film de Chaplin. |
| J'**étais** à Paris... | ...quand une lettre **est arrivée.** |
| [Allez-y! B] | |
| **4.** *Physical or mental states of being (general description)* | *Changes in an existing physical or mental state at a precise moment, or for a particular isolated cause* |
| Ma nièce **avait** peur des chiens. | Ma nièce **a eu** peur quand le chien a aboyé (*barked*). |

---

*Remember the role of the definite article with days of the week: **le dimanche** (*on Sundays*); **dimanche** (*on Sunday*).

## Grammaire interactive

For more on the uses of the **imparfait** and the **passé composé**, watch the corresponding Grammar Tutorial and take a brief practice quiz at **Connect French.**

www.mhconnectfrench.com

**3.** In summary, the **imparfait** is generally used for *descriptions* in the past, and the **passé composé** is generally used for the *narration* of specific events in the past. The **imparfait** also often sets the stage for an event expressed with the **passé composé.** Look over the following passages with these points in mind.

| IMPARFAIT | PASSÉ COMPOSÉ |
|---|---|
| Il **faisait** beau; le ciel (*sky*) **était** clair; les terrasses des cafés **étaient** pleines (*filled*) de gens; c'**était** un beau jour de printemps à Paris. | J'**ai continué** tout droit dans la rue Mouffetard, j'**ai traversé** le boulevard de Port-Royal et j'**ai descendu** l'avenue des Gobelins jusqu'à la place d'Italie. |

**4.** The following indicators of tense can help you determine whether to use the **passé composé** or the **imparfait.**

| IMPARFAIT | PASSÉ COMPOSÉ |
|---|---|
| autrefois (*formerly*) d'habitude de temps en temps le lundi (le mardi... ) le week-end pendant que | au moment où lundi (mardi... ) plusieurs fois soudain (*suddenly*) tout à coup (*suddenly*) un jour un week-end une fois (*once*), deux fois... |
| **D'habitude,** nous **étudiions** à la bibliothèque. | **Un jour,** nous **avons étudié** au café. |
| Quand j'**étais** jeune, nous **allions** à la plage **le week-end.** | **Un week-end,** nous **sommes allés** à la montagne. |

 *Allez-y!*

**A.** **Un dimanche pas comme les autres.** Votre voisin Marc Dufour était une personne routinière, mais un dimanche, il a changé ses habitudes. Voici son histoire.

> **MODÈLE:** le dimanche matin / dormir en général jusqu'à huit heures / mais ce dimanche-là / dormir jusqu'à midi →
> Le dimanche matin, il dormait en général jusqu'à huit heures, mais ce dimanche-là, il a dormi jusqu'à midi.

**1.** normalement au petit déjeuner / prendre des céréales et une tasse de café / mais ce matin-là / prendre un petit déjeuner copieux

2. après le petit déjeuner / faire toujours du jogging dans le parc / mais ce jour-là / rester longtemps au téléphone
3. souvent l'après-midi / regarder le match de football à la télé / mais cet après-midi-là / lire des poèmes dans le jardin
4. d'habitude le soir / sortir avec ses copains / mais ce soir-là / sortir avec une jeune fille
5. parfois / aller au cinéma ou / lire un roman / mais ce soir-là / inviter son amie à un restaurant élégant
6. normalement / rentrer chez lui assez tôt / mais ce dimanche-là / danser jusqu'au petit matin (*early morning*)

À votre avis, est-ce que Marc est malade (*sick*)? amoureux (*in love*)? déprimé (*depressed*)?... Justifiez votre réponse. Et vous, est-ce qu'il y a des choses que vous faisiez autrefois que vous ne faites plus maintenant? Expliquez.

Au jardin du Luxembourg, à Paris. Est-ce que vous aimiez les parcs quand vous étiez petit(e)?

**B. Interruptions.** Anne était à la maison hier soir. Elle voulait faire plusieurs choses, mais il y a eu toutes sortes d'interruptions. Décrivez-les.

MODÈLE:  étudier... téléphone / sonner $\rightarrow$
Anne étudiait quand le téléphone a sonné.

1. parler au téléphone / un ami... l'employé / couper la ligne (*to cut the line*)
2. écouter / iPod... son voisin / commencer à faire / bruit (*m., noise*)
3. lire / journal... le propriétaire / venir demander / argent
4. faire / devoirs... un ami / arriver
5. regarder / informations à la télé... son frère / changer de chaîne
6. dormir... quelqu'un / frapper (*to knock*) à la porte

**C. Une année à l'université de Caen.** Jérémie a passé un an à Caen, une des grandes villes de Normandie. Il raconte son histoire. Choisissez l'imparfait ou le passé composé pour les verbes suivants.

Mon année en Normandie a été vraiment super, mais j'ai dû passer beaucoup de temps à étudier. Je (avoir)[1] cours le matin de 8 h à 11 h. L'après-midi, je (étudier)[2] en général à la bibliothèque. Le week-end, avec des amis, nous (faire)[3] du tourisme. Le samedi, nous (rester)[4] en ville et le dimanche, nous (aller)[5] à la campagne. En octobre, nous (faire)[6] une excursion à Rouen. Ce (être)[7] très intéressant. Pour Noël, je (rentrer)[8] chez mes parents. En février, je (faire)[9] du ski dans les Alpes. Nous (avoir)[10] de la chance car (*because*) il (faire)[11] très beau et je (rentrer)[12] bien bronzé (*tanned*). De temps en temps, je (manger)[13] chez les Levergeois, des amis français très sympathiques. Pendant ces dîners entre amis, je (perfectionner)[14] mon français. Finalement, au début du mois de mai, je (devoir)[15] quitter Caen. Je (être)[16] triste de partir.

Marguerite Yourcenar

**D. Biographie de Marguerite Yourcenar.** Voici quelques faits (*facts*) importants de la vie de cette romancière (*novelist*) et historienne de langue française. Mettez-les dans l'ordre chronologique et utilisez les adverbes de temps des **Mots clés.**

**1.** Elle est allée aux États-Unis en 1958.
**2.** Elle a écrit son fameux livre *L'Œuvre au noir* en 1968.
**3.** Elle est née à Bruxelles en 1903.
**4.** Elle est morte en 1987 à l'âge de 84 ans dans le Maine, aux États-Unis.
**5.** Elle a été la première femme élue à l'Académie française, en 1980.

Maintenant, faites brièvement (*briefly*) votre autobiographie. Utilisez des adverbes de temps.

**E. Conversation.** Posez les questions suivantes à un(e) camarade pour découvrir ce qui s'est passé dans sa vie l'année dernière. Ensuite, changez de rôle.

**1.** Où étais-tu? Où as-tu étudié? Qu'est-ce que tu as étudié?
**2.** Qu'est-ce que tu as fait pendant tes vacances? As-tu fait un voyage? Où es-tu allé(e)? Comment était le voyage?
**3.** Et tes amis, où étaient-ils l'année dernière? Qu'est-ce qu'ils ont fait pendant les vacances?

**F. Il était une fois...** (*Once upon a time . . .*) Racontez une histoire que vous avez vécue (*lived*) ou une histoire fantastique (inventez-la!). Utilisez les éléments suggérés pour organiser votre histoire et choisissez le temps convenable (passé composé ou imparfait).

**Suggestions:** l'heure, le temps, la description de la scène, la description des personnages, la description des sentiments...

**Expressions utiles:** soudain, tout à coup, d'habitude, en général, puis, ensuite, enfin, alors, autrefois, quand, souvent, parfois, toujours...

## Mots clés

**Mettre les événements par ordre chronologique**

**d'abord** *first of all*
**puis** *next*
**ensuite** *and then*
**après** *after that*
**enfin** *finally*

**Puis** and **ensuite** can be used interchangeably.

**DÉPANNAGE** (*Emergency Repair*)
**D'abord,** j'ai garé (*parked*) la voiture.
**Puis,** j'ai téléphoné à un garage dans le quartier.
**Ensuite,** j'ai tout expliqué au mécanicien.
**Après,** j'ai attendu dans la voiture.
**Enfin,** il est arrivé. Maintenant, le carburateur fonctionne à merveille.

# Les pronoms d'objet indirect

*Speaking Succinctly*

## Cannes en été

*Hector et Hassan discutent au café.*

HECTOR: Juliette et Léa **nous** proposent de les rejoindre[1] pour un week-end à Cannes.

HASSAN: Je sais: Elles **m'**ont téléphoné…

HECTOR: Qu'est-ce que tu **leur** as répondu?

HASSAN: Que je devais **te** parler avant de prendre une décision!

HECTOR: Pour moi, c'est «oui»!

HASSAN: Pour moi, c'est «non». Parce que Cannes en été, c'est la foule[2] dans les rues, dans les restaurants, sur la plage. C'est infernal!

[1]*join, accompany*   [2]*crowd*

Cannes: un mythe et une délicieuse réalité

Trouvez, dans le dialogue, la phrase équivalente.

1. Hector dit à Hassan qu'ils sont invités pour le week-end à Cannes.
2. Hassan le sait: Juliette et Léa lui ont téléphoné.
3. Hector veut connaître la réponse d'Hassan.
4. Hassan a dit à Juliette et à Léa qu'il voulait consulter Hector.

## Indirect Objects

1. As you know, direct object nouns and pronouns answer the question *what?* or *whom?* Indirect object nouns and pronouns usually answer the question *to whom?* or *for whom?* In English, the word *to* is frequently omitted: I gave the book *to Paul.* → I gave *Paul* the book. In French, the preposition **à** is *always* used before an indirect object noun.

| | |
|---|---|
| J'ai donné des informations **à** Paul. | *I gave information to Paul.* |
| Elle a écrit une lettre **au** maire. | *She wrote a letter to the mayor.* |
| Nous montrons l'article **aux** journalistes. | *We show the article to the journalists.* |
| Elle prête les photos **à** son frère. | *She lends the photos to her brother.* |

2. If a sentence has an indirect object, it usually has a direct object as well. Some French verbs, however, take only an indirect object. These include **téléphoner à, parler à,** and **répondre à.**

| | |
|---|---|
| Je téléphone / parle souvent **à** mes amis. | *I often phone / speak to my friends.* |
| Elle a répondu **au** professeur. | *She answered the instructor.* |

## Indirect Object Pronouns

1. Indirect object pronouns replace indirect object nouns. They are identical in form to direct object pronouns, except for the third-person forms, **lui** and **leur.**

| INDIRECT OBJECT PRONOUNS | | | |
|---|---|---|---|
| me, m' | *(to/for) me* | nous | *(to/for) us* |
| te, t' | *(to/for) you* | vous | *(to/for) you* |
| **lui** | *(to/for) him, her* | **leur** | *(to/for) them* |

**Grammaire interactive**

For more on indirect object pronouns, watch the corresponding Grammar Tutorial and take a brief practice quiz at **Connect French.**

**connect**
|FRENCH
www.mhconnectfrench.com

2. The placement of indirect object pronouns is identical to that of direct object pronouns. However, the past participle does not agree with a preceding indirect object.

Je **lui** ai montré la réception. — *I showed him (her) the (front) desk.*

On **m'**a demandé l'adresse de l'auberge de jeunesse. — *They asked me for the address of the youth hostel.*

Valérie **nous** a envoyé un texto. — *Valérie sent us a text message.*

Nous allons **leur** téléphoner maintenant. — *We're going to telephone them now.*

Je **leur** ai emprunté* la voiture. — *I borrowed the car from them.*

Ils **m'**ont prêté de l'argent. — *They loaned me some money.*

3. In negative sentences, the object pronoun immediately precedes the auxiliary verb in the **passé composé.** If the pronoun is the indirect object of an infinitive, it is placed directly before the infinitive.

Elle **ne lui** a **pas** téléphoné. — *She hasn't telephoned him (her).*

Je **ne** vais **pas leur** écrire. — *I am not going to write to them.*

 **Allez-y!**

A. **L'après-midi d'Elsa.** Elsa va tous les vendredis après-midi chez sa grand-mère qui habite dans son quartier. Elle nous raconte ce qu'elle a fait vendredi dernier. Complétez son histoire avec les pronoms qui correspondent: **me, te, lui, nous, vous, leur.**

Après les cours, j'ai pris un café avec des amies. Je _____¹ ai montré mon nouvel iPad. Un peu plus tard, j'ai rendu visite à ma grand-mère. Je _____² ai apporté ses magazines préférés. Elle était très contente et elle _____³ a dit: «Je vais _____⁴ préparer un bon

---

*Emprunter (quelque chose) à (quelqu'un)** means *to borrow* (*something*) *from* (*someone*).

goûter.» En fin d'après-midi, mon frère est arrivé. Il _____⁵ a raconté ses aventures avec sa nouvelle moto. Nous avons bien ri. (*We laughed a lot.*)

Au moment de partir, ma grand-mère _____⁶ a demandé (à mon frère et à moi): «Je vous revois la semaine prochaine, les enfants?» Nous _____⁷ avons répondu, «Bien sûr, à vendredi prochain!»

**B. N'oublie pas...** Au moment de dire au revoir, la grand-mère d'Elsa se rappelle (*remembers*) plusieurs questions qu'elle voulait lui poser. Jouez le rôle d'Elsa et répondez-lui, en utilisant les pronoms complément d'objet indirect.

**1.** As-tu téléphoné à ton oncle? **2.** Tu as écrit à ta tante Céline?
**3.** Tu as donné le plan de la ville à ton frère pour son voyage?
**4.** As-tu répondu à M. et Mᵐᵉ Morin en Espagne? **5.** Est-ce que tu as souhaité (*wished*) «bon anniversaire» à ton petit cousin?
**6.** Est-ce que tu as rendu à Nicolas et Virginie le livre qu'ils nous ont prêté?

**C. Êtes-vous communicatif / communicative?** Posez les questions suivantes à un(e) camarade et créez de nouvelles questions sur le même sujet.

**1.** À qui as-tu écrit la semaine dernière? Qu'est-ce que tu lui as écrit? Pourquoi? En général, écris-tu souvent?
**2.** À qui as-tu téléphoné hier soir? Qu'est-ce que tu lui as dit?
**3.** Tu envoies souvent des textos? À quelle occasion? À qui?

Ensuite, dites à la classe si votre camarade est très ou peu communicatif / communicative. Qui est la personne la plus communicative de la classe?

## Un peu plus...

**Le Trocadéro.**
Où trouver, à Paris, un endroit où l'on peut visiter plusieurs grands musées, se rendre dans un théâtre national et profiter d'une vue impressionnante de la tour Eiffel? Place du Trocadéro, bien sûr! Le Trocadéro est une grande place située en face de la tour Eiffel, sur la Rive droite de la Seine. Sur cette place se trouve le Palais de Chaillot qui abrite (*houses*) le musée national de la Marine, le musée de l'Homme et la Cité de l'architecture et du patrimoine. C'est aussi le lieu du Théâtre National de Chaillot.

◄ *Le Trocadéro au crépuscule (dusk).*
*Décrivez la scène.*

# Le blog de Juliette

## «Ajoutez deux lettres à Paris: c'est le Paradis.»

—(Jules Renard)

**mardi 21 juillet**

Vous rêvez de Paris? Moi, j'y[1] habite depuis trois ans!

Avant, je visitais la capitale comme une touriste: je connaissais[2] tous les monuments, les musées, les promenades, les restaurants.

Maintenant, je sais[3] utiliser les transports en commun et lire un plan; je passe sans problème des cafés de la Rive gauche aux grands magasins de la Rive droite; je fréquente les petits restaurants bobos[4] du 11e. Je connais aussi le vieux Paris, avec ses lieux secrets pleins[5] de charme.

J'ai toujours aimé les grandes villes. Après mon Master, dans un an, je veux aller travailler dans une capitale à l'étranger. Déjà, l'an dernier, j'ai fait un stage[6] de trois mois dans une entreprise à Londres.

Vous avez compris: la banlieue ou les petites villes de province, ce n'est pas ma passion (ou ce n'est pas ma tasse de thé, comme disent les Anglais!).

Bisous quand même[7] à tous les banlieusards[8] et à tous les provinciaux[9]!

Juliette

Vous voyez, la campagne à Paris, c'est une réalité!

. . . . . . . . . . . . . . . . . . . . . . . . . . . . . . . . . . . . . . . . . . . . . . . . . . . . . . . . . . . . . . . . . . . . . . . . . . . . . . . . . . . .

## COMMENTAIRES

**Alexis**

Moi, j'ai passé toute mon enfance à Québec et je connais New York, Chicago, Miami. J'ai aussi visité Rome, Barcelone et Varsovie. Eh bien, je vais te dire: j'aime mieux Versailles! Quand je suis arrivé ici, j'ai compris que je préférais le charme à la grandeur…

**Trésor**

Hypocrite! Et le château, c'est du charme ou de la grandeur?

**Poema**

Personnellement, je suis très attachée à Papeete, la ville de mon enfance. Cette petite capitale de la Polynésie française n'a que 100 000 habitants! Avec ses bateaux à voile blancs, ses palmiers du bord de mer, elle ressemble à une cité balnéaire[10] de la Côte d'Azur.[11]

**Mamadou**

Vous connaissez Dakar, ma ville natale? On y trouve plein de[12] choses à faire.

**Charlotte**

C'est vrai! À Dakar, on trouve des bars, des restaurants, et aussi des musées, une université, des bibliothèques, des galeries d'art, des cinémas! Je le sais, j'y suis allée!

[1]y = *there*  [2]*was familiar with*  [3]*know how to*  [4]*hipster (from* **bo**urgeois-**bo**hème)  [5]*full*  [6]*internship*
[7]quand… *nevertheless*  [8]*people living in the suburbs (pej.)*  [9]*city dwellers in other regions of France (as opposed to Paris) (fam.)*  [10]cité.. *summer resort town*  [11]Côte… *French Riviera*  [12]plein… *plenty of*

## Jolis villages de France

Ils sont pittoresques, charmants, perdus dans la nature ou installés au sommet d'une montagne comme une cerise[1] sur un gâteau: Ce sont les 32 000 villages de la campagne française. L'existence y est simple et tranquille. On y vit au milieu des moutons, des vaches et des poules.[2]

Riquewihr: charme et histoire

Dans un village typique de France, on trouve toujours une église, une mairie, une école, un cimetière, une salle des fêtes. Très anciens, les jolis villages de France ont des visages multiples: villages-forteresses organisés autour d'un château, villages-jardins, villages de pêcheurs,[3] villages-labyrinthes… Chaque village raconte une page de l'histoire de France et définit l'identité d'une région. Par exemple, **Riquewihr**, situé à quelques kilomètres de Colmar dans l'est de la France, est un village médiéval typiquement alsacien. Il est célèbre pour ses maisons aux colombages[4] sculptés, pour ses petites rues tortueuses, pour ses vieux puits[5] et ses fontaines. **Gordes**, avec son château monumental construit au centre du village, est situé au milieu de champs de lavande et des vignes. C'est un centre culturel et artistique qui attire des visiteurs amoureux de la Provence. Dans les Hautes-Alpes, **Saint-Véran** est un adorable village de montagne situé à 2 042 m[6] d'altitude. L'hiver, il se transforme en station de ski; l'été, il propose de merveilleuses randonnées aux amoureux de la nature.

Certains villages construisent leur réputation sur leur production locale: vins, cidres, champagnes, fromages, pâtés, miel,[7] gâteaux, bonbons… Allez à **Pérouges**, près de Lyon: c'est un minuscule village du XIIe siècle, célèbre pour ses galettes[8] au sucre absolument exquises. Arrêtez-vous à **La Roque-Gageac**, ravissant village du Sud-Ouest, construit le long de la Dordogne: On y déguste[9] un foie gras fabuleux fabriqué dans la région. À **Hauvillers**, village du Nord-Est surnommé[10] «La Perle du Champagne», on boit du champagne! Et on visite l'abbaye où repose, pour l'éternité, le fameux moine[11] Dom Pérignon. C'est lui qui a donné son nom à l'un des meilleurs champagnes français: le Dom Pérignon.

Aujourd'hui, les jolis villages vivent essentiellement du tourisme. Avec leurs églises, leurs châteaux, leurs abbayes, leurs fermes et leurs maisons bourgeoises, ils proposent une expérience authentique aux visiteurs. Prendre un petit café au soleil, manger un poulet fermier[12] dans le restaurant local, acheter des œufs frais et des fruits de saison à l'épicerie, se promener dans les rues tranquilles et dire bonjour à tout le monde, voilà les plaisirs uniques qu'on découvre dans les jolis petits villages de France.

[1]*cherry*  [2]*chickens*  [3]*fishermen*  [4]*half-timbers*  [5]*wells*  [6]*6,636 feet*  [7]*honey*  [8]*tarts*  [9]*tastes*  [10]*nicknamed*  [11]*monk*  [12]*farm-raised*

À vous!

1. Décrivez un petit village typiquement français selon le *Reportage*.
2. Qu'est-ce qu'on trouve dans tous les petits villages typiques de France?
3. Quel village en France est célèbre pour ses galettes? son champagne? son foie gras?
4. Décrivez plusieurs endroits que les touristes aiment visiter dans les petits villages.

Parlons-en!

1. Travaillez à deux ou en petits groupes. Allez sur le site Internet de l'association «Les plus beaux villages de France». Parmi les 156 villages remarquables de son répertoire, sélectionnez un village que vous trouvez particulièrement charmant.
2. Situez votre village sur une carte de France. Précisez dans quelle région il se trouve (la Bourgogne, le Centre, la Lorraine…), si c'est un village de campagne, de montagne ou de pêcheurs, s'il propose une activité particulière, etc.
3. Expliquez pourquoi ce village vous intéresse.

# Leçon 3

STRUCTURES

## Les verbes *savoir* et *connaître*

*Expressing What and Whom You Know*

### Les mystères du château de Versailles

*Alexis téléphone à Poema.*

ALEXIS: **Tu connais** le château de Versailles?
POEMA: **Qui ne connaît pas** le château de Versailles?
**Nous connaissons** tous le château: c'est un symbole de la France!
ALEXIS: **Tu sais** qu'il reçoit des millions de visiteurs par an?
POEMA: **Je sais**! C'est un monument national. Comme le musée du Louvre ou la tour Eiffel.
ALEXIS: Moi, **je connais** les mystères du château... Si tu veux, je te montre un passage secret entre la chambre du Roi et la chambre de la Reine...
POEMA: Tu crois qu'on va rencontrer le fantôme de Marie-Antoinette?

Versailles: la chambre somptueuse de la reine Marie-Antoinette

Faites des phrases complètes pour montrer que vous avez compris le dialogue. Choisissez le verbe approprié. **Attention!** il y a parfois plusieurs réponses possibles.

| Tout le monde | ⎧ sait ⎫ | le château de Versailles. |
| Alexis | ⎨ ⎬ | que c'est un monument national. |
| Poema | ⎩ connaît ⎭ | les mystères du château. |

The verbs **savoir** and **connaître** both correspond to the English verb *to know,* but they are used differently.

## Forms of *savoir* and *connaître*

| PRESENT TENSE OF **savoir** | | | |
|---|---|---|---|
| je | **sais** | nous | **savons** |
| tu | **sais** | vous | **savez** |
| il/elle/on | **sait** | ils/elles | **savent** |
| *Past participle:* **su** | | | |

| PRESENT TENSE OF **connaître** | |
|---|---|
| je **connais** | nous **connaissons** |
| tu **connais** | vous **connaissez** |
| il/elle/on **connaît** | ils/elles **connaissent** |

| *past participle:* **connu** |
|---|

## Uses of *savoir* and *connaître*

**1. Savoir** means *to know* or *to have knowledge of* a fact, *to know by heart,* or *to know how to* do something. It is frequently followed by an infinitive or by a subordinate clause introduced by **que, quand, pourquoi,** and so on.

| **Sais**-tu l'heure qu'il est? | *Do you know what time it is?* |
|---|---|
| **Savez**-vous où est le bureau de poste le plus proche d'ici? | *Do you know where the closest post office is?* |
| Je **sais** que le bureau de poste du boulevard Haussmann est fermé. | *I know that the post office on Boulevard Haussmann is closed.* |

**2.** In the **passé composé, savoir** means *learned* or *found out.*

| **J'ai su** hier que la mairie allait être démolie. | *I learned yesterday that the city hall is going to be demolished.* |
|---|---|

**3. Connaître** means *to know* or *to be familiar (acquainted) with* someone or something. **Connaître**—never **savoir**—means *to know a person or a place.* **Connaître** is always used with a direct object; it cannot be followed directly by an infinitive or by a subordinate clause.

| —**Connais**-tu Lucille? | *Do you know Lucillle?* |
|---|---|
| —Non, je ne la **connais** pas. | *No, I don't know her.* |

| Ils **connaissent** très bien Dijon. | *They know Dijon very well.* |
|---|---|

**4.** In the **passé composé, connaître** means *met for the first time.* It is the equivalent of the **passé composé** of **faire la connaissance de.**

| **J'ai connu** Didier à l'université. | *I met Didier at the university.* |
|---|---|

Cagnes-sur-mer, un petit village de la Côte d'Azur. Connaissez-vous la Côte d'Azur? Voulez-vous la visiter? Pourquoi?

 *Allez-y!*

**A. Dialogue.** Complétez les phrases avec **connaître** ou **savoir.**

M^ME DUPUY: _____^1-vous Paris, monsieur?

M. STEIN: Je _____^2 seulement que c'est la capitale de la France.

M^ME DUPUY: _____^3-vous quelle est la distance entre Paris et Marseille?

M. STEIN: Non, mais je _____^4 une agence de voyages où on doit le _____^5. Dans cette agence, ils _____^6 très bien le pays.

M^ME DUPUY: _____^7-vous s'il y a d'autres villes intéressantes à visiter?

M. STEIN: Comme je l'ai dit, je ne _____^8 pas bien ce pays, mais hier j'ai fait la connaissance d'un homme qui _____^9 où aller pour passer de bonnes vacances.

M^ME DUPUY: Je voudrais bien _____^10 cet homme. _____^11-vous où il travaille?

**B. Et toi, connais-tu Paris?** Avec un(e) camarade, posez des questions et répondez-y.

**MODÈLE:** l'Opéra-Bastille →

VOUS: Connais-tu l'Opéra-Bastille?

VOTRE CAMARADE: Non, je ne le connais pas, mais je sais qu'on y va pour écouter de la musique.

### ENDROITS

l'Opéra-Bastille
Notre-Dame de Paris
le Louvre
le Palais de l'Élysée
la tour Eiffel
la Bibliothèque nationale
le Quartier latin
la Pyramide

### DÉFINITIONS

C'est le quartier des étudiants à Paris.
Le président y habite.
On y va pour écouter de la musique.
On y trouve une vaste collection de livres.
C'est une église située dans l'île de la Cité.
C'est la structure en verre (*glass*) devant le Louvre.
On y trouve une riche collection d'art.
Elle a 320 mètres de haut (*tall*) et elle est en fer (*iron*).

## Le parler jeune

| | |
|---|---|
| **une balade** | une promenade |
| **se balader** | se promener |
| **une manif** | une manifestation |
| **quartier bobo** | quartier bourgeois-bohème |
| **quartier branché** | quartier à la mode |

Une **balade** à vélo, ça t'intéresse?

J'aime bien **me balader** sur la croisette (*boardwalk*) à Cannes.

À Paris, les grandes **manifs** populaires passent par République.

Le XIᵉ arrondissement? C'est le **quartier bobo** de Paris.

Le haut Marais, c'est le nouveau **quartier branché** de Paris.

### Un peu plus...

**L'Opéra-Garnier.**
Cet opéra est l'un des édifices les plus somptueux de Paris. L'intérieur est fait de différents marbres et décoré de nombreuses sculptures. La salle de concert est rouge et or. C'est Napoléon III qui a fait construire l'Opéra du palais Garnier. Son décor flamboyant devait représenter le luxe, l'art et le plaisir. De nos jours, on y présente de grands spectacles de danse.

Aimez-vous le luxe? Expliquez.

▶ *Les luxes de la ville: le grand escalier de l'Opéra de Paris.*

**C. Vos connaissances.** Utilisez ces phrases pour interviewer un(e) camarade. Dans les réponses, utilisez le verbe **savoir** ou **connaître**.

1. Nomme deux choses que tu sais faire.
2. Nomme deux choses que tu veux savoir faire un jour.
3. Nomme deux domaines (*fields*) où tu es plus ou moins compétent(e). (Je connais / ne connais pas bien… )
4. Nomme une personne que tu as connue récemment.
5. Nomme quelqu'un que tu aimerais (*would like*) connaître.

**D. Une ville.** Donnez le nom d'une ville que vous connaissez bien. Ensuite, racontez ce que vous savez sur cette ville.

> **MODÈLE:** Je connais New York. Je sais qu'il y a d'immenses gratte-ciel (*skyscrapers*).

# Les pronoms *y* et *en*

*Speaking Succinctly*

## Le musée Picasso

*Juliette et Léa discutent au café.*

JULIETTE: Tu as un plan d'Antibes sur toi?

LÉA: J'**en** ai un sur mon iPhone. Qu'est-ce que tu cherches?

JULIETTE: Le musée Picasso.

LÉA: C'est au château Grimaldi, dans la vieille ville, face à la mer. J'**y** suis déjà allée.

JULIETTE: J'ai deux billets gratuits.[1] Tu **en** veux un?

LÉA: Si j'**en** veux un? Bien sûr!

JULIETTE: Tu veux **y** retourner?

LÉA: Sans hésitation! C'est tellement[2] beau! On **y** va ensemble!

[1]*free*  [2]*so*

Trouvez, dans le dialogue, des phrases équivalentes.

1. J'ai un plan d'Antibes sur mon iPhone.
2. Je suis déjà allée au musée Picasso.
3. Tu veux un billet?
4. Tu veux retourner au musée Picasso?
5. On va ensemble au musée Picasso.

Pour les amateurs d'art

## The Pronoun y

1. The pronoun **y** can refer to a place that has already been mentioned. It replaces a prepositional phrase, and its English equivalent in such cases is *there*.

| | |
|---|---|
| —Est-ce que Nathalie est déjà allée **au parc Montsouris**? | *Has Nathalie already gone to Montsouris Park?* |
| —Non, mais elle **y** va samedi. | *No, but she is going there Saturday.* |
| —Est-ce que Myriam va **au festival** avec elle? | *Is Myriam going to the festival with her?* |
| —Non, elle n'**y** va pas avec elle. | *No, she isn't going (there) with her.* |
| —Vont-elles **chez Nathalie** ce week-end? | *Are they going to Nathalie's this weekend?* |
| —Oui, elles **y** vont ensemble. | *Yes, they're going (there) together.* |

Note that *there* is often implied in English, whereas **y** must always be expressed in French.

2. **Y** can replace the combination **à** + *noun* when the noun refers to a place or thing. This substitution most often occurs after certain verbs that are followed by **à: répondre à, réfléchir à, réussir à, penser à** (*to think about someone or something*), **jouer à.** It is not usually applied to the **à** + *noun* combination when the noun refers to a person; in these cases, a stressed or indirect object pronoun is used.

| | |
|---|---|
| —As-tu répondu **au texto de ta sœur**? | *Did you answer your sister's text message?* |
| —Oui, j'**y** ai répondu. | *Yes, I answered it.* |
| —Elle pense déjà **au voyage à Marseille**? | *Is she already thinking about the trip to Marseille?* |
| —Non, elle n'**y** pense pas encore. | *No, she's not thinking about it yet.* |

**BUT**

| | |
|---|---|
| —As-tu téléphoné **à ta mère?** | *Did you call your mother?* |
| —Non, je ne **lui** ai pas téléphoné, mais je pense à **elle.** | *No, I didn't call her, but I'm thinking about her.* |

3. The placement of **y** is identical to that of object pronouns: It precedes a conjugated verb, an infinitive, or an auxiliary verb in the **passé composé.**

| | |
|---|---|
| La ville de Nice? Nous **y** cherchons une maison. | *The city of Nice? We're looking for a house there.* |
| Mon mari va **y** aller jeudi. | *My husband will go there on Thursday.* |
| Est-ce qu'il **y** est allé en train ou en avion? | *Did he go there by train or by plane?* |

[Allez-y! A]

# The Pronoun *en*

**1. En** can replace a combination of a partitive article (**du, de la, de l'**) or indefinite article (**un, une, des**) plus a noun; **en** is then equivalent to English *some* or *any*. Again, whereas these expressions can often be omitted in English, **en** must always be used in French. Like other object pronouns, **en** is placed directly before the verb that refers to it. In the **passé composé,** it is placed directly before the auxiliary verb.

| | |
|---|---|
| —Est-ce qu'il y a **des musées intéressants** à Avignon? | *Are there interesting museums in Avignon?* |
| —Oui, il y **en** a. | *Yes, there are (some).* |
| —Est-ce que vous avez visité **des sites touristiques** à Avignon? | *Did you visit any tourist attractions in Avignon?* |
| —Oui, nous y **en** avons visité. | *Yes, we visited some (there).* |
| —Avez-vous acheté **des souvenirs**? | *Did you buy souvenirs?* |
| —Non, nous n'**en** avons pas acheté. | *No, we didn't buy any.* |
| —Voici **du vin d'Avignon. En** veux-tu? | *Here's some wine from Avignon. Do you want some?* |
| —Non merci. Je n'**en** veux pas. | *No, thanks, I don't want any.* |

**2. En** can also replace a noun modified by a number or by an expression of quantity such as **beaucoup de, un kilo de, trop de, deux,** and so on. Only **en** (*of it, of them*) and the number or expression of quantity are used in place of the noun.

| | |
|---|---|
| —Avez-vous **une chambre**? | *Do you have a room?* |
| —Oui, j'**en** ai **une.*** | *Yes, I have one.* |
| —Vous avez **beaucoup de chambres** disponibles? | *Do you have a lot of rooms available?* |
| —Oui, j'**en** ai **beaucoup.** | *Yes. I have a lot.* |
| —**Combien de lits** voudriez-vous? | *How many beds would you like?* |
| —J'**en** voudrais **deux.** | *I'd like two.* |

**3. En** is also used to replace **de** plus a noun and its modifiers (unless the noun refers to people) in sentences with verbs or expressions that use **de: parler de, avoir envie de,** and so on.

| | |
|---|---|
| —Avez-vous besoin **de ce guide**? | *Do you need this guidebook?* |
| —Oui, j'**en** ai besoin. | *Yes, I need it.* |
| —Parliez-vous **des ruines romaines**? | *Were you talking about the Roman ruins?* |
| —Non, nous n'**en** parlions pas. | *No, we weren't talking about them.* |

[Allez-y! B-C]

---

*In a negative answer to a question containing **un(e)**, the word **un(e)** is not repeated:
**Je n'en ai pas.**

## Y and *en* Together

The combination of **y en** is very common with the expression **il y a.**

—Combien de terrains de
camping est-ce qu'il y a?
*How many campgrounds are
there?*
—Il **y en** a sept.
*There are seven (of them).*
—Combien de campeurs y
avait-il?
*How many campers were
there?*
—Il **y en** avait à peu près cent
cinquante.
*There were about a hundred
fifty (of them).*

[Allez-y! D-E]

 *Allez-y!*

**A. Roman policier.** Paul Marteau est détective. Il file (*trails*) une suspecte, Pauline Dutour. Doit-il aller partout (*everywhere*) où elle va?

MODÈLE: Pauline Dutour va à Paris. →
Marteau y va aussi. (*ou* Marteau n'y va pas.)

1. La suspecte entre dans un magasin de vêtements.
2. Elle va au cinéma.
3. Elle entre dans une pharmacie.
4. Pauline reste longtemps dans un bistro.
5. La suspecte monte dans un taxi.
6. Elle va chez le coiffeur (*hairdresser*).
7. Elle entre dans un hôtel.
8. La suspecte va au bar de l'hôtel.
9. Finalement, elle va en prison.

Maintenant, racontez les aventures de Marteau au passé composé.

**B. Un dîner chez Maxim.** Un(e) camarade vous interroge sur votre choix.

MODÈLE: pâté →
É1: Tu as envie de manger du pâté? (Prends-tu du pâté?)
É2: Oui, j'ai envie d'en manger. (Oui, j'en prends.)
(*ou* Non, je n'ai pas envie d'en manger. / Non, je n'en prends pas.)

1. hors-d'œuvre   3. escargots   5. légumes   7. dessert
2. soupe   4. viande   6. vin   8. café

**C. Mél à ma mère.** Lisez le mél et répondez aux questions suivantes. Utilisez le pronom **en** dans vos réponses.

1. Est-ce qu'Audrey a trouvé un appartement?
2. Combien de pièces est-ce qu'il y a?
3. Est-ce qu'Audrey et sa copine parlent souvent de la vie parisienne?
4. Quand va-t-elle acheter un vélo?
5. Pourquoi ne veut-elle pas de voiture?

ENVOYER | Enregistrer | Supprimer | Libellés ▾

À: Christinemom@wanadoo.com
Ajouter un champ Cc Ajouter un champ Cci
Objet: Paris!!
Joindre un fichier **Insérer** : Invitation

Chère Maman,
Je suis à Paris depuis trois jours. J'ai déjà trouvé un appartement dans le 15ᵉ. J'ai une chambre, un salon et une petite cuisine. Ma copine me parle souvent de la vie parisienne. C'est une ville fascinate. Je vais acheter un vélo la semaine prochaine pour me promener sur les bords* du canal Saint-Martin. Je ne veux pas de voiture. C'est trop dangereux ici. Je t'embrasse très fort. À bientôt.

Ta fille adorée,
Audrey

*me... *ride along the banks*

**D. Votre ville.** Imaginez qu'un(e) touriste vous pose des questions sur votre ville. Jouez les rôles avec un(e) camarade. Utilisez dans vos réponses le pronom **en** et un nombre ou une expression de quantité. Donnez aussi le plus de détails possible.

> **MODÈLE:** É1: Il y a des grands magasins dans votre ville?
> É2: Oui, il y en a beaucoup—Saks, Macy's, Nordstrom...
> (Il y en a seulement deux, Macy's et Saks.)

1. Avez-vous une université dans votre ville?
2. Il y a des musées intéressants à visiter?
3. Combien de cinémas et de théâtres avez-vous?
4. Est-ce qu'on peut y faire beaucoup de sport?
5. Combien d'habitants est-ce qu'il y a dans votre ville?
6. On y rencontre beaucoup d'étrangers?

**Résumez!** Maintenant, votre camarade décrit votre ville à la classe. Il/Elle commence par «Mon/Ma camarade est de _____. Il y a beaucoup de grands magasins à _____... » Est-ce que tout le monde est d'accord avec cette description? Comparez les descriptions d'une même ville. Qui a donné le plus de détails? Qui a été le plus précis / la plus précise?

La Grande Arche à la Défense, le centre d'affaires de Paris. Est-ce qu'il y a une arche comme celle-ci (*this one*) dans votre ville?

**E. Échange d'opinions.** Avec un(e) camarade, donnez des opinions sur des sujets divers. Utilisez les **Mots clés.**

**Suggestions:** les chauffeurs de taxi, les grandes villes américaines, les monuments, les musées, les touristes, les transports en commun...

> **MODÈLE:** É1: Que penses-tu des voitures japonaises?
> É2: Elles sont jolies (trop petites, pratiques)... Et toi, qu'en penses-tu?
> É1: Je (ne) les aime (pas). Elles (ne) sont (pas)...

## Mots clés

**Demander à quelqu'un son opinion**

**Que pensez-vous / penses-tu de...***
*What do you think of...*

**Qu'en pensez-vous / penses-tu?**
*What do you think about that?*

**À votre/ton avis,...**
*In your opinion,...*

**Donnez son opinion**

**Je pense que...**
*I think that...*

*****Penser de** is normally used to ask a person's opinion about something or someone; **penser à** means to think about (to have on one's mind) something or someone.

Prononcez bien!

**Nasal vowels** (page 291)

**A. Un anniversaire au restaurant.** Pour fêter l'anniversaire d'Isabelle, vous allez au restaurant avec elle, ses amis et votre camarade de classe. Vous venez de réviser les voyelles nasales en cours de français, alors vous faites attention à leur prononciation pendant que vos amis passent leur commande (*place their order*).

1. Écoutez Isabelle et écrivez les mots contenant la voyelle [ɔ̃] comme dans **bon**.

   a. _____   b. _____

2. Écoutez Louis et écrivez les mots contenant la voyelle [ɑ̃] comme dans **plan**.

   a. _____   b. _____   c. _____

3. Écoutez Hugo et écrivez les mots contenant la voyelle [ɛ̃] comme dans **chemin**.

   a. _____   b. _____

**B. Un anniversaire au restaurant (suite).** Maintenant, votre camarade et vous passez votre commande. Choisissez au moins trois choses sur le menu ci-dessous.

VOUS: Moi, je vais prendre…
VOTRE CAMARADE: Et pour moi…

---

## Aujourd'hui, le chef vous propose…

### Entrées
Pâté de campagne • Assiette de jambon • Champignons à la grecque • Saucisson

### Plats principaux
Gratin de pommes de terre • Bœuf bourguignon[1] • Saumon au vin blanc
• Canard à l'orange

### Desserts
Macarons aux amandes • Meringue à la framboise • Far breton[2] • Tarte tatin[3]

### Boissons
• Saint-Émilion (vin rouge) • Sancerre (vin blanc) • Champagne
Jus d'orange • Bouteille d'Évian

[1]Bœuf… Beef stew with red wine sauce  [2]Far… traditional cake from Brittany
[3]Tarte… Upside down apple tart

---

Lecture

### Avant de lire

**Reading poetry (Part 1).** Up until this chapter, you have been reading narrative texts. Depending on the text type, you have used a variety of strategies to facilitate comprehension: anticipating context by the use of titles and visuals, guessing from context, scanning for the gist, and so on.

Reading poetry, on the other hand, requires different skills. To identify these skills, it will be helpful for you to first clarify your expectations in reading poetry. Which of the following statements are true for you?

Poetry _____.

- ☐ is hard to read and understand
- ☐ uses abstract and figurative language
- ☐ must rhyme
- ☐ is written for the ear as well as for the eye
- ☐ should be read for the literal meaning
- ☐ creates a mood
- ☐ tells a story

Based on your answers, which of the following strategies would be most useful to read poetry effectively and pleasurably?

- ☐ Poetry should be read aloud.
- ☐ Be alert to both the literal and figurative meaning of a word.
- ☐ Skip unimportant details and concentrate on the main idea.
- ☐ Both the meaning of words and the shape of the text contribute to understanding.
- ☐ Because poetry is difficult to read, it helps to paraphrase the text.

**À propos de la lecture...**
«Le chat abandonné» est un poème inédit de Paul Degray, poète et instituteur français contemporain.

# «Le chat abandonné»

Je suis le chat de ton quartier
On me dit abandonné.
Ne cherche pas à m'attraper
Car mes griffes sont acérées.[1]

Je me promène sur les toits
Qu'il fasse nuit, qu'il fasse froid.[2]
Je n'ai pas peur de tomber
Car la Lune sait me guider.

Pour manger au restaurant
Je n'ai pas besoin d'argent
Je me sers dans les poubelles[3]
Et ne fais jamais d'vaisselle.

Je suis le chat de ton quartier
On me dit abandonné
Ça ne me fait pas pleurer
Car mon nom est Liberté.

[1]Car... *For my claws are sharp*  [2]Qu'il... *Whether it's night, whether it's cold*  [3]*garbage cans*

Poème inédit de Paul Degray in Christian Lamblin, *Poésies et Jeux de langage CP/CE1*, Éd. Retz, 2003

«Mon nom est Liberté»

### *Compréhension*

Complétez les phrases suivantes selon votre compréhension du poème.
Justifiez vos réponses.

1. Le chat du quartier est _____.
   a. abandonné
   b. content de sa vie
   c. triste
   d. attrapé

2. La nuit, le chat a _____.
   a. froid
   b. des difficultés à voir les toits
   c. la Lune pour le guider
   d. peur de se promener

3. Pour manger, le chat cherche _____.
   a. un endroit protégé de la pluie
   b. un refuge dans une maison du quartier
   c. un repas dans une poubelle
   d. un restaurant ouvert

4. Le chat du quartier se sent _____.
   a. abandonné
   b. libre
   c. sans amis
   d. énergique

 # Écriture

The writing activities **Par écrit** and **Journal intime** can be found in
the Workbook/Laboratory Manual to accompany *Vis-à-vis*.

# Pour s'amuser

Conduire dans Paris c'est une question de vocabulaire.

—Michel Audiard

# Le vidéoblog de Juliette

## En bref

Dans cet épisode, Juliette et Hector font une promenade au jardin du Luxembourg. Les deux amis parlent de leur ville natale et de leur vie actuelle (*present*) à Paris. Dans son vidéoblog, Juliette présente le côté «villageois» de Paris et Hector nous fait visiter son village à la Martinique.

## Vocabulaire en contexte

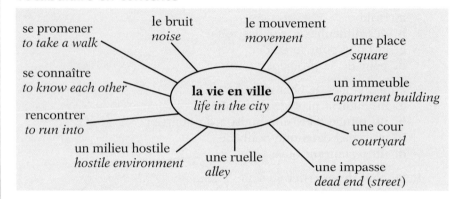

se promener
*to take a walk*

se connaître
*to know each other*

rencontrer
*to run into*

un milieu hostile
*hostile environment*

le bruit
*noise*

le mouvement
*movement*

une place
*square*

un immeuble
*apartment building*

une cour
*courtyard*

une impasse
*dead end (street)*

une ruelle
*alley*

**la vie en ville**
*life in the city*

L'église aux Anses d'Arlet, à la Martinique

## Note culturelle

Le long des côtes de la Martinique, on trouve de nombreux villages de pêcheurs[1] dans de très petites baies appelées «anses». L'Anse Dufour est un village de pêcheurs qui a gardé tout son charme d'origine; les Trois-Îlets tiennent[2] leur nom des trois petits îlots rocheux[3] qui émergent au large de[4] la pointe aux Pères; le village des Anses d'Arlet est célèbre pour ses deux plages superbes: la grande Anse et la Petite Anse.

[1]villages… *fishing villages*  [2]*take*
[3]îlots… *rocky islands*  [4]au… *offshore from*

## Visionnez!

Est-ce que les phrases suivantes décrivent Paris ou les Anses d'Arlet à la Martinique?

| | Paris | les Anses d'Arlet |
|---|---|---|
| 1. Il y a toujours du bruit, du mouvement. | ☐ | ☐ |
| 2. On rencontre toujours les mêmes gens. | ☐ | ☐ |
| 3. On vit (*makes a living*) de la pêche. | ☐ | ☐ |
| 4. On est toujours près de la nature. | ☐ | ☐ |
| 5. Au cœur (*heart*) de la capitale, il y a de vrai villages. | ☐ | ☐ |
| 6. Il y a des villas, des lofts et des ateliers d'artistes. | ☐ | ☐ |

## Analysez!

1. Hector nous dit qu'aux Anses d'Arlet, tout est «à l'échelle (*scale*) humaine». Expliquez pourquoi il a ce sentiment.
2. Quels aspects d'une petite ville trouve-t-on même à Paris?

## Comparez!

Décrivez votre ville natale. S'agit-il d'une commune (*town*) rurale ou d'une grande ville? Qu'a-t-elle en commun avec les Anses d'Arlet? Et avec Paris? Regardez encore une fois les parties culturelles de la vidéo: Dans quelle sorte de lieu désirez-vous vivre plus tard (*later*)? Expliquez.

# Vocabulaire

## Verbes

**annuler** to cancel
**connaître** to know, be familiar with
**emprunter (à)** to borrow (from)
**penser à** to think of (about)
**penser de** to think of (about) (to have an opinion about)
**poser une question (à)** to ask a question
**prêter (à)** to lend (to)
**savoir** to know (how, a fact)

À REVOIR: **écrire, envoyer, montrer, prendre, réfléchir (à), rendre visite (à), réussir (à), traverser**

## Substantifs

**l'arrondissement** (*m.*) district, section (*of Paris*)
**la banlieue** suburbs
**le bâtiment** building
**le bois** forest, woods
**le boulevard** boulevard
**le café-tabac** bar-tobacconist
**le carrefour** intersection
**la carte** map (*of a region, country*)
**le centre-ville** downtown
**le château** castle, château
**le chemin** way (road)
**le coin** corner
**le commissariat** police station
**l'église** (*f.*) church
**l'île** (*f.*) island
**la mairie** town hall

**le marché en plein air** open-air market
**la piscine** swimming pool
**la place** square
**le plan** map (*of a city*)
**le poste de police** police station
**la Rive droite** the Right Bank (*in Paris*)
**la Rive gauche** the Left Bank (*in Paris*)
**le syndicat d'initiative** tourist information bureau
**la tour** tower

À REVOIR: **la bibliothèque, le bureau de poste, le jardin, la librairie, la pièce, le quartier, le restaurant, la rue**

## Les nombres ordinaux

**le premier (la première), le/la deuxième,... , le/la cinquième,... , le/la huitième, le/la neuvième,... , le/la onzième,** etc.

## Les expressions temporelles

**au moment où** at the time when
**autrefois** formerly
**d'abord** first, first of all, at first
**enfin** finally
**ensuite** then, next
**pendant que** while
**puis** then, next
**soudain** suddenly

**tout à coup** suddenly
**une fois** once

À REVOIR: **de temps en temps, un week-end**

## Mots et expressions divers

**À votre (ton) avis,... ?** In your opinion, . . . ?
**de nouveau** (*adv.*) again
**en** (*pron.*) of them; of it; some; any (*in negatives*)
**gratuit** (*adj.*) free
**jusqu'à** up to, as far as
**partout** (*adv.*) everywhere
**plusieurs** several
**Qu'en penses-tu / pensez-vous?** What do you think of that?
**Que penses-tu / pensez-vous de... ?** What do you think about . . . ?
**tellement** (*adv.*) so
**tout droit** (*adv.*) straight ahead
**y** (*pron.*) there

À REVOIR: **à droite, à gauche**

## Mots apparentés

*Verbes:* **continuer, tourner, traverser**
*Substantifs:* **la banque, l'hôpital** (*m.*)**, l'hôtel** (*m.*)**, le monument, le musée, le parc, la pharmacie, la station (de métro)**
*Adjectifs:* **municipal(e), public / publique**

# La passion pour les arts

Les dossiers de Juliette

Juliette

➤ 📁 Mes photos
  ➤ 📁 *Le Penseur*, de Rodin
  ➤ 📁 Grand stabile rouge
  ➤ 📁 Au musée d'Orsay

*Le Penseur* de Rodin, dans le jardin du musée Rodin avec, à l'arrière, le dôme des Invalides

# Dans ce chapitre...

## OBJECTIFS COMMUNICATIFS

- talking about artistic and historical heritage
- emphasizing and clarifying
- speaking succinctly
- expressing actions
- talking about how things are done
- learning to distinguish between and pronounce selected sounds in French

Grand stabile rouge de Calder, sur l'esplanade de la Défense

## PAROLES (Leçon 1)

- Le patrimoine historique
- Les œuvres d'art et de littérature
- Les verbes **suivre, vivre** et **habiter**

## STRUCTURES (Leçons 2 et 3)

- Les pronoms accentués
- La place des pronoms personnels
- Les verbes suivis de l'infinitif
- Les adverbes

Le musée d'Orsay

## CULTURE

- Le blog de Juliette: *Pour les amateurs d'art*
- Reportage: *Les musées parisiens*
- Lecture: «Déjeuner du matin» (poème de Jacques Prévert) (Leçon 4)

www.mhconnectfrench.com

# Leçon 1

## Le patrimoine historique°

*Le... Historical heritage*

Les arènes d'Arles, monument de l'époque romaine (59 av. J.-C.*–V$^e$ siècle)

La cathédrale d'Amiens, chef-d'œuvre (*masterpiece*) du Moyen Âge (l'époque médiévale: V$^e$–XV$^e$ siècles)

_____
*avant Jésus-Christ

**PAROLES**

Chenonceaux, château de la Renaissance (XVIᵉ siècle)

Versailles, château de l'époque classique (XVIIᵉ siècle)

### Allez-y!

**A. Définitions.** Regardez les quatre photos et complétez les phrases.

1. Une période historique, c'est une _____.
2. Une durée de cent ans, c'est un _____.
3. On a bâti (*built*) la cathédrale d'Amiens à l'époque _____.
4. L'époque historique qui se situe entre le Vᵉ et le XVᵉ siècles s'appelle le _____.
5. Le château de Chenonceaux a été bâti au _____.
6. Le château de Versailles date de l'époque _____.
7. Les arènes d'Arles datent de l'époque _____.

**B. Leçon d'histoire.** Indiquez dans une phrase en quel siècle et à quelle époque chacun des événements suivants s'est passé (*took place*). Remplacez les éléments en italique par des pronoms.

**MODÈLE:** *Guillaume, duc de Normandie,* a conquis *l'Angleterre* en 1066. → Il l'a conquise au XIᵉ siècle, à l'époque du Moyen Âge.

1. *Blaise Pascal* a inventé *la première machine à calculer* en 1642.
2. On a bâti *les arènes de Nîmes* au premier siècle.
3. *La ville de Paris* s'appelait Lutèce du IIᵉ siècle av. J.-C. jusqu'au IVᵉ siècle après J.-C.
4. *Jacques Cartier* a pris possession *du Canada* au nom de la France en 1534.
5. *Jeanne d'Arc* a essayé de prendre *la ville de Paris* en 1429.
6. *René Descartes* a écrit *sa «Géométrie»* en 1637.
7. *Charlemagne* est devenu roi (*king*) en 768.

**C. À vous!** Imaginez que votre classe de français est en visite à Paris. Votre guide vous propose trois sites à visiter. En groupes de trois ou quatre personnes, choisissez un site parmi les suggestions suivantes. Vous devez présenter votre choix à la classe et le justifier. Finalement, on vote pour choisir un seul site pour toute la classe.

**Les arènes de Lutèce**

**Histoire:** des arènes romaines de 15 000 places avec une arène séparée pour les combats des gladiateurs

**Aujourd'hui:** un jardin public très agréable où on peut flâner (*stroll*), pique-niquer ou rêver

**À proximité:** le Quartier latin

**Le palais du Louvre**

**Histoire:** ancienne résidence royale commencée au XIIIᵉ siècle

**Aujourd'hui:** un magnifique musée d'art

**À proximité:** le quartier élégant de l'Opéra

**La cathédrale de Notre-Dame**

**Histoire:** Le grand chef-d'œuvre du Moyen Âge. Commencée en 1163 et finie en 1345. Son architecture de style gothique crée une atmosphère de mystère et de beauté.

**Aujourd'hui:** Toujours une église catholique. On peut monter les 387 marches (*steps*) jusqu'au sommet de sa tour et prendre de splendides photos de Paris.

**À proximité:** le Quartier latin, l'île Saint-Louis, l'Hôtel de Ville (*City Hall*) de Paris

# Les œuvres d'art et de littérature

### La littérature

une pièce de théâtre

un poème
la poésie

un roman

un écrivain, une femme écrivain

### La sculpture

une sculpture

un sculpteur, une femme sculpteur

### La peinture

un tableau

un peintre, une femme peintre

### La musique

un musicien, une musicienne

### Le cinéma

une actrice

un acteur

un/une cinéaste

**AUTRES MOTS UTILES**

| | |
|---|---|
| **un auteur dramatique** | playwright |
| **un comédien, une comédienne** | stage actor / actress |
| **un compositeur, une compositrice** | composer |
| **une œuvre** | work, composition |
| **un recueil** | collection |

## Allez-y!

**A. Qui sont-ils?** Retrouvez la profession de ces artistes. Si vous ne savez pas, devinez ou faites des recherches.

**MODÈLE:** Jean-Paul Sartre → C'est un écrivain.

1. Audrey Tautou
2. Auguste Rodin
3. Pierre Auguste Renoir
4. Simone de Beauvoir
5. Louis Malle
6. Camille Claudel
7. Claude Debussy
8. Mary Cassatt*
9. Henri Matisse
10. Catherine Deneuve

acteur / actrice
cinéaste
écrivain / femme écrivain
musicien(ne) et compositeur / compositrice
peintre / femme peintre
sculpteur / femme sculpteur

**B. Littérature.** Complétez les phrases avec la forme correcte des mots suivants: **acteur, écrivain, pièce de théâtre, poème, poésie, roman.**

1. *L'Étranger* est un _____ d'Albert Camus.
2. Molière était un _____ et un _____. Il a écrit des _____.
3. La vie de Verlaine a été turbulente, mais ses _____ font partie des chefs-d'œuvre de la _____ française.
4. Simone de Beauvoir a écrit des _____ et des essais sur la condition féminine.
5. *Les Fleurs du mal* est un recueil de _____ de Charles Baudelaire.

**C. Les goûts artistiques.** Posez les questions à un(e) camarade.

1. Quel est ton roman préféré? C'est de qui?
2. Qui est ton peintre préféré? Pourquoi?
3. Connais-tu des artistes français? Lesquels (*Which ones*)?
4. Est-ce que tu écoutes de la musique classique? Qui est ton compositeur préféré / ta compositrice préférée?
5. Aimes-tu la poésie? Quels poètes anglais ou américains aimes-tu? Connais-tu un poème par cœur (*by heart*)? Lequel?
6. Vas-tu quelquefois au théâtre? Quelle pièce as-tu vue récemment?
7. Aimes-tu aller au cinéma? Quel film as-tu vu récemment?

Maintenant, décrivez les goûts artistiques de votre camarade à la classe.

### Le parler jeune

| | |
|---|---|
| **un bouquin** | un livre |
| **faire un bide** | ne pas réussir (pour décrire un spectacle) |
| **faire un carton, cartonner** | avoir du succès (pour décrire un spectacle) |
| **un navet** | un mauvais film |
| **un tube** | une chanson à succès |

Lire un **bouquin** sur un écran? Pourquoi pas?

Avec un mauvais scénario, on est sûr de **faire un bide.**

Le prochain film de Tarantino va **cartonner** en Europe.

À ton avis, c'est un bon film ou **un navet**?

Tu l'aimes, le dernier **tube** de Camille?

---

*Mary Cassatt est née à Pittsburgh, mais elle a vécu (*lived*) à Paris et a participé au mouvement impressionniste.

# Les verbes *suivre* et *vivre*

| suivre (*to follow*) | |
|---|---|
| je **suis** | nous **suivons** |
| tu **suis** | vous **suivez** |
| il/elle/on **suit** | ils/elles **suivent** |
| *Past participle:* **suivi** | |

| vivre (*to live*) | |
|---|---|
| je **vis** | nous **vivons** |
| tu **vis** | vous **vivez** |
| il/elle/on **vit** | ils/elles **vivent** |
| *Past participle:* **vécu** | |

**Suivre** and **vivre** are irregular verbs, and they have similar conjugations in the present tense. **Suivre un cours** means *to take a course.*
**Poursuivre** (*to pursue*) is conjugated like **suivre.**

| | |
|---|---|
| Combien de cours d'art **suis**-tu? | *How many art courses are you taking?* |
| **Suivez** mes conseils! | *Follow my advice!* |
| Monet **a vécu** de nombreuses années à Giverny. | *Monet lived many years in Giverny.* |
| Est-ce qu'il **a poursuivi** ses études de musique? | *Did he pursue his musical studies?* |

## Allez-y!

**A. Van Gogh.** Complétez cette biographie en utilisant les verbes suivants: **suivre, poursuivre, vivre, habiter.** Mettez tous les verbes, excepté le numéro 7, au présent.

Vincent Van Gogh est né en 1853 à Groot-Zundert, aux Pays-Bas. En 1877, il _____[1] des cours pour devenir pasteur (*preacher*), mais malheureux, il change d'avis. Il _____[2] des études de dessin anatomique parce qu'il veut devenir artiste. Après des séjours en Belgique et aux Pays-Bas, où il peint *Les Mangeurs de pommes de terre*, il _____[3] à Paris, où il fait la connaissance des peintres impressionnistes comme Monet. C'est Pissarro qui le convainc d'utiliser des couleurs vives (*bright*). À Paris, Van Gogh ne vend aucun* tableau; il _____[4] dans la misère (*poverty*). De 1888 jusqu'à sa mort, Van Gogh _____[5] le sud de la France où il _____[6] sa passion pour la peinture. De plus en plus tourmenté, il se suicide en 1890. Il _____[7] (*passé composé*) seulement jusqu'à l'âge de 37 ans et n'a vendu qu'un seul tableau pendant sa vie.

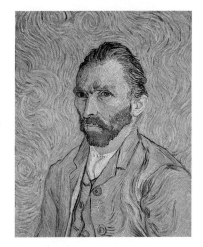

Vincent Van Gogh: *Autoportrait,* 1889–1890 (Musée d'Orsay, Paris)

---

*ne... aucun(e)** is a negative expression meaning *no, not one.*

**B. Conversation.** Avec un(e) camarade, répondez aux questions suivantes.

1. Quelle carrière veux-tu poursuivre? Suis-tu déjà des cours qui mènent à (*lead to*) cette carrière?
2. Est-ce que la plupart (*majority*) des gens basent leur choix de carrière sur ce qui les intéresse? Sinon, comment la choisissent-ils?
3. Comment veux-tu vivre dans dix ans? Dans le luxe en ville, par exemple, ou très simplement à la campagne? Dans quelle sorte de logement veux-tu habiter?
4. À ton avis, est-il plus important de suivre ses passions dans la vie ou de poursuivre la fortune? Pourquoi?

## Un peu plus...

**Claude Monet. (1840–1926)**

Comme ils ne sont pas acceptés dans les galeries traditionnelles, Monet et ses amis peintres décident, en 1874, d'organiser leur propre exposition. La technique de Monet vise (*aims*) à suggérer une expression spontanée de la nature par une application de couleurs vives. C'est la naissance du mouvement impressionniste qui sera (*will be*) reconnu plus tard comme l'un des plus importants mouvements d'art moderne. Vous aimez l'impressionnisme? Expliquez.

▶ *Claude Monet: Impression, soleil levant, 1873*
*(Musée Marmottan Monet, Paris)*

# Leçon 2

STRUCTURES

## Les pronoms accentués

*Emphasizing and Clarifying*

### Savoir parler d'amour

*Hassan, Hector, Juliette et Léa discutent chez Hector.*

HASSAN: **Moi**, j'aime la sculpture. Je passe des heures au musée Rodin.

JULIETTE: **Moi**, j'ai une passion pour la peinture, surtout pour Kandinsky. Je le trouve joyeux. Picasso, **lui**, est moins[1] gai.

LÉA: Et **toi**, Hector, qu'est-ce que tu aimes?

HECTOR: **Moi**, j'adore la danse: c'est ma passion, mon métier[2] et ma raison de vivre.[3]

LÉA: **Vous**, vous êtes différents de **moi**. Parce que **moi**, j'aime la poésie et les poètes.

JULIETTE: Pourquoi les poètes?

LÉA: Parce que **eux**, ils savent parler d'amour!

[1]*less*  [2]*profession*  [3]raison... *reason for living*

*Complétez les phrases suivantes en utilisant* **moi**, **toi**, **lui**, **vous** *ou* **eux**.

1. Et _____, vous aimez la sculpture?
2. _____, tu as une passion pour la peinture?
3. Kandinsky est joyeux, Picasso, _____, est moins gai.
4. _____, j'adore la danse.
5. Et _____, tu aimes la poésie et les poètes?
6. Les poètes, _____, ils savent parler d'amour.

Wassily Kandinsky: *Balançant,* 1925 (Tate Gallery, Londres)

## Forms of Stressed Pronouns

Stressed pronouns (**les pronoms accentués**) are used as objects of prepositions or for clarity or emphasis. The following chart shows their forms. Note that several are identical in form to subject pronouns.

| STRESSED PRONOUNS | | | |
|---|---|---|---|
| **moi** | *I, me* | **nous** | *we, us* |
| **toi** | *you* | **vous** | *you* |
| **lui** | *he, him* | **eux** | *they, them (m.)* |
| **elle** | *she, her* | **elles** | *they, them (f.)* |
| **soi\*** | *oneself* | | |

\*****Soi** corresponds to the subjects **on, tout le monde,** and **chacun** (*each one*).

## Uses of Stressed Pronouns

Stressed pronouns are used:

**1.** As objects of prepositions

| | |
|---|---|
| Nous allons travailler chez **toi** ce soir. | *We're going to work at your house tonight.* |
| Après **vous**! | *After you!* |
| Après le concert, tout le monde rentre chez **soi.** | *After the concert, everybody goes back home.* |

**2.** As part of compound subjects

| | |
|---|---|
| **Clara et elle** ont lu *À la recherche du temps perdu\** en entier. | *She and Clara read the entire* In Search of Lost Time. |
| **Robin et moi** avons joué ensemble une sonate de Debussy. | *Robin and I played a Debussy sonata together.* |

**3.** With subject pronouns, to emphasize the subject

| | |
|---|---|
| Et **lui,** écrit-il un roman? | *What about him? Is he writing a novel?* |
| **Eux,** ils ont de la chance. | *As for them, they are lucky.* |
| Tu es brillant, **toi**! | *You're brilliant!* |

When stressed pronouns emphasize the subject, they can be placed at the beginning or the end of the sentence.

[Allez-y! A]

**4.** After **ce** + **être**

| | |
|---|---|
| —C'est **vous,** Monsieur Lemaître? | *Is it you, Mr. Lemaître?* |
| —Oui, c'est **moi.** | *Yes, it's me (it is I).* |
| C'est **lui** qui donnait le cours sur Proust. | *He's the one who was teaching the course on Proust.* |

**5.** In sentences without verbs, such as one-word answers to questions and tag questions

| | |
|---|---|
| —Qui a visité le musée Delacroix? | *Who has visited the Delacroix Museum?* |
| —**Toi!** | *You!* |
| —As-tu pris mon livre d'art? | *Did you take my art book?* |
| —**Moi?** | *Me?* |
| Nous allons visionner une vidéo sur la peinture moderne. Et **lui?** | *We're going to see a video on modern painting. What about him?* |

---

\*Long novel by Marcel Proust, in seven volumes. The original English translation was titled *Remembrance of Things Past.* A 2003 translation is called *In Search of Lost Time.*

**6.** In combination with **même(s)** for emphasis

Préparent-ils la vidéo **eux-mêmes**?     *Are they preparing the video themselves?*

Allez-vous choisir les images **vous-même**?     *Are you going to choose the pictures yourself?*

[Allez-y! B-C]

### Allez-y!

**A. Au théâtre.** Vos amis et vous avez présenté une pièce de théâtre devant la classe. Décrivez le comportement des acteurs / actrices avant le commencement de la pièce, à l'aide des pronoms accentués.

> **MODÈLE:** nous / fatigués → Nous, nous étions fatigués.

**1.** je / préoccupé(e)      **4.** Jessica et Anaïs / sérieuses
**2.** Alice / anxieuse      **5.** Marc et Angela / calmes
**3.** Louis / agité      **6.** nous / heureux

**B. Pour monter la pièce.** (*To prepare the play.*) D'autres étudiants vous ont aidé(e) à monter la pièce de l'exercice précédent. Dites ce qu'ils ont fait. Remplacez les mots en italique par des pronoms qui correspondent aux mots entre parenthèses. Faites attention à la conjugaison du verbe.

**1.** Qui a fait les costumes? C'est *moi* qui ai fait les costumes. (Sandrine, Bruno, Pierre et Nassim)
**2.** Vous avez écrit le scénario vous-mêmes? Oui, *nous* l'avons écrit *nous*-mêmes. (je, une amie et moi, Richard et Florent, les acteurs)

**C. Êtes-vous indépendant(e)?** Est-ce que vos camarades et vous faites des choses intéressantes, utiles ou inhabituelles? Renseignez-vous sur les activités de quatre camarades. Utilisez les pronoms accentués + **même(s)** et les verbes de la liste suivante.

**Verbes utiles:** acheter, aller, bâtir* (*to build*), devoir, faire, gagner, jouer, lire, pouvoir, préparer, réparer, travailler, vendre, venir, voir, vouloir

> **MODÈLES:** Moi, je fais toujours le pain moi-même pour les repas à la maison.
> J'ai une camarade qui, elle, répare elle-même sa voiture.

---

*conjugated like **finir**

# La place des pronoms personnels

*Speaking Succinctly*

## Pas d'argent entre nous!

*Alexis contacte Poema sur sa page Facebook (Messagerie instantanée).*

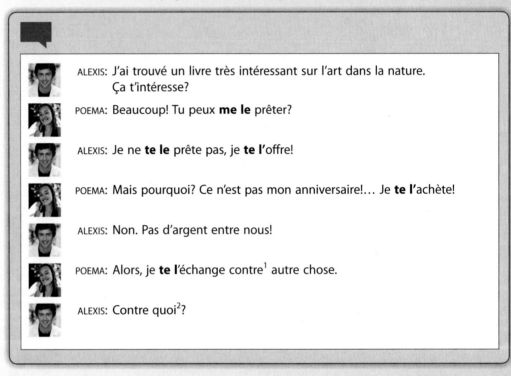

ALEXIS: J'ai trouvé un livre très intéressant sur l'art dans la nature. Ça t'intéresse?

POEMA: Beaucoup! Tu peux **me le** prêter?

ALEXIS: Je ne **te le** prête pas, je **te l'**offre!

POEMA: Mais pourquoi? Ce n'est pas mon anniversaire!... Je **te l'**achète!

ALEXIS: Non. Pas d'argent entre nous!

POEMA: Alors, je **te l'**échange contre[1] autre chose.

ALEXIS: Contre quoi[2]?

[1]échange... *trade for*  [2]*what*

Trouvez, dans le dialogue, la phrase équivalente.

**1.** Tu peux me prêter ton livre?
**2.** Je ne te prête pas mon livre.
**3.** Je t'offre mon livre.
**4.** Je t'achète le livre.
**5.** Je t'échange le livre.

## Order of Object Pronouns in Declarative Statements

When two or more pronouns are used in a declarative sentence, they follow a fixed order. The direct object pronoun is usually **le, la,** or **les. Me, te, nous,** and **vous** precede **le, la,** and **les; lui** and **leur** follow them. The pronouns **y** and **en,** in that order, come last.

| DIRECT OR INDIRECT OBJECT | DIRECT OBJECT | INDIRECT OBJECT | **y / en** |
|---|---|---|---|
| me<br>te<br>nous<br>vous | le<br>la<br>les | lui<br>leur | y / en |

| | |
|---|---|
| —Le guide vous a expliqué la théorie des peintres impressionnistes?<br>—Oui, il **nous l'**a expliquée. | *Did the guide explain the theory of the Impressionist painters to you?*<br>*Yes, he explained it to us.* |
| —Avez-vous montré le tableau de Manet aux étudiants américains?<br>—Oui, je **le leur** ai montré. | *Did you show the Manet painting to the American students?*<br>*Yes, I showed it to them.* |
| —Est-ce que le guide a donné des livrets sur l'impressionnisme aux autres étudiants?<br>—Oui, il **leur en** a donné. | *Did the guide give booklets on Impressionism to the other students?*<br>*Yes, he gave them some.* |

It might help you to remember this formula: First and second person before third; direct object before indirect object. Apply the first part if it is relevant, then the second.

**1.** When the pronouns are objects of an infinitive, they are placed immediately before the infinitive. The same order rules apply.

| | |
|---|---|
| —Quand est-ce que tu vas donner le cadeau à Line?<br>—Je vais **le lui** donner à Noël. | *When are you going to give Line the gift?*<br>*I am going to give it to her at Christmas.* |

**2.** In negative sentences with object pronouns, **ne** precedes the pronouns; when the negative sentence is in the **passé composé, pas** follows the conjugated verb (the auxiliary) and precedes the past participle.

| | |
|---|---|
| —Ils nous ont envoyé les horaires des autres musées de Paris?<br>—Non, ils **ne nous les** ont **pas** envoyés. | *Did they send us the schedules of the other museums in Paris?*<br>*No, they didn't send them to us.* |

[Allez-y! A-B]

## Commands with One or More Object Pronouns

**1.** The order of object pronouns in a negative command is the same as the order in declarative sentences: the pronouns precede the verb.

| | |
|---|---|
| N'**en** parlons pas! | *Let's not talk about it!* |
| N'**y** pense pas! | *Don't think about it!* |
| Ne **me** donnez pas le tableau! | *Don't give me the painting!* |
| Ne **me le** donnez pas! | *Don't give it to me!* |
| Ne **leur** dites pas que vous êtes venus! | *Don't tell them you came!* |
| Ne **le leur** dites pas! | *Don't tell them!* |

**2.** In affirmative commands with one object pronoun, the pronoun follows the verb and is attached with a hyphen. When **me** and **te** come at the end of the expression, they become **moi** and **toi.**

| | |
|---|---|
| La lettre? **Écrivez-la!** | *The letter? Write it!* |
| Voici du papier. **Prenez-en!** | *Here's some paper.* |
| | *Take some!* |
| Tes amis? **Donne-leur** des billets! | *Your friends? Give them some tickets!* |
| **Parle-moi** des concerts! | *Tell me about the concerts!* |

As you know, the final **-s** is dropped from the **tu** form of regular **-er** verbs and of **aller** to form the **tu** imperative: **Parle de tes problèmes! Va à la maison!** However, the -s is *not* dropped before **y** or **en** in the affirmative imperative: **Parles-*en*! Vas-*y*!**

**3.** When there is more than one pronoun in an affirmative command, however, all direct object pronouns precede indirect object pronouns, followed by **y** and **en,** in that order. All pronouns follow the command form of the verb and are attached by hyphens. The forms **moi** and **toi** are used except before **y** and **en,** where **m'** and **t'** are used.

| DIRECT OBJECT | INDIRECT OBJECT | | **y / en** |
|---|---|---|---|
| le | moi (m') | nous | |
| la | toi (t') | vous | y / en |
| les | lui | leur | |

| | |
|---|---|
| —Voulez-vous ma carte d'entrée au musée? | *Do you want my museum entrance card?* |
| —Oui, **donnez-la-moi.** | *Yes, give it to me.* |
| —Je t'apporte du papier? | *Shall I bring you some paper?* |
| —Oui, **apporte-m'en.** | *Yes, bring me some.* |
| —Tu veux que je cherche l'horaire du musée? | *Do you want me to look for the museum schedule?* |
| —Oui, **cherche-le-moi.** | *Yes, look for it for me.* |
| —Est-ce que je dis aux autres que l'entrée est gratuite? | *Shall I tell the others that admission is free?* |
| —Oui, **dites-le-leur.** | *Yes, tell them that (lit., tell it to them).* |

[Allez-y! C-D-E]

## Allez-y!

**A. Travail d'équipe.** Audrey et ses camarades préparent un exposé sur la Fondation Maeght, un musée d'art moderne au sud de la France. Transformez les phrases selon le modèle.

**MODÈLE:** Audrey donne <u>ses notes</u> <u>à Anaïs.</u> →
Elle les lui donne.

**1.** Elle prête <u>le livre sur Chagall</u> <u>à Sylvie</u>.
**2.** Anaïs envoie <u>des photos de la cour Giacometti</u> <u>à Audrey</u>.
**3.** La prof explique <u>les sculptures de Miró</u> <u>aux trois filles</u>.
**4.** Sylvie parle <u>à sa prof</u> <u>de l'exposition sur Braque</u>.
**5.** Audrey et ses camarades présentent <u>leur exposé</u> <u>aux autres étudiants du cours</u>.

**B. Détails pratiques.** Vous faites une visite artistique de Paris. Répondez par *oui* ou *non* et utilisez des pronoms.

> **MODÈLE:** Achetez-vous vos guides (*guidebooks*) à la librairie?
> Oui, je les y achète. (Non, je ne les y achète pas.)

**1.** Prenez-vous vos repas dans les musées?
**2.** Achetez-vous vos cartes postales au musée?
**3.** Emmenez-vous vos amis au musée?
**4.** Il y a des sculptures au musée du Louvre?
**5.** Avez-vous rencontré vos amis au ciné-club?
**6.** Apportez-vous votre appareil photo au musée?
**7.** Est-ce qu'il y avait beaucoup de visiteurs à l'exposition du Grand-Palais?

**C. Pour devenir un écrivain célèbre.** Dans les phrases suivantes, remplacez les mots en italique par des pronoms.

> **MODÈLES:** Lisez *beaucoup de romans*. →
> Lisez-en beaucoup!
>
> Montrez *vos œuvres à vos amis*. →
> Montrez-les-leur!

**1.** N'oubliez jamais *vos cahiers à la maison*.
**2.** Prenez *des notes*.
**3.** Révisez *votre travail*.
**4.** Envoyez *votre roman à l'éditeur*.
**5.** Invitez *votre éditeur* à dîner.
**6.** Après la publication du roman, demandez *à vos amis* d'acheter un exemplaire (*copy*).

**D. Situations.** Vous entendez des fragments de conversation. Imaginez la situation.

> **MODÉLE:** N'y touche pas! →
> La mère de Tristan vient de faire un gâteau, et Tristan essaie d'en manger un morceau.

**1.** Vas-y! **2.** N'y touche pas! **3.** Ne m'en donne pas! **4.** Ne les regardez pas! **5.** Donne-la-lui! **6.** Ne lui parle pas si fort! **7.** Montre-les-moi! **8.** Ne le lui dis pas!

**E. Interview.** Interrogez un(e) camarade sur une ville ou une région que vous pensez visiter. Suivez le modèle.
**Mots utiles:** une cathédrale, le cinéma, un musée, la musique, une pièce de théâtre, la sculpture, les tableaux; des acteurs / actrices célèbres, des compositeurs / compositrices, des cinéastes, des écrivains

> **MODÈLE:** É1: Est-ce qu'il y a une belle cathédrale à Strasbourg?
> É2: Oui, il y en a une.

---

## Mots clés

**Les verbes *apporter* et *emmener***

**Apporter** (*to bring something*) is used only with objects.

> Il apporte ses tableaux à la galerie d'art.

**Emmener** (*to take someone along; to invite*) is used with people or animals.

> Je t'emmène au cinéma?

# Le blog de Juliette

## Pour les amateurs d'art

samedi 2 août

**J'aime l'art.**

J'ai commencé à aimer la peinture vers[1] l'âge de 12 ans, quand ma mère m'a emmenée voir une exposition du peintre Kandinsky, le peintre des compositions abstraites et des jeux de couleurs.

Ensuite, j'ai appris à peindre. Je rêvais de créer une œuvre, je voulais être le Mozart de la peinture! Mais rapidement, j'ai accepté de reconnaître une vérité absolue: je n'ai aucun talent[2]…

Alors, je me contente[3] d'admirer les œuvres des autres, de voir des expositions et d'explorer des musées. La semaine dernière, par exemple, j'ai visité les musées en plein air[4] de Paris: les œuvres sont exposées dans des lieux publics, sous le vent, la pluie[5] et le soleil! C'est une expérience unique!

Malheureusement, je ne serai jamais[6] une artiste… Je dois l'accepter. Mais j'ai décidé de promouvoir[7] les chefs-d'œuvre des jeunes artistes…

Je vais donc créer une galerie d'art virtuelle sur le net pour encourager les jeunes peintres et sculpteurs à montrer leurs œuvres.

Mes amis du blog sont les premiers informés!

Juliette

Grand stabile rouge de Calder sur l'esplanade à la Défense

.......................................................

### COMMENTAIRES

**Alexis**

Franchement Juliette, c'est une bonne idée. Mais des galeries virtuelles, il y en a déjà beaucoup sur le Web. Pourtant, si tu veux faire la promotion des jeunes peintres québécois, je peux t'aider…

**Charlotte**

Juliette, je te conseille de poursuivre ton projet. Il faut seulement créer un site différent et original. Toi, tu as une double expertise et tu peux inventer un concept génial: tu connais parfaitement le multimédia et tu connais l'art.

**Mamadou**

Pourquoi ne pas organiser des expositions d'art africain d'avant-garde? Évidemment, tout le monde connaît les masques, les statuettes et les tissus[8] africains traditionnels, mais en Afrique, il y a aussi des artistes contemporains vraiment exceptionnels. Moi-même, j'en connais et je peux te les présenter.

**Poema**

La plupart des artistes polynésiens ont des difficultés pour exposer leurs tableaux en Europe. Tu peux les aider à réussir sur le marché français!

[1]*around*   [2]*Je… I have no talent whatsoever*   [3]*me… am satisfied*   [4]*musées… open-air museums*   [5]*rain*
[6]*ne… will never be*   [7]*promote*   [8]*fabrics*

## Les musées parisiens

Où se trouve *Le Penseur,* la plus fameuse sculpture d'Auguste Rodin? À Paris, au musée Rodin, qui était autrefois l'hôtel Biron où l'artiste a passé beaucoup de temps pendant les dernières années de sa vie. Le jardin qui entoure[1] le musée est une petite merveille. Flânez dans les allées et découvrez les chefs-d'œuvre du grand maître exposés en plein air.

Ensuite, visitez le musée. Imaginez une sorte de petit palais avec des parquets cirés.[2] D'une pièce à l'autre, vous découvrez des sculptures remarquables: *Le Baiser,*[3] *La Main de Dieu*[4]…

Vous sortez de ce musée fasciné par la blancheur du marbre, charmé par ces corps et ces visages[5] sculptés dans la pierre[6] éternelle.

Pour continuer votre visite des musées parisiens, vous devez, bien sûr, aller au Louvre: cette ancienne demeure[7] des rois de France est une pièce majeure du patrimoine français et l'un des plus grands musées d'art du monde. On y trouve notamment la célèbre *Joconde*[8] au sourire mystérieux. Le musée d'Orsay, très riche en tableaux impressionnistes, mérite aussi une visite.

Mais si vous voulez sourire, il faut aller au musée Grévin, qui présente plus de 450 personnages célèbres… en cire,[9] ou au musée de la Poupée,[10] qui va vous rappeler votre enfance. Et si vous aimez la littérature, vous devez absolument visiter la maison de Balzac et la maison de Victor Hugo: dans ces murs, des œuvres immortelles sont nées.

C'est dans l'ancienne gare d'Orsay que le musée d'Orsay s'est installé. Ce bâtiment magnifique, classé monument historique, date de 1900. Construit pour l'Exposition Universelle, il réunit aujourd'hui des chefs-d'œuvre de l'impressionnisme et du post-impressionnisme français, comme *Femme à l'ombrelle* de Monet ou *La Danseuse* de Renoir.

[1]*surrounds*   [2]parquets… *waxed wood floors*   [3]*Kiss*   [4]*Main… Hand of God*   [5]*faces*   [6]*stone*   [7]*residence*   [8]*Mona Lisa*   [9]en… *in wax*   [10]*Doll*

1. Avez-vous envie de visiter le musée Rodin ou un autre musée parisien? Expliquez pourquoi.
2. Est-ce que vous avez visité, aux États-Unis ou dans d'autres pays, des musées originaux et surprenants? Racontez une de ces expériences et expliquez vos réactions.

1. Travaillez à deux ou en petits groupes. Préparez un circuit (*tour*) de trois petits musées originaux à Paris. Aidez-vous d'Internet.
2. Pour chaque musée, trouvez deux mots-clés pouvant expliquer votre sélection. Par exemple, pour le musée de la Vie romantique: «ambiance, Chopin».
3. Avec votre camarade ou votre groupe, présentez et expliquez votre circuit de musées à la classe. N'oubliez pas de mentionner les mots clés.

Quel est le musée le plus intéressant? Votez!

# Leçon 3

## Les verbes suivis de l'infinitif

*Expressing Actions*

### Provocation?

*Mamadou contacte Léa sur sa page Facebook (Messagerie instantanée).*

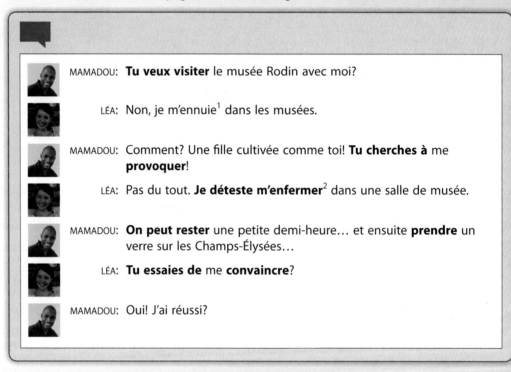

MAMADOU: **Tu veux visiter** le musée Rodin avec moi?

LÉA: Non, je m'ennuie[1] dans les musées.

MAMADOU: Comment? Une fille cultivée comme toi! **Tu cherches à** me **provoquer**!

LÉA: Pas du tout. **Je déteste m'enfermer**[2] dans une salle de musée.

MAMADOU: **On peut rester** une petite demi-heure… et ensuite **prendre** un verre sur les Champs-Élysées…

LÉA: **Tu essaies de** me **convaincre**?

MAMADOU: Oui! J'ai réussi?

[1]*je… I get bored*   [2]*shut myself up*

Dans le dialogue, trouvez les verbes à l'infinitif qui suivent les verbes conjugués.

1. Tu veux _____ le musée Rodin avec moi?
2. Tu cherches à me _____?
3. Je déteste _____ dans une salle de musée.
4. On peut _____ une petite demi-heure.
5. Tu essaies de me _____?

1. Some verbs can be followed by an infinitive without an intervening preposition. Among the most common:

| | | | |
|---|---|---|---|
| **aimer** | **détester** | **falloir (il faut)** | **savoir** |
| **aller** | **devoir** | **pouvoir** | **venir** |
| **désirer** | **espérer** | **préférer** | **vouloir** |

Je **déteste chanter.** Mais je **sais**
très bien **jouer** de la guitare.

*I hate singing, but I know how
to play the guitar very well.*

Sophie **ne peut pas aller** au
cinéma samedi soir. Elle **doit
aller voir** sa grand-mère.

*Sophie cannot go to the movies
on Saturday evening. She has
to visit her grandmother.*

When **penser** is followed by an infinitive, it means *to count or plan
on doing something.*

Je **pense rester** chez moi ce
week-end.

*I'm planning on staying home
this weekend.*

2. Other verbs require the preposition **à** directly before the infinitive.
These include:

| | | | |
|---|---|---|---|
| **aider à** | **chercher à** | **continuer à** | **réussir à** |
| **apprendre à** | **commencer à** | **enseigner à** | |

J'**ai commencé à fumer** quand
j'avais 16 ans. Caroline m'**a
aidé à arrêter.**

*I started to smoke when I was
16. Caroline helped me quit.*

La semaine prochaine, je vais
**apprendre à jouer** au
tennis et je **continue à
prendre** des cours de yoga
deux fois par semaine.

*Next week I will learn how to
play tennis, and I will
continue to take yoga classes
twice a week.*

3. Still other verbs require the preposition **de** directly before the infinitive.

| | | | |
|---|---|---|---|
| **accepter de** | **décider de** | **finir de** | **rêver de** |
| **arrêter de** | **demander de** | **oublier de** | **venir de** |
| **choisir de** | **empêcher de** | **permettre de** | |
| **conseiller de** | **essayer de** | **refuser de** | |

Rachid **a décidé de prendre**
des cours d'art dramatique.
Il **rêve de devenir** acteur. Il
**vient de jouer** un petit rôle
dans *Le Cid* à l'université.
L'année prochaine, il va
**essayer d'entrer** au
Conservatoire de Paris.

*Rachid has decided to take
drama classes. He dreams of
becoming an actor. He just
played a small role in* Le
Cid *at the university. Next
year, he is going to try to get
into the Paris Conservatory.*

4. A few verbs change in meaning with different prepositions. **Commencer** regularly takes **à** before an infinitive; **finir** normally takes **de** before an infinitive. However, they can both take **par. Commencer par** is used to talk about what one did first in a series of things; **finir par** means *to end up by doing something.*

Grégoire **a commencé par** jouer un petit rôle dans une comédie à l'université. Il **a fini par** devenir acteur à Hollywood.

5. Note that the meaning of **venir** changes depending on whether it is followed directly by an infinitive or by **de** plus an infinitive. **Ils viennent dîner** means *They are coming to dinner.* **Ils viennent de dîner** means *They've just had dinner.*

### Allez-y!

**A. Au cabaret de la Contrescarpe.** Deborah, Chuck et Jacques arrivent à la Contrescarpe, dans le quartier Montmartre, à Paris. Classez leurs activités par ordre chronologique de 1 à 8.

_____ Ils décident de commander du champagne.

_____ Ils finissent par s'endormir dans le séjour.

_____ Ils demandent au serveur de leur apporter l'addition.

_____ Ils choisissent de s'asseoir à une table près de la scène.

_____ Ils commencent par regarder la salle.

_____ Ils commencent à chanter en rentrant chez eux.

_____ Ils arrêtent de parler quand le spectacle commence.

_____ Ils n'oublient pas de laisser un pourboire au serveur.

**B. Projets et activités.** Posez des questions à vos camarades pour vous informer de leurs projets et de leurs activités.

> **MODÈLE:** aller / faire / ce soir →
> É1: Qu'est-ce que tu vas faire ce soir?
> É2: Je vais sortir avec mes amis.

1. vouloir / faire / ce week-end
2. aller / faire / l'été prochain
3. devoir / faire / demain
4. aimer / faire / après les cours
5. penser / faire / la semaine prochaine
6. détester / faire / le soir
7. espérer / faire / ce soir

**C. Résolutions du Nouvel An.** Énumérez quelques-unes de vos résolutions à vos camarades. Complétez les phrases suivantes avec un infinitif.

> **MODÈLE:** Cette année, je vais finir... →
> Cette année, je vais finir de lire *La Vie mode d'emploi* de Georges Perec.*

1. Je voudrais apprendre...
2. Je vais commencer...
3. J'ai aussi décidé...
4. En plus, je vais arrêter...
5. Enfin, je rêve...
6. Mais je refuse...

**D. Interview.** Posez les questions suivantes—en français, s'il vous plaît—à un(e) camarade de classe. Puis faites un résumé de ses réponses. Demandez à votre camarade...

1. what he/she likes to do in the evening
2. what he/she hates to do in the house
3. if he/she is learning to do something interesting, and what it is
4. if he/she has decided to continue to study French
5. what he/she has to do after class
6. if he/she prefers going to a play or to a movie
7. if he/she has just read a good book, and what it was
8. what he/she knows how to do well
9. what he/she tries, but does not always succeed in doing well
10. if he/she forgot to do something this morning, and what it was
11. if he/she has stopped doing something recently, and what it was
12. ?

---

*Perec (1936–1982) était un artiste et écrivain français. *La Vie mode d'emploi,* fruit de neuf années de travail, retrace l'histoire d'un immeuble parisien et de ses habitants.

# Les adverbes

*Talking About How Things Are Done*

## L'art et le foot

*Léa et Mamadou discutent au café.*

Le célèbre Fouquet's sur les Champs-Élysées

LÉA: Une heure au musée, c'est **vraiment** le maximum pour moi!

MAMADOU: Dis la vérité: tu as **beaucoup** aimé les sculptures. Tu étais fascinée!

LÉA: **Franchement,** j'ai apprécié la lumière* naturelle sur les œuvres.

MAMADOU: Tu vois: il faut **toujours** aller au musée avec moi!

LÉA: Et **maintenant,** qu'est-ce qu'on fait?

MAMADOU: On va d'**abord** prendre un verre au Fouquet's.

LÉA: Et **ensuite**?

MAMADOU: **Ensuite,** je t'emmène à un match de foot!

*light

Répondez aux questions en utilisant les adverbes du dialogue.

1. Est-ce que deux heures au musée, c'est le maximum pour Léa?
2. Est-ce que Mamadou pense qu'elle a aimé les sculptures?
3. Qu'est-ce qu'elle a apprécié?
4. Avec qui faut-il aller au musée?
5. Qu'est-ce qu'ils vont faire après leur visite du musée?

## Forms of Adverbs

Adverbs (**les adverbes,** *m.*) modify a verb, an adjective, or another adverb: She learns *quickly*. He is *extremely* hardworking. They see each other *quite often*. You have already learned a number of adverbs, such as **souvent, parfois, bien, mal, beaucoup, trop, peu, très, vite, d'abord, puis, ensuite, après,** and **enfin.**

1. Most adverbs are formed by adding **-ment** (often corresponding to *-ly* in English) to the feminine form of an adjective.

| FEMININE ADJECTIVE | ADVERB | |
|---|---|---|
| franche | **franchement** | *frankly* |
| active | **activement** | *actively* |
| (mal)heureuse | **(mal)heureusement** | *(un)fortunately* |

**2.** If the masculine form of the adjective ends in a vowel, **-ment** is usually added directly to it.

| MASCULINE ADJECTIVE | ADVERB | |
|---|---|---|
| absolu | **absolument** | *absolutely* |
| poli | **poliment** | *politely* |
| rapide | **rapidement** | *quickly* |
| vrai | **vraiment** | *truly, really* |

**3.** If the masculine form of the adjective ends in **-ent** or **-ant,** the corresponding adverbs have the endings **-emment** and **-amment,** respectively. The two endings have the same pronunciation.

| MASCULINE ADJECTIVE | ADVERB | |
|---|---|---|
| différent | **différemment** | *differently* |
| évident | **évidemment** | *evidently, obviously* |
| constant | **constamment** | *constantly* |
| courant | **couramment** | *fluently* |

One exception to this rule is **lent,** which adds **-ment** to the feminine adjective to form **lentement.**

Note: In English, the adverbial forms of *good* and *bad* are *well* and *badly.* In French, the adverb forms of **bon** and **mauvais** are both irregular.

**bon** → **bien**         Sonia est une **bonne** actrice; elle joue **bien** son rôle.

**mauvais** → **mal**         Normand est un **mauvais** cinéaste; il dirige **mal** ses acteurs.

[Allez-y! A-B]

## Position of Adverbs

**1.** When adverbs qualify adjectives or other adverbs, they usually precede them.

Elle est **très** intelligente.         *She is very intelligent.*
Il va au cinéma **assez** souvent.         *He goes to the movies fairly often.*

**2.** When a verb is in the present or imperfect tense, the qualifying adverb usually follows it. In negative constructions, the adverb comes after **pas.**

Je travaille **lentement.**         *I work slowly.*
Elle voulait **absolument** devenir écrivain.         *She absolutely wanted to become a writer.*
Vous ne l'expliquez pas **bien.**         *You aren't explaining it well.*

**3.** Short adverbs usually precede the past participle when the verb is in a compound form; they usually follow **pas** in a negative construction.

J'ai **beaucoup** voyagé cette année.

*I've traveled a lot this year.*

Il a **déjà** visité le Louvre.

*He has already visited the Louvre.*

Elle n'est pas **souvent** allée en Bretagne.

*She has not often been to Brittany.*

Je n'ai pas **très** faim.*

*I'm not very hungry.*

**4.** Adverbs ending in **-ment** follow a verb in the present or imperfect tense, and usually follow the past participle when the verb is in the **passé composé.**

Tu parles **couramment** le français.

*You speak French fluently.*

Il était **vraiment** travailleur.

*He was really hardworking.*

Paul n'a pas répondu **intelligemment.**

*Paul didn't respond intelligently.*

[Allez-y! C-D]

Des menhirs préhistoriques à Carnac, en Bretagne: ces pierres dressées (*standing stones*) sont vraiment mystérieuses!

 **Allez-y!**

**A. Ressemblances.** Donnez l'équivalent adverbial de chacun des adjectifs suivants.

**MODÈLE:** franc → franchement

1. heureux
2. actif
3. long
4. vrai
5. différent
6. naturel
7. certain
8. constant
9. absolu
10. admirable
11. poli
12. intelligent

---

*In idiomatic expressions with **avoir,** one often uses an adverb: **J'ai très soif; Elle a très chaud,** and so on.

**B. Carrières.** Complétez les paragraphes suivants avec des adverbes logiques.

1. Le linguiste

**Adverbes:** bien, bientôt, couramment, ensuite, évidemment, probablement, vite

Jean-Luc parle _____¹ l'anglais. Il a vécu aux États-Unis. Il est allé au lycée (à l'école secondaire) à New York et il a très _____² appris la langue pendant son séjour. _____³, à l'université il a choisi la section langues étrangères. Il va _____⁴ passer sa licence d'anglais. _____⁵, il doit _____⁶ choisir entre la traduction (*translation*) littéraire et l'enseignement. Ses parents sont professeurs et je pense qu'il va _____⁷ choisir de devenir professeur.

2. L'actrice

**Adverbes:** absolument, beaucoup, constamment, fréquemment, rarement, seulement, souvent, très

Marie veut _____¹ devenir une artiste célèbre. Elle travaille _____² pour y arriver: le matin, elle arrive _____³ au Théâtre National de Chaillot après six heures et elle y reste _____⁴ jusqu'à neuf heures du soir. Dans la journée, elle travaille _____⁵ et prend _____⁶ quinze minutes pour déjeuner. _____⁷, elle est fatiguée le soir. Mais je pense qu'elle va réussir parce qu'elle est _____⁸ travailleuse et ambitieuse.

Le Théâtre National de Chaillot se trouve au Palais de Chaillot, à Paris. Décrivez cette photo comme si c'était une œuvre d'art.

**C. Interview.** Interviewez un(e) camarade de classe sur ses préférences et ses habitudes. Votre camarade doit utiliser dans sa réponse un adverbe basé sur les mots entre parenthèses. Décidez ensuite quelle sorte de personne il/elle est (calme, énergique, patiente, pratique, travailleuse, et cetera).

**MODÈLE:** Comment déjeunes-tu d'habitude? (rapide / lent) →
Je déjeune lentement pour me reposer. *ou* Je déjeune rapidement parce que je suis toujours pressé(e).

1. Quand fais-tu la sieste? (fréquent / rare)
2. Comment attends-tu le résultat de ton examen? (patient / impatient)
3. Regardes-tu souvent ta montre? (constant / fréquent / rare / jamais)
4. Comment travailles-tu en général? (bon / mal)
5. Lis-tu souvent les romans policiers? (fréquent / rare / jamais)

Maintenant décrivez le caractère de votre camarade.

**D. Qu'en pensez-vous?** Posez les questions suivantes à des camarades. Ils vont répondre en utilisant des adverbes.

**Suggestions:** absolument, admirablement, constamment, couramment, diligemment, évidemment, franchement, heureusement, intelligemment, lentement, malheureusement, poliment, souvent, tranquillement, vite

**MODÉLE:**  É1: Qu'est-ce qu'on doit faire pour avoir de bonnes notes?
 É2: On doit étudier constamment.
 É1: On doit travailler intelligemment.

1. Qu'est-ce qu'on doit faire pour être un bon professeur?
2. Qu'est-ce qu'on doit faire pour devenir président(e) des États-Unis?
3. Qu'est-ce qu'on doit faire pour courir dans un marathon?
4. Qu'est-ce qu'on doit faire pour devenir riche?
5. Qu'est-ce qu'on doit faire pour avoir de bons rapports (*a good relationship*) avec une autre personne?

E. **Opinions et habitudes.** Posez ces questions à un(e) camarade. Dans sa réponse il/elle doit employer des adverbes.

1. À ton avis, est-ce qu'on doit beaucoup travailler pour réussir?
2. Quel est l'aspect le plus important de ta carrière future?
3. Est-ce que l'argent fait le bonheur?
4. Est-ce que l'amitié est plus importante que la réussite?
5. Est-ce que tu rêves de quitter ton pays pour aller vivre sur une île tropicale?

### Un peu plus...

**Paul Gauguin. (1848–1903)**
Après plus de dix ans comme agent de change (*stockbroker*) à Paris, où il fait la connaissance de Camille Pissarro et découvre l'impressionnisme, Gauguin quitte la Bourse (*stock exchange*) pour se consacrer à la peinture. Il privilégie les couleurs vives et les contours clairement démarqués, comme son ami Van Gogh. En 1888, Gauguin et Van Gogh passent neuf semaines ensemble à Arles mais l'amitié tourne mal et se termine avec le drame de l'oreille coupée de Van Gogh. Quelques années plus tard, Gauguin s'installe à Tahiti où il s'inspire de la culture polynésienne et des mythes anciens pour peindre ses plus fameux tableaux. Vous aimez les tableaux de Gauguin? Pourquoi ou pourquoi pas?

◀ *Paul Gauguin: Femmes de Tahiti, 1891 (Musée d'Orsay, Paris)*

# Prononcez bien!

**The vowel sound in *sculpture*** (page 323)

**A.** **Un bruit bizarre...** Vous regardez la télévision avec Hugo quand vous entendez un bruit bizarre. Hugo vous rassure. Sélectionnez les phrases qu'il dit.

1. **a.** Tout va bien. C'est Pierre, notre voisin. Il a sûrement laissé tomber un objet.
   **b.** Tu vas bien. C'est Pierre, notre voisin. Il a sûrement laissé tomber un objet.

2. **a.** Il habite au-dessous de chez nous.
   **b.** Il habite au-dessus de chez nous.

3. **a.** Isabelle et moi, nous l'avons rencontré pendant notre cours l'année dernière.
   **b.** Isabelle et moi, nous l'avons rencontré pendant notre cure (*vacation at the hot springs*) l'année dernière.

4. **a.** C'est quelqu'un qui est très sourd (*deaf*). Alors, ne t'inquiète pas!
   **b.** C'est quelqu'un qui est très sûr (*reliable*). Alors, ne t'inquiète pas!

**B.** **Des photos.** Hugo vous montre les photos de ses vacances d'été. Jouez la scène suivante avec votre camarade de classe en faisant attention à la prononciation de [u] comme dans **vous** et de [y] comme dans **sculpture**.

VOUS: C'est qui ça?
HUGO: Ah, c'est Luc, mon cousin.
VOUS: Qu'est-ce qu'il a sur la figure (*face*)?
HUGO: Des gouttes (*drops*) de jus de prune (*plum*). Il faisait très chaud ce jour-là. Une vraie canicule (*heat wave*)! Nous avons beaucoup bu.
VOUS: Et sur cette photo, on dirait qu'il fume.
HUGO: Oui, mais il a arrêté récemment parce qu'il toussait (*was coughing*) beaucoup.
VOUS: Voilà une bonne nouvelle!

# Leçon 4

 Lecture

### *Avant de lire*

**Reading poetry (Part 2).** Poetry often remains popular for decades and even centuries. One of the reasons is that it is often based on emotions that are universal over time such as happiness, sadness, love, sorrow, jealousy, fear, and anger. Effective poetry engages the reader emotionally and often articulates one of those inner feelings for him or her. The impact of the poem is often derived from the sounds and the repetition of those sounds along with the rhythm and rhyming used.

In *Déjeuner du matin*, Prévert uses much repetition.

Find...

1. which phrase is repeated at least six times.
2. which phrases contain the word **sans**. Note which ones are repeated more than one time.
3. which verb tense is used repeatedly throughout the poem.

Glance through the text to determine which inner feeling will be engaged. Use the following information to help you guess.

Find out...

1. how many people are involved.
2. where the scene is taking place.
3. what the weather is like.
4. what one character does at the very end.

# «Déjeuner du matin»

Le poète Jacques Prévert

Il a mis le café
Dans la tasse
Il a mis le lait
Dans la tasse de café
Il a mis le sucre
Dans le café au lait
Avec la petite cuiller
Il a tourné
Il a bu le café au lait
Et il a reposé[1] la tasse
Sans me parler
Il a allumé[2]
Une cigarette
Il a fait des ronds
Avec la fumée
Il a mis les cendres

Dans le cendrier
Sans me parler
Sans me regarder
Il s'est levé[3]
Il a mis
Son chapeau sur sa tête
Il a mis
Son manteau de pluie
Parce qu'il pleuvait
Et il est parti
Sous la pluie
Sans une parole
Sans me regarder
Et moi j'ai pris
Ma tête dans ma main
Et j'ai pleuré.[4]

[1]a... *put down again*   [2]a... *lit*   [3]s'est... *got up*   [4]j'ai... *I cried*

"Déjeuner du matin" in *Paroles* by Jacques Prévert, © Éditions GALLIMARD

## Compréhension

**Qu'en pensez-vous?** Dites si les phrases suivantes reflètent votre inter-
prétation du poème. Sinon, reformulez-les pour mieux exprimer votre
opinion. Justifiez votre point de vue en citant des extraits du poème.

1. Dans ce poème, une mère raconte son petit déjeuner avec
   son fils.
2. Ces personnes se connaissent (*know each other*) depuis
   longtemps.
3. On a l'impression que c'est un repas typique entre ces deux
   personnes.
4. Le narrateur / La narratrice est très satisfait(e) de sa vie.
5. Le poète crée une ambiance de joie.

 Écriture

The writing activities **Par écrit** and **Journal intime** can be found in
the Workbook/Laboratory Manual to accompany *Vis-à-vis*.

# Pour s'amuser

Un jeune peintre se passionne pour l'abstraction.

—Ce que les gens préfèrent dans mes tableaux, c'est l'imagination.
—Vraiment?
—Oui. Après avoir regardé mes œuvres, beaucoup me disent: «Si vous appelez ça de l'art, vous avez beaucoup d'imagination!»

Marc Chagall*: *Le Cantique des cantiques IV,* 1958 (Musée National Message Biblique Marc Chagall, Nice)

---

*Marc Chagall (1887–1985) est un artiste et peintre né en Bélarussie. Il a vécu principalement en France.

# Le vidéoblog de Juliette

## En bref

Dans cet épisode, Juliette rencontre Léa sur le pont près du musée d'Orsay. Comme il faut faire la queue pour y entrer, les deux amies décident de passer l'après-midi à découvrir les œuvres des musées «en plein air».

### Vocabulaire en contexte

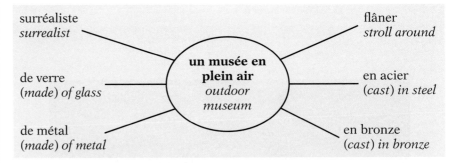

surréaliste
*surrealist*

de verre
(*made*) *of glass*

de métal
(*made*) *of metal*

**un musée en plein air**
*outdoor museum*

flâner
*stroll around*

en acier
(*cast*) *in steel*

en bronze
(*cast*) *in bronze*

*Tête monumentale* dans le musée en plein air de la Défense

## Visionnez!

Trouvez la description qui correspond à chaque œuvre d'art.

| ŒUVRES D'ART | DESCRIPTIONS |
|---|---|
| 1. \_\_\_\_\_ *Le Pouce* (*The Thumb*) | a. un homme qui marche sur une boule de métal |
| 2. \_\_\_\_\_ *Stabile* | b. une œuvre qui célèbre l'amour |
| 3. \_\_\_\_\_ *Le Somnambule* | c. un énorme insecte en acier rouge |
| 4. \_\_\_\_\_ *Deux personnages fantastiques* | d. une composition surréaliste |
| 5. \_\_\_\_\_ *Tête monumentale* | e. une reproduction en bronze par l'artiste César |
| 6. \_\_\_\_\_ *Le mur des «je t'aime»* | f. un visage (*face*) sans émotion par l'artiste Mitoraj |

## Analysez!

1. Comment imaginez-vous un musée parisien typique? Comment est-ce que ces musées en plein air diffèrent de (*differ from*) cette image?
2. Est-ce que les œuvres du musée en plein air à la Défense reflètent bien le quartier dans lequel (*in which*) elles se trouvent? Expliquez pourquoi (pas).

## Comparez!

Regardez encore une fois la partie culturelle de la vidéo. Y a-t-il des musées d'art dans votre ville? Trouve-t-on des sculptures à l'extérieur (dans les parcs ou devant les bâtiments, par exemple)? Quelle œuvre présentée dans la vidéo aimeriez-vous (*would you like*) voir dans votre ville? Expliquez.

**J'aimerais voir** \_\_\_\_\_ **parce que...**

## Note culturelle

Le monument «la Défense de Paris», qui commémore les soldats défenseurs de la ville pendant la guerre[1] franco-allemande de 1870, a donné son nom au quartier.

L'œuvre *Tête monumentale* se trouve aujourd'hui sur le parvis[2] de la Défense. Elle est accompagnée d'une soixantaine d'œuvres d'art contemporain, fresques et sculptures monumentales qui forment un musée en plein air.

[1]*war* [2]*square*

# Vocabulaire

## Verbes

**bâtir** to build
**dater (de)** to date from
**deviner** to guess
**emmener** to take someone along; to invite
**flâner** to stroll
**peindre** to paint
**poursuivre** to pursue
**suivre** to follow; to take (*a course*)
**vivre** to live

À REVOIR: **apporter, habiter**

## Verbes suivis de l'infinitif

**accepter (de)** to accept (to)
**aider (à)** to help (to)
**arrêter (de)** to stop
**chercher à** to try to
**commencer par** to begin by (*doing something*)
**conseiller (de)** to advise (to)
**continuer (à)** to continue (to)
**décider (de)** to decide (to)
**empêcher (de)** to prevent (from)
**enseigner (à)** to teach (to)
**essayer (de)** to try (to)
**finir par** to end up (*doing something*)
**permettre (de)** to permit, allow (to)
**refuser (de)** to refuse (to)
**réussir (à)** to succeed (in)

À REVOIR: **aimer, aller, apprendre à, choisir de, commencer à, demander de, désirer, détester, devoir, espérer, finir de, il faut, oublier de, penser, pouvoir, préférer, rêver de, savoir, venir, venir de, vouloir**

## Substantifs

**l'acteur / l'actrice** actor
**les arènes** (*f. pl.*) arena
**l'artiste** (*m., f.*) artist

**l'auteur dramatique** (*m.*) playwright
**la cathédrale** cathedral
**le chef-d'œuvre** (*pl.* **les chefs-d'œuvre**) masterpiece
**le/la cinéaste** filmmaker
**le comédien / la comédienne** stage actor
**le compositeur / la compositrice** composer
**la conférence** lecture
**l'écrivain** (*m.*) **/ la femme écrivain** writer
**l'époque** (*f.*) period (*of history*)
**l'événement** (*m.*) event
**l'exposition** (*f.*) exhibit
**l'horaire** (*m.*) schedule
**le Moyen Âge** Middle Ages
**le/la musicien(ne)** musician
**l'œuvre** (*f.*) **(d'art)** work (of art)
**le palais** palace
**le patrimoine** legacy, heritage
**le peintre / la femme peintre** painter
**la peinture** painting
**la pièce de théâtre** play
**la place** seat
**le poème** poem
**la poésie** poetry
**le poète / la femme poète** poet
**le recueil** collection
**la reine** queen
**la Renaissance** Renaissance
**le roi** king
**le sculpteur / la femme sculpteur** sculptor
**la sculpture** sculpture
**le siècle** century
**le tableau** painting
**le théâtre** theater

À REVOIR: **le cadeau, la carte postale, le château, le cinéma, la littérature, la musique, le roman**

## Adjectifs

**actif / active** active
**absolu(e)** absolute

**classique** classical
**constant(e)** constant
**courant(e)** common; standard
**évident** evident, obvious
**franc(he)** frank
**gothique** Gothic
**historique** historical
**lent(e)** slow
**magnifique** magnificent
**malheureux / malheureuse** unhappy; unfortunate
**médiéval(e)** medieval
**poli(e)** polite
**rapide** fast, rapid
**romain(e)** Roman

À REVOIR: **bon(ne), différent(e), heureux / heureuse, mauvais(e), vrai(e)**

## Adverbes

**activement** actively
**absolument** absolutely
**constamment** constantly
**couramment** fluently
**différemment** differently
**évidemment** evidently, obviously
**franchement** frankly
**heureusement** fortunately
**lentement** slowly
**malheureusement** unfortunately
**poliment** politely
**rapidement** rapidly
**récemment** recently
**vraiment** really

À REVOIR: **après, beaucoup, bien, d'abord, enfin, ensuite, mal, parfois, peu, puis, souvent, très, trop, vite**

## Mots et expressions divers

**la plupart de** the majority
**moi-même** myself
  **toi-même, lui-même...**
**par cœur** by heart

# Bienvenue...

## Un coup d'œil sur Genève, en Suisse

LA SUISSE
•Genève

Vous avez sans doute déjà entendu parler de Genève, en Suisse, notamment lorsqu'on parle des Conventions de Genève ou du Comité international de la Croix-Rouge.

Genève est une belle ville située dans la partie francophone* de la Suisse, au pied des Alpes.

La Suisse, qui est une des plus anciennes démocraties du monde et un pays politiquement stable et neutre, est donc un lieu privilégié pour de nombreuses organisations internationales. Genève, en particulier, est le siège des Nations Unies en Europe, de l'Assemblée de l'Organisation mondiale de la Santé et du CERN[†] (Centre européen de recherches nucléaires).

### PORTRAIT **Henri Dunant (1828–1910)**

▲ Genève avec, à l'arrière, le mont Blanc, le plus haut sommet des Alpes

L'une des organisations internationales les plus importantes du monde, le Comité international de la Croix-Rouge, a été fondée à Genève par un Genevois, Henri Dunant.

À l'âge de 18 ans, Henri Dunant allait déjà visiter les pauvres, les malades et les prisonniers. Plus tard, en 1859, alors qu'il se trouvait à Solférino, en Italie du Nord, le lendemain d'une terrible bataille entre 100 000 Français et Italiens d'une part[1] et 100 000 Autrichiens qui occupaient l'Italie[‡] d'autre part, Dunant a été horrifié quand il a vu les nombreux hommes blessés, mourants ou morts, abandonnés sur le champ de bataille. Il a immédiatement organisé le secours aux blessés des deux camps avec l'aide des habitants du village.

Il a décrit cette terrible expérience dans son livre, *Un souvenir de Solférino*, et a proposé la création d'une organisation neutre qui apporterait[2] de l'aide à *tous* les soldats blessés, quelle que soit[3] leur nationalité. Une commission a adopté le projet de Dunant et un comité international de secours aux militaires blessés a été créé en 1863. Ce comité est ensuite devenu le Comité international de la Croix-Rouge.

Dunant s'est battu toute sa vie pour ses idées humanitaires. En 1901, il a reçu le premier prix Nobel de la paix pour son rôle dans la fondation du Comité international de la Croix-Rouge et dans la première Convention de Genève, qui, en cas de guerre, protège les militaires blessés ou malades, les ambulances et hôpitaux militaires et le personnel sanitaire. Cette première convention a été le point de départ d'un vaste mouvement humanitaire.

[1]d'une part... d'autre part *on the one hand . . . on the other hand*   [2]*would bring*   [3]quelle... *regardless of*

*There is no language called "Swiss." Switzerland has four official languages: German (63.7%), French (20.4%), Italian (6.5%), and Romanche (0.5%).
[†]A scientist at CERN invented the "World-Wide Web" in 1989 to enable the sharing of academic and scientific information. Today, many physicists at CERN research the state of matter at the beginning of the universe, using the largest particle accelerators and detectors in the world.
[‡]Austria had occupied Italy. The Italians fought back against the Austrian occupation and were aided in the fight by the French.

▲ Henri Dunant, foundateur de la Croix-Rouge

# en Europe francophone

## Un coup d'œil sur Bruxelles, en Belgique

Capitale du Royaume de Belgique, Bruxelles est aussi l'une des villes-phares[1] de la francophonie depuis le Moyen Âge. On y parle flamand—surtout dans les quartiers historiques du centre—et français. En fait, les Bruxellois se composent de deux groupes linguistiques: les Wallons (ceux[2] qui parlent français) et les Flamands (ceux pour qui le flamand est la langue maternelle). Les Bruxellois sont donc souvent bilingues.

À Bruxelles, le temps est souvent gris, mais on dit que ses habitants ont le soleil dans le cœur. Vous y serez[3] accueilli avec chaleur[4] et bonne humeur. Ses musées, ses églises, ses petites rues commerçantes et ses passages couverts où sont installés confiseries,[5] chocolateries et magasins de dentelles font de Bruxelles une ville de culture et de commerce. Les fêtes se succèdent[6] été comme hiver; à ces occasions, les cortèges,[7] comme celui de Carnaval, convergent vers la Grand-Place, ou *Grote Markt* en flamand. Beaucoup de belles demeures anciennes de la Grand-Place sont maintenant des restaurants où vous pouvez trouver des spécialités culinaires comme les moules-frites ou le célèbre waterzoï.[8] Bruxelles est aussi la capitale politique de l'Union européenne, siège du Parlement européen, ce qui lui donne un caractère cosmopolite.

▲ Le triple Arc de Triomphe domine le parc du Cinquantenaire, à Bruxelles.

[1]*beacons*  [2]*those*  [3]*will be*  [4]*warmth*  [5]*candy stores*  [6]*se... follow each other*
[7]*processions*  [8]*Belgian speciality made from fish or meat in a cream sauce*

## PORTRAIT  René Magritte (1898–1967)

René Magritte est le peintre surréaliste par excellence. Ce Belge rivalise dans cet art du XXe siècle avec l'Espagnol Salvador Dali. Ses nombreuses œuvres nous ouvrent un monde inconnu[1] où se mélangent le rêve et une réalité transposée par l'artiste. Il crée des associations étranges et conçoit[2] des personnages extraordinaires et des paysages fabuleux. Son univers est imprévisible,[3] énigmatique, absurde, ironique.

[1]*unknown*  [2]*conceives*  [3]*unpredictable*

▲ René Magritte: *Le Maître d'école*, 1954 (collection particulière, Genève)

Watch the *Bienvenue en Europe francophone* video segments to learn more about Brussels and Geneva.

# CHAPITRE **13**

# La vie quotidienne

Les dossiers d'Hector

Hector

➤ Mes photos
    ➤ Des amoureux en Corse
    ➤ Devant la pharmacie
    ➤ La mer des Caraïbes

Deux jeunes amoureux passent un après-midi sous le soleil en Corse

# Dans ce chapitre...

## OBJECTIFS COMMUNICATIFS

➤ talking about love, marriage, the human body, and daily life

➤ expressing actions

➤ reporting everyday events

➤ expressing reciprocal actions

➤ talking about the past

➤ giving commands

➤ learning to distinguish between and pronounce selected sounds in French

## PAROLES (Leçon 1)

➤ L'amour et le mariage

➤ Le corps humain

➤ Les activités de la vie quotidienne

## STRUCTURES (Leçons 2 et 3)

➤ Les verbes pronominaux (première partie)

➤ Les verbes pronominaux (deuxième partie)

➤ Les verbes pronominaux (troisième partie)

➤ Les verbes pronominaux (quatrième partie)

## CULTURE

➤ Le blog d'Hector: *Discipline!**

➤ Reportage: *La Martinique au quotidien*

➤ Lecture: «Pour toi mon amour» (poème de Jacques Prévert) (Leçon 4)

Devant la pharmacie. Les jours de grande fatigue, j'achète des vitamines.

La mer des Caraïbes

McGraw Hill Education **connect** |FRENCH

www.mhconnectfrench.com

*In **Chapitres 13–16** you will read Hector Clément's blog about his life as a dancer, what he likes to do in his spare time, his efforts to find a new job, and his feelings about the problems of the world.

**PAROLES**

## L'amour et le mariage

**1.** Ils se rencontrent.
Ils tombent amoureux.

**2.** Ils se fiancent.

Les amoureux:
le coup de foudre*

*\*\*\*\*\**

Le couple:
les fiançailles (*f. pl.*)

*\*\*\*\*\**

**3.** Ils se marient.

**4.** Mais ils ne s'entendent pas toujours.

Le couple:
la cérémonie

Les nouveaux mariés:
parfois, ils se disputent.

## Le parler jeune

| | |
|---|---|
| **draguer** | essayer de séduire |
| **un dragueur** | un séducteur |
| **être accro à** | être incapable de vivre sans |
| **être mordu** | être amoureux |
| **kiffer** | adorer, être fou de |
| **un rencard** | rendez-vous |

Moi, je ne **drague** pas: je parle d'amour.

Comment décourager un **dragueur**?

Je **suis accro à** Jérôme.

Pour la première fois de ma vie, je suis vraiment **mordu.**

Tu la **kiffes,** Léa?

Ce soir, j'ai un **rencard** avec Juliette.

**AUTRES MOTS UTILES**

| | |
|---|---|
| **l'amitié** (*f.*) | friendship |
| **le/la célibataire** | single person |
| **divorcer** | to divorce |
| **le voyage de noces** | honeymoon |

 *Allez-y!*

**A. Pour commencer...** Quelles phrases de la colonne de droite correspondent aux étapes traditionnelles qui précèdent le mariage?

———
*\*love at first sight* (lit., *flash of lightning*)

1. la rencontre *a meeting*
2. le coup de foudre
3. les rendez-vous
4. les fiançailles
5. la cérémonie
6. l'installation (*setting up house*)

a. Ils se marient.
b. Ils sortent ensemble. *dating*
c. Ils tombent amoureux.
d. Ils se rencontrent. *to meet*
e. Ils s'installent.
f. Ils se fiancent.

**B. Conversation.** Posez les questions suivantes à un(e) camarade.

1. Est-ce que tu préfères sortir seul(e), avec un ami / une amie ou avec d'autres couples?
2. Selon toi, est-ce que les jeunes d'aujourd'hui tombent trop vite ou trop souvent amoureux?
3. Est-ce que tu crois au coup de foudre? Pourquoi ou pourquoi pas?
4. Est-ce que tout le monde doit se marier? Pourquoi ou pourquoi pas? Si oui, à quel âge?

# Le corps humain

**Prononcez bien!**

**The vowels in *le* and *la***

Remember to make a clear distinction between [ə] in **le** and [a] in **la**. For **le,** pronounce a brief and tense sound while closing your mouth and rounding your lips. For **la,** open your mouth wide and stretch your lips in a semi-smile.

[ə]: **je, ne, me, de**

[a]: **passif, va, ça, ma**

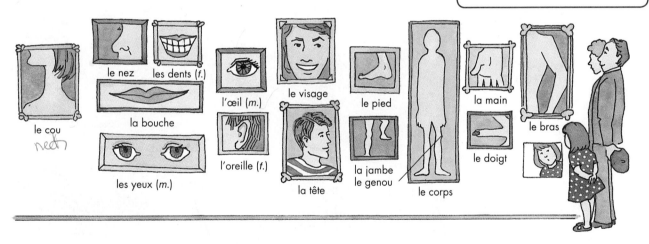

le nez    les dents (*f.*)
la bouche
le cou    *neck*
les yeux (*m.*)
l'œil (*m.*)
l'oreille (*f.*)
le visage
la tête
le pied
la jambe
le genou
le corps
la main
le doigt
le bras

**AUTRES MOTS UTILES**

| | |
|---|---|
| avoir mal (à) | to hurt, have a pain (in) |
| J'ai mal à la tête. | My head hurts. (I have a headache.) |
| le cœur | heart |
| le dos | back |
| la gorge | throat |
| la santé | health |
| le ventre | abdomen; stomach |
| être malade | to be sick |

 *Allez-y!*

**A. Exercice d'imagination.** Où ont-ils mal? Répondez d'après le modèle.

> **MODÈLE:** Il y a beaucoup de bruit chez Judith. →
> Elle a mal à la tête / aux oreilles.

1. Vous portez des colis très lourds (*heavy*).
2. Les nouvelles chaussures d'Aurélien sont trop petites.
3. J'ai mangé trop de chocolat.
4. Vous apprenez à jouer de la guitare.
5. Anouk a marché très longtemps.
6. La cravate de Patrice est trop serrée (*tight*).
7. Ils font du ski et il y a beaucoup de soleil.
8. Il fait extrêmement froid et vous n'avez pas de gants (*gloves*).
9. Aïcha va chez le dentiste.
10. Clément chante depuis deux heures.

Une pharmacie française. Qu'est-ce que les clientes achètent? Pourquoi? Imaginez.

 **B. Devinettes.** Pensez à une partie du corps et donnez-en une définition au reste de la classe. Vos camarades vont deviner de quelle partie il s'agit.

> **MODÈLE:** Vous en avez une. On fait la bise avec cette partie du corps. →
> C'est la bouche!

# Les activités de la vie quotidienne

Ils se réveillent et ils se lèvent.

Ils se brossent les dents.

Il se rase et elle se maquille.

Ils se peignent.

Ils s'habillent.

Ils s'en vont.

Ils se couchent.

Ils s'endorment.

## Allez-y!

**A. Et votre journée?** Décrivez votre journée en employant le vocabulaire des illustrations.

> **MODÈLE:** À _____ heures, je me _____. → À 7 heures, je me réveille.*

**B. Habitudes quotidiennes.** Dites dans quelles circonstances on utilise les objets suivants.

**Mots utiles:** se brosser, se coucher, s'en aller, s'endormir, s'habiller, se lever, se maquiller, se peigner, se raser, se réveiller

> **MODÈLE:** une voiture → On utilise une voiture pour s'en aller.

1. un réveil
2. une brosse à dents
3. des vêtements
4. un lit
5. un peigne
6. du rouge à lèvres (*lipstick*)
7. un rasoir (*razor*)
8. un pyjama

---

*The verbs introduced here are called *pronominal verbs*. To conjugate the **je** form of pronominal verbs, place the pronoun **me** before the first-person conjugation of the verb.

# Leçon 2

## Les verbes pronominaux (*première partie*)

*Expressing Actions*

### Allô, docteur?

*Hector téléphone à Hassan.*

HECTOR: Hassan, est-ce que tu as un bon médecin?
HASSAN: Excellent. Tu es malade?
HECTOR: J'ai très mal au genou. **Je me demande** si je n'ai pas une tendinite.
HASSAN: Prends rendez-vous! **Le cabinet médical se trouve**[1] au Quartier latin.
HECTOR: Comment **s'appelle le docteur**?
HASSAN: **Il s'appelle** Guy Levi. Il vient juste de **s'installer**.
HECTOR: Je n'ai peut-être pas besoin d'une consultation. Si **je me repose** pendant deux jours…
HASSAN: Quel raisonnement[2] infantile! **Dépêche-toi**[3] de lui téléphoner!
HECTOR: Tu viens avec moi? J'ai peur des piqûres[4]!

**Docteur Guy LEVI**
Chirurgie Orthopédique et Traumatologique

Tél : 01 45 49 34 09

Heureusement, les médecins sont là pour nous soigner!

[1]*Le… the doctor's office is located*  [2]*reasoning*  [3]*Hurry up*  [4]*injections*

Trouvez, dans le dialogue, les phrases qui répondent aux questions suivantes.

1. Quelle question se pose Hector (*does Hector ask himself*)?
2. Où est situé le cabinet médical?
3. Quel est le nom du docteur?
4. Est-ce que le médecin est dans le quartier depuis longtemps?
5. Hector ne veut pas voir le docteur. Quelle est sa solution? Que dit-il?
6. Qu'est-ce qu'Hassan ordonne (*recommend*) à Hector?

Certain French verbs are conjugated with an object pronoun in addition to the subject; consequently, they are called *pronominal verbs* (**les verbes pronominaux**). The object pronoun agrees with the subject of the verb. **Se reposer** (*To rest*) and **s'amuser** (*to have fun*) are two pronominal verbs.

| se reposer | | | | s'amuser | | | |
|---|---|---|---|---|---|---|---|
| je | **me** repose | nous | **nous** reposons | je | **m'**amuse | nous | **nous** amusons |
| tu | **te** reposes | vous | **vous** reposez | tu | **t'**amuses | vous | **vous** amusez |
| il/elle/on | **se** repose | ils/elles | **se** reposent | il/elle/on | **s'**amuse | ils/elles | **s'**amusent |

—Est-ce que tu **t'amuses**
en général avec tes grands-
parents?

*Do you usually have fun with
your grandparents?*

—Oui, on **s'amuse** bien
ensemble.

*Yes, we have a good time
together.*

1. Note that the object pronouns **me, te,** and **se** become **m', t',** and **s'**
before a vowel or a nonaspirate **h.**

2. Common pronominal verbs include:

| | |
|---|---|
| **s'amuser** *to have fun* | **s'excuser** *to apologize* |
| **s'appeler** *to be named* | **s'installer** *to settle down,* |
| **s'arrêter** *to stop* | *settle in* |
| **se demander** *to wonder* | **se rappeler** *to remember* |
| **se dépêcher** *to hurry* | **se reposer** *to rest* |
| **se détendre** *to relax* | **se souvenir (de)** *to remember* |
| **s'entendre (avec)** *to get along* | **se tromper** *to make a mistake* |
| *(with)* | **se trouver** *to be located* |

Où **se trouve** l'arrêt d'autobus?
L'autobus **s'arrête** devant
mon immeuble.

*Where is the bus stop?*
*The bus stops in front of my
building.*

3. Note that word order in the negative and infinitive forms follows the
usual word order for pronouns: the object pronoun precedes the
main verb.

Antoine ne **se souvient** pas à
quelle heure le musée ouvre.
Je vais **me dépêcher** pour
arriver à l'heure.

*Antoine doesn't remember
what time the museum opens.*
*I'm going to hurry to arrive on
time.*

 *Allez-y!*

**A. Questions d'amour.** Trouvez dans la colonne de droite une réponse
logique aux phrases de la colonne de gauche.

1. Je dis que le mariage précède
les fiançailles.
2. Demain c'est l'anniversaire de
ma femme et je n'ai encore
rien acheté.
3. Arthur et moi, nous nous
disputons tout le temps.
Nous travaillons trop et ne
nous amusons jamais.
4. Quelle est la date de
l'anniversaire de mariage
de vos parents?
5. Toi et moi, nous aimons les
mêmes choses! Nous ne nous
disputons presque jamais.

a. Désolé(e), mais je ne m'en
souviens plus.
b. Tu te trompes!
c. Oui, nous nous entendons
bien.
d. Je me demande pourquoi
tu n'y as pas pensé!
e. Il faut vous arrêter pour
respirer un peu. Prenez le
temps de vivre!

B. **Départ à la hâte.** C'est l'heure de partir pour Chartres, mais vous avez un petit problème. Remplacez l'expression en italique par un des verbes pronominaux suivants: **se demander, se dépêcher, se rappeler, se tromper, se trouver.**

Où *est*[1] mon sac à dos? Je ne *me souviens*[2] plus où je l'ai mis. En plus, je dois *faire vite*[3], je suis en retard. Mais je ne peux pas aller à Chartres sans mon appareil photo. Je *veux savoir*[4] si Jean-François l'a mis dans sa valise. Il peut facilement *faire une erreur*[5] quand il est en retard.

C. **Trouvez quelqu'un qui...** Circulez dans la classe pour trouver quelqu'un qui fait une des activités suivantes. Ensuite, trouvez quelqu'un qui fait l'activité suivante et ainsi de suite (*so on*).

1. veut s'installer à l'étranger
2. se souvient de son premier jour de classe à l'université
3. se trompe souvent dans ses calculs
4. se détend en regardant (*while watching*) des matchs de foot
5. s'entend bien avec ses frères ou ses sœurs
6. se repose en écoutant (*while listening*) de la musique classique
7. s'arrête tous les jours au café
8. se rappelle son meilleur ami / sa meilleure amie à l'école primaire

# Les verbes pronominaux (*deuxième partie*)

*Reporting Everyday Events*

## Tout va bien!

*Léa téléphone à Hector.*

LÉA: Alors Hector, **tu te sens**[1] mieux?

HECTOR: **Je me sens** très bien; je suis presque guéri[2]!

LÉA: Tu vois: parfois, **on se repose** pendant 24 heures et hop! **La douleur**[3] **s'en va**!

HECTOR: **Tu te trompes. Se détendre** ne suffit pas.[4] J'ai eu une piqûre de cortisone dans le genou... terrible... abominable!

LÉA: Oh! Pauvre Hector! Mais tu peux marcher[5] maintenant?

HECTOR: Je peux marcher, courir[6] et danser!

LÉA: Alors, on va **se promener**[7] ce soir?

**Diprostène®**
dipropionate de bétaméthasone,
phosphate disodique de bétaméthasone

suspension injectable en seringue pré-remplie

Voie injectable intramusculaire ou voie injectable locale
1 seringue pré-remplie avec 2 aiguilles stériles

MSD

Médicament autorisé n° 3400932005093

1 seringue
pré-remplie de 1 ml

Un anti-inflammatoire pour guérir Hector

[1]*te... feel*  [2]*cured*  [3]*pain*  [4]*ne... isn't enough*  [5]*walk*  [6]*run*  [7]*se... to take a walk*

Répondez aux questions selon le dialogue.

1. Hector se sent mieux?
2. Selon Léa, que faut-il faire pendant 24 heures pour aller mieux?
3. Selon Léa, après 24 heures de repos, qu'arrive-t-il?
4. Est-ce qu'Hector pense que Léa a raison ou qu'elle se trompe?
5. Quelle est la théorie d'Hector?
6. Que propose Léa?

# Reflexive Pronominal Verbs

**1.** In reflexive constructions, the action of the verb reflects or refers back to the subject: *The child dressed* **himself.** *Did you hurt* **yourself?** *She talks to* **herself.** In these examples, the subject and the object are the same person. In French, common reflexive pronominal verbs include:

| | |
|---|---|
| **se baigner** *to bathe; to swim* | **se maquiller** *to put on makeup* |
| **se brosser** *to brush* | **se peigner** *to comb one's hair* |
| **se coucher** *to go to bed* | **se raser** *to shave* |
| **se doucher** *to take a shower* | **se regarder** *to look at oneself* |
| **s'habiller** *to get dressed* | **se réveiller** *to wake up* |
| **se laver** *to wash oneself* | **se sentir** *to feel* |
| **se lever** *to get up* | |

Zoé **se réveille** à 6 h.
Théo **se douche** et **se rase** pendant que Sarah **se maquille.**

*Zoé wakes up at 6:00.*
*Théo showers and shaves while Sarah puts on makeup.*

**2.** Most reflexive pronominal verbs can also be used nonreflexively.

Aujourd'hui, Théo **lave** la voiture.
Le bruit **réveille** tout le monde.

*Today, Théo is washing his car.*
*The noise wakes everyone up.*

**3.** Some reflexive pronominal verbs can have two objects, one direct and one indirect; this frequently occurs with the verbs **se brosser** and **se laver** plus a part of the body. The definite article—not the possessive adjective, as in English—is used with the part of the body.

Lisa se brosse **les** dents.
Je me lave **les** mains.

*Lisa is brushing her teeth.*
*I'm washing my hands.*

Mon dentifrice, c'est du Docteur Pierre.
Et le vôtre?

## Idiomatic Pronominal Verbs

When certain verbs are used with reflexive pronouns, their meaning changes.

| | | | |
|---|---|---|---|
| **aller** *to go* | → | **s'en aller** *to go away* | |
| **appeler** *to call* | → | **s'appeler** *to be named* | |
| **demander** *to ask* | → | **se demander** *to wonder* | |
| **endormir** *to put to sleep* | → | **s'endormir** *to fall asleep* | |
| **ennuyer** *to bother* | → | **s'ennuyer** *to be bored* | |
| **entendre** *to hear* | → | **s'entendre** *to get along* | |
| **fâcher** *to make angry* | → | **se fâcher** *to get angry* | |
| **installer** *to install* | → | **s'installer** *to settle in* (*to a new house*) | |
| **mettre** *to place, put* | → | **se mettre à** *to begin* | |
| **perdre** *to lose* | → | **se perdre** *to get lost* | |
| **promener** *to (take for a) walk* | → | **se promener** *to take a walk* | |
| **tromper** *to deceive* | → | **se tromper** *to be mistaken* | |
| **trouver** *to find* | → | **se trouver** *to be located* | |

### Mots clés

**Vous parlez français?**

You are now at a point where you can answer this question with something else besides **Un peu.** Here are some suggestions:

Je me débrouille.     (*I can get by.*)
Oui, couramment.
Bien sûr! Je suis bilingue.

Les jeunes mariés **s'en vont** en voyage de noces.

*The newlyweds are going away on their honeymoon trip.*

Après cela, Véronique va **se mettre à** chercher un appartement.

*Afterward, Véronique is going to start looking for an apartment.*

Tu **te trompes**! Elle en a déjà trouvé un.

*You're wrong! She's already found one.*

Où est-ce qu'il **se trouve**?

*Where is it?*

 **Allez-y!**

**A.  La routine.** Que font les membres de la famille Duteil?

**MODÈLE:**   Annick se lave les mains.

Le matin...

1.

2.

3.

4.

Plus tard...

**5.**    **6.**    **7.**    **8.**

Et vous, parmi ces activités, lesquelles faites-vous régulièrement?

**B. Habitudes matinales.** Qui dans votre famille a les habitudes suivantes? Faites des phrases complètes. Puis comparez leurs habitudes aux vôtres (*to yours*). Commencez par «Moi aussi, je... » ou «Mais moi, je... ».

| | |
|---|---|
| mon père | se regarder longtemps dans le miroir |
| ma mère | se lever souvent du pied gauche* |
| ma sœur | se réveiller toujours très tôt |
| mon frère | s'habiller rapidement / lentement |
| le chien | se maquiller / se raser très vite |
| le chat | se préparer à la dernière minute |
| | s'en aller sans prendre de petit déjeuner |
| | se laver les cheveux tous les jours |
| | se fâcher quand il n'y a plus de lait |
| | se tromper de chaussures |

**C. Synonymes.** Racontez l'histoire suivante. Remplacez l'expression en italique par un verbe pronominal.

À sept heures du matin, Sylvie *ouvre les yeux*,[1] elle *sort de son lit*,[2] *fait sa toilette*[3] (*washes up*) et *met ses vêtements*[4]. À huit heures, elle *quitte la maison*.[5] Au travail, elle *commence à*[6] parler au téléphone. Sylvie *finit de*[7] travailler vers 18 h; elle *fait une promenade*[8] et parfois ses amies et elle vont *nager*[9] à la piscine. Le soir, elle *va au lit*[10] et elle *trouve le sommeil*[11] très vite!

**D. Interview.** Interrogez un(e) camarade sur une de ses journées typiques à l'université. Posez-lui des questions avec les verbes **se réveiller, s'habiller, se dépêcher, s'en aller, s'amuser, s'ennuyer, se reposer, se promener** et **se coucher.** Ensuite, comparez votre journée et celle de votre camarade et présentez les résultats à la classe.

**E. Vos habitudes.** Comparez vos habitudes avec celles de vos camarades. Trouvez quelqu'un qui...

1. se lève dix minutes avant de partir
2. s'en va sans prendre de petit déjeuner
3. se réveille avant dix heures
4. se lève souvent du pied gauche
5. se promène souvent le soir
6. se douche avant de se coucher
7. se couche souvent après minuit
8. a souvent du mal à[†] s'endormir

---

*Se lever du pied gauche** is the equivalent of *to get up on the wrong side of the bed.*
[†]**Avoir du mal à** means *to have difficulty* (*doing something*). It should not be confused with **avoir mal à,** meaning *to have an ache or pain* (*in a part of the body*).

# Le blog d'Hector

## Discipline!

**vendredi 3 juillet**

Salut les amis!

Qui suis-je? Je suis Hector. Je commence mon blog.

Je suis danseur. Danseur, c'est un beau métier, n'est-ce pas? Mais il faut soigner[1] son corps, suivre un régime, avoir de la discipline…

Mes journées sont réglées[2]: je me réveille vers 10 heures. Je me lève, je prends ma douche et je me rase, puis je m'habille. Ensuite, je m'installe devant un petit déjeuner léger avec du thé, des fruits. Si mes colocataires sont là, on s'amuse et on se raconte notre vie! C'est bon pour le moral!

Vers midi, je commence mon entraînement[3] au studio de danse. Quand j'arrive, je mets immédiatement mon tee-shirt et mes collants,[4] puis je m'échauffe[5] seul avant le début du cours de ballet ou la répétition du spectacle.

Je danse jusqu'à 18 heures, mais je m'arrête régulièrement pour manger et pour boire: il faut renouveler[6] les calories et s'hydrater.

Ensuite, je me change et je rentre chez moi. Je me détends avant le spectacle ou je sors avec mes potes. Les jours de grande fatigue, j'achète des vitamines à la pharmacie. Et je retrouve mon énergie.

Elle est belle ma vie d'artiste! C'est vrai. Mais parfois, je désire tout changer et essayer d'autres modes de vie. Mon copain Hassan me parle souvent du Maroc et il me fait rêver…

Hector

Devant la pharmacie. Les jours de grande fatigue j'achète des vitamines.

. . . . . . . . . . . . . . . . . . . . . . . . . . . . . . . . . . . . . . . . . . . . .

### COMMENTAIRES

**Alexis**

Tout le monde a sa petite routine. Chaque jour, Trésor règle mon train-train.[7] Le matin, il m'appelle: ouah ouah! Impossible de me reposer! Le soir, après mes cours, je me dépêche de rentrer. Il se fâche si j'arrive tard!

**Trésor**

Alexis, je m'ennuie tout seul à la maison!

**Charlotte**

Ma routine est celle[8] d'une mère de famille: je me prépare très tôt le matin; j'accompagne ma fille Gilberte à l'école et je m'en vais au travail. Le soir, mon mari se débrouille[9] pour faire les courses. On se met à table vers 19 h et puis on s'installe devant la télé après avoir couché Gilberte. C'est pas très glamour, tout ça!

---

[1]*take care of*  [2]*well-ordered*  [3]*practice*  [4]*tights*  [5]*warm up*  [6]*replenish*  [7]*daily routine*  [8]*that*  [9]*se… manages*

## La Martinique au quotidien°

*daily life*

Vivre dans l'Hexagone[1] ou à la Martinique, est-ce réellement différent? Élisa, qui travaille à Fort-de-France, est catégorique: «Non, car la Martinique est un département d'outre-mer: elle fait partie du territoire français et fonctionne sous la loi[2] française. Ici, nous sommes en France; la vie quotidienne d'un Martiniquais est celle d'un Français du continent: le matin, tout le monde se lève pour aller travailler; les élèves[3] se dépêchent sur le chemin de l'école; les étudiants s'en vont à l'université; les magasins ouvrent[4] leur porte; les ménagères[5] font leurs courses.

Débutant(e) ou certifié(e) en plongée libre (*snorkeling*) ou avec bouteille (*scuba diving*), vous pouvez découvrir les eaux cristallines et la faune (*animal life*) de la mer des Caraïbes. Vous êtes accueilli(e) par des bancs de poissons multicolores, des barrières de corail (*coral reefs*) intactes et des variétés d'organismes marins uniques.

Mais le week-end, on tire avantage[6] du climat tropical. Comme sur la Côte d'Azur, on reste dehors[7] pour profiter du soleil et de la chaleur.[8] On se promène dans les rues animées de Fort-de-France ou des petits villages cachés[9] dans l'île; on s'installe sur la plage, en famille et avec ses amis; on se repose, on s'amuse, on se baigne, on pique-nique.

Et le soir, on sort, comme à Paris, à Bordeaux ou à Marseille: on va au restaurant goûter quelques plats traditionnels ou manger… un hamburger! Et ensuite, on va au théâtre, au cinéma ou… en boîte. Les Martiniquais adorent la musique: jazz, rock, variétés françaises ou antillaises.

Comme la Guadeloupe, sa voisine,[10] la Martinique réunit[11] tous les ingrédients d'une vie quotidienne tout à fait[12] française sous le soleil des Caraïbes!

[1]*continental France (so called due to its shape)* [2]*law* [3]*pupils* [4]*open* [5]*housewives* [6]*tire… take advantage* [7]*outside* [8]*heat* [9]*hidden* [10]*neighbor* [11]*unites* [12]*tout… completely*

1. Est-ce qu'il y a une différence majeure entre le style de vie d'un Français du continent et d'un Français de la Martinique? Comment vivent-ils leur quotidien?
2. Présentez une journée typique de votre quotidien. Êtes-vous satisfait(e) de votre vie? Que voulez-vous changer?
3. Que faites-vous pour vous détendre? Faites-vous des sports nautiques comme le jeune homme sur la photo? Racontez.

1. Nommez un(e) secrétaire chargé(e) d'écrire au tableau.
2. Quels mots associez-vous au mot «Martinique»? Donnez spontanément vos idées pendant que le/la secrétaire de la classe les enregistre au tableau (ex: «soleil»).
3. Avec tous ces mots, créez, en commun, un petit poème à la gloire de la Martinique.

# Leçon 3

## Les verbes pronominaux (*troisième partie*)

*Expressing Reciprocal Actions*

### L'amour fou

*Poema contacte Alexis sur sa page Facebook (Messagerie instantanée).*

POEMA: Qu'est-ce que tu penses du mariage, Alexis?

ALEXIS: **On se rencontre,** on a le coup de foudre, **on se marie** et **on se quitte**…

POEMA: Quel cynisme! Il y a pourtant* des couples éternels…

ALEXIS: Ah oui, dans les romans: Tristan et Yseult, Roméo et Juliette…

POEMA: Écoute, ma sœur et mon beau-frère sont mariés depuis huit ans. **Ils s'adorent** comme au premier jour.

ALEXIS: Vraiment? **Ils** ne **se disputent** jamais?

POEMA: **Ils se disputent**, comme tout le monde. Mais **ils se réconcilient**. Parce qu'**ils s'aiment**.

ALEXIS: Parlons-en dans dix ans…

*nevertheless

Répondez aux questions en utilisant les verbes du dialogue.

**1.** Que pense Alexis du mariage?
**2.** Que dit Poema sur la relation amoureuse de sa sœur et de son beau-frère?

The plural reflexive pronouns **nous, vous,** and **se** can be used to show that an action is reciprocal or mutual in which two or more subjects interact. Almost any verb that can take a direct or indirect object can be used reciprocally with **nous, vous,** and **se.**

| | |
|---|---|
| Ils **se** rencontrent par hasard. | *They meet by chance.* |
| Ils **s'**aiment. | *They love each other.* |
| Allons-nous **nous** téléphoner demain? | *Are we going to phone each other tomorrow?* |
| Vous ne **vous** quittez jamais. | *You are inseparable (never leave each other).* |
| Vous **vous** disputez souvent? | *Do you argue often?* |

 **Allez-y!**

**A. Une amitié sincère.** M^me Chabot raconte l'amitié qui unit sa famille à la famille Marnier. Complétez son histoire au présent.

Éva Marnier et moi, nous _____¹ depuis plus de quinze ans. Nous _____² tous les jours et nous parlons longtemps. Nous _____³ souvent en ville. Quand nous partons en voyage, nous _____⁴ des cartes postales.

Nos maris _____⁵ aussi très bien. Nos enfants _____⁶ surtout pendant les vacances quand ils jouent ensemble. Parfois ils _____,⁷ mais comme ils _____⁸ bien, ils oublient vite leurs différends (*disagreements*).

| |
|---|
| **s'aimer** |
| **se connaître** |
| **se disputer** |
| **s'écrire** |
| **s'entendre** |
| **se rencontrer** |
| **se téléphoner** |
| **se voir** |

**B. Une brève rencontre.** Racontez au présent l'histoire un peu triste d'un jeune homme et d'une jeune fille qui ne forment pas le couple idéal. Dites quand et où chaque action a lieu.

**MODÈLE:** se voir → Ils se voient un dimanche matin (au jardin du Luxembourg, à l'Opéra-Garnier, à la gare de Lyon)...

1. se voir
2. se rencontrer
3. se donner rendez-vous
4. se téléphoner
5. s'écrire souvent
6. se revoir
7. se disputer
8. (ne plus) s'entendre
9. se détester
10. se quitter

**C. Rapports familiaux.** Posez les questions suivantes à un(e) camarade de classe.

1. Avec qui est-ce que tu t'entends bien dans ta famille?
2. Tes parents et toi, quand est-ce que vous vous téléphonez?
3. Tes frères et sœurs et toi, combien de fois par semaine, par mois, par an est-ce que vous vous voyez?
4. Est-ce que tu te disputes souvent avec tes frères et tes sœurs? Quand et pourquoi vous disputez-vous?
5. Tes cousins et toi, est-ce que vous vous connaissez bien? Pourquoi ou pourquoi pas?

### Un peu plus...

**Les Berbères.**
On retrouve les traces de ce groupe de peuple à diverses époques, de l'Égypte jusqu'à l'Atlantique et du Niger à la Méditerranée. Aussi loin qu'on remonte (*go back*) dans le passé, l'Afrique du Nord est occupée par ce peuple autochtone (*native*). Pasteurs (*Shepherds*), agriculteurs, ils vivaient divisés en tribus; la division reste un fait constant et essentiel de l'histoire berbère.

▶ *Des époux (married couple) berbères, au Maghreb. Comparez-les aux époux nord-américains.*

# Les verbes pronominaux (*quatrième partie*)

*Talking About the Past and Giving Commands*

## Des petits mots d'amour

*Appel vidéo entre Charlotte et Juliette.*

| | |
|---|---|
| CHARLOTTE: | Tu es mariée, Juliette? |
| JULIETTE: | Non. Et je ne suis même pas amoureuse! |
| CHARLOTTE: | Moi **je me suis mariée** il y a 10 ans… J'avais 20 ans! |
| JULIETTE: | **Vous vous êtes rencontrés** à la fac? |
| CHARLOTTE: | **On s'est rencontrés** à la bibliothèque. |
| JULIETTE: | **Vous vous êtes aimés** tout de suite? |
| CHARLOTTE: | Pas du tout. **Ne t'imagine pas** que nous avons eu le coup de foudre! Je le trouvais prétentieux et autoritaire! |
| JULIETTE: | Et alors, comment **ça s'est passé?** |
| CHARLOTTE: | C'est inexplicable: **nous nous sommes** tellement **détestés** que nous avons fini par nous aimer! |
| JULIETTE: | Ce sont les paradoxes de l'amour… |

▼ AUDIO & VIDEO

MESSAGE    VIDEO ●

Répondez aux questions suivantes.

1. À quel âge Charlotte s'est-elle mariée?
2. Où Charlotte et son futur mari se sont-ils rencontrés?
3. Est-ce qu'ils se sont aimés tout de suite?

## *Passé composé* of Pronominal Verbs

**1.** All pronominal verbs are conjugated with **être** in the **passé composé.** The past participle agrees with the reflexive pronoun in number and gender when the pronoun is the *direct* object of the verb.

| PASSÉ COMPOSÉ OF **se baigner** | | | |
|---|---|---|---|
| je | me suis baigné(e) | nous | nous sommes baigné(e)s |
| tu | t'es baigné(e) | vous | vous êtes baigné(e)(s) |
| il | s'est baigné | ils | se sont baignés |
| elle | s'est baignée | elles | se sont baignées |
| on | s'est baigné(e)(s) | | |

| | |
|---|---|
| Nous **nous sommes mariés** en octobre. | *We got married in October.* |
| Vos parents **se sont fâchés**? | *Did your parents get angry?* |
| Vous ne **vous êtes** pas **vus** depuis Noël? | *You haven't seen each other since Christmas?* |

**2.** Here are some of the more common pronominal verbs whose past participles do not agree with the pronoun: **se demander, se dire, s'écrire, s'envoyer, se parler, se téléphoner.** The reflexive pronoun of these verbs is *indirect* (**demander à, parler à,** and so on).

| | |
|---|---|
| Elles se sont **écrit** des textos. | *They wrote text messages to each other.* |
| Ils se sont **téléphoné** hier soir? | *Did they phone each other last night?* |
| Vous êtes-vous **dit** bonjour? | *Did you say hello to each other?* |

[Allez-y! A-B-D]

## Imperative of Pronominal Verbs

Reflexive pronouns follow the rules for the placement of object pronouns. In the affirmative imperative, they follow and are attached to the verb with a hyphen; **toi** is used instead of **te.** In the negative imperative, reflexive pronouns precede the verb.

| AFFIRMATIVE | | NEGATIVE | |
|---|---|---|---|
| Lève-**toi.** | *Get up.* | Ne **te** lève pas. | *Don't get up.* |
| Dépêchons-**nous.** | *Let's hurry.* | Ne **nous** dépêchons pas. | *Let's not hurry.* |
| Habillez-**vous.** | *Get dressed.* | Ne **vous** habillez pas. | *Don't get dressed.* |

[Allez-y! C]

### Grammaire interactive

For more on pronominal verbs, watch the corresponding Grammar Tutorial and take a brief practice quiz at **Connect French.**

**|FRENCH**

www.mhconnectfrench.com

 *Allez-y!*

**A. Avant la soirée.** Hier, il y avait une fête à la Maison des Jeunes (*youth center*). Décrivez les activités de ces jeunes gens. Faites des phrases complètes au passé composé.

**MODÈLE:** Fabien / se raser / avant de partir →
Fabien s'est rasé avant de partir.

1. Fabrice / s'habiller / avec soin (*care*)
2. Christine et toi, vous / se reposer
3. Nadia et Thomas / s'amuser / à écouter de la musique
4. Sylvie / s'endormir / sur le canapé
5. David et moi, nous / s'installer / devant la télévision
6. je / se promener / dans le jardin

**B. Souvenirs.** Rebecca retrouve un vieil album de photos. Lisez son histoire, puis racontez-la au passé composé.

**MODÈLE:** Rebecca s'interroge sur son passé. →
Rebecca s'est interrogée sur son passé.

1. Elle s'installe pour regarder son album de photos. **2.** Elle s'arrête à la première page. **3.** Elle se souvient de son premier amour. **4.** Elle ne se souvient pas de son nom. **5.** Elle se trompe de personne. **6.** Elle se demande où il est aujourd'hui. **7.** Elle s'endort sur la page ouverte.

**C. Un rendez-vous difficile.** Bruno a rendez-vous avec quelqu'un qu'il ne connaît pas. Il est très nerveux. Donnez-lui des conseils et utilisez l'impératif.

**MODÈLE:** Je ne *me suis* pas encore *préparé.* (vite) →
Prépare-toi vite!

1. À quelle heure est-ce que je dois *me réveiller*? (à 5 h)
2. Je n'ai pas envie de *m'habiller*. (tout de suite)
3. Je ne *me souviens* pas de la rue. (rue Mirabeau)
4. J'ai peur de *me tromper*. (ne... pas)
5. Je dois *m'en aller* à 6 h. (maintenant)

Maintenant, utilisez **vous.**

**MODÈLE:** Je ne *me suis* pas encore *préparé.* (vite) →
Préparez-vous vite!

**D. Tête-à-tête.** Posez les questions suivantes à un(e) camarade. Ensuite, faites une observation intéressante sur votre camarade.

1. Est-ce que tu t'entends bien avec tes amis? avec tes professeurs? avec tes camarades de chambre? (Si votre camarade ne s'entend pas bien avec eux, demandez-lui pourquoi.)
2. Tu as déjà rencontré une personne qui t'a beaucoup impressionné(e)? Comment s'appelle cette personne? De quels traits physiques (yeux, visage, cheveux, taille, et cetera) te souviens-tu?
3. Est-ce que tu te rappelles le moment où tu es tombé(e) amoureux/ amoureuse pour la première fois? C'était à quel âge, et avec qui? Ça a été le coup de foudre? C'était l'amour?
4. Tu veux te marier un jour? À quel âge? Où est-ce que tu veux t'installer avec ton mari (ta femme)?

## Prononcez bien!

**The vowels in *le* and *la*** (page 355)

**A.** **Mariage.** Hugo est allé à un mariage ce week-end. Il montre les photos à Isabelle. Écoutez ce qu'ils disent et choisissez l'option appropriée.

ISABELLE: Oh! _____¹ a l'air très jeune!

HUGO: Oui, _____² aussi: Ils ont tous les deux 22 ans.

ISABELLE: Qui est cette personne?

HUGO: C'est _____³ de l'ami(e) de mon frère.

ISABELLE: Et où est _____⁴?

HUGO: Là… Ça, c'est une photo de tous les célibataires qui étaient au mariage. _____⁵ à gauche des mariés a rencontré _____⁶ à leur droite. Ça a été le coup de foudre. Ah! Il y avait beaucoup d'amour dans l'air ce jour-là!

1. **a.** La mariée    **b.** Le marié
2. **a.** la mariée    **b.** le marié
3. **a.** la fiancée    **b.** le fiancé
4. **a.** la fiancée    **b.** le fiancé
5. **a.** la célibataire    **b.** le célibataire
6. **a.** la célibataire    **b.** le célibataire

**B.** **Le jeu de la description.** Vous êtes chez le médecin avec votre ami(e). Sur les murs, il y a des dessins représentant des personnes avec des traits physiques particuliers. Complétez les phrases suivantes à voix haute en utilisant les articles **le** ou **la** et les parties du corps. Faites bien attention à la forme des adjectifs. Votre camarade va identifier le dessin que vous décrivez.

**a.**

**c.**

**b.**

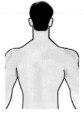

**d.**

1. La personne dans ce dessin a _____ plat(e) (*flat*) et _____ très rond(e).
2. La personne dans ce dessin a _____ pointu et _____ pulpeux(se) (*fleshy*).
3. La personne dans ce dessin a _____ très long(ue) et _____ très large (*wide*).
4. La personne dans ce dessin a _____ souriant(e) (*smiling*) et _____ large.

# Leçon 4

**À propos de la lecture…**
Ce poème est tiré du recueil *Paroles* (1946) par Jacques Prévert.

 Lecture

### Avant de lire

**Scanning (Part 2).** As noted in **Chapitre 4**, it is helpful to scan a text for specific information before you read it. Scanning is a reading skill that readers use almost every day. The overview you receive from scanning allows you to understand the text better during the first, more thorough reading. Scan the poem to determine the following:

1. *Tense:* Which verb tense is used the most often? What expression is repeated several times?
2. *Structure of the poem:* Which lines are the longest? How do they differ from each other?
3. *Objects:* How many gifts does the author buy for his love? What are those gifts?
4. *Narrative style of the poem:* Is the narrator speaking directly to his love or is he talking about her? How do you know?

## «Pour toi mon amour»

Je suis allé au marché aux oiseaux
Et j'ai acheté des oiseaux
Pour toi
mon amour
Je suis allé au marché aux fleurs
Et j'ai acheté des fleurs
Pour toi
mon amour
Je suis allé au marché à la ferraille[1]
Et j'ai acheté des chaînes
De lourdes chaînes
Pour toi
mon amour
Et puis je suis allé au marché aux esclaves[2]
Et je t'ai cherchée
Mais je ne t'ai pas trouvée
mon amour

[1]*scrap iron, metal*  [2]*marché… slave market*

"Pour toi mon amour" in *Paroles* by Jacques Prévert, © Éditions GALLIMARD

## Compréhension

1. Quels cadeaux le poète a-t-il achetés pour son amour?
2. À votre avis, qu'est-ce que chaque cadeau symbolise?
3. Pourquoi est-ce que le poète n'a pas trouvé son amour à la fin du poème?
4. Quel commentaire fait le poète sur les relations entre les hommes et les femmes?

 # Écriture

The writing activities **Par écrit** and **Journal intime** can be found in the Workbook/Laboratory Manual to accompany *Vis-à-vis*.

## Pour s'amuser

LE MARI: On est mariés depuis cinq ans, et on n'est jamais arrivés à être d'accord sur quelque chose.

LA FEMME: Tu as tort, on est mariés depuis six ans.

# Le vidéoblog d'Hector

## En bref

Dans cet épisode, Hassan rencontre Hector devant une pharmacie. Comme Hector ne se sent pas bien, Hassan lui suggère de modifier sa façon de vivre. Il évoque «l'art de vivre» au Maroc.

## Vocabulaire en contexte

Qu'est-ce que vous faites pour maintenir (*maintain*) votre santé physique et mentale? Indiquez vos préférences.

☐ prendre des **médicaments** (*medications*)
☐ ne pas trop **faire la fête** (*to party*)
☐ s'arrêter dans un café, un salon de thé
☐ boire des jus de fruits
☐ se coucher tôt et dormir huit heures

☐ prendre des **vitamines**
☐ se promener
☐ faire du sport, de la gym
☐ s'amuser avec des amis
☐ **économiser** (*to save, conserve*) son énergie

Un Marocain lit le journal le matin au café à Marrakech, au Maroc.

## Visionnez!

Choisissez la bonne réponse.

1. Hector se sent fatigué parce qu'il _____.
   **a.** **s'entraîne** (*practice*) beaucoup
   **b.** fait trop la fête
2. Hassan lui conseille _____.
   **a.** de consulter un médecin
   **b.** d'aller se détendre à la campagne
3. Hassan est content parce qu'il _____ cette semaine.
   **a.** a du **temps libre** (*free time*)
   **b.** ferme son restaurant
4. Hassan **trouve que** (*thinks that*) la vie au Maroc est plus (*more*) _____ qu'à Paris.
   **a.** agréable et **douce** (*gentle*)
   **b.** ennuyeuse

## Analysez!

Répondez aux questions.

1. Quels sont les éléments de «l'art de vivre» au Maroc? Que fait-on, par exemple, pour se détendre le matin, l'après-midi et le soir?
2. À votre avis, est-ce que le climat a une très grande influence sur l'art de vivre au Maroc? Expliquez.

## Comparez!

Quels sont les critères de qualité de vie (une vie agréable, douce) dans votre pays? Selon cette définition, avez-vous vous-même une bonne qualité de vie? Regardez encore une fois la partie culturelle de la vidéo: préférez-vous l'art de vivre *à l'américaine* ou *à la marocaine*? Expliquez.

## Note culturelle

En France, on distingue les pharmacies des parapharmacies. Les premières sont autorisées à distribuer des médicaments sur présentation d'une ordonnance[1] et à proposer des équivalents génériques. Elles vendent aussi des médicaments accessibles sans ordonnance (ex: l'aspirine) et des produits de santé (ex: un thermomètre). Signalées par une grande croix verte,[2] elles sont, pour certaines, ouvertes[3] la nuit. Les parapharmacies ne peuvent pas vendre de médicaments. Elles distribuent des produits de confort et de beauté (ex: les produits de toilette pour les bébés et pour les femmes). À noter: la publicité pour les médicaments est interdite par la loi.[4]

[1]prescription  [2]croix… *green cross*  [3]*open*
[4]interdite… *prohibited by law*

# Vocabulaire

## Verbes

**s'amuser (à)** to have fun
**s'appeler** to be named
**s'arrêter** to stop
**avoir mal (à)** to have pain;
  to hurt
**se baigner** to bathe; to swim
**se brosser (les cheveux, les
  dents)** to brush (one's hair,
  one's teeth)
**courir** to run
**se coucher** to go to bed
**se débrouiller** to manage
**se demander** to wonder
**se dépêcher** to hurry
**se détendre** to relax
**se disputer** to argue
**divorcer** to divorce
**se doucher** to take a shower
**s'embrasser** to kiss
**s'en aller** to go away,
  go off (*to work*)
**s'endormir** to fall asleep
**s'ennuyer** to be bored
**s'entendre (avec)** to get along
  (with)
**s'excuser** to apologize
**se fâcher** to get angry
**se fiancer** to get engaged
**s'habiller** to get dressed
**s'installer** to settle down, settle in
**se laver** to wash oneself
**se lever** to get up
**se maquiller** to put on makeup
**marcher** to walk
**se marier (avec)** to get
  married (to)
**se mettre à** (+ *inf.*) to begin to
  (*do something*)
**se peigner** to comb one's hair

**se perdre** to get lost
**se préparer** to get ready
**se promener** to take a walk
**se rappeler** to remember
**se raser** to shave
**se regarder** to look at oneself, at
  each other
**se rencontrer** to meet
**se reposer** to rest
**se réveiller** to awaken, wake up
**se souvenir (de)** to remember
**tomber amoureux / amoureuse
  (de)** to fall in love (with)
**se tromper** to make a mistake
**se trouver** to be located

## Substantifs

**l'amitié** (*f.*) friendship
**l'amour** (*m.*) love
**l'amoureux / l'amoureuse** lover,
  sweetheart
**la bouche** mouth
**le bras** arm
**la brosse** brush
  **la brosse à cheveux** hairbrush
  **la brosse à dents** toothbrush
**le cabinet médical** doctor's office
**le/la célibataire** single person
**la cérémonie** ceremony
**le cœur** heart
**le corps** body
**le cou** neck
**le coup de foudre** flash of
  lightning; love at first sight
**le couple** (engaged, married)
  couple
**la dent** tooth
**le doigt** finger
**le dos** back
**la douleur** pain

**les fiançailles** (*f. pl.*) engagement
**le genou** knee
**la gorge** throat
**la jambe** leg
**la main** hand
**le mariage** marriage
**le nez** nose
**les nouveaux mariés** (*m. pl.*)
  newlyweds
**l'œil** (*m.*) **(les yeux)** eye(s)
**l'oreille** (*f.*) ear
**les pantoufles** (*f.*) slippers
**le peigne** comb
**le pied** foot
**la piqûre** injection, shot
**le rasoir** razor
**la rencontre** meeting, encounter
**le rendez-vous** date
**le rouge à lèvres** lipstick
**la santé** health
**la tête** head
**le ventre** abdomen; stomach
**le visage** face
**le voyage de noces** honeymoon

À REVOIR: **les cheveux** (*m. pl.*),
  **le réveil**

## Adjectifs

**amoureux / amoureuse** loving,
  in love
**guéri(e)** cured, healed
**malade** sick
**quotidien(ne)** daily, everyday

## Mots et expressions divers

**Allez-vous-en!** Go away!
**Va-t'en!** Go away!

# Sur le marché du travail

Les dossiers d'Hector

Hector

➤ 📁 Mes photos
   ➤ 📁 Les vendanges
   ➤ 📁 Pomme Cannelle
   ➤ 📁 Au CIDJ

Les vendanges (*Grape harvest*) en Bourgogne

# Dans ce chapitre...

## OBJECTIFS COMMUNICATIFS
- ➤ talking about jobs and professions
- ➤ talking about banking and finances
- ➤ talking about the future
- ➤ linking ideas
- ➤ making comparisons
- ➤ learning to distinguish between and pronounce selected sounds in French

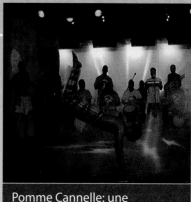

Pomme Cannelle: une troupe de danse antillaise

## PAROLES (Leçon 1)
- ➤ Les métiers et professions
- ➤ À la banque
- ➤ Le budget
- ➤ Le verbe **ouvrir**

## STRUCTURES (Leçons 2 et 3)
- ➤ Le futur simple (première partie)
- ➤ Le futur simple (deuxième partie)
- ➤ Les pronoms relatifs
- ➤ La comparaison de l'adjectif qualificatif

Au CIDJ on propose des milliers (*thousands*) offres d'emploi pour l'été en France

## CULTURE
- ➤ Le blog d'Hector: *Pas facile, la vie d'artiste!*
- ➤ Reportage: *Étudiants: la chasse aux stages et aux petits boulots*
- ➤ Lecture: *Des métiers pas ordinaires* (Leçon 4)

www.mhconnectfrench.com

# Leçon 1

## Au travail

**1. Les fonctionnaires:** ils travaillent pour l'État.

*[handwritten: Civil servant]*

M. Merel,
agent de
police*

M<sup>lle</sup> Drouet,
secrétaire‡ de
mairie

M. Barbier,
facteur*

M<sup>me</sup> Lambert,
professeur
des écoles‡

M<sup>me</sup> Guilloux,
employée† à
la SNCF

**2. Les travailleurs\* salariés:**
ils travaillent pour
une entreprise.

M. Dufour,
chef* d'entreprise → *[handwritten: CEO]*

**LES CADRES**\*
*[handwritten: executive ↗]* M. Geslot,
directeur*
commercial

M<sup>me</sup> Dumur,
ingénieur‡

**LES EMPLOYÉS**
M<sup>lle</sup> Cadet,
secrétaire

M. Tessier,
comptable‡

**LES
OUVRIERS**\*

---

\**Feminine forms*: un agent, une factrice, une travailleuse, un cadre, un chef, une directrice,
une ouvrière
†*Masculine form*: un employé
‡**Secrétaire, professeur,** and **comptable** can be either masculine or feminine.
**Ingénieur** is always masculine, even for a woman.

**3. Les travailleurs indépendants:** ils travaillent **à leur compte**.

- **Les artisans**

M. Lepape,
plombier*

Mᵐᵉ Ngalla,
coiffeuse†

| AUTRES MOTS UTILES | |
|---|---|
| **un entretien** | job interview |
| **un chômeur /** | unemployed |
| **une chômeuse** | person |
| **un C.V.** | curriculum vitae, résumé |
| **le marché du travail** | job market |
| **un stage** | internship |

- **Les commerçants**

M. Thétiot,
boucher‡

M. Lefranc,
marchand‡ de vin

- **Les professions de la santé**

M. Morin,
pharmacien‡

Mˡˡᵉ Wong,
dentiste*

Mᵐᵉ Bouakaz,
femme médecin†

- **D'autres professions**

Mᵐᵉ Aubry,
avocate†

M. Leconte,
architecte*

M. Colin,
agriculteur‡

Mˡˡᵉ Cossec,
artiste,* peintre*

M. Kalubi,
journaliste*

---

*__Plombier__ is always masculine, even for a woman, but **dentiste, architecte, artiste, peintre,**
and **journaliste** can all be either masculine or feminine.
†*Masculine forms*: un coiffeur, un médecin, un avocat
‡*Feminine forms*: une bouchère, une marchande, une pharmacienne, une agricultrice

## Allez-y!

A. **Définitions.** Quelle est la profession des personnes suivantes?

**MODÈLES:** Elle enseigne à l'école primaire. → Elle est professeur des écoles.
Il écrit des articles pour des journaux. → Il est journaliste.

1. Elle soigne les dents de ses patients.
2. Il travaille à la campagne.
3. Il règle la circulation automobile.
4. Elle vend des billets de train.
5. Elle s'occupe de (*takes care of*) la santé de ses patients.
6. Il distribue des lettres et des colis.
7. Il vend de la viande aux clients.
8. Elle coupe (*cuts*) les cheveux des clients.
9. Elle tape des lettres sur un ordinateur.
10. Il vend des vins et des liqueurs.
11. Il prépare et vend des médicaments.
12. Elle fait des portraits et des paysages (*landscapes*).

B. **Stéréotypes.** Voici quelques dessins du caricaturiste français Jean-Pierre Adelbert. Choisissez la profession qui, selon vous, correspond le mieux à chaque dessin. Expliquez pourquoi.

**Professions:** architecte, artiste, caricaturiste, chef d'entreprise, chômeur/chômeuse, coiffeur/coiffeuse, comptable, critique de cinéma, critique de cuisine, journaliste de mode, peintre, plombier, vendeur/vendeuse… ?

C. **Projets d'avenir.** Découvrez les futures professions de vos camarades de classe. Interviewez cinq étudiant(e)s pour découvrir quel métier ils/elles désirent faire après avoir terminé leurs études. Ensuite, analysez les résultats. En général, avez-vous des ambitions différentes ou semblables (*similar*)?

**MODÈLE:** É1: Que veux-tu faire après tes études?
É2: Je veux / Je voudrais devenir avocat(e).
É1: Et pourquoi?…

# À la banque

Rebecca Johnson est une architecte américaine.
Elle vient de s'installer en France et va à la banque.

**1.** Elle ouvre (*opens*) **un compte bancaire** et **un compte d'épargne** pour pouvoir **faire des économies** (*f.*) **(économiser) pour l'avenir** [m.]. Elle a accès à ses comptes sur Internet et peut les gérer (*manage them*) à distance.

**2.** Elle prend aussi **une carte bancaire.***

**3.** Elle regarde **le cours du jour (le taux de change)** et change ses dollars en euros.

| CHANGES | Monnaies | Cours du jour |
|---------|----------|---------------|
| États-Unis.... | 1 USD | 0,792 € |

**4.** Quelques jours plus tard, elle va au **guichet automatique.** Avec sa carte bancaire, elle **retire** du **liquide** et **dépose** un chèque.

**AUTRES MOTS UTILES**

**un bureau de change** exchange office
**compter** to count
**contrôler ses relevés** (*m.*) check one's bank statements
**une dépense** expenditure
**un emprunt** loan
**des frais** (*m. pl.*) expenses, costs

**la monnaie** change; currency
**un montant** sum
**payer par prélèvement automatique** to make automatic payments
**réaliser un virement** to transfer money
**un reçu** receipt
**toucher** to cash (a check)

 *Allez-y!*

**A. Les services bancaires.** Assane, un étudiant sénégalais, vient d'obtenir un permis de travail (*work permit*) en France. Complétez les phrases suivantes en utilisant le vocabulaire que vous venez d'apprendre.

   **1.** Pour changer ses francs sénégalais en euros, il consulte _____.
   **2.** Il va à la banque pour ouvrir un _____ et un _____ afin de (*in order to*) pouvoir faire des économies.
   **3.** Quand il veut retirer du _____ ou _____ un chèque sur son compte, il peut aller au _____ et utiliser sa _____.

---

*Carte bancaire is a general term that refers to both **cartes de crédit** and **cartes de débit.**

**B. Une globe-trotter.** Audrey vient d'arriver à Paris. Elle est à l'aéroport Charles-de-Gaulle et veut changer de l'argent. Indiquez dans quel ordre elle doit faire les choses suivantes.

_____ prendre sa carte bancaire et du liquide avec elle

_____ prendre le reçu

_____ compter l'argent

_____ se présenter à un bureau de change avec son passeport

_____ vérifier le montant sur le reçu

_____ dire combien d'argent elle veut changer

# Le budget de Marc Convert

Voulez-vous travailler dans une petite société ou une grande entreprise?

Marc travaille dans une petite **société** (*company*) près de Marseille où il est responsable (*director*) commercial.

Il **gagne** 1 800 euros par mois.

Il **dépense** presque tout ce qu'il gagne pour vivre; le **coût de la vie** est très **élevé** dans les villes françaises. Mais il espère avoir une **augmentation de salaire** dans six mois. En ce moment, il lui est difficile de **faire des économies** pour acheter une maison.

Marc est content de son travail. Il sait qu'il a de la chance **car le taux de chômage** est très élevé en France: 10,4% en juillet 2013.

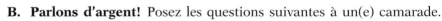 **Allez-y!**

**A. Frais et revenus.** Complétez les phrases en utilisant le vocabulaire que vous venez d'apprendre.

1. Manon _____ pour acheter une voiture.
2. Les employés demandent souvent des _____.
3. Le _____ est moins élevé dans les petites villes.
4. Dayan est très économe: il _____ très peu.
5. M^me Reich? Elle travaille dans une _____ d'assurance (*insurance*).
6. Irène a un emploi sympa; elle est contente même si elle _____ relativement peu.

**B. Parlons d'argent!** Posez les questions suivantes à un(e) camarade.

1. Est-ce que tu travailles en ce moment? Si oui, qu'est-ce que tu fais comme travail?
2. Est-ce que tu as un compte bancaire, un compte d'épargne, une carte de crédit?
3. Est-ce que tu gères tes comptes à distance?
4. Comment est-ce que tu paies ton électricité et ton loyer? par prélèvement automatique? par chèque?
5. Qu'est-ce que tu fais pour économiser de l'argent?
6. Est-ce que tu as un budget ou est-ce que tu vis au jour le jour (*from day to day*)? Pourquoi?

# Le verbe *ouvrir*

| PRESENT TENSE OF **ouvrir** (*to open*) | |
| --- | --- |
| j' **ouvre** | nous **ouvrons** |
| tu **ouvres** | vous **ouvrez** |
| il/elle/on **ouvre** | ils/elles **ouvrent** |
| *Past participle: ouvert* | |

The verb **ouvrir** is irregular. Verbs conjugated like **ouvrir** include **couvrir** (*to cover*), **découvrir** (*to discover*), **offrir** (*to offer*), and **souffrir** (*to suffer*). Note that these verbs are conjugated in the present tense like **-er** verbs.

The opposite of **ouvrir** is **fermer** (*to close*).

«J'aimerais ouvrir un compte, s'il vous plaît.» Avez-vous un compte bancaire?

## Allez-y!

**A. Finances.** Ce mois-ci, Jason a des problèmes d'argent. Racontez cette histoire en utilisant les verbes suivants: **ouvrir, couvrir, découvrir, offrir, souffrir.** Utilisez le passé composé (*p.c.*) où c'est indiqué.

Le mois dernier, Jason _____¹ (*p.c.*) un compte bancaire et un compte d'épargne. Sa grand-mère lui _____² toujours de l'argent pour son anniversaire, mais il l'utilise pour ses frais scolaires. Jason est très économe. Il _____³ toujours ses dépenses. Mais ce mois-ci, il a acheté une nouvelle moto et il _____⁴ parce qu'il ne peut pas sortir aussi souvent. Alors, il _____⁵ les plaisirs de la lecture!

**B. Profil psychologique.** Demandez à un(e) camarade _____.

1. s'il / si elle a un compte bancaire
2. s'il / si elle couvre toujours ses dépenses
3. s'il / si elle fait des économies et pourquoi
4. s'il / si elle souffre quand il/elle est obligé(e) de faire des économies
5. combien de fois par semaine, ou par mois, il/elle doit retirer de l'argent de son compte et combien de fois il/elle doit déposer de l'argent
6. si quelqu'un lui a récemment offert de l'argent et ce qu'il/elle en a fait

Maintenant, dites ce que vous avez découvert et faites un petit portrait psychologique de votre camarade. Ou si vous préférez, lisez l'histoire de Jason dans l'exercice précédent et faites un portrait psychologique de Jason.

**Mots utiles:** économe, impulsif/impulsive, généreux/généreuse, (im)prudent(e), un magnat des affaires (*tycoon*)

STRUCTURES

# Leçon 2

## Le futur simple (*première partie*)

*Talking About the Future*

### La vie d'artiste

*Appel vidéo entre Juliette et Hector,*

JULIETTE: Tu as signé un nouveau contrat?

HECTOR: Non. Avec la crise,[1] les artistes ont la vie dure[2]! Si ça continue, **je changerai** de métier!

JULIETTE: Tu as des idées?

HECTOR: Oui! **J'enseignerai.** Avec mes potes,[3] **on proposera** des cours de hip-hop pour les enfants. Les gosses[4] adorent ça!

JULIETTE: Alors **tu travailleras** à ton compte?

HECTOR: Exactement. Et **je serai** enfin indépendant.

▼ AUDIO & VIDEO

MESSAGE    VIDEO ●

[1]*crisis*   [2]*la… a hard life*   [3]*buddies, pals*   [4]*kids*

Dans les phrases suivantes, identifiez les verbes au futur proche. Puis remplacez-les par les verbes au futur utilisés dans le dialogue.

1. Je vais changer de métier.
2. Je vais enseigner.
3. On va proposer des cours de hip-hop.
4. Tu vas travailler à ton compte?
5. Je vais être indépendant.

### Expressing the Future in French

In French, there are three ways of expressing future actions or events:

| | | |
|---|---|---|
| PRESENT | J'**arrive** à 2 h. | *I arrive at 2:00.* |
| NEAR FUTURE | Je **vais arriver** demain. | *I'm going to arrive tomorrow.* |
| FUTURE TENSE | J'**arriverai** en janvier. | *I will arrive in January.* |

## Verbs with Regular Future Stems

The future is a simple tense, formed with the infinitive plus the endings **-ai, -as, -a, -ons, -ez, -ont.** The final **-e** of the infinitive of **-re** verbs is dropped.

| parler | finir | vendre |
|---|---|---|
| je parler**ai** | je finir**ai** | je vendr**ai** |
| tu parler**as** | tu finir**as** | tu vendr**as** |
| il/elle/on parler**a** | il/elle/on finir**a** | il/elle/on vendr**a** |
| nous parler**ons** | nous finir**ons** | nous vendr**ons** |
| vous parler**ez** | vous finir**ez** | vous vendr**ez** |
| ils/elles parler**ont** | ils/elles finir**ont** | ils/elles vendr**ont** |

Demain nous **parlerons** avec le conseiller d'orientation.
Il te **donnera** des conseils.
Ces conseils t'**aideront** peut-être à trouver du travail.
La réunion **finira** vers cinq heures.

*Tomorrow we will talk with the job counselor.*
*He will give you some advice.*
*Maybe this advice will help you find a job.*
*The meeting will end around five o'clock.*

### Prononcez bien!

**The consonant r**

Pronounce [ʀ] as you would an *h* in English, but raise the back of your tongue so that the distance between it and the back of your palate is much narrower than for *h*. When in between two vowels, **r** is pronounced more softly than when it occurs next to a consonant sound, especially [p], [t], and [k].

**aide<u>r</u>ons, <u>arriver</u>, étudi<u>era</u>, Pa<u>r</u>is**

BUT

he<u>r</u>be, Ma<u>r</u>seille, p<u>r</u>ès, se<u>cr</u>et, su<u>cr</u>e, <u>tr</u>avail

### *Allez-y!*

**A. Stratégies.** Marie cherche du travail pour cet été. Elle doit se présenter demain à un entretien. Dites ce qu'elle fera.

*interview*

**MODÈLE:** se lever très tôt → Elle se lèvera très tôt.

1. se coucher tôt ce soir
2. s'habiller avec soin
3. prendre un petit déjeuner léger
4. mettre son curriculum vitæ dans sa serviette (*briefcase*)
5. prendre le métro pour éviter les embouteillages (*traffic jams*)
6. y arriver un peu en avance
7. se présenter brièvement
8. parler calmement
9. répondre avec précision aux questions de l'employeur
10. remercier l'employeur avant de partir

Maintenant répétez l'exercice en utilisant le sujet **Marie et Loïc.**

**MODÈLE:** se lever très tôt → Ils se lèveront très tôt.

L'architecture: un travail de précision. Est-ce que vous travaillerez comme architecte? comme professeur? comme cadre?

**B. Jeu de société.** À une soirée, vous jouez à la voyante (*fortune-teller*) et prédisez la carrière de chacun(e) de vos ami(e)s. Choisissez le verbe convenable pour présenter vos prévisions.

**Verbes:** écrire, enseigner, jouer, s'occuper, participer, travailler, vendre, voyager

1. Vous _____ des bijoux à Alger.
2. Vous _____ le rôle de Hamlet à Londres.
3. Vous _____ à la construction d'un stade à Mexico.
4. Vous _____ des articles pour le *New York Times*.
5. Vous _____ souvent à l'étranger.
6. Vous _____ des malades à Dakar.
7. Vous _____ dans une école primaire à Seattle.
8. Vous _____ comme cosmonaute.

# Le futur simple (*deuxième partie*)

*Talking About the Future*

## La grande aventure

*Léa téléphone à Juliette.*

LÉA: Quand est-ce que **tu feras** ton stage de fin d'études?
JULIETTE: En janvier prochain.
LÉA: **Tu seras** en stage combien de temps?
JULIETTE: Six mois. Ensuite, **je devrai** trouver un emploi. Je veux être chef de projet multimédia.
LÉA: **Tu obtiendras** peut-être un poste dans l'entreprise où **tu feras** ton stage... C'est fréquent, tu sais!
JULIETTE: C'est possible, mais je veux travailler à l'étranger. **J'enverrai** des C.V. dès[1] février.
LÉA: Au Canada, il y a plein d'opportunités[2]! Et on parle français!
JULIETTE: Oui, mais je rêve d'une grande aventure: **j'irai** en Australie! **Tu viendras** me voir?

L'avenir appartient aux champions du Web

[1]*beginning in*   [2]plein... *lots of opportunities*

Dans les phrases suivantes, identifiez les verbes au futur proche. Puis remplacez-les par les verbes au futur utilisés dans le dialogue.

1. Tu vas faire ton stage?
2. Tu vas être en stage combien de temps?
3. Ensuite, je vais devoir trouver un emploi.
4. Tu vas peut-être obtenir un poste dans l'entreprise où tu vas faire ton stage.
5. Je vais envoyer des C.V. dès février.
6. Je vais aller en Australie. Tu vas venir me voir?

## Verbs with Irregular Future Stems

Some verbs have irregular future stems.

| | | | | | |
|---|---|---|---|---|---|
| aller: | **ir-** | faire: | **fer-** | recevoir: | **recevr-** |
| avoir: | **aur-** | falloir: | **faudr-** | savoir: | **saur-** |
| devoir: | **devr-** | mourir: | **mourr-** | venir: | **viendr-** |
| envoyer: | **enverr-** | pleuvoir: | **pleuvr-** | voir: | **verr-** |
| être: | **ser-** | pouvoir: | **pourr-** | vouloir: | **voudr-** |

| | |
|---|---|
| J'**irai** au travail la semaine prochaine. | *I'll go to work next week.* |
| Et toi, quand **enverras**-tu ta demande d'emploi? | *And you? When will you send in your job application?* |
| Pas de problème! J'**aurai** bientôt un poste. | *No problem! I will have a position soon.* |
| Alors, vous **devrez** tous les deux vous lever très tôt le matin. | *So both of you will have to get up very early in the morning.* |
| C'est vrai. Mais demain on **devra** célébrer cela! | *It's true. But tomorrow we should celebrate!* |

Verbs with spelling irregularities in the present tense also have irregularities in the future tense. These include verbs such as **acheter, appeler,** and **payer.** See Appendix B: **-er** Verbs with Spelling Changes, at the end of the book.

## Uses of the Future Tense

**1.** As you can see from the preceding examples, the use of the future tense parallels that of English. This is also true of the tense of verbs after an *if*-clause in the present tense.

| | |
|---|---|
| Si je pose ma candidature pour ce poste, j'**aurai** peut-être des chances de l'obtenir. | *If I apply for this position, I may (will maybe) have some chance of getting it.* |
| Mais si tu ne te présentes pas, tu ne l'**auras** sûrement pas! | *But if you don't apply in person, you surely will not get it!* |

**2.** However, in dependent clauses following words such as **quand, lorsque** (*when*), **dès que** (*as soon as*), or **aussitôt que** (*as soon as*), the future tense is used in French if the action is expected to occur at a future time. English uses the present tense in this case.

| | |
|---|---|
| Je te **téléphonerai** *dès que* j'**arriverai.** | *I'll phone you as soon as I arrive.* |
| Nous **pourrons** en discuter *lorsque* l'avocat **sera** là. | *We'll be able to discuss it when the lawyer arrives.* |
| La discussion **commencera** *dès que* tout le monde **sera** prêt. | *The discussion will begin as soon as everyone is ready.* |

### Mots clés

**Exprimer le futur**

All the expressions mentioned in the **Mots clés** of **Chapitre 5, Leçon 2** are also applicable to the **futur simple.** The following expressions are mostly used with the **futur simple:**

**à l'avenir** *from now on; in the future*
**un jour** *some day*
**à partir de maintenant** *from now on*

**À l'avenir,** nous ferons des économies.
**Un jour,** nous n'aurons plus de dettes.
**À partir de maintenant,** je te montrerai toutes mes dépenses.

3. The **futur simple** can also be used to politely express a command, a request, or a piece of advice.

Tu me **donneras** ton adresse
avant de partir.

*Give me your address before
you leave.*

Vous **finirez** de taper ces
documents pour demain.

*Finish typing these documents
for tomorrow.*

 *Allez-y!*

A. **Les exigences du milieu de travail.** Transformez les phrases en utilisant le futur simple.

MODÈLE: Téléphone à ton collègue! →
Tu téléphoneras à ton collègue!

1. Va poster ce colis!
2. Venez nous voir pendant les vacances!
3. Sois patient(e) avec tes collègues!
4. Envoyez des références!
5. Fais ton possible!

B. **Problème urgent.** Les membres d'une équipe au travail organisent une réunion pour essayer de trouver une solution à un problème. Utilisez le futur.

MODÈLE: (vous) expliquer le problème / quand / tout le monde / être là →
Vous expliquerez le problème quand tout le monde sera là.

1. (tu) commencer la réunion / dès que / la patronne / arriver
2. (Nils) montrer les photos / aussitôt que / il / les recevoir
3. (nous) discuter nos options / quand / le problème / être clair pour tous
4. (je) téléphoner au client / quand / nous / pouvoir répondre à ses questions
5. (Nathalie et Octave) écrire une lettre au client / dès que / nous / être tous d'accord

C. **Interview.** Vous voulez savoir ce que votre camarade pense de l'avenir, et vous lui posez les questions suivantes. Mais malheureusement, il/elle ne vous prend pas au sérieux! L'interviewé(e) utilise toute son imagination et tout son humour pour répondre. À la fin, inversez les rôles.

MODÈLE: dès que tu auras ton diplôme →
É1: Qu'est-ce que tu feras dès que tu auras ton diplôme?
É2: Moi, plus tard, je vendrai des légumes biologiques (*organic*) à Athènes.

1. quand tu seras vieux/vieille
2. si un jour tu es acteur/actrice
3. dans dix ans
4. lorsque tu te marieras
5. dès que tu pourras réaliser un de tes rêves
6. si tu n'obtiens pas tout ce que tu veux
7. lorsque tu auras des enfants

À votre avis, parmi toutes les réponses, laquelle (*which one*) est la plus originale, la plus amusante et la plus bizarre?

| le blé, le fric | l'argent |
| --- | --- |
| **bosser** | travailler |
| **un boulot** | un travail |
| **claquer** | dépenser |
| **être fauché** | ne plus avoir d'argent |

Pour gagner du **blé**, il faut éviter les métiers intellectuels.

Je préfère **bosser** la nuit.

Moi, j'aime mon **boulot**.

Je viens de **claquer** 100 euros en DVD!

Depuis les vacances, Delphine **est** complètement **fauchée**.

**D. Conversation.** Posez les questions suivantes à un(e) camarade, qui vous les posera à son tour.

L'été prochain, _____?

1. qu'est-ce que tu écriras?
2. qu'est-ce que tu liras?
3. qu'est-ce que tu achèteras?
4. qui verras-tu?
5. où iras-tu?
6. que feras-tu? Auras-tu un job?

**E. Interview.** Posez les questions suivantes à un(e) camarade de classe.

1. Qu'est-ce que tu feras quand l'année scolaire sera terminée? Continueras-tu tes études, iras-tu en vacances ou travailleras-tu?
2. Qu'est-ce que tu feras après tes études? Tu choisiras une profession indépendante? salariée? Seras-tu fonctionnaire? commerçant(e)? artisan(e)?
3. Tu voyageras souvent? Si oui, dans quels pays? Pour quelles raisons?
4. Tu gagneras beaucoup d'argent? Est-ce que cela sera important pour toi?
5. Où est-ce que tu vivras si tu en as le choix? Pourquoi?

Être professeur: une profession prestigieuse et satisfaisante. Avez-vous un professeur que vous aimez beaucoup? Expliquez.

# Le blog d'Hector

## Pas facile, la vie d'artiste!

lundi 6 juillet

La semaine commence mal… Je suis angoissé[1]!

Quelquefois, je regrette de ne pas être plombier, dentiste, ou comptable! Ces professions sont moins fatigantes et plus rassurantes que le métier de danseur. Parce que, vous savez, c'est beau, la vie d'artiste, mais c'est avant tout des concessions, des efforts, des sacrifices, beaucoup de discipline et de courage.

Je ne suis pas un travailleur salarié. Je suis un danseur moderne indépendant. Alors, j'ai toujours des incertitudes[2] sur mon avenir; je me pose mille questions: «Est-ce que j'aurai un contrat cet été? Qu'est-ce que je ferai si je n'ai pas de contrat? Comment est-ce que je paierai mes frais? Serai-je obligé d'emprunter de l'argent à ma banque?»

Dans ma profession, le taux de chômage est élevé et il faut savoir faire des économies pour les mauvais jours. Il faut aussi avoir une bonne relation avec son banquier en cas de problème!

Je vais envoyer une candidature à la troupe antillaise Pomme Cannelle pour un poste de Directeur de spectacles. Je rêve d'un emploi stable et j'aimerais bien partir travailler au soleil: ça me changerait les idées[3]!

Hector

Pomme Cannelle: une troupe de danse antillaise

. . . . . . . . . . . . . . . . . . . . . . . . . . . . . . . . . . . . . . . . . . . . . . . . . . . . . . . . . . . . . . . . . . . . . . .

## COMMENTAIRES

**Alexis**
Salut, Hector!
Dans ta prochaine vie, tu seras fonctionnaire! Tu seras moins angoissé!

**Trésor**
Mon métier, c'est d'être le chien d'Alexis. Ce n'est pas toujours facile non plus…

**Poema**
Les problèmes dont tu parles ne sont pas spécifiques aux artistes. Les travailleurs indépendants n'ont aucune sécurité d'emploi! Je le sais parce que mon père est dentiste.

**Mamadou**
Poema, les gens auront toujours mal aux dents, et ils auront toujours besoin d'un dentiste!

**Charlotte**
Hector, si tu obtiens ton poste de Directeur de spectacles, tu pourras retourner aux Antilles. Et tu seras un artiste salarié: c'est l'idéal, non?

[1]*anxious*  [2]*uncertainties*  [3]*ça… that would give me a change of pace*

## REPORTAGE

## Étudiants: la chasse aux stages et aux petits boulots

En France, l'accès à l'université est gratuit.[1] Mais ensuite, comment couvrir vos dépenses et gagner l'argent du loyer, de la nourriture, des livres, des sorties et des vacances? Il n'y a qu'une solution: trouver un petit boulot.

Vous voulez un travail intéressant, pas trop fatigant et, en plus, bien payé? Première règle: si vous désirez travailler en été, commencez vos recherches dès le mois de janvier. Deuxième règle: faites l'inventaire des entreprises qui embauchent[2] des étudiants; parlez de vos projets à votre boucher, à votre dentiste, à votre facteur, à votre pharmacien, aux membres de votre famille, à tout le monde. Troisième règle: envoyez des lettres de motivation personnalisées et des C.V. attractifs qui mettent en valeur[3] vos points forts.

Attention, il ne faut pas confondre petit boulot et stage en entreprise. Aurélie, qui vient de terminer un stage de relations publiques chez Air France, explique: «Un stage en entreprise vous donne une compétence professionnelle. Souvent obligatoire, il complète votre formation universitaire dans le domaine de vos études. Et s'il dure plus de huit semaines, il donne droit à une indemnité.[4] C'est le meilleur argument sur un C.V. au moment de la recherche d'un emploi.» Comment a-t-elle trouvé son stage? «J'ai consulté les petites annonces du CIDJ (Centre d'information et de documentation de la jeunesse) sur Internet et j'ai posé ma candidature sur des sites spécialisés comme Apec.fr et Letudiant.fr. À la fin, j'ai eu plusieurs propositions!»

Le CIDJ propose aux étudiants plus de des milliers offres d'emplois pour l'été en France et dans les autres pays d'Europe. Tous les secteurs sont représentés: la vente, l'hôtellerie, le sport, les nouvelles technologies… N'hésitez pas à consulter son site Internet. Comme ce jeune homme, vous y trouverez sûrement le stage ou le petit boulot de vos rêves!

[1]free  [2]hire  [3]mettent… *emphasize*  [4]*compensation*

1. En France, quel est le meilleur moyen de trouver un petit boulot pour l'été? En Amérique, comment procédez-vous?
2. Expliquez la différence entre un petit boulot et un stage en entreprise.
3. Avez-vous l'expérience de petits boulots? Avez-vous déjà fait un stage en entreprise? Décrivez votre expérience. Sinon, décrivez l'expérience d'un ami / d'une amie.
4. Quel emploi cherche le jeune homme sur la photo? Imaginez.

1. Travaillez en groupes de quatre et rédigez (*write up*) une proposition de stage destinée à un étudiant qui vient de terminer ses études. (Vous pouvez vous inspirer des petites annonces publiées sur le site du CIDJ.)
2. Dans votre petite annonce, présentez l'entreprise, précisez la durée du stage et la rémunération. Énumérez, au futur, les tâches à accomplir.
3. Lisez votre offre devant la classe. Vos camarades discuteront les détails de l'offre.
4. Demandez qui, parmi vos camarades, est intéressé par votre stage et pourquoi.
5. Les camarades qui ne sont pas intéressés expliqueront leur point de vue.

Qui propose le stage le plus intéressant? Votez!

# Leçon 3

## Les pronoms relatifs

*Linking Ideas*

### Ça m'intéresse!

*Appel vidéo entre Mamadou et Léa.*

MAMADOU: Léa, tu veux toujours écrire des articles pour la presse?

LÉA: Bien sûr! Tu connais un journal **qui** cherche des journalistes en free-lance?

MAMADOU: Oui…

LÉA: Les C.V. **que** j'ai envoyés n'ont pas eu de succès… Si tu as une piste,[1] ça m'intéresse!

MAMADOU: Le journal **dont** je te parle veut une rédactrice[2] **qui** maîtrise parfaitement[3] la langue française: C'est toi!

LÉA: Tu es bien indulgent… Mais donne-moi des précisions: les articles **qu'**il faudra écrire concernent la littérature? la mode[4]? l'actualité[5]?

MAMADOU: Non. Le football.

LÉA: Tu te moques de[6] moi?

▼ AUDIO & VIDEO

MESSAGE  VIDEO ●

[1]*lead*  [2]*editor*  [3]*maîtrise… has a command of*  [4]*fashion*  [5]*current events*  [6]*Tu… You're making fun of*

Trouvez, dans le dialogue, les phrases équivalentes.

1. Tu connais un journal cherchant (*looking for*) des journalistes?
2. Mes C.V. envoyés n'ont pas eu de succès.
3. Le journal en question veut une rédactrice.
4. Le journal veut une rédactrice maîtrisant (*with a command of*) la langue française.
5. Les articles à écrire concernent la littérature?

A relative pronoun (*who, that, which, whom, whose*) links a dependent (relative) clause to a main clause. A dependent clause is one that cannot stand by itself—for example, the italicized parts of the following sentences: The suitcase *that he is carrying* is mine; There is the store *in which we met.*

|  | PERSON | THING |
|---|---|---|
| *subject* | qui | qui |
| *object* | que | que |
| *with preposition* | qui | lequel* |
| *with* **de** | dont | dont |

## Qui

**1.** The relative pronoun used as a subject of a dependent clause is **qui** (*who, that, which*). It can refer to both people and things.

> J'ai un emploi. **Il** me plaît.
>
> J'ai un emploi **qui** me plaît.
>
> Je vois la femme. **Elle** vous a parlé.
>
> Je vois la femme **qui** vous a parlé.

In the first example, **qui** replaces the subject **il** in the dependent clause. Because it is the subject of the clause, **qui** will always be followed by a conjugated verb (**qui... plaît**). Note that in the second example, **vous** is not a subject but an object pronoun; **elle** is the subject of **a parlé**.

**2. Qui** does not elide when followed by a vowel sound.

> L'architecte **qui** est arrivé ce matin vient du Japon.

**3. Qui** can also be used as the object of a preposition to refer to people.

| | |
|---|---|
| Le comptable **avec qui** je travaille est agréable. | *The accountant with whom I work is pleasant.* |
| L'ouvrier **à qui** j'ai donné du travail est très spécialisé. | *The worker to whom I gave some work is highly specialized.* |

[Allez-y! A]

## Que

**1.** The relative pronoun used as a direct object of a dependent clause is **que** (*whom, that, which*). It also can refer to both people and things.

> C'est une entreprise. Je connais bien **cette entreprise.**
>
> C'est une entreprise **que** je connais bien.
>
> Voici une amie. J'ai rencontré **cette amie** au travail.
>
> Voici une amie **que** j'ai rencontrée au travail.

In the second example, **que** replaces the direct object **cette amie. Que** is always followed by a subject and a conjugated verb (**que j'ai rencontrée**). Note that the past participle agrees with the preceding feminine direct object **que** (**une amie**). You may want to review the section on the agreement of past participles in **Chapitre 10, Leçon 3.**

---

*Lequel** is not discussed in this chapter. Refer to **Chapitre 15, Leçon 2** and Appendix E.

**2. Que** elides with a following vowel sound.

L'architecte **qu'**elle a rencontré vient du Japon.

## Dont

1. The pronoun **dont** is used to replace the preposition **de (du, de la, de l', des)** plus its object. If the verb of the dependent clause requires the preposition **de** (as in **parler de, avoir besoin de,** etc.) before an object, use **dont.**

| | |
|---|---|
| Où est le reçu? J'ai besoin **du reçu.** | *Where is the receipt? I need the receipt.* |
| Où est le reçu **dont** j'ai besoin? | *Where is the receipt that I need?* |

2. **Dont** is also used to express possession.

| | |
|---|---|
| C'est la passagère. Ses valises sont à la douane. | *That's the passenger. Her suitcases are at the customs office.* |
| C'est la passagère **dont** les valises sont à la douane. | *That's the passenger whose suitcases are at the customs office.* |
| Aziz est écrivain. On peut acheter ses livres à la librairie. | *Aziz is a writer. You can buy his books at the bookstore.* |
| Aziz est l'écrivain **dont** on peut acheter les livres à la librairie. | *Aziz is the writer whose books you can buy at the bookstore.* |

When **dont** is used, there is no need for a possessive adjective. Note the use of the definite article (**les**).

## Où

**Où** is the relative pronoun of time and place. It can mean *where, when,* or *which.*

| | |
|---|---|
| Le guichet **où** vous changez votre argent est là-bas. | *The window where you change your money is over there.* |
| Le 1ᵉʳ janvier, c'est le jour **où** je commence mon nouveau travail. | *The first of January, that's the day (when) I begin my new job.* |
| L'aéroport d'**où** vous êtes partis est maintenant fermé. | *The airport from which you departed is closed now.* |

[Allez-y! B-C-D-E]

 *Allez-y!*

A. **À la recherche d'un emploi.** Max raconte comment il a passé sa semaine à chercher du travail. Reliez les phrases suivantes avec **qui.**

**MODÈLE:** Dimanche, j'ai téléphoné à une amie. Elle est directrice d'un journal. →
Dimanche, j'ai téléphoné à une amie qui est directrice d'un journal.

1. Lundi, j'ai déjeuné avec un ami. Il connaît beaucoup de comptables.
2. Mardi, j'ai eu un entretien à la BNP (Banque Nationale de Paris) Paribas. Elle est près de la place de la Concorde.
3. Mercredi, j'ai parlé à un employé du Crédit Agricole. Il m'a beaucoup encouragé.
4. Jeudi, j'ai pris rendez-vous avec un membre de la Chambre de commerce. Il est expert-comptable.
5. Enfin samedi, j'ai reçu une lettre d'une société belge. Elle m'offre un poste de comptable à Bruxelles.
6. Et aujourd'hui, je prends l'avion. Il me conduit vers ma nouvelle vie.

**B. Promenade sur la Seine.** Cet été, Clarisse travaille comme guide sur un bateau-mouche* à Paris. Complétez ses explications avec les pronoms relatifs **qui, que** et **où**.

*La Vénus de Milo* au Louvre

Ce bâtiment _____¹ vous voyez à présent dans l'île de la Cité, c'est la Conciergerie. Autrefois une prison, c'est l'endroit _____² Marie-Antoinette a passé ses derniers jours. Et cette église _____³ se trouve en face de nous, c'est Notre-Dame. Voici le musée d'Orsay _____⁴ vous pourrez admirer les peintres impressionnistes et _____⁵ je vous recommande de visiter. Et un peu plus loin, le musée du Louvre _____⁶ vous trouverez *la Joconde* et *la Vénus de Milo*. Et enfin, voici la tour Eiffel _____⁷ est le symbole de notre ville. Est-ce que vous voyez cette statue _____⁸ ressemble à la Liberté éclairant (*lighting*) le monde? Eh bien, c'est l'original de la statue _____⁹ la France a donnée aux Américains.

**C. Photos de vacances.** Jade a passé un mois dans un village d'artistes dans le Midi. Elle y a rencontré beaucoup de gens intéressants. Elle montre maintenant ses photos de vacances à ses amis.

**MODÈLE:** Voici un artisan. Ses poteries sont très chères. →
Voici un artisan **dont les** poteries sont très chères.

1. Charlie est un jeune artiste. On peut admirer ses tableaux au musée de Marseille.
2. Voici Yann. Ses sculptures sont déjà célèbres dans le milieu artistique.
3. Et voilà Clara. On vend ses bijoux à Saint-Tropez.
4. Octave est un jeune écrivain. Son premier roman vient d'être publié.

---

*The **bateaux-mouches** are cruise boats that take tourists along the Seine in Paris, offering historical commentaries on the various monuments that can be seen during the trip. They serve about five million passengers per year.

**D. Travail et vacances.** Racontez les projets de Sabine en reliant les deux phrases avec un pronom relatif. Le symbole ▲ indique le début (*beginning*) d'une proposition relative.

**MODÈLE:** Je travaille au tribunal (*court*). ▲ Je suis avocate au tribunal. →
Je travaille au tribunal où je suis avocate.

1. Je prendrai bientôt des vacances. ▲ J'ai vraiment besoin de ces vacances.
2. Ma camarade de chambre ▲ viendra avec moi. Elle s'appelle Élise.
3. Elle travaille avec des comptables. ▲ Ces comptables sont très exigeants (*demanding*).
4. Nous irons à Genève. ▲ Les parents d'Elise ont une maison à Genève.
5. Hier Élise a téléphoné à son père. ▲ Le père d'Élise nous a invitées.
6. Élise a envie de voir sa mère. ▲ Elle pense souvent à sa mère.
7. J'ai acheté une nouvelle valise. ▲ Je mettrai tous mes vêtements de ski dans cette valise.
8. Nous resterons deux jours à Strasbourg. ▲ Nous visiterons le Palais de l'Europe à Strasbourg.
9. Nous rentrerons trois semaines plus tard, prêtes à reprendre le travail. ▲ Ce travail se sera accumulé (*piled up*).

Maintenant, cherchez l'information demandée dans le récit de Sabine.

1. saison
2. durée des vacances
3. nationalité probable d'Élise
4. état d'esprit (*mental state*) de Sabine

**E. Énigme.** Décrivez un objet, une personne ou un endroit à vos camarades. Utilisez des pronoms relatifs. Vos camarades vont essayer d'identifier la chose dont vous parlez.

**Catégories suggérées:** une classe, un gâteau, un pays, une personne, un plat, une profession, une ville…

**MODÈLE:** É1: Je pense à un gâteau qui est français et dont le nom commence par un *é*.
É2: Est-ce que c'est un éclair?

Maintenant, continuez ce jeu avec une différence. Cette fois, vous ne donnez que la catégorie d'un objet ou d'une personne. Vos camarades vous demandent des précisions. Répondez-leur par *oui* ou *non*.

**Autres catégories suggérées:** un acteur / une actrice, un chanteur / une chanteuse, une émission de télévision, un film, une pièce de théâtre…

**MODÈLE:** É1: Je pense à un film.
É2: C'est un film que tu as vu il y a longtemps?
C'est un film dont l'action se passe à New York?
C'est un film où un animal a joué le rôle principal?
C'est un film dont l'action se déroule (*takes place*) en 1933?
C'est *King Kong*.

# La comparaison de l'adjectif qualificatif

*Making Comparisons*

## Vie professionnelle ou développement personnel?

*Poema et Alexis discutent au café.*

POEMA: Tu travailleras en France ou au Québec après ton diplôme?

ALEXIS: Au Québec. Le marché de l'emploi y est **meilleur**[1] qu'en France et les salaires y sont **plus élevés**.[2]

POEMA: Oui, mais les conditions de travail y sont **moins bonnes**: en France, tu travailles 35 heures par semaine et tu as cinq semaines de vacances payées!

ALEXIS: Je sais. Mais moi, je trouve que **le plus important**, c'est d'aimer son travail. Je ne compterai pas mes heures de présence si j'occupe un poste intéressant.

POEMA: Tu es **plus idéaliste** que moi! Je considère que la vie professionnelle est **moins essentielle** que le développement personnel.

Montréal, au Québec: un marché de l'emploi très dynamique

[1]*better* [2]*plus... higher*

Choisissez la bonne réponse selon le dialogue.

1. Au Québec, le marché de l'emploi est <u>meilleur</u> / <u>moins bon</u> qu'en France.
2. Les salaires y sont <u>plus bas</u> / <u>plus élevés</u>.
3. Les conditions de travail sont <u>meilleures</u> / <u>moins bonnes</u>.
4. Alexis considère que <u>le plus important</u> / <u>le moins important</u>, c'est d'aimer son travail.
5. Poema trouve Alexis <u>plus</u> / <u>moins</u> idéaliste qu'elle.
6. Elle pense que la vie professionnelle est <u>plus</u> / <u>moins</u> essentielle que le développement personnel.

## Comparison of Adjectives

**1.** In French, the following constructions can be used with adjectives to express a comparison. It is not always necessary to state the second term of the comparison.

> **plus... que** (*more . . . than*)

Chez l'épicier, les produits sont **plus** chers (**qu'**à Carrefour*). 

*The products at the grocer's are more expensive (than at Carrefour).*

---

*supermarché très populaire

> **moins... que** *(less . . . than)*

| | |
|---|---|
| Franck pense que Carrefour est **moins** cher (**que** Trouvetout). | *Franck thinks Carrefour is less expensive (than Trouvetout).* |

> **aussi... que** *(as . . . as)*

| | |
|---|---|
| Pour Laure, l'accueil est **aussi** important **que** la qualité des produits. | *For Laure, the friendly service is as important as the quality of the products.* |

**2.** Stressed pronouns (**Chapitre 12, Leçon 2**) are used after **que** when a pronoun is required.

| | |
|---|---|
| Elle est plus intelligente que **lui.** | *She is more intelligent than he is.* |

[Allez-y! A]

## Superlative Form of Adjectives

**1.** To form the superlative of an adjective, use the appropriate definite article with the comparative form of the adjective.

Deborah est frisée. → Juliette est plus frisée que Deborah. → Alice est **la** plus frisée des trois.

OU

Alice est frisée. → Juliette est moins frisée qu'Alice. → Deborah est **la** moins frisée des trois.

**2.** Superlative adjectives normally follow the nouns they modify, and the definite article is repeated.

| | |
|---|---|
| Alice est **la** femme **la plus** frisée des trois. | *Alice is the woman with the curliest hair of the three.* |

**3.** Adjectives that usually precede the nouns they modify can either precede or follow the noun in the superlative construction. If the adjective follows the noun, the definite article must be repeated.

> **la** plus petite maison
>
> > OU
>
> **la** maison **la** plus petite

**4.** The preposition **de** expresses *in* or *of* in a superlative construction.

> Alice et Grégoire habitent la plus belle maison **du** quartier.
>
> *Alice and Grégoire live in the most beautiful house in the neighborhood.*
>
> C'est le quartier le plus cher **de** la ville.
>
> *It's the most expensive neighborhood in town.*

## Irregular Comparative and Superlative Forms

The adjective **bon(ne)** has irregular comparative and superlative forms. **Mauvais(e)** has both regular and irregular forms.

| | COMPARATIVE | SUPERLATIVE |
|---|---|---|
| bon(ne) | meilleur(e) | le meilleur / la meilleure |
| mauvais(e) | plus mauvais(e) pire | le plus mauvais / la plus mauvaise le/la pire |

> Les légumes à Carrefour sont bons, mais les légumes à Trouvetout sont **meilleurs.**
>
> *The vegetables at Carrefour are good, but the vegetables at Trouvetout are better.*
>
> Ce grand magasin est **le meilleur** de la ville.
>
> *This department store is the best (one) in town.*
>
> Ce détergent-ci est **plus mauvais (pire)** que ce détergent-là.
>
> *This detergent is worse than that detergent.*
>
> C'est **le plus mauvais (le pire)** des produits.
>
> *It's the worst of products.*

[Allez-y! B-C-D]

Ces pâtisseries sont les meilleures du quartier!

*Allez-y!*

**A. Comparaisons.** Regardez les deux dessins et répondez aux questions suivantes.

> **MODÈLE:** Qui est moins nerveux, le jeune homme ou la jeune fille?
> La jeune fille est moins nerveuse (que le jeune homme).

1. Qui est plus grand, le jeune homme ou la jeune fille? Qui est plus mince?
2. Est-ce que la jeune fille a l'air aussi dynamique et sympathique que le jeune homme?
3. Qui est plus timide? plus bavard (*talkative*)?
4. Est-ce que le jeune homme est aussi studieux que la jeune fille?
5. Est-ce que le jeune homme est plus ou moins travailleur que la jeune fille?
6. Qui est le plus ambitieux des deux? Qui est le plus sportif des deux?

**B. Un couple de francophiles.** M. et M^me Cohen adorent tout ce qui est français, et ils ont tendance à exagérer. Donnez leur opinion en transformant les phrases selon le modèle.

> **MODÈLE:** Le français est une très belle langue. →
> Le français est la plus belle langue du monde.

1. La cuisine française est bonne.
2. Les vins de Bourgogne sont sophistiqués.
3. La civilisation française est très avancée.
4. Paris est une ville intéressante.
5. Les Français sont un peuple cultivé.
6. La France est un beau pays.

**C. Opinions.** Changez les phrases suivantes, si nécessaire, pour indiquer votre opinion personnelle: **plus / moins / aussi... que; meilleur(e) / plus mauvais(e) que.** Regardez d'abord les expressions de **Mots clés.** Utilisez ces mots et justifiez vos opinions.

1. Le sport est aussi important que les études.
2. Les rapports humains sont aussi importants que les bonnes notes.
3. Grâce à la technologie, la vie des étudiants est meilleure qu'il y a vingt ans.
4. Les cours universitaires sont plus intéressants que les cours à l'école secondaire.
5. Comme étudiant(e), je suis plus sérieux/sérieuse que la plupart de mes ami(e)s.

**D. Mais ce n'est pas possible!** Vous aimez exagérer. Donnez votre opinion sur les sujets suivants. Pour chaque catégorie, proposez aussi d'autres exemples si possible.

1. Le président _____ / bon ou mauvais / président / le XX^e ou XXI^e siècle
2. Les Américains / les gens / généreux / le monde
3. Le manque (*lack*) d'éducation / le problème / sérieux / le monde actuel
4. _____ / le problème / grand / ma vie
5. _____ / la nouvelle / intéressant / l'année
6. _____ / l'athlète / bon / l'année

## Mots clés

**Pour insister**

Like **très,** the adverbs **bien** (*much*) and **fort** (*very, mostly*) are used to emphasize a point.

Faire des économies est **bien** plus important qu'on le pense.

Cette employée a une personnalité **fort** agréable.

## Prononcez bien!

**The consonant *r*** (page 385)

**A. La famille d'Hugo (1).** Hugo vous parle de sa famille. Complétez chaque phrase avec le mot qui manque et décidez si le premier *r* dans ce mot est un *r* doux ou un *r* fort.

|  | *r* doux | *r* fort |
|---|---|---|
| **1.** Mon père travaille dans un _____. | ☐ | ☐ |
| **2.** Ma mère aussi: elle y est _____. | ☐ | ☐ |
| **3.** C'est une petite _____. | ☐ | ☐ |
| **4.** Il n'y a que dix _____. | ☐ | ☐ |
| **5.** Le _____ est un homme honnête et juste. | ☐ | ☐ |
| **6.** Mais il est un peu _____. | ☐ | ☐ |
| **7.** Mais dans l'ensemble, mes _____ sont satisfaits de leur métier. | ☐ | ☐ |

**B. La famille d'Hugo (2).** Hugo vous parle encore de sa famille. Avec votre camarade, répétez ce qu'il dit. Faites bien attention à la prononciation des *r* dans les mots **en caractères gras**. Dans les phrases 1 et 2, ils sont forts; dans les phrases 3 et 4, ils sont doux.

**1.** Je suis le plus jeune de la famille! **Patrick,** mon **frère**, a **trente-quatre** ans. Il est **peintre**.

**2.** Et **Christelle**, ma sœur, a **trente-trois** ans. Elle **travaille** dans le monde de la **traduction**: elle est **interprète**.

**3.** Mes **parents** sont **mariés** depuis **quarante** ans! Ils vont fêter **leur** long **mariage** à **Paris** dans deux semaines.

**4.** Il y **aura** beaucoup de gens (*people*) à cette fête. Nous allons bien manger. Et nous **boirons** beaucoup aussi! Je pense que ça **plaira** à mes **parents** de passer la **soirée** avec tout ce monde!

On fête le long mariage des parents d'Hugo. Félicitations!

# Leçon 4

 Lecture

### *Avant de lire*

**Using the dictionary.** As you know, you can figure out from context the meaning of many unfamiliar words that you encounter in readings. Sometimes, however, you will need to consult a dictionary. When you do, keep in mind the following guidelines.

1. If possible, use a good hardback French–English dictionary; paperback dictionaries often do not provide all the common equivalents for a word, nor do they offer examples of usage.
2. Read through *all* the meanings and examples. Make sure the meaning you choose corresponds to the part of speech (noun, verb, etc.) of the French word you are looking for and, of course, that it makes sense in context.
3. Later on, try consulting a monolingual dictionary: one in which French words are defined in French. This may present a bit of a challenge at first, but you will find it of great benefit in terms of vocabulary enrichment and increased range of expression.

The following sentence appears in the middle of the third paragraph of the reading selection: "Au XVIIᵉ siècle, à l'abbaye d'Hautvillers, le moine bénédictin Dom Pérignon perfectionne la création d'un vin qui mousse,… " Look for the meaning of **mousser** in the following excerpt from the *Larousse French Dictionary* (bilingual dictionary):

> **mousser** [muse] *vi* [écumer-champagne, cidre] to bubble, to sparkle; [bière] to froth; [savon, crème à raser] to lather; [détergent, shampooing] to foam, to lather

Which meaning is closest to the use of **mousser** in the sentence quoted from the article? Now, take a look at the definition of **mousser** from the *Nouveau Petit Robert* (monolingual dictionary):

> **1♦** Produire de la mousse. *Boisson qui mousse. Shampooing qui mousse beaucoup.*
> **2♦** Fig. et Fam. *Faire mousser:* vanter, mettre exagérément en valeur (une personne, une chose) → **valoir.** *Se faire mousser.*

What extra information did you get from the monolingual dictionary?

PERSPECTIVES

# Des métiers pas ordinaires

Les métiers originaux, il y en a plus que vous ne pensez! En voilà quelques exemples.

## *Si le vin vous intéresse…*

Un œnologue est un spécialiste des vins. Il les goûte, les évalue et les classe. Il partage[1] son temps entre le vignoble,[2] la cave[3] et le laboratoire. Conseiller des producteurs, des marchands et des restaurateurs, c'est un expert formé à l'université: quatre ans d'études après le bac sont nécessaires pour obtenir le Diplôme National d'Œnologie.

### *Le père du champagne*
Au XVII$^e$ siècle, à l'abbaye d'Hautvillers, le moine[4] bénédictin Dom Pérignon perfectionne la création d'un vin qui mousse, le prestigieux champagne. L'abbaye doit sa prospérité à cet œnologue subtil et au «seul vin qui rend les femmes plus belles après qu'elles l'aient bu», selon la Marquise de Pompadour.[5]

Les œnologues dans leur cave, à Bourgogne, en France. Que feront ces hommes après leur travail?

## *Si vous préférez les parfums, devenez aromaticien!*

Comme l'œnologue, l'aromaticien doit faire confiance à son nez. D'ailleurs, on l'appelle aussi un «Nez». C'est lui qui invente des parfums. Le «Nez» a fait des études de chimie, mais il a surtout une mémoire des odeurs et un instinct de création extrêmement rares. C'est pourquoi il n'y a que 250 «Nez» dans le monde.

### *Un «Nez» et un parfum célèbres*
Le «Nez» en question s'appelle Ernest Beaux. En 1920, il propose à sa patronne, Coco Chanel, différentes créations qu'il a numérotées. Le numéro 5 plaît à Mademoiselle. Elle décide de ne pas changer son nom. Le parfum le plus célèbre du monde, Chanel N°5, vient de naître!

Le parfum le plus célèbre du monde. Aimez-vous les parfums?

[1]*divides* [2]*vineyard* [3]*cellar* [4]*monk* [5]*Marquise… la confidente du roi Louis XV, connue pour sa beauté et son esprit au XVIII$^e$ siècle*

Comment trouvez-vous cette robe en chocolat du Salon du Chocolat 2013?

### *Un autre parfum: le chocolat*

Qui dit chocolat dit chocolatier. Un chocolatier est un spécialiste diplômé d'un lycée professionnel. Il peut devenir célèbre s'il gagne le concours[6] annuel du Meilleur Ouvrier de France. Pour réussir, l'artisan chocolatier doit être aussi doué[7] et travailleur qu'imaginatif.

### *La mode au chocolat*

Le chocolat a toujours inspiré les passions. Sous Louis XIV, on disait «La Reine a deux passions, le Roi et… le chocolat!» La passion du chocolat a aujourd'hui son propre Salon. Une fois par an, au Salon du Chocolat de Paris, des chocolatiers s'associent avec de grands couturiers pour créer une mode absolument délicieuse. Le défilé des robes en chocolat fait fondre[8] les spectateurs de plaisir!

[6]*competition*   [7]*gifted*   [8]*fait… melts*

### *Compréhension*

**Un métier pour vous?** Répondez aux questions suivantes.

1. Combien d'années d'études sont nécessaires pour devenir œnologue?
2. Qui est Dom Pérignon? Qu'est-ce qu'il a fait?
3. Qu'est-ce que l'aromaticien étudie à l'université?
4. Pourquoi est-ce que le chocolat est aussi populaire en France?

 # Écriture

The writing activities **Par écrit** and **Journal intime** can be found in the Workbook/Laboratory Manual to accompany *Vis-à-vis*.

# *Pour s'amuser*

Un jeune diplômé se présente pour un poste de cadre dans une entreprise. Le directeur des Ressources humaines insiste:

—Pour ce poste, nous avons besoin d'une personne très responsable.

—C'est parfait! Dans mon poste précédent, chaque fois qu'il se passait quelque chose, on disait que c'était moi!

# Le vidéoblog d'Hector

## En bref

Dans cet épisode, Hector parle au téléphone à Léa d'un emploi qu'il veut obtenir chez Pomme Cannelle. Son entretien s'est bien passé et il attend maintenant un coup de fil du directeur. Pendant leur conversation, Léa et Hector regardent un extrait du spectacle de Pomme Cannelle sur leur site Web.

La musique et la danse sont essentielles à la vie antillaise.

## Vocabulaire en contexte

Mettez les étapes de la recherche d'un emploi en ordre chronologique en les numérotant de 1 à 7.

### Étapes de la recherche d'un emploi

_____ poser sa candidature
_____ négocier son salaire
_____ accepter le rendez-vous de l'employeur
_____ rédiger (*to write*) un bon C.V.

_____ faire bonne impression sur le patron (*boss*)
_____ envoyer une lettre de remerciement
_____ recevoir une proposition d'embauche (*job offer*)

## Visionnez!

Choisissez le mot ou l'expression qui complète le mieux chaque phrase.

1. Hector est <u>optimiste</u> / <u>pessimiste</u> en ce qui concerne (*about*) cet emploi.
2. Pomme Cannelle présente son spectacle <u>en France</u> / <u>dans le monde entier</u>.
3. Pomme Cannelle a un style <u>traditionnel</u> / <u>particulier</u>.
4. Hector gagnerait (*would earn*) au minimum <u>1 200</u> / <u>1 800</u> euros par mois.
5. Si Hector n'obtient pas ce poste, il <u>restera à Paris</u> / <u>repartira pour la Martinique</u>.

## Analysez!

1. Décrivez les étapes qu'Hector a suivies pour obtenir son poste chez Pomme Cannelle.
2. Quel numéro de Pomme Cannelle vous plaît (*do you like*) le plus ou le moins? Expliquez.

## Comparez!

Regardez encore une fois la partie culturelle de la vidéo. Y a-t-il des troupes de danse traditionnelle ou des groupes de musique traditionnelle comme Pomme Cannelle dans votre pays ou dans votre culture? Décrivez-les. Où montent-ils leurs spectacles? Qui va les voir? Est-ce que vous aimez ces spectacles? Expliquez.

## Note culturelle

La musique et la danse sont essentielles à la culture des îles. Elles traduisent des influences européennes, africaines et américaines. Inspirée du rythme des orchestres de jazz de La Nouvelle Orléans, la biguine[1] symbolise aujourd'hui les sons et les rythmes des Antilles françaises. Mais depuis 1980, le zouk a pris la première place dans le folklore euro-antillais. Très rythmé, très sensuel, il existe aussi en version douce[2] et lente: on l'appelle le «zouk-love»!

[1]*une danse*   [2]*soft, gentle*

## Vocabulaire

### Verbes

**changer** to change
**compter** to count
**contrôler** to check, monitor
**couvrir** to cover
**découvrir** to discover
**dépenser** to spend (*money*)
**déposer** to deposit
**diriger** to direct
**économiser** to save money
**faire des économies** (*f. pl.*) to save (up) money
**faire un chèque** to write a check
**fermer** to close
**gagner** to earn; to win
**gérer** to manage
**intéresser** to interest
**maîtriser** to master, have a command
**se moquer de** to make fun of
**offrir** to offer
**ouvrir** to open
**poser sa candidature** to apply
**proposer** to propose
**réaliser** to make (happen), carry out
**recruter** to recruit
**retirer** to withdraw
**soigner** to treat
**souffrir** to suffer
**toucher** to touch; to cash (*a check*)
**travailler à son compte** to be self-employed

### Substantifs

**l'actualité** (*f.*) current events
**l'argent** (*m.*) **liquide** cash
**l'augmentation** (*f.*) increase
  **l'augmentation de salaire** raise
**l'avenir** (*m.*) future
**le bijou** jewel
**le budget** budget

**le bureau de change** money exchange (office)
**la carte bancaire** bank (ATM/credit) card
**la carte de crédit** credit card
**la carte de débit** debit card
**le chèque** check
**le chômage** unemployment
**le chômeur / la chômeuse** unemployed person
**le compte bancaire** bank
**le compte d'épargne** savings account
**le cours** exchange rate
**le coût de la vie** cost of living
**le curriculum vitæ (C.V.)** résumé
**la demande d'emploi** job application
**la dépense** expense
**l'emploi** (*m.*) job
**l'emprunt** (*m.*) loan
**l'entreprise** (*f.*) company
**l'entretien** (*m.*) job interview
**le guichet automatique** automatic teller machine (ATM)
**les frais** (*m. pl.*) expenses, costs
**le marché de l'emploi** job market
**le métier** trade, profession
**la monnaie** change; currency
**le montant** sum, amount
**la piste** lead
**le prélèvement automatique** automatic payment/withdrawal
**le reçu** receipt
**le relevé** bank statment
**le salaire** salary
**la societé** company
**le stage** internship
**le taux de change** exchange rate
**le taux de chômage** unemployment rate
**le virement** transfer (money)

À REVOIR: **l'horaire** (*m.*), **la santé**

### Les professions

**l'agent** (*m.*) **de police** police officer
**l'agriculteur / l'agricultrice** farmer
**l'architecte** (*m., f.*) architect
**l'artisan(e)** artisan, craftsperson
**l'artiste** (*m., f.*) artist
**l'avocat(e)** lawyer
**le boucher / la bouchère** butcher
**le cadre** middle or upper manager
**le chef d'entreprise** company head, top manager, boss
**le coiffeur / la coiffeuse** hairdresser
**le/la commerçant(e)** shopkeeper
**le/la comptable** accountant
**le/la dentiste** dentist
**le directeur / la directrice** manager, head
**le directeur / la directrice commercial(e)** business manager
**l'employé(e)** employee
**le facteur / la factrice** letter carrier
**le/la fonctionnaire** civil servant
**l'ingénieur** (*m.*) engineer
**le/la journaliste** reporter
**le marchand / la marchande (de vin)** (wine) merchant
**le médecin / la femme médecin** doctor
**l'ouvrier / l'ouvrière** (manual) worker, laborer
**le/la peintre** painter
**le/la pharmacien(ne)** pharmacist
**le plombier** plumber
**le/la professeur des écoles** primary school teacher

**le rédacteur / la rédactrice**
editor
**le/la secrétaire** secretary
**le travailleur / la travailleuse**
worker
> **le travailleur indépendant**
> self-employed worker
> **le travailleur salarié**
> salaried worker

À REVOIR: **l'acteur / l'actrice;
l'écrivain / la femme
écrivain; le serveur / la
serveuse**

**Mots et expressions divers**

**à l'avenir** from now on, in the
future
**à partir de maintenant** from
now on
**à son compte** for oneself
**aussi... que** as . . . as
**aussitôt que** as soon as
**car** because
**dès que** as soon as
**dont** whose, of whom, of which
**élevé(e)** high

**fort** (*adv.*) very
**un jour** someday
**lorsque** when
**meilleur(e)** better
**moins... que** less . . . than
**où** where; when
**parfaitement** perfectly
**pire** worse
**plus... que** more . . . than
**que** whom, that, which
**qui** who, that, which

À REVOIR: **quand**

# Les loisirs

Les dossiers d'Hector

Hector

➤ Mes photos
   ➤ Du théâtre à Avignon
   ➤ Paris-Plages en été
   ➤ Deux amies s'amusent au café

Une pièce de théâtre en plein air sur la place du Palais des Papes à Avignon

# Dans ce chapitre...

## OBJECTIFS COMMUNICATIFS

- ➤ talking about leisure-time activities
- ➤ getting information
- ➤ being polite
- ➤ speculating
- ➤ making comparisons
- ➤ talking about quantity
- ➤ learning to distinguish between and pronounce selected sounds in French

Paris-Plages en été, c'est un vrai bonheur

## PAROLES (Leçon 1)

- ➤ Les loisirs
- ➤ Les verbes **courir** et **rire**

## STRUCTURES (Leçons 2 et 3)

- ➤ Les pronoms interrogatifs
- ➤ Le présent du conditionnel
- ➤ La comparaison de l'adverbe et du nom
- ➤ Les adjectifs et les pronoms indéfinis

## CULTURE

- ➤ Le blog d'Hector: *Le temps de vivre*
- ➤ Reportage: *Étudier ou s'amuser?*
- ➤ Lecture: *Traversée de l'Atlantique en solitaire* (Leçon 4)

www.mhconnectfrench.com

Deux amies s'amusent au café

# Leçon 1

## Quelques loisirs°

*(m.) leisure activities*

**Les spectacles** (*m.*)
le spectacle de
  variétés
le cinéma
l'opéra (*m.*)
le théâtre

**Les activités** (*f.*) **de plein air**
le pique-nique   la marche
la pétanque*   le ski
la pêche

**Les sports** (*m.*)
le football
le cyclisme
les matchs (*m.*)
  (de football)

**Les jeux** (*m.*)
les jeux de hasard
les jeux de société

**Le bricolage**
le jardinage

**Les passe-temps** (*m.*)
la lecture
les collections (*f.*)
la peinture

Qu'est-ce qu'on est en train de faire? Est-ce qu'on fait un pique-nique?
Est-ce qu'on joue au football? Est-ce qu'on assiste à† un concert?

**AUTRES MOTS UTILES**

| | |
|---|---|
| **bricoler** | to putter around, do odd jobs |
| **une chanson**‡ | song |
| **une équipe** | team |

*La pétanque** is a Provençal game similar to Italian bocce ball.
†**Assister à** means *to attend;* **aider** means *to assist, help.*
‡**Une chanson de variété** is a popular song, frequently associated with a particular singer
and sung in a music hall or a small nightclub.

## Allez-y!

**A. Catégories.** Le ballet et l'opéra sont des spectacles. Dans quelle(s) catégorie(s) de distractions classez-vous _____?

**MODÈLE:** la marche → La marche, c'est une activité de plein air.

1. un match de football
2. une collection de timbres
3. le jardinage
4. la pêche
5. la roulette
6. la lecture
7. un pique-nique
8. le poker
9. le cinéma
10. la pétanque
11. le cyclisme
12. un concert de jazz

**B. Interview.** Posez les questions suivantes à un(e) camarade. Demandez-lui _____.

1. quelles sortes de chansons il/elle aime (les chansons d'amour, les chansons folkloriques, le rap, le hip hop?)
2. s'il / si elle a déjà joué à la pétanque
3. à quelles sortes de spectacles il/elle assiste souvent et à quel spectacle il/elle a assisté récemment
4. s'il / si elle préfère faire du sport ou assister à des manifestations sportives; à quel événement sportif il/elle a assisté récemment
5. quel jeu de société il/elle préfère (le bridge, le Scrabble, le Monopoly?)
6. à quels jeux de hasard il/elle a joué, où il/elle y a joué et combien il/elle a gagné ou perdu
7. s'il / si elle aime bricoler et quels objets il/elle a réparés ou fabriqués
8. s'il / si elle collectionne quelque chose

**Résumez!** D'après ses réponses, parlez brièvement du caractère ou de la personnalité de votre camarade.

**Expressions utiles:** actif/active, adroit/adroite, audacieux/audacieuse, créateur/créatrice, énergique, être un homme (une femme) à tout faire (*handy*), (im)prudent(e), (n')avoir (pas) le goût du risque, paresseux/paresseuse, (peu) doué(e) (*gifted*) pour les sports, sentimental(e), sportif/sportive, terre à terre (= prosaïque, ordinaire), et cetera

Du travail ou du bricolage? À vous de décider! Expliquez votre réponse.

# Les verbes *courir* et *rire*

*vive la détente!*

| PRESENT TENSE OF **courir** (*to run*) | | **rire** (*to laugh*) | |
|---|---|---|---|
| je | cour**s** | je | ri**s** |
| tu | cour**s** | tu | ri**s** |
| il/elle/on | cour**t** | il/elle/on | ri**t** |
| nous | cour**ons** | nous | ri**ons** |
| vous | cour**ez** | vous | ri**ez** |
| ils/elles | cour**ent** | ils/elles | ri**ent** |
| *Past participle:* | **couru** | | **ri** |
| *Future stem:* | **courr-** | | **rir-** |

A verb conjugated like **rire** is **sourire** (*to smile*).

## IIII *Allez-y!*

**A. Sondage sur le jogging.** De plus en plus de gens sont des adeptes du jogging.

**1.** Demandez à un(e) camarade s'il / si elle fait du jogging.

Si oui, demandez-lui _____.

**2.** combien de fois par semaine il/elle court
**3.** pendant combien de temps il/elle court ou combien de kilomètres il/elle fait (1 mile = 1,6 kilomètres)
**4.** depuis quand il/elle fait du jogging

Sinon, demandez-lui _____.

**5.** pourquoi il/elle ne court pas
**6.** s'il / si elle pratique un autre sport
**7.** ce qu'il/elle pense des gens qui font du jogging régulièrement

**B. Le rire.** Le rire est le passe-temps préféré de beaucoup de gens. Et vous? Aimez-vous rire? Avec un(e) camarade, répondez aux questions suivantes. Chaque fois que vous répondez que oui, donnez un exemple.

**1.** Racontez-vous des blagues (*jokes*)? **2.** Faites-vous souvent des jeux de mots (*puns*)? **3.** Avez-vous un comique préféré / une comique préférée? **4.** Est-ce qu'il y a un film ou une pièce de théâtre que vous trouvez particulièrement intéressant(e)? **5.** Est-ce que vous riez quelquefois en cours de français? Quand et pourquoi?

# Leçon 2

## Les pronoms interrogatifs

*Getting Information*

### C'est quoi, le temps libre?

*Juliette téléphone à Charlotte.*

JULIETTE: **Que** fais-tu pendant ton temps libre[1]?

CHARLOTTE: C'est **quoi** le temps libre? Je n'ai pas une minute à moi!

JULIETTE: **Qu'est-ce que** tu racontes[2]? **Qu'est-ce qui** t'empêche de prendre quelques heures par semaine pour toi? Il faut être un peu égoïste[3] dans la vie!

CHARLOTTE: Mais **qui** va s'occuper de[4] la maison?

JULIETTE: Charlotte, c'est une blague! J'ai l'impression d'entendre mon arrière-grand-mère! Réserve un après-midi pour toi.

CHARLOTTE: **Lequel**[5]? Je suis super occupée.

JULIETTE: Le samedi après-midi, par exemple: tu pourras faire du sport, du shopping, prendre un café avec une copine...

CHARLOTTE: Tu as raison! Je dois penser à moi.

[1]*free*  [2]*Qu'est-ce que... What are you talking about?*  [3]*selfish*  [4]*s'occuper... take care of*
[5]*Which one*

Père et fille sur la plage

Trouvez, dans le dialogue, les questions qui correspondent aux situations suivantes.

1. Juliette interroge Charlotte sur ses loisirs.
2. Charlotte ne comprend pas l'expression «temps libre».
3. Juliette demande des précisions à Charlotte.
4. Charlotte demande comment la maison va fonctionner sans elle.
5. Charlotte demande quel après-midi elle pourrait libérer.

## Forms of Interrogative Pronouns

Interrogative pronouns—in English, *who? whom? which? what?*—are used to ask questions. They can play several roles in questions, serving as subjects, as objects of verbs, or as objects of prepositions. You are already familiar with the French interrogative pronouns **qui** and **qu'est-ce que.** Following is a more detailed list of French interrogative pronouns. Note that different pronouns are used for people and for things, and that several pronouns have a short and a long form.

| USE | PEOPLE | THINGS |
|---|---|---|
| *Subject of a question* | qui<br>qui est-ce qui | _____<br>qu'est-ce qui |
| *Object of a question* | qui<br>qui est-ce que | que<br>qu'est-ce que |
| *Object of a preposition* | à qui | à quoi |

## Interrogative Pronouns as the Subject of a Question

As the *subject* of a question, the interrogative pronoun that refers to people has both a short and a long form. The pronoun that refers to things has only one form. Note that **qui** is always followed by a singular verb.

**PEOPLE**

**Qui** fait du jogging ce matin?
**Qui est-ce qui** fait du jogging ce matin?

**THINGS**

**Qu'est-ce qui** se passe? (*What's happening?*)

## Interrogative Pronouns as the Object of a Question

As the *object* of a question, the interrogative pronouns referring to people, as well as those referring to things, have both a long and a short form.

**1.** Long forms

PEOPLE: **Qui est-ce que**
THINGS: **Qu'est-ce que** + *subject* + *verb* + (*other elements*)?

**Qui est-ce que** tu as vu sur le court de tennis ce matin?
*Whom did you see on the tennis court this morning?*

**Qu'est-ce que** Marie veut faire ce soir?
*What does Marie want to do this evening?*

Remember that **qu'est-ce que (qu'est-ce que c'est que)** is a set phrase used to ask for a definition: *What is _____?*

**Qu'est-ce que la pétanque?**
*What is pétanque?*

**2.** The short form **qui** can follow the subject and verb in questions using an intonation change.

Tu cherches **qui?**
*You're looking for whom?*

Aurélien a vu **qui** au théâtre?
*Whom did Aurélien see at the theater?*

The short form **qui** can also be followed by an inverted subject and verb.

**Qui** (+ *noun subject*) + *verb-pronoun* + (*other elements*)?

**Qui as-tu vu** au club de gym?
*Whom did you see at the gym?*

**Qui Marie a-t-elle vu** sur le court de tennis?
*Whom did Marie see on the tennis court?*

**3.** The short form **que** is followed by an inverted subject and verb. This is true for both noun and pronoun subjects.

> **que** + *verb* + *subject* (*noun or pronoun*) + (*other elements*)?

> **Que cherches-tu?**      *What are you looking for?*
> **Que cherche Justine?**      *What is Justine looking for?*

[Allez-y! A]

## Use of *qui* and *quoi* after Prepositions

After a preposition or as a one-word question, **qui** is used to refer to people, and **quoi** is used to refer to things.

> **À qui** est-ce que Djamel parle?      *Whom is Djamel speaking to?*
> **De qui** est-ce que tu parles?      *Whom are you talking about?*
> **À quoi** est-ce que Raphaëlle réfléchit?      *What is Raphaëlle thinking about?*
> **De quoi** est-ce que vous parlez?      *What are you talking about?*

[Allez-y! B-C-D]

## *Lequel*

**Lequel, laquelle, lesquels,** and **lesquelles** (*which one[s]?*) are used to ask about a person or thing that has already been mentioned. These pronouns agree in gender and number with the nouns to which they refer.

> —Avez-vous vu cet opéra?      *Have you seen this (that) opera?*
> —**Lequel?**      *Which one?*

> —Vous rappelez-vous cette pièce de théâtre?      *Do you remember this (that) play?*
> —**Laquelle?**      *Which one?*

> —**Lequel** des chanteurs américains préférez-vous?      *Which American singer do you prefer?*

[Allez-y! E]

**Prononcez bien!**

**The consonant *l***

To pronounce a French **l** [l], remember to keep the body of your tongue flat and shifted to the front of your mouth, with the tip pressing against your upper front teeth. Refrain from (1) lowering the back of your tongue, (2) letting it shift to the back of your mouth, and (3) curling up the tip of your tongue, especially when you pronounce a final **-l.**

[l]: **i**l**, **l**eque**l**, pâ**l**e, Ju**l**es, so**l**

**A. À la Maison des jeunes et de la culture.**\* Posez des questions sur les activités des jeunes à la MJC. Utilisez **qui** ou **qui est-ce qui,** en remplaçant les mots en italique.

> **MODÈLE:** *Pierrot* apprend à jouer du piano. →
> Qui (Qui est-ce qui) apprend à jouer du piano?

**1.** *Astrid* est en train de lire (*is reading*) un roman.
**2.** *Hakim* apprend à faire un portrait dans le cours de peinture.
**3.** *Alexandre* écoute un concert de musique vietnamienne.
**4.** *Le professeur* choisit les meilleures œuvres à exposer.

---

\*The **Maison des jeunes et de la culture (MJC)** is a recreational center supported by the French government. **MJC**s offer courses in many hobbies and sports and sponsor cultural events.

Maintenant, posez des questions avec **que** ou **qu'est-ce que.**

> **MODÈLE:** Colombe regarde *un film de François Truffaut* au ciné-club. →
> Que regarde Colombe au ciné-club? (Qu'est-ce que Colombe regarde au ciné-club?)

**5.** Les jeunes font *des vases* dans le cours de poterie.
**6.** On joue *un air de Jacques Brel* dans le cours de guitare.
**7.** Grégory a fabriqué *des étagères* dans l'atelier de bricolage.
**8.** Marie a travaillé *son service* pendant son cours de tennis.

**B. Exposition à la MJC.** Vous êtes chargé(e) d'organiser une exposition à votre MJC, et vous donnez des instructions à un groupe de volontaires. Quelles questions vous posent-ils? Choisissez l'interrogatif correct.

> **MODÈLE:** (qui / qu'est-ce que) William nous prêtera une... →
> Qu'est-ce que William nous prêtera?

**1.** (qui / qu'est-ce qui) le directeur a invité...
**2.** (qui / qu'est-ce que) Joséphine va nous apporter une...
**3.** (qui / qui est-ce qui) nous devons téléphoner à...
**4.** (à quoi / de quoi) vous voulez nous parler...
**5.** (qui est-ce qui / qui) Aurore viendra avec son...
**6.** (quoi / que) vous pensez beaucoup à la...

**C. Une matinée de bricolage.** Ce matin, il y a eu beaucoup d'animation chez les Fontanet. À son retour de la maternelle (*kindergarten*), la petite Émilie veut tout savoir. À l'aide des mots en italique, formulez les questions.

> **MODÈLE:** Papa a invité *un ami.* →
> Qui est-ce que papa a invité?

**1.** *Maman* fabriquait une petite table.
**2.** Florent faisait *de la poterie.*
**3.** Papa parlait avec *son ami.*
**4.** *Florent* a ouvert la porte.
**5.** Le chien a vu *le facteur.*
**6.** Maman a crié après *le chien.*
**7.** Le chien a couru après *le facteur.*
**8.** *La poterie* est tombée par terre.
**9.** *Papa* a rattrapé (*caught*) le chien.
**10.** Le chien a cassé (*broke*) *la petite table de maman.*

**D. Interview.** Avec un(e) camarade de classe, posez des questions et répondez-y à tour de rôle.

> **MODÈLE:** acteurs comiques: Will Ferrell, Steve Carell →
> É1: Lequel de ces acteurs comiques préfères-tu, Will Ferrell ou Steve Carell?
> É2: Je préfère Steve Carell. Et toi, lequel préfères-tu?
> É1: Je préfère...

1. actrices: Angelina Jolie, Jennifer Lawrence
2. peintres: le Français Gauguin, l'Espagnol Picasso
3. chanteuses: Taylor Swift, Alicia Keys
4. loisirs: le bricolage, le jardinage
5. spectacles: les manifestations sportives, les spectacles de variétés
6. chansons: les chansons de Green Day, de Coldplay

Que pouvez-vous dire des goûts de votre camarade?

# Le présent du conditionnel

*Being Polite, Speculating*

## Qu'est-ce qu'on pourrait faire?

*Alexis contacte Poema sur sa page Facebook (Messagerie instantanée).*

 ALEXIS: Poema, qu'est-ce qu'**on pourrait** faire ce week-end?

 POEMA: Si j'avais le choix,[1] **j'aimerais** bien aller à la pêche.

 ALEXIS: Ah non! Attendre le poisson toute la journée: **Je m'ennuierais** à mourir! Tu as d'autres idées?

 POEMA: **J'adorerais** aller pique-niquer au bord de la Seine. **Nous mangerions** plein de bonnes choses. Après, si tu voulais, **nous irions** nous promener dans la nature. **Trésor viendrait** avec nous…

 ALEXIS: Bof… Manger sur l'herbe,[2] c'est assez inconfortable… Si on allait plutôt[3] à la piscine? **On nagerait** et **on bronzerait.**

 POEMA: Non: Je n'aime pas bronzer: c'est mauvais pour la peau.[4]

 ALEXIS: Finalement, **je préférerais** faire quelque chose de culturel: un musée, un film, une exposition…

 POEMA: Je ne suis pas d'accord: la culture, c'est pour les jours de pluie[5]! Et ce week-end, il va faire beau!

 ALEXIS: Alors, qu'est-ce qu'on fait?

[1]*choice*  [2]*sur… on the grass*  [3]*instead*  [4]*skin*  [5]*rain*

Répondez aux questions en utilisant des phrases du dialogue.

1. Que demande Alexis?
2. Quelles sont les suggestions de Poema?
3. Quelles activités préfère Alexis?

## Forms of the Conditional

**1.** In English, the conditional is a compound verb form consisting of *would* plus the infinitive: *He would travel, we would go.* In French, the **conditionnel** is a simple verb form. The imperfect-tense endings **-ais, -ais, -ait, -ions, -iez, -aient** are added to the infinitive. The final **-e** of **-re** verbs is dropped before the endings are added.

| parler | | finir | | vendre | |
|---|---|---|---|---|---|
| je | parler**ais** | je | finir**ais** | je | vendr**ais** |
| tu | parler**ais** | tu | finir**ais** | tu | vendr**ais** |
| il/elle/on | parler**ait** | il/elle/on | finir**ait** | il/elle/on | vendr**ait** |
| nous | parler**ions** | nous | finir**ions** | nous | vendr**ions** |
| vous | parler**iez** | vous | finir**iez** | vous | vendr**iez** |
| ils/elles | parler**aient** | ils/elles | finir**aient** | ils/elles | vendr**aient** |

| | |
|---|---|
| Elle **passerait** son temps à faire de la peinture. | *She'd spend her time painting.* |
| Elle **habiterait** dans une grande maison à la campagne. | *She'd live in a big house in the country.* |

**2.** Verbs with irregular stems in the future tense (**Chapitre 14, Leçon 2**) have the same irregular stems in the conditional.

| | |
|---|---|
| S'il ne pleuvait pas, nous **irions** tous à la pêche. | *If it weren't raining, we would all go fishing.* |
| Elle **voudrait** venir avec nous. | *She would like to come with us.* |
| Est-ce que tu **aurais** le temps de m'aider à tout préparer? | *Would you have time to help me prepare everything?* |

## Uses of the Conditional

**1.** In both English and French, the conditional is used to make polite requests or inquiries. It gives a softer, more deferential tone to statements that might otherwise seem abrupt (see **Mots clés** of **Chapitre 6, Leçon 2** and **Chapitre 7, Leçon 3**).

| | |
|---|---|
| **Auriez**-vous la gentillesse de m'aider? | *Would you be so kind as to help me?* |
| Je **pourrais** poser une question? | *Could I ask a question?* |
| Jean **voudrait** venir avec moi. | *Jean would like to come with me.* |
| Tu **devrais** faire plus de sport. | *You should be more active.* |
| Nous **aimerions** commander. | *We would like to order.* |

[Allez-y! A-B]

**2.** The conditional is used in the main clause of sentences containing **si** (*if*) clauses to express what *would* happen if the hypothesis of the *if*-clause were true. The imperfect is used in the *if*-clause.

| | |
|---|---|
| Si j'**avais** le temps, je **jouerais** au tennis. | *If I had time, I would play tennis.* |
| Si nous **pouvions** pique-niquer tous les jours, nous **serions** contents. | *If we could go on a picnic every day, we would be happy.* |
| Elle **irait** avec vous au bord de la mer si elle **savait** nager. | *She would go to the seashore with you if she knew how to swim.* |

The **si** clause containing the condition is sometimes understood and not directly expressed.

| | |
|---|---|
| Je **viendrais** avec grand plaisir... (si tu m'invitais, si j'avais le temps, et cetera). | *I would like to come . . . (if you invited me, if I had the time, etc.).* |

**3.** Remember that an *if*-clause in the present expresses a condition that, if fulfilled, will result in a certain action (stated in the future).

| | |
|---|---|
| Si j'**ai** le temps, je **jouerai** au tennis cet après-midi. | *If I have the time, I'll play tennis this afternoon.* |

Note that the future and the conditional are *never* used in the dependent clause (after **si**) of an *if*-clause sentence.

**4.** The present conditional of the verb **devoir** is used to give advice and corresponds to the English *should*.

| | |
|---|---|
| —J'aime bien les jeux de hasard. | *I like games of chance.* |
| —Vous **devriez** aller à Monte-Carlo. | *You should go to Monte-Carlo.* |
| —Elle a besoin d'exercice. | *She needs some exercise.* |
| —Elle **devrait** faire du jogging. | *She should go jogging.* |

[Allez-y! C-D-E-F]

### Mots clés

**Exprimer un désir et suggérer**

The construction **si** + **imparfait** (without the conditional) is used to express a wish or to make a suggestion.

**Si** seulement **j'étais** riche!
*If only I were rich!*

**Si on dansait?**
*Shall we dance?*

---

# ||||| *Allez-y!*

**A. S'il vous plaît.** Michael passe ses vacances en France. Il a rencontré une jeune Française et veut l'inviter à sortir avec lui. Il veut faire bonne impression au téléphone. Aidez-le en mettant ses phrases au conditionnel et en ajoutant **s'il vous plaît / s'il te plaît** quand c'est possible.

MODÈLE: Bonjour, madame. Puis-je parler à Manon? →
Bonjour, madame. Pourrais-je parler à Manon, s'il vous plaît?

**1.** Je veux inviter votre fille à venir avec moi au cinéma.
**2.** Pouvez-vous lui dire que je suis au téléphone?...
**3.** Salut Manon. Est-ce que tu veux aller voir un film ce soir?
**4.** Est-ce que nous pouvons partir vers 18 h?
**5.** Tes parents préfèrent peut-être faire ma connaissance...
**6.** Tu peux me donner ton adresse?

**B. Soyons diplomates.** Vous avez un ami / une amie qui donne toujours des ordres. Indiquez-lui deux façons de demander la même chose, mais poliment.

MODÈLE: L'AMI(E): Dites-moi à quelle heure le film commence!
VOUS: Non! Pourriez-vous me dire à quelle heure le film commence? (Je voudrais savoir à quelle heure le film commence.)

1. Donnez-moi un billet!
2. Expliquez-moi pourquoi les billets sont si chers.
3. Faites-moi de la monnaie de cinquante euros.
4. Dites-moi dans quelle salle on passe ce film.
5. Dites-moi si je dois réserver des places pour le film.

**C. Un après-midi de loisir.** Si vous pouviez choisir, laquelle de ces activités feriez-vous cet après-midi? Posez les questions à un(e) camarade.

MODÈLE: faire une promenade en ville ou à la campagne →
É1: Est-ce que tu ferais une promenade en ville ou à la campagne?
É2: Je ferais une promenade à la campagne.

1. jouer au tennis ou au football
2. aller au cinéma ou au café
3. passer une heure au musée ou au parc
4. manger une pizza ou un sandwich
5. boire un café ou un coca-cola
6. faire des courses ou la sieste
7. écouter de la musique classique ou du rock
8. acheter des vêtements ou des livres
9. lire des bandes dessinées ou un roman
10. se reposer ou faire du sport

**D. À l'office du tourisme.** Vous êtes de passage dans une ville que vous ne connaissez pas, et vous demandez à l'employé(e) de l'office de tourisme de vous donner des idées de choses à faire. Complétez ses phrases de façon logique.

MODÈLE: VOUS: J'aime profiter de la nature tôt le matin.
L'EMPLOYÉ(E): À votre place, j'irais à la pêche. Il y a un beau lac pas très loin.

1. VOUS: En milieu de matinée, j'aime faire des courses.
L'EMPLOYÉ(E): Si j'étais vous, _____.
2. VOUS: À midi, j'aime manger dehors quand il fait beau.
L'EMPLOYÉ(E): À votre place, _____.
3. VOUS: Quand j'ai fini de manger, j'aime faire un peu de sport.
L'EMPLOYÉ(E): À mon avis, _____.
4. VOUS: L'après-midi, j'aime bien faire quelque chose de culturel.
L'EMPLOYÉ(E): Selon notre guide, _____.
5. VOUS: Et pour entendre de la bonne musique, que me suggérez-vous?
L'EMPLOYÉ(E): À mon avis, _____.
6. VOUS: J'ai besoin de rencontrer des gens le soir, sinon je me sens seul(e).
L'EMPLOYÉ(E): À votre place, _____.

**E. Nommez trois choses...** Donnez par écrit votre réaction spontanée aux questions suivantes. Écrivez des phrases complètes. Puis, comparez vos réponses avec celles d'un(e) camarade de classe. Lesquelles sont identiques?

**1.** Nommez trois choses que vous feriez si vous étiez riche.
**2.** Donnez trois raisons pour lesquelles vous vous battriez (*you would fight*) si c'était nécessaire.
**3.** Nommez trois instruments de musique dont vous aimeriez jouer.
**4.** Nommez trois sports que vous aimeriez bien pratiquer.
**5.** Nommez trois personnes qui vous font souvent rire.
**6.** Nommez trois chanteurs (ou chanteuses) que vous admirez.
**7.** Nommez trois choses que vous feriez ce week-end si vous aviez le temps.

**F. De beaux rêves.** Imaginez ce que vous feriez dans les situations suivantes. Justifiez vos choix.

**MODÈLE:** si vous gagniez un voyage →
Si je gagnais un voyage, j'irais à Tahiti.

**1.** si vous receviez un chèque de 100 000 dollars **2.** si vous deviez vivre dans une autre ville **3.** si vous pouviez avoir la maison de vos rêves **4.** si vous preniez de longues vacances **5.** si vous veniez de finir vos études

**Un peu plus...**

**En Provence.**
La lavande est une plante indigène de la région des Alpes, et différentes variétés poussent (*grow*) partout en Provence. Les fleurs de lavande s'épanouissent (*bloom*) de juin à octobre et colorent de violet les champs (*fields*). Ces fleurs peuvent être séchées (*dried*) et utilisées en cuisine ou pour parfumer le linge (*laundry*). On utilise l'essence de lavande dans les parfums et les savons.

Nommez une plante indigène de votre région.

◀ *Et si on allait en Provence? Que ferait-on?*

# Le blog d'Hector

## Le temps de vivre

**jeudi 9 juillet**

Si j'avais du temps à moi, qu'est-ce que je ferais?

Il y a un Hector paresseux qui dit: «Je resterais des journées entières devant la télé; je surferais toute la nuit sur Internet; je bavarderais pendant des heures au téléphone.»

Il y a un Hector aventurier qui rêve: «Je jouerais au poker, je ferais le commerce des diamants.»

Il y a un Hector intellectuel qui jure[1]: «J'irais au cinéma, au théâtre, à l'opéra; je lirais deux livres par semaine; j'écouterais plus de musique classique que de musique techno; je jouerais du saxophone et j'écrirais des poèmes!»

Il y a un Hector raisonnable qui pense: «Je ferais du bricolage dans l'appartement; je téléphonerais plus souvent à mes parents; je dépenserais moins d'argent… »

Paris-Plages en été, c'est un vrai bonheur!

Il y a un Hector généreux qui promet: «Je ferais du bénévolat[2] aussi souvent que possible et je donnerais mon temps à des associations de défense de l'environnement.»

Et pour dire la vérité, il y avait, ce week-end, un Hector particulièrement glandeur[3] qui est allé se détendre à Paris-Plages avec Léa. Ce soir, le même Hector assistera au concert en plein air du chanteur Corneille: «Tant mieux[4] pour Hector!»

Hector

..........................................................................

## COMMENTAIRES

**Poema**
Corneille, c'est le plus beau, le plus généreux, le moins prétentieux des chanteurs francophones. Si je pouvais, je l'écouterais 24 heures sur 24.

**Mamadou**
Poema, j'ai deux billets pour le concert de Corneille: ça te dirait de venir avec moi?

**Alexis**
Qui est-ce qui apprécie Isabelle Boulay? C'est la plus sublime des chanteuses québécoises! Elle va passer à l'Olympia cet automne. Je pourrais avoir des billets…

**Trésor**
Houuuu! Alexis est amoureux de la belle Isabelle!

**Charlotte**
Si j'habitais Paris, j'aimerais bien aller au concert de Corneille ou à Paris-Plages.

[1]*swears*   [2]*volunteer work*   [3]*idle* (fam.)   [4]Tant… *So much the better*

## REPORTAGE

### Étudier ou s'amuser?

Est-ce qu'on a le temps de se détendre quand on est étudiant? Entre les cours, les révisions et les examens, peut-on se permettre des loisirs?

«Il n'y a pas que les études dans la vie», répond Élisabeth avec conviction. Cette étudiante brillante concilie[1] sans problème études et loisirs: «Je travaille un maximum pendant la semaine. Mais le week-end, je m'éclate[2]! Il faut savoir faire la fête, non?» À la question «Quelles sont vos activités de loisirs?», elle répond: «Je fais les boutiques avec mes copines, je pratique le judo, j'écoute de la musique rap, je vais en boîte et j'écris des poèmes!»

Deux amies s'amusent au café

«Évidemment, je pourrais ne pas lever la tête de mes livres et rester scotché devant mon ordinateur, mais ça ne serait pas efficace,[3] ajoute Saïd, étudiant en médecine. En fait, chacun s'organise en fonction de sa personnalité. Certains travaillent sept jours sur sept et attendent les vacances pour se détendre. D'autres, pour être plus performants, ont besoin de se détendre pendant une heure ou deux chaque jour. C'est mon cas. Alors un jour je vais au ciné, un autre jour je me réserve une soirée avec mes potes. Quand c'est possible, je vais à un concert. Et toutes les semaines, j'ai mon entraînement au foot… Je dois dire aussi que je suis accro[4] aux jeux vidéo… »

Une vie d'étudiant à cent à l'heure[5] n'empêche pas[6] la détente et les loisirs. Quels loisirs? Les jeunes passent leur temps libre avec leurs amis. Ils font du sport, ils écoutent de la musique et ils font la fête. Mais surtout, ils passent des heures sur Internet!

[1]*reconciles*   [2]*have fun (lit. blow up)*   [3]*effective, efficient*   [4]*hooked, addicted*   [5]*à cent… at 100 miles per hour*   [6]*n'empêche… doesn't preclude*

---

**À vous!**

1. Comment Élisabeth organise-t-elle son temps? Quels sont ses loisirs?
2. Comment Saïd se détend-il?
3. Parmi les loisirs préférés des jeunes Français, lequel préférez-vous? Pourquoi?
4. Pour se détendre, que font les deux étudiantes représentées sur la photo?

**Parlons-en!**

1. Dites quelles activités vous pratiquez pendant votre temps libre. Un(e) étudiant(e) va les inscrire au tableau.
2. Quelle est l'activité la plus populaire auprès des étudiants de la classe? Quelle est la moins pratiquée? La plus originale?
3. Imaginez que vous avez 40 ans. Quels seront alors vos loisirs préférés? Un(e) étudiant(e) va les inscrire au tableau.
4. Discutez: quel changement majeur observez-vous?

# Leçon 3

## La comparaison de l'adverbe et du nom

*Making Comparisons*

### Et si on essayait?

*Hector, Hassan, Juliette et Léa discutent au restaurant.*

Le Duplex: une boîte de nuit pour les jeunes

LÉA: On va en boîte[1] samedi?

HECTOR: J'aime **mieux** une fête à la maison **qu'**une sortie en boîte: Déjà, ça coûte moins cher.

LÉA: Oui, mais en boîte, on rencontre **plus de gens que** dans une fête privée.

HASSAN: C'est vrai mais, **le plus souvent,** les gens qu'on rencontre en boîte n'ont aucun intérêt[2]…

JULIETTE: Hassan, tu as **plus de préjugés que** d'expérience: Il y a **autant de**[3] **gens** bien dans une boîte **qu'**ailleurs.[4] Moi, j'ai rencontré des gens supers en boîte. Des gens comme nous…

HASSAN: Des gens beaux, intelligents et drôles comme nous? C'est impossible! (*Il rit.*)

HECTOR: Moi, j'avoue[5] que j'irais **plus facilement** dans un bar sympa pour boire un coup entre potes…

JULIETTE: **Le mieux,** c'est d'essayer! On va au Duplex!

[1]en… *to a club*  [2]n'ont… *are of no interest*  [3]autant… *as many*
[4]*anywhere else*  [5]*admit*

Vrai ou faux? Découvrez les phrases fausses et remplacez-les par les phrases du dialogue.

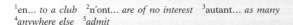

1. Hector préfère une sortie en boîte à une fête à la maison.
2. Hector pense qu'une fête à la maison coûte plus cher.
3. Hassan trouve que, la plupart du temps, les gens qui vont en boîte ne sont pas intéressants.
4. Hassan a moins d'expérience que de préjugés.
5. Selon Juliette, il y a des gens bien partout.
6. Hector irait plus facilement dans un bar.
7. Juliette propose d'essayer une sortie en boîte.

## Comparative and Superlative Forms of Adverbs

**1.** The same constructions you learned in **Chapitre 14, Leçon 3** for the comparative forms of adjectives are used for the comparative forms of adverbs.

|  |  |
|---|---|
| Jeanne écoute du jazz **plus** souvent (**que** moi). | *Jeanne listens to jazz music more often (than I).* |
| On écoute la musique **moins** attentivement dans les boîtes de nuit **que** dans les bars de jazz. | *People listen to the music less attentively at discos than at jazz bars.* |
| Nous allons danser **aussi** souvent **que** possible. | *We go dancing as often as possible.* |

> **plus... que** (*more . . . than*)
>
> **moins... que** (*less . . . than*)
>
> **aussi... que** (*as . . . as*)

[Allez-y! C]

**2.** To form the superlative of an adverb, place **le** in front of the comparative form (**le plus...** or **le moins...** ). Because adverbs are invariable, the definite article will always be **le.**

Romain s'en va tard. Louis s'en va plus tard. Sacha s'en va **le plus tard.**

## *Bien* and *mal*

The comparative and superlative forms of **bien** are irregular. The comparative and superlative forms of **mal** are regular.*

|  | COMPARATIVE | SUPERLATIVE |
|---|---|---|
| bien | mieux | le mieux |
| mal | plus mal | le plus mal |

|  |  |
|---|---|
| Tu parles français **mieux** que moi. | *You speak French better than I.* |
| Mais c'est Mehdi qui le parle **le mieux.** | *But Mehdi speaks it best.* |
| Augustin joue **plus mal** au tennis que moi. | *Augustin plays tennis worse than I.* |
| Mais c'est Marc qui y joue **le plus mal.** | *But Marc plays the worst.* |

[Allez-y! A]

### Mots clés

**Tant mieux, tant pis**

The expressions **tant mieux** (*so much the better*) and **tant pis** (*that's too bad*) are commonly used in everyday conversation.

Si tu viens, **tant mieux;** si tu ne viens pas, **tant pis.**

Il ne veut pas nous accompagner? **Tant pis** pour lui!

*Irregular comparative and superlative forms of **mal (pis, le pis)** exist, but the regular forms are much more commonly used.

## Comparisons with Nouns

**Plus de... (que)**, **moins de... (que)**, and **autant de... (que)** express quantitative comparisons with nouns.

Ils ont **plus d'**argent (**que** nous), mais nous avons **moins de** problèmes (**qu'**eux).
Je suis **autant de** cours **que** toi ce semestre.

*They have more money (than we do), but we have fewer problems (than they do).*
*I'm taking as many courses as you this semester.*

[Allez-y! B-C]

*Allez-y!*

A. **Les comparaisons.** Formez des phrases pour comparer ces personnes célèbres en vous aidant des signes donnés. Mettez les verbes au présent.

   **Signes:**    + plus    = aussi    − moins

   **MODÈLE:**  Beyoncé / danser / + bien / Fergie →
              Beyoncé danse mieux que Fergie.

   1. Steven Spielberg / aller au cinéma / = souvent / Woody Allen
   2. Taylor Swift / chanter / − bien / Beyoncé
   3. Ronaldo / jouer / + bien / au football / David Beckham
   4. Josh Groban / chanter / = bien / Plácido Domingo
   5. Tout le monde / jouer / − bien / au basket-ball / LeBron James

B. **Les Français et les loisirs.** Regardez le tableau et faites au moins trois comparaisons entre les hommes et les femmes en ce qui concerne les loisirs.

| Des millions d'artistes | | |
|---|---|---|
| Pratiques artistiques amateurs au cours des douze derniers mois par sexe et âge (en % de la population de 15 ans et plus): | | |
|  | Hommes | Femmes |
| Jouer d'un instrument musical | 15 | 11 |
| Faire de la musique en groupe | 11 | 9 |
| Tenir un journal | 6 | 11 |
| Écrire des poèmes, nouvelles, romans | 5 | 7 |
| Faire de la peinture, sculpture, gravure | 9 | 11 |
| Faire de la poterie, céramique, reliure, artisanat d'art | 3 | 5 |
| Faire du théâtre | 2 | 2 |
| Faire du dessin | 16 | 16 |
| Faire de la danse | 5 | 10 |

**MODÈLE:**  Les hommes font moins de danse que les femmes, mais ils font plus de musique en groupe que les femmes.

C. **Interview.** Posez les questions suivantes en français à un(e) camarade. Ensuite, résumez ses réponses.

   1. Who in class has more leisure time than you? Why?
   2. What sport would you like to be able to play better?
   3. Which American plays tennis best?
   4. Which athlete (**athlète,** *m., f.*) would you like to speak to the most?
   5. Who in the class runs faster than you? How do you know?
   6. Who in the class goes to the library as often as you?
   7. Who in the class needs to study the least in order to (**pour**) have good grades (**notes,** *f.*)?

**D. Les habitudes.** Demandez à un(e) camarade combien de fois par semaine, par jour, par mois ou par an il/elle fait quelque chose, puis comparez sa réponse avec vos propres habitudes.

**Possibilités:** faire du sport, lire le journal, partir en voyage, regarder la télévision…

**MODÈLE:**   É1: Combien de fois par semaine vas-tu au cinéma?
   É2: Une ou deux fois par semaine.
   É1: J'y vais plus (moins, aussi) souvent que toi.

# Les adjectifs et les pronoms indéfinis

*Talking About Quantity*

## L'influence du soleil

*Mamadou téléphone à Léa.*

MAMADOU: Alors, ces vacances avec Juliette?

LÉA: **Tout** s'est très bien passé. Après **quelques** heures à Londres, nous sommes allées chercher le beau temps sur la Côte d'Azur.

MAMADOU: Vous vous êtes bien amusées?

LÉA: On a fait **chaque** jour **quelque chose** de différent: un jour la plage, **un autre** les musées, et **plusieurs** fois des randonnées.

MAMADOU: **Tout** est super dans le Midi[1]! Les gens sont tellement cools!

LÉA: Ça, c'est un cliché! Il y a des gens désagréables même sous le soleil de la Côte d'Azur et surtout en été: **certains** sont exaspérés par les touristes, **d'autres** sont furieux à cause des embouteillages.[2] **Les uns** protestent parce qu'il faut faire la queue dans les supermarchés, **les autres** détestent la foule[3] sur la plage…

MAMADOU: Je suis sûr que ce sont des Parisiens!

[1]*South (of France)*   [2]*à… because of the traffic jams*   [3]*crowds*

Sculpture sous le soleil de la Côte d'Azur (Fondation Maeght, Saint-Paul-de-Vence)

Répondez aux questions en utilisant les expressions du dialogue.

**1.** Qu'est-ce qui s'est bien passé?
**2.** Combien de temps Juliette et Léa sont-elles restées à Londres?
**3.** Qu'est-ce qu'elles ont fait sur la Côte d'Azur?
**4.** Pour Mamadou, qu'est-ce qui est super dans le Midi?
**5.** Que font les gens désagréables sur la Côte d'Azur?

## Forms and Uses of *tout*

**1.** The adjective **tout (toute, tous, toutes)**

As an adjective, **tout** can be followed by an article, a possessive adjective, or a demonstrative adjective.

| | |
|---|---|
| Nous avons marché **toute la journée** pour arriver au sommet du volcan. | *We hiked all day to reach the summit of the volcano.* |
| Nous étions là-haut avec **tous nos amis**. | *We were up there with all our friends.* |
| Tu as apporté **toutes ces provisions**? | *Did you bring all those supplies?* |

[Allez-y! A]

**2.** The pronoun **tout**

As a pronoun (masculine singular), **tout** means *all, everything.*

| | |
|---|---|
| **Tout** va bien! | *Everything is fine!* |
| **Tout** est possible dans ce pays. | *Everything is possible in this country.* |

**3. Tous** and **toutes** mean *everyone, every one (of them), all of them.* When **tous** is used as a pronoun, the final **-s** is pronounced: **tous** [tus].

| | |
|---|---|
| Tu vois ces jeunes gens? Ils veulent **tous** faire une danse traditionnelle. | *Do you see those young people? They all want to do a traditional dance.* |
| Ces photos sont magnifiques! Sur **toutes**, on voit des costumes traditionnaux. | *These photos are gorgeous! In all of them, you see traditional costumes.* |

## Other Indefinite Adjectives and Pronouns

Indefinite adjectives and pronouns refer to unspecified things, people, or qualities. They are also used to express sameness (the same one) and difference (another). Here is a list of the most frequently used indefinite adjectives and pronouns in French.

| ADJECTIVES | PRONOUNS | |
|---|---|---|
| **quelques*** (+ *noun*) *some, a few* | **quelqu'un** (*invariable*) | *someone, anyone* |
| | **quelqu'un de** (+ *masc. adj.*) | *someone, anyone* (+ *adj.*) |
| | **quelque chose** | *something, anything* |
| | **quelque chose de** (+ *masc. adj.*) | *something, anything* (+ *adj.*) |
| | **quelques-uns / quelques-unes** (*pl.*) | *some, a few* |
| **chaque** (+ *noun*) *each, every* | **chacun(e)** | *each (one)* |

| EXPRESSIONS USED AS ADJECTIVES AND PRONOUNS | |
|---|---|
| **un(e) autre** *another* | **certain(e)s*** *certain, some* |
| **d'autres**† *other(s)* | **le/la même; les mêmes** *the same* |
| **l'autre / les autres** *the other(s)* | **plusieurs (de)** *several (of )* |

---

*****Quelques** and **certain(e)s** can both mean *some* but are used in different ways. **Quelques** is used to indicate a small, non-specific number. **Certain(e)s** is more often used to indicate *some* as opposed to others. Compare these two examples:

    Je lis généralement **quelques** poèmes (*some / a few poems*) avant de m'endormir.

    Il y a **certains** poèmes (*some specific poems*) que je lis tous les soirs avant de m'endormir.

†Note that **de** is used without an article before **autres** whether **autres** modifies a noun or stands alone as a pronoun.

| ADJECTIVES | PRONOUNS |
|---|---|
| J'ai **quelques** amis à Tahiti. | **Quelques-uns** sont agriculteurs. **Quelqu'un** m'a envoyé un livre sur Tahiti. |
| Nous avons **plusieurs** choix. → | **Plusieurs** de ces choix sont extrêmement difficiles. |
| **Chaque** voyageur voudrait un circuit différent. → | **Chacun** des voyageurs visitera une île différente. |
| Tu veux **une autre** tasse de thé? → | Non, si j'en prenais **une autre,** je ne pourrais pas dormir. |
| Où est **l'autre** autocar? → | **L'autre** est parti. |
| **Les autres** passagers sont partis. → | **Les autres** sont partis. |
| J'ai **d'autres** problèmes. → | J'en ai **d'autres.** |
| Ce sont **les mêmes** voyageurs. → | **Les mêmes** sont en retard. |

The indefinite pronouns **quelqu'un** and **quelque chose** are singular and masculine. Remember that adjectives that modify these pronouns follow them and are introduced by **de.**

| | |
|---|---|
| Je connais **quelqu'un d'intéressant** dans la capitale. | *I know someone interesting in the capital.* |
| Il a toujours **quelque chose de drôle** à dire. | *He always has something amusing to say.* |

[Allez-y! B-C-D]

 *Allez-y!*

**A. À Dakar.** Jeanne-Marie a passé quelque temps à Dakar, capitale du Sénégal. Jouez le rôle de Jeanne-Marie et répondez aux questions avec **tout, toute, tous** ou **toutes.**

> **MODÈLE:** Tu as visité les marchés? → Oui, j'ai visité tous les marchés.

1. Tu as vu le musée anthropologique?
2. Tu as photographié les églises de la ville?
3. Est-ce que tu as visité les bâtiments de l'université?
4. Tu as vu la vieille ville?
5. Tu as lu l'histoire du Sénégal?
6. Est-ce que tu as fait le tour des plantations?

**B. L'île de la Martinique.** Estelle a passé de nombreuses années à la Martinique. Elle y pense toujours avec nostalgie. Complétez les phrases.

J'aime la Martinique. On y trouve encore (quelques / d'autres)[1] belles maisons coloniales. (Chacun / Certains)[2] jours, à Fort-de-France, je me promenais dans les marchés en plein air, près du port. (Certaines / D'autres)[3] fois, je restais sur la place de la Savane pendant de longues heures. Il y a, tout près de la place, (quelques / quelques-unes)[4] maisons décorées avec du fer forgé (*wrought iron*) qui me rappellent La Nouvelle-Orléans.

(Certaines / Quelques)[5] choses ont changé, il est vrai, mais on trouve encore les (plusieurs / mêmes)[6] gommiers (*gum trees*) et ces bateaux pittoresques aux couleurs vives, que Gauguin* aimait tant.

**C. Projets de vacances.** Complétez le dialogue suivant avec un des adjectifs ou des pronoms indéfinis à droite.

JULIEN: _____[1] les ans, c'est la _____[2] chose. _____[3] fois que je propose un voyage au Sénégal, tu as d' _____[4] suggestions.

BÉNÉDICTE: Mais j'ai rencontré _____[5] qui m'a dit que _____[6] touristes ont eu des problèmes de santé au Sénégal. D'ailleurs, cette année je voudrais faire _____[7] de différent. J'aimerais faire de l'alpinisme en Suisse.

JULIEN: De l'alpinisme! Mais c'est très dangereux! Bon, eh bien, cette année _____[8] fera ce qu'il voudra. Moi, je pars au Sénégal.

**autres**

**chaque**

**même**

**tous**

**chacun**

**plusieurs**

**quelque chose**

**quelqu'un**

Une maison coloniale à la Martinique. Décrivez-la.

---

*Le peintre français Paul Gauguin a vécu brièvement à la Martinique et plus tard à Tahiti.

**D. La première chose qui vient à l'esprit** (*mind*). Avec un(e) camarade de classe, posez des questions—en français, s'il vous plaît—à partir des indications suivantes. Votre camarade doit donner la première réponse qui lui vient à l'esprit.

MODÈLE: *someone important* →
  É1: Est-ce que tu as déjà rencontré quelqu'un d'important?
  É2: Non, mais une fois mon frère a rencontré le Président.

1. *something important*
2. *something stupid*
3. *something funny*
4. *someone funny*
5. *all the large cities in Quebec*
6. *a few of the Francophone countries in Africa*
7. *several French cities*
8. *other French cities*
9. *another Canadian city*

 # Prononcez bien!

**The consonant *l*** (page 415)

**A. Isabelle.** Vous parlez d'Isabelle avec un autre étudiant étranger. Avec votre camarade, lisez la description d'Isabelle en faisant bien attention à la prononciation du **l**.

1. Ma meilleure amie ici s'appelle Isabelle. C'est l'amie idéale! Elle vient de Montréal.
2. Elle parle le français, l'anglais, et l'espagnol.
3. C'est elle qui est venue me chercher à l'hôtel et qui m'a montré la ville quand je suis arrivé(e) ici.
4. En avril, nous allons partir en Italie pour un week-end. J'ai hâte!

**B. Virelangue.** (*Tongue twister.*) Isabelle vous apprend le virelangue suivant. Écoutez Isabelle et puis, avec votre camarade, entraînez-vous à le prononcer.

«Lulu a lu la lettre à Lyon et Lola a lu le livre à Lille où Lala liait[1] le lilas.[2]»

[1]*was binding*  [2]*lilac*

# Leçon 4

##  Lecture

### *Avant de lire*

**Reading journalistic texts.** News reporting, as found in the daily paper and news sites on the Internet, represents a special kind of text. Because of their focus on detail, these texts require intensive reading skills in order to respond to the so-called five questions: *Who* is newsworthy? *What* is the event itself? *Where* and *when* did the event occur? and *Why* did it occur?

The first paragraph of this reading answers four of the five questions. Read through this paragraph and supply these details:

- Who is the person creating the news event?
- What is the news event?
- Where did it take place?
- When did the event occur?

As you read the text, locate other details that deepen your understanding of the event—in particular, the answer to the question *why?*

**À propos de la lecture...**
Cet article est tiré et adapté d'un article sur le site Web d'**An Tour Tan,** le serveur de la diaspora bretonne.

Anne Quéméré dans son bateau «Connétable»

Le voyage d'Anne Quéméré dans un bateau à rame, 2004

## Traversée de l'Atlantique en solitaire

### *Anne Quéméré: une championne*

Le lundi 30 août 2004 à 5 h 15 (heure locale), Anne Quéméré a franchi[1] la ligne d'arrivée, près de Rochefort, après avoir traversé l'Atlantique nord à la rame[2] en solitaire et sans assistance en 87 jours, 12 heures et 15 minutes. Elle avait déjà le record féminin de traversée de l'Atlantique sud depuis 2003; elle a maintenant le record féminin de la traversée de l'Atlantique nord.

### *La traversée*

Partie de Chatham (Cape Cod, USA) le 3 juin à 15 h GMT, elle a parcouru environ 5 052 kilomètres (3,139 miles) dans des conditions météo difficiles. Pour mettre toutes les chances de son côté, Anne Quéméré avait préparé[3] avec précision une route idéale. Avec des vents d'ouest dominants et un Gulf Stream qui devait l'aider à progresser, cette route avait plusieurs avantages, mais aussi de nombreux inconvénients: une eau extrêmement froide près de Terre-Neuve, des tempêtes violentes et fréquentes et des vents contraires

[1]a... *crossed*  [2]à... *rowing in a rowboat*  [3]avait... *had prepared*

susceptibles de faire reculer[4] ou chavirer[5] le bateau. Les conditions météorologiques l'ont d'ailleurs forcée à modifier ses plans. Elle a eu des moments difficiles, particulièrement pendant l'ouragan Alex. «J'ai vu défiler ma vie»,[6] dit-elle avec encore beaucoup d'émotion.

## L'arrivée

«J'ai ramé comme une cinglée[7] les derniers 67 km,[8] heureusement aidée par un bon vent de nord-ouest qui m'a permis d'atteindre la ligne d'arrivée. Mon bonheur immédiat a tout effacé,[9] jusqu'au souvenir des heures difficiles.» Accueillie[10] dans le port de Tréboul comme une reine, incapable de se tenir debout seule, Anne Quéméré, très émue, a retrouvé sa petite fille, qui est restée juste à côté de sa maman toute l'après-midi.

Anne Quéméré recherchait la confrontation avec des réalités fondamentales et authentiques: la mer, les vents, le risque de chavirer… Ce dialogue difficile avec la nature lui a permis d'apprendre de nouvelles leçons et de porter un regard différent sur l'existence. Tout est possible: Anne l'a fait et le refera encore, parole de Bretonne!

[4]*move backward*  [5]*capsize*  [6]*J'ai… I saw my life pass in front of me*  [7]*fool, crazy person*  [8]*approx. 41 miles*
[9]*tout… wiped it all away*  [10]*Welcomed*

---

## Compréhension

**Les cinq questions.**  Testez votre compréhension du texte en utilisant les cinq questions comme points de départ.

1. Qui a établi la route du Connétable? Qui en particulier a accueilli Anne à son retour?
2. Qu'est-ce qu'Anne a trouvé comme obstacles pendant son voyage? Qu'est-ce qui a aidé Anne à arriver à sa ligne d'arrivée?
3. D'où est-elle partie? Où se trouvait la ligne d'arrivée?
4. Quand (À quels moments) Anne s'est-elle sentie désespérée?
5. Selon le texte, pourquoi Anne a-t-elle entrepris un tel voyage? À votre avis, est-ce qu'il s'agit d'un acte purement égoïste?

 # Écriture

The writing activities **Par écrit** and **Journal intime** can be found in the Workbook/Laboratory Manual to accompany *Vis-à-vis*.

## Pour s'amuser

Le travail, c'est la santé; ne rien faire c'est la conserver.  —Henri Salvador

# Le vidéoblog d'Hector

Un café à Paris-Plages, au bord de la Seine

## En bref

Dans cet épisode, Hector et Léa voudraient passer l'après-midi ensemble, mais ils ont du mal à choisir une activité. Ils finissent par décider d'aller à Paris-Plages, un grand événement de l'été à Paris.

### Vocabulaire en contexte

Imaginez qu'un ami / une amie vous propose les activités suivantes. Indiquez les activités que vous feriez volontiers (avec plaisir) et expliquez pourquoi les autres ne vous tentent pas.

**Activités**
☐ aller sur une belle plage de **sable** (*sand*) blanc
☐ aller au ciné l'après-midi
☐ aller **prendre un verre**
☐ **se baigner** à la piscine
☐ **se balader** (*stroll*) à vélo

☐ se faire **bronzer** (*to tan*)
☐ faire de **l'escalade** (*rock/wall climbing*)
☐ faire un jogging au parc
☐ pique-niquer
☐ **se promener** au bord de l'eau

## Visionnez!

Pourquoi Hector ne veut-il pas faire les activités suivantes? Choisissez la bonne réponse.

1. Il ne veut pas aller au ciné parce qu'il _____.
   **a.** n'a plus d'argent
   **b.** préfère être dehors l'après-midi
2. Il ne veut pas faire un jogging parce qu'il _____.
   **a.** ne veut pas courir après un repas
   **b.** ne trouve pas ses tennis
3. Il ne veut pas faire du vélo et aller prendre un verre parce qu'il _____.
   **a.** n'aime pas le vin
   **b.** fait trop chaud
4. Il ne veut pas aller à la piscine parce qu'il _____.
   **a.** y aura trop d'enfants
   **b.** ne sait pas nager

## Analysez!

Répondez aux questions.

1. Quelles activités font de Paris-Plages une vraie plage?
2. À quoi bon (*What good is it*) avoir une plage en centre-ville? Pourquoi, à votre avis, la Mairie de Paris organise-t-elle ce grand événement de l'été?

## Comparez!

Y a-t-il beaucoup d'endroits dans votre ville ou votre région où vous pouvez vous amuser? Est-il plus facile de passer son temps libre à l'intérieur (dans un cinéma ou un musée) ou à l'extérieur? Regardez encore une fois la partie culturelle de la vidéo: est-ce que votre ville ou votre région a besoin d'organiser quelque chose comme Paris-Plages?

## Note culturelle

Depuis 2001, la Ville de Paris organise avec succès «Paris-Plages» le long de la Seine. Cette opération municipale, qui coûte plus de 1,5 millions d'euros, est financée par la Ville et par des sponsors privés. En 2012, «Paris-Plages» a attiré[1] presque 5 millions de visiteurs, dont 50 % parisiens. L'opération a nécessité 2 plages de 800 mètres; 5 000 tonnes de sable; 900 pièces de mobilier (matelas,[2] transats,[3] parasols, tables, chaises, etc.); 44 palmiers et 74 oriflammes[4]; 60 secouristes[5] et 55 plagistes.[6]

[1]*attracted*   [2]*(air) mattresses*   [3]*beach chairs*
[4]*banners*   [5]*first aid workers*   [6]*beach attendants*

# Vocabulaire

**Verbes**

**assister à** to attend
**bricoler** to putter, do odd jobs
**courir** to run
**désirer** to desire, want
**indiquer** to show, point out
**se passer** to happen, take place
**rire** to laugh
**sourire** to smile

À REVOIR: **aider, emmener, faire du sport, gagner, jouer à, jouer de, perdre**

**Substantifs**

**les activités** (f.) **de plein air** outdoor activities
**la bande dessinée** cartoon
**la blague** joke
**le bricolage** do-it-yourself work, puttering around
**la chanson** song
  **la chanson de variété** popular song
**la collection** collection
**le cyclisme** cycling
**l'équipe** (f.) team
**la foule** crowd
**le jardinage** gardening
**le jeu (les jeux)** game
  **le jeu de mot** pun
  **le jeu de hasard** game of chance
  **le jeu de société** board game

**la lecture** reading
**les loisirs** (m.) leisure activities
**la manifestation sportive** sporting event
**la marche** walking
**le match** game
**l'opéra** (m.) opera
**le passe-temps** hobby
**la pêche** fishing
**la pétanque** bocce ball, lawn bowling
**le pique-nique** picnic
**le spectacle** show, performance
  **le spectacle de variétés** variety show; floor show (in a restaurant)
**le temps libre** free time

À REVOIR: **le théâtre**

**Expressions interrogatives**

**lequel, laquelle, lesquels, lesquelles, qu'est-ce qui, qui est-ce que, qui est-ce qui, qui, quoi**

**Adjectifs et pronoms indéfinis**

**un(e) autre** another
**d'autres** other(s)
**l'autre / les autres** the other(s)
**certain(e)(s)** certain, some
**chacun(e)(s)** each (one)
**chaque** each

**le/la même (les mêmes)** the same one(s)
**plusieurs (de)** several
**quelque chose (de)** something
**quelques** (adj.) some, a few
**quelqu'un** someone, anyone
**quelques-uns / quelques-unes** (pron.) some, a few
**tout(e)** all, everything
**tous / toutes** everyone, every one (of them), all of them

**Mots et expressions divers**

**à ta place...** if I were you . . .
**aller en boîte** to go clubbing
**autant (de)... que** as much (many) . . . as
**bien, mieux, le mieux** well, better, best
**en train de** in the process of; in the middle of
**je devrais** I should
**Qu'est-ce que tu racontes / vous racontez?** What are you talking about?
**Qu'est-ce qui se passe?** What's happening? What's going on?
**tant mieux** so much the better
**tant pis** that's too bad

À REVOIR: **je pourrais**

# Qu'en pensez-vous?

Les dossiers d'Hector

Hector

- Mes photos
  - On danse sur le volcan?
  - Une affiche à Fort-de-France
  - Une amitié multiculturelle

Des réacteurs nucléaires à Cattenom, en Lorraine: On danse sur le volcan?

## Dans ce chapitre...

Une affiche à Fort-de-France

### OBJECTIFS COMMUNICATIFS

➤ talking about environmental and social problems

➤ expressing attitudes, wishes, necessity, possibility, emotions, doubt, and uncertainty

➤ learning to distinguish between and pronounce selected sounds in French

### PAROLES (Leçon 1)

➤ L'environnement

➤ Les problèmes de la société moderne

### STRUCTURES (Leçons 2 et 3)

➤ Le subjonctif (première partie)

➤ Le subjonctif (deuxième partie)

➤ Le subjonctif (troisième partie)

➤ Le subjonctif (quatrième partie)

Une amitié multiculturelle

### CULTURE

➤ Le blog d'Hector: *Moi d'abord?*

➤ Reportage: *La France multiculturelle*

➤ Lecture: *La Réclusion solitaire* (extrait) de Tahar Ben Jelloun (Leçon 4)

www.mhconnectfrench.com

# Leçon 1

## L'environnement

le gaspillage[1] des sources d'énergie
la pollution de l'atmosphère

les déchets[2] (*m*) industriels

**ne** gaspillez pas les sources d'énergie

CONTRÔLEZ LES DÉCHETS INDUSTRIELS!

NE POLLUEZ PAS L'ATMOSPHÈRE!

Il faut conserver les sources d'énergie!

IL FAUT DÉVELOPPER L'ÉNERGIE SOLAIRE

IL FAUT RECYCLER

PROTÉGEZ LA NATURE

la conservation des sources d'énergie

le recyclage

le développement de l'énergie solaire

la protection de la nature

[1]*wasting*   [2]*waste, refuse*

**AUTRES MOTS UTILES**

| | |
|---|---|
| **une centrale nucléaire** | nuclear power plant |
| **consommer** | to consume |
| **le covoiturage** | carpooling |
| **épuiser** | to use up, exhaust |
| **le réchauffement de la planète** | global warming |
| **sauver** | to save |
| **la surpopulation** | overpopulation |
| **une voiture hybride** | hybrid car |

 *Allez-y!*

**A. Association de mots.** Quels problèmes écologiques associez-vous
avec les verbes suivants?

> **MODÈLE:** gaspiller → le gaspillage des sources d'énergie

> **1.** conserver  **2.** protéger  **3.** polluer  **4.** recycler  **5.** développer

**B. Remèdes.** Expliquez quelles sont les actions nécessaires pour sauver
notre planète. Utilisez **Il faut** ou **Il ne faut pas** suivi d'un infinitif.

> **MODÈLES:** le contrôle des déchets industriels →
> Il faut contrôler les déchets industriels.
> le gaspillage de l'énergie →
> Il ne faut pas gaspiller l'énergie.

> **1.** la pollution de l'environnement
> **2.** la protection de la nature
> **3.** le développement de l'énergie solaire
> **4.** la conservation des sources d'énergie
> **5.** le gaspillage des ressources naturelles
> **6.** le développement des transports en commun

**C. Rendez-vous des Verts.** Vous êtes pour une ville plus verte où il y
a moins de voitures et plus de gens qui circulent à pied ou à vélo.
En résumant le plaidoyer (*defense*) dans le *Manuel du cycliste urbain*,
faites une petite présentation pour comparer les voitures aux vélos.
Parlez des avantages du vélo, mais n'oubliez pas ses inconvénients.

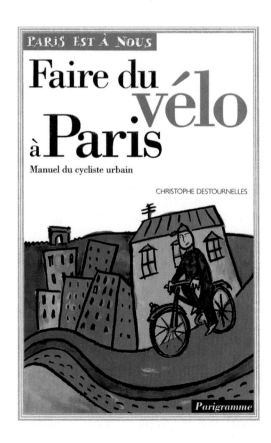

### Petit plaidoyer pour le vélo à Paris

*Il ne pollue pas*
*Il est silencieux*
*Il est très maniable[1]*
*Il occupe un espace restreint*
*Il ne demande pas beaucoup d'infrastructures*
*Il est économique (il revient en moyenne à 100 euros*
*par an, quand une voiture réclame 800 euros par mois,*
*et une Carte orange 125 euros chaque année)*
*Il se gare[2] relativement facilement*
*(adieu les soucis de stationnement gênant, les PV,[3]*
*les parkings et les horodateurs[4]... )*
*Il est très bien adapté aux petits parcours en ville[5]*
*Il est bon pour la santé*
*Il est bon pour le moral*
*Il n'est pas aussi dangereux qu'on veut bien le dire*
*Il expose moins à la pollution*
*que l'habitacle[6] d'une voiture*
*Il permet de découvrir Paris...*

[1]*easy to steer*  [2]*se... is parked*  [3]*tickets*  [4]*parking ticket machines*
[5]*parcours... trips around town*  [6]*interior*

# Les problèmes de la société moderne

Voici les résultats d'une enquête réalisée pour le journal *Le Monde*.

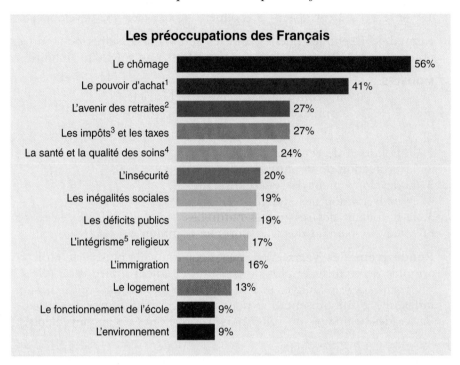

**Les préoccupations des Français**

| | |
|---|---|
| Le chômage | 56% |
| Le pouvoir d'achat[1] | 41% |
| L'avenir des retraites[2] | 27% |
| Les impôts[3] et les taxes | 27% |
| La santé et la qualité des soins[4] | 24% |
| L'insécurité | 20% |
| Les inégalités sociales | 19% |
| Les déficits publics | 19% |
| L'intégrisme[5] religieux | 17% |
| L'immigration | 16% |
| Le logement | 13% |
| Le fonctionnement de l'école | 9% |
| L'environnement | 9% |

Source: Adapté d'une enquête IPSOS / CGI Business Consulting pour *Le Monde*, Fondation Jean Jaurès et le Cevipof. Janvier 2013.

Les Français sont préoccupés. Le futur leur semble incertain; la crise économique crée un climat d'instabilité qui affecte toute la société.

- Le gros problème de la France, c'est le chômage. «Mes enfants font de longues études: est-ce qu'ils trouveront du travail?» se demandent avec angoisse[6] les parents. Rien de moins sûr car, avec la récession, les entreprises n'embauchent pas.[7]
- Le pouvoir d'achat et les retraites inquiètent. Tout le monde s'interroge: «Comment maintenir mon niveau de vie[8]?» En réalité, les Français sont obligés de réduire leur consommation parce que les impôts augmentent massivement, mais pas les salaires. Et les seniors savent que le montant[9] de leurs retraites diminuera. Pourquoi? Parce qu'il faut, en priorité, réduire un déficit public colossal.
- On a peur aussi de devoir sacrifier le meilleur système social du monde notamment l'accès gratuit à la santé et à l'école, et les aides au logement.[10]
- Dans une société en pleine mutation, les Français perdent leurs repères[11]: les inégalités sociales s'amplifient, l'insécurité et l'intégrisme religieux créent une névrose[12] collective; l'immigration pose le problème de l'identité française.
- Enfin l'environnement devient une question sensible: on sait qu'il faut modifier les comportements et encourager le développement durable[13] pour préserver les ressources naturelles.

---

[1]pouvoir... *purchasing power* [2]*pensions* [3]*taxes* [4]*care* [5]*fundamentalism* [6]avec... *anxiously* [7]n'embauchent... *aren't hiring* [8]niveau... *standard of living* [9]*amount* [10]aides... *housing subsidies* [11]perdent... *are losing their points of reference* [12]*neuroses* [13]développement... *sustainable development*

**AUTRES MOTS UTILES**

**le citoyen / la citoyenne** citizen
**les droits** (*m.*) **civils** civil rights
**l'écologiste** (*m., f.*) environmentalist
**l'électeur / l'électrice** voter
**l'élection** (*f.*) election
**la guerre** war
**l'homme / la femme politique** politician
**les idées extrémistes** extremist ideas
**les impôts** (*m.*) taxes
**le parti** political party
**la politique** politics; policy
**la réussite** success
**le/la sans-abri** homeless person

**le terrorisme** terrorism
**augmenter** to raise, increase
**diminuer** to lower, reduce
**élire** to elect
**s'engager (dans)** to get involved (in) (*a public issue, cause*)
**exiger** to require; to demand
**exprimer une opinion** to express an opinion
**faire grève** to strike
**manifester (pour/contre)** to demonstrate (for/against)
**poser sa candidature** to run for elected office; to apply (for a job)
**soutenir** to support

 *Allez-y!*

**A. Autrement dit.** Choisissez la bonne définition.

_____ **1.** exiger
_____ **2.** la grève
_____ **3.** soutenir
_____ **4.** élire
_____ **5.** s'engager
_____ **6.** manifester
_____ **7.** la guerre
_____ **8.** le/la sans-abri

**a.** prendre publiquement position
**b.** encourager
**c.** participer à une manifestation
**d.** demander, réclamer
**e.** la cessation collective du travail
**f.** une personne sans domicile
**g.** choisir
**h.** le contraire de la paix

**B. L'actualité.** Lisez à la page précédente les résultats de l'enquête faite pour *Le Monde*. Puis répondez aux questions.

1. Quelles sont les préoccupations des citoyens de votre pays?
2. Parmi ces préoccupations, laquelle considérez-vous comme la plus importante ou la moins importante?
3. Sélectionnez trois problèmes qui, selon vous, affectent gravement la société dans laquelle vous vivez. Proposez des solutions pour les résoudre.
4. Quels autres problèmes pourrait-on ajouter au sondage français?

**C. À mon avis.** Choisissez une des expressions des **Mots clés** pour exprimer votre point de vue.
   **MODÈLE:** possible / contrôler le problème des déchets nucléaires →
   Personnellement, je crois qu'il est (qu'il n'est pas) possible de contrôler le problème des déchets nucléaires, parce que...

1. essentiel / développer de nouvelles sources d'énergie
2. impossible / empêcher les accidents nucléaires
3. important / respecter l'image de la femme dans les publicités
4. indispensable / faire attention aux problèmes de la jeunesse
5. inutile / limiter l'immigration
6. essentiel / augmenter les impôts
7. utile / aider les chômeurs (les gens qui sont au chômage)
8. essentiel / protéger et maintenir (*maintain*) les droits civils

## Mots clés

**Exprimer son opinion**

To express a personal point of view, use the following expressions:

| Moi, Pour ma part, Personnellement, | je crois que... je pense que... j'estime que... je trouve que... |
|---|---|

**À mon avis...**
**Selon moi...**

Your point will be more convincing if you give examples or refer to other people's opinions. Use the following expressions:

**Par exemple...**
**On dit que...**
**J'ai entendu dire que...**

# Leçon 2

## Le subjonctif (*première partie*)

*Expressing Attitudes*

### Je rêve, n'est-ce pas?

*Juliette téléphone à Charlotte.*

JULIETTE: Pourquoi as-tu choisi de travailler pour l'OMS[1] plutôt que pour une administration suisse?

CHARLOTTE: Par idéalisme, je crois. **Je veux que** tous les pays **coordonnent** leurs efforts pour le bien commun;[2] **je désire que** la santé **soit** une priorité universelle. Je rêve, n'est-ce pas?

JULIETTE: Mais non, tu ne rêves pas! La santé est un droit fondamental. Moi aussi, **j'aimerais que** nous **soyons** tous égaux[3] devant la maladie!

CHARLOTTE: À l'OMS, **nous souhaitons**[4] **que** chaque enfant **arrive** à l'âge adulte en bonne santé. **Nous insistons pour que** tous les pays du tiers-monde[5] **établissent** une excellente politique de santé publique.

JULIETTE: C'est un des grands défis[6] du XXIe siècle. Mais moi je parle, je fais des commentaires... alors que toi, tu agis! Cela me fait réfléchir...

CHARLOTTE: J'ai toujours été engagée dans des causes humanitaires. À mon petit niveau,[7] **je veux que** mon travail **puisse** aider les plus vulnérables. C'est juste, non?

L'OMS: la santé pour tous

[1]Organisation Mondiale de la Santé *WHO (World Health Organization)*  [2]le... *the common good*  [3]*equal*
[4]*hope*  [5]*third world*  [6]*challenges*  [7]À... *In my small way*

Trouvez, dans le dialogue, la phrase équivalente.

1. Les pays doivent coordonner leurs efforts pour le bien commun.
2. La santé doit être une priorité universelle.
3. Nous devons tous être égaux face à la maladie.
4. Tous les enfants doivent arriver à l'âge adulte avec un bon capital santé.
5. Les pays du tiers-monde doivent établir une très bonne politique de santé publique.
6. Mon travail doit aider les gens défavorisés.

## The Subjunctive Mood

The verb tenses you have learned so far have been in the *indicative* mood (**présent, passé composé, imparfait, futur**), in the *imperative* mood (used for direct commands or requests), or in the *conditional* mood (used to express hypothetical situations). In this chapter, you will learn about the *subjunctive* mood.

The subjunctive is used to present actions or states as subjective or doubtful, instead of as facts. It appears most frequently in dependent clauses, and is used infrequently in English. Compare the following examples.

| INDICATIVE | SUBJUNCTIVE |
|---|---|
| He *goes* to Paris. | I insist that he *go* to Paris for the meeting. |
| We *are* on time. | They ask that we *be* on time. |
| She *is* the president. | She wishes that she *were* the president of the group. |

In French, the subjunctive is used more frequently than it is in English. It almost always appears in a dependent clause introduced by **que.** In such cases, the main clause contains a verb expressing desire, emotion, uncertainty, or some other subjective view of the action in the dependent clause. For now, you will focus on the use of the subjunctive in dependent clauses introduced by **que** after verbs of volition (wanting), including **aimer bien, désirer, insister (pour), préférer, souhaiter** (*to want, to wish*), and **vouloir.**

nucléocrates
cessez de
mettre en péril
l'avenir de
nos enfants !

**Un peu plus...**

**Les manifestations.**
En France, 75 % de l'énergie nécessaire aux entreprises et aux particuliers (*individuals*) est produite par des centrales nucléaires. Bien que les Français soient généralement en faveur de la production d'énergie nucléaire, le problème des déchets nucléaires les inquiète. Dans les années 80, de violentes émeutes (*riots*) ont éclaté (*broke out*) dans les régions rurales où l'on voulait enfouir (*to bury*) ces déchets. Aujourd'hui, le gouvernement cherche une solution.

◀ *Pour ou contre l'énergie nucléaire? Et vous?*

Usually, the subjects of the main and dependent clauses are different.

| MAIN CLAUSE<br>*Indicative* | DEPENDENT CLAUSE<br>*Subjunctive* |
| --- | --- |
| Je veux | **que** vous **partiez.** |

Note that French constructions with the subjunctive have many possible English equivalents.

**que je parle** → *that I speak, that I'm speaking, that I do speak, that I may speak, that I will speak, me to speak*

| | |
| --- | --- |
| De quoi veux-tu **que je parle**? | *What do you want me to talk about?* |
| Il préfère **que je parle** des déchets nucléaires. | *He prefers that I speak about nuclear waste.* |
| L'agent ne croit pas **que le suspect parle.** | *The police officer doesn't believe that the suspect will speak.* |

## Forms of the Present Subjunctive

For most verbs, including many irregular verbs (e.g., **conduire, connaître, écrire, lire, ouvrir, mettre, suivre**) the stem for the forms of the subjunctive is found by dropping the **-ent** of the third-person plural (**ils/elles**) form of the present indicative and by adding the subjunctive endings: **-e, -es, -e, -ions, -iez,** and **-ent.**

| | parler | finir | vendre | sortir |
| --- | --- | --- | --- | --- |
| | (ils) **parl**/ent | (ils) **finiss**/ent | (ils) **vend**/ent | (ils) **sort**/ent |
| ...que je | parl**e** | finiss**e** | vend**e** | sort**e** |
| ...que tu | parl**es** | finiss**es** | vend**es** | sort**es** |
| ...qu'il/elle/on | parl**e** | finiss**e** | vend**e** | sort**e** |
| ...que nous | parl**ions** | finiss**ions** | vend**ions** | sort**ions** |
| ...que vous | parl**iez** | finiss**iez** | vend**iez** | sort**iez** |
| ...qu'ils/elles | parl**ent** | finiss**ent** | vend**ent** | sort**ent** |

## Verbs with Two Stems in the Subjunctive

Some verbs that have two stems in the present indicative also have two stems in the subjunctive: One stem is taken from the **ils** form of the present (for **je, tu, il/elle/on,** and **ils/elles**), and the other, from the **nous** form (for **nous** and **vous**). Some verbs of this type are **acheter, apprendre, boire, préférer, prendre,** and **venir.**

| boire | |
| --- | --- |
| **ils boivent** | |
| **nous buvons** | |
| ...que je **boiv**e | ...que nous **buv**ions |
| ...que tu **boiv**es | ...que vous **buv**iez |
| ...qu'il/elle/on **boiv**e | ...qu'ils/elles **boiv**ent |

[Allez-y! A-B]

## Irregular Subjunctive Verbs

Some verbs have irregular subjunctive stems. The endings themselves are all regular, except for some endings of **avoir** and **être.**

| | aller<br>*aill-/all-* | faire<br>*fass-* | pouvoir<br>*puiss-* | savoir<br>*sach-* | vouloir<br>*veuill-/voul-* | avoir<br>*ai-/ay-* | être<br>*soi-/soy-* |
| --- | --- | --- | --- | --- | --- | --- | --- |
| ...que je/j' | aille | fasse | puisse | sache | veuille | aie | sois |
| ...que tu | ailles | fasses | puisses | saches | veuilles | aies | sois |
| ...qu'il/elle/on | aille | fasse | puisse | sache | veuille | ait | soit |
| ...que nous | allions | fassions | puissions | sachions | voulions | a**yons** | so**yons** |
| ...que vous | alliez | fassiez | puissiez | sachiez | vouliez | a**yez** | so**yez** |
| ...qu'ils/elles | aillent | fassent | puissent | sachent | veuillent | aient | soient |

Le professeur veut que nous **allions** au débat.

Son parti veut que le gouvernement **fasse** des réformes.

Le président préfère que les sénateurs **soient** présents.

*The professor wants us to go to the debate.*

*His (Her) party wants the government to make reforms.*

*The president prefers the senators to be there.*

[Allez-y! C-D-E]

 **Prononcez bien!**

**The subjunctive of *aller* and *avoir***

When using the subjunctive, be sure to distinguish between the pronunciation of **aller** and **avoir.** For the **je, tu, il,** and **ils** forms of **aller,** pronounce [aj], somewhat like the English pronoun *I.*

[aj]: ...que j'**aille,** tu **ailles,** il **aille**

For the corresponding persons for **avoir,** pronounce a single sound [ɛ], as in **est.**

[ɛ]: ...que j'**aie,** tu **aies,** elle **ait**

Remember that the **nous** and **vous** forms start with the sound [a] for **aller** and [ɛ] for **avoir.**

[aljɔ̃]: ...que nous **allions**

[alje]: ...que vous **alliez**

[ɛjɔ̃]: ...que nous **ayons**

[ɛje]: ...que vous **ayez**

### Allez-y!

**A. Stratégie électorale.** Laure accepte de poser sa candidature au Conseil universitaire. Avec un groupe d'étudiants, elle prépare sa campagne. Que veut Laure?

**MODÈLE:** Elle veut que les étudiants / choisir / des délégués responsables →
Elle veut que les étudiants choisissent des délégués responsables.

1. Elle veut que tout le monde / réfléchir / aux problèmes de l'université
2. Elle aimerait que nous / préparer / tout de suite / une stratégie électorale
3. Elle préfère que vous / finir / les affiches aujourd'hui
4. Elle veut que Luc et Simon / organiser / un débat
5. Elle souhaite que la trésorière / établir / un budget
6. Elle insiste pour que je / convoquer (*to ask to attend*) / tous les bénévoles (*volunteers*) ce soir

**B. Discours politique.** Ce soir, Laure fait son premier discours de la campagne électorale. Voici ce qu'elle dit aux étudiants.

**MODÈLE:** Je voudrais que nous / trouver / tous ensemble des solutions à nos problèmes →
Je voudrais que nous trouvions tous ensemble des solutions à nos problèmes.

1. Je veux que le Conseil universitaire / agir / en faveur des étudiants
2. Je souhaite que vous / participer / aux décisions du Conseil
3. Je préfère que nous / discuter / librement des mesures à prendre
4. Je désire que l'université / prendre / nos inquiétudes / en considération
5. Je voudrais que les professeurs / comprendre / nos positions
6. Je souhaite enfin que tous les candidats / se réunir / bientôt pour mieux exposer leurs idées

**C. Revendications.** (*Demands.*) Les délégués du Conseil universitaire donnent leurs directives aux étudiants. Remplacez les sujets en italique par **vous,** puis par **les étudiants** et faites tous les changements nécessaires.

Nous ne voulons pas que *tu* ailles[1] en cours aujourd'hui. Nous préférons que *tu* sois[2] présent(e) à la manifestation et que *tu* fasses[3] grève. Nous désirons que *tu* aies[4] une affiche lisible (*legible*). Naturellement, nous voudrions que *tu* puisses[5] exprimer tes opinions librement.

**D. Engagement politique.** Les Legrand ont des opinions libérales. Quels conseils donnent-ils à leurs enfants? Suivez les modèles.

> **MODÈLES:** Arnaud / être réactionnaire →
> Nous ne voulons pas que tu sois réactionnaire.
> Arnaud et Fabrice / être courageux →
> Nous voulons que vous soyez courageux.

1. Jacob / être actif en politique
2. Albane et Jacob / avoir le courage de leurs opinions
3. vous / avoir des amis intolérants
4. Arnaud / être bien informé
5. Joachim / être violent
6. vous / être tolérant
7. Fabrice / avoir de l'ambition politique
8. Arnaud et Joachim / avoir des idéaux pacifistes

**E. Exprimez-vous!** Composez votre propre slogan. Complétez les phrases suivantes et donnez votre opinion. Commencez avec **Je voudrais que.**

1. notre gouvernement _____
2. les écologistes _____
3. les hommes et les femmes politiques _____
4. nous _____
5. les pays industrialisés _____
6. ?

# Le subjonctif (*deuxième partie*)

*Expressing Wishes, Necessity, and Possibility*

## Un petit coin de paradis

*Appel vidéo entre Hassan et Hector.*

HASSAN: **Il est possible que** je **vienne** fin août à la Martinique! Je vais fermer mon restaurant une semaine et j'ai envie d'aller dans les Caraïbes.[1]

HECTOR: Ça serait génial[2]! Mais une semaine, c'est trop court! **Je préfère que** tu **restes** plus longtemps! Il y a tellement de choses à voir et à faire sur cette île sublime!

HASSAN: Oh, tu sais… **Il est** surtout **essentiel que** je **me repose**… Je veux vivre quelques jours loin de la civilisation et de la pollution: pas d'ordinateur, pas de téléphone… l'air pur… le silence…

HECTOR: La plage… la mer transparente… À la Martinique, il y a 22 000 hectares[3] d'espaces naturels protégés! On trouve des zones très solitaires où on peut vivre comme Robinson Crusoé!

HASSAN: **Il faut** absolument **que** tu m'**indiques** quelques endroits secrets.

HECTOR: Je connais un petit coin de paradis…Tu veux savoir où c'est?

HASSAN: Qui dirait non au Paradis? Pas moi!

[1]*Caribbean* [2]*great* [3]*hectare (One hectare is slightly less than 2.5 acres.)*

Trouvez, dans le dialogue, la phrase équivalente.

1. Hassan va peut-être venir une semaine à la Martinique.
2. Hector conseille à Hassan de rester plus longtemps.
3. Hassan veut essentiellement se reposer.
4. Il demande à Hector de lui indiquer de beaux endroits secrets.

## The Subjunctive with Verbs of Volition

1. When someone expresses a desire for someone else to behave in a certain way, or for a particular thing to happen, the verb in the subordinate clause is usually in the subjunctive. The following construction is used.

| | |
|---|---|
| Mon père **veut que je fasse** les études aux USA. | *My father wants me to study in the USA.* |
| Ma mère **préfère que j'étudie** en France. | *My mother prefers that I study in France.* |

Note that an infinitive construction is sometimes used in English to express such a desire.

**2.** Verbs of volition are followed by an infinitive in French when there is no change in subject, as in the first example.

| | |
|---|---|
| **Je veux finir** mes études. | *I want to finish my studies.* |
| Et **ma mère veut** aussi **que** je les **finisse.** | *And my mother wants me to finish them too.* |

**3.** Verbs expressing desires include **aimer bien, désirer, exiger, insister (pour), préférer, souhaiter, vouloir,** and **vouloir bien.** These verbs take the subjunctive. The verb **espérer,** however, takes the indicative.

| | |
|---|---|
| **Je souhaite que** tu **aies** de bonnes vacances. | *I hope you have a good vacation.* |
| **J'espère que** tu **as** mon numéro de téléphone. | *I hope you have my telephone number.* |

[Allez-y! A]

## The Subjunctive with Impersonal Expressions

**1.** An impersonal expression is one in which the subject does not refer to any particular person or thing. In English, the subject of an impersonal expression is usually *it: It is important that I go to class.* In French, many impersonal expressions—especially those that express will, necessity, judgment, possibility, or doubt—are followed by the subjunctive in the dependent clause.

| IMPERSONAL EXPRESSIONS USED WITH THE SUBJUNCTIVE | |
|---|---|
| WILL OR NECESSITY | POSSIBILITY, JUDGMENT, OR DOUBT |
| il est essentiel que | il est normal que |
| il est important que | il est peu probable que† |
| il est indispensable que | il est possible / impossible que |
| il est nécessaire que | il se peut que (*it's possible that*) |
| il est préférable que | il semble que (*it seems that*) |
| il faut que* | |
| il vaut mieux que* | |
| (*it's better that*) | |

| | |
|---|---|
| **Il est important que** le racisme **disparaisse.** | *It's important that racism disappear.* |
| **Il faut que** vous **soyez** au courant de la politique. | *You must (It's necessary that you) keep up with politics.* |
| **Il est peu probable que** le sexisme **soit** tout à fait éliminé. | *It's not likely that sexism will be (is) totally eliminated.* |
| **Il se peut que** d'autres pays **possèdent** des armes nucléaires. | *It's possible that other countries possess nuclear weapons.* |

**Grammaire interactive**

For more on the subjunctive with **il faut,** watch the corresponding Grammar Tutorial and take a brief practice quiz at **Connect French.**

**www.mhconnectfrench.com**

---

*The infinitive of the verb conjugated in the expression **il faut que** is **falloir** (*to be necessary*). The infinitive of the verb in **il vaut mieux que** is **valoir** (*to be worth*).
†Although **il est peu probable que** takes the subjunctive because it conveys a lack of certainty, the expression **il est probable que** takes the indicative because it conveys probability or more certainty. For more information on this difference, see page 458.

Except for **il faut que, il vaut mieux que,** and **il semble que,** these impersonal expressions are usually limited to writing and formal discourse.

2. When no specific person or thing is mentioned, impersonal expressions are followed by the infinitive instead of the subjunctive. Compare the following sentences.

| | |
|---|---|
| Il vaut mieux **attendre.** | *It's better to wait.* |
| Il vaut mieux **que nous attendions.** | *It's better for us to wait.* |
| Il est important **de voter.** | *It's important to vote.* |
| Il est important **que vous votiez.** | *It's important for you to vote.* |

Note that the preposition **de** is used before the infinitive after impersonal expressions that contain **être.**

[Allez-y! B-C-D-E]

## *Allez-y!*

A. **À la table de négociations.** Faites des phrases pour exprimer des souhaits et des exigences.

> MODÈLE: les écologistes / vouloir / le gouvernement / contrôler les déchets industriels →
> Les écologistes veulent que le gouvernement contrôle les déchets industriels.

1. les hommes politiques / vouloir (*cond.*) / nous / payer plus d'impôts
2. les Verts / exiger / on / consommer moins d'essence
3. je / aimer (*cond.*) / tout le monde / faire du recyclage
4. vous / vouloir bien (*cond.*) / il y avoir moins de pollution atmosphérique
5. nous / vouloir / les richesses mondiales / être partagées

B. **Comment gagner?** Donnez des conseils à Jeanne Laviolette, candidate à la mairie de Dijon, en suivant le modèle.

> MODÈLE: Il est important de savoir écouter les gens. →
> Il est important que vous sachiez écouter les gens.

1. Pour être maire, il faut être dynamique et responsable.
2. Il est essentiel de ne pas avoir peur d'agir.
3. Il est nécessaire de rester calme en toutes circonstances.
4. Il est préférable de parler souvent aux électeurs.
5. Il faut faire attention aux problèmes des jeunes.
6. Il est indispensable de gagner la confiance des commerçants.

**C. La routine de tous les jours.** Posez des questions à un(e) camarade de classe. Suivez le modèle.

**MODÈLE:** nécessaire / faire la cuisine chaque soir
É1: Est-il nécessaire que tu fasses la cuisine chaque soir?
É2: Oui, il est nécessaire que je fasse la cuisine chaque soir. (Non, il n'est pas nécessaire que je fasse la cuisine chaque soir; mes copains m'aident souvent.)

1. vaut mieux / aller au cours de français tous les jours
2. préférable / faire ton lit chaque matin
3. faut / nettoyer ta chambre tous les jours
4. normal / pouvoir dormir tard le matin
5. indispensable / étudier chaque soir
6. important / lire le journal chaque jour

**D. Problèmes contemporains.** Discutez des problèmes suivants avec un(e) camarade. Suggérez des solutions en utilisant les expressions suivantes: **il est important que, il faut que, il est nécessaire que, il est indispensable que, il est essentiel que, il est préférable que.**

1. l'immigration clandestine dans votre pays
2. l'abus de la drogue chez les jeunes
3. la pollution
4. le chômage
5. le gaspillage des sources d'énergie
6. la violence dans votre pays
7. le terrorisme
8. l'intégrisme

**E. Nécessités et probabilités.** Quelle sera votre vie? Répondez aux questions suivantes. Dans chaque réponse, utilisez une de ces expressions: **il se peut que, il est peu probable que, il est impossible que, il est possible que, il est essentiel que, il faut que, il est nécessaire que.**

**MODÈLE:** Ferez-vous une découverte (*discovery*) importante? →
Il est peu probable que je fasse une découverte importante.

1. Vous marierez-vous?
2. Apprendrez-vous une langue étrangère?
3. Voyagerez-vous beaucoup?
4. Deviendrez-vous célèbre?
5. Serez-vous riche?
6. Saurez-vous jouer du piano?
7. Écrirez-vous un roman?
8. Ferez-vous la connaissance d'un homme / d'une femme d'état?
9. Irez-vous en Chine?
10. Vivrez-vous jusqu'à l'âge de cent ans?

Maintenant, utilisez ces questions pour interviewer un(e) camarade de classe.

**MODÈLE:** É1: Feras-tu une découverte importante?
É2: Oui, il est possible que je fasse une découverte importante. (Non, il est peu probable que je fasse une découverte importante.)

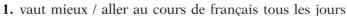

**le parler jeune**

| furax | furieux |
| **le hic** | le problème |
| kif-kif | équivalent |
| **ne pas mâcher** | dire ce que |
| **ses mots** | l'on pense |
| **râler** | protester |

Le sondage révèle que les électeurs sont **furax** contre le gouvernement.

**Le hic,** c'est que les voitures électriques sont trop chères.

En réalité, la «droite» et la «gauche», c'est **kif-kif.**

Tu as entendu son discours sur les droits de l'homme? Il **n'a pas mâché ses mots!**

Arrête de **râler** tout le temps!

# Le blog d'Hector

## Moi d'abord?

lundi 13 juillet

Salut les amis!

Est-ce que nous sommes tous fous, vous, moi et nos hommes politiques?

J'ai 25 ans, et j'appartiens à la génération «Moi d'abord!»: Ce qui compte avant tout, c'est mon plaisir et comme tous les Français, je veux «profiter de la vie» surtout maintenant que je suis à la Martinique! Mais l'autre jour, j'ai vu une émission à la télé qui m'a fait froid dans le dos. C'était sur l'état du monde dans 50 ans. J'aurai 75 ans. Eh bien, savez-vous ce qui attend le «Senior» Hector?

Le tri sélectif[3]: une façon d'être un bon citoyen!

Il est certain que la terre aura épuisé la majeure partie de ses ressources naturelles en pétrole et en gaz. Il est probable que nos réserves d'eau seront très insuffisantes. Il est sûr que le réchauffement de la planète aura changé nos climats et notre géographie: les glaciers auront fondu,[1] Venise sera sous les eaux, il fera aussi chaud à Paris qu'au Sahara. Dans le monde, le choc des cultures et des religions aura provoqué des conflits apocalyptiques.

Alors, qu'est-ce qu'on fait? On réagit ou on danse sur le volcan? Dites-moi ce que vous pensez de tout ça: votre opinion m'intéresse!

Hector

. . . . . . . . . . . . . . . . . . . . . . . . . . . . . . . . . . . . . . . . . . . . . . . . . . . . . . . . . . . . . . . . . . . . . . . . . . . . . . . .

### COMMENTAIRES

**Alexis**

Il se peut que ces prévisions[2] soient complètement fausses! Dansons!

**Charlotte**

Il faut qu'on réagisse: je propose que chacun fasse attention à sa consommation d'eau et d'électricité. Il faut qu'on arrête de gaspiller l'essence et qu'on prenne les transports en commun. C'est ça être un bon citoyen.

**Poema**

Tu as raison, Charlotte! Exprimer publiquement son opinion, manifester, faire la grève pour soutenir les grandes causes internationales, c'est inutile. Il semble que nos hommes politiques soient incapables de prendre des décisions radicales. Nous devons nous engager individuellement pour sauver notre belle planète!

**Mamadou**

En France, nous avons plus de 1 000 associations engagées dans des actions en faveur de l'écologie du développement durable.

[1]*melted*   [2]*predictions*   [3]*tri… sorting of household trash (for recycling)*

## La France multiculturelle

Corneille est une star de la chanson française. Il est né au Rwanda. Grâce au chanteur algérien Cheb Khaled, le raï, musique populaire algérienne, a donné au public français le goût des sons et des rythmes orientaux. Dans des salles de spectacles archi-comble,[1] des humoristes de talent comme Gad El Maleh, Smaïn ou Jamel Debbouze font la satire de la société française. Au stade de France, Mapou Yangambiva, né en République centrafrique, ou Steve Mandanda, qui vient de la République démocratique du Congo, font la fierté[2] de l'équipe de France de football.

En littérature, Shan Sa, auteur de *La joueuse de go,* et Dai Sijie, qui a écrit *Balzac et la petite tailleuse chinoise*, sont devenus des écrivains célèbres. Nés en Chine, ils apportent à la littérature française une inspiration asiatique. Avant eux, le Russe Andreï Makine a donné à la littérature de l'Hexagone des œuvres de première qualité comme *Le Testament français* (1995).

Une amitié multiculturelle. Oui, la France multiculturelle est une réalité!

En hommage à la France, ces écrivains ont écrit leurs œuvres… en français. Mixité,[3] mélange, altérité,[4] diversité: tous ces termes nobles traduisent la réalité de la société française. Regardez les rues de Paris, de Lyon, de Marseille: on y rencontre toutes les nationalités, on y entend tous les accents. La rue française est algérienne, tunisienne, marocaine, turque, sénégalaise, ivoirienne, chinoise, vietnamienne, polonaise… La France multiculturelle existe: elle associe à ses traditions, des manières de penser, d'agir et de créer complètement nouvelles.

Mais elle veut, avant tout, que les immigrés qui ont choisi de vivre sur son territoire s'assimilent à la société française, seule garantie pour que les différentes communautés vivent en paix les unes avec les autres. Car il n'est pas toujours facile de vivre ensemble. Et il arrive que la diversité ethnique crée en France des tensions difficiles à gérer. Mais au pays des Droits de l'homme, il est important que le désir de s'unir pour un enrichissement mutuel soit plus fort que la tentation de l'exclusion. Et face aux problèmes du monde contemporain, n'est-il pas évident que l'on est plus forts si l'on est unis? C'est ce que pensent les sages…

[1]*full of people*   [2]*pride*   [3]*Mix of populations*   [4]*otherness*

1. Qu'est-ce que «la France multiculturelle»? Donnez une image globale de la société française à partir du **Reportage.**
2. Comment la France accueille-t-elle (*welcome*) les immigrés? Que demande-t-elle aux immigrés qui ont choisi de vivre en France?
3. Comment vivent les immigrés en Amérique du Nord? Gardent-ils les coutumes de leur pays d'origine? Citez quelques exemples.

1. Travaillez en petits groupes. Chacun à votre tour, citez, au choix, un personnage représentatif de la France ou de l'Amérique multiculturelle—un artiste, un chanteur, un musicien, un acteur, un sportif, un écrivain, un homme ou une femme politique. Précisez son domaine d'excellence.
2. D'après (*Based on*) cette liste, comment le multiculturalisme transforme-t-il une société? Discutez!

# Leçon 3

## Le subjonctif (*troisième partie*)

*Expressing Emotion*

### Le job de mes rêves

*Hassan, Hector, Juliette et Léa discutent au restaurant.*

HASSAN: Le chômage, c'est quand même[1] le problème essentiel de la société française. **Il est injuste que** nous **fassions** des études et **que** nous ne **trouvions** pas d'emploi!

HECTOR: Toi Hassan, tu as trouvé la solution: tu es ton propre patron.

HASSAN: Oui, et **je regrette que** la plupart des jeunes diplômés **veuillent** devenir fonctionnaires!

JULIETTE: L'époque est difficile! Moi, **je ne suis** pas **étonnée que** les jeunes **cherchent** un emploi stable et un salaire garanti.

HASSAN: Personnellement, j'ai l'âme[2] d'un entrepreneur! **Je suis heureux que** mon avenir ne **soit** pas dessiné à l'avance.

HECTOR: Tu es indépendant, travailleur, audacieux: c'est exactement le profil d'un créateur d'entreprise!

HASSAN: **Je suis content que** tu **penses** ça! **Et je regrette que** si peu de jeunes Français **prennent** des risques.

JULIETTE: Mais les jeunes ne refusent pas l'aventure! **Il est bizarre que** tu ne le **saches** pas! Par exemple, beaucoup partent à l'étranger. Moi-même, j'ai l'intention d'aller travailler en Australie!

LÉA: **Nous sommes tristes que** tu **partes,** Juliette… Dans les nouvelles technologies, tu pourrais aussi bien trouver un emploi en France…

JULIETTE: C'est sans[3] doute vrai, mais **il est bon que** les jeunes diplômés **jouent** la carte de l'international. Après tout, on est dans la mondialisation, non?

Le Pôle Emploi: un établissement public chargé de mettre en relation demandeurs et offreurs d'emplois

[1]quand… *even so, anyway*   [2]*soul*   [3]*without*

Complétez les phrases selon le dialogue.

1. Pour Hassan, il est injuste que les jeunes _____ des études et qu'ils ne _____ pas d'emploi.
2. Hassan regrette que la plupart des jeunes diplômés _____ devenir fonctionnaires.
3. Juliette n'est pas étonnée que les jeunes _____ un emploi dans la fonction publique.
4. Hassan est heureux que son avenir ne _____ pas dessiné à l'avance.
5. Il est content qu'Hector _____ qu'il a le profil d'un créateur d'entreprise. Et il regrette que peu de Français _____ des risques.
6. Juliette s'étonne qu'Hassan ne _____ pas que beaucoup de jeunes acceptent l'aventure.
7. Léa et ses amis sont tristes que Juliette _____.
8. Mais selon Juliette, il est bon qu'on _____ la carte de l'international.

**1.** The subjunctive is frequently used after expressions of emotion.

| EXPRESSIONS OF EMOTION |
| --- |
| *happiness:* **être content(e), être heureux / heureuse** |
| *regret:* **être désolé(e), être triste, regretter** (*to be sorry*) |
| *surprise:* **être surpris(e), être étonné(e)** |
| *fear:* **avoir peur** |
| *relief:* **être soulagé(e)** |
| *anger:* **être furieux / furieuse** |

| | |
| --- | --- |
| Le président **est content** que les électeurs **aient** confiance en lui. | *The president is pleased that the voters have confidence in him.* |
| Les électeurs **ont peur** que l'inflation **soit** un problème insoluble. | *The voters are afraid that inflation is an insurmountable problem.* |
| Les écologistes **sont furieux** que les lois contre la pollution des forêts et des rivières **soient** tellement faibles. | *The environmentalists are angry that the laws against polluting the forests and rivers are so weak.* |

**2.** As with verbs of volition, there must be different subjects in the main and dependent clauses. Otherwise, an infinitive is used.

| | |
| --- | --- |
| **Le président est content de rencontrer** le Premier ministre du Canada. | *The president is happy to meet the prime minister of Canada.* |

**3.** The subjunctive is also used following impersonal expressions of emotion.

| IMPERSONAL EXPRESSIONS OF EMOTION | |
| --- | --- |
| il est bizarre que | il est juste / injuste que |
| il est bon que* | il est stupide que* |
| il est dommage que (*it's too bad that*) | il est utile / inutile que |

| | |
| --- | --- |
| **Il est dommage que** la guerre y **continue.** | *It's too bad that war is continuing there.* |
| **Est-il bon que** les enfants aussi **expriment** leurs opinions? | *Is it good that children also express their opinions?* |
| **Il est stupide que** tant de citoyens ne **votent** pas. | *It is stupid that so many citizens do not vote.* |

*In everyday conversation, the French often say **c'est stupide que, c'est bon que,** and so on.

 *Allez-y!*

**A. Opinions.** Complétez chaque phrase de façon logique en mettant une des expressions en italique au subjonctif.

> **MODÈLE:** Nous sommes furieux / *les leaders politiques se sentent responsables face aux électeurs* / *la télévision n'analyse pas les problèmes actuels.* →
> Nous sommes furieux que la télévision n'analyse pas les problèmes actuels.

1. Je suis vraiment désolé(e) / *les grandes puissances mondiales ne sont pas d'accord sur la protection de l'environnement* / *le gouvernement prend des mesures pour encourager le développement de l'énergie solaire.*
2. Les gens ont peur / *les hommes politiques font de mauvais choix* / *les hommes politiques prennent de bonnes décisions.*
3. Je regrette / *il y a encore des dictateurs dans certains pays* / *on donne tant d'importance à la liberté dans ce pays.*
4. Mon amie Gaëlle est soulagée / *les Européens sont de plus en plus sensibles* (more and more sensitive) *aux questions liées à la protection de l'environnement* / *le taux de chômage en Europe est élevé cette année.*
5. Les sénateurs sont étonnés / *le public ne veut pas payer plus d'impôts* / *le public veut payer plus d'impôts.*

**B. Le journal.** Voici des titres (*headlines*) adaptés de divers journaux français. Donnez votre réaction à chaque situation en utilisant les expressions suivantes: **être content(e), heureux / heureuse, désolé(e), triste, surpris(e), étonné(e), soulagé(e), fâché(e), furieux / furieuse, regretter, avoir peur, il est stupide (bizarre, bon, dommage, juste, injuste, utile, inutile) que.**

> **MODÈLE:** Les femmes et les chômeurs fument davantage (*more*) →
> Il est dommage que les femmes et les chômeurs fument davantage.

1. **Le Club Méditerranée ouvre son premier village en Chine**
2. **L'Europe aime la France** (La majorité des Européens choisiraient la France comme terre d'accueil [*country where they would settle*].)
3. **Le froid tue** (*kills*) **5 sans-abri** (Des centres d'hébergement [*shelters*] exceptionnels ont ouvert leurs portes aux victimes du froid.)
4. **Les Français disent «non» à la drogue** (68 % des Français sont favorables au maintien de l'interdiction totale des ventes et de la consommation de drogues, selon un sondage.)
5. **L'industrie textile va supprimer** (*to eliminate*) **un emploi sur sept** (L'industrie textile a annoncé qu'elle comptait supprimer 750 emplois.)

**C. Émotions.** Donnez votre opinion personnelle sur les problèmes de la société américaine.

> **MODÈLE:** Je suis heureux / heureuse que... →
> Je suis heureux / heureuse que les États-Unis aident plusieurs pays en voie de développement (*developing*).

1. Je suis heureux / heureuse que…
2. Je regrette que…
3. Il est injuste que…
4. Il est bon que…
5. Il est bizarre que…
6. Il est stupide que…

**D. Encore des émotions.** Reprenez les *trois premières* phrases de l'exercice C. Maintenant demandez à cinq camarades comment ils/ elles ont complété ces phrases. Pouvez-vous trouver quelqu'un qui a les mêmes opinions que vous?

> **MODÈLE:** É1: Qu'est-ce qui te rend heureux/heureuse?
> É2: Je suis heureux/heureuse que le maire fasse quelque chose pour aider les sans-abri.

# Le subjonctif (*quatrième partie*)

*Expressing Doubt and Uncertainty*

## Parlons de la Francophonie

*Mamadou contacte Léa sur sa page Facebook (Messagerie instantanée).*

MAMADOU: **Crois-tu que** la Francophonie **ait** un bel avenir?

LÉA: J'en suis sûre; elle est si belle la langue française!

MAMADOU: Je ne suis pas aussi optimiste que toi. Avec la mondialisation, on uniformise tout: on parle anglais partout!

LÉA: **Je ne pense pas que** tout le monde **veuille** ressembler à tout le monde… La Francophonie, c'est un refus d'uniformiser la planète.

MAMADOU: **Je ne suis pas certain que** les 220 millions de Francophones **tiennent à**[1] être différents du reste du monde. Ils parlent français sans se poser des questions, tout simplement parce que c'est la langue de leur pays.

LÉA: Tu as tort! La Francophonie, c'est bien plus qu'un idiome[2] commun: c'est une culture, c'est un idéal, c'est une passion!

[1]tiennent… *are keen about*   [2]*langue*

Trouvez, dans le dialogue, les phrases équivalentes.

1. Mamadou demande si la Francophonie a un bel avenir.
2. Léa pense que les gens veulent être différents les uns des autres.
3. Selon Mamadou, les Francophones ne sont pas attachés à leur singularité.

1. The subjunctive is used—with a change of subject—after expressions of doubt and uncertainty, such as **je doute, je ne suis pas sûr(e),** and **je ne suis pas certain(e).**

Beaucoup de femmes **ne sont pas sûres** que leur statut **soit** égal au statut des hommes.

*Many women aren't sure that their status is equal to the status of men.*

Les jeunes **doutent** souvent que les hommes et les femmes politiques **soient** honnêtes.

*Young people often doubt that politicians are honest.*

2. In the affirmative, verbs such as **penser** and **croire** are followed by the indicative. In the negative and interrogative, they express a degree of doubt and uncertainty and can then be followed by the subjunctive. In spoken French, however, the indicative is more commonly used.

Je **pense** que la presse **est** libre.

*I think the press is free.*

**Pensez**-vous que la presse **soit** libre?
**Pensez**-vous que la presse **est** libre?

*Do you think the press is free?*

Je **ne crois pas** que la démocratie **soit** en danger.
Je **ne crois pas** que la démocratie **est** en danger.

*I don't think that democracy is in danger.*

3. The following impersonal expressions are followed by the *indicative* because they imply certainty or probability.*

| IMPERSONAL EXPRESSIONS USED WITH THE INDICATIVE | |
|---|---|
| il est certain que | il est probable que |
| il est clair que | il est sûr que |
| il est évident que | il est vrai que |

**Il est probable que** l'Europe et les États-Unis **feront** plus d'échanges culturels et commerciaux.

*It's probable that Europe and the U.S. will engage in more cultural and commercial exchanges.*

**Il est vrai que** les Québécois **veulent** préserver leur propre identité.

*It's true that the Quebecois want to preserve their own identity.*

---

*In everyday conversation, you will often hear **c'est,** rather than **il est,** with these expressions.

## Allez-y!

**A. Réflexions sur l'Afrique francophone.** Complétez les phrases avec le subjonctif ou l'indicatif des verbes, selon le cas.

1. Il est sûr que le Burkina Faso _____ (être) un pays très, très pauvre.
2. Pensez-vous que le Mali _____ (être) un pays où l'intervention militaire est justifiée?
3. Les observateurs diplomatiques ne croient pas que l'assistance étrangère _____ (pouvoir) améliorer la crise économique et sociale de l'Afrique centrale.
4. On ne doute pas que les Sénégalais _____ (vouloir) multiplier les échanges commerciaux avec les pays voisins.
5. Il est évident que la République de Guinée _____ (avoir) des ressources minières importantes.
6. Je ne crois pas que les autres nations _____ (devoir) intervenir dans les affaires africaines.

**B. Discussion.** Avec un(e) camarade, discutez des idées suivantes. Choisissez une phrase et posez une question. Votre camarade répond selon sa conviction.

MODÈLE: L'homme politique est honnête. →
    É1: Crois-tu que l'homme politique soit honnête?
    É2: Oui, je crois qu'il est honnête. (Non, je ne crois pas qu'il soit honnête.)

Idées à discuter:

1. Nous avons besoin d'une armée plus moderne.
2. Les citoyens de ce pays savent voter intelligemment.
3. Le gouverneur de votre état/province a de bonnes idées.
4. On doit limiter l'immigration dans ce pays.
5. L'enseignement bilingue est une bonne idée.

**C. Opinions et croyances.** Complétez les phrases de façon logique. Exprimez une opinion personnelle.

**Vocabulaire utile:** le covoiturage, les droits civils, la guerre, les impôts, le recyclage, les sans-abris

MODÈLE: Je ne pense pas que... →
    Je ne pense pas que les jeunes soient informés sur la contraception.

1. C'est vrai que... 2. Personne ne croit que... 3. Je ne suis pas sûr(e) que... 4. Il est probable que... 5. Beaucoup d'étudiants trouvent que...

---

## Mots clés

### Éviter l'emploi du subjonctif

**Espérer,** followed by the indicative, can be used instead of **souhaiter** and other constructions that require the subjunctive.

    J'**espère** qu'il gagnera les élections.

**Devoir** + infinitive can sometimes be used instead of **il faut que** and **il est nécessaire que.**

    Tu **dois** afficher les prospectus.

In general statements, the infinitive can replace the subjunctive.

    Il faut que nous contrôlions les déchets industriels.

    Il faut **contrôler** les déchets industriels.

Prononcez bien!

**The subjunctive of *aller* and *avoir***   (page 445)

**A.** **Cet après-midi.** Hugo et Isabelle discutent de leurs projets pour l'après-midi. Écoutez leur conversation et indiquez si les verbes au subjonctif sont une forme du verbe **aller** ou du verbe **avoir**.

1. **a.** ☐ aille       **b.** ☐ aie
2. **a.** ☐ ailles       **b.** ☐ aies
3. **a.** ☐ ailles       **b.** ☐ aies
4. **a.** ☐ allions       **b.** ☐ ayons
5. **a.** ☐ alliez       **b.** ☐ ayez

**B.** **Ce soir.** Hugo veut aussi faire des projets pour la soirée. D'abord, complétez les phrases avec la forme appropriée des verbes **aller** et **avoir** au subjonctif. Ensuite, avec votre camarade, lisez la conversation à voix haute, en faisant bien attention à la prononciation de ces verbes.

HUGO: Est-ce que ton frère et toi, vous allez dîner ici ce soir?

ISABELLE: Oui, si tu veux bien.

HUGO: Bien sûr! Mais j'aimerais que vous _____¹ au supermarché pour acheter de la salade. Nous n'en avons plus.

ISABELLE: Pas de problème! Ce serait bien qu'ils _____² de la romaine. C'est ma salade préférée.

HUGO: D'accord. Je préfère que vous _____³ ce que vous aimez!

ISABELLE: Hmmm, finalement, je pense que ce serait mieux que nous _____⁴ à l'épicerie: elle est sur notre chemin.

HUGO: Comme vous voulez. À tout à l'heure!

 ## Lecture

### Avant de lire

**Inferring an author's point of view.** Approximately 8% of the French population is composed of immigrants, chiefly from former French colonies in North and West Africa, as well as Spain, Portugal, and Eastern European countries. These immigrants came to France to seek greater economic opportunities and social freedoms. However, immigrants have not been universally welcomed. Some of the French have associated immigration with increased violence and crime and with a disruption of the French way of life.

You will be reading an excerpt from the novel *La Réclusion solitaire*, written in 1976 by the Moroccan novelist and poet Tahar Ben Jelloun (1944– ). In this work, Ben Jelloun draws on his personal experience to describe the sometimes difficult conditions Arabs experience in French society. The narrator, a North African worker, lives in a room with three others. In this excerpt, he describes some of the arbitrary and discriminatory rules imposed upon the residents.

Examine carefully the wording of these rules, as illustrated in the following examples. Which words and structures are repeated?

Il est interdit de faire son manger dans la chambre…
Il est interdit de recevoir des femmes; […]

The repetition of the impersonal expression **Il est interdit de** followed by the infinitive is an example of parallelism.

Now compare the following two rules. You will note that although they are parallel in structure, they do not express parallel ideas. (In what ways are the ideas dissimilar?)

Il est interdit d'écouter la radio à partir de neuf heures.
Il est interdit de vous peindre en bleu, en vert ou en mauve.

In the first case, the restriction is of a realistic nature, a rule one might find in places such as workers' housing. In the second, the rule is absurd, a behavior that would never occur and consequently expresses a useless regulation.

As you read the text, pay particular attention to the nature of the behavior forbidden by the repeated formula **Il est interdit de.** Which rules are plausible? Which seem ridiculous? Which criticize the behaviors of immigrants? Which express hostility toward the presence of immigrants in French society?

**PERSPECTIVES**

**À propos de la lecture...**
Cet extrait est tiré du roman *La Réclusion solitaire* de Tahar Ben Jelloun.

# *La Réclusion solitaire* (extrait) de Tahar Ben Jelloun

À l'entrée du bâtiment, on nous a donné le règlement:
—Il est interdit de faire son manger dans la chambre (il y a une cuisine au fond du couloir);

—Il est interdit de recevoir des femmes;...

—Il est interdit d'écouter la radio à partir de neuf heures;

—Il est interdit de chanter le soir, surtout en arabe ou en kabyle;[1]

—Il est interdit d'égorger[2] un mouton dans le bâtiment;...

—Il est interdit de faire du yoga dans les couloirs;

—Il est interdit de repeindre les murs, de toucher aux meubles, de casser les vitres,[3] de changer d'ampoule,[4] de tomber malade, d'avoir la diarrhée, de faire de la politique, d'oublier d'aller au travail, de penser à faire venir sa famille,... de sortir en pyjama dans la rue, de vous plaindre[5] des conditions objectives et subjectives de vie,... de lire ou d'écrire des injures[6] sur les murs, de vous disputer, de vous battre,[7] de manier[8] le couteau, de vous venger.

—Il est interdit de mourir dans cette chambre, dans l'enceinte de[9] ce bâtiment (allez mourir ailleurs: chez vous, par exemple, c'est plus commode);

—Il est interdit de vous suicider (même si on vous enferme à Fleury-Mérogis[10]): votre religion vous l'interdit, nous aussi;

—Il est interdit de monter dans les arbres;

—Il est interdit de vous peindre en bleu, en vert ou en mauve;

—Il est interdit de circuler en bicyclette dans la chambre, de jouer aux cartes, de boire du vin (pas de champagne);

—Il est aussi interdit de... prendre un autre chemin pour rentrer du boulot. Vous êtes avertis. Nous vous conseillons de suivre le règlement, sinon,... ce sera le séjour dans un camp d'internement en attendant votre rapatriement.

Tahar Ben Jelloun

[1]*language spoken in Kabylia, a rugged mountain region in northeastern Algeria*  [2]*slit the throat of*
[3]*windows*  [4]*lightbulb*  [5]*vous... complain*  [6]*insults*  [7]*vous... fight*  [8]*wield*  [9]*dans... within the boundary of*
[10]*prison près de Paris*

*Compréhension*

**Classez.** Choisissez sept des règles énumérées dans le texte. Ensuite, classez-les en utilisant les catégories suivantes.

C'est une règle...

- qui convient à la situation.
- qui exprime le racisme.
- qui semble critiquer des pratiques musulmanes.
- ridicule.
- qui exprime de l'hostilité envers la présence maghrébine.
- qui suggère que les Maghrébins sont impliqués dans la criminalité.

 Écriture

The writing activities **Par écrit** and **Journal intime** can be found in the Workbook/Laboratory Manual to accompany *Vis-à-vis*.

# *Pour s'amuser*

Quelques mots sur les hommes politiques:

«Le mois de l'année où le politicien dit le moins de conneries (*stupid things, tr. fam.*), c'est le mois de février, parce qu'il n'y a que vingt-huit jours.»
—Coluche

«En politique, on succède à des imbéciles et on est remplacé par des incapables.»

—Georges Clémenceau

# Le vidéoblog d'Hector

Une belle plage martiniquaise

## En bref

Dans cet épisode, Léa, Juliette, et Hassan discutent de la protection de l'environnement. À la fin de leur conversation, ils regardent le blog d'Hector sur la Martinique.

## Vocabulaire en contexte

Indiquez ce que vous faites ou ce que vous avez fait pour protéger l'environnement.

### Comment protéger l'environnement

☐ **créer** un groupe ou organiser une journée «environnement»
☐ écrire aux sénateurs/députés de votre état pour **lutter** (*fight*) contre **la pollution**
☐ faire du bénévolat (*volunteer*) pendant une journée «Plages **propres** (*clean*)»
☐ participer à une manifestation contre la pollution

☐ participer à la **Journée mondiale de la biodiversité**
☐ imprimer vos dissertations des deux côtés d'une feuille de papier
☐ prendre des douches rapides pour économiser l'eau
☐ recycler vos bouteilles, vos boîtes, le papier, le plastique, et cetera
☐ réduire vos déchets
☐ rouler à vélo ou aller à pied pour économiser l'essence

## Visionnez!

Quel personnage dans la vidéo dirait les phrases suivantes?

|  | Léa | Hassan | Juliette | Hector |
|---|---|---|---|---|
| 1. «Il est préférable de rouler à vélo.» | ☐ | ☐ | ☐ | ☐ |
| 2. «Il est essentiel de prendre des douches très rapides.» | ☐ | ☐ | ☐ | ☐ |
| 3. «Il vaut mieux recycler le verre et le papier.» | ☐ | ☐ | ☐ | ☐ |
| 4. «Il est important de nettoyer (*clean*) nos plages.» | ☐ | ☐ | ☐ | ☐ |
| 5. «Il faut lutter contre la pollution de l'eau.» | ☐ | ☐ | ☐ | ☐ |

## Analysez!

1. Des quatre camarades, quelle est la personne la plus «verte»? Expliquez.

2. Hector est très engagé dans la protection de la nature. Qu'est-ce qu'il fait personnellement? Imaginez pourquoi.

## Comparez!

Qu'est-ce qu'on fait dans votre pays pour protéger l'environnement? Y a-t-il des endroits qui ont particulièrement besoin d'être protégés? Quelles actions ont été organisées? Est-ce que vous êtes plus (ou moins) «vert(e)» que les quatre blogueurs? Expliquez.

## Note culturelle

En 1971, la France a créé[1] un Ministère de l'environnement. Il est devenu le Ministère de l'Écologie, du Développement durable et de l'Énergie. Ses principaux objectifs sont les suivants: la lutte contre le changement climatique; la préservation de la biodiversité, de l'environnement et des ressources; la cohésion sociale et la solidarité entre territoires et entre générations; les modes de production et de consommation[2] responsables. Initiée par Jacques Chirac, la «Charte de l'environnement» est, en France, un texte à valeur constitutionnelle stipulant le droit[3] de chacun à vivre dans un environnement favorable.

[1]*created*  [2]*consumption*  [3]*right*

# Vocabulaire

## Verbes

**abolir** to abolish
**augmenter** to raise, increase
**conserver** to conserve
**consommer** to consume
**contrôler** to inspect, monitor
**développer** to develop
**diminuer** to lower, reduce, diminish
**douter** to doubt
**élire** to elect
**embaucher** to hire
**s'engager (dans)** to get involved (in) (*a public issue, cause*)
**épuiser** to use up, exhaust
**estimer** to consider; to believe; to estimate
**établir** to establish
**exiger** to require; to demand; to necessitate
**exprimer une opinion** to express an opinion
**faire grève** to strike
**gaspiller** to waste
**manifester (pour/contre)** to demonstrate (for/against)
**paraître** to appear
**polluer** to pollute
**poser sa candidature** to run for elected office; to apply (*for a job*)
**protéger** to protect
**reconnaître** to recognize
**recycler** to recycle
**regretter** to regret, be sorry
**sauver** to save, rescue
**souhaiter** to wish, desire
**soutenir** to support
**tenir à** to be keen about
**valoir** to be worth

## Substantifs

**le bien commun** the common good
**la centrale nucléaire** nuclear power plant
**le citoyen / la citoyenne** citizen
**le covoiturage** carpooling
**les déchets** (*m. pl.*) waste (*material*)

**le défi** challenge
**les droits** (*m.*) **civils** civil rights
**l'écologiste** (*m., f.*) environmentalist
**l'électeur / l'électrice** voter
**le gaspillage** wasting
**la grève** strike
**la guerre** war
**l'homme / la femme politique** politician
**les idées** (*f.*) **extrémistes** extremist ideas
**les impôts** (*m. pl.*) taxes
**l'intégrisme** fundamentalism
**la mondialisation** globalization
**le niveau de vie** standard of living
**le parti** political party
**la politique** politics; policy
**le pouvoir d'achat** purchasing power
**le réchauffement de la planète** global warming
**le recyclage** recycling
**la retraite** pension
**la réussite** success
**le/la sans-abri** homeless person
**le sondage** survey
**la surpopulation** overpopulation
**une voiture hybride** hybrid car

À REVOIR: **la banlieue, l'essence**

## Substantifs apparentés

**l'accident** (*m.*), **l'atmosphère** (*f.*), **le budget (militaire), le développement, l'élection** (*f.*), **l'énergie** (*f.*) **nucléaire / solaire, l'environnement** (*m.*), **le gouvernement, l'inflation** (*f.*), **la légalisation, la liberté d'expression, les médias** (*m.*), **la nature, l'opinion** (*f.*) **publique, la pollution, le problème, le progrès, la prolifération, la protection, la réduction, la réforme, les ressources naturelles, le rythme, la sécurité, le sexisme, la solitude, la source, le terrorisme**

## Adjectifs

**désolé(e)** sorry
**égal(e)** equal
**étonné(e)** surprised
**fâché(e)** angry
**furieux / furieuse** furious
**grave** serious
**industriel(le)** industrial
**préoccupé(e)** preoccupied
**soulagé(e)** relieved
**sûr(e)** sure, certain
**surpris(e)** surprised

## Expressions impersonnelles

**il est...** it is . . .
**il est vrai que...** it's true that . . .
**dommage** too bad
**étrange** strange
**fâcheux** unfortunate
**(in)utile** useless / useful
**il se peut que...** it is possible that . . .
**il semble que...** it seems that . . .
**il vaut mieux (que)...** it is better (that) . . .

## Expressions impersonnelles apparentées

**il est... certain, clair, essentiel, évident, important, (im)possible, indispensable, (in)juste, nécessaire, normal, peu probable, préférable, probable, stupide, sûr, urgent**

## Mots et expressions divers

**j'ai entendu dire que...** I heard that . . .
**par exemple** for example
**personnellement** personally
**pour ma part** in my opinion, as for me
**quand même** even so, anyway
**sans doute** without a doubt

# Bienvenue...

## Un coup d'œil sur Papeete, en Polynésie française

La Polynésie, composée de 118 îles et atolls au cœur de l'océan Pacifique, devient une colonie de la France en 1880 et un «Territoire d'Outre-mer» en 1946, ce qui lui donne plus d'indépendance. En 2004, elle devient encore plus autonome. Elle est maintenant un «Pays d'Outre-mer au sein de[1] la République» et se gouverne librement et démocratiquement.

Papeete est la capitale de Tahiti, la plus grande île de la Polynésie. C'est aussi le centre économique de l'île. Malgré d'importants problèmes de pollution, Papeete est une ville agréable à vivre. Le marché de Papeete est un endroit animé et authentique: on peut y trouver de la nourriture, des fleurs, de l'artisanat,[2] des tissus,[3] et même des tatoueurs[4] qui exercent leur art dans des petits studios. Les grandes festivités du *Heiva i Tahiti* (Jeux de Tahiti) ont lieu en juillet. Les compétitions sportives, les chants, les danses polynésiennes et la foire[5] artisanale attirent[6] un grand nombre d'habitants des différentes îles de la Polynésie française. Un événement annuel à ne pas manquer!

La ville de Papeete

[1]au... *within*  [2]*crafts*  [3]*fabrics*  [4]*tattooers*  [5]*fair*  [6]*attract*

## PORTRAIT **Pouvanaa a Oopa (1895–1977)**

Né en 1895 en Polynésie, Pouvanaa a Oopa participe à la Première Guerre mondiale aux côtés de la France et joue un rôle important dans le ralliement[1] de la Polynésie à la France libre en 1940. Mais il accuse vite l'Administration française de ne pas respecter les droits des Polynésiens. Il consacre alors le reste de sa vie à lutter en faveur de l'autonomie du territoire polynésien.

Élu député en 1949, il encourage le «Non» lors du[2] référendum de 1958 sur l'attachement de la Polynésie à la France, mais la population vote «Oui». Peu après, il est accusé d'avoir ordonné un incendie[3] à Papeete. Rien n'est prouvé, mais il est condamné à l'exil jusqu'en 1968. Il devient sénateur en 1971 et continue à proclamer son innocence pour les faits de 1958. Pouvanaa meurt avant que la France n'accorde[4] le statut d'autonomie de gestion[5] à la Polynésie française le 12 juillet 1977. Considéré comme le «Metua», ou «Père» des Polynésiens, il reste aujourd'hui encore un symbole du nationalisme polynésien.

Une statue de Pouvanaa a Oopa à Papeete

[1]*uniting*  [2]lors... *at the time of the*  [3]*fire*  [4]avant... *before France granted*  [5]autonomie... *self-government*

## Un coup d'œil sur Fort-de-France, à la Martinique

**LA MARTINIQUE**
Fort-de-France ★

Tournée vers[1] la mer des Caraïbes, Fort-de-France est la capitale de «l'île aux Fleurs» découverte par Christophe Colomb en 1502. C'est un port où font escale[2] les bateaux de croisière[3] venus d'Amérique et d'Europe. La Martinique est un département français depuis 1946. Le souffle bienfaisant[4] des vents alizés[5] vous accueille pour une visite du centre-ville, avec le marché aux poissons près du canal Levassor, la bibliothèque Schœlcher (du nom de l'abolitionniste du XIXe siècle) dans la rue de la Liberté et la Cathédrale Saint-Louis dans la rue Schœlcher. Ces deux bâtiments sont construits en fer et en acier,[6] comme la tour Eiffel à Paris!

La bibliothèque Schœlcher à Fort-de-France

Ici le créole est la langue maternelle et tout le monde apprend le français à l'école, même les Békés. Les Békés, qui sont les descendants blancs des premiers colons français, contrôlent à peu près toute l'économie de l'île. Ils possèdent plus de 50 % des richesses de l'île et sont les propriétaires des plantations de canne à sucre, qu'on appelle des «habitations». Mais la vraie richesse de la Martinique vient de sa culture ainsi que[7] de ses femmes et de ses hommes qui forment une société solidaire.

[1]Tournée... *Facing*  [2]font... *stop over*  [3]bateaux... *cruise ships*  [4]souffle... *refreshing breath*
[5]vents... *trade winds*  [6]*steel*  [7]ainsi... *as well as*

## PORTRAIT Aimé Césaire (1913–2008)

Poète et homme politique (Maire de Fort-de-France pendant cinquante ans), il personnifie la théorie de la «négritude».* La littérature mondiale lui doit des œuvres majeures comme *Cahier d'un retour au pays natal*, écrit après sa rencontre avec Léopold Sédar Senghor,[†] et *La Tragédie du roi Christophe*, sur les difficultés de la libération psychologique des anciens esclaves devenus maîtres[1] d'Haïti.

[1]*masters*

 Watch the *Bienvenue dans les îles francophones* video segments to learn more about Fort-de-France and Papeete.

Aimé Césaire

*Négritude* was the movement to restore the cultural identity of Africans around the world by rejecting European values and affirming the history and personality of African peoples.
[†]Léopold Senghor (1906–2001): poet and founding president of Senegal who was an early leader of the Black consciousness movement and who coined the term *négritude*.

# Appendix A

## Glossary of Grammatical Terms

**ACCORD** (*m.*) (*AGREEMENT*) There is agreement when a word takes the gender and the number of another word it modifies. Articles and adjectives agree with the noun they modify, as do past participles of verbs conjugated with **être**.

C'est **une femme indépendante.**
*She is an independent woman.*
**Elles sont arrivées** à temps.
*They arrived in time.*

---

**ADJECTIF** (*m.*) (*ADJECTIVE*) A word that describes a noun or a pronoun. It agrees in number and gender with the word it modifies.

**Adjectif démonstratif** (*Demonstrative adjective*) An adjective that points out a particular noun.

**ce** garçon, **ces** livres
*this* boy, *these* books

**Adjectif interrogatif** (*Interrogative adjective*) An adjective used to form questions.

**Quelles** affiches cherchez-vous?
*What posters are you looking for?*
**Quel** livre?
*Which book?*

**Adjectif possessif** (*Possessive adjective*) An adjective that indicates possession or a special relationship.

**leur** voiture, **ma** sœur
*their car, my sister*

**Adjectif qualificatif** (*Descriptive adjective*) An adjective that specifies size, color, or other qualities.

Elles sont **intelligentes.**
*They are smart.*
C'est une **grande** maison.
*It's a big house.*

---

**ADVERBE** (*m.*) (*ADVERB*) A word that describes an adjective, a verb, or another adverb.

Il écrit **très bien.** Elle est **plus** efficace.
*He writes very well. She is more efficient.*

**Adverbe interrogatif** (*Interrogative adverb*) An adverb that introduces a question about time, place, manner, or quantity (amount).

**Combien** ça coûte?
*How much is it?*
**Quand** est-ce que vous partez?
*When are you leaving?*

---

**ANTÉCÉDENT** (*m.*) A word, usually a noun, that is replaced by a pronoun in the same or a subsequent sentence. In the example, **Manon** is the antecedent of **elle,** and **un gant** is the antecedent of **le.**

**Manon** a perdu **un gant** et **elle** ne **le** retrouve plus.
*Manon lost a glove, and she can't find it anymore.*

| | |
|---|---|
| **ARTICLE** (*m.*) A determiner that sets off a noun. | |
| **Article défini** (*Definite article*) An article that indicates a specific noun. | **le** pays, **la** chaise, **les** femmes<br>*the country, the chair, the women* |
| **Article indéfini** (*Indefinite article*) An article that indicates an unspecified noun. | **un** garçon, **une** ville, **des** carottes<br>*a boy, a city, some carrots* |
| **Article partitif** (*Partitive article*) In French, an article that denotes part of a whole. *Some* is not always expressed in English, but the partitive is almost always expressed in French. | **du** chocolat, **de la** tarte, **de l'**eau<br>(***some***) *chocolat,* (***some***) *pie,* (***some***) *water* |
| **COMPARATIF** (*m.*) (*COMPARATIVE*) The form of adjectives and adverbs used to compare two nouns or actions. | Léa est **moins** bavarde **que** Julien.<br>*Léa is **less** talkative **than** Julien.*<br>Elle court **plus** vite **que** lui.<br>*She runs **faster than** he does.* |
| **CONDITIONNEL** (*m.*) (*CONDITIONAL*) | *See* **Mode.** |
| **CONJUGAISON** (*f.*) (*CONJUGATION*) The different forms of a verb for a particular tense or mood. A present indicative conjugation: | je parle        *I speak*<br>tu parles      *you speak*<br>il/elle/on parle   *he/she/it/one speaks*<br>nous parlons    *we speak*<br>vous parlez     *you speak*<br>ils/elles parlent   *they speak* |
| **CONJONCTION** (*f.*) (*CONJUNCTION*) An expression that connects words, phrases, or clauses. | Christophe **et** Diane<br>*Christophe **and** Diane*<br>Il fait froid, **mais** il fait beau.<br>*It's cold, **but** nice.* |
| **CONTRACTION** (*f.*) (*CONTRACTION*) Two words combine to form one. In French, this phenomenon happens with **à** and **de** combined with the definite articles **le** or **les**. | Ils parlent **aux** étudiants.<br>*He's talking to the students.*<br>C'est le livre **du** professeur.<br>*It's the teacher's book.* |
| **ÉLISION** (*f.*) (*ELISION*) The replacement of the final vowel of a word by an apostrophe before the initial vowel or vowel sound of the following word. | Il arrive à **l'**université à 8 h.<br>*He arrives at the university at 8:00.*<br>J'ai compris **qu'**il reviendrait.<br>*I understood that he would come back.* |
| **GENRE** (*m.*) (*GENDER*) A grammatical category of words. In French, there are two genders: feminine and masculine. Gender applies to nouns, articles, adjectives, and pronouns. |               masc.     fem.<br>articles and nouns   **le** film     **la** vidéo<br>adjectives         **lent, beau**   **lente, belle**<br>pronouns         **il, celui**    **elle, celle** |

| | |
|---|---|
| **IMPARFAIT** (*m.*) (*IMPERFECT*) In French, a verb tense that expresses a past action with no specific beginning or end. | Nous **nagions** souvent. <br> *We **used to swim** often.* |
| **IMPÉRATIF** (*m.*) (*IMPERATIVE*) | *See* **Mode.** |
| **INDICATIF** (*m.*) (*INDICATIVE*) | *See* **Mode.** |
| **INFINITIF** (*m.*) (*INFINITIVE*) | *See* **Mode.** |
| **LIAISON** (*f.*) (*LIAISON*) A speech-sound redistribution in which an otherwise silent final consonant is articulated with the initial vowel or vowel sound of the following word. | C'est\_un\_animal. <br> [sɛtœ̃nanimal] <br> aux\_États-Unis <br> [ozetazyni] |
| **MODE** (*m.*) (*MOOD*) A set of categories for verbs indicating the attitude of the speaker toward what he or she is saying. | |
| **Mode conditionnel** (*Conditional mood*) A verb form conveying possibility. | J'**irais** si j'avais le temps. <br> *I **would go** if I had time.* |
| **Mode impératif** (*Imperative mood*) A verb form expressing a command. | **Allez**-y! <br> ***Go** ahead!* |
| **Mode indicatif** (*Indicative mood*) A verb form denoting actions or states considered facts. | Je **vais** à la bibliothèque. <br> *I **am going** to the library.* |
| **Mode infinitif** (*Infinitive mood*) A verb form introduced in English by *to*. In French dictionaries, this form appears as the main entry. | **jouer, vendre, venir** <br> ***to play, to sell, to come*** |
| **Mode subjonctif** (*Subjunctive mood*) A verb form, uncommon in English, used primarily in subordinate clauses after expressions of desire, doubt, or emotion. French constructions with the subjunctive have many possible English equivalents. | Je veux que vous y **alliez**. <br> *I want you to go there.* <br> J'ai peur qu'elle **dise** non. <br> *I'm afraid she will say no.* |
| **MOT APPARENTÉ** (*m.*) (*COGNATE*) In two languages, words spelled similarly with similar meaning. | **état, ordre, sérieux** <br> ***state, order, serious*** |
| **NOM** (*m.*) (*NOUN*) A word that denotes a person, place, thing, or idea. Proper nouns are capitalized names. | **avocat, journal, ville, Louise** <br> ***lawyer, newspaper, city, Louise*** |
| **NOMBRE** (*m.*) (*NUMBER*) A grammatical category of words. It indicates whether a noun, article, adjective, or pronoun is singular (**singulier**) or plural (**pluriel**). | singular: Le fromage est bon. <br> plural: Les fromages sont bons. |
| **Nombre cardinal** (*Cardinal number*) A number that expresses an amount. | **deux** bureaux, **quatre** ans <br> ***two** desks, **four** years* |
| **Nombre ordinal** (*Ordinal number*) A number that indicates position in a series. | le **deuxième** bureau, la **quatrième** année <br> *the **second** desk, the **fourth** year* |

| | |
|---|---|
| **PARTICIPE PASSÉ** (*m.*) (*PAST PARTICIPLE*) The form of a verb used in a compound tense (such as the **passé composé**) with forms of *to have* in English, and with **avoir** and **être** in French. | **mangé, fini, perdu**<br>*eaten, finished, lost* |
| **PASSÉ COMPOSÉ** (*m.*) In French, a verb tense that expresses a past action with a definite ending. It consists of the present indicative of the auxiliary verb (**avoir** or **être**) and the past participle of the conjugated verb. There are several equivalent forms in English. | **J'ai mangé**<br>*I ate, I did eat, I have eaten*<br>Elle **est tombée**<br>*She fell, she did fall, she has fallen* |

**PERSONNE** (*f.*) (*PERSON*) The form of a pronoun or a verb that indicates the person involved in an action.

| | singular | plural |
|---|---|---|
| 1st pers. | je / *I* | nous / *we* |
| 2nd pers. | tu / *you* | vous / *you* |
| 3rd pers. | il, elle, on / *he, she, one, it* | ils, elles / *they* |

| | |
|---|---|
| **PRÉPOSITION** (*f.*) (*PREPOSITION*) A word or phrase that specifies the relationship of a word (usually a noun or a pronoun) to another. The relationship is usually spatial or temporal. | **près de** l'aéroport, **avec** lui, **avant** 11 h<br>*near the airport, with him, before 11:00* |
| **PRONOM** (*m.*) (*PRONOUN*) A word used in place of one or more nouns. | |
| **Pronom accentué ou disjoint** (*Stressed or disjunctive pronoun*) In French, a pronoun used for emphasis or as the object of a preposition. | **Toi,** tu es incroyable!<br>*You are unbelievable!*<br>Je travaille avec **lui.**<br>*I work with **him.*** |
| **Pronom complément (d'objet)** (*Object pronoun*) A pronoun that replaces a direct object noun or an indirect object noun. | direct: Je vois Alain. Je **le** vois.<br>*I see Alain. I see **him.***<br>indirect: Je donne le livre à Daniel. Je **lui** donne le livre.<br>*I give the book to Daniel. I give **him** the book.* |
| **Pronom démonstratif** (*Demonstrative pronoun*) A pronoun that singles out a particular person or thing. | Voici deux livres: **celui-ci** est intéressant, mais **celui-là** est ennuyeux.<br>*Here are two books: **this one** is interesting, but **that one** is boring.* |
| **Pronom interrogatif** (*Interrogative pronoun*) A pronoun used to ask a question. | **Qui** parle? **Qu'est-ce que** vous voulez?<br>***Who** is speaking? **What** do you want?* |
| **Pronom réfléchi** (*Reflexive pronoun*) A pronoun that represents the same person as the subject of the verb. | Je **me** regarde dans le miroir.<br>*I am looking at **myself** in the mirror.* |
| **Pronom relatif** (*Relative pronoun*) A pronoun that introduces an independent clause and denotes a noun already mentioned. | On parle à la femme **qui** habite ici.<br>*We're talking to the woman **who** lives here.*<br>C'est le stylo **que** vous cherchez?<br>*Is it the pen (**that**) you're looking for?* |
| **Pronom sujet** (*Subject pronoun*) A pronoun representing the person or thing performing the action of the verb. | **Ils** travaillent bien ensemble.<br>***They** work well together.* |

| | |
|---|---|
| **PROPOSITION** (*f.*) (*CLAUSE*) A construction that contains a subject and a verb. | |
| **Proposition principale** (*Main clause*) A clause that stands on its own and expresses a complete idea. | **Je cherche la femme** qui joue au tennis. *I'm looking for the woman who plays tennis.* |
| **Proposition subordonnée** (*Subordinate clause*) A clause that cannot stand on its own because it does not express a complete idea. | Je cherche la femme **qui joue au tennis.** *I'm looking for the woman who plays tennis.* |
| **SUJET** (*m.*) (*SUBJECT*) The word(s) denoting the person, place, or thing performing an action or existing in a state. | **Mon ordinateur** est là-bas. *My computer is over there.* **Marc** arrive demain. *Marc arrives tomorrow.* |
| **SUBJONCTIF** (*m.*) (*SUBJUNCTIVE*) | *See* **Mode.** |
| **SUPERLATIF** (*m.*) (*SUPERLATIVE*) The form of adjectives or adverbs used to compare three or more nouns or actions. In English, the superlative is expressed by using *most* or *-est*. | Elle a choisi la robe **la plus** chère. *She chose the most expensive dress.* Béatrice court **le plus** vite. *Béatrice runs the fastest.* |
| **TEMPS** (*m.*) (*TENSE*) The form of a verb indicating time: present, past, or future. | |
| **VERBE** (*m.*) (*VERB*) A word that reports an action or state. | Elle **est arrivée** hier. *She arrived yesterday.* Elle **était** fatiguée. *She was tired.* |
| **Verbe auxiliaire** (*Auxiliary verb*) A verb used in conjunction with an infinitive or a participle to convey distinctions of tense and mood. In French, the main auxiliaries are **avoir** and **être.** | J'**ai** fait mes devoirs. *I did my homework.* Nous **sommes** allés au cinéma. *We went to the movies.* |
| **Verbe impersonnel** (*Impersonal verb*) Always accompanied by the impersonal pronoun **il,** impersonal verbs are divided into two categories: verbs reporting natural phenomena and verbs with special meaning. | **Il fait** beau aujourd'hui. *It is nice today.* **Il faut** travailler fort. *One has to work hard.* |
| **Verbe pronominal** (*Pronominal verb*) In French, a verb with a reflexive pronoun as well as a subject pronoun in its conjugated form. Its infinitive is preceded by **se.** | **se souvenir, je me souviens** *to remember, I remember* **Il se coupe** quand **il se rase.** *He cuts himself when he shaves (himself).* |

# Verb Charts

More complete verb charts that include the conjugations of the pluperfect and the past conditional are available at **Connect French** (**www.mhconnectfrench.com**). The formation of these tenses and other perfect tenses are explained in **Appendix C.**

## Verbes réguliers

### 1. chercher — cherchant

| | PRÉSENT | PASSÉ COMPOSÉ | IMPARFAIT | FUTUR | CONDITIONNEL | SUBJONCTIF | IMPÉRATIF |
|---|---|---|---|---|---|---|---|
| je / j' | cherche | ai cherché | cherchais | chercherai | chercherais | que je cherche | cherche |
| tu | cherches | as cherché | cherchais | chercheras | chercherais | que tu cherches | |
| il/elle/on | cherche | a cherché | cherchait | cherchera | chercherait | qu'il/elle/on cherche | |
| nous | cherchons | avons cherché | cherchions | chercherons | chercherions | que nous cherchions | cherchons |
| vous | cherchez | avez cherché | cherchiez | chercherez | chercheriez | que vous cherchiez | cherchez |
| ils/elles | cherchent | ont cherché | cherchaient | chercheront | chercheraient | qu'ils/elles cherchent | |

### 2. répondre — répondant

| | PRÉSENT | PASSÉ COMPOSÉ | IMPARFAIT | FUTUR | CONDITIONNEL | SUBJONCTIF | IMPÉRATIF |
|---|---|---|---|---|---|---|---|
| je / j' | réponds | ai répondu | répondais | répondrai | répondrais | que je réponde | réponds |
| tu | réponds | as répondu | répondais | répondras | répondrais | que tu répondes | |
| il/elle/on | répond | a répondu | répondait | répondra | répondrait | qu'il/elle/on réponde | |
| nous | répondons | avons répondu | répondions | répondrons | répondrions | que nous répondions | répondons |
| vous | répondez | avez répondu | répondiez | répondrez | répondriez | que vous répondiez | répondez |
| ils/elles | répondent | ont répondu | répondaient | répondront | répondraient | qu'ils/elles répondent | |

### 3. finir — finissant

| | PRÉSENT | PASSÉ COMPOSÉ | IMPARFAIT | FUTUR | CONDITIONNEL | SUBJONCTIF | IMPÉRATIF |
|---|---|---|---|---|---|---|---|
| je / j' | finis | ai fini | finissais | finirai | finirais | que je finisse | finis |
| tu | finis | as fini | finissais | finiras | finirais | que tu finisses | |
| il/elle/on | finit | a fini | finissait | finira | finirait | qu'il/elle/on finisse | |
| nous | finissons | avons fini | finissions | finirons | finirions | que nous finissions | finissons |
| vous | finissez | avez fini | finissiez | finirez | finiriez | que vous finissiez | finissez |
| ils/elles | finissent | ont fini | finissaient | finiront | finiraient | qu'ils/elles finissent | |

### 4. dormir* — dormant

| | PRÉSENT | PASSÉ COMPOSÉ | IMPARFAIT | FUTUR | CONDITIONNEL | SUBJONCTIF | IMPÉRATIF |
|---|---|---|---|---|---|---|---|
| je / j' | dors | ai dormi | dormais | dormirai | dormirais | que je dorme | dors |
| tu | dors | as dormi | dormais | dormiras | dormirais | que tu dormes | |
| il/elle/on | dort | a dormi | dormait | dormira | dormirait | qu'il/elle/on dorme | |
| nous | dormons | avons dormi | dormions | dormirons | dormirions | que nous dormions | dormons |
| vous | dormez | avez dormi | dormiez | dormirez | dormiriez | que vous dormiez | dormez |
| ils/elles | dorment | ont dormi | dormaient | dormiront | dormiraient | qu'ils/elles dorment | |

### 5. se laver† — (se) lavant

| | PRÉSENT | PASSÉ COMPOSÉ | IMPARFAIT | FUTUR | CONDITIONNEL | SUBJONCTIF | IMPÉRATIF |
|---|---|---|---|---|---|---|---|
| je | me lave | me suis lavé(e) | me lavais | me laverai | me laverais | que je me lave | lave-toi |
| tu | te laves | t'es lavé(e) | te lavais | te laveras | te laverais | que tu te laves | |
| il/elle/on | se lave | s'est lavé(e) | se lavait | se lavera | se laverait | qu'il/elle/on se lave | |
| nous | nous lavons | nous sommes lavé(e)s | nous lavions | nous laverons | nous laverions | que nous nous lavions | lavons-nous |
| vous | vous lavez | vous êtes lavé(e)(s) | vous laviez | vous laverez | vous laveriez | que vous vous laviez | lavez-vous |
| ils/elles | se lavent | se sont lavé(e)s | se lavaient | se laveront | se laveraient | qu'ils/elles se lavent | |

*Traditionally, only verbs ending in **-ir** like **finir** are considered one of the three regular verb groups. However, verbs like **dormir** also end in **-ir** and are conjugated following their own "regular" pattern, though they are many fewer in number than **-ir** verbs like **finir**. Verbs from this group include: **s'endormir, mentir, partir, sentir,** and **sortir.** Note that **s'endormir, partir,** and **sortir** are conjugated with **être** in the compound tenses.

†All pronominal verbs are conjugated with **être** in the compound tenses.

## Verbes réguliers avec changements orthographiques

| INFINITIF ET PARTICIPE PRÉSENT | PRÉSENT | | PASSÉ COMPOSÉ | IMPARFAIT | FUTUR | CONDITIONNEL | SUBJONCTIF | IMPÉRATIF | AUTRES VERBES |
|---|---|---|---|---|---|---|---|---|---|
| 1. **commencer** commençant | je commence<br>tu commences<br>il/elle/on commence | nous commençons<br>vous commencez<br>ils/elles commencent | j'ai commencé | je commençais<br>nous commencions | je commencerai | je commencerais | que je commence<br>que nous commencions | commence<br>commençons<br>commencez | divorcer, lancer, remplacer |
| 2. **manger** mangeant | je mange<br>tu manges<br>il/elle/on mange | nous mangeons<br>vous mangez<br>ils/elles mangent | j'ai mangé | je mangeais<br>nous mangions | je mangerai | je mangerais | que je mange<br>que nous mangions | mange<br>mangeons<br>mangez | changer, encourager, engager, exiger, mélanger, nager, partager, voyager |
| 3. **préférer** préférant | je préfère<br>tu préfères<br>il/elle/on préfère | nous préférons<br>vous préférez<br>ils/elles préfèrent | j'ai préféré | je préférais | je préférerai | je préférerais | que je préfère<br>que nous préférions | préfère<br>préférons<br>préférez | espérer, répéter, s'inquiéter, sécher |
| 4. **payer** payant | je paie<br>tu paies<br>il/elle/on paie | nous payons<br>vous payez<br>ils/elles paient | j'ai payé | je payais | je paierai | je paierais | que je paie<br>que nous payions | paie<br>payons<br>payez | employer, envoyer, essayer |
| 5. **appeler** appelant | j'appelle<br>tu appelles<br>il/elle/on appelle | nous appelons<br>vous appelez<br>ils/elles appellent | j'ai appelé | j'appelais | j'appellerai | j'appellerais | que j'appelle<br>que nous appelions | appelle<br>appelons<br>appelez | s'appeler, se rappeler |
| 6. **acheter** achetant | j'achète<br>tu achètes<br>il/elle/on achète | nous achetons<br>vous achetez<br>ils/elles achètent | j'ai acheté | j'achetais | j'achèterai | j'achèterais | que j'achète<br>que nous achetions | achète<br>achetons<br>achetez | se lever, se promener |

## Verbes irréguliers

| INFINITIF ET PARTICIPE PRÉSENT | PRÉSENT | | PASSÉ COMPOSÉ | IMPARFAIT | FUTUR | CONDITIONNEL | SUBJONCTIF | IMPÉRATIF | AUTRES VERBES |
|---|---|---|---|---|---|---|---|---|---|
| 1. **aller*** allant | je vais<br>tu vas<br>il/elle/on va | nous allons<br>vous allez<br>ils/elles vont | je suis allé(e) | j'allais | j'irai | j'irais | que j'aille<br>que nous allions | va<br>allons<br>allez | |
| 2. **avoir** ayant | j' ai<br>tu as<br>il/elle/on a | nous avons<br>vous avez<br>ils/elles ont | j'ai eu | j'avais | j'aurai | j'aurais | que j'aie<br>que nous ayons | aie<br>ayons<br>ayez | |
| 3. **boire** buvant | je bois<br>tu bois<br>il/elle/on boit | nous buvons<br>vous buvez<br>ils/elles boivent | j'ai bu | je buvais | je boirai | je boirais | que je boive<br>que nous buvions | bois<br>buvons<br>buvez | |
| 4. **conduire** conduisant | je conduis<br>tu conduis<br>il/elle/on conduit | nous conduisons<br>vous conduisez<br>ils/elles conduisent | j'ai conduit | je conduisais | je conduirai | je conduirais | que je conduise<br>que nous conduisions | conduis<br>conduisons<br>conduisez | construire, détruire, produire, réduire, traduire |
| 5. **connaître** connaissant | je connais<br>tu connais<br>il/elle/on connaît | nous connaissons<br>vous connaissez<br>ils/elles connaissent | j'ai connu | je connaissais | je connaîtrai | je connaîtrais | que je connaisse<br>que nous connaissions | connais<br>connaissons<br>connaissez | apparaître, disparaître, paraître, reconnaître |

*Verbs followed by an asterisk * are conjugated with **être** in the compound tenses.

# Verbes irréguliers

| INFINITIF ET PARTICIPE PRÉSENT | PRÉSENT | | PASSÉ COMPOSÉ | IMPARFAIT | FUTUR | CONDITIONNEL | SUBJONCTIF | IMPÉRATIF | AUTRES VERBES |
|---|---|---|---|---|---|---|---|---|---|
| 6. **croire** croyant | je crois / tu crois / il/elle/on croit | nous croyons / vous croyez / ils/elles croient | j'ai cru | je croyais | je croirai | je croirais | que je croie / que nous croyions | crois / croyons / croyez | |
| 7. **devoir** devant | je dois / tu dois / il/elle/on doit | nous devons / vous devez / ils/elles doivent | j'ai dû | je devais | je devrai | je devrais | que je doive / que nous devions | dois / devons / devez | |
| 8. **dire** disant | je dis / tu dis / il/elle/on dit | nous disons / vous dites / ils/elles disent | j'ai dit | je disais | je dirai | je dirais | que je dise / que nous disions | dis / disons / dites | |
| 9. **écrire** écrivant | j'écris / tu écris / il/elle/on écrit | nous écrivons / vous écrivez / ils/elles écrivent | j'ai écrit | j'écrivais | j'écrirai | j'écrirais | que j'écrive / que nous écrivions | écris / écrivons / écrivez | décrire |
| 10. **être** étant | je suis / tu es / il/elle/on est | nous sommes / vous êtes / ils/elles sont | j'ai été | j'étais | je serai | je serais | que je sois / que nous soyons | sois / soyons / soyez | |
| 11. **faire** faisant | je fais / tu fais / il/elle/on fait | nous faisons / vous faites / ils/elles font | j'ai fait | je faisais | je ferai | je ferais | que je fasse / que nous fassions | fais / faisons / faites | |
| 12. **falloir** | il faut | | il a fallu | il fallait | il faudra | il faudrait | qu'il faille | — | |
| 13. **lire** lisant | je lis / tu lis / il/elle/on lit | nous lisons / vous lisez / ils/elles lisent | j'ai lu | je lisais | je lirai | je lirais | que je lise / que nous lisions | lis / lisons / lisez | |
| 14. **mettre** mettant | je mets / tu mets / il/elle/on met | nous mettons / vous mettez / ils/elles mettent | j'ai mis | je mettais | je mettrai | je mettrais | que je mette / que nous mettions | mets / mettons / mettez | permettre, promettre |
| 15. **mourir*** mourant | je meurs / tu meurs / il/elle/on meurt | nous mourons / vous mourez / ils/elles meurent | je suis mort(e) | je mourais | je mourrai | je mourrais | que je meure / que nous mourions | meurs / mourons / mourez | |

*Verbs followed by an asterisk * are conjugated with **être** in the compound tenses.

## Verbes irréguliers (*suite*)

| INFINITIF ET PARTICIPE PRÉSENT | PRÉSENT | | | PASSÉ COMPOSÉ | IMPARFAIT | FUTUR | CONDITIONNEL | SUBJONCTIF | IMPÉRATIF | AUTRES VERBES |
|---|---|---|---|---|---|---|---|---|---|---|
| 16. **naître\*** naissant | je nais tu nais il/elle/on naît | nous naissons vous naissez ils/elles naissent | | je suis né(e) | je naissais | je naîtrai | je naîtrais | que je naisse que nous naissions | nais naissons naissez | |
| 17. **ouvrir** ouvrant | j' ouvre tu ouvres il/elle/on ouvre | nous ouvrons vous ouvrez ils/elles ouvrent | | j'ai ouvert | j'ouvrais | j'ouvrirai | j'ouvrirais | que j'ouvre que nous ouvrions | ouvre ouvrons ouvrez | couvrir, découvrir; offrir; souffrir |
| 18. **plaire** plaisant | je plais tu plais il/elle/on plaît | nous plaisons vous plaisez ils/elle plaisent | | j'ai plu | je plaisais | je plairai | je plairais | que je plaise que nous plaisions | plais plaisons plaisez | |
| 19. **pleuvoir** pleuvant | il pleut | | | il a plu | il pleuvait | il pleuvra | il pleuvrait | qu'il pleuve | — | |
| 20. **pouvoir** pouvant | je peux† tu peux il/elle/on peut | nous pouvons vous pouvez ils/elles peuvent | | j'ai pu | je pouvais | je pourrai | je pourrais | que je puisse que nous puissions | — | |
| 21. **prendre** prenant | je prends tu prends il/elle/on prend | nous prenons vous prenez ils/elles prennent | | j'ai pris | je prenais | je prendrai | je prendrais | que je prenne que nous prenions | prends prenons prenez | apprendre, comprendre |
| 22. **recevoir** recevant | je reçois tu reçois il/elle/on reçoit | nous recevons vous recevez ils/elles reçoivent | | j'ai reçu | je recevais | je recevrai | je recevrais | que je reçoive que nous recevions | reçois recevons recevez | |
| 23. **savoir** sachant | je sais tu sais il/elle/on sait | nous savons vous savez ils/elles savent | | j'ai su | je savais | je saurai | je saurais | que je sache que nous sachions | sache sachons sachez | |
| 24. **suivre** suivant | je suis tu suis il/elle/on suit | nous suivons vous suivez ils/elles suivent | | j'ai suivi | je suivais | je suivrai | je suivrais | que je suive que nous suivions | suis suivons suivez | poursuivre |
| 25. **venir\*** venant | je viens tu viens il/elle/on vient | nous venons vous venez ils/elles viennent | | je suis venu(e) | je venais | je viendrai | je viendrais | que je vienne que nous venions | viens venons venez | appartenir, contenir; devenir;\* obtenir; revenir;\* tenir |
| 26. **vivre** vivant | je vis tu vis il/elle/on vit | nous vivons vous vivez ils/elles vivent | | j'ai vécu | je vivais | je vivrai | je vivrais | que je vive que nous vivions | vis vivons vivez | survivre |
| 27. **voir** voyant | je vois tu vois il/elle/on voit | nous voyons vous voyez ils/elles voient | | j'ai vu | je voyais | je verrai | je verrais | que je voie que nous voyions | vois voyons voyez | revoir |
| 28. **vouloir** voulant | je veux tu veux il/elle/on veut | nous voulons vous voulez ils/elles veulent | | j'ai voulu | je voulais | je voudrai | je voudrais | que je veuille que nous voulions | veuille veuillons veuillez | |

\*Verbs followed by an asterisk \* are conjugated with **être** in the compound tenses.
†If **je peux** is inverted to form a question, it becomes **puis-je… ?**

# Appendix C

## Perfect Tenses

In addition to the **passé composé,** French has several other perfect verb tenses (conjugated forms of **avoir** or **être** + the past participle of a verb). Following are the most common perfect tenses.

**Le plus-que-parfait** (*The Pluperfect*)
The pluperfect tense (also called the past perfect) is formed with the imperfect of the auxiliary verb (**avoir** or **être**) + the past participle of the main verb.

| | **parler** | | **sortir** | | **se réveiller** |
|---|---|---|---|---|---|
| j' | avais parlé | j' | étais sorti(e) | je | m'étais réveillé(e) |
| tu | avais parlé | tu | étais sorti(e) | tu | t'étais réveillé(e) |
| il/elle/on | avait parlé | il/elle/on | était sorti(e) | il/elle/on | s'était réveillé(e) |
| nous | avions parlé | nous | étions sorti(e)s | nous | nous étions réveillé(e)s |
| vous | aviez parlé | vous | étiez sorti(e)(s) | vous | vous étiez réveillé(e)(s) |
| ils/elles | avaient parlé | ils/elles | étaient sorti(e)s | ils/elles | s'étaient réveillé(e)s |

The pluperfect is used to indicate an action or event that occurred before another past action or event, either stated or implied: *I had already left for the country* (*when my friends arrived in Paris*).

Quand j'ai téléphoné aux Dupont, ils **avaient** déjà **décidé** d'acheter la ferme.

Marie **s'était réveillée** avant moi. Elle **était** déjà **sortie** à sept heures.

*When I phoned the Duponts, they had already decided to buy the farm.*

*Marie had awakened before me. She had already left by seven o'clock.*

**Le futur antérieur** (*The Future Perfect*)
The future perfect is formed with the future of the auxiliary verb (**avoir** or **être**) + the past participle of the main verb.

| | **parler** | | **sortir** | | **se réveiller** |
|---|---|---|---|---|---|
| j' | aurai parlé | je | serai sorti(e) | je | me serai réveillé(e) |
| tu | auras parlé | tu | seras sorti(e) | tu | te seras réveillé(e) |
| il/elle/on | aura parlé | il/elle/on | sera sorti(e) | il/elle/on | se sera réveillé(e) |
| nous | aurons parlé | nous | serons sorti(e)s | nous | nous serons réveillé(e)s |
| vous | aurez parlé | vous | serez sorti(e)(s) | vous | vous serez réveillé(e)(s) |
| ils/elles | auront parlé | ils/elles | seront sorti(e)s | ils/elles | se seront réveillé(e)s |

The future perfect is used to express a future action that will already have taken place when another future action occurs. The subsequent action is always expressed by the simple future.

| | |
|---|---|
| Je publierai mes résultats quand j'**aurai terminé** cette expérience. | *I'll publish the results when I finish this experiment.* |
| Aussitôt que mes collègues **seront revenus,** ils liront mon rapport. | *As soon as my colleagues return, they'll read my report.* |

**Le conditionnel passé** (*The Past Conditional*)

**A. Formation of the Past Conditional**

The past conditional (or conditional perfect) is formed with the conditional of the auxiliary verb (**avoir** or **être**) + the past participle of the main verb.

| parler | | sortir | | se réveiller | |
|---|---|---|---|---|---|
| j' | aurais parlé | je | serais sorti(e) | je | me serais réveillé(e) |
| tu | aurais parlé | tu | serais sorti(e) | tu | te serais réveillé(e) |
| il/elle/on | aurait parlé | il/elle/on | serait sorti(e) | il/elle/on | se serait réveillé(e) |
| nous | aurions parlé | nous | serions sorti(e)s | nous | nous serions réveillé(e)s |
| vous | auriez parlé | vous | seriez sorti(e)(s) | vous | vous seriez réveillé(e)(s) |
| ils/elles | auraient parlé | ils/elles | seraient sorti(e)s | ils/elles | se seraient réveillé(e)s |

The past conditional is used to express an action or event that would have occurred if some set of conditions (stated or implied) had been present: *We would have worried (if we had known).*

**B. Uses of the Past Conditional**

The past conditional is used in the main clause of an *if*-clause sentence when the verb of the *if*-clause is in the pluperfect.

| | |
|---|---|
| Si j'**avais eu** le temps, j'**aurais visité** Nîmes. | *If I had had the time, I would have visited Nîmes.* |
| Si les Normands n'**avaient** pas **conquis** l'Angleterre en 1066, l'anglais **aurait été** une langue très différente. | *If the Normans had not conquered England in 1066, English would have been a very different language.* |

The underlying set of conditions (the *if*-clause) is sometimes not stated.

| | |
|---|---|
| À ta place, j'**aurais parlé** au guide. | *If I were you, I would have spoken to the guide.* |
| Nous **serions allés** au lac. | *We would have gone to the lake.* |

## C. The Past Conditional of *devoir*

The past conditional of **devoir** means *should have* or *ought to have.* It expresses regret about something that did not take place in the past.

| | |
|---|---|
| J'**aurais dû prendre** l'autre chemin. | *I should have taken the other road.* |
| Nous **aurions dû acheter** un plan. | *We should have bought a map.* |

### Le subjonctif passé (*The Past Subjunctive*)

The past subjunctive is formed with the present subjunctive of the auxiliary verb (**avoir** or **être**) + the past participle of the main verb.

| PAST SUBJUNCTIVE OF **parler** | | PAST SUBJUNCTIVE OF **venir** | |
|---|---|---|---|
| que j' | aie parlé | que je | sois venu(e) |
| que tu | aies parlé | que tu | sois venu(e) |
| qu'il/elle/on | ait parlé | qu'il/elle/on | soit venu(e) |
| que nous | ayons parlé | que nous | soyons venu(e)s |
| que vous | ayez parlé | que vous | soyez venu(e)(s) |
| qu'ils/elles | aient parlé | qu'ils/elles | soient venu(e)s |

| | |
|---|---|
| Je suis content que tu **aies parlé** avec **Léa**. | *I'm glad you spoke with Léa.* |
| Il est dommage qu'elle ne **soit** pas encore **venue**. | *It's too bad that she hasn't come yet.* |

The past subjunctive is used following the same expressions as the present subjunctive except that it indicates that the action or situation described in the dependent clause occurred *before* the action or situation described in the main clause. Compare these sentences:

| | |
|---|---|
| Je suis content que tu **viennes**. | *I'm happy that you are coming.* |
| Je suis content que tu **sois venu(e)**. | *I'm happy that you came.* |
| | |
| Je doute qu'ils le **comprennent**. | *I doubt that they understand it.* |
| Je doute qu'ils l'**aient compris**. | *I doubt that they have understood it.* |

# Appendix D

## Le passé simple

**1.** The **passé simple** is a past tense often used in literary texts; it is not a conversational tense. Verbs that would be used in the **passé composé** in informal speech or writing are in the **passé simple** in formal writing. You may want to learn to recognize the forms of the **passé simple** for reading purposes. The **passé simple** of regular **-er** verbs is formed by adding the endings **-ai, -as, -a, -âmes, -âtes, -èrent** to the verb stem. The endings for **-ir** and **-re** verbs are: **-is, -is, -it, -îmes, -îtes, -irent**. The endings for **-oir** verbs are: **-us, -us, -ut, -ûmes, -ûtes, -urent**.

| parler | | finir | | perdre | | vouloir | |
|---|---|---|---|---|---|---|---|
| je | parlai | je | finis | je | perdis | je | voulus |
| tu | parlas | tu | finis | tu | perdis | tu | voulus |
| il/elle/on | parla | il/elle/on | finit | il/elle/on | perdit | il/elle/on | voulut |
| nous | parlâmes | nous | finîmes | nous | perdîmes | nous | voulûmes |
| vous | parlâtes | vous | finîtes | vous | perdîtes | vous | voulûtes |
| ils/elles | parlèrent | ils/elles | finirent | ils/elles | perdirent | ils/elles | voulurent |

**2.** Here are the third-person forms (**il, elle, on; ils, elles**) of some verbs that are irregular in the **passé simple**.

| INFINITIVE | PASSÉ SIMPLE |
|---|---|
| avoir | il eut, ils eurent |
| dire | il dit, ils dirent |
| être | il fut, ils furent |
| faire | il fit, ils firent |

# Appendix E

## Les pronoms

**Les pronoms démonstratifs** (*Demonstrative Pronouns*)
Demonstrative pronouns such as *this one* and *that one* refer to a person, thing, or idea that has been mentioned previously. In French, they agree in gender and number with the nouns they replace.

|  | | SINGULAR | | PLURAL |
|---|---|---|---|---|
| *Masculine* | **celui** | *this one, that one, the one* | **ceux** | *these, those, the ones* |
| *Feminine* | **celle** | *this one, that one, the one* | **celles** | *these, those, the ones* |

French demonstrative pronouns cannot stand alone. They must be:

1. used with the suffix **-ci** (to indicate someone or something located close to the speaker) or **-là** (for someone or something more distant from the speaker)

   | | |
   |---|---|
   | Voici deux affiches. Préférez-vous **celle-ci** ou **celle-là**? | *Here are two posters. Do you prefer this one or that one?* |

2. followed by a prepositional phrase (often a construction with **de**)

   | | |
   |---|---|
   | Quelle époque t'intéresse, **celle** du Moyen Âge ou **celle** de la Renaissance? | *Which period interests you, that of the Middle Ages or that of the Renaissance?* |

3. followed by a dependent clause introduced by a relative pronoun

   | | |
   |---|---|
   | On trouve des villages anciens dans plusieurs parcs: **ceux** qui sont dans le Parc de la Brière sont en ruine; **ceux** qui sont dans les parcs de la Lorraine et du Morvan ont été restaurés. | *One finds very old villages in several parks: Those that are in Brière Park are in ruins; those that are in the Lorraine and Morvan parks have been restored.* |

**Indefinite Demonstrative Pronouns**
**Ceci** (*this*), **cela** (*that*), and **ça** (*that,* informal) are indefinite demonstrative pronouns; they refer to an idea or thing with no definite antecedent. They do not show gender or number.

| | |
|---|---|
| **Cela (Ça)** n'est pas important. | *That's not important.* |
| Regarde **ceci** de près. | *Look at this closely.* |
| Qu'est-ce que c'est que **ça**? | *What's that?* |

**Les pronoms relatifs** (*Relative Pronouns*)
**A.** *Ce qui* **and** *ce que*
**Ce qui** and **ce que** are indefinite relative pronouns similar in meaning to **la chose qui (que)** or **les choses qui (que);** the first serves as the subject of a dependent clause, and the second as the object. They refer to an idea or a subject that is unspecified and has neither gender nor number, often expressed as *what.*

| | |
|---|---|
| —Dites-moi **ce qui** est arrivé au touriste américain. | *Tell me what happened to the American tourist.* |
| —Je ne sais pas **ce qui** lui est arrivé. | *I don't know what happened to him.* |
| —Dites-moi **ce que** vous avez fait à Reims. | *Tell me what you did in Reims.* |
| —Je n'ai pas le temps de vous dire tout **ce qu'**on a fait. | *I don't have time to tell you everything we did.* |

**B.** *Lequel*
**Lequel (laquelle, lesquels, lesquelles)** is the relative pronoun used as an object of a preposition to refer to things and people. **Lequel** and its forms contract with **à** and **de**.

| | |
|---|---|
| Où est l'agence de voyages **devant laquelle** il attend? | *Where is the travel agency in front of which he's waiting?* |
| L'hôtel **auquel** j'écris est à la Guadeloupe. | *The hotel to which I am writing is in Guadeloupe.* |
| Je connais bien l'homme **près duquel** elle est assise. | *I know well the man next to whom she is sitting.* |

**Les pronoms possessifs** (*Possessive Pronouns*)
Possessive pronouns replace nouns that are modified by a possessive adjective
or other possessive construction. In English, the possessive pronouns are *mine,
yours, his, hers, its, ours,* and *theirs.* In French, the appropriate definite article
is always used with the possessive pronoun.

| | SINGULAR | | PLURAL | |
| | MASCULINE | FEMININE | MASCULINE | FEMININE |
|---|---|---|---|---|
| *mine* | le mien | la mienne | les miens | les miennes |
| *yours* | le tien | la tienne | les tiens | les tiennes |
| *his/hers/its* | le sien | la sienne | les siens | les siennes |
| *ours* | le nôtre | la nôtre | les nôtres | |
| *yours* | le vôtre | la vôtre | les vôtres | |
| *theirs* | le leur | la leur | les leurs | |

| POSSESSIVE CONSTRUCTION + NOUN | | POSSESSIVE PRONOUN |
|---|---|---|
| Où sont **leurs bagages**? | $\longrightarrow$ | **Les leurs** sont ici. |
| C'est **mon frère** là-bas. | $\longrightarrow$ | Ah oui? C'est **le mien** à côté de lui. |
| La **voiture de Frédérique** est plus rapide que **ma voiture**. | $\longrightarrow$ | Ah oui? **La sienne** est aussi plus rapide que **la mienne**. |

# Lexiques

## Lexique français-anglais

This end vocabulary provides contextual meanings of French words used in this text. It does not include proper nouns (unless presented as active vocabulary or unless the French equivalent is quite different in spelling from English), most abbreviations, exact cognates, most near cognates, past participles used as adjectives if the infinitive is listed, or regular adverbs formed from adjectives listed. Adjectives are listed in the masculine singular form; feminine endings or forms are included when irregular. An asterisk (*) indicates words beginning with an aspirate *h*. Active vocabulary is indicated by the number of the chapter in which it is activated.

### ABBREVIATIONS

| | | | | | |
|---|---|---|---|---|---|
| *A.* | archaic | *indic.* | indicative (mood) | *p.p.* | past participle |
| *ab.* | abbreviation | *inf.* | infinitive | *prep.* | preposition |
| *adj.* | adjective | *interj.* | interjection | *pron.* | pronoun |
| *adv.* | adverb | *interr.* | interrogative | *Q.* | Quebec usage |
| *art.* | article | *inv.* | invariable | *s.* | singular |
| *colloq.* | colloquial | *irreg.* | irregular | *s.o.* | someone |
| *conj.* | conjunction | *m.* | masculine noun | *s.th.* | something |
| *fam.* | familiar or colloquial | *n.* | noun | *subj.* | subjunctive |
| *f.* | feminine noun | *neu.* | neuter | *tr. fam.* | very colloquial, slang |
| *Gram.* | grammatical term | *pl.* | plural | *v.* | verb |

**à** *prep.* to; at; in (2); by, on (*bicycle, horseback, foot*) (9); **à bientôt** see you soon (1); **à côté de** beside (4); **à destination de** to, for (9); **à droite (de)** on the right (of) (4); **à gauche (de)** on the left (of) (4); **à l'est/ l'ouest** to the east/west (9); **à l'étranger** abroad, in a foreign country (9); **à l'heure** on time (9); **à pied** on foot (9); **à son compte** for oneself (14); **au nord/sud** to the north/south (9); **au printemps** in spring (5); **au revoir** good-bye (1); **à vélo** by bike (9)

**abandonné** *adj.* abandoned

**abats** *m. pl.* giblets, offal

**abbaye** *f.* abbey

**abîme** *m.* abyss

**abolir** to abolish (16)

**abominable** *adj.* appalling

**abondance** *f.* abundance

**abonnement** *m.* subscription

**abonner** to subscribe

**abord: d'abord** *adv.* first, first of all, at first (11)

**abordable** *adj.* approachable; reasonable

**aboutissement** *m.* end, outcome

**aboyer (il aboie)** to bark (*dog*)

**abréger (j'abrège, nous abrégeons)** to cut short, shorten

**abréviation** *f.* abbreviation

**abri** *m.* shelter; **sans-abri** *m., f.* homeless person (16)

**abriter** to house

**absolu** *adj.* absolute

**abstrait** *adj.* abstract

**abus** *m.* abuse, misuse

**académicien(ne)** *m., f. member of the* **Académie française**

**Académie française** *f.* French Academy (*official body that rules on language questions*)

**accéder (j'accède)** to access

**accent** *m.* accent; **accent aigu (grave, circonflexe)** acute (grave, circumflex) accent

**accentué: pronom accentué** *Gram.* stressed or disjunctive pronoun

**accepter (de)** to accept (to) (12); to agree to

**accès** *m.* access; **fournisseur** (*m.*) **d'accès** (*Internet*) service provider (ISP)

**accessoire** *m.* accessory

**acclamé** *adj.* cheered

**accompagner** to accompany, go along (with)

**accomplir** to perform, accomplish, carry out

**accord** *m.* agreement; **d'accord** all right, O.K., agreed (2); **être d'accord** to agree, be in agreement

**accorder** to grant, bestow, confer

**accourir** to run, rush up

**accro à** *inv., fam.* addicted to **être un accro de** to be addicted to

**accrocher** to hang

**accroître** (*p.p.* **accru**) *irreg.* to increase, add to

**accueil** *m.* greeting, welcome; **page** (*f.*) **d'accueil** homepage; **terre** (*f.*) **(pays** [*m.*]) **d'accueil** country of settlement (*immigration*)

**accueillir** (*p.p.* **accueilli**) *irreg.* to greet, welcome

**acculer** to drive (*s.o.*) back

**s'accumuler** to accumulate

**acéré** *adj.* sharp

**achat** *m.* purchase; **pouvoir** (*m.*) **d'achat** purchasing power (16)

**acheter (j'achète)** to buy (8)

**acheteur/euse** *m., f.* buyer, purchaser

**s'achever (il s'achève)** to end; to come to an end

**acier** *m.* steel

**acquérir** (*like* **conquérir**) *irreg.* to acquire

**acteur/trice** *m., f.* actor, actress (12)

**actif/ive** *adj.* active; working

**action** *f.* action; gesture

**activé** *adj.* activated

**activité** *f.* activity; **activités de plein air** outdoor activities (15)

**actualisé** *adj.* updated

**actualité** *f.* piece of news; present-day event; current events (14)

**actuel(le)** *adj.* present, current

**actuellement** *adv.* currently, at the present time

**adapter** to adapt; **s'adapter à** to adapt oneself to

**addition** *f.* bill, check (*in a restaurant*) (7)

**adepte** *m., f.* enthusiast, follower

**adieu** *interj.* good-bye

**adjectif** *m., Gram.* adjective

**admettre** (*like* **mettre**) *irreg.* to admit, accept

**administratif/ive** *adj.* administrative; **assistant(e)** (*m., f.*) **administratif/ive** administrative assistant

**administration** *f.* administration; Civil Service

**admirer** to admire

**adolescent(e)** *m., f., adj.* adolescent, teenager

**adopter** to adopt
**adorer** to love, adore (2)
**adresse** *f.* address (10)
**s'adresser (à)** to be intended (for), aimed (at)
**ADSL** DSL
**adulte** *m., f., adj.* adult; **âge** (*m.*) **adulte** adulthood
**adverbe** *m., Gram.* adverb
**adverse** *adj.* opposing; opposite
**aérobic** *f.* aerobics; **faire de l'aérobic** to do aerobics (5)
**aéroport** *m.* airport (9)
**affaire** *f.* affair; business matter; *pl.* belongings; business; **chiffre** (*m.*) **d'affaires** turnover (*in business*); **classe** (*f.*) **affaires** business class (9); **homme (femme) d'affaires** *m., f.* businessman (-woman)
**affectueux/euse** *adj.* affectionate; fond
**affiche** *f.* poster; billboard (4)
**afficher** to post, put up; to display, show; **s'afficher** to be displayed
**affirmatif/ive** *adj.* affirmative
**affirmation** *f.* declaration
**affirmer** to affirm, state
**affreux/euse** *adj.* awful
**afin de** *prep.* to, in order to
**africain** *adj.* African; **Africain(e)** *m., f.* African (*person*)
**Afrique** *f.* Africa; **Afrique de l'ouest (Afrique occidentale)** West Africa; **Afrique du Nord** North Africa
**âge** *m.* age; epoch; **Moyen Âge** *m. s.* Middle Ages (12); **quel âge avez-vous?** how old are you?
**agence** *f.* agency; **agence de voyages** travel agency
**agenda** *m.* engagement book, pocket calendar
**agitation** *f.* bustle
**agent** *m.* agent; **agent de police** police officer (14)
**agir** to act (4); **il s'agit de** it's about, it's a question of
**agité** *adj.* agitated, restless; rough, choppy (*sea*)
**agneau: côte** (*f.*) **d'agneau** lamb chop
**agrandir** to make bigger
**agréable** *adj.* agreeable, pleasant, nice (3)
**agricole** *adj.* agricultural
**agriculteur/trice** *m., f.* farmer (14)
**ah bon?** *interj.* oh, really?
**aide** *f.* help, assistance; **à l'aide de** with the help of
**aider** to help (12)
**aigreur** *f.* sourness; bitterness
**aigu: accent** (*m.*) **aigu** acute accent (é)
**aiguille** *f.* needle
**ail** *m.* garlic (7)
**ailleurs** elsewhere; **d'ailleurs** besides, moreover
**aimable** *adj.* likable, friendly
**aimer** to like; to love (2); **aimer bien** to like; **aimer mieux** to prefer (2); **j'aimerais +** *inf.* I would like (*to do s.th.*); **je n'aime... pas du tout** I don't like . . . at all
**ainsi** *conj.* thus, so; **ainsi que** as well as; **et ainsi de suite** and so on
**air** *m.* air; look; tune; **activités** (*f. pl.*) **de plein air** outdoor activities (15); **avoir l'air (de)** to seem, look (like) (3); **de plein air** outdoor; **en plein air** outdoors, in the open air; **hôtesse** (*f.*) **de l'air** flight attendant (9)

**aise: à l'aise** at ease
**ajouter** to add
**album** *m.* (photo) album; picture book
**alcool** *m.* alcohol
**alcoolisé** *adj.* alcoholic
**Alger** Algiers
**Algérie** *f.* Algeria (2, 8)
**algérien** *adj.* Algerian; **Algérien(ne)** *m., f.* Algerian (*person*) (2)
**aligné: faire du patin à roues alignées** to do in-line skating
**aliment(s)** *m.* food, nourishment (6)
**alimentaire** *adj.* alimentary, pertaining to food
**alimentation** *f.* food, feeding, nourishment; **magasin** (*m.*) **d'alimentation** food store
**alizé: vent** (*m.*) **alizé** trade wind
**allée** *f.* path, walk
**allégé** *adj.* light, low-fat (*foods*)
**Allemagne** *f.* Germany (2, 8)
**allemand** *adj.* German; *m.* German (*language*) (2); **Allemand(e)** *m., f.* German (*person*) (2)
**aller** *irreg.* to go (5); **aller +** *inf.* to be going (*to do s.th.*) (5); **aller à la pêche** to go fishing (8); **aller en boîte** to go clubbing (15); **aller mal** to feel bad (ill) (4); **allez-vous-en!** go away! (13); **allez-y!** go ahead!; **billet** (*m.*) **aller-retour** round-trip ticket; **ça peut aller** all right, pretty well (1); **ça va?** how's it going? (1); **ça va** fine (things are going well) (1); **ça va bien (mal)** fine (bad[ly]) (things are going well [badly]) (1); **comment allez-vous? (comment vas-tu?)** how are you? (1); **s'en aller** to go away, go off (*to work*) (13); **va-t'en!** go away! (13)
**allergique** *adj.* allergic
**allier** to combine
**allô** *interj.* hello (*phone greeting*) (10)
**allumer** to light
**alors** *adv.* so; then, in that case (4)
**alouette** *f.* lark
**alpin** *adj.* Alpine; **ski** (*m.*) **alpin** downhill skiing (8)
**alpinisme** *m.* mountaineering, mountain climbing; **faire de l'alpinisme** to go mountain climbing (8)
**alsacien(ne)** *adj.* Alsatian
**altérité** *f.* otherness
**amande** *f.* almond
**amants** *m. pl.* lovers
**amateur** (*m.*) **de** lover of
**ambiance** *f.* atmosphere, surroundings
**ambitieux/euse** *adj.* ambitious
**âme** *f.* soul; spirit
**amélioration** *f.* improvement
**améliorer** to improve, better
**amener (j'amène)** to bring (along)
**américain** *adj.* American; **à l'américaine** American-style; **Américain(e)** *m., f.* American (*person*) (2)
**Amérique** *f.* America
**ameublement** *m. s.* furnishings
**ami(e)** *m., f.* friend (2); **petit(e) ami(e)** *m., f.* boyfriend, girlfriend
**amical** *adj.* (*m. pl.* **amicaux**) friendly
**amitié** *f.* friendship (13)
**amour** *m.* love (13); love affair
**amoureux/euse** *adj.* loving, in love (13); *m., f.* lover, sweetheart, person in love (13); **tomber amoureux/euse (de)** to fall in love (with) (13); **vie** (*f.*) **amoureuse** love life

**amphithéâtre** (*fam.* **amphi**) *m.* lecture hall, amphitheater (2)
**ampoule** *f.* light bulb
**amusant** *adj.* amusing, fun (3)
**s'amuser (à)** to have fun, have a good time (13)
**an** *m.* year; **avoir (vingt) ans** to be (twenty) years old (3); **l'an dernier (passé)** last year; **par an** per year, each year
**analyser** to analyze
**ananas** *m.* pineapple
**ancêtre** *m., f.* ancestor
**ancien(ne)** *adj.* old, antique; former (4); ancient; **anciens** *n. m. pl.* elders
**ange** *m.* angel; **je suis aux anges** I'm in seventh heaven
**anglais** *adj.* English; *m.* English (*language*) (2); **Anglais(e)** *m., f.* Englishman (-woman) (2)
**Angleterre** *f.* England (2, 8)
**angoissé** *adj.* anxious, anxiety-prone
**animal** *m.* animal; **animal domestique** pet
**animateur/trice** *m., f.* host, hostess (*radio, TV*); motivator (*in marketing*)
**animé** *adj.* animated
**année** *f.* year; **l'année prochaine (dernière [passée])** next (last) year; **les années (cinquante)** the decade (era) of the (fifties) (8)
**anniversaire** *m.* anniversary; birthday; **bon anniversaire** *interj.* happy birthday; **carte** (*f.*) **d'anniversaire** birthday card
**annonce** *f.* announcement, ad; **petites annonces** (classified) ads (10)
**annoncer (nous annonçons)** to announce, declare; **s'annoncer** to look; to promise to be
**annuaire** *m.* telephone directory (10); **annuaire électronique** online (telephone) directory (10); **consulter l'annuaire** to look up a phone number (10)
**annuel(le)** *adj.* annual
**annuler** to cancel (11)
**anonyme** *adj.* anonymous
**anorak** *m.* (ski) jacket, wind-breaker (8)
**anticiper (sur)** to anticipate
**anticonformiste** *m., f.* nonconformist
**antillais** *adj.* West Indian; **Antillais(e)** *m., f.* West Indian (*person*)
**Antilles** *f. pl.* West Indies
**antipathique** *adj.* disagreeable, unpleasant (3)
**anxieux/euse** *adj.* anxious
**août** August (1)
**apaiser** to appease; to soothe
**aperçu** *adj.* noticed
**apéritif** (*fam.* **apéro**) *m.* cocktail
**apparaître** (like **connaître**) *irreg.* to appear
**appareil** *m.* apparatus (10); device; appliance; telephone (10); **appareil (photo) numérique** *m.* (still) digital camera (10); **qui est à l'appareil?** who's calling? (10)
**apparemment** *adv.* apparently
**apparence** *f.* appearance
**apparenté** *adj.* related; **mot** (*m.*) **apparenté** cognate (*word*)
**apparition** *f.* appearance
**appartement** (*fam.* **appart**) *m.* apartment (4)
**appartenir** (like **tenir**) **à** *irreg.* to belong to
**appel** *m.* call; **faire appel à** to appeal to; to require, call for
**appeler (j'appelle)** to call (10); to name; **comment s'appelle... ?** what's . . . name?; **comment vous appelez-vous? (comment t'appelles-tu?)** what's your name? (1); **je m'appelle...** my name is . . . (1); **s'appeler** to be named (13)

**appétit** *m.* appetite; **bon appétit** *interj.* enjoy your meal

**appliquer** to apply

**apporter** to bring, carry; to furnish (6)

**apprécier** to appreciate, value

**apprendre** (*like* **prendre**) *irreg.* to learn; to teach (6); **apprendre à** to learn (how) to

**apprentissage** (*m.*) **des langues** language learning

**approcher** to approach

**approprié** *adj.* appropriate

**après** *prep.* after (2); afterward (5); **après avoir (être)...** after having . . . ; **d'après** *prep.* according to

**après-midi** *m.* or *f.* afternoon; **cet après-midi** this afternoon (5); **de l'après-midi** in the afternoon (6); **tous les après-midi** every afternoon (10)

**arabe** *m.* Arabic (*language*)

**arachide** *f.* peanut(s)

**arbre** *m.* tree (5)

**archéologique** *adj.* archeological

**archéologue** *m., f.* archeologist

**archi-comble** full of people

**architecte** *m., f.* architect (14)

**arène(s)** *f.* (*pl.*) arena, bullring (12)

**argent** *m.* money (7); silver; **argent liquide** cash (14)

**argot** *m.* slang

**arme** *f.* weapon, arm

**armée** *f.* army; **armée de métier** professional army

**armoire** *f.* wardrobe; closet (4)

**aromaticien(ne)** *m., f.* perfume maker

**arranger** to arrange

**arrêter (de)** to stop, cease (12); **s'arrêter** to stop (*oneself*) (13)

**arrière** *adv.* back; **arrière-grand-parent** *m.* great-grandparent (5)

**arrivant(e)** *m., f.* newcomer

**arrivée** *f.* arrival (9)

**arriver** to arrive, come (3); to happen

**arrondissement** *m.* district, section (*of Paris*) (11)

**arroser** to water (*plants*)

**art** *m.* art; **œuvre** (*f.*) **d'art** work of art (12)

**artichaut** *m.* artichoke

**artifice: feux** (*m. pl.*) **d'artifice** fireworks

**artisan(e)** *m., f.* artisan, craftsperson (14)

**artisanal** *adj.* craft

**artisanat** *m.* handicrafts, arts and crafts

**artiste** *m., f.* artist (12)

**artistique** *adj.* artistic

**ascenseur** *m.* elevator

**Asiatique** *m., f.* person from Asia

**Asie** *f.* Asia

**aspiré** *adj.* aspirate

**asseoir** (*p.p.* **assis**) *irreg.* to seat; **s'asseoir** to sit down

**asservi** *adj.* enslaved

**assez** *adv.* somewhat (3); rather, quite; **assez de** *adv.* enough (6)

**assiette** *f.* plate (6)

**assise** *f.* foundation

**assistance** *f.* assistance, help; audience

**assistant(e)** *m., f.* assistant; **assistant(e) administratif/ive** administrative assistant

**assisté** *adj.* supported, assisted

**assister à** to attend, go to (*concert, etc.*) (15)

**associer** to associate

**assortiment** *m.* assortment

**assurance** *f.* assurance; insurance; **assurances-automobile** *pl.* car insurance

**assurer** to insure; to assure; to ensure

**atelier** *m.* workshop; (*art*) studio

**athlète** *m., f.* athlete

**atmosphère** *f.* atmosphere (16)

**atours** *m. pl.* finery, attire

**atout** *m.* asset

**attacher** to attach

**attaquer** to attack

**atteindre** (*like* **craindre**) *irreg.* to reach, attain

**attendre** to wait, wait for (5)

**attention** *f.* attention; **faire attention (à)** to pay attention (to); to be careful (of), watch out (for) (5)

**attentivement** *adv.* attentively

**attirer** to attract

**attrait** *m.* attraction, lure; charm

**attraper** to catch

**attribuer** to attribute

**auberge** *f.* inn; **auberge de jeunesse** youth hostel (9)

**aucun(e) (ne... aucun[e])** *adj., pron.* none; no one, not one, not any; anyone; any

**audace** *f.* daring innovation

**audacieux/euse** *adj.* daring

**auditeur/trice** *m., f.* listener

**auditoire** *m.* audience

**augmentation** *f.* increase (14); **augmentation de salaire** salary raise (14)

**augmenter** to increase (16)

**aujourd'hui** *adv.* today (1); nowadays

**auprès de** *prep.* with, to

**aurore** *f.* dawn

**aussi** *adv.* also; so; as; **aussi... que** as . . . as (14); **moi aussi** me too (3)

**aussitôt** *conj.* immediately, at once; **aussitôt que** as soon as (14)

**Australie** *f.* Australia

**autant (de)** *adv.* as much, so much, as many, so many; **autant (de)... que** as much (many) . . . as (15); **autant que** as much as

**auteur** *m.* author; **auteur dramatique** playwright (12)

**authentique** *adj.* authentic, genuine

**autobus** (*fam.* **bus**) *m.* (*city*) bus (5)

**autocar** *m.* (*interurban*) bus (9)

**automatique** *adj.* automatic; **consigne** (*f.*) **automatique** coin locker (9); **guichet** (*m.*) **automatique** automatic teller machine (ATM) (14)

**automne** *m.* autumn, fall; **en automne** in the autumn (5)

**automobile** (*fam.* **auto**) *f., adj.* automobile, car

**autonome** autonomous

**autoportrait** *m.* self-portrait

**autorisé** permitted

**autoritaire** *adj.* authoritarian

**autoroute** *f.* highway, freeway (9)

**autour de** *prep.* around

**autre** *adj., pron.* other (4); another; *m., f.* the other; *pl.* the others, the rest; **autre chose** something else (7); **d'autres** other(s) (15); **entre autres** among other things; **l'autre / les autres** the other(s) (15); **un(e) autre** another (15)

**autrefois** *adv.* formerly, in the past (11)

**autrement** *adv.* otherwise; **autrement dit** in other words

**Autriche** *f.* Austria

**auxiliaire** *m., Gram.* auxiliary (verb)

**avaleur/euse** (*m., f.*) **de feu** fire swallower

**avance** *f.* advance; **à l'avance** beforehand; **en avance** early (6)

**avancé** *adj.* advanced

**avant** *adj.* before (*in time*); *prep.* before, in advance of; *m.* front; **avant de** + *inf.* (*prep.*) before; **avant-goût** *m.* foretaste; **avant-hier** *adv.* the day before yesterday (7); **avant tout** *prep.* above all

**avantage** *m.* advantage, benefit; **tirer avantage de** to take advantage of

**avare** *adj.* stingy, tightfisted

**avec** *prep.* with (2)

**avenir** *m.* future (14); **à l'avenir** from now on, in the future (14)

**aventure** *f.* adventure; **partir à l'aventure** to leave with no itinerary

**aventurier/ière** *m., f.* adventurer (adventuress)

**averti** *adj.* warned; informed

**avertir** to warn

**aveugle** *adj.* blind; **dégustation** (*f.*) **à l'aveugle** blind tasting

**avion** *m.* airplane (9); **billet** (*m.*) **d'avion aller-retour** round-trip plane ticket; **en avion** by plane

**avis** *m.* opinion; **à votre (ton) avis** in your opinion (11); **changer d'avis** to change one's mind

**avocat(e)** *m., f.* lawyer (14)

**avoir** (*p.p.* **eu**) *irreg.* to have (3); **avoir (vingt) ans** to be (twenty) years old (3); **avoir besoin de** to need (3); **avoir chaud** to be warm (hot) (3); **avoir confiance en** to have confidence in; **avoir de la chance** to be lucky (3); **avoir de la fièvre** to have a fever; **avoir droit à** to have a right to; **avoir du mal à** to have trouble (difficulty); **avoir envie de** to feel like; to want (3); **avoir faim** to be hungry (3); **avoir froid** to be (feel) cold (3); **avoir honte (de)** to be ashamed (of) (3); **avoir horreur de** to hate; **avoir l'air (de)** to seem, look (like) (3); **avoir le temps (de)** to have the time (to); **avoir lieu** to take place; **avoir mal (à)** to have pain; to hurt (13); **avoir peur (de)** to be afraid (of) (3); **avoir raison** to be right (3); **avoir rendez-vous avec** to have a meeting (date) with (3); **avoir soif** to be thirsty (3); **avoir sommeil** to be sleepy (3); **avoir tort** to be wrong (3); **il n'y a pas de quoi** you're welcome (7); **il y a** there is, there are (1); ago (8); **j'aurai droit à quoi** I'll be entitled to what

**avouer** to confess, admit

**avril** April (1)

**Azur: Côte** (*f.*) **d'Azur** French Riviera

**babouche** *f.* (Turkish) slipper

**baccalauréat** (*fam.* **bac**) *m.* baccalaureate (*French secondary school degree*)

**badiner** to banter, joke

**bafouille** *f., fam.* letter

**bagages** *m. pl.* luggage

**bagarre** *f.* fight, brawl

**bagnole** *f., fam.* car, jalopy

**baguette (de pain)** *f.* French bread, baguette (6)

**baie** *f.* bay

**baigner: ça baigne** it's chill, it's going great

**se baigner** to bathe (*oneself*) (13); to swim (13)

**bain** *m.* bath; swim; **maillot** (*m.*) **de bain** swimsuit (3); **salle** (*f.*) **de bains** bathroom (5)

**baiser** *m.* kiss

**baisse** *f.* lowering, reduction

**baisser: faire baisser** to lower

**bal** *m.* dance, ball
**balade** *f., fam.* walk, drive, outing
**se balader** *fam.* to go for a walk (drive, outing)
**balancer: se balancer** to sway
**balayé** *adj.* swept away
**balcon** *m.* balcony (5)
**balle** *f.* (*small*) ball; tennis ball
**ballon** *m.* (*soccer, basket*) ball; balloon; **ballon à air chaud** hot-air balloon
**balnéaire** *adj.* seaside
**banal** *adj.* commonplace
**banane** *f.* banana (6)
**banc** *m.* bench
**bancaire** *adj.* banking, bank; **carte** (*f.*) **bancaire** bank (ATM/credit) card (14); **compte** (*m.*) **bancaire** bank account
**bande** *f.* band; group; gang; (*cassette, video*) tape; **bande dessinée** comic strip, cartoon (15); *pl.* comics
**banlieue** *f.* suburbs (11); **en banlieue** in the suburbs
**banlieusard** *m., f.* suburbanite, commuter
**banque** *f.* bank (11)
**baptiser** to baptize; to name
**bar** *m.* bar; snack bar; pub
**barde** *f.* bard (*layer of bacon on a roast*)
**barreau** *m.* bar (*of a cage*)
**barrer** to bar, block; **se barrer** *fam.* to run off, clear out
**barrière** *f.* gate, fence; barrier
**bas(se)** *adj.* low; **à bas...** down with . . . ; **là-bas** *adv.* over there (10); **Pays-Bas** *m. pl.* the Netherlands, Holland
**base** *f.* base; basis, foundation; **base de données** database; **être à la base de** to be at the root of
**base-ball** *m.* baseball; **jouer au base-ball** to play baseball
**baser** to base; **se baser sur** to be based on
**basilique** *f.* basilica
**basket-ball** (*fam.* **basket**) *m.* basketball; **jouer au basket** to play basketball
**bassin** *m.* ornamental pond
**bassiste** *m., f.* bass guitarist; bass player
**bataille** *f.* battle
**bateau** *m.* boat (8); **bateau à voile** sailboat (8); **bateau de croisière** cruise ship; **bateau-mouche** *m. tourist boat on the Seine;* **en bateau** by boat, in a boat; **faire du bateau** to go boating (8)
**bâtiment** *m.* building (11)
**bâtir** to build (12)
**battre** (*p.p.* **battu**) *irreg.* to beat; to battle with; **se battre** to fight
**bavard** *adj.* talkative
**bavardage** *m.* chattering
**bavarder** to chat; to talk
**bavaroise** *f.* mousse (*dessert*)
**bavette: bifteck** (*m.*) **bavette** sirloin of beef
**beau** (**bel, belle** [**beaux, belles**]) *adj.* handsome; beautiful (3); **à la belle étoile** under the stars; **beau-frère** *m.* brother-in-law; stepbrother (5); **beau-père** *m.* father-in-law; stepfather (5); **belle-mère** *f.* mother-in-law; stepmother (5); **belle-sœur** *f.* sister-in-law; stepsister (5); **il fait beau** it's nice (weather) out (5)
**beaucoup (de)** *adv.* very much, a lot (1); much, many (6)
**beauté** *f.* beauty
**bébé** *m.* baby
**bécane** *f., fam.* bike

**becquée** *f.* beakful
**beignet** *m.* doughnut; fritter
**belette** *f.* weasel
**belge** *adj.* Belgian; **Belge** *m., f.* Belgian (*person*) (2)
**Belgique** *f.* Belgium (2, 8)
**belle** (see **beau**)
**bénédiction** *f.* blessing
**bénéficier (de)** to profit, benefit (from)
**bénévolat** *m.* volunteerism
**bénévole** *m., f., adj.* volunteer
**béquille** *f.* crutch
**béret** *m.* beret (3)
**besoin** *m.* need; **avoir besoin de** to need (3)
**bête** *f.* animal, beast
**beur** *m., f.* second-generation North African living in France
**beurre** *m.* butter (6)
**beurré** *adj.* buttered
**bibliothèque** (*fam.* **bibli**) *f.* library (2)
**bicentenaire** *m.* bicentennial
**bicyclette** *f.* bicycle (8); **faire de la bicyclette** to go bicycling (8)
**bide: faire un bide** *fam.* to flop; to bomb (as a theatre production)
**bien** *adv.* well (1); (*fam.*) good, quite; much; comfortable; **aimer bien** to like; **bien** (*m.*) **commun** common good (16); **bien sûr** *interj.* of course; **ça va bien** (things are going well) (1); **eh bien** *interj.* well (10); **je vais bien** I'm fine; **s'amuser bien** to have a good time; **s'entendre bien** to get along (well); **très bien** very well (good) (1); **vouloir bien** to be willing; to agree
**bien-être** *m.* well-being; welfare
**bienfaisant** *adj.* refreshing; beneficial
**bientôt** *adv.* soon (5); **à bientôt** *interj.* see you soon (1)
**bienvenu(e)** *adj., interj.* welcome
**bière** *f.* beer (6)
**bifteck** *m.* steak (6)
**bijou** *m.* jewel (14); piece of jewelry
**bilingue** *adj.* bilingual
**billet** *m.* bill (*currency*); ticket (9); **billet aller-retour** round-trip ticket; **billet d'avion (de train)** plane (train) ticket; **composter son billet** to stamp (punch) one's ticket
**biologie** *f.* biology (2)
**biologique** *adj.* (*fam.* **bio**) biological; organic
**bip** *m.* beep (*answering machine*)
**biscuit (sec)** *m.* cookie
**bise** *f., fam.* kiss, smack; **faire la bise** to kiss on both cheeks (*in greeting*); **(grosses) bises** love and kisses
**bisou** *m., fam.* kiss (*child's language*); **(gros) bisous** love and kisses
**bistro** *m.* bar, pub; neighborhood restaurant
**bizarre** *adj.* strange, odd; **il est bizarre que** + *subj.* it's strange (bizarre) that
**blaff** *m.* broth (in Martinique)
**blague** *f.* joke (15)
**blanc(he)** *adj.* white (3); **coup** (*m.*) **à blanc** blank shot
**blancheur** *f.* whiteness
**blé** *m.* wheat; *fam.* cash
**blessé** wounded
**bleu** *adj.* blue (3)
**blog** *m.* blog
**blogueur/blogueuse** *m., f.* blogger
**blond(e)** *m., f., adj.* blond (3)
**bloqué** *adj.* stuck, held up (*in traffic*); **être bloqué** to have a mental block

**blouson** *m.* windbreaker; jacket (3)
**bobo** *adj.* hipster
**bœuf** *m.* beef (6); **consommé** (*m.*) **de bœuf** beef consommé; **filet** (*m.*) **de bœuf** beef fillet; **rôti** (*m.*) **de bœuf** roast beef
**bof** *interj.* I dunno; not really; so-so
**boire** (*p.p.* **bu**) *irreg.* to drink (6); **boire un coup** to have a drink
**bois** *m.* forest, woods (11); wood
**boisson** *f.* drink, beverage (6); **boisson gazeuse** soft drink
**boîte** *f.* box; can; nightclub (15); **boîte (de conserve)** can (*of food*) (7); **boîte aux lettres** mailbox (10); **boîte de nuit** nightclub; **boîte vocale** voice mail (10)
**bol** *m.* wide cup; bowl (6)
**bombe: faire la bombe** *fam.* to celebrate, have a party
**bon(ne)** *adj.* good (4); right, correct; *f.* maid, chambermaid; **ah bon?** oh, really?; **bon anniversaire** *interj.* happy birthday; **bon appétit** *interj.* enjoy your meal; **bon marché** *adj., inv.* inexpensive; **bon voyage** *interj.* have a good trip; **bonne chance** *interj.* good luck; **bonne route** *interj.* have a good trip; **de bonne heure** early (6); **il est bon que** + *subj.* it's good that (16)
**bonbon** *m.* (*piece of*) candy
**bonheur** *m.* happiness
**bonjour** *interj.* hello, good day (1)
**bonsoir** *interj.* good evening (1)
**bonté** *f.* kindness
**bord** *m.* board; edge, bank, shore; **à bord** on board; **au bord de** on the banks (shore, edge) of
**bordé** *adj.* edged, lined
**bordelais** *adj.* Bordeaux-style
**border** to line, edge
**borne** *f.* terminal; pay point
**borné** *adj.* limited; restricted
**Bosnie-Herzégovine** *f.* Bosnia-Herzegovina
**bosser** *fam.* to work
**bottes** *f. pl.* boots (3)
**boubou** *m. long tunic worn by black North Africans*
**bouche** *f.* mouth (13)
**boucher/ère** *m., f.* butcher (14)
**boucherie** *f.* butcher shop (7); **boucherie-charcuterie** *f.* combination butcher and deli
**boucler** to buckle
**bouddhisme** *m.* Buddhism
**bouffe** *f.* (*fam.*) food, grub; **faire une petite bouffe** have a light meal
**bouger (nous bougeons)** to move, budge
**bougie** *f.* candle
**bouillabaisse** *f. fish chowder typical of southern France*
**bouillir** (*p.p.* **bouilli**) *irreg.* to boil; **faire bouillir** to bring to a boil
**boulangerie** *f.* bakery (7); **boulangerie-pâtisserie** *f.* bakery-pastry shop
**boule** *f.* ball
**boulot** *m., fam.* job; work
**bouquin** *m., fam.* book
**bouquiniste** *m., f.* secondhand bookseller (*especially along the Seine in Paris*)
**bourgeois** *adj.* bourgeois; middle-class
**Bourgogne** *f.* Burgundy
**bourguignon(ne)** *adj.* from Burgundy; **bœuf bourguignon** beef stew with red wine sauce

**bourse** (*f.*) **d'études** scholarship, study grant; **Bourse** *f.* stock exchange

**bout** *m.* end; **au bout de** to the end of; **jusqu'au bout** until the very end

**bouteille** *f.* bottle (6)

**boutique** *f.* shop, store

**bouton** *m.* button; push-button

**branché** *adj., fam.* trendy

**brancher** to connect (up); **se brancher (sur)** to link oneself (with); to go online (on the Internet)

**bras** *m. s., pl.* arm (13)

**brasser** to mix, stir

**brasserie** *f.* bar, brasserie

**bref/ève** *adj.* short, brief; *adv.* in short, in brief

**Brésil** *m.* Brazil (8)

**Bretagne** *f.* Brittany

**breton(ne)** *adj.* Breton; **Breton(ne)** *m., f.* Breton (*person*); **Far** (*m.*) **breton** traditional cake from Brittany

**bribes** *f. pl.* scraps, snippets

**bricolage** *m.* do-it-yourself work, puttering around (15)

**bricoler** to putter around, do odd jobs (15)

**brièvement** *adv.* briefly

**brillant** *adj.* brilliant; shining

**briller** to shine, gleam

**brique** *f.* brick

**briser** to break

**bronchite** *f.* bronchitis

**bronzer** to get a suntan (8)

**brosse** *f.* brush (13); **brosse à dents** toothbrush

**brosser** to brush; **se brosser les cheveux (les dents)** to brush one's hair (teeth) (13)

**brousse** *f.* (*African, Australian*) bush (country)

**bru** *f.* daughter-in-law (5)

**bruit** *m.* noise (5)

**brûlant** *adj.* burning; urgent

**brûlé** *adj.* burned, burnt; **crème** (*f.*) **brûlée** *custard topped with caramelized sugar*

**brumeux/euse** *adj.* foggy, misty

**brun** brown; **la sauce brune** gravy

**brutal** *adj.* violent, rough

**Bruxelles** Brussels

**bûche** *f.* log; **bûche de Noël** Yule log (*pastry*)

**bûcheron(ne)** *m., f.* woodcutter

**budget** *m.* budget (14); **budget militaire** military budget (16)

**buée** *f.* condensation; steam

**buffet** (*m.*) **de la gare** train station restaurant (9)

**bureau** *m.* desk (1); office (2), study (5); **bureau de change** money exchange (office) (14); **bureau de poste** post office (10); **bureau de tabac** (*government-licensed*) tobacconist (10)

**bus** *m.* (*city*) bus

**but** *m.* goal; objective; **ligne** (*f.*) **de but** goal, goal line (*soccer*)

**ça** *pron.* this, that; it (7); **ça cloche** things aren't going right; **ça m'est égal** it's all the same to me; **ça peut aller** all right, pretty well (1); **ça va?** how's it going? (1); **ça va** fine (things are going well) (1); **ça va bien (mal)** things are going well (badly) (1); **comme ci, comme ça** so-so (1)

**cabine** *f.* cabin; booth; **cabine téléphonique** telephone booth

**cabinet** *m.* office; **cabinet medical** doctor's office (13)

**câble** *m.* cable; cable TV (10); **télévision** (*f.*) **par câble** cable TV

**câblé** *adj.* wired; equipped for cable TV

**cachemire** *m.* cashmere

**cacher** to hide

**cacheter (je cachette)** to seal (*envelope*)

**cadeau** *m.* present, gift (10)

**cadien(ne)** *adj.* Cajun

**cadre** *m.* frame; setting, framework; middle (upper) manager (14)

**café** *m.* café (2); (cup of) coffee (2); coffee-flavored; **café au lait** coffee with milk; **café-tabac** *m.* bar- tobacconist (*government-licensed*) (11)

**cafetière** *f.* coffeepot, coffeemaker

**cahier** *m.* notebook (1); workbook

**caisse** *f.* cash register

**calcul** *m.* calculation; arithmetic; calculus; **faire des calculs** to do calculations

**calculer** to calculate, figure; **machine** (*f.*) **à calculer** adding machine

**calendrier** *m.* calendar

**Californie** *f.* California

**californien(ne)** *adj.* Californian

**calme** *m., adj.* calm (3)

**calmer** to calm (down)

**calorique** *adj.* caloric; **très (peu) calorique** high (low) in calories

**camarade** *m., f.* friend, companion; **camarade de chambre** roommate (3); **camarade de classe** classmate, schoolmate

**Cameroun** *m.* Cameroon

**caméscope (numérique)** *m.* (digital) camcorder, video camera (10)

**camion** *m.* truck (9)

**camp** (*m.*) **de travail forcé** forced laber camp

**campagne** *f.* country(side) (8); campaign; **à la campagne** in the country; **campagne électorale** election campaign; **pain** (*m.*) **de campagne** country-style bread, wheat bread (7); **pâté** (*m.*) **de campagne** terrine, (country-style) pâté (7)

**camper** to camp

**campeur/euse** *m., f.* camper

**camping** *m.* camping (8); **faire du camping** to go camping (8)

**Canada** *m.* Canada (2, 8)

**canadien** *adj.* Canadian; **Canadien(ne)** *m., f.* Canadian (*person*) (2)

**canal** (*pl.* **canaux**) *m.* channel; canal

**canapé** *m.* sofa, couch (4)

**canard** *m.* duck; *tr. fam.* newspaper; **confit** (*m.*) **de canard** duck conserve

**canari** *m.* canary

**cancre** *m.* dunce

**candélabre** *m.* candelabra

**candidat(e)** *m., f.* candidate; applicant

**candidature** *f.* candidacy; **poser sa candidature** to apply (14)

**caniche** *m.* poodle

**canicule** *f.* heat wave

**canne** (*f.*) **à sucre** sugarcane

**cannelle** *f.* cinnamon

**canon** *adj., fam.* sexy, gorgeous (*a woman*)

**cap** *m.* cape (*strip of land*)

**capitale** *f.* capital (*city*)

**capter** to pick up (a radio signal)

**car** *conj.* for, because

**caractère** *m.* character (*personality*)

**caractériser** to characterize; **se caractériser par** to be characterized (distinguished) by

**caractéristiques** *f.* characteristics

**carafe** *f.* carafe; pitcher (6)

**Caraïbes** *f. pl.* Caribbean (*islands*)

**caravane** *f.* caravan; (camping) trailer

**carburateur** *m.* carburetor

**cardiaque** *adj.* cardiac

**cardinal: points** (*m. pl.*) **cardinaux** compass points, directions

**cargaison** *f.* cargo

**caricaturiste** *m., f.* caricaturist, cartoonist

**carnaval** *m.* carnival

**carnet** *m.* booklet; **carnet d'adresses** address book; **carnet de chèques** checkbook (14)

**carotte** *f.* carrot (6)

**carré** *adj.* square (*geometry*)

**carreau** *m.* tile, window pane; **à carreaux** checkered, checked

**carrefour** *m.* intersection; crossroads (11)

**carrière** *f.* career

**cartable** *m.* schoolbag

**carte** *f.* card (3); menu (7); map (*of region, country*) (11); *pl.* (playing) cards; **carte bancaire** bank (ATM/credit) card (14); **carte d'anniversaire** birthday card; **carte de crédit** credit card (14); **carte de débit** debit card (14); **carte d'embarquement** boarding pass (9); **carte d'étudiant** student ID card; **carte d'identité** ID card (8); **carte postale** postcard (10); **carte routière** road map; **jouer aux cartes** to play cards (3)

**carton** *m.* box

**cartonner** *fam.* to score a success

**cas** *m.* case; **dans ce cas** in this case (situation); **en cas de** in case of; **en tout cas** in any case, at any rate; **selon le cas** as the case may be

**casque** *m.* helmet (8); headset

**casquette** *f.* cap; baseball cap (3)

**casser** to break; **se casser** *fam.* to leave (a place)

**casserole** *f.* saucepan

**casse-dalle** *m., fam.* sandwich

**casse-tête** *m.* puzzle, riddle game

**cassette** *f.* cassette tape (*video or audio*); **cassette vidéo** videotape; **lecteur** (*m.*) **de cassettes** cassette deck, cassette player

**cata: c'est la cata!** *fam.* It's a catastrophe!

**catégorie** *f.* category, class

**catégorique** *adj.* categorical, flat

**cathédrale** *f.* cathedral (12)

**cauchemar** *m.* nightmare

**cause: à cause de** because of

**cave** *f.* cellar

**CD (les CD)** *m.* CD (4); **lecteur** (*m.*) **de CD** compact disc player (4)

**ce (c')** **(cet, cette, ces)** *pron., adj.* this, that (7); **ce week-end** this weekend; **c'est-à-dire (que)** that is, I mean (10); **c'est moi.** It's me. (10); **c'est un(e)...** it's a (an) . . . ; **cet après-midi (ce matin, ce soir)** this afternoon (morning, evening) (5); **qu'est-ce que c'est?** what is it? (1); **qui est-ce?** who is it? (1)

**cédérom (CD-ROM)** *m.* CD-ROM

**cédille** *f.* cedilla (ç)

**ceinture** *f.* belt; **ceinture de sécurité** seat belt

**cela (ça)** *pron.* this, that

**célèbre** *adj.* famous

**célébrer (je célèbre)** to celebrate (6)

**célébrité** *f.* celebrity

**céleri** *m.* celery

**célibataire** *adj.* single (*person*) (5); *n. m., f.* single person (13)

**cellulaire** *m.* cellular phone

**celui (ceux, celle, celles)** *pron.* the one, the ones; this one, that one; these, those

**cendres** *f. pl.* ashes

**cendrier** *m.* ashtray

**censé: être censé(e)** + *inf.* to be supposed to (*do s.th.*)

**cent** *adj.* one hundred

**centaine** *f.* about one hundred

**centrale** *f.* power station; **centrale nucléaire** nuclear power plant (16)

**centre** *m.* center; **centre d'hébergement** shelter; **centre-ville** *m.* downtown (11)

**cependant** *conj.* however, nevertheless

**céramique** *f.* pottery, ceramics

**cercle** *m.* circle

**céréales** *f. pl.* cereal; grains

**cérémonie** *f.* ceremony (13)

**cerise** *f.* cherry

**cerné de** surrounded by

**certain** *adj.* sure; particular; certain (15); *pl., pron.* certain ones, some people; **il est certain que** + *indic.* it's certain that (16)

**certificat** *m.* certificate, diploma

**ces** (see **ce**)

**cesser** to stop, cease

**c'est-à-dire** *conj.* that is to say, I mean

**cet** (see **ce**)

**chacun(e)** *m., f., pron.* each (one), every one (15)

**chagrin** *m.* grief

**chaîne** *f.* television channel; network (10); chain

**chair** *f.* meat; flesh

**chaise** *f.* chair (1)

**chaleur** *f.* heat; warmth

**chaleureux/euse** *adj.* warm; friendly

**chambre** *f.* room; bedroom (4); hotel room; **camarade** (*m., f.*) **de chambre** roommate (3); **chambre de bonne** (4) garret; maid's room

**chameau** *m.* camel

**champ** *m.* field

**champagne** *m.* champagne, sparkling wine (*from Champagne*)

**champignon** *m.* mushroom (6)

**champion(ne)** *m., f.,* champion

**chance** *f.* luck; possibility; opportunity; **avoir de la chance** to be lucky (3); **bonne chance** *interj.* good luck; **pas de chance** no luck; **quelle chance** what luck

**chancelant** unsteady, faltering

**chandail** *m.* sweater

**change** *m.* currency exchange; **bureau** (*m.*) **de change** money exchange (office) (14); **taux** (*m.*) **de change** exchange rate (14)

**changement** *m.* change

**changer (nous changeons)** to change; to exchange (*currency*) (14); **changer d'avis** to change one's mind; **changer de l'argent** to exchange currency

**chanson** *f.* song (15); **chanson de variété** popular song (15)

**chant** *m.* song

**chanter** to sing

**chanteur/euse** *m., f.,* singer

**chantilly** *f.* whipped cream; **à la chantilly** with whipped cream

**chapeau** *m.* hat (3)

**chapitre** *m.* chapter

**chaque** *adj.* each, every (4)

**charbon** *m.* coal; charcoal

**charcuterie** *f.* deli; cold cuts; pork butcher's shop, delicatessen (7); **boucherie-charcuterie** *f.* combination butcher and deli

**charge** (*f.*); **charges comprises** utilities included; **pris/en/charge par** taken care of by

**chargé (de)** *adj.* in charge (of), responsible (for); heavy, loaded (with); busy

**chargement** *m.* loading; shipping; **gare** (*f.*) **de chargement** loading dock

**charger (nous chargeons)** to load; **charger de** to ask (*s.o. to do s.th.*); **se charger de** to take responsibility for, take care of

**charlotte** *f.* charlotte (*cake with whipped cream and fruit*)

**charmant** *adj.* charming (3)

**charmer** to charm, enchant

**charmeur** (*m.*) **de serpents** snake charmer

**charolais** *adj.* of (from) Charolais

**charte** *f.* charter, title

**chasse** *f.* hunt, hunting

**chasser** to hunt; to chase away

**chat(te)** *m., f.* cat (4)

**châtain** *adj.* brown, chestnut-colored (*hair*) (3)

**château** *m.* castle, chateau (11)

**chatier** to punish

**chaud** *adj.* warm; hot; **avoir chaud** to be warm (hot) (3); **il fait chaud** it's hot (5)

**chauffeur/euse** *m., f.,* chauffeur; driver; **chauffeur/euse de taxi** taxi(cab) driver

**chaussée** *f.* pavement; **rez-de-chaussée** *m.* ground floor (5)

**chaussettes** *f. pl.* socks (3)

**chaussures** *f. pl.* shoes (3); **chaussures de ski (de montagne)** ski (hiking) boots (8)

**chavirer** to capsize

**chef** *m.* leader; head; chef, head cook; **chef d'entreprise** company head, top manager, boss (14)

**chef-d'œuvre** *m.* (*pl.* **chefs-d'œuvre**) masterpiece (12)

**chemin** *m.* way (road) (11); path; **chemin de fer** railroad

**chemise** *f.* shirt (3)

**chemisier** *m.* (*woman's*) shirt, blouse (3)

**chèque** *m.* check (14); **carnet** (*m.*) **de chèques** checkbook (14); **chèque de voyage** traveler's check; **compte-chèques** *m.* checking account (14); **déposer un chèque** to deposit a check; **encaisser (toucher) un chèque** to cash a check; **faire un chèque** to write a check (14)

**cher/ère** *adj.* expensive; dear (3)

**chercher** to look for (2); to pick up (*a passenger*); **chercher à** to try to (12)

**chéri(e)** *m., f.,* darling

**cheval** (*pl.* **chevaux**) *m.* horse (8); **à cheval** on horseback; **faire du cheval** to go horseback riding (8); **queue** (*f.*) **de cheval** ponytail

**cheveux** *m. pl.* hair (3); **se brosser les cheveux** to brush one's hair (13)

**chèvre** *f.* (she-) goat

**chez** at the home (establishment) of (5); **chez moi** at my place

**chic** *adj., often inv.* chic, stylish (3)

**chien(ne)** *m., f.,* dog (4)

**chiffre** *m.* number, digit; **chiffre d'affaires** turnover (*in business*); **chiffre record** record number

**chimie** *f.* chemistry (2)

**chimique** *adj.* chemical; **produit** (*m.*) **chimique** chemical

**chimiste** *m., f.* chemist

**Chine** *f.* China (2, 8)

**chinois** *adj.* Chinese; *m.* Chinese (*language*) (2); **Chinois(e)** *m., f.* Chinese (*person*) (2)

**choc** *m.* clash; shock; jolt

**chocolat** *m.* chocolate; hot chocolate (6); **éclair** (*m.*) **au chocolat** chocolate eclair; **mousse** (*f.*) **au chocolat** chocolate mousse; **pain** (*m.*) **au chocolat** chocolate croissant

**chocolaterie** *f.* chocolate shop

**chocolatier/ière** *m., f.* chocolate maker

**choisir (de)** to choose (to) (4)

**choix** *m.* choice

**chômage** *m.* unemployment (14); **taux** (*m.*) **de chômage** unemployment rate (14)

**chômeur/euse** *m., f.,* unemployed person (14)

**choquer** to shock

**chose** *f.* thing; **autre chose** something else (7); **quelque chose** something (9); **quelque chose de** + *adj.* something + *adj.* (15)

**chou** *m.* cabbage; (*fam.*) darling; **chou-fleur** (*pl.* **choux-fleurs**) *m.* cauliflower

**choucroute** *f.* sauerkraut

**chrétien(ne)** *adj.* Christian

**chronique** *adj.* chronic

**chronologique** *adj.* chronological

**ci: comme ci, comme ça** so-so (1); **ci-dessous** *adv.* below; **ci-dessus** *adv.* above, previously

**ciboulette** *f.* chive(s)

**cidre** *m.* cider

**ciel** *m.* sky; **gratte-ciel** *m. inv.* skyscraper

**cigare** *m.* cigar

**cils** *m. pl.* eyelashes

**cimetière** *m.* cemetery

**cinéaste** *m., f.* filmmaker (12)

**ciné-club** *m.* film club

**cinéma** (*fam.* **ciné**) *m.* movies; movie theater (2)

**cinglé(e)** *m., f.* lunatic, crazy person

**cinq** *adj.* five (1)

**cinquante** *adj.* fifty (1); **les années** (*f. pl.*) **cinquante** the decade (era) of the fifties

**cinquième** *adj.* fifth (11)

**circonflexe** *m.* circumflex (*accent*) (**ê**)

**circonstance** *f.* circumstance

**circuit** *m.* organized tour

**circulation** *f.* traffic; circulation

**circuler** to circulate; to travel

**cire** *f.* wax

**ciré** *adj.* polished; waxed

**cirque** *m.* circus

**cirrhose** *f.* cirrhosis

**citadin(e)** *m., f.* city-dweller

**citation** *f.* quotation

**cité** *f.* area in a city; **cité universitaire** (*fam.* **cité-U**) university dormitory (2)

**citer** to cite, name; to quote

**citoyen(ne)** *m., f.* citizen (16)

**citron** *m.* lemon; **citron pressé** fresh lemon juice; **citron vert** lime (*fruit*)

**cive** *f.* chive

**civil: état** (*m.*) **civil** marital (civil) status

**clair** *adj.* light, bright; light-colored; clear; evident; **il est clair que** + *indic.* it's clear that (16)

**clandestin** *adj.* clandestine, secret

**claquer** *fam.* spend

**clarinette** *f.* clarinet

**classe** *f.* class; classroom; *adj., fam.* chic, stylish; **camarade** (*m., f.*) **de classe** classmate; **classe affaires (économique)** business (tourist) class (9); **première (deuxième [seconde]) classe** first (second) class (9); **salle** (*f.*) **de classe** classroom (1)

**classement** *m.* classification

**classer** to classify; to sort; to rate; **se classer** to come in; to rank

**classique** *adj.* classical; classic; **musique** (*f.*) **classique** classical music

**clavier** *m.* keyboard (10)

**clé, clef** *f.* key (5); **mot clé** *m.* key word

**clic** *m.* click

**client(e)** *m., f.* customer, client

**clientèle** *f.* clientele, customers

**climat** *m.* climate

**climatisé** *adj.* air-conditioned

**cliquer (sur)** to click (on) (10)

**cloche** *f.* bell

**clocher** *fam.* to be cockeyed; to go wrong; **ça cloche** things are going wrong

**clos** *m.* field

**clou** (*m.*) **de girofle** clove

**club** *m.* club (*social, athletic*); **ciné-club** *m.* film club

**coca** *m., fam.* cola drink

**cocasse** *adj.* comical, funny

**cocher** to check off (*list*)

**coco: noix** (*f.*) **de coco** coconut; **lait** (*m.*) **de coco** coconut milk

**cocotier** *m.* coconut tree

**cocotte** *f.* stewpot, casserole

**code** *m.* code; **code postal** postal (zip) code

**cœur** *m.* heart (13); **au cœur de** at the heart (source) of; **par cœur** by heart (12)

**coexister** to coexist

**coffre** *m.* trunk (*of car*) (9)

**coffret** *m.* box; lunch box

**coiffeur/euse** *m., f.* hairdresser; barber (14)

**coiffure** *f.* hair style; **salon** (*m.*) **de coiffure** beauty salon

**coin** *m.* corner (11)

**colis** *m.* package, parcel (10)

**collant** *m.* pantyhose

**collectif/ive** *adj.* collective

**collectionner** to collect

**collège** *m.* (*French*) *secondary school*

**collègue** *m., f.* colleague

**colocataire** (*fam.* **coloc**) *m., f.* housemate, roommate

**colocation** *f.* house or apartment sharing

**colombage** *m.* half-timbers

**Colombie** *f.* Colombia; **Colombie-Britannique** *f.* British Columbia

**colonie** *f.* colony

**colonisateur/trice** *m., f.* colonizer

**colonisé** *adj.* colonized

**colonne** *f.* column

**combatif/ive** *adj.* fighting, combative

**combattre** (*like* **battre**) *irreg.* to fight

**combien (de)?** *adv.* how much? (1), how many? (4); **c'est combien?** how much is it? (1) **depuis combien de temps... ?** (for) how long . . . ? (9); **pendant combien de temps... ?** (for) how long . . . ? (9)

**combinaison** *f.* combination

**combiner** to combine

**comédie** *f.* comedy

**comédien(ne)** *m., f.* stage actor; comedian (12)

**comète** *f.* comet

**comique** *m., f.* comedian, comic; *adj.* funny, comical, comic

**commande** *f.* order (*in business, restaurant*)

**commandement** *m.* command (*military leadership*)

**commander** to order (*in a restaurant*) (6)

**comme** *adv.* as, like, how; **comme ci, comme ça** so-so (1)

**commencement** *m.* beginning

**commencer (nous commençons) (à)** to begin (to) (2); **commencer par** to begin by (*doing s.th.*)

**comment** *adv.* how; **comment** what, how (1); **comment allez-vous? (comment vas-tu?)** how are you? (1); **comment ça va?** how are you?, how's it going? (1); **comment dit-on... en français?** how do you say . . . in French?; **comment est-il/elle?** what's he/she/it like?; **comment s'appelle-t-il/elle?** what's his/her name?; **comment vous appelez-vous? (comment t'appelles-tu?)** what's your name? (1)

**commentaire** *m.* remark, comment; commentary

**commenter** to comment on

**commerçant(e)** *m., f.* shopkeeper (14); *adj.* commercial, shopping

**commerce** *m.* business (2)

**commercial** *adj.* commercial, business; **directeur/trice** (*m., f.*) **commercial(e)** business manager (14)

**commissariat** *m.* police station (11)

**commission** *f.* commission; errand

**commode** *f.* chest of drawers (4); *adj.* convenient

**commun** *adj.* ordinary, common; shared; **bien** (*m.*) **commun** common good (16); **en commun** in common; **transports** (*m. pl.*) **en commun** public transportation

**communauté** *f.* community

**commune** *f.* district

**communicatif/ive** *adj.* communicative

**communication** *f.* communication; phone call

**communiquer** to communicate

**compact: disque** (*m.*) **compact** compact disc

**compagnie** *f.* company

**compagnon/compagne** *m., f.* companion

**comparaison** *f.* comparison

**comparer** to compare

**compartiment** *m.* compartment (9)

**compatriote** *m., f.* fellow countryman (-woman)

**complément** *m.* complement; **pronom** (*m.*) **complément d'objet (in)direct** *Gram.* (in)direct object pronoun

**complémentaire** *adj.* complementary

**complet/ète** *adj.* complete; whole

**compléter (je complète)** to complete, finish

**compliqué** *adj.* complicated

**comportement** *m.* behavior

**composé** *adj.* composed; **passé** (*m.*) **composé** *Gram.* compound past tense

**composer** to compose; to make up; **composer le numéro** to dial the (phone) number (10)

**compositeur/trice** *m., f.* composer (12)

**composter** to stamp (*date*); to punch (*ticket*)

**compréhensif/ive** *adj.* understanding

**compréhension** *f.* understanding

**comprendre** (*like* **prendre**) *irreg.* to understand; to comprise, include (6); **je ne comprends pas** I don't understand (1)

**comprimé** *m.* tablet, pill

**compris** *adj.* included (7); **tout compris** all inclusive

**comptabilité** *f.* accounting

**comptable** *m., f.* accountant (14); **expert(e)-comptable** *m., f.* certified public accountant

**compte** *m.* account; **à son compte** for oneself (14); **compte bancaire** bank account; **compte d'épargne** savings account (14); **travailler pour (à) son compte** to be self-employed (14)

**compter** to plan (to do something); to intend; to count (14); to have; to include; **compter sur** to count on, rely on (s.o. or s.th.)

**concentrer** to concentrate

**concerner** to concern; **en ce qui concerne** concerning

**concevoir** (*like* **recevoir**) *irreg.* to conceive, design

**concierge** *m., f.* caretaker, super, janitor; concierge

**concilier** to reconcile

**conclu** (*p.p. of* **conclure**) *adj.* settled, agreed upon

**concours** *m. s.* competition; competitive exam

**conçu** (*p.p. of* **concevoir**) *adj.* designed, devised, conceived

**concurrence** *f.* competition; trading

**concurrencer** to rival, compete with

**concurrent(e)** *m., f.* competitor

**condamner** to condemn

**condition** *f.* condition; situation; **à condition de** provided, providing

**conditionnel** *m., Gram.* conditional

**conducteur/trice** *m., f.* driver (9); engineer (*train*)

**conduire** (*p.p.* **conduit**) *irreg.* to drive (9); to take; to lead; **permis** (*m.*) **de conduire** driver's license

**conduite** *f.* behavior, conduct

**confection** *f.* making (*clothing*)

**conférence** *f.* lecture (12); conference

**confiance** *f.* confidence; **avoir confiance en** to have confidence in; to trust; **faire confiance à** to trust in

**confié (à)** *adj.* entrusted (to)

**confirmer** to confirm

**confiserie** *f.* candy store

**confit** (*m.*) **de canard** duck conserve

**confiture** *f.* jam

**conflit** *m.* conflict (16)

**confondre** to mix up, confuse

**confondu** *adj.* mixed, confused

**conformiste** *m., f., adj.* conformist (3)

**confort** *m.* comfort; amenities

**confortable** *adj.* comfortable

**congé** *m.* vacation, leave (*from work*)

**Congo** *m.* Congo (8); **République** (*f.*) **Démocratique du Congo** Democratic Republic of Congo (8)

**congolais** *adj.* Congolese; **Congolais(e)** *m., f.* Congolese (*person*)

**congrès** *m.* meeting, convention

**conjugaison** *f., Gram.* (verb) conjugation

**conjuguer** to conjugate

**connaissance** *f.* knowledge; acquaintance; **faire connaissance** to get acquainted; **faire la connaissance de** to meet (*for the first time*), make the acquaintance of (5)

**connaisseur/euse** *m., f.* connoisseur

**connaître** (*p.p.* **connu**) *irreg.* to know, be familiar with (11); **se connaître** to know one another; to meet

**connecté** logged on, connected (*to the Internet*)

**connerie** *f.*, *tr. fam.* stupid mistake

**connexion** *f.* link, connection; **connexion ADSL** DSL connection/line (10)

**connu** *adj.* known; famous

**conquérir** (*p.p.* **conquis**) *irreg.* to conquer

**consacrer** to devote

**se consacrer à** to devote oneself to

**conscience** *f.* conscience; **prendre conscience de** to become aware of

**conseil** *m.* (piece of) advice; council; **donner des conseils à** to give advice to

**conseiller (à, de)** to advise; to suggest (12)

**conseiller/ère** *m.*, *f.* adviser; **conseiller/ère d'orientation** guidance counselor

**conservation** *f.* conserving; preservation (16)

**conservatoire** *m.* conservatory

**conserve** *f.* preserve(s), canned food; *pl.* canned goods (7); **boîte** (*f.*) **de conserve** can of food (7)

**conserver** to conserve, preserve (16)

**considération: prendre en considération** to take into consideration

**considérer (je considère)** to consider (6)

**consigne** *f.* instruction(s); **consigne (automatique)** coin locker (9)

**consommateur/trice** *m.*, *f.* consumer

**consommation** *f.* consumption; consumerism

**consommé** *m.* clear soup, consommé

**consommer** to consume (16)

**conspirer à** to conspire to

**constamment** *adv.* constantly (12)

**constater** to notice; to remark

**constituer** to constitute

**constructeur** *m.* maker; constructor

**constructif/ive** *adj.* constructive

**construire** (*like* **conduire**) *irreg.* to construct, build (9)

**consulter** to consult; **consulter l'annuaire** to look up a phone number (10)

**contacter** to contact

**conte** *m.* tale, story; **conte de fée** fairy tale

**contempler** to contemplate, meditate upon

**contemporain** *adj.* contemporary

**contenir** (*like* **tenir**) *irreg.* to contain

**content** *adj.* happy, pleased (3); **être content(e) de** (+ *inf.*) to be happy about (to); **être content(e) que** + *subj.* to be happy that

**contenter** to please

**contenu** *m.* content

**contester** to dispute; to answer

**conteur/euse** *m.*, *f.* storyteller

**continuer (à)** to continue (to) (11)

**contracter** to get, contract (*a disease*)

**contraire: vent** (*m.*) **contraire** headwind

**contrairement à** contrary to, unlike

**contrat** *m.* contract

**contravention** *f.* traffic ticket

**contre** *prep.* against; **le pour et le contre** the pros and cons; **manifester contre** to demonstrate against (16)

**contrôle** *m.* control, overseeing; inspection

**contrôler** to inspect, monitor (14)

**contrôleur/euse** *m.*, *f.* ticket collector; conductor

**convaincant** *adj.* convincing

**convaincre** (*p.p.* **convaincu**) *irreg.* to convince

**convenable** *adj.* proper; appropriate

**convenir** (*like* **venir**) *irreg.* to be suitable

**converger (nous convergeons) (vers)** to converge (on), lead (toward)

**convertisseur** *m.* converter

**convoquer** to summon, invite, convene

**coordonner** to coordinate

**copain (copine)** *m.*, *f.*, *fam.* friend, pal (7); boyfriend (girlfriend) (7)

**copier** to copy

**copieux/euse** *adj.* copious, abundant

**coq** *m.* rooster; **coq au vin** coq au vin (*chicken prepared with red wine*)

**coquelicot** *m.* poppy

**coquillages** *m. pl.* seashells

**corbeau** *m.* crow

**corps** *m. s.* body (13)

**correctement** *adv.* correctly

**correspondance** *f.* correspondence

**correspondant(e)** *m.*, *f.* newspaper correspondent; *adj.* corresponding

**correspondre** to correspond

**corriger (nous corrigeons)** to correct

**Corse** *f.* Corsica

**cortège** *m.* procession

**cortisone** *f.* cortisone

**cosmopolite** *adj.* cosmopolitan

**costumé** *m.* (*man's*) suit; costume (3)

**costumé: soirée** (*f.*) **costumée** costume party

**costumier/ière** *m.*, *f.* costume designer

**côte** *f.* coast; chop (7); rib; rib steak; side; **côte d'agneau (de porc)** lamb (pork) chop; **Côte d'Azur** (French) Riviera; **Côte d'Ivoire** *f.* Cote d'Ivoire (2, 8)

**côté** *m.* side; **(d')à côté** (from) next door; **à côté (de)** *prep.* by, near; beside, next to (4); at one's side; **mettre de côté** to set aside

**coton** *m.* cotton

**cou** *m.* neck (13)

**couchage: sac** (*m.*) **de couchage** sleeping bag (8)

**coucher** to put to bed; **se coucher** to go to bed (13)

**couchette** *f.* berth (*train*) (9)

**coucou** *interj.*, *fam.* peek-a-boo

**coudre** (*p.p.* **cousu**) *irreg.* to sew; **machine** (*f.*) **à coudre** sewing machine

**coulé** *adj.* cast

**couleur** *f.* color; **de quelle couleur est… ?** what color is . . . ?; **en couleur(s)** in color; colored

**coulis** *m.* purée

**couloir** *m.* hall(way) (4)

**coup** *m.* blow; **boire un coup** to have a drink; **coup à blanc** blank shot; **coup de foudre** flash of lightning (13); love at first sight (13); **coup de pouce** little push (in the right direction); **coup de téléphone** telephone call; **coup d'œil** glance, quick look; **tout à coup** *adv.* suddenly (11)

**coupe** *f.* trophy, cup; ice cream sundae; **Coupe d'Europe** European Cup (*soccer*); **Coupe du Monde** World Cup (*soccer*)

**couper** to cut (off, up); **couper la ligne** to cut off (*phone call*)

**couple** *m.* (*engaged, married*) couple

**cour** *f.* court (*legal, royal*)

**courage** *m.* courage; spirit; **bon courage** *interj.* cheer up, be brave

**courageux/euse** *adj.* courageous (3)

**couramment** *adv.* fluently (12)

**courant** *adj.* general, everyday; **être au courant de** to be up (to date) with

**coureur/euse** *m.*, *f.* runner; **coureur/euse cycliste** bicycle racer

**courir** (*p.p.* **couru**) *irreg.* to run (13)

**couronne** *f.* crown; royalty

**couronné** *adj.* crowned

**courriel** *m.*, *fam.* e-mail message (10)

**courrier** *m.* mail (10); **courrier électronique** e-mail (*in general*)

**cours** *m. s.* course (2); class; exchange rate (14); price; **au cours de** during; **cours d'eau** river, waterway; **cours du jour** today's exchange rate; **suivre un cours** to take a course

**course** *f.* race; errand; **faire les courses** to do errands; to shop (5)

**court** *adj.* short (3); *m.* (tennis) court; **à court terme** in the short term (run)

**court-bouillon** *m.* broth

**couscous** *m.* couscous (*North African cracked-wheat dish*)

**couscoussier** *m.* couscous pan (*with steamer*)

**cousin(e)** *m.*, *f.* cousin (5)

**coût** *m.* cost; **coût de la vie** cost of living (14)

**couteau** *m.* knife (6)

**coûter** to cost

**coutume** *f.* custom, tradition

**couture** *f.* sewing; clothes design; *\**haute couture** high fashion

**couturier/ière** *m.*, *f.* clothes designer; dressmaker

**couvert (de)** *adj.* covered (with); *m.* table setting; **mettre le couvert** to set the table (10)

**couverture** *f.* coverage; cover

**couvrir** (*like* **ouvrir**) *irreg.* to cover (14)

**covoiturage** *m.* carpooling (16)

**crabe** *m.* crab (*seafood*)

**craindre** (*p.p.* **craint**) *irreg.* to fear

**craquer** to crack, snap

**cravate** *f.* tie (3)

**crayon** *m.* pencil (1)

**créateur/trice** *m.*, *f.* creator

**créativité** *f.* creativity

**crèche** *f.* day-care center

**crédit** *m.* credit; **carte** (*f.*) **de crédit** credit card (14)

**credo** *m.* creed, system of beliefs

**créer** to create

**crème** *f.* cream (6); *m.* coffee with cream; **crème brulée** *custard topped with caramelized sugar*; **crème fraîche** clotted cream, crème fraîche; **crème glacée** *Q.* ice cream; **crème solaire** suntan lotion (8)

**crêpe** *f.* crepe, French pancake

**crevé** *adj.*, *fam.* exhausted, wiped out

**crevette** *f.* shrimp

**cri** *m.* cry, shout

**crier** to cry out; to shout

**crise** *f.* crisis; **crise économique** recession; depression

**critère** *f.* criterion

**critique** *m.*, *f.* critic

**critiquer** to criticize

**croire** (*p.p.* **cru**) **(à/en)** *irreg.* to believe (in) (10); **croire que** to believe that

**croisière** *f.* cruise; **bateau** (*m.*) **de croisière** cruise ship

**croissant** *m.* croissant (*roll*) (6); *adj.* growing

**croisé: mers croisées** *choppy seas, waves*

**croix** *f.* cross
**croyance** *f.* belief
**cru** *adj.* raw; *m.* vintage; vineyard or wine-producing region; **lait** (*m.*) **cru** unpasteurized milk
**crustacé** *m.* crustacea, shellfish
**cuillère** *f.* spoon (6); **cuillère à soupe** soup spoon, tablespoon (6); **petite cuillère** teaspoon
**cuillerée** *f.* spoonful (*measure*)
**cuir** *m.* leather; **en cuir** (*made of*) leather
**cuire: faire cuire** to cook (*food*)
**cuisine** *f.* cooking (6); food, cuisine; kitchen (5); **faire la cuisine** to cook (5); **nouvelle cuisine** light (low-fat) cuisine
**cuisiner** to cook
**cuisinette** *f.* kitchenette
**cuisinier/ière** *m., f.* cook, chef
**cuisse** *f.* leg; thigh
**cuisson** *f.* cooking (*process*)
**cuit** *adj.* cooked
**culinaire** *adj.* culinary, cooking
**culotte** *f.* breeches
**cultivé** *adj.* educated; cultured
**cultiver** to cultivate; to grow (*crops*)
**culture** *f.* education; culture
**culturel(le)** *adj.* cultural
**cure** *f.* course of treatment
**curieux/euse** *adj.* curious (3)
**curiosité** *f.* curiosity
**curriculum** (*m.*) **vitæ** résumé (14)
**cybercafé** *m.* Web (Internet) café
**cybermarché** *m.* Web (Internet) market
**cyclable: piste** (*f.*) **cyclable** bike path
**cyclisme** *m.* cycling (15)
**cycliste** *m., f.* cyclist, bicycle rider
**cynique** *adj.* cynical
**cynisme** *m.* cynicism

**d'abord** *adv.* first, first of all, at first (11)
**d'accord** *interj.* all right, O.K., agreed (2)
**dalle: avoir la dalle** to be hungry; **casse-dalle** *m.* sandwich
**dame** *f.* lady, woman; **messieurs dames** *colloq.* ladies and gentlemen
**Danemark** *m.* Denmark
**dangereux/euse** *adj.* dangerous
**dans** *prep.* within, in (2); **dans quatre jours** in four days (from now)
**danse** *f.* dance; dancing
**danser** to dance (2)
**danseur/euse** *m., f.* dancer
**darne** *f.* steak (*fish*)
**date** *f.* date (*time*); **quelle est la date (d'aujourd'hui)?** what's today's date? (1)
**dater de** to date from (12)
**datte** *f.* date (*fruit*)
**d'autres** *pron.* others (15)
**davantage** *adv.* more
**de (d')** *prep.* of, from, about (2); **de nouveau** again (11); **de rien** not at all; don't mention it; you're welcome (1); **de temps en temps** from time to time (2)
**débarquement** *m.* disembarkation, landing
**débarquer** to land
**débat** *m.* debate
**débit: carte de débit** debit card (14)
**débouché** *m.* opening, (job) prospect
**déboucher** to come out, lead to
**debout** *adj., inv., adv.* standing up
**se débrouiller** to manage (13)
**début** *m.* beginning; **au début (de)** in (at) the beginning (of)

**débutant(e)** *m., f.* beginner, novice
**débuter** to begin, start
**décapotable** *f.* convertible (*car*)
**décembre** December (1)
**décevoir** to disappoint
**déchets** *m. pl.* waste (material) (16); **déchets industriels** industrial waste; debris; **déchets nucléaires** nuclear waste
**déchirer** to rip; *fam.* to be the height of fashion
**décidément** *adv.* decidedly; definitely
**décider (de)** to decide (to) (12)
**décision** *f.* decision; **prendre une décision** to make a decision
**déclencher** to release, activate
**déclin** *m.* decline
**déconseillé** *adj.* not recommended
**décor** *m.* setting
**décoratif/ive** *adj.* decorative
**décorer (de)** to decorate (with)
**découler** to follow from; to ensue
**découper** to cut up
**découragé** *adj.* discouraged
**décourager** to discourage
**découverte** *f.* discovery
**découvrir** (*like* **ouvrir**) *irreg.* to discover (14)
**décrire** (*like* **écrire**) *irreg.* to describe (10)
**décrocher** *fam.* to get, receive
**déçu** *adj.* disappointed
**dédié** *adj.* consecrated, dedicated
**défaite** *f.* defeat
**défaut** *m.* defect, fault
**défavoriser** to penalize, put at a disadvantage
**défendre** to defend; to prohibit, disallow
**défenseur** *m.* defender, champion
**défi** *m.* challenge (16)
**défiance** *f.* mistrust
**défilé** *m.* fashion show
**défiler** to file past; to unwind
**défini: article** (*m.*) **défini** *Gram.* definite article
**définir** to define
**définitif/ive** *adj.* definitive, permanent
**déforestation** (*f.*) **tropicale** tropical rainforest deforestation (16)
**dégager (nous dégageons)** to release; to clear; to bring out
**dégâts** *m. pl.* damage, harm
**dégénérer (je dégénère)** to degenerate
**dégouliner** to drip
**dégourdir** to bring the circulation back to; to warm up
**degré** *m.* degree
**déguiser** to disguise
**dégustation** *f.* tasting
**déguster** to taste (*wine*)
**dehors** *adv.* outdoors; outside; **en dehors de** *prep.* outside
**déjà** *adv.* already; ever (9)
**déjeuner** to have lunch (6); *m.* lunch (6); **petit déjeuner** breakfast (6)
**delà: au-delà de** *prep.* beyond
**délai** *m.* wait, time period
**délégué(e)** *m., f.* delegate
**délice** *m.* delight
**délicieux/euse** *adj.* delicious
**délinquance** *f.* criminality
**délire: en délire** ecstatic; *adj., fam.* great, fantastic
**demain** *adv.* tomorrow (5)
**demande** (*f.*) **d'emploi** job application (14)

**demander (de)** to ask (for, to), request (2); **se demander** to wonder (13)
**se démarquer (par)** to stand out, distinguish oneself
**déménagement** *m.* move out (of a home)
**déménager (nous déménageons)** to move out (*change residence*) (4)
**demeure** *f.* residence
**demeurer** to remain
**demi** *adj.* half; **demi-frère** *m.* half brother; stepbrother (5); **demi-sœur** *f.* half sister; stepsister (5); **et demi(e)** half past (the hour) (6)
**démocratie** *f.* democracy
**démocratique: République** (*f.*) **Démocratique du Congo** Democratic Republic of Congo (8)
**démodé** *adj.* old-fashioned
**démolir** to demolish, destroy
**démonstratif/ive** *adj.* demonstrative
**dénoncer (nous dénonçons)** to denounce
**dent** *f.* tooth (13); **brosse** (*f.*) **à dents** toothbrush; **se brosser les dents** to brush one's teeth (13)
**dentelle** *f.* lace
**dentiste** *m., f.* dentist (14)
**dépannage** *m.* emergency repair
**départ** *m.* departure (9); **point** (*m.*) **de départ** starting point
**se dépêcher** to hurry (13); **dépêche-toi!** hurry up! (6)
**dépendant** *adj.* dependent
**dépendre de** to depend on
**dépense** *f.* expense; spending (14)
**dépenser** to spend (*money*) (10)
**dépit: en dépit de** *prep.* in spite of
**déporté** *adj.* deported
**déposer** to deposit (14); **déposer de l'argent (un chèque)** to deposit money (a check) (14); **déposer la monnaie** to deposit change (10)
**dépôt-vente** *m.* resale store
**dépravation** *f.* depravity
**dépression** *f.* depression, breakdown
**déprime** *f., fam.* blues
**déprimé** *adj.* depressed
**depuis** *prep.* since, for (9); **depuis combien de temps... ?** (for) how long . . . ? (9); **depuis longtemps** for a long time; **depuis quand... ?** since when . . . ? (9)
**député** *m.* delegate, deputy
**déranger (nous dérangeons)** to disturb, bother
**dernier/ière** *adj.* last (4, 7); most recent; past; **la dernière fois** the last time; **l'an dernier (l'année dernière)** last year
**dernièrement** *adv.* recently
**se dérouler** to take place, happen
**derrière** *prep.* behind (4)
**dès** *prep.* from (*then on*); **dès que** *conj.* as soon as (14)
**désaccord** *m.* disagreement
**désagréable** *adj.* disagreeable, unpleasant (3)
**désavantage** *m.* disadvantage
**descendre** to go down (*street, river*) (5); to get off (5); to take down; **descendre à (sur)** to go down (*south*) to; **descendre de** to get down (from), get off
**déséquilibre** *m.* imbalance
**désert** *m.* desert; wilderness
**déserter** to desert; to run away
**désertique** *adj.* desert; barren; arid

**désespéré** *adj.* desperate

**désespoir** *m.* despair, hopelessness

**désigner** to designate

**désir** *m.* desire

**désirer** to desire, want (15)

**désolé** *adj.* sorry (16); **(je suis) désolé(e)** I'm sorry

**désordonné** *adj.* disorganized

**désordre** *m.* disorder, confusion; **en désordre** disorderly; disheveled (4)

**désormais** *adv.* henceforth

**dessert** *m.* dessert (6)

**dessin** *m.* drawing

**dessiné: bande** (*f.*) **dessinée** comic strip, cartoon (15); *pl.* comics

**dessiner** to draw (10)

**dessous: au-dessous de** *prep.* below; **ci-dessous** *adv.* below

**dessus: au-dessus de** *prep.* above; **ci-dessus** *adv.* above, previously

**destin** *m.* destiny

**destination** *f.* destination; **à destination de** to, for (9); in the direction of; heading for

**destinée** *f.* destiny, future

**détail** *m.* detail; **en détail** in detail

**détaillé** *adj.* detailed

**détecteur** *m.* detector

**se détendre** to relax (13)

**détente** *f.* relaxation

**déterminer** to determine

**détester** to detest; to hate (2)

**détour** *m.* detour

**détruire** (*like* **conduire**) *irreg.* to destroy (9)

**dette** *f.* debt

**deux** *adj.* two (1); **tous (toutes) les deux** both (of them)

**deuxième** *adj.* second (11); **deuxième classe** *f.* second class; **deuxième étage** third floor (*in the U.S.*) (5)

**devant** *prep.* before, in front of (4)

**développé** *adj.* developed; industrialized

**développement** *m.* development (16); developing (*photo*); **développement durable** sustainable development; **pays** (*m.*) **en voie de développement** developing country

**développer** to develop (16); **se développer** to develop

**devenir** (*like* **venir**) *irreg.* to become (8)

**deviner** to guess (12)

**devinette** *f.* riddle, conundrum

**dévoiler** to reveal, disclose

**devoir** (*p.p.* **dû**) *irreg.* to owe; to have to, be obliged to (7); *m.* duty; *m. pl.* homework; **faire ses devoirs** to do one's homework (5); **je devrais** I should (15)

**dévorant** *adj.* all-consuming

**d'habitude** *adv.* habitually, usually (5)

**diagnostic** *m.* diagnosis; prognosis

**diapositive** *f.* (*photographic*) slide

**dicter** to dictate

**dictionnaire** *m.* dictionary (2)

**diététique** *adj.* dietetic

**Dieu** *m.* God; **croire en Dieu** to believe in God

**différemment** *adv.* differently

**différend** *m.* disagreement

**différent** *adj.* different (3)

**difficile** *adj.* difficult (3)

**difficulté** *f.* difficulty

**diffuser** to broadcast; to disseminate

**digne** *adj.* worthy

**dignité** *f.* dignity

**diligemment** *adv.* diligently

**dimanche** *m.* Sunday (1); **le dimanche** on Sundays (5)

**diminuer** to lessen, diminish, lower (16)

**dinde** *f.* turkey

**dîner** to dine, have dinner (6); *m.* dinner (6)

**diplomate** *m., f.* diplomat; *adj.* diplomatic, tactful

**diplomatique** *adj.* diplomatic (*of the diplomatic corps*)

**diplôme** *m.* diploma

**diplômé(e)** *m., f.* graduate; holder of a diploma

**dire** (*p.p.* **dit**) *irreg.* to say; to tell, relate (10); **c'est-à-dire que** that is to say, namely, I mean (10); **entendre dire que** to hear that; **que veut dire... ?** what does . . . mean?; **se dire** to say to one another; **vouloir dire** to mean

**direct** *adj.* direct; **en direct** live (*broadcasting*); **pronom** (*m.*) **(complément) d'objet direct** *Gram.* direct object pronoun

**directeur/trice** *m., f.* manager, head (14); **directeur/trice commercial(e)** business manager (14)

**direction** *f.* direction; steering (*auto*)

**directives** *f. pl.* rules of conduct, directives

**diriger** (**nous dirigeons**) to direct (14); to govern, control

**discothèque** (*fam.* **disco**) *f.* discothèque

**discours** *m. s.* discourse; speech

**discret/ète** *adj.* discreet

**discuter (de)** to discuss

**disparaître** (*like* **connaître**) *irreg.* to disappear

**disparition** *f.* disappearance; **en voie de disparition** endangered (*species*)

**disponible** *adj.* available

**disposer** to arrange

**dispute** *f.* quarrel

**disputer** to contest; to play; to fight (over); **se disputer** to argue (13)

**disque** *n.* record, recording; **disque compact** compact disc

**dissertation** *f.* essay, term paper

**dissimuler** to hide

**dissiper** to dissipate; to dispel

**distance** *f.* distance; **mettre à distance** to separate

**distinguer** to differentiate; **se distinguer** to distinguish oneself

**distraction** *f.* recreation; entertainment; distraction

**se distraire** (*p.p.* **distrait**) *irreg.* to have fun, amuse oneself

**distribuer** to distribute

**distributeur** *m.* distributor; **distributeur automatique** automatic teller machine (ATM)

**divers** *adj.* varied, diverse (1)

**se diversifier** to diversify

**se divertir** to amuse oneself, have a good time

**divertissant** *adj.* amusing

**divisé (par)** *adj.* divided (by)

**divorcé** *adj.* divorced (5)

**divorcer** (**nous divorçons**) to get a divorce, divorce

**dix** *adj.* ten (1); **dix-sept (-huit, -neuf)** *adj.* seventeen (eighteen, nineteen) (1)

**dixième** *adj.* tenth

**dizaine** *f.* about ten

**djellaba** *f.* djellaba (hooded Moroccan robe for men)

**docteur** *m.* doctor

**doctorat** *m.* doctorate

**documentaire** *m.* documentary (*film*) (10)

**doigt** *m.* finger (13)

**domaine** *m.* domain; specialty

**domestique** *m., f.* servant; *adj.* domestic; **animal** (*m.*) **domestique** pet

**dominant: vent** (*m.*) **dominant** prevailing wind

**dominer** to dominate

**dommage!** *interj.* too bad! (16); **il est dommage que** + *subj.* it's too bad that (16)

**don** *m.* gift

**donc** *conj.* then; therefore (4)

**données: base** (*f.*) **de données** database

**donner** to give (2); **donner des conseils** to give advice; **donner rendez-vous à** to make an appointment with; **donner sur** to overlook

**dont** whose, of whom, of which (14)

**dorer: faire dorer** to brown (*in cooking*); **se dorer au soleil** to sunbathe

**dormir** *irreg.* to sleep (8)

**dortoir** *m.* dormitory

**dos** *m. s., pl.* back (13); **sac** (*m.*) **à dos** backpack (3)

**dossier** *m.* document; file

**douane** *f.* customs (*at the border*)

**doubler** to double; to pass (*in a car*)

**douche** *f.* shower (*bath*) (4); **prendre une douche** to take a shower

**se doucher** to take a shower (13)

**doudou** *f., fam.* (*West Indies*) girlfriend

**doué** *adj.* gifted, talented

**douleur** *f.* pain, ache (13); grief

**douleureux/euse** *adj.* painful, unhappy

**doute** *m.* doubt; **sans doute** probably

**douter** to doubt (16); **douter de** to be suspicious of

**doux (douce)** *adj.* sweet; **à feu doux** over a low flame (*cooking*); **petits pois** (*m. pl.*) **doux** sweet peas

**douzaine** *f.* dozen; about twelve

**douze** *adj.* twelve (1)

**douzième** *adj.* twelfth

**draguer** *fam.* to come on to, flirt with

**dragueur/euse** *m., f.* flirt

**dramatique: art** (*m.*) **dramatique** theater, theater arts

**drame** *m.* drama

**drap** *m.* sheet (*bed*)

**drapeau** *m.* flag

**dresser** to set up

**drogue** *f.* drug(s)

**droit** *m.* law (2); right (*legal*); **droits civils** civil rights (16); **droit d'entrée** entrance fee

**droit** *adj.* right; straight; **Rive** (*f.*) **droite** Right Bank (*in Paris*) (11); **tout droit** *adv.* straight ahead (11)

**droite** *f.* right, right-hand; **à droite (de)** *prep.* on (to) the right (of) (4)

**drôle** *adj.* funny, odd (3)

**duc** *m.* duke

**dur** *adj.* hard

**durable** lasting, enduring; **développement** (*m.*) **durable** sustainable development

**durant** *prep.* during

**durée** *f.* duration, length

**durer** to last, continue; to endure; to last a long time

**DVD** *m.* DVD (1); **lecteur** (*m.*) **de DVD** DVD player (1)

**dynamique** *adj.* dynamic (3)

**eau** *f.* water (6); **cours** (*m.*) **d'eau** river, waterway; **eau minérale** mineral water (6)
**ébène** *f.* ebony
**ébloui** *adj.* dazzled
**ébranlé** *adj.* shaken, shattered
**écart** *m.* gap; difference
**écarté** *adj.* removed
**échange** *m.* exchange
**échanger (nous échangeons)** to exchange (10)
**échapper (à)** to get away (from); **s'echapper** to escape
**s'échauffer** to warm up
**échec** *m.* failure; *pl.* chess (3)
**échelle** *f.* scale; ladder
**échouer** to fail
**éclair** *m.* éclair (*pastry*) (7)
**éclaircie** *f.* clearing (*in weather*)
**éclairer** to light, illuminate
**éclater** to break out (*war*); **s'éclater** *fam.* to have a great time, have fun
**école** *f.* school (10); **école primaire (secondaire)** primary (secondary) school
**écolier/ière** *m., f.* pupil, schoolchild
**écologie** *f.* ecology
**écologique** (*fam.* **écolo**) *adj.* ecological
**écologiste** *m., f.* ecologist, environmentalist (16); *adj.* ecological
**économe** *adj.* thrifty, economical
**économie** *f.* economics (2); economy; *pl.* savings; **faire des économies** to save (up) money (14)
**économique** *adj.* economic; financial; economical; **classe** (*f.*) **économique** tourist class (9); **sur le plan économique** economically speaking
**économiser** to save (*money*) (14)
**Écosse** *f.* Scotland; **Nouvelle-Écosse** *f.* Nova Scotia
**écoute** *f.* listening; **à l'écoute** tuning in
**écouter** to listen to (2)
**écran** *m.* screen (1, 10); monitor (10); **écran solaire** sunblock (8); **le petit écran** television
**écraser** to crush
**écrevisse** *f.* crayfish (7)
**écrire** (*p.p.* **écrit**) **(à)** *irreg.* to write (to) (10)
**écriture** *f.* writing; handwriting
**écrivain (femme écrivain)** *m., f.* writer (12)
**écumoire** *f.* skimmer (*in cooking*)
**édifice** *m.* (public) building
**éditeur/trice** *m., f.* editor; publisher
**édition** *f.* publishing; edition; **maison** (*f.*) **d'édition** publisher, publishing house
**éducatif/ive** *adj.* educational
**éducation** *f.* upbringing; breeding; education
**éduqué** *adj.* educated; brought up
**effacer** to erase, wipe out; **s'effacer (nous nous effaçons)** to fade; to stay in the background
**effectif/ive** *adj.* effective
**effectuer** to carry out, make
**effet** *m.* effect; **en effet** as a matter of fact, indeed
**efficace** *adj.* efficient
**effort** *m.* effort, attempt; **faire des efforts pour** to try (make an effort) to
**égal** *adj.* equal (16); **cela (ça) m'est égal** I don't care, it's all the same to me
**également** *adv.* equally; likewise, also
**égaler** to equal
**égalité** *f.* equality
**égard** (*m.*): **à cet égard** in this respect

**égaré** *adj.* scattered, lost
**église** *f.* church (11)
**égoïste** *adj.* selfish (3)
**égorger (nous égorgeons)** to slit the throat of
**Égypte** *f.* Egypt
**eh bien** *interj.* well, well then (10)
**élaborer** to refine; to develop
**s'élancer (nous nous élançons)** to rush out
**électeur/trice** *m., f.* voter (16)
**électoral** *adj.* election, electoral
**électricité** *f.* electricity
**électrique** *adj.* electric
**électronique: adresse** (*f.*) **électronique** e-mail address; **courrier** (*m.*) **électronique** e-mail; **message** (*m.*) **électronique** e-mail message
**élégant** *adj.* elegant (3)
**élève** *m., f.* pupil, student
**élevé** *adj.* high; raised, built
**éliminé** *adj.* eliminated
**élire** (*like* **lire**) *irreg.* to elect (16)
**elle** *pron., f. s.* she; her; it; **elle-même** *pron., f. s.* herself (12); **elles** *pron., f. pl.* they; them
**élu** *adj.* elected
**emancipé** *adj.* emancipated
**embarquement: carte** (*f.*) **d'embarquement** boarding pass (9)
**embarquer** to embark, get on
**embarrassé** *adj.* embarrassed; ill-at-ease; bothered
**embauche** *f.* hiring; **entretien** (*m.*) **d'embauche** job interview
**embaucher** to hire (16)
**embouteillage** *m.* traffic jam
**embrassade** *f.* hugging and kissing, embrace
**embrasser** to kiss; to embrace; **je t'embrasse** love (*closing of letter*); **s'embrasser** to kiss; to embrace (13)
**émérite** *adj.* highly skilled; emeritus
**émettre** (*like* **mettre**) *irreg.* to broadcast
**émeute** *f.* riot
**émigré(e)** *m., f.* émigré, expatriate
**émission** *f.* program; broadcast (10); **émission de musique** music program (10); **émission de télé réalité** reality show (10)
**emménager (nous emménageons)** to move in (4)
**emmener (j'emmène)** to take (*s.o. somewhere*); to take along (12)
**empêcher (de)** to prevent (from) (12); to preclude
**empereur** *m.* emperor
**emplacement** *m.* location
**emploi** *m.* use; job, position (14); **demande** (*f.*) **d'emploi** job application (14); **marché** (*m.*) **de l'emploi** job market (14); **offre** (*f.*) **d'emploi** job offer
**employé(e)** *m., f.* employee (14); white-collar worker; (sales) clerk; **employé(e) de** s.o. employed by
**employer (j'emploie)** to use; to employ
**employeur/euse** *m., f.* employer
**emporter** to take (*s.th. somewhere*); to take out (*food*); to carry away
**emprunt** *m.* loan (14)
**emprunter (à)** to borrow (from) (11)
**ému** *adj.* moved
**en** *prep.* in (2); in, by (*train, plane, bus*) (9); to; like; in the form of; *pron.* of them; of it; some, any (11); **de temps en temps** from time to time (2); **en automne** in autumn (5); **en avance** early (6); **en dehors de**

outside; **en effet** indeed; **en été** in summer (5); **en face de** across from (4); **en général** in general (2); **en hiver** in winter (5); **en profondeur** in depth; **en retard** late (6); **en train de** in the process of; **qu'en penses-tu?** what do you think of that? (11)
**encadrement** *m.* training, supervision; framework
**encaisser** to cash (*a check*)
**enceinte** *f.* enclosure; **dans l'enceinte de** within (the boundary of)
**encens** *m.* incense
**encercler** to circle, encircle
**enchaîné** *adj.* chained, fettered
**enchanté** *adj.* enchanted; pleased (to meet you)
**enchère** *f.* bid; **vente** (*f.*) **aux enchères** auction
**enchérir** to bid
**encore** *adv.* still (9); again; yet; even; more; **encore de** more; **encore un peu** a little more; **ne... pas encore** not yet (9); **ou encore** or else
**encourager (nous encourageons) (à)** to encourage (to)
**encyclopédie** *f.* encyclopedia
**endormir** (*like* **dormir**) *irreg.* to put to sleep; **s'endormir** to fall asleep (13)
**endroit** *m.* place, spot (8)
**énergie** *f.* energy; **énergie nucléaire (solaire)** nuclear (solar) energy (16)
**énergique** *adj.* energetic
**énervant** *adj.* aggravating, irritating
**énervé** *adj.* on edge, nervous
**enfance** *f.* childhood
**enfant** *m., f.* child (5); **petit-enfant** *m.* grandchild (5)
**enfer** *m.* hell
**enfermer** to lock up
**enfin** *adv.* finally, at last (11)
**enflammer** to kindle (*imagination*)
**enfouir** to bury
**engagé** *adj.* involved, politically active, politically committed
**engagement** *m.* (*political*) commitment
**engager (nous engageons)** to begin, start; **s'engager (dans)** to get involved (*in a public issue*) (16)
**énigme** *f.* riddle, enigma
**enlever (j'enlève)** to remove, take off
**ennemi(e)** *m., f.* enemy
**ennui** *m.* trouble; problem (9); worry; boredom
**ennuyer (j'ennuie)** to bother; to bore; **s'ennuyer** to be bored (13); **s'ennuyer à mourir** to be bored to death
**ennuyeux/euse** *adj.* boring; annoying
**énoncé** *m.* statement, utterance
**énorme** *adj.* enormous, huge
**énormément** *adv.* enormously, tremendously
**enquête** *f.* survey, poll
**enregistrer** to record; to check in
**enrichissement** *m.* enrichment
**enseignant(e)** *m., f.* teacher, instructor
**enseignement** *m.* teaching; education
**enseigner (à)** to teach (to) (12)
**ensemble** *adv.* together (8); *m.* ensemble; whole
**ensoleillé** *adj.* sunny
**ensuite** *adv.* then, next (11)
**entendre** to hear (5); **entendre dire que** to hear that; **entendre parler de** to hear about; **s'entendre (avec)** to get along (with) (13)

**entente** f. (mutual) understanding
**enterré** adj. buried
**enthousiasme** m. enthusiasm
**enthousiaste** adj. enthusiastic (3)
**entier/ière** adj. entire, whole, complete; **en entier** in its entirety
**entourer (de)** to surround (with)
**entraînement** m. practice, training
**entraîner** to bring about, lead to; **s'entraîner** to train, work out
**entraîneur/euse** m., f. trainer
**entre** prep. between, among (4)
**entrecôte** f. rib steak
**entrée** f. entrance, entry; admission; first course (meal) (7); **droit** (m.) **d'entrée** entrance fee
**entreprendre** to undertake
**entrepreneur/euse** m., f. entrepreneur
**entreprise** f. business, company (14); **chef** (m.) **d'entreprise** company head, top manager, boss (14)
**entrer (dans)** to enter (8)
**entretien** m. maintenance; conversation; **entretien (d'embauche)** job interview (14)
**énumérer (j'énumère)** to spell out, recite; to list, enumerate
**envahir** to invade
**enveloppe** f. envelope (10)
**envers** prep. toward
**envie** f. desire; **avoir envie de** to want; to feel like (3)
**environ** adv. about, approximately; m. pl. environs; **dans les environs** in the vicinity
**environnement** m. environment (16)
**envoi** m. sending
**envoyer (j'envoie) (a)** to send (to) (10)
**éolienne** f. windmill; windpump
**épais** adj. thick
**s'épanouir** to bloom
**épargne: compte** (m.) **d'épargne** savings account (14)
**s'éparpiller** to scatter
**épaule** f. shoulder
**épice** f. spice
**épicé** adj. spicy
**épicerie** f. grocery store (7)
**épicier/ière** m., f. grocer
**épinards** m. pl. spinach
**époque** f. period (of history) (12); **à l'époque (de)** at the time (of); **meubles** (m. pl.) **d'époque** antique furniture
**épouser** to marry
**époux (épouse)** m., f. husband; wife; **époux** m. pl. married couple
**épreuve** f. test; event (sports)
**éprouver** to feel; to experience
**épuiser** to use up, exhaust (16)
**équilibre** m. equilibrium, balance
**équipage** m. crew
**équipe** f. team (15); **sports** (m. pl.) **d'équipe** team sports; **travail** (m.) **d'équipe** teamwork
**équipé** adj. equipped
**équipement** m. equipment; gear
**s'équiper** to equip oneself
**équitation** f. horseback riding (8); **faire de l'équitation** to go horseback riding
**erreur** f. error; mistake
**erroné** adj. wrong, erroneous
**escalade** f. (mountain) climbing
**escalader** to climb, scale
**escale: faire escale à** to stop over at
**escalier** m. stairs, stairway (5)

**escalope** f. (veal) scallop
**escargot** m. snail; escargot (7)
**escarpement** m. steep slope
**esclavage** m. slavery
**esclave** m., f. slave
**espace** m. space; **espaces verts** open spaces, greenbelts
**espadrilles** f. pl. fabric sandals, espadrilles
**Espagne** f. Spain (2, 8)
**espagnol** adj. Spanish; m. Spanish (language) (2); **Espagnol(e)** m., f. Spaniard (person) (2)
**espèces** f. pl. species
**espérer (j'espère)** to hope (6)
**espoir** m. hope
**esprit** m. mind; spirit; wit
**essai** m. attempt, try; **mariage** (m.) **à l'essai** trial marriage
**essaimer** to spread, expand
**essayer (j'essaie) (de)** to try (to) (12)
**essence** f. gasoline, gas (9); **faire le plein (d'essence)** to fill the tank (9)
**essentiel(le)** adj. essential (3); **il est essentiel que** + subj. it's essential that (16)
**essentiellement** adv. largely, mainly
**est** m. east; **à l'est** to the east (9)
**estampe** f. engraving
**esthétique** adj. aesthetic
**estimer** to consider; to believe; to estimate (16)
**et** conj. and (2); **et demi(e)** half past (the hour) (6); **et puis** and (then), next (7); **et quart** quarter past (the hour); **et vous? (et toi?)** and you?; how about you? (1)
**établir** to establish, set up (16)
**établissement** m. establishment
**étage** m. floor (of building); **premier (deuxième) étage** second (third) floor (in the U.S.) (5)
**étagère** f. shelf (4)
**étape** f. stage; stopping place
**état** m. state (8); condition; **état civil** marital (civil) status; **États-Unis** m. pl. United States (of America) (2, 8); **homme (femme) d'état** statesman (-woman)
**été** m. summer; **en été** in summer (5); **job** (m.) **d'été** summer job
**s'étendre** to sprawl
**étendue** f. area, expanse
**éternel(le)** adj. eternal
**éternité** f. eternity
**étincelle** f. sparkle, sparkling
**étiquette** f. label
**étoile** f. star; **à la belle étoile** in the open air
**étonné** adj. surprised; astonished (16)
**étouffer** to suffocate
**étrange** adj. strange; **il est étrange que** + subj. it's strange that (16)
**étranger/ère** adj. foreign; m., f. stranger; foreigner; **à l'étranger** abroad, in a foreign country (9); **langue** (f.) **étrangère** foreign language
**être** (p.p. **été**) irreg. to be (2); **c'est (ce n'est pas)** it's (it isn't) (1); **c'est combien?** how much is it? (1); **comment est-il/elle?** what's he/she like?; **être en train de** to be in the process of, be in the middle of (15); **il est... heure(s)** it is . . . o'clock (6); **n'est-ce pas?** isn't it (so)?, isn't that right? (3); **nous sommes lundi (mardi...)** it's Monday (Tuesday . . . ) (1); **peut-être** adv. perhaps, maybe; **quel jour sommes-nous (est-ce)?** what day is it? (1); **quelle heure**

**est-il?** what time is it? (6); **qui est-ce?** who is it? (1)
**étroit** adj. narrow
**étude** f. study; pl. studies; **bourse** (f.) **d'études** scholarship, study grant; **faire des études** to study
**étudiant(e)** m., f., adj. student (1); **carte** (f.) **d'étudiant** student ID card
**étudier** to study (2)
**euh...** interj. uhmm . . . (10)
**euphorisant** m. producing a sense of euphoria
**euro** m. euro (European currency)
**Europe** f. Europe; **coupe** (f.) **d'Europe** European Cup (soccer)
**européen(ne)** adj. European; **Européen(ne)** m., f. European (person); **Union** (f.) **européenne (UE)** European Union (EU)
**eux** pron., m. pl. them; **eux-mêmes** pron., m. pl. themselves (12)
**s'évader** to escape
**évaluer** to appraise, evaluate
**s'éveiller** to wake up
**événement** m. event (12)
**évidemment** adv. evidently, obviously (12)
**évident** adj. obvious, clear; **il est évident que** + indic. it is clear that (16)
**éviter** to avoid
**évoluer** to evolve, advance, develop
**évoquer** to evoke, call to mind
**exact** adj. precise, true; **oui, c'est exact** yes, that's correct
**exactement** adv. exactly
**exagérer (j'exagère)** to exaggerate
**examen** (fam. **exam**) m. test, exam (2); examination; **passer un examen** to take an exam (4); **réussir à un examen** to pass a test
**examiner** to inspect, examine
**exaspérant** adj. exasperating
**exaspéré** adj. exasperated
**excéder (j'excède)** to exceed
**excellent** adj. excellent (3)
**excentricité** f. eccentricity
**excentrique** adj. eccentric (3)
**excepté** prep. except
**exceptionnel(le)** adj. exceptional
**excès** m. excess
**excitant** adj. exciting
**excité** adj. excited
**exclamer** to exclaim
**exclu(e)** m., f. excluded (people)
**exclure** (p.p. **exclu**) irreg. to exclude, rule out
**exclusivement** adv. exclusively
**exclusivité** f. exclusive rights, coverage
**excursion** f. excursion, outing; **faire une excursion** to go on an outing
**s'excuser** to apologize (13); **excusez-moi (excuse-moi)** excuse me, pardon me (1)
**exemplaire** adj. exemplary; m. copy
**exemple** m. example; **par exemple** for example (16)
**exercer (nous exerçons)** to exercise, exert (control, influence)
**exercice** m. exercise
**exigeant** adj. demanding; difficult
**exigence** f. demand
**exiger (nous exigeons)** to require; to demand (16)
**exil** m. exile
**exilé** adj. exiled
**exister** to exist
**exode** m. exodus

**expatrié** *adj.* expatriated

**s'expatrier** to leave one's country

**expédition** *f.* trip

**expérience** *f.* experience; experiment

**expert(e)** *m., f.* expert; **expert(e)-comptable** *m., f.* certified public accountant

**explication** *f.* explanation

**expliquer** to explain

**exploité** *adj.* exploited

**exploiter** to make use of, make the most of

**explorateur/trice** *m., f.* explorer

**explorer** to explore

**exportation** *f.* export(s)

**s'exporter** to be exported

**exposé** *m.* presentation, exposé; *adj.* displayed

**exposer** to expose, show; to display

**exposition** *f.* exhibition; show (12)

**expression** *f.* expression; term (1); **liberté** (*f.*) **d'expression** freedom of expression (16)

**exprimer** to express; **exprimer une opinion** to express an opinion (16); **s'exprimer** to express oneself

**exquis** *adj.* exquisite

**extraire** to extract

**extrait** *m.* excerpt; extract

**extraordinaire** *adj.* extraordinary (3)

**extrasensoriel(le)** *adj.* extra-sensory

**extrêmement** *adv.* extremely

**extrémiste: idées** (*f.*) **extremistes** extremist ideas (16)

**fabrication** *f.* manufacture, making

**fabriquer** to manufacture, make

**fabuleux/euse** *adj.* fabulous

**fac** *f., fam.* **(faculté)** university department or school

**façade** *f.* façade, face (*of a building*)

**face: en face (de)** *prep.* opposite, facing, across from (4); **face à** facing; **face à face** face to face

**fâché** *adj.* angry (16)

**fâcher** to anger; **se fâcher** to get angry (13)

**fâcheux/euse** *adj.* unfortunate; troublesome; **il est fâcheux que** + *subj.* it is unfortunate that (16)

**facile** *adj.* easy (3)

**facilité** *f.* ease, easiness

**faciliter** to facilitate, make easier

**façon** *f.* way, manner, fashion; **de façon (logique)** in a (logical) way

**facteur/trice** *m., f.* factor; letter carrier (14)

**faculté** *f.* ability; (*fam.* **fac**) division (*academic*) (2); **faculté des lettres** School of Arts and Letters; **faculté des sciences** School of Science

**faible** *adj.* weak; small

**failli: j'ai failli...** I nearly . . .

**faim** *f.* hunger; **avoir faim** to be hungry (3)

**faire** (*p.p.* **fait**) *irreg.* to do; to make (5); to form; to be; **faire appel à** to appeal to; to require, call for; **faire attention (à)** to pay attention (to) (5); to watch out (for); **faire baisser** to lower; **faire beau (il fait beau)** to be good weather (it's nice out) (5); **faire bouillir** to boil; **faire chaud (il fait chaud)** to be warm, be hot (out) (it's warm, it's hot) (5); **faire confiance à** to trust; **faire connaissance** to get acquainted; **faire cuire** to cook; **faire de la bicyclette** to cycle, go (bi)cycling (8); **faire de la peinture (de la musique, de la poterie)** to paint (play music, do ceramics); **faire de la planche à voile** to go windsurfing; **faire de la plongée sous-marine** to go scuba diving (8); **faire de la politique** to go in for politics; **faire de la voile** to go sailing (5); **faire de l'aérobic** to do aerobics (5); **faire de l'alpinisme** to go mountain climbing (8); **faire de l'équitation** to go horseback riding (8); **faire des économies** to save (up) money (14); **faire des études** to study; **faire des glissades** *Q.* to go tobogganing; **faire des moulinets avec les bras** to whirl one's arms about; **faire des projets** to make plans; **faire des recherches** to do research; **faire dorer** to brown (*in cooking*); **faire du bateau** to go boating (8); **faire du bruit** to make noise; **faire du camping** to camp, go camping; **faire du cheval** to go horseback riding (8); **faire du covoiturage** to carpool, rideshare; **faire du jogging** to run, jog (5); **faire du magasinage** *Q.* to go shopping; **faire du patin à glace** to go ice-skating; **faire du patin à roues alignées** to do in-line skating; **faire du recyclage** to recycle; **faire du shopping** to go shopping; **faire du ski (alpin)** to ski (downhill) (5); **faire du ski de fond** to go cross-country skiing; **faire du ski nautique** to go waterskiing; **faire du snowboard** to go snowboarding; **faire du soleil (il fait du soleil)** to be sunny (it's sunny) (5); **faire du sport** to play, do sports (5); **faire du théâtre** to act; **faire du tourisme** to go sightseeing; **faire du vélo (de montagne)** to go cycling (mountain biking) (5); **faire du vent (il fait du vent)** to be windy (it's windy) (5); **faire escale à** to stop over at; **faire faire** to have done, make (*s.o.*) do (*s.th.*); **faire frais (il fait frais)** to be cool (out) (it's cool) (5); **faire froid (il fait froid)** to be cold (out) (it's cold) (5); **faire grève** to strike, go on strike (16); **faire la bise** to kiss on both cheeks (*in greeting*); **faire la connaissance de** to meet (*for the first time*) (5); **faire la cuisine** to cook (5); **faire la fête** to party; **faire la lessive** to do the laundry (5); **faire la queue** to stand in line (5); **faire la sieste** to take a nap; **faire la vaisselle** to wash (do) the dishes (5); **faire le lit** to make the bed; **faire le marché** to do the shopping, go to the market (5); **faire le ménage** to do the housework (5); **faire le plein** to fill it up (gas tank) (9); **faire le tour de** to go around; to tour; **faire les courses** to do errands (5); **faire les valises** to pack one's bags; **faire mauvais (il fait mauvais)** to be bad weather (out) (it's bad out) (5); **faire partie de** to belong to; **faire preuve de** to show; **faire ses devoirs** to do one's homework (5); **faire son possible** to do one's best; **faire un chèque** to write a check (14); **faire un pique-nique** to go on a picnic; **faire un safari** to go on a safari; **faire un temps pourri** *fam.* to be rotten weather; **faire un tour (en voiture)** to take a walk (ride) (5); **faire un voyage** to take a trip (5); **faire une erreur** to make a mistake; **faire une excursion** to go on an outing; **faire une promenade** to take a walk (5); **faire une randonnée (pédestre)** to go hiking (8); **faire une réservation** to make a reservation; **faire une visite** to pay a visit; **quel temps fait-il?** how's the weather? (5)

**fait** *m.* fact; *adj.* made; **tout à fait** *adv.* completely, entirely

**falaise** *f.* cliff

**falloir** (*p.p.* **fallu**) *irreg.* to be necessary (8); to be lacking; **il faut** + *inf.* it is necessary to, one must; one needs (8)

**fameux/euse** *adj.* famous

**familial** *adj.* family

**famille** *f.* family (5); **en famille** with one's family; **fonder une famille** to start a family

**fanatique** (*fam.* **fan**) *m., f.* fan; fanatic, zealot

**fanatisme** *m.* fanaticism

**fantaisie: bijoux** (*m. pl.*) **fantaisie** costume jewelry

**fantaisiste** *adj.* fanciful, whimsical

**fantôme** *m.* ghost

**Far** (*m.*) **breton** traditional cake from Brittany

**farine** *f.* flour

**fascinant** *adj.* fascinating

**fasciné** *adj.* fascinated

**fatal** *adj.* fatal; unlucky; fateful

**fatigant** *adj.* tiring

**fatigué** *adj.* tired (3)

**fauché** *adj., fam.* broke, without money

**se faufiler** to creep; to thread one's way; to sidle

**faut (il)** it is necessary to, one must; one needs (8)

**faute** *f.* fault, mistake

**fauteuil** *m.* armchair

**faux (fausse)** *adj.* false (4)

**faveur: en faveur de** in favor of

**favorable: être favorable à** to be in favor of (favorably disposed to)

**favori(te)** *adj.* favorite

**favoriser** to further, favor

**fax** *m.* fax (10)

**fée** *f.* fairy; **conte** (*m.*) **de fée** fairy tale

**félicitations** *f. pl.* congratulations

**féminin** *adj.* feminine; female

**femme** *f.* woman (2); wife (5); **femme d'affaires** businesswoman; **femme d'état** stateswoman; **femme écrivain** writer (12); **femme médecin** doctor, physician (14); **femme peintre** painter (12); **femme poète** poet (12); **femme politique** politician; **femme sculpteur** sculptor (12); **jeune femme** young woman (3)

**fenêtre** *f.* window (1)

**fente** *f.* slot

**fer** *m.* iron; **chemin** (*m.*) **de fer** railroad

**ferme** *f.* farm

**fermer** to close

**fermeture** *f.* closing

**fermier/ière** *m., f.* farmer

**ferraille** *f.* scrap iron, metal

**ferroviaire** *adj.* rail, railroad

**fête** *f.* holiday; celebration, party (7); saint's day, name day; *pl.* Christmas season; **faire la fête** to party; **fête des patrons** saint's day; **fête des Rois** Feast of the Magi, Epiphany; **jour** (*m.*) **de fête** holiday

**fêter** to celebrate; to observe a holiday

**feu** (*pl.* **feux**) *m.* fire; traffic light; **à feu doux** on low heat (*cooking*); **feux d'artifice** fireworks

**feuille** *f.* leaf

**feuilleté** *adj.* flaky (*pastry*)

**feuilleton** *m.* soap opera (10)

**fève** *f.* bean
**février** February (1)
**fez** *m.* fez (*feltcap*)
**fiable** *adj.* reliable
**fiançailles** *f. pl.* engagement (13)
**fiancé(e)** *m., f.* fiancé, fiancée
**se fiancer (nous nous fiançons)** to get engaged (13)
**fibre** *f.* fiber, filament
**fiche** *f.* index card; form (to fill out); deposit slip
**fichier** *m.* file (10)
**fictif/ive** *adj.* fictitious; imaginary
**fier/ière** *adj.* proud (3)
**fierté** *f.* pride
**fièvre** *f.* fever
**figure** *f.* figure, important person
**figurer** to appear
**fil** *m.*: **coup** (*m.*) **de fil** telephone call
**filer** to trail, follow
**filet** *m.* fillet (*fish, meat*) (7); **filet de porc (de bœuf)** pork (beef) fillet
**filiale** *f.* subsidiary; branch (*office*)
**fille** *f.* girl (3); daughter (5); **jeune fille** girl, young lady; **petite-fille** granddaughter (5)
**film** *m.* movie, film (2)
**fils** *m.* son (5); **petit-fils** grandson (5)
**filtrage** *m.* filtration, filtering
**fin** *f.* end; **à la fin de** at the end of; **en fin d'après-midi** in the late afternoon; **fin 1996** at the end of 1996; *adj.* fine, delicate; **extra-fin** *adj.* superfine; **mi-fin** *adj.* medium-cut (*vegetables*)
**finalement** *adv.* finally
**finaliser** to complete
**finance** *f.* finance; *pl.* finances
**financier/ière** *adj.* financial, monetary
**finir (de)** to finish (4); **finir par** to end (finish) by (*doing s.th.*) (4)
**Finlande** *f.* Finland
**firme** *f.* firm, company
**fiscalité** *f.* tax system, taxes
**fixer** to fasten; to make firm
**flacon** *m.* small bottle (*with stopper*)
**flamand** *m.* Flemish (*language*)
**flâner** to stroll (12)
**flash (d'informations)** *m.* newsbrief
**flatté** *adj.* flattered
**fleur** *f.* flower (4); **chou-fleur** *m.* cauliflower; **fleur de lys** fleur de lis, trefoil
**fleurette** *f.* floret
**fleurir** to flower; to flourish
**fleuve** *m.* (*large*) river (8)
**Floride** *f.* Florida
**flûte** *f.* flute
**foie** *m.* liver; **pâté** (*m.*) **de foie gras** goose liver pâté
**foire** *f.* fair, exhibition; marketplace
**fois** *f.* time, occasion; times (*arithmetic*); **à la fois** at the same time; **la première (dernière) fois** the first (last) time; **une fois** once (11); **une fois par semaine** once a week (5)
**folklorique** *adj.* traditional; folk (*music, etc.*)
**foncé** *adj.* dark
**fonction** *f.* function, use
**fonctionnaire** *m., f.* civil servant (14)
**fonctionner** to function, work
**fond** *m.* bottom; background; back; **ski** (*m.*) **de fond** cross-country skiing (8)
**fondamental** *adj.* fundamental, basic
**fondateur/trice** *m., f.* founder
**fondation** *f.* founding, inception

**fonder** to found; **fonder une famille** to start a family
**fonds** *m. pl.* fund
**fondre** to melt
**fondue** *f.* fondue (*Swiss melted cheese dish*)
**fontaine** *f.* fountain
**fonte** *f.* cast iron
**football** (*fam.* **foot**) *m.* soccer; **football américain** football; **match** (*m.*) **de foot** soccer game
**footballeur/euse** *m., f.* soccer player
**footing** *m.* jogging
**force** *f.* strength; **à force de** as a result of; **en force** in force; **force est de** + *inf.* one must
**forcément** *adv.* necessarily
**forcer (nous forçons)** to force, compel
**forêt** *f.* forest (8)
**forgé: fer** (*m.*) **forgé** wrought iron
**formalité** *f.* formality
**formation** *f.* education, training
**forme** *f.* form; shape; figure; **en (bonne, pleine) forme** physically fit; **en forme de** in the form of; **sous forme de** in the form of
**formel(le)** *adj.* formal
**formellement** *adv.* positively, categorically
**former** to form, shape; to train
**formidable** terrific, great
**formule** *f.* formula; plan
**formuler** to formulate, make up
**fort** *adj.* strong; heavy; *adv.* strongly; loudly; very (14); **parler fort** to speak loudly
**fortifier** to fortify
**fou (fol, folle)** *adj.* crazy, mad; **fou (folle)** *m., f.* insane (crazy) person
**foudre** *f.* lightning; **coup** (*m.*) **de foudre** flash of lightning (13); love at first sight (13)
**foulard** *m.* scarf
**foule** *f.* crowd (15)
**fourchette** *f.* fork (6)
**fournir** to furnish, supply
**fournisseur** (*m.*) **d'accès** service provider (*Internet*)
**foyer** *m.* hearth; home; student residence; **femme** (*f.*) **au foyer** homemaker
**frais** *m., pl.* expenses, costs (14); **frais de scolarité** school, university (tuition) fees
**frais (fraîche)** *adj.* cool; fresh (6); **crème fraîche** clotted cream, crème fraîche; **faire frais (il fait frais)** to be cool (out) (it's cool) (5); **produits** (*m.*) **frais** fresh products (6)
**fraise** *f.* strawberry (6)
**framboise** *f.* raspberry
**franc(he)** *adj.* frank; fruitful; honest
**français** *adj.* French; *m.* French (*language*); **Français(e)** *m., f.* Frenchman (-woman) (2)
**France** *f.* France (2, 8)
**franchement** *adv.* frankly (12)
**franchir** to cross
**francophile** *m., f.* Francophile (*person who admires France or the French*)
**francophone** *adj.* French-speaking
**francophonie** *f.* French-speaking world
**frangin(e)** *m., f. fam.* brother (sister)
**frapper** to strike
**fraternité** *f.* brotherhood, fraternity
**fredonner** to hum
**freinage** *m.* braking system (*auto*)
**fréquemment** *adv.* frequently, often
**fréquent** *adj.* frequent, common
**fréquenter** to go to often

**frère** *m.* brother (5); **beau-frère** brother-in-law (5); **demi-frère** half brother; stepbrother (5)
**fric** *m., fam.* money
**fricassée** *f.* (chicken) stew; fricassee
**frigo** *m., fam.* fridge, refrigerator
**fringue** *f., fam.* clothes
**fripe** *f. s.* secondhand clothing
**frisé** *adj.* curly
**frites** *f. pl.* French fries (6); **moules** (*f.*)**-frites** mussels with French fries; **steak** (*m.*)**-frites** steak with French fries
**froid** *adj.* cold; *m.* cold; **avoir froid** to be cold (3); **faire froid (il fait froid)** to be cold (out) (it's cold) (5)
**fromage** *m.* cheese (6)
**front** *m.* forehead
**frontière** *f.* border
**frotter** to rub
**fruit** *m.* fruit (6); **jus** (*m.*) **de fruit** fruit juice
**fumer** to smoke (2)
**fumeur/euse** *m., f.* smoker; **zone** (*f.*) **fumeurs (non-fumeurs)** smoking (nonsmoking) section
**furax** *adj., fam.* angry, furious
**furieux/euse** *adj.* furious (16)
**fusée** *f.* rocket
**fût** *m., fam.* pair of pants
**futur** *m., Gram.* future (*tense*); *adj.* future
**futuriste** *adj.* futuristic

**gabarit** *m.* size, stature
**gagner** to win; to earn (14); **gagner du temps** to save time
**gai** *adj.* cheerful
**galère: C'était la galère!** *fam.* It was hell!
**galerie** *f.* gallery; roof rack (*auto*)
**galette** *f.* pancake; tart, pie
**gant** *m.* glove (8)
**garagiste** *m., f.* mechanic, garage owner
**garanti** *adj.* guaranteed
**garçon** *m.* boy (3); café waiter
**garder** to keep, retain; **garder la ligne** to keep one's figure
**gardien(ne)** *m., f.* guard
**gare** *f.* station; train station (9); **buffet** (*m.*) **de la gare** train station restaurant (9); **gare de chargement** loading dock
**garer** to park; **se garer** to be parked
**gars** *m., fam.* guy; boy
**gaspillage** *m.* wasting, waste (16)
**gaspiller** to waste (16)
**gastronome** *m., f.* gourmet
**gastronomie** *f.* gastronomy, good food
**gastronomique** *adj.* gastronomic
**gâteau** *m.* cake (6)
**gâter** to spoil
**gauche** *adj.* left; *f.* left; **à gauche (de)** *prep.* on the (to the) left (of) (4); **Rive** (*f.*) **gauche** Left Bank (*in Paris*) (11); **se lever du pied gauche** to get up on the wrong side of the bed
**gaz** *m.* gas
**gazeux/euse: boisson** (*f.*) **gazeuse** soft drink (6)
**gênant** *adj.* bothersome, annoying
**gendre** *m.* son-in-law (5)
**généalogique** *adj.* genealogical; family
**général** *m., adj.* general; **en général** generally (2); **quartier** (*m.*) **général** headquarters
**généraliste** *m., f.* general practitioner (MD)
**générer (je génère)** to generate

**généreux/euse** *adj.* generous

**génétique** *adj.* genetic

**Genève** Geneva

**génial** *adj.* brilliant, inspired; *fam.* neat, delightful, cool

**génie** *m.* genius; engineering (2)

**genou** (*pl.* **genoux**) *m.* knee (13)

**genre** *m.* type, style, kind

**gens** *m. pl.* people; **jeunes gens** young men; young people

**gentil(le)** *adj.* nice, pleasant; kind (3)

**gentillesse** *f.* kindness, niceness

**gentiment** *adv.* nicely

**géographe** *m., f.* geographer

**géographie** (*fam.* **géo**) *f.* geography (2)

**géographique** *adj.* geographical

**géologie** *f.* geology (2)

**géométrie** *f.* geometry

**Géorgie** *f.* Georgia (*country*)

**gerbe: donner la gerbe à** (**qqn**) to make (*s.o.*) want to vomit

**gérer** (**je gère**) to manage (14)

**geste** *m.* gesture

**gestion** *f.* management

**gigantesque** *adj.* gigantic

**gingembre** *m.* ginger

**girofle** *m.* cloves

**glace** *f.* ice cream (6); ice; mirror; **patin** (*m.*) **à glace** ice-skating

**glacé: crème** (*f.*) **glacée** *Q.* ice cream

**glissade: faire des glissades** *Q.* to go tobogganing

**se glisser** to slip into

**gloire** *f.* glory

**glorieux/euse** *adj.* glorious

**glorifier** to glorify

**golfe** *m.* gulf

**gomme** *f.* eraser

**gommier** *m.* gum tree

**gorge** *f.* throat (13); gorge; **avoir mal à la gorge** to have a sore throat (13)

**gosse** *m., f. fam.* kid, child

**gothique** *adj.* Gothic (12)

**gourmand(e)** *adj.* gluttonous, greedy; *m., f.* glutton, gourmand

**gousse** (*m.*): **gousse d'ail** clove of garlic

**goût** *m.* taste; **avant-goût** *m.* foretaste

**goûter** *m.* afternoon snack (6); *v.* to taste; to eat (7)

**goutte** *f.* drop (*liquid*)

**gouvernement** *m.* government (16)

**gouverner** to rule; to govern

**gouverneur** *m.* governor

**grâce** *f.* grace; pardon; **jour** (*m.*) **d'action de grâce** Thanksgiving Day; **grâce à** thanks to

**gramme** *m.* gram

**grammaire** *f.* grammar

**grand** *adj.* great; large, tall; big (3); **arrière-grand-parent** *m.* great-grandparent; **grand magasin** *m.* department store; **grand-maman** *f.* grandma, granny; **grand-mère** *f.* grandmother (5); **grand-parent** (*pl.* **grands-parents**) *m.* grandparent (5); **grand-père** *m.* grandfather (5); **grande surface** *f.* mall; superstore; **grandes écoles** *f. pl. French government graduate schools*; **grandes vacances** *f. pl.* summer vacation (from school); **Train** (*m.*) **à grande vitesse (TGV)** (*French high-speed*) bullet train

**grandeur** *f.* size

**grandir** to grow; to grow up

**gras(se)** *adj.* fat; oily; rich; **en caractères gras** in boldface print; **pâté** (*m.*) **de foie gras** goose liver pâté

**gratin** *m.* gratin, cheese-topped dish

**gratte-ciel** *m., inv.* skyscraper

**gratuit** *adj.* free (*of charge*) (11)

**grave** *adj.* grave, serious; **accent** (*m.*) **grave** grave accent (**è**)

**gravure** *f.* printing, engraving

**Grèce** *f.* Greece (8)

**grec(que)** *adj.* Greek

**greffe** *f.* transplant

**grenouille** *f.* frog

**grève** *f.* strike, walkout (16); **faire grève** to strike (16)

**griffe** *f.* claw

**grille** *f.* grid

**grillé** *adj.* toasted; grilled; broiled

**griller: faire griller** to broil; to toast

**grimpeur/euse** *m., f.* climber

**grippe** *f.* flu, influenza

**gris** *adj.* gray (3)

**gros(se)** *adj.* large; fat; thick (4); **grosses bises** (**gros bisous**) *fam.* hugs and kisses (*closing of letter*)

**grossir** to gain weight

**guéri** *adj.* cured, healed (13)

**guérison** *f.* recovery

**guerre** *f.* war (16); **Première (Deuxième [Seconde]) Guerre mondiale** First (Second) World War

**guetter** to watch out for, be on the lookout for

**guichet** *m.* (ticket) window (9); counter, booth; **guichet automatique** automatic teller machine (ATM) (14)

**guide** *m., f.* guide; *m.* guidebook; instructions

**Guinée** *f.* Guinea

**guirlande** *f.* garland; Christmas lights

**guitare** *f.* guitar (4); **jouer de la guitare** to play the guitar

**Guyane** *f.* Guyana

**gym** (*ab.* **gymnastique**) *f.* fitness training

**gymnase** *m.* gymnasium (2)

**habilement** *adv.* skillfully

**s'habiller** to get dressed (13)

**habit** *m.* clothing, dress

**habitacle** *m.* passenger compartment

**habitant(e)** *m., f.* inhabitant; resident

**habitation** *f.* lodging, housing; **habitations à loyer modéré (H.L.M.)** *publicly subsidized apartment blocks* (*France*)

**habiter** to live (2)

**habitude** *f.* habit; **d'habitude** *adv.* usually, habitually (5)

**habitué (à)** *adj.* accustomed (to)

**habituel(le)** *adj.* usual

***hacher** to chop (up)

**haïr** to hate

**Haïti** *m.* Haiti (8)

***harceler** to harass, torment

***hardi** *adj.* bold, daring

***haricot** *m.* bean; **haricots** (*pl.*) **mange-tout** string beans; sugar peas; **haricots verts** green beans (6)

***harissa** *m., f.* hot chili sauce

***hasard** *m.* chance, luck; **jeux** (*m. pl.*) **de hasard** games of chance (15); **par hasard** by accident, by chance

***hasardeux/euse** *adj.* dangerous, hazardous

***hâte** *f.* haste; **à la hâte** hastily

***haut** *adj.* high; higher; tall; upper; *m.* top; height; **à voix haute** *adv.* in a loud voice, aloud; **de haut** high (*in measuring*); **du haut de** from the top of; **haute couture** *f.* high fashion; **là-haut** *adv.* up there

***hauteur** *f.* height

**hébergement** *m.* lodging, accommodations; shelter

**héberger** (**nous hébergeons**) to shelter

**hectare** *m.* hectare (slightly less than 2.5 acres)

**hein?** *interj.* eh?

**hélas** *interj.* alas

**hépatite** *f.* hepatitis

**herbe** *f.* herb

**héritage** *m.* legacy, inheritance

**héritier** *m.* heir

***héros** *m.* (*f.* **héroïne**) hero, heroine

**hésiter (à)** to hesitate (to)

**heure** *f.* hour; time; **à l'heure** on time (9); per hour; **à n'importe quelle heure** at any time; **à quelle heure... ?** (at) what time . . . ? (6); **à tout à l'heure** see you soon; **dans une heure** in one hour; **de bonne heure** early (6); **de l'heure** an hour, per hour; **demi-heure** *f.* half hour; **il est... heure(s)** it is . . . o'clock (6); **il est l'heure de** + *inf.* it's time to . . . ; **quelle heure est-il?** what time is it? (6); **tout à l'heure** in a while (5)

**heureusement** *adv.* fortunately, luckily

**heureux/euse** *adj.* happy; fortunate (3)

**Hexagone** *m.* (metropolitan) France

**hic** *m., fam.* snag, problem

**hier** *adv.* yesterday (7); **avant-hier** day before yesterday (7); **hier matin** yesterday morning; **hier soir** last night (7)

**histoire** *f.* history (2); story

**historien(ne)** *m., f.* historian

**historique** *adj.* historical (12)

**hiver** *m.* winter; **en hiver** in the winter (5)

**H.L.M. (habitations à loyer modéré)** *f. pl. publicly subsidized apartment blocks* (*France*)

**hollandais** *adj.* Dutch

***homard** *m.* lobster

**hommage** *m.* homage, respects; **en hommage à** in recognition of

**homme** *m.* man (2); **homme d'affaires** businessman; **homme politique** politician; **jeune homme** young man (3)

**honnête** *adj.* honest

**honorer** to honor

***honte** *f.* shame; **avoir honte (de)** to be ashamed (of) (3)

**hop: et hop!** *interj.* bingo!

**hôpital** *m.* hospital (11)

**horaire** *m.* schedule (12)

**horodateur** *m.* parking ticket machine

**horreur** *f.* horror; **avoir horreur de** to hate, detest; **j'ai horreur de...** I can't stand . . .

***hors de** *prep.* outside, beyond

***hors-d'œuvre** *m. inv.* appetizer (7)

**hospitalier/ière** *adj.* hospitable

**hôtel** *m.* hotel (11); **hôtel de ville** town hall, city hall

**hôtellerie** *f.* hotel business or management

**hôtesse** *f.* hostess; **hôtesse de l'air** flight attendant (9)

**huile** *f.* oil; **huile de tournesol** sunflower seed oil; **huile d'olive** olive oil (7); **sardines** (*f. pl.*) **à l'huile** sardines in oil (7)

***huit** *adj.* eight (1)

***huitième** *m.* one-eighth; *adj.* eighth (11)

**huître** *f.* oyster (7)

**humain** *adj.* human; *m.* human being; **corps** (*m.*) **humain** human body; **sciences** (*f. pl.*) **humaines** social sciences
**humanitaire** *adj.* humanitarian
**humeur** *f.* mood; temperament
**humidité** *f.* humidity, dampness
**humour** *m.* humor
**hybride** *adj.* hybrid; **voiture** (*f.*) **hybride** hybrid car (16)
**s'hydrater** to become hydrated
**hymne** *m.* hymn
**hypocrisie** *f.* hypocrisy
**hypocrite** *adj.* hypocritical (3)

**ici** *adv.* here (2)
**idéal** *m.* ideal; *adj.* ideal (3)
**idéaliste** *m., f.* idealist; *adj.* idealistic (3)
**idée** *f.* idea; **idées extrémistes** extremist ideas (16)
**identifier** to identify
**identité** *f.* identity; **carte** (*f.*) **d'identité** ID card (8)
**idiome** *m.* language
**ignorer** to not know; to have no experience of
**il** *pron., m. s.* he; it; there; **il faut** + *inf.* it is necessary to; one needs (8); **il n'y a pas de quoi** *interj.* you're welcome (7); **il y a** there is/are (1); ago; **il y a... que** for (*period of time*); it's been . . . since; **y a-t-il... ?** is/are there . . . ? (1)
**île** *f.* island (11)
**illimité** *adj.* unlimited
**illuminer** to light up
**illustrer** to illustrate
**ils** *pron., m. pl.* they
**image** *f.* picture, image
**imaginer** to imagine
**imiter** to imitate
**immédiatement** *adv.* immediately
**immeuble** *m.* apartment or office building (4)
**immigré(e)** *m., f.* immigrant
**imparfait** *m., Gram.* imperfect (*verb tense*)
**impatience** *f.* impatience; **avec impatience** impatiently
**impératif** *m., Gram.* imperative, command
**impératrice** *f.* empress
**imperméable** *m.* raincoat (3)
**impersonnel(le)** *adj.* impersonal
**s'implanter** to take hold
**impliqué** *adj.* implicated, involved
**important** *adj.* important (3); large, great; **il est important que** + *subj.* it's important that (16)
**importer** to import; to matter; **n'importe (où)** any(where)
**imposer** to impose
**impossible** *adj.* impossible; **il est impossible que** + *subj.* it's impossible that (16)
**impôts** *m. pl.* (*direct*) taxes (16)
**impressionnant** *adj.* impressive
**impressionné** *adj.* impressed
**impressionnisme** *m.* impressionism (*art*)
**impressionniste** *m., f., adj.* impressionist (*art*)
**imprévisible** *adj.* unpredictable
**imprimante** *f.* (*computer*) printer (10)
**imprimer** to print
**improviste: à l'improviste** unexpectedly, without warning
**inacceptable** *adj.* unacceptable
**inaugurer** to unveil
**incarner** to embody
**incendie** *f.* blaze, fire

**incertitude** *f.* uncertainty
**inclure** (*p.p.* **inclus**) *irreg.* to include
**inconfortable** *adj.* uncomfortable
**inconnu** *adj.* unknown
**incontestablement** *adv.* unquestionably
**inconvénient** *m.* disadvantage
**incorporer** to incorporate
**incroyable** *adj.* unbelievable, incredible
**Inde** *f.* India
**indéfini** *adj.* indefinite; **pronom** (*m.*) **indéfini** *Gram.* indefinite pronoun
**indéniable** *adj.* undeniable
**indépendance** *f.* independence; **fête** (*f.*) **de l'Indépendance** Independence Day
**indépendant** *adj.* independent; **travailleur/euse** (*m., f.*) **indépendant(e)** self-employed worker (14)
**indicatif** *m., Gram.* indicative
**indication** *f.* instruction(s)
**indice** *m.* indication, sign
**indicible** *adj.* inexpressible
**indiquer** to show, point out (15)
**indirect** *adj.* indirect; **pronom** (*m.*) **d'objet indirect** *Gram.* indirect object pronoun
**indiscret** *adj.* indiscreet
**indispensable** *adj.* indispensable; **il est indispensable que** + *subj.* it's indispensable that (16)
**individu** *m.* individual
**individualisé** *adj.* individualized
**individualiste** *adj.* individualistic, nonconformist (3)
**industrialisé** *adj.* industrialized
**industrie** *f.* industry
**industriel(le)** *adj.* industrial (16); *m.* manufacturer; **déchets** (*m. pl.*) **industriels** toxic waste (16)
**inédit** *adj.* original
**inégalité** *f.* inequality
**inertie** *f.* inertia
**inexact** *adj.* incorrect
**inférer** (**j'infère**) to infer
**infernal** *adj.* terrible
**infini** *adj.* infinite
**infinitif** *m., Gram.* infinitive
**infirmier/ière** *m., f.* (hospital) nurse
**influencer** (**nous influençons**) to influence
**infographie** *f.* computer graphics
**informaticien(ne)** *m., f.* computer scientist
**information** *f.* (*fam.* **info**) information; *pl.* (*fam.* **infos**) news (broadcast) (10); **flash** (*m.*) **d'informations** newsbrief
**informatique** *f., adj.* computer science (2)
**informé** *adj.* informed; **bien (mal) informé** well (badly) informed
**informel(le)** *adj.* informal
**informer** to inform
**ingénieur** *m.* engineer (14)
**inhabituel(le)** *adj.* unusual
**initiateur/trice** *m., f.* innovator, pioneer
**initiation** *f.* initiation, introduction
**initiative: syndicat** (*m.*) **d'initiative** (local) chamber of commerce; tourist information bureau (11)
**initier (à)** to introduce (*s.o.*) (to) (*activity, sport, cuisine, etc.*)
**injure** *f.* insult
**injuste** *adj.* unjust, unfair; **il est injuste que** + *subj.* it's unfair that (16)
**innovant** *adj.* innovative
**inondation** *f.* flood
**inoubliable** *adj.* unforgettable

**inquiéter** (**j'inquiète**) to trouble, concern, worry; to threaten
**inquiétude** *f.* worry
**inscription** *f.* inscription; matriculation; registration
**inscrire** (*like* **écrire**) *irreg.* to inscribe; **s'inscrire (à)** to join; to enroll; to register
**insister** to insist; **insister sur** to stress; to emphasize
**insolite** *adj.* unusual
**inspirer** to inspire; **s'inspirer de** to be inspired by
**installation** *f.* moving in; installation
**installer** to install; to set up; **s'installer** to settle down, settle in (13); to settle in (*to a new house*)
**instant** *m.* moment
**instantané** *adj.* instant
**instituer** to institute, set up
**instituteur/trice** *m., f.* elementary (primary) school teacher
**instructeur/trice** *m., f.* instructor
**instrument** *m.* instrument; **jouer d'un instrument** to play a musical instrument (3)
**insuffisant** *adj.* insufficient
**insupportable** *adj.* unbearable, insufferable
**intègre** *adj.* honest, upright
**s'intégrer** (**je m'intègre**) **(à)** to integrate oneself, get assimilated (into)
**intégrisme** *m.* fundamentalism (16)
**intellectuel(le)** *adj.* intellectual (3); *m., f.* intellectual (*person*)
**intelligemment** *adv.* intelligently
**intempéries** *f. pl.* bad weather
**intention** *f.* intention; meaning; **avoir l'intention de** to intend to
**interdiction** *f.* prohibition
**interdire** (*like* **dire, vous interdisez**) *irreg.* to forbid; to prohibit
**interdit** *adj.* forbidden; prohibited
**intéressant** *adj.* interesting (3)
**intéresser** to interest (14); **s'intéresser à** to be interested in
**intérêt** *m.* interest, concern
**interlocuteur/trice** *m., f.* speaker, interlocutor
**internaute** *m., f.* Internet user
**Internet** *m.* Internet (10); **sur Internet** on the Internet (10)
**interprète** *m., f.* singer, performer
**interrogatif/ive** *adj., Gram.* interrogative
**interroger (sur)** (**nous interrogeons**) to question, ask (about)
**intervenir** (*like* **venir**) *irreg.* to intervene
**intervention** *f.* intervention; speech; operation
**interview** *f.* interview (*journalism*)
**interviewé(e)** *m., f.* interviewee
**interviewer** to interview
**intime** *adj.* intimate; private; **journal** (*m.*) **intime** private diary
**intimité** *f.* intimacy
**intouchable** *adj.* untouchable
**introduire** to introduce
**intrus(e)** *m., f.* intruder
**inutile** *adj.* useless; **il est inutile que** + *subj.* it's useless that (16)
**inventaire** *m.* inventory
**inventer** to invent
**inverser** to reverse
**investir** to invest; **s'investir** to invest oneself
**invité(e)** *m., f.* guest, invitee
**inviter** to invite
**iPod** *m.* iPod (4)
**ironie** *f.* irony

**irrégulier/ière** *adj.* irregular
**irrésistible** *adj.* compelling
**irrité** *adj.* irritated, sore
**islamiste** *m., f.* Islamist, Muslim
**isolé** *adj.* isolated, alone
**isolement** *m.* isolation, loneliness
**issu** *adj.* stemming from
**Italie** *f.* Italy (2, 8)
**italien** *adj.* Italian; *m.* Italian (*language*) (2);
 **Italien(ne)** *m., f.* Italian (*person*) (2)
**italique** *m.* italic; **en italique** in italics
**itinéraire** *m.* itinerary; **tracer un itinéraire**
 to map out an itinerary
**ivoire** *m.* ivory; **Côte d'Ivoire** *f.* Cote d'Ivoire
**ivoirien(ne)** *adj.* of (from) the Ivory Coast
 Republic; **Ivoirien(ne)** *m., f.* native (inhabitant) of the Ivory Coast Republic

**jamais** *adv.* ever; **ne... jamais** *adv.* never (9)
**jambe** *f.* leg (13)
**jambon** *m.* ham (6)
**janvier** January (1)
**Japon** *m.* Japan (2, 8)
**japonais** *adj.* Japanese; *m.* Japanese (*language*) (2); **Japonais(e)** *m., f.* Japanese person (2)
**jardin** *m.* garden (5)
**jardinage** *m.* gardening (15); **faire du jardinage** to garden
**jaune** *adj.* yellow (3)
**je (j')** *pron., s.* I
**jean(s)** *m.* (*blue*) jeans (3)
**jésuite** *adj., m.* Jesuit
**jeter (je jette)** to throw, throw away; **ne je-
 tez plus** don't throw away any more
**jeu** (*pl.* **jeux**) *m.* game; game show; **jeu de
 mots** pun, play on words (15); **jeu télévisé**
 game show (10); **jeux de \*hasard** games of
 chance (15); **jeux de société** board games,
 group games (15); **jeux vidéo** video games
**jeudi** *m.* Thursday (1); **le jeudi** on Thursdays
 (5)
**jeune** *adj.* young (4); *m. pl.* young people,
 youth; **jeune femme** *f.* young woman (3);
 **jeune fille** *f.* girl, young lady; **jeune
 homme** *m.* young man (3); **jeunes gens** *m.
 pl.* young men; young people; **jeunes mariés** *m. pl.* newlyweds, newly married
 couple
**jeunesse** *f.* youth, young people; **auberge** (*f.*)
 **de jeunesse** youth hostel (9)
**job** *m.* job; odd job; **job d'été** summer job
**Joconde: la Joconde** *Mona Lisa*
**jogging** *m.* jogging; **faire du jogging** to run,
 jog (5)
**joie** *f.* joy
**joindre** (*p.p.* **joint**) *irreg.* to join; to reach; to
 attach; to add
**joint** *adj.* connected, reachable
**joli** *adj.* pretty (4)
**jouer** to play (3); **jouer à** to play (*a sport or
 game*) (3); to play at (*being*); **jouer de** to
 play (*a musical instrument*) (3); **jouer un
 rôle** to play a role
**jouet** *m.* toy
**joueur/euse** *m., f.* player
**jour** *m.* day (1); **au jour le jour** from day to
 day; **chaque jour** every day; **dans quatre
 jours** in four days (5); **de nos jours** these
 days, nowadays, currently; **du jour** today's
 (*menu, exchange rate*); **jour d'action de
 grâce** Thanksgiving Day; **par jour** per day,
 each day; **plat** (*m.*) **du jour** today's special

(*restaurant*); **quel jour est-ce (aujourd'hui)?** what day is it today? (1); **quel
 jour sommes-nous?** what day is it? (1); **quinze jours** two weeks; **tous les jours**
 every day (5); **un jour** someday (14)
**journal** (*pl.* **journaux**) *m.* newspaper (2);
 **journal intime** private journal, diary;
 **journal télévisé** television news
 program (10)
**journaliste** *m., f.* reporter, journalist (2)
**journée** *f.* (*whole*) day (6)
**joyau** *m.* jewel
**joyeux** *adj.* joyful, merry
**juger** to judge
**Juif/Juive** *m., f.* Jewish person
**juillet** July (1)
**juin** June (1)
**jupe** *f.* skirt (3); **minijupe** *f.* miniskirt
**jurer** to swear
**jus** *m.* juice; **jus de fruit** fruit juice; **jus
 d'orange** orange juice (6)
**jusqu'à (jusqu'en)** *prep.* up to, as far as (11);
 until
**juste** *adj.* just; right, exact; *adv.* just, preci-
 sely; accurately; **il est juste que** + *subj.* it's
 fair (equitable) that (16)
**justifier** to justify

**kabyle** *m.* Kabylian (*language*)
**kaki** *adj. inv.* khaki
**kasbah** *m.* casbah (walled citadel of some
 Arab cities)
**kawa** *m., fam.* coffee
**kif-kif: c'est kif-kif** *fam.* (it's) all the same
**kiffer** *fam.* to like
**kilo(gramme) (kg)** *m.* kilogram (7)
**kilomètre (km)** *m.* kilometer
**kiosque** *m.* kiosk; newsstand (10)
**KO** *adj. inv.* exhausted

**la (l')** *art., f. s.* the; *pron., f. s.* it, her
**là** *adv.* there; **là-bas** *adv.* over there (10); **oh,
 là, là** *interj.* good heavens, my goodness
**laboratoire** (*fam.* **labo**) *m.* laboratory; **laboratoire de langues** language lab (2)
**lac** *m.* lake (8); **au bord du lac** on the
 lakeshore
**lâcher** to let go
**laisser** to let; to leave (*behind*) (7); **laisser** +
 *inf.* to let, allow
**lait** *m.* milk (6); **café** (*m.*) **au lait** coffee with
 hot milk
**laitier/ière** *adj.* dairy, milk
**laitue** *f.* lettuce (6)
**lampe** *f.* lamp (4); flashlight; **lampe torche**
 flashlight
**lancer (nous lançons)** to launch; to start up;
 **se lancer dans** to take on, embark on
**langage** *m.* language (system of symbols)
**langue** *f.* language; tongue; **apprentissage**
 (*m.*) **des langues** language learning; **laboratoire** (*m.*) **de langues** language lab (2);
 **langue étrangère** foreign language;
 **langue maternelle** native language; **langues vivantes** modern languages
**lapin** *m.* rabbit
**large** *adj.* wide; extensive; **au large de Dakar** off (of) Dakar
**larme** *f.* tear (drop)
**las(se)** weary (16)
**latin: Quartier** (*m.*) **latin** Latin Quarter (*in
 Paris*)
**lauréat(e)** *m., f.* (award) winner

**laurier** *m.* laurel, bay; **feuille** (*f.*) **de laurier**
 bay leaf
**lavabo** *m.* bathroom sink (4)
**lavande** *f.* lavender
**lave-vaisselle** *m.* (*automatic*) dishwasher
**laver** to wash; **se laver** to wash (*oneself*) (13);
 **se laver les mains** to wash one's hands
**laveuse** *f.* washing machine
**le (l')** *art., m. s.* the; *pron., m. s.* it, him
**leçon** *f.* lesson
**lecteur/trice** *m., f.* reader; *m.* disk drive;
 **lecteur de DVD** DVD player (1)
**lecture** *f.* reading (15)
**légalisation** *f.* legalization (16)
**légendaire** *adj.* legendary
**légende** *f.* legend
**léger/ère** *adj.* light; lightweight; slight; mild
**légume** *m.* vegetable (6)
**lendemain** *m.* day after
**lent** *adj.* slow
**lequel (laquelle, lesquels, lesquelles)** *pron.*
 which one, who, whom, which (15)
**les** *art., pl., m., f.* the; *pron., pl., m., f.* them
**lessive** *f.* laundry; **faire la lessive** to do the
 laundry (5)
**lettre** *f.* letter (10); *pl.* literature; humanities;
 **arts** (*m.*) **et lettres** humanities; **boîte** (*f.*)
 **aux lettres** mailbox (10); **faculté** (*f.*) **des
 lettres** School of Arts and Letters; **mettre
 une lettre à la poste** to mail a letter (10);
 **poster une lettre** to mail a letter
**leur** *adj., m., f.* their; *pron., m., f.* to them;
 **le/la/les leur(s)** *pron.* theirs
**lever (je lève)** to raise, lift; **levez la main**
 raise your hand; **se lever** to get up; to get
 out of bed (13)
**levier** *m.* lever
**lèvres** *f. pl.* lips; **rouge** (*m.*) **à lèvres**
 lipstick (13)
**lézard** *m.* lizard
**liaison** *f.* liaison; love affair
**Liban** *m.* Lebanon (2, 8)
**libanais** *adj.* Lebanese; **Libanais(e)** *m., f.*
 Lebanese person (2)
**libéral** *adj.* liberal; **professions** (*f. pl.*)
 **libérales** professions (*private practice*)
**libérer (je libère)** to free
**liberté** *f.* freedom; **liberté d'expression**
 freedom of expression (16)
**librairie** *f.* bookstore (2)
**libre** *adj.* free; available; vacant; **plongée** (*f.*)
 **libre** snorkeling (8); **temps** (*m.*) **libre** leisure time (15); **union** (*f.*) **libre** cohabita-
 tion, common-law marriage
**libre-service** *m. inv.* self-service
**Libye** *f.* Libya
**licence** *f.* French university degree (*U.S.
 bachelor's degree*)
**lien** *m.* tie, bond, link
**lier** to link
**lieu** *m.* place (2); **au lieu de** *prep.*
 instead of, in the place of; **avoir lieu** to
 take place
**ligne** *f.* line; bus line; figure; **couper la ligne**
 to cut off (*phone call*); **en ligne** online;
 **garder la ligne** to keep one's figure; **ligne
 de but** goal, goal line; **ligne fixe**
 (telephone) landline
**lilas** *m. inv.* lilac
**limite** *f.* limit, deadline; **limite de vitesse**
 speed limit
**limiter** to limit
**limonade** *f.* lemonade; soft drink

**linge** *m.* laundry
**linguiste** *m., f.* linguist
**linguistique** *f.* linguistics (2)
**liqueur** *f.* liquor; liqueur
**liquide** *m., adj.* liquid; cash; **argent** (*m.*) **liquide** cash (14)
**lire** (*p.p.* **lu**) *irreg.* to read (10)
**liseuse** *f.* e-reader (10)
**lisible** *adj.* legible
**liste** *f.* list
**lit** *m.* bed (4); **faire son lit** to make one's bed; **wagon-lit** *m.* sleeping car
**litre** *m.* liter
**littéraire** *adj.* literary
**littérature** *f.* literature (2)
**livraison** *f.* delivery
**livre** *m.* book (1); **livre numérique** e-book (10); **livre papier** print book (10)
**locataire** *m., f.* renter
**location** *f.* rental; rent (4)
**logement** *m.* lodging(s), place of residence (4)
**loger** to reside, live
**logiciel** *m.* software (program) (10); **logiciel de navigation** browser
**logique** *m.* logic; *adj.* logical
**loi** *f.* law
**loin** *adv.* far; **loin de** *prep.* far from (4)
**loisir** *m.* leisure; *pl.* leisure activities (15)
**Londres** London
**long(ue)** *adj.* long (3); **le long de** (all) along; **tout au long de** throughout
**longtemps** *adv.* (for) a long time; **il y a longtemps** a long time ago
**lors de** at the time of
**lorsque** *conj.* when
**loterie** *f.* lottery
**loto** *m.* lottery
**louer** to rent (4); to reserve; **à louer** for rent
**Louisiane** *f.* Louisiana
**loup** *m.* wolf
**lourd** *adj.* heavy
**loyer** *m.* rent (*payment*)
**ludique** *adj.* playful
**lui** *pron., m., f.* he; it; to him; to her; to it; **lui-même** *pron., m. s.* himself (12)
**lumière** *f.* light; **Siècle** (*m.*) **des lumières** Age of Enlightenment
**lumineux: voyant lumineux** *m.* indicator light
**lundi** *m.* Monday (1); **le lundi** on Mondays (5)
**lune** *f.* moon
**lunettes** *f. pl.* (eye)glasses (8); **lunettes de ski** ski goggles (8); **lunettes de soleil** sunglasses (8)
**lutter** to fight
**luxe** *m.* luxury
**luxueux/euse** *adj.* luxurious
**lycée** *m.* lycée (*French secondary school*)
**lycéen(ne)** *m., f.* secondary school student
**lyonnais** *adj.* of (from) Lyon
**lyrique** *adj.* lyrical
**lys: fleur** (*f.*) **de lys** fleur de lis, trefoil

**ma** *adj., f. s.* my; **pour ma part** in my opinion, as for me (16)
**mâcher** to chew
**machine** *f.* machine; **machine à café** coffee-maker; **machine à calculer** calculator; **machine à coudre** sewing machine
**madame (Mme)** (*pl.* **mesdames**) *f.* Madam, Mrs. (ma'am) (1)
**mademoiselle (Mlle)** (*pl.* **mesdemoiselles**) *f.* Miss (1)

**magasin** *m.* store, shop (3); **grand magasin** department store; **magasin d'alimentation** food store
**magasinage** *m., Q.* shopping; **faire du magasinage** to go shopping
**magazine** *m.* (*illustrated*) magazine (4)
**Maghreb** *m.* Maghreb, North Africa
**maghrébin** *adj.* from the Maghreb; North African
**magique** *adj.* magic, magical
**magnifique** *adj.* magnificent (12)
**mai** May (1)
**maillot** *m.* jersey, T-shirt; **maillot de bain** swimsuit (3); **maillot jaune** yellow jersey (*worn by current leader in the Tour de France*)
**main** *f.* hand (13); **sac** (*m.*) **à main** handbag, purse (3); **se laver les mains** to wash one's hands; **se serrer la main** to shake hands
**maintenant** *adv.* now (2); **à partir de maintenant** from now on (14)
**maintenir** to maintain
**maintien** *m.* keeping, upholding
**maire** *m.* mayor
**mairie** *f.* town (city) hall (11)
**mais** *conj.* but (2); **mais non** (but) of course not; **mais si** of course (*affirmative answer to negative question*)
**maison** *f.* house, home (4); company, firm; **à la maison** at home; **Maison-Blanche** *f.* White House; **maison d'édition** publishing company; **repas** (*m.*) **fait maison** home-made meal
**maître (maîtresse)** *m., f.* master (mistress)
**maîtriser** to master, have a command of (14)
**majestueux/euse** *adj.* majestic, stately
**majoritairement** *adv.* mostly, in the majority
**majorité** *f.* majority
**mal** *adv.* badly (1); *m.* evil; pain (*pl.* **maux**); **aller mal** to feel bad (ill); **avoir du mal à** to have trouble (difficulty); **avoir mal (à)** to hurt, have a pain; **avoir mal à la tête (au ventre)** to have a headache (stomachache) (13); **ça va mal** bad(ly) (things are going badly) (1); **(le) plus mal** worse (worst); **pas mal** not bad(ly) (1); **pas mal de** a lot of
**malade** *m., f.* sick person; patient; *adj.* sick (13)
**maladie** *f.* illness, disease; **assurances** (*f. pl.*) **maladie** health insurance
**malaise** *m.* uneasiness
**malchance** *f.* bad luck, misfortune
**mâle** *adj.* male
**malgré** *prep.* in spite of
**malheur** *m.* unhappiness
**malheureusement** *adv.* unfortunately; sadly
**malheureux/euse** *adj.* unhappy; miserable
**maltraité** *adj.* mistreated
**maman** *f., fam.* mom, mommy
**mamie** *f., fam.* grandma
**mamours: se faire des mamours** (*m. pl., fam.*) to bill and coo, neck, sweet-talk
**mandat** *m.* mandate, term in office
**mange-tout:** *°***haricots** (*m. pl.*) **mange-tout** string beans; sugar peas
**manger (nous mangeons)** to eat (2); *n. m.* food; **salle** (*f.*) **à manger** dining room (5)
**mangeur/euse** *m., f.* eater
**mangue** *f.* mango
**maniable** *adj.* easy to handle, manageable
**manier** to wield; to handle

**manière** *f.* manner, way; **bonnes manières** good manners
**manifestation** (*fam.* **manif**) *f.* (*political*) demonstration; **manifestation sportive** sporting event (15)
**manifester (pour, contre)** to demonstrate (for, against) (16)
**manne** *f.* manna, godsend
**mannequin** *m.* fashion model
**manque** *m.* lack, shortage
**manquer** to lack; **manquer à** to be missed by
**manteau** *m.* coat, overcoat (3)
**se maquiller** to put on makeup (13)
**marais** *m.* marsh, swamp
**marbre** *m.* marble
**marchand(e)** *m., f.* merchant, shopkeeper; **marchand(e) de vin** wine merchant (14)
**marchander** to bargain
**marche** *f.* walking (15); step (*stair*)
**marché** *m.* market; deal, transaction; **bon marché** *adj. inv.* cheap, inexpensive; **faire le marché** to do the shopping, go to the market (5); **marché aux puces** flea market; **marché de l'emploi** job market (14); **marché en plein air** outdoor market
**marcher** to walk (13); to work (*machine, object*)
**mardi** *m.* Tuesday (1); **le mardi** on Tuesdays (5)
**mari** *m.* husband (5)
**mariage** *m.* marriage; wedding (13); **mariage à l'essai** trial marriage
**marié** *adj.* married (5); **nouveaux mariés** *m. pl.* newlyweds, newly married couple (13)
**se marier (avec)** to get married (to) (13)
**marin** *adj.* maritime, of the sea; **plongée** (*f.*) **sous-marine** scuba diving (8); **sous-marin** (*m.*) submarine
**marmite** *f.* soup pot
**Maroc** *m.* Morocco (2, 8)
**marocain** *adj.* Moroccan; **Marocain(e)** *m., f.* Moroccan (*person*) (2)
**marque** *f.* trade name, brand, make
**marquer** to mark; to indicate
**marrant** *adj., fam.* funny, hilarious
**marre: avoir marre de** *fam.* to be fed up with
**se marrer** to have a good time
**marron** *adj. inv.* brown (3); *m.* chestnut; **dinde** (*f.*) **aux marrons** turkey with chestnuts
**mars** March (1)
**martiniquais** *adj.* Martinican; **Martiniquais(e)** *m., f.* Martinican (*person*)
**masculin** *adj.* masculine
**masque** *m.* mask
**masqué** *adj.* masked
**master** *m.* masters degree (*in France*)
**mât** *m.* pole, climbing pole
**match** *m.* game (15); **match de foot(ball) (de rugby)** soccer game (rugby match)
**matérialiste** *adj.* materialistic
**matériau** (*pl.* **matériaux**) *m.* material; building material
**matériel** *m.* material(s); **matériel(le)** *adj.* material
**maternel(le)** *adj.* maternal; (**école**) (*f.*) **maternelle** nursery school, preschool; **langue** (*f.*) **maternelle** native language
**maternité** *f.* maternity, childbearing
**mathématiques** (*fam.* **maths**) *f. pl.* mathematics (2)

**matière** *f.* academic subject (2); material; **en matière de** in the matter of, as far as . . . is concerned

**matin** *m.* morning; **ce matin** this morning (5); **du matin** in the morning (6); **petit matin** early morning; **tous les matins** every morning (10)

**matinal** *adj.* morning

**matinée** *f.* morning (*duration*) (7)

**mauvais** *adj.* bad (4); **il fait mauvais** it's bad (weather) out (5); **le/la plus mauvais(e)** the worst; **plus mauvais(e)** worse

**me (m')** *pron., s.* me, to me, for me

**mec** *m., fam.* guy

**mécanicien(ne)** *m., f.* mechanic

**mécanisme** *m.* mechanism

**médaille** *f.* medal

**médecin (femme médecin)** *m., f.* doctor, physician (14); **médecin généraliste** general practitioner

**médias** *m. pl.* media (16)

**médicament** *m.* medication; drug

**médiéval** *adj.* medieval (12)

**médina** *f.* medina (old part of city in Morocco)

**méditer** to meditate

**mégalithique** *adj.* megalithic

**meilleur** *adj.* better (14); **le/la/les meilleur(e)(s)** the best

**mél** *m.* e-mail (10)

**mélange** *m.* mixture

**mélanger (nous mélangeons)** to mix

**mêlée** *f.* scrum (*rugby*)

**se mêler** to mingle

**membre** *m.* member

**même** *adj.* same (8); itself; very same; *adv.* even (8); **de même** *adv.* likewise; **en même temps** at the same time; **le/la/les même(s)** the same one(s) (15); **moi-même** *pron.* myself (12); **quand même** anyway, even so

**mémoire** *m.* memory; *pl.* memoirs

**ménage** *m.* housekeeping; household; **faire le ménage** to do the housework (5); **scène** (*f.*) **de ménage** domestic squabble

**ménager/ère** *adj.* household; **tâches** (*f. pl.*) **ménagères** household tasks

**mener (je mène) (à)** to lead (to)

**mensuel(le)** *adj.* monthly

**menthe** *f.* mint (*leaves*)

**mentionner** to mention

**menton** *m.* chin

**menu** *m.* menu; fixed-price menu (7)

**mer** *f.* sea, ocean (8); **au bord de la mer** at the seashore

**merci** *interj.* thank you (1); **merci beaucoup** thank you very much (1)

**mercredi** *m.* Wednesday (1); **le mercredi** on Wednesdays (5)

**mère** *f.* mother (5); **belle-mère** mother-in-law; stepmother (5); **grand-mère** grandmother (5)

**méridien** *m.* meridian

**mérite** *m.* merit, worth

**mériter** to deserve, be worth

**merveille** *f.* marvel; **à merveille** *adv.* marvelously

**merveilleux/euse** *adj.* wonderful

**mes** *adj., m., f., pl.* my

**mesdames** *f., pl.* ladies

**message** (*m.*) **électronique** e-mail message

**messager/ère** *m., f.* messenger

**messe** *f.* (*Catholic*) Mass

**messieurs dames** ladies and gentlemen

**mesure** *f.* measure; **dans une moindre mesure** to a lesser extent; **prendre des mesures** to take measures; **sur mesure** custom-made

**météo** *f., fam.* weather forecast (5)

**méthode** *f.* method

**métier** *m.* trade, profession (14); **armée** (*f.*) **de métier** professional army

**métissage** *m.* mixing of races

**mètre** *m.* meter

**métro** *m.* subway (*train, system*) (9); **station** (*f.*) **de métro** metro station (11)

**métropole** *m.* metropolis

**métropolitain** *adj.* metropolitan; from (of) mainland France

**mets** *m. s.* food, dish

**metteur/euse** (*m., f.*) **en scène** producer; film or theater director

**mettre** (*p.p.* **mis**) *irreg.* to place, put (10); to put on (10); to turn on; to take (*time*); to admit, grant; **mettre à mort** to put to death; **mettre en valeur** to emphasize; **mettre la table (le couvert)** to set the table (10); **mettre ses vêtements** to get dressed; **mettre une lettre à la poste** to mail a letter (10); **se mettre à** to begin to (*do s.th.*) (13)

**meuble** *m.* piece of furniture (5); **meubles d'époque** antique furniture

**meublé** *adj.* furnished

**meuf** *f., fam.* chick, woman, girl

**meule** *f., fam.* moped

**meurs, meurt** (see **mourir**)

**mexicain** *adj.* Mexican; **Mexicain(e)** *m., f.* Mexican (*person*) (2)

**Mexico** Mexico City

**Mexique** *m.* Mexico (2, 8)

**mi-:** (**à la**) **mi-juin** (in) mid-June

**micro-ordinateur** (*fam.* **micro**) *m.* desktop computer (10)

**midi** noon; **Midi** *m. south-central region of France*; **après-midi** *m.* or *f.* afternoon; **de l'après-midi** in the afternoon (6); **il est midi** it's noon (6)

**miel** *m.* honey

**mien(ne)(s) (le/la/les)** *pron., m., f.,* mine

**mieux** *adv.* better (15); **aimer mieux** to prefer (2); **il vaut mieux que** + *subj.* it's better that (16); **mieux (le mieux)** better (the best) (15); **tant mieux** so much the better (15)

**mièvrerie** *f.* sentimentality, soppiness, mush

**mijoter** to simmer

**milieu** *m.* environment; milieu, setting; middle; **au milieu de** in the middle of

**militaire** *adj.* military; **budget** (*m.*) **militaire** military budget (16)

**militairement** *adv.* militarily

**militer pour (contre)** to militate, argue for (against)

**mille** *adj.* thousand (7)

**millénaire** *m.* one thousand; millennium; *adj.* millennial

**milliard** *m.* billion (7)

**milliardaire** *m., f.* billionaire

**millier** *m.* (around) a thousand

**million** *m.* million (7)

**mince** *adj.* thin; slender

**minceur** *f.* leanness, slenderness

**mine** *f.* appearance, demeanor; mine; **vous n'avez pas bonne mine** you don't look well

**minéral: eau** (*f.*) **minérale** mineral water (6)

**minier/ière** *adj.* mining

**minijupe** *f.* miniskirt

**ministre** *m.* minister; **premier ministre** prime minister

**minuit** midnight; **il est minuit** it's midnight (6)

**minute** *f.* minute; **dans dix minutes** in ten minutes

**miraculeux/euse** *adj.* miraculous

**miroir** *m.* mirror (4)

**mise** *f.* placement; **mise à distance** separating; **mise en circulation** putting into circulation; **mise en place** placement

**misère** *f.* misery, poverty

**missionnaire** *m., f.* missionary

**mixeur** *m.* mixer

**mixité** *f.* diversity

**mixte** *adj.* mixed

**mobile** *m.* cell phone (10)

**mobiliser** to mobilize

**mobilité** *f.* mobility

**mobylette** *f.* moped

**mode** *f.* fashion, style; *m.* form, mode; *adj.* fashionable; **à la mode** in style; **créateur/trice** (*m., f.*) **de mode** fashion designer

**modèle** *m.* model; pattern

**modéré** *adj.* moderate; **habitations** (*f. pl.*) **à loyer modéré (H.L.M.)** *publicly subsidized apartment blocks* (*France*)

**modernité** *f.* modernity

**modeste** *adj.* modest, humble (3)

**modifié** *adj.* modified

**moi** *pron. s.* I, me; **c'est moi.** it's me (10); **chez moi** at my place; **excusez-moi** excuse me; **moi aussi** me too (3); **moi-même** *pron.* myself (12); **moi non plus** me neither (3); **selon moi** in my view

**moindre** *adj.* less, lesser; **dans une moindre mesure** to a lesser extent; **le/la/les moindre(s)** the least

**moine** *m.* monk

**moins** *adv.* less; minus; **au moins** at least; **le moins** the least; **moins de...** fewer than (*with numbers*); **moins le quart** quarter to (the hour) (6); **moins... que** less . . . than (14); **plus ou moins** more or less

**mois** *m.* month (1); **par mois** per month

**moitié** *f.* half

**môme** *m., f., fam.* kid

**moment** *m.* moment; **au dernier moment** at the last moment; **au moment de partir** upon leaving; **en ce moment** now, currently; **pour le moment** for the moment

**momie** *f.* mummy

**mon** *adj., m. s.* my

**monde** *m.* world (8); people; society; **Coupe** (*f.*) **du Monde** World Cup (*soccer*); **Tiers-Monde** *m.* Third World; **tour** (*m.*) **du monde** trip around the world; **tout le monde** everybody, everyone (7)

**mondial** *adj.* world; worldwide; **Première (Deuxième [Seconde]) Guerre** (*f.*) **mondiale** First (Second) World War

**mondialement** *adv.* throughout the world

**mondialisation** *f.* globalization (16)

**monétaire** *adj.* monetary

**moniteur** *m.* monitor; screen (10)

**monnaie** *f.* coins, change (10); currency (*units*); **déposer la monnaie** to deposit change (10)

**monsieur (M.)** (*pl.* **messieurs**) *m.* Mister; gentleman; sir (1); **croque-monsieur** *m. grilled ham and cheese sandwich*

**montagne** *f.* mountain (8); **à la montagne** in the mountains; **chaussures** (*f.*) **de montagne** hiking boots (8); **faire du vélo de montagne** to go mountain biking

**montant** *m.* sum, amount (14); total

**monter (dans)** to set up, organize; to put on; to carry up; to go up; to climb (into) (8); **en montant à bord** embarking, getting on board

**montre** *f.* watch; wristwatch

**montrer** to show (3)

**monumental** *adj.* huge

**moquer: se moquer de** to make fun of (14)

**moqueur/euse** *adj.* mocking

**moral** *m.* morale, spirits

**morale** *f.* moral philosophy

**moralement** in one's morale; morally

**moralité** *f.* morals, morality

**morceau** *m.* piece (7); **morceau de gâteau** piece of cake

**mordre** to bite; **être mordu de** to be crazy about, smitten with

**morosité** *f.* gloominess, moroseness

**morphinique** *adj.* containing morphine

**mort** *f.* death; *adj.* dead; **mettre à mort** to put to death; **mort de fatigue** dead-tired; **nature** (*f.*) **morte** still life

**mosaïque** *f.* mosaic

**mosquée** *f.* mosque

**mot** *m.* word (1); **jeu** (*m.*) **de mots** pun, play on words (15); **mot apparenté** related word, cognate; **mot clé** key word

**moteur** (*m.*) **de recherche** search engine

**motivation** *f.* motive; **lettre** (*f.*) **de motivation** cover letter, letter in support of one's application

**motivé** *adj.* motivated

**motocyclette** (*fam.* **moto**) *f.* motorcycle (9)

**mouche** *f.* fly, housefly; **bateau-mouche** (*pl.* **bateaux-mouches**) *m. tourist boat on the Seine*

**moudre** to grind

**moule** *f.* mussel (*seafood*)

**moulinet: faire des moulinets avec les bras** to whirl one's arms about

**mourant** *adj.* dying

**mourir** (*p.p.* **mort**) *irreg.* to die (8); **s'ennuyer à mourir** to be bored to death

**mousse** (*f.*) **au chocolat** chocolate mousse

**mousser** to bubble; to sparkle

**moustique** *m.* mosquito

**mouton** *m.* sheep

**mouvement** *m.* movement

**moyen** *m.* mean(s); way; **moyen de transport** means of transportation (9); **un bon (meilleur) moyen** a good (better) way

**moyen(ne)** *adj.* average; all right (*in response to* **comment vas-tu?**) **cadre** (*m.*) **moyen** middle manager; **des classes** (*f.*) **moyennes** middle classes; **de taille moyenne** of medium height (3); **Moyen Âge** *m. s.* Middle Ages (12)

**moyennant** *prep.* in return for (which)

**moyenne** *f.* average; **en moyenne** on (an) average

**mp3** *m.* mp3 player (10)

**muet(te)** *adj.* mute

**multinationale** *f.* multinational (corporation)

**multiplier** to multiply

**mur** *m.* wall (4)

**muraille** *f.* wall

**musée** *m.* museum (11)

**musical** (*pl.* **musicaux**) *adj.* musical

**Musicien(ne)** *m., f.* musician (12)

**musique** *f.* music (2); **musique classique** classical music

**Musulman(e)** *m., f.* Muslim

**mutation** *f.* change, alteration

**myrtille** *f.* huckleberry; blueberry

**mystère** *m.* mystery

**nacre** *f.* mother-of-pearl; *m.* pearly (*color*)

**nager (nous nageons)** to swim (8)

**naïf/ïve** *adj.* naive (3); simple

**naissance** *f.* birth

**naissant** *adj.* emerging

**naître** (*p.p.* **né**) *irreg.* to be born (8)

**nana** *f., fam.* babe (pretty girl)

**nappe** *f.* tablecloth (6)

**narrateur/trice** *m., f.* narrator

**natal** *adj.* native

**natation** *f.* swimming

**nation** *f.* nation; **Organisation des Nations Unies (ONU)** United Nations (UN)

**nationaliste** *m., f.* nationalist; *adj.* nationalistic, nationalist

**nationalité** *f.* nationality (2)

**nature** *f.* nature (16); **nature morte** still life

**naturel(le)** *adj.* natural; **ressources** (*f. pl.*) **naturelles** natural resources (16); **sciences** (*f. pl.*) **naturelles** natural sciences (2)

**nautique** *adj.* nautical; **ski** (*m.*) **nautique** water-skiing (8)

**navarin** *m.* stew; lamb stew

**navet** *m., fam.* bad film, flop

**navigateur** *m.* browser (10)

**navigation: logiciel** (*m.*) **de navigation** browser (*Internet*)

**naviguer** to navigate, to browse (10)

**navire** *m.* ship

**n'dolé** *m.* hearty soup of Cameroon

**ne (n')** *adv.* no; not; **ne... aucun(e)** none, not one; **ne... jamais** never, not ever (9); **ne... ni... ni** neither . . . nor; **ne... pas** no; not; **ne... pas du tout** not at all (9); **ne... pas encore** not yet (9); **ne... personne** no one, nobody (9); **ne... plus** no more, no longer (9); **ne... que** only (9); **ne... rien** nothing (9); **n'est-ce pas?** isn't it (so)?, isn't that right? (3)

**néanmoins** *adv.* nevertheless

**nécessaire** *adj.* necessary; **il est nécessaire que** + *subj.* it's necessary that (16)

**nécessité** *f.* need

**nécessiter** to require, necessitate

**né(e)** (see **naître**)

**néfaste** *adj.* harmful

**négatif/ive** *adj.* negative

**négativement** *adv.* negatively

**négociateur/trice** *m., f.* negotiator

**négocier** to negotiate

**nègre (négresse)** *m., f.* Negro (Negress)

**négrier/ière: traite** (*f.*) **négrière** slave trade

**négritude** *f.* Negritude (*1930s Black consciousness movement*)

**neige** *f.* snow; **surf** (*m.*) **des neiges** snowboarding

**neiger (il neigeait)** to snow; **il neige** it's snowing (5)

**nénuphar** *m.* water lily

**nerveux/euse** *adj.* nervous (3)

**net(te)** *adj.* clear; net (*price*)

**nettoyer (je nettoie)** to clean

**neuf** *adj.* nine (1)

**neuf (neuve)** *adj.* new, brand-new; **quoi de neuf?** what's new?; **remettre à neuf** to restore; **Terre-Neuve** *f.* Newfoundland

**neutre** *adj.* neutral

**neuvième** *adj.* ninth (11)

**neveu** *m.* nephew (5)

**nez** *m.* nose (13)

**ni** *conj.* neither; nor; **ne... ni... ni** neither . . . nor

**niçois(e)** *adj.* of/from Nice

**nièce** *f.* niece (5)

**niveau** *m.* level; **niveau de vie** standard of living (16)

**noces: repas** (*m.*) **de noces** wedding meal/party; **voyage** (*m.*) **de noces** honeymoon trip

**Noël** *m.* Christmas; **bûche** (*f.*) **de Noël** Yule log (*pastry*); **père** (*m.*) **Noël** Santa Claus; **réveillon** (*m.*) **de Noël** midnight Christmas dinner

**noir** *adj.* black (3)

**noisette** *f.* hazel nut

**noix** *f.* nut; **noix de coco** coconut

**nom** *m.* noun; name; **au nom de** in the name of

**nombre** *m.* number (1); quantity; **nombres** (*pl.*) **ordinaux** ordinal numbers

**nombreux/euse** *adj.* numerous; **famille** (*f.*) **nombreuse** large family

**nommer** to name; to appoint

**non** *interj.* no; not (1); **moi non plus** me neither (3); **non plus** neither, not . . . either

**nord** *m.* north; **Amérique** (*f.*) **du Nord** North America; **au nord** to the north (9); **Nord-américain(e)** *m., f.* North American (*person*); **nord-est** *m.* northeast; **nord-ouest** *m.* northwest

**normal** *adj.* normal; **il est normal que** + *subj.* it's normal that (16)

**normalement** *adv.* usually

**normand** *adj.* Norman; **à la normande** in the Norman style

**Normandie** *f.* Normandy

**Norvège** *f.* Norway

**nos** *adj., m., f., pl.* our

**notamment** *adv.* notably; especially

**note** *f.* note; grade (*academic*); **bonnes (mauvaises) notes** good (bad) grades; **prendre des notes** to take notes

**noter** to notice; to note, write down

**notre** *adj., m., f., s.* our

**nôtre(s): le/la/les nôtre(s)** *pron., m., f.* ours; our own

**nourrir** to nourish

**nourrissant** *adj.* nourishing

**nourriture** *f.* food (6)

**nous** *pron., pl.* we; us; **nous-mêmes** *pron., pl.* ourselves (12); **nous sommes lundi (mardi...)** it's Monday (Tuesday . . . ) (1); **quel jour sommes-nous?** what day is it? (1)

**nouveau (nouvel, nouvelle [nouveaux, nouvelles])** *adj.* new (3); **à nouveau** once more; **de nouveau** again (11); **nouveaux mariés** *m. pl.* newlyweds, newly married couple (13); **la nouvelle cuisine** lighter, low-fat cooking style; **La Nouvelle-Orléans** New Orleans; **Nouveau-Brunswick** *m.* New Brunswick; **Nouveau-Mexique** *m.* New Mexico; **Nouvel An** *m.* New Year's; **Nouvelle-Écosse** *f.* Nova Scotia

**nouveauté** *f.* novelty

**nouvelle** *f.* piece of news; short story; *pl.* news, current events; **bonne (mauvaise) nouvelle** good (bad) news

**novembre** November (1)

**nu** *adj.* naked

**nuage** *m.* cloud

**nuageux/euse** *adj.* cloudy; **le temps est nuageux** it's cloudy (5)

**nucléaire** *adj.* nuclear; **armes** (*f. pl.*) **nucléaires** nuclear weapons; **centrale** (*f.*) **nucléaire** nuclear power plant; **déchets** (*m. pl.*) **nucléaires** nuclear waste (16); **énergie** (*f.*) **nucléaire** nuclear power (16)

**nuit** *f.* night (7); **boîte** (*f.*) **de nuit** nightclub, club; **de nuit** at night

**nul(le)** *adj.,* null; worthless; *fam.* no good

**numérique** digital; **appareil** (*m.*) **(photo) numérique** digital camera (10); **livre** (*m.*) **numérique** e-book (10); **télévision** (*f.*) **numérique terrestre (la TNT)** high-definition television (10)

**numéro** *m.* number (10); **composer le numéro** to dial the number (10); **numéro de téléphone** telephone number (10)

**numéroter** to number

**nuque** *f.* nape, back of the neck

**nymphéa** *m.* white water lily

**obéir** to obey

**objectif** *m.* goal, objective

**objet** *m.* object; objective; **pronom** (*m.*) **complément d'objet direct (indirect)** *Gram.* direct (indirect) object pronoun

**obligatoire** *adj.* obligatory; mandatory; **service** (*m.*) **(militaire) obligatoire** mandatory military service

**obligatoirement** *adv.* necessarily, obligatorily

**obligé** *adj.* obliged, required; **être obligé de** to be obliged to

**observateur/trice** *m., f.* observer

**observer** to observe

**obsolète** *adj.* obsolete, outdated

**obtenir** (*like* **tenir**) *irreg.* to obtain, get (8)

**obtention** *f.* obtaining; achieving

**occasion** *f.* opportunity; occasion; bargain

**occident** *m.* the west

**occidental** *adj.* (*pl.* **occidentaux**) western, occidental; **Afrique** (*f.*) **occidentale** western Africa; **Virginie-Occidentale** *f.* West Virginia

**occupé** *adj.* occupied; busy

**occuper** to occupy; **s'occuper de** to look after, take care of

**océan** *m.* ocean, sea; **océan Atlantique** Atlantic Ocean

**Océanie** *f.* Oceania, the South Sea Islands

**ocre** *adj.* ochre (yellow-earth color)

**octobre** October (1)

**odeur** *f.* odor, smell

**odorat** *m.* sense of smell

**œil** (*pl.* **yeux**) *m.* eye (13); **coup** (*m.*) **d'œil** glance, quick look

**œnologue** *m., f.* oenologist, wine expert

**œuf** *m.* egg (6)

**œuvre** *f.* work; artistic work; **chef-d'œuvre** (*pl.* **chefs-d'œuvre**) *m.* masterpiece (12); ***hors-d'œuvre** *m. inv.* appetizer (7); **œuvre d'art** work of art (12)

**officiel(le)** *adj.* official

**offre** *f.* offer; **offre d'emploi** job offer

**offrir** (*like* **ouvrir**) *irreg.* to offer (14)

**oie** *f.* goose; **la Mère l'Oie** Mother Goose

**oignon** *m.* onion (7); **soupe** (*f.*) **à l'oignon** (French) onion soup

**oiseau** *m.* bird

**olive** *f.* olive; **huile** (*f.*) **d'olive** olive oil (7)

**olivier** *m.* olive tree

**ombre** *f.* shadow; shade

**ombrelle** *f.* parasol

**omelette** *f.* omelet

**on** *pron. s.* one, they, we

**oncle** *m.* uncle (5)

**onze** *adj.* eleven (1)

**onzième** *adj.* eleventh (11)

**opéra** *m.* opera (15)

**opérateur** *m.* operator **opérateur de téléphonie mobile** cell phone service provider

**opinion** *f.* opinion; **exprimer une opinion** to express an opinion (16); **opinion publique** public opinion (16)

**opposé** *m.* the opposite

**opter pour** to opt for, choose

**optimiste** *m., f.* optimist; *adj.* optimistic (3)

**or** *m.* gold

**orage** *m.* storm

**orageux/euse** *adj.* stormy; **le temps est orageux** it's stormy (5)

**orange** *adj. inv.* orange (3); *m.* orange (*color*); *f.* orange (*fruit*) (6); **jus** (*m.*) **d'orange** orange juice (6)

**orchestre** *m.* orchestra; band

**ordinaire** *adj.* ordinary, regular (3)

**ordinal** *adj.* ordinal; **nombres** (*m. pl.*) **ordinaux** ordinal numbers

**ordinateur** (*fam.* **ordi**) *m.* computer (1); **micro-ordinateur** *m.* desktop computer; **ordinateur de bureau (de table)** desktop computer (10); **ordinateur portable** (*fam.* **portable** *m.*) laptop computer (10)

**ordonner** to order (*s.o. to do s.th.*)

**ordre** *m.* order; command; **dans le bon ordre** in the right order; **dans l'ordre chronologique** in chronological order; **en ordre** orderly, neat (4)

**oreille** *f.* ear (13)

**organique** *adj.* organic

**organiser** to organize

**organisme** *m.* organization, institution; organism

**oriental** (*pl.* **orientaux**) *adj.* Oriental

**orientation** *f.* orientation; direction; **conseiller/ère** (*m., f.*) **d'orientation** guidance counselor

**s'orienter** to orient oneself, get one's bearings

**oriflamme** *f.* banner, standard (*flag*)

**originaire** (*adj.*) **de** native to

**original** (*pl.* **originaux**) *adj.* original; eccentric

**originalité** *f.* originality, imagination

**origine** *f.* origin; **d'origine algérienne** of Algerian origin (background); **pays** (*m.*) **d'origine** native country, nationality

**ornement** *m.* ornament; embellishment, adornment

**orteil** *m.* toe

**os** *m.* bone

**ou** *conj.* or; either (2); **ou bien** or else

**où** *adv.* where (4); *pron.* where, in which, when (14); **où est... ?** where is . . . ?

**ouah ouah!** bow-wow!, woof!

**oublier (de)** to forget (to) (8)

**ouest** *m.* west; **à l'ouest** to the west (9); **Afrique** (*f.*) **de l'ouest** West Africa; **nord-ouest** *m.* northwest; **ouest-africain** *adj.* West African; **sud-ouest** *m.* southwest

**ouf** *interj.* phew, whew

**oui** *interj.* yes (1); **oui, mais...** yes, but . . . (10)

**ouïe** *f.* sense of hearing

**ouragan** *m.* hurricane

**outil** *m.* tool

**ouvert** *adj.* open; frank

**ouverture** *f.* opening

**ouvrier/ière** *m., f.* (*manual*) worker, laborer (14)

**ouvrir** (*p.p.* **ouvert**) *irreg.* to open (14)

**pacifiste** *adj.* pacifistic

**pacsé** *adj.* legally joined by a PACS

**page** (*f.*) **d'accueil** homepage

**pager** *m.* pager

**pain** *m.* bread (6); **baguette** (*f.*) **de pain** (French) bread, baguette; **pain au chocolat** chocolate croissant; **pain de campagne** country-style bread, wheat bread (7)

**pair: au pair** au pair (*child care by foreign student*)

**paix** *f.* peace

**palais** *m.* palace (12)

**palier** *m.* (stair) landing; **voisin(e)** (*m., f.*) **de palier** neighbor living on the same landing

**palmarès** *m.* record of achievement

**palmeraie** *f.* palm grove

**palmier** *m.* palm tree

**pamplemousse** *m.* grapefruit

**Paname** *m. fam.* Paris

**pané** *adj.* fried in breadcrumbs

**panier** *m.* basket

**panne** *f.* (*mechanical*) breakdown; **en panne de débouchés** faced with an absence of job openings

**panneau** *m.* billboard, sign

**panoramique** *adj.* with a panoramic view

**pantalon** *m.* (pair of) pants (3)

**pantoufle** *f.* slipper (13)

**papa** *m., fam.* dad, daddy

**papier** *m.* paper; **livre** (*m.*) **papier** print book (10)

**papy** *m., fam.* grandpa

**Pâques** *f. pl.* Easter

**paquet** *m.* package

**par** *prep.* by, through, with (4, 12); **commencer (finir) par** to begin (end up) by; **par avion** air-mail; **par cœur** by heart (12); **par exemple** for example (16); **par *hasard** by chance; **par jour (semaine, etc.)** per day (week, etc.); **par ordre chronologique** in chronological order; **par rapport à** in comparison with, in relation to; **par terre** on the ground (4); **une fois par semaine** once a week (5)

**paradis** *m.* paradise

**paradoxalement** *adv.* paradoxically

**paradoxe** *m.* paradox

**paragraphe** *m.* paragraph

**paraître** (*like* **connaître**) *irreg.* to appear (16)

**paralysé** *adj.* paralyzed; strike-bound

**parapluie** *m.* umbrella (8)

**parasol** *m.* beach umbrella; parasol

**parc** *m.* park (11); **parc d'attraction** theme park

**parce que** *conj.* because (4)

**parcourir** (*like* **courir**) *irreg.* to cover, travel; to skim

**parcours** *m. s.* distance, journey, course

**pardon** *interj.* pardon (me) (1)

**pareil(le)** *adj.* the same, similar

**parent(e)** *m., f.* parent; relative (5); **arrière-grand-parent** *m.* great-grandparent (5); **grand-parent** grandparent (5); **parent(e) proche** close relative

**parenthèse** *f.* parenthesis; **entre parenthèses** in parentheses

**paresseux/euse** *adj.* lazy (3)

**parfait** *adj.* perfect

**parfaitement** *adv.* perfectly (14)

**parfois** *adv.* sometimes (9)

**parfum** *m.* perfume; flavor

**parfumé** *adj.* fragrant; flavorful

**pari** *m.* bet, wager; **pari perdu** lost bet

**parier** to bet, wager

**parisien(ne)** *adj.* Parisian (3); **Parisien(ne)** *m., f.* Parisian (*person*)

**parking** *m.* parking lot

**parlement** *m.* parliament

**parler (à, de)** to speak (to, of) (2); to talk (2); *m.* speech

**parmi** *prep.* among

**parole** *f.* word; *pl.* lyrics

**parquet** *m.* wooden (parquet) floor

**part** *f.* share, portion; **à part** besides; separately; **c'est de la part de X** X is calling; **de ma part** for me, on my behalf; **pour ma part** in my opinion, as for me (16); **quelque part** somewhere

**partager (nous partageons)** to share

**partenaire** *m., f.* partner

**partenariat** *m.* partnership

**parti** *m.* (*political*) party (16)

**participant(e)** *m., f.* participant

**participe** *m., Gram.* participle

**participer à** to participate in

**particulier/ière** *adj.* particular, special; **en particulier** in particular

**partie** *f.* part; **faire partie de** to be part of

**partir** (*like* **dormir**) (**à, pour, de**) *irreg.* to leave (for, from) (8); **à partir de** *prep.* starting from; **à partir de maintenant** from now on (14); **partir à l'aventure** to leave with no itinerary; **partir en vacances** to leave on vacation

**partisan(e)** *m., f.* supporter, advocate

**partitif/ive** *adj., Gram.* partitive

**partout** *adv.* everywhere (11)

**parvenir** (*like* **venir**) **à** *irreg.* to succeed in

**pas** (**ne... pas**) not; **ne... pas du tout** not at all (9); **ne... pas encore** not yet (9); **n'est-ce pas?** isn't it (so)?, isn't that right? (3); **pas à pas** step-by-step; **pas du tout** not at all; **pas mal** not bad(ly) (1)

**passage** *m.* passage; passing; **lieu** (*m.*) **de passage** crossing point, passageway

**passager/ère** *m., f.* passenger (9)

**passant(e)** *m., f.* passerby

**passé** *m.* past; *adj.* past, gone, last (7); **l'année** (*f.*) **passée** last year; **participe** (*m.*) **passé** *Gram.* past participle; **passé composé** *Gram.* compound past tense; **passé simple** *Gram.* past tense (*literary*)

**passeport** *m.* passport (8)

**passer** to pass, spend (*time*) (6); to put through to (*by phone*); to show, play (*a film, record*); **passer (par)** to pass (by, through) (8); **passer sur** to go over; **passer les vacances** to spend one's vacation; **passer un examen** to take an exam (4); **qu'est-ce qui se passe?** what's happening?, what's going on? (15); **se passer** to happen, take place (15); to go

**passe-temps** *m. inv.* pastime, hobby (15)

**passionné(e)** *m., f.* enthusiast; *adj.* enthusiastic; passionate

**se passionner pour** to be excited about

**pasteur** *m.* (*Protestant*) minister

**pastilla** *f.* pastilla (*Moroccan pastry and meat dish*)

**patate** *f., fam.* potato

**pâté** *m.* liver paste, pâté; **pâté de campagne** (country-style) pâté (7); **pâté de foie gras** goose liver pâté

**paternel(le)** *adj.* paternal

**pâtes** *f. pl.* pasta, noodles (7)

**patience** *f.* patience; **avoir de la patience** to be patient; **perdre patience** to lose patience

**patient** *m., f.* (*hospital*) patient; *adj.* patient (3)

**patienter** to wait (patiently)

**patin** *m.* skate, ice skate; **faire du patin à glace** to go ice-skating; **faire du patin à roues alignées** to do in-line skating

**patiner** to skate

**pâtisserie** *f.* pastry; pastry shop (7); **boulangerie-pâtisserie** *f.* bakery-pastry shop

**pâtissier/ière** *m., f.* pastry shop owner; pastry chef

**patrie** *f.* native land

**patrimoine** *m.* legacy; heritage (12)

**patron(ne)** *m., f.* boss, employer; **fête** (*f.*) **des patrons** saint's day

**pause** *f.* pause, break

**pauvre** *adj.* poor; unfortunate (3)

**pauvreté** *f.* poverty

**pavillon** *m.* house, lodge

**payé** *adj.* paid, paying

**payer (je paie)** to pay, pay for (10)

**pays** *m.* country, nation (2); **pays en voie de développement** developing nation; **Pays-Bas** *m. pl.* Netherlands, Holland; **pays d'origine** native country

**paysage** *m.* landscape; scenery

**paysan(ne)** *m., f.* peasant, farmworker

**peau** *f.* skin

**pêche** *f.* peach; fishing (15); **aller à la pêche** to go fishing (8); **avoir la pêche** *fam.* to feel great, like a million bucks

**pêcheur/euse** *m., f.* fisherman (woman)

**pécule** *m., fam.* savings

**pédagogique** *adj.* pedagogical, teaching

**pédaler** to pedal

**pédestre** *adj.* pedestrian; **randonnée** (*f.*) **pédestre** hike; hiking

**peigne** *m.* comb (13)

**se peigner** to comb one's hair (13)

**peindre** (*like* **craindre**) *irreg.* to paint (12)

**peintre (femme peintre)** *m., f.* painter (12)

**peinture** *f.* painting (12); paint(s); **faire de la peinture** to paint

**peler** to peel

**peloton: en peloton** *m.* in a pack (*of people*)

**pendant** *prep.* for, during (9); **pendant combien de temps... ?** (for) how long . . . ? (9); **pendant les vacances** during vacation; **pendant que** *conj.* while

**pénible** *adj.* painful; hard, difficult

**péniche** *f.* barge

**Pennsylvanie** *f.* Pennsylvania

**pensée** *f.* thought; idea

**penser** to think (10); to reflect; to expect, intend; **je ne pense pas** I don't think so; **penser** + *inf.* to plan on (*doing s.th.*); **penser à** to think of, think about (11); **penser de** to think of, have an opinion about (11);

**qu'en penses-tu?** what do you think about it? (11); **que pensez-vous de... ?** what do you think of . . . ? (11)

**penseur/euse** *m., f.* thinker

**pensif/ive** *adj.* pensive, thoughtful

**perception** (*f.*) **extrasensorielle** extrasensory perception (ESP)

**perché** *adj.* perched, sitting (on)

**perdre** to lose; to waste (5); **perdre patience** to lose patience; **se perdre** to get lost (13)

**père** *m.* father (5); **beau-père** father-in-law; stepfather (5); **grand-père** grandfather (5)

**perfectionner** to perfect

**performant** *adj.* competitive; highly capable

**péril** *m.* danger; **mettre en péril** to endanger

**période** *f.* period (of time)

**péripétie** *f.* adventure; event, episode

**perle** *f.* pearl

**permanence: en permanence** *adv.* permanently

**permettre** (*like* **mettre**) (**de**) *irreg.* to permit, allow (to), let (12)

**permis** *m.* permit, license; **permis de conduire** driver's license; **permis de travail** work permit

**perruque** *f.* wig

**persévérant** *adj.* persevering, dogged (3)

**persil** *m.* parsley

**personnage** *m.* (*fictional*) character; personality, celebrity

**personnalisé** *adj.* personalized

**personnalité** *f.* personality

**personne** *f.* person (3); **ne... personne** nobody, no one (9)

**personnel(le)** *adj.* personal

**personnellement** *adv.* personally (16)

**perspective** *f.* view; perspective

**persuader** to persuade, convince

**perte** *f.* loss

**peser** to weigh

**pessimiste** *adj.* pessimistic (3)

**pétanque** *f.* bocce ball, lawn bowling (*southern France*) (15)

**pétiller** to fizz

**petit** *adj.* little; short (3); very young; *m. pl.* young ones; little ones; **petit(e) ami(e)** *m., f.* boyfriend, girlfriend; **petit déjeuner** *m.* breakfast (6); **petit écran** *m.* television; **petit matin** *m.* early morning; **petit-enfant** *m.* grandchild (5); **petit-fils** *m.* grandson (5); **petite cuillère** *f.* teaspoon; **petite-fille** *f.* granddaughter (5); **petites annonces** *f. pl.* classified ads (10); **petits pois** *m. pl.* peas; **un petit peu** a little (bit)

**pétrole** *m.* oil, petroleum

**peu** *adv.* little; few; not very; hardly (3); **à peu près** *adv.* nearly; **encore un peu** a little more; **il est peu probable que** + *subj.* it's doubtful that (16); **peu à peu** little by little; **peu calorique** low in calories; **peu de** few (6); **un peu** a little (3); **un peu (de)** a little (of) (6)

**peuple** *m.* nation; people (*of a country*)

**peuplé (de)** *adj.* filled (with), full (of); populated

**peur** *f.* fear; **avoir peur (de)** to be afraid (of) (3)

**peut-être** *adv.* perhaps, maybe (5)

**pharaon** *m.* Pharaoh

**phare** *m.* beacon

**pharmacie** *f.* pharmacy, drugstore (11)

**pharmacien(ne)** *m., f.* pharmacist (14)

**phénomène** *m.* phenomenon
**philanthrope** *m., f.* philanthropist
**philosophe** *m., f.* philosopher
**philosophie** (*fam.* **philo**) *f.* philosophy (2)
**philosophique** *adj.* philosophical
**photocopieur** *m.* photocopy machine (10)
**photographe** *m., f.* photographer
**photo(graphie)** *f.* picture, photograph;
  **appareil (photo) numérique** *m.* digital
  camera (10); **prendre des photos** to take
  photos
**photographique** *adj.* photographic
**phrase** *f.* sentence
**physique** *f.* physics (2); *adj.* physical
**piano** *m.* piano; **jouer du piano** to play
  the piano
**pianoter** to tap away on
**piaule** *f., fam.* digs, place (*residence*)
**pièce** *f.* piece; room (*of a house*) (5); coin;
  **monter une pièce** to put on a play; **pièce
  de collection** collector's item; **pièce de
  monnaie** coin; **pièce de théâtre**
  (*theatrical*) play (12)
**pied** *m.* foot (13); **à pied** on foot (9); **se lever
  du pied gauche** to get up on the wrong
  side of the bed
**piège** *f.* trap, trick
**pierre** *f.* stone
**pieu** *m., fam.* bed
**pile** *f.* battery; stack; support
**pilote** *m., f.* pilot (9); driver
**piment** *m.* chili, pepper
**pinard** *m., fam.* wine
**pincée** *f.* pinch, dash (*cooking*)
**pique-nique** *m.* picnic (15); **faire un
  pique-nique** to go on a picnic
**pique-niquer** to have a picnic
**piqûre** *f.* injection, shot (13)
**pire** *adj.* worse (14); **le/la/les pire(s)**
  the worst
**pirogue** *f.* dugout canoe
**pis** *adv.* worse; **le pis** the worst; **tant pis**
  too bad (15)
**piscine** *f.* swimming pool (11)
**piste** *f.* path, trail; course; slope; lead (14);
  **piste cyclable** bicycle path
**pitchoune** *f., fam.* girl
**pittoresque** *adj.* picturesque
**place** *f.* place; position; (public) square (11);
  seat (12); **à votre (ta) place** in your place,
  if I were you (15); **mise** (*f.*) **en place**
  placement
**placer (nous plaçons)** to place, put
**plafond** *m.* ceiling
**plage** *f.* beach (8); **serviette** (*f.*) **de plage**
  beach towel (8)
**plaidoyer** *m.* defense, plea
**se plaindre (de)** (*like* **craindre**) *irreg.* to
  complain (about)
**plaine** *f.* plain
**plaire** (*p.p.* **plu**) **à** *irreg.* to please; **en
  français, s'il vous plaît** in French, please;
  **s'il te (vous) plaît** *interj.* please (1)
**plaisir** *m.* pleasure
**plan** *m.* plan; diagram; map (*of a city*) (11);
  **sur le plan économique** economically
  speaking
**planche** *f.* board; **faire de la planche à
  voile** to windsurf; **planche à voile**
  windsurfer (8)
**plancher** *m.* floor
**planète** *f.* planet
**planifier** to plan

**plante** *f.* plant
**planter** to plant
**planteur** *m.* planter, plantation owner
**plaque** *f.* package (*of frozen food*); **plaque
  tournante** linchpin; hub
**plaquer** to tackle (*U.S. football*)
**plat** *m.* dish (*type of food*); course (*meal*) (7);
  *adj.* flat; **plat de résistance** main course,
  dish; **plat du jour** today's special
  (*restaurant*); **plat principal** main course,
  main dish (7)
**plein (de)** *adj.* full (of); complete; **activités**
  (*f. pl.*) **de plein air** outdoor activities (15);
  **faire le plein** to fill it up (gas tank) (9);
  **marché** (*m.*) **en plein air** outdoor market;
  **plein de** a lot of
**plénitude** *f.* plenitude; richness
**pleurer** to cry, weep
**pleuvoir** (*p.p.* **plu**) *irreg.* to rain (7); **il pleut**
  it's raining (5)
**plier** to fold
**plombier** *m.* plumber (14)
**plongée** *f.* diving; **faire de la plongée
  libre** to go snorkeling (8); **faire de la
  plongée sous-marine** to go scuba
  diving (8)
**plonger (nous plongeons)** to
  dive, plunge
**pluie** *f.* rain
**plumard** *m., fam.* bed
**plumer** to pluck
**plupart: la plupart (de)** most (of), the
  majority (of) (12)
**pluriel** *m., Gram.* plural
**plus (de)** *adv.* more; plus; **de plus en plus**
  more and more; **en plus** in addition; **le
  plus** + *adv.* most; **le/la/les plus** + *adj.*
  most; **moi non plus** me neither; **ne...
  plus** no longer, no more (9); **plus... que**
  more . . . than (14); **plus tard** later
**plusieurs (de)** *adj., pron.* several (of) (6)
**plutôt** *adv.* instead; rather
**poche** *f.* pocket (10)
**poème** *m.* poem (12)
**poésie** *f.* poetry (12)
**poète (femme poète)** *m., f.* poet (12)
**poétique** *adj.* poetic, poetry
**poids** *m.* weight
**poignée** (*f.*) **de main** handshake
**point** *m.* point; spot; **être sur le point
  de** + *inf.* to be on the verge of; **point
  cardinal** compass point; **point de départ**
  starting point; **point de rencontre**
  meeting point; **point de vue** point of
  view; **point fort** strong point; *adv.* **ne...
  point** not at all
**pointe** *f.* point, tip; *pl.* headlands
**pointillisme** *m.* pointillism (*style
  of painting*)
**pointu** *adj.* pointed, sharp
**pointure** *f.* (shoe) size
**poire** *f.* pear (6)
**pois** *m. pl.* peas; dots; **à pois** polka-dotted;
  **petits pois** peas
**poisson** *m.* fish (6)
**poissonnerie** *f.* fish market (7)
**poivrade: sauce** (*f.*) **poivrade** vinaigrette
  *dressing with pepper*
**poivre** *m.* pepper (6); **steak** (*m.*) **au poivre**
  pepper steak
**poivrer** to pepper
**poivron** *m.* bell pepper
**poli** *adj.* polite (12); polished

**police** *f.* police; **agent** (*m.*) **de police** police
  officer (14); **poste** (*m.*) **de police** police
  station (11)
**policier/ière** *adj.* pertaining to the police; *m.*
  police officer; **roman** (*m.*) **policier**
  detective novel
**poliomyélite** *f.* polio(myelitis)
**politicien(ne)** *m., f.* politician
**politique** *f.* politics; policy (16); *adj.* political;
  **faire de la politique** to go in for politics;
  **homme (femme) politique** *m., f.*
  politician (16)
**Polononais(e)** *m., f.* Polish person
**polonais** *adj.* Polish
**polyvalent** *adj.* multipurpose; versatile
**polluant** *adj.* polluting
**polluer** to pollute (16)
**Polynésie** (*f.*) **française** French Polynesia
**pomme** *f.* apple (6); **jus** (*m.*) **de pomme**
  apple juice; **pomme de terre** potato (6);
  **tarte** (*f.*) **aux pommes** apple tart
**pompe** *f., fam.* shoe
**pompier** *m.* fire fighter
**ponctuation** *f.* punctuation
**ponctuel** *adj.* punctual
**pont** *m.* bridge
**populaire** *adj.* popular; common; of the
  people
**popularité** *f.* popularity
**porc** *m.* pork (6); **côte** (*f.*) **de porc** pork chop
**portable** *m.* laptop computer (1, 10);
  **téléphone portable** cell phone (10)
**porte** *f.* door (1); stop, exit (*metro*); gate
**porter** to wear; to carry (3); **prêt-à-porter** *m.*
  ready-to-wear (*clothing*)
**porto** *m.* port (wine)
**portugais** *adj.* Portuguese
**Portugal** *m.* Portugal (8)
**poser** to put (down); to state, pose; to ask;
  **poser sa candidature** to apply; to run
  (*for office*) (14); **poser une question** to ask
  a question (1)
**positif/ive** *adj.* positive
**positionnement** *m.* positioning
**posséder (je possède)** to possess (10)
**possesseur/euse** *m., f.* owner
**possessif/ive** *adj.* possessive
**possession** *f.* possession; **prendre possession
  de** to take possession of
**possibilité** *f.* possibility
**possible** *adj.* possible; **aussi souvent que
  possible** as often as possible; **faire son
  possible** to do one's best; **il est possible
  que** + *subj.* it's possible that (16)
**postal** *adj.* postal, post; **carte** (*f.*) **postale**
  postcard (10); **code** (*m.*) **postal** postal
  code, zip code
**poste** *m.* position; employment; *f.* mail (10);
  **bureau** (*m.*) **de poste** post office (10); **La
  Poste** post office; postal service (10); **poste**
  (*m.*) **de police** police station (11)
**poster** to mail (10)
**postuler** to apply (*for a job*)
**potasser** *fam.* to study
**pote** *m., fam.* buddy
**poterie** *f.* pottery
**poubelle** *f.* garbage can
**pouce** *m.* thumb; inch; **coup** (*m.*) **de pouce**
  little push (in the right direction)
**poudre: en poudre** *f.* powdered
**poule** *f.* hen
**poulet** *m.* chicken (6)
**poupée** *f.* doll

**pour** *prep.* for, in order to (2); **le pour et le contre** the pros and cons; **manifester pour** to demonstrate for (16); **pour ma part** in my opinion, as for me (16); **pour que** + *subj.* in order to

**pourboire** *m.* tip, gratuity (7)

**pourcentage** *m.* percentage

**pourquoi** *adv., conj.* why (4)

**pourri: faire un temps pourri** *fam.* to be rotten weather

**poursuivre** (*like* **suivre**) *irreg.* to pursue (12)

**pourtant** *adv.* yet, nevertheless

**pousser** to push; to grow; to move (*s.o. to do s.th.*)

**poutine** *f.* poutine (Quebec dish of French fries with cheese and gravy)

**pouvoir** (*p.p.* **pu**) *irreg.* to be able to, can (7); *m.* power, strength; **ça peut aller** all right, pretty well (1); **il se peut que** + *subj.* it's possible that (16); **je pourrais** I could (7); **pouvoir** (*m.*) **d'achat** purchasing power (16)

**pratique** *adj.* practical; *f.* practice; use; **travaux** (*m. pl.*) **pratiques** hands-on learning

**pratiquer** to play, perform (*sport, activity*)

**préalablement** *adv.* beforehand

**préavis: sans donner de préavis** without notice

**précaire** fragile, precarious

**précédent** *adj.* preceding

**précéder (je précède)** to precede

**précieusement** *adv.* preciously

**précipiter** to rush, hurry

**précieux/euse** *adj.* precious

**précis** *adj.* precise, accurate (3)

**préciser** to clarify, specify

**précision** *f.* precision; piece of information

**précoce** *adj.* precocious

**prédiction** *f.* prediction, forecast

**prédilection** *f.* partiality, predilection

**prédire** (*like* **dire, vous prédisez**) *irreg.* to predict, foretell

**préférable** *adj.* preferable, more advisable; **il est préférable que** + *subj.* it's preferable that (16)

**préféré** *adj.* favorite, preferred (5)

**préférence** *f.* preference; **de préférence** preferably

**préférer (je préfère)** to prefer, like better (6)

**préfrit** *adj.* pre-fried

**préjugé** *m.* prejudice

**prélèvement** (*m.*) **automatique** automatic payment/withdrawal (14)

**premier/ière** *adj.* first (4); *f.* opening night, premiere; **le premier janvier** the first of January; **premier étage** *m.* second floor (*in the U.S.*) (5); **premier ministre** *m.* prime minister; **première classe** *f.* first class (9)

**prendre** (*p.p.* **pris**) *irreg.* to take (6); to have (to eat, to drink) (6); to order (6); **prendre au sérieux** to take seriously; **prendre conscience de** to realize, become aware of; **prendre des notes** to take notes; **prendre des vacances** to take vacation; **prendre du temps** to take a long time (6); **prendre l'avion** to take a plane; **prendre possession de** to take possession of; **prendre rendez-vous** to make an appointment (date); **prendre son temps** to take one's time (6); **prendre un repas** to have a meal (6); **prendre un verre** *fam.* to have a drink (*with s.o.*) (6); **prendre une douche**

to take a shower; **prendre une photo** to take a photo; **se prendre pour** to believe oneself to be

**prénom** *m.* first name, Christian name

**préoccupé** *adj.* worried, preoccupied (16)

**préoccuper** to concern; **se préoccuper de** to concern, preoccupy oneself with; to worry about

**préparatifs** *m. pl.* preparations

**préparer** to prepare (5); **préparer un examen** to study for an exam; **se préparer (à)** to prepare oneself, get ready (for) (13)

**près (de)** *adv.* near, close to (4); **à peu près** nearly; **tout près** very near

**présence** *f.* presence; attendance

**présent** *m.* present (*time*); *adj.* present; **à présent** now, at the present time

**présentement** *adv.* presently, currently

**présenter** to present; to introduce; to put on (*a performance*); **je vous (te) présente...** I want you to meet . . . ; **se présenter** to run for office; to introduce oneself

**préserver** to preserve

**président(e)** *m., f.* president

**présidentiel(le)** *adj.* presidential

**présider** to preside

**presque** *adv.* almost, nearly

**presse** *f.* press (*media*)

**pressé** *adj.* in a hurry, rushed; **citron** (*m.*) **pressé** fresh lemon juice

**prestigieux/ieuse** *adj.* prestigious

**prêt** *adj.* ready (3); **prêt-à-porter** *m.* ready-to-wear clothing

**prétendre** to claim (to be); **prétendre à** to lay claim to

**prétentieux/euse** *adj.* pretentious

**prêter (à)** to lend (to) (11)

**prétexte** *m.* pretext, excuse

**preuve** *f.* proof; **faire preuve de** to show

**prévision** *f.* prediction

**prévoir** (*like* **voir**) *irreg.* to foresee, anticipate

**prévu** *adj.* expected, anticipated; **comme prévu** as planned

**prier** to pray; to beg, entreat; to ask (*s.o.*); **je vous (t')en prie** please; you're welcome (7)

**primaire** *adj.* primary; **école** (*f.*) **primaire** primary school

**principal** *adj.* principal, main, most important; **plat** (*m.*) **principal** main course (7)

**principe** *m.* principle

**printanier/ière** *adj.* spring(like); with vegetables (*in cooking*)

**printemps** *m.* spring; **au printemps** in the spring (5)

**priorité** *f.* priority

**pris** (see **prendre**)

**prise** *f.* taking

**prisme** *m.* prism

**prisonnier/ière** *m., f.* prisoner

**privé** *adj.* private

**privilégié** *adj.* privileged

**privilégier** to favor

**prix** *m.* price (7); prize

**probabilité** *f.* probability

**probable** *adj.* probable; **il est peu probable que** + *subj.* it's doubtful that (16); **il est probable que** + *indic.* it's probable that (16)

**problématique** *f.* problem, issue

**problème** *m.* problem (16)

**procédé** *m.* process, method

**procéder (je procède)** to proceed

**processus** *m.* process

**prochain** *adj.* next; coming; **à la prochaine** until next time; **la rentrée prochaine** beginning of next academic year; **la semaine prochaine** next week (5)

**prochainement** *adv.* soon, shortly

**proche (de)** *adj., adv.* near, close; *m. pl.* close relatives; **futur** (*m.*) **proche** *Gram.* immediate (near) future

**producteur/trice** *m., f.* producer

**produire** (*like* **conduire**) *irreg.* to produce (9)

**produit** *m.* product (6); **produit chimique** chemical; **produits frais** fresh products (6)

**professeur** (*fam.* **prof**) *m.* professor, instructor (*male or female*) (1); **professeur des écoles** *m., f.* primary school teacher (14)

**professionnel(le)** *adj.* professional

**profil** *m.* profile; outline; cross section

**profiter de** to take advantage of, profit from; **profitez-en donc** take advantage of it

**profiterole** *f.* profiterole (*small cream puff*)

**profond** *adj.* deep

**profondément** *adv.* deeply, profoundly

**profondeur: en profondeur** in depth

**programme** *m.* program; agenda

**programmer** to program; to plan

**progrès** *m. s.* progress

**progresser** to advance, make progress

**projection** *f.* projection, showing

**projet** *m.* project; *pl.* plans (5); **projets d'avenir** future plans

**prolifération** *f.* proliferation (16)

**promenade** *f.* walk; ride; **faire une promenade** to take a walk (5)

**promener (je promène)** to take out walking, take for a walk; **se promener** to go for a walk (drive, ride), take a walk (13)

**promesse** *f.* promise

**promettre** (*like* **mettre**) (**de**) *irreg.* to promise (to)

**promotion** *f.* promotion; sale, store special; **en promotion** on special

**promouvoir** (*p.p.* **promu**) *irreg.* to promote

**pronom** *m., Gram.* pronoun; **pronom accentué (indéfini, interrogatif, personnel, relatif)** *Gram.* disjunctive, stressed (indefinite, interrogative, personal, relative) pronoun; **pronom complément d'objet direct (indirect)** *Gram.* direct (indirect) object pronoun

**pronominal** *adj., Gram.* pronominal; **verbe** (*m.*) **pronominal** *Gram.* pronominal (reflexive) verb

**prononcé** *adj.* pronounced

**prononcer** to pronounce

**prononciation** *f.* pronunciation

**propagation** *f.* spread

**propos** *m.* talk; utterance; **à propos** by the way; **à propos de** about

**proposer** to propose; to offer (14)

**proposition** *f.* proposal; offer

**propre** *adj.* own; clean; **propre à** characteristic of

**propriétaire** (*fam.* **proprio**) *m., f.* owner; landlord

**propriété** *f.* property

**prospectus** *m.* handbill, leaflet

**protéger (je protège, nous protégeons)** to protect (16)

**prouver** to prove

**provenir** (*like* **venir**) *irreg.* to come (descend) from

**province** *f.* province; **ville** (*f.*) **de province** country town
**provincial** *adj.* small-town; *n. m.* small-town person
**provision** *f.* supply; *pl.* groceries
**provoquer** to provoke
**proximité** *f.* proximity, closeness; **à proximité de** near
**prudent** *adj.* careful; cautious
**prune** *f.* plum
**psychiatre** *m., f.* psychiatrist
**psychologie** (*fam.* **psycho**) *f.* psychology (2)
**psychologique** *adj.* psychological
**psychologue** *m., f.* psychologist
**public (publique)** *adj.* public (11); *m.* public; audience; **opinion** (*f.*) **publique** public opinion (16); **télévision** (*f.*) **publique** government-owned television (10)
**publicité** (*fam.* **pub**) *f.* commercial, advertisement; advertising (10)
**publier** to publish
**puce** *f.* flea; **marché** (*m.*) **aux puces** flea market; **excité comme une puce** as excited as a flea (at a cat show)
**puériculteur/trice** *m., f.* daycare teacher, nursery nurse
**puis** *adv.* then, next (11); besides (7); **et puis** and then; and besides (7)
**puissance** *f.* power, strength
**puissant** *adj.* powerful; **tout-puissant** *adj.* all-powerful
**puit** *m.* well
**pull-over** (*fam.* **pull**) *m.* sweater (3)
**pulpeux/euse** *adj.* fleshy
**pur** *adj.* pure
**purée** *f.* purée (*e.g., mashed potatoes*)
**pureté** *f.* purity
**puzzle** *m.* puzzle
**pyjama** *m. s.* pajamas

**quai** *m.* quay; platform (*train station*) (9)
**qualificatif/ive** *adj.* qualifying
**qualité** *f.* quality; characteristic
**quand** *adv., conj.* when (4); **depuis quand** since when (9); **quand même** even so; anyway (16)
**quant à** *adv.* as for; regarding
**quantité** *f.* quantity
**quarantaine** *f.* quarantine
**quarante** *adj.* forty (1)
**quart** *m.* quarter; fourth; quarter of an hour; **et quart** quarter past (the hour) (6); **moins le quart** quarter to (the hour) (6); **un quart de vin** a quarter liter carafe of wine
**quartier** *m.* quarter, neighborhood (2); **quartier général** headquarters; **Quartier latin** Latin Quarter (district) (*in Paris*)
**quasi-totalité** *f.* nearly all
**quatorze** *adj.* fourteen (1)
**quatorzième** *adj.* fourteenth
**quatre** *adj.* four (1)
**quatre-vingts** *adj.* eighty
**quatrième** *adj.* fourth
**que (qu')** what (4); that, which; whom (14); **ne... que** *adv.* only (9); **parce que** because (4); **que pensez-vous de... ?** what do you think about . . . ? (11); **que veut dire... ?** what does . . . mean?; **qu'en penses-tu?** what do you think of that? (11); **qu'est-ce que** what (*object*) (4); **qu'est-ce que c'est?** what is it? (1); **qu'est-ce qui** what (*subject*) (15); **qu-est-ce qui se passe?** what's happening?, what's going on? (15)

**Québec** *m.* Quebec (*province*); (2, 8); **Québec** Quebec (*city*)
**québécois** *m.* Quebecois (*language*); *adj.* from (of) Quebec; **Québécois(e)** *m., f.* Quebecois (*person*)
**quel(le)(s)** *interr. adj.* what, which (7); what a; **à quelle heure... ?** (at) what time . . . ? (6); **quel âge avez-vous?** how old are you?; **quel jour sommes-nous (est-ce)?** what day is it? (1); **quel temps fait-il?** how's the weather? (5); **quelle est la date?** what is the date? (1); **quelle heure est-il?** what time is it? (6)
**quelque(s)** *adj.* some, any; a few (15); **quelque chose** *pron.* something (9); **quelque chose de** + *adj.* something + *adj.* (15); **quelque part** *adv.* somewhere
**quelquefois** *adv.* sometimes (2)
**quelques-uns/unes** *pron., pl.* some, a few (15)
**quelqu'un** *pron., neu.* someone, somebody (9)
**question** *f.* question; **poser une question (à)** to ask a question (11)
**quête** *f.* quest, search
**queue** *f.* line (*of people*); **faire la queue** to stand in line (5); **queue de cheval** ponytail
**qui** *pron.* who, whom (4); who, that, which (14); **qu'est-ce qui** what (*subject*); **qui est à l'appareil?** who's calling? (10); **qui est-ce** who is it? (1); **qui est-ce que** whom (*object*) (15); **qui est-ce qui** who (*subject*) (9)
**quiche** *f.* quiche (*egg custard pie*); **quiche lorraine** *egg custard pie with bacon*
**quinze** *adj.* fifteen (1); **quinze jours** two weeks
**quinzième** *adj.* fifteenth
**quitter** to leave (*s.o. or someplace*) (8); **se quitter** to separate, leave one another
**quoi (à quoi, de quoi)** *pron.* which; what; **à quoi sert-il?** what is it for? (7); **il n'y a pas de quoi** you're welcome (7); **j'aurai droit à quoi** I'll be entitled to what; **n'importe quoi** anything; no matter what
**quotidien(ne)** *adj.* daily, everyday (13); *n. m.* daily life; **dépenses** (*f. pl.*) **du quotidien** everyday living expenses

**raccrocher** to hang up (the telephone)
**racine** *f.* root
**racisme** *m.* racism
**raconter** to tell, relate (a story) (10); **qu'est-ce que tu racontes / vous racontez?** what are you talking about? (15)
**rage: faire rage** to rage; to be fierce
**ragoût** *m.* meat stew, ragout
**raï** *m.* raï (type of Moroccan music)
**raide** *adj.* stiff; straight (*hair*) (3)
**raideur** *f.* stiffness
**raisin** *m.* grape
**raison** *f.* reason; **avoir raison** to be right (3)
**raisonnable** *adj.* reasonable; rational (3)
**raisonnement** *m.* (logical) argument, reasoning
**raisonneur/euse** *adj.* argumentative; reasoning
**râler** *fam.* to complain
**ralliement** *m.* rallying
**rallonger (nous rallongeons)** to prolong, lengthen
**rame** *f.* oar; paddle
**ramener (je ramène)** to bring back
**ramer** to row

**randonnée** *f.* hike; **faire une randonnée (pédestre)** to go hiking (8)
**rang** *m.* rank, ranking; row
**ranger** to put away, tidy up
**rapatriement** *m.* repatriation
**raper** to grate
**rapide** *adj.* rapid, fast; **restauration** (*f.*) **rapide** fast food
**rapidement** *adv.* quickly
**rappeler (je rappelle)** to remind; **se rappeler** to recall, remember (13)
**rapport** *m.* relation; **rapports familiaux** family relationships; **par rapport à** in comparison with, in relation to
**rapporter** to bring back; to return; to report
**rapprocher** to relate; **se rapprocher (de)** to draw nearer (to)
**rarement** *adv.* rarely (2)
**raser** to raze, demolish; **se raser** to shave (oneself) (13)
**rasoir** *m.* razor (13)
**rassembler** to put back together, reassemble; to gather together, assemble
**rassurant** *adj.* reassuring
**rassurer** to reassure
**rater** to miss, not find
**rationnellement** *adv.* reasonably, rationally
**rattraper** to recapture
**ravi** *adj.* delighted
**ravissant** *adj.* charming, delightful; beautiful
**rayé** *adj.* striped
**rayon** (*m.*) **de soleil** ray of light
**réactionnaire** *adj.* reactionary, very conservative
**réagir** to react
**réaliser** to carry out, fulfill; to create (14)
**réaliste** *adj.* realistic (3)
**réalité** *f.* reality; **en réalité** actually
**rebondir** to bounce (back)
**récemment** *adv.* recently, lately (12)
**recensement** *m.* census
**récent** *adj.* recent, new, late
**réception** *f.* hotel (lobby) desk; receiving, receipt
**recette** *f.* recipe
**recevoir** (*p.p.* **reçu**) *irreg.* to receive (10)
**rechange: ampoule** (*f.*) **de rechange** spare lightbulb
**rechargement** *m.* recharging; refilling
**réchauffement** (*m.*) **de la planète** global warming (16)
**recherche** *f.* (*piece of*) research; search; **à la recherche de** in search of; **faire des recherches** to do research; **moteur** (*m.*) **de recherche** search engine
**rechercher** to research; to seek out; to strive for; **recherché** *adj.* sought after
**réclamer** to call for, demand
**récolte** *f.* harvest
**récolter** to harvest
**recommandation** *f.* recommendation
**recommander** to recommend
**recommencer (nous recommençons)** to start again
**réconcilier** to reconcile; **se réconcilier** to make up (*with somebody*)
**reconnaître** (like **connaître**) *irreg.* to recognize (16)
**reconnu** *adj.* known, recognized
**recours: avoir recours à** to have recourse, turn to
**recruter** to recruit (14)
**reçu** *m.* receipt (14); (see **recevoir**)

**recueil** *m.* collection (12)

**reculer** to move backward; to recoil; to delay

**récupérer (je récupère)** to recover, get back

**recyclage** *m.* recycling (16)

**recycler** to recycle (16)

**rédacteur/trice** *m., f.* writer; editor (14)

**rédaction** *f.* writing, preparing (*documents*)

**rédiger (nous rédigeons)** to write, write up, compose

**redoutable** *adj.* formidable, fearsome

**réduction** *f.* reduction; discount

**réduire (*like* conduire)** *irreg.* to reduce (9)

**réduit** *adj.* reduced; discounted

**rééducation** *f.* rehabilitation

**réel(le)** *adj.* real, actual

**référence** *f.* reference

**réfléchir (à)** to reflect (upon); to think (about) (4)

**reflet** *m.* reflection

**refléter (je reflète)** to reflect, mirror

**réflexion** *f.* reflection, thought

**réforme** *f.* reform (16)

**réformer** to reform

**reformuler** to reformulate

**refrain** *m.* chorus, refrain

**refus** *m.* refusal

**refuser (de)** to refuse (to) (12)

**se régaler** to feast on, treat oneself

**regard: porter un regard (sur)** to have a viewpoint (about)

**regarder** to look at, watch (2); **se regarder** to look at oneself, look at each other (13)

**régime** *m.* diet; régime (7)

**régional (*pl.* régionaux)** *adj.* local, of the district

**règle** *f.* rule

**règlement** *m.* rules, regulations

**régler (je règle)** to regulate, adjust; to settle

**règne** *m.* reign

**regretter** to regret, be sorry (16)

**regrouper** to regroup

**régulier/ière** *adj.* regular

**régulièrement** *adv.* regularly

**reine** *f.* queen (12)

**rejoindre (*like* craindre)** *irreg.* to (re)join

**réjouissance** *f.* rejoicing

**relatif/ive** *adj.* relative; **pronom** (*m.*) **relatif** *Gram.* relative pronoun

**relation** *f.* relation; relationship; **en relation avec** in contact with

**relativement** *adv.* relatively

**relevé** *m.* bank statment

**se relaxer** to relax

**relier** to tie, link

**religieux/euse** *adj.* religious

**reliure** *f.* bookbinding

**remarquable** *adj.* remarkable, outstanding

**remarquer** to notice

**remède** *m.* remedy; treatment

**remercier (de)** to thank (for); **(je ne sais pas) comment vous (te) remercier** I don't know how to thank you

**remerciements** *m. pl.* thanks

**remettre (*like* mettre)** *irreg.* to hand in; to replace; to deliver; **remettre à neuf** to restore

**rempart** *m.* wall (of a city)

**remplacer (nous remplaçons)** to replace

**rempli** *adj.* filled, full

**remplir** to fill (in, out, up)

**remporter** to win

**rémunéré** *adj.* compensated, paid

**Renaissance** *f.* Renaissance (12)

**rencard** *m.* date; appointment

**rencontre** *f.* meeting, encounter (13); **point** (*m.*) **de rencontre** meeting point

**rencontrer** to meet, encounter; **se rencontrer** to meet; to get together (13)

**rendez-vous** *m.* meeting, appointment; date (13); meeting place; **avoir rendez-vous avec** to have a meeting (date) with (3); **donner rendez-vous à** to make an appointment with

**rendre** to give (back), return; to hand in (5); to render, make; **rendre visite à** to visit (*s.o.*) (5); **se rendre à** to go to

**renoncer** to reject; to give up (*s.th.*)

**renouveler (je renouvelle)** to renew

**rénover** to renew

**renseignement** *m.* (*piece of*) information

**se renseigner sur** to make inquiries about

**rentrée** *f.* going back to school; **rentrée prochaine** beginning of next academic year

**rentrer** to return, go home (8)

**réparation** *f.* repair

**réparer** to repair

**réparti** *adj.* spread out

**repartir (*like* partir)** *irreg.* to leave (again)

**répartition** *f.* dividing up; distribution

**repas** *m.* meal (6); **repas fait maison** homemade meal

**repeindre (*like* craindre)** *irreg.* to repaint

**repérer (je repère)** to spot, locate, find

**répertoire** *m.* directory (*Internet*)

**répéter (je répète)** to repeat; **répétez (répète)** repeat (1)

**réplique** *f.* replica

**répondeur (téléphonique)** *m.* answering machine

**répondre (à)** to answer, respond (5)

**réponse** *f.* answer, response

**reportage** *m.* reporting; commentary

**repos** *m.* rest

**reposant** *adj.* restful

**reposer** to put down, set down; **se reposer** to rest (13)

**reprendre (*like* prendre)** *irreg.* to take (up) again; to have more (*food*)

**représentant(e)** *m., f.* representative

**représentatif/ive** *adj.* representative

**représenter** to represent

**reprise: à plusieurs reprises** several times

**reprocher** to reproach (*s.o. for s.th.*)

**reproduire (*like* conduire)** *irreg.* to reproduce, copy

**république** *f.* republic; **République Démocratique du Congo** Democratic Republic of Congo (2, 8)

**répudié** *adj.* repudiated, renounced

**réputé** *adj.* famous

**réseau** *m.* network

**réservation** *f.* reservation; **faire une réservation** to make a reservation

**réservé (à)** *adj.* reserved (for)

**réserver** to reserve; to keep in store

**résidence** *f.* residence; apartment building; **résidence universitaire** dormitory building

**résider** to reside

**résistance: plat** (*m.*) **de résistance** main dish, course

**résister à** to resist

**résolument** *adv.* resolutely, steadfastly

**résonner** to resonate, reverberate, resound

**résoudre (*p.p.* résolu)** *irreg.* to solve, resolve

**respecter** to respect, have regard for

**respectueux/euse** *adj.* respectful

**respirer** to breathe

**responsabilité** *f.* responsibility

**responsable** *m., f.* supervisor; staff member; *adj.* responsible

**ressemblance** *f.* resemblance

**ressembler à** to resemble; **se ressembler** to look alike, be similar

**ressentir (*like* dormir)** *irreg.* to feel

**ressource** *f.* resource; **ressources naturelles** natural resources (16)

**restaurant (*fam.* resto)** *m.* restaurant (2); **restaurant universitaire (*fam.* resto-U)** university cafeteria (2)

**restaurateur/trice** *m., f.* restaurant owner

**restauration** *f.* restoration; restaurant business; **restauration rapide** fast food

**reste** *m.* rest, remainder

**rester** to stay, remain (5); to be remaining; **il nous reste encore...** we still have . . .

**restituer** to return, restore

**restreint** *adj.* limited, restrained

**résultat** *m.* result

**résulter de** to stem from, result from

**résumé** *m.* summary, résumé

**rétablir** to reestablish

**retard** *m.* delay; **en retard** late (6)

**retirer** to withdraw (14); to derive, gain

**retour** *m.* return; **au retour** upon returning; **billet** (*m.*) **aller-retour** round-trip ticket

**retourner** to return; to go back (8)

**retraite** *f.* retirement; pension (16)

**retraité(e)** *m., f.* retiree, retired person

**retransmission** *f.* broadcast; rebroadcast (10); **retransmission sportive** sports broadcast (10)

**retrouver** to find (again); to regain; **se retrouver** to meet (again)

**réunion** *f.* meeting; reunion

**réunir** to collect, gather together; **se réunir** to get together; to hold a meeting

**réussir (à)** to succeed (at), be successful (in); to pass (*a test*) (4)

**réussite** *f.* success, accomplishment

**revanche** *f.* revenge

**rêve** *m.* dream; **un emploi** (*m.*) **de rêve** a "dream" job

**réveil** *m.* alarm clock (4)

**réveiller** to wake, awaken (*s.o.*); **se réveiller** to awaken, wake up (13)

**Réveillon** *m.* Christmas Eve (New Year's Eve) dinner

**révéler** to reveal

**revendication** *f.* demand; claim

**revenir (*like* venir)** *irreg.* to return; to come back (*someplace*) (8)

**revenus** *m. pl.* personal income

**rêver (de, à)** to dream; to dream (about, of) (2)

**réviser** to review, revise

**révision** *f.* review; revising

**revivre (*like* vivre)** *irreg.* to relive

**revoir (*like* voir)** *irreg.* to see again (10); **au revoir** good-bye (1)

**révolte** *f.* rebellion, revolt

**révolutionnaire** *adj.* revolutionary

**révolutionner** to revolutionize

**revue** *f.* magazine; review; journal (10)

**rez-de-chaussée** *m.* ground floor, first floor (5)

**rhume** *m.* (head) cold

**riad** (*see* ryad)

**riche** *adj.* rich (3)

**richesse** *f.* wealth; blessing

**rideau** (*pl.* **rideaux**) *m.* curtain (4)
**ridicule** *adj.* ridiculous
**rien (ne... rien)** *pron.* nothing (9); **de rien** *interj.* not at all, don't mention it; you're welcome (1)
**rigoler** *fam.* to amuse, entertain; to be kidding
**rire** (*p.p.* **ri**) *irreg.* to laugh (15); *m.* laughter
**risette** *f.*, *fam.* smile
**risque** *m.* risk
**risquer** to risk
**rissoler** to brown (*cooking*)
**rivage** *m.* shore, beach coast
**rivaliser avec** to rival, compete with
**rive** *f.* (river)bank; **Rive gauche (droite)** the Left (Right) Bank (*in Paris*) (11)
**rivière** *f.* river, tributary
**riz** *m.* rice
**robe** *f.* dress (3)
**robinet** *m.* faucet, tap
**rocheux/euse** *adj.* rocky
**roi** *m.* king (12); **fête** (*f.*) **des Rois** Feast of the Magi, Epiphany
**rôle** *m.* part, character, role; **à tour de rôle** in turn, by turns; **jouer le rôle de** to play the part of
**romain** *adj.* Roman (12)
**roman** *m.* novel (10); **roman de science-fiction** science fiction novel; **roman policier** detective novel
**romancier/ière** *m.*, *f.* novelist
**romantique** *m.*, *f.*, *adj.* romantic
**romantisme** *m.* romanticism
**rompre (avec)** (*p.p.* **rompu**) *irreg.* to break (with)
**rond** *adj.* round; *m.* (smoke) ring
**rondelle** *f.* round slices
**rose** *adj.* pink (3); *f.* rose
**rôti** *m.* roast (7)
**roue** *f.* wheel; **faire du patin à roues alignées** to do in-line skating
**rouge** *adj.* red (3); **rouge** (*m.*) **à lèvres** lipstick (13)
**roulé** *adj.* rolled (up)
**rouler** to travel (*in a car, on a bike*) (9); to roll (along)
**route** *f.* road, highway (8); **en route** on the way, en route
**routier/ière** *adj.* (pertaining to the) road; **carte** (*f.*) **routière** road map; **sécurité** (*f.*) **routière** highway safety
**routinier/ière** *adj.* routine, following a routine
**roux (rousse)** *m.*, *f.* redhead; *adj.* redheaded; red (*hair*) (3)
**royaume** *m.* kingdom
**rubrique** *f.* headline; section
**rue** *f.* street (4)
**ruelle** *f.* alley; narrow street; lane
**ruine** *f.* ruin; decay; collapse
**ruiné** *adj.* ruined
**russe** *adj.* Russian; *m.* Russian (*language*); **Russe** *m.*, *f.* Russian (*person*) (2)
**Russie** *f.* Russia (2, 8)
**ryad** *m.* Moroccan villa
**rythme** *m.* rhythm (16)

**sa** *adj.*, *f. s.* his; her; its; one's
**sable** *m.* sand
**sac** *m.* sack; bag; handbag; **sac à dos** backpack (3); **sac à main** handbag (3); **sac de couchage** sleeping bag (8)
**sachet** *m.* packet

**sacré** *adj.* sacred; *fam.* darn
**sacrifier** to sacrifice
**safran** *m.* saffron
**saharien(ne)** *adj.* saharan
**sage** *m.* wise man; *adj.* good, well-behaved
**saignant** *adj.* rare (*meat*)
**Saint-Sylvestre** *f.* New Year's Eve
**saison** *f.* season
**saisonnier/ière** *adj.* seasonal
**salade** *f.* salad; lettuce (6)
**salaire** *m.* salary (14); **augmentation** (*f.*) **de salaire** salary raise (14)
**salarié(e)** *m.*, *f.* salaried employee; **travailleur/euse** (*m.*, *f.*) **salarié(e)** salaried worker (14)
**saler** to salt
**salle** *f.* room; auditorium; **salle à manger** dining room (5); **salle de bains** bathroom (5); **salle de classe** classroom (1, 5); **salle de sports** gymnasium
**salon** *m.* salon; living room; **salon de coiffure** hairdresser, beauty salon
**saltimbanque** *m.*, *f.* acrobat; traveling performer
**saluer** to greet; **se saluer** to greet each other
**salut** *m.* health; *interj.* hi; bye (1)
**salutation** *f.* greeting
**samedi** *m.* Saturday (1); **le samedi** on Saturdays (5)
**sandales** *f. pl.* sandals (3)
**sans** *prep.* without; **sans-abri (sans-domicile)** *m.*, *f. inv.* homeless (*person, people*) (16); **sans doute** probably (16)
**santé** *f.* health (13); **à votre (ta) santé** *interj.* cheers, to your health
**sardines** (*f. pl.*) **(à l'huile)** sardines (in oil) (7)
**satellite: télévision** (*f.*) **satellite** satellite television (10)
**satisfaisant** *adj.* satisfying
**satisfait** *adj.* satisfied; pleased
**sauce** *f.* sauce; gravy; salad dressing
**saucisse** *f.* sausage (7)
**saucisson** *m.* (hard) salami
**sauf** *prep.* except
**saumon** *m.* salmon (7); **darne** (*f.*) **de saumon** salmon steak
**sauté** *adj.* pan-fried, sautéed
**sauter** to jump
**sauve-qui-peut** *m.*, *inv.* stampede
**sauver** to save, rescue (16)
**savane** *f.* savanna
**saveur** *f.* flavor
**savoir** (*p.p.* **su**) *irreg.* to know (how, a fact) (11)
**savon** *m.* soap
**scandaleux/euse** *adj.* scandalous
**scanner** *m.* scanner (10)
**scénario** *m.* screenplay, script
**scène** *f.* stage; scenery; scene; **scène de ménage** domestic squabble
**science** *f.* science; **faculté** (*f.*) **des sciences** School of Science; **science-fiction** science fiction; **sciences humaines** humanities; **sciences naturelles** natural sciences (2)
**scientifique** *m.*, *f.* scientist; *adj.* scientific
**scolaire** *adj.* pertaining to schools, school, academic; **frais** (*m. pl.*) **scolaires** tuition, fees; **zone** (*f.*) **scolaire** school zone
**scolarité: frais** (*m. pl.*) **de scolarité** tuition, fees
**scotché (à)** *adj.*, *fam.* glued (to)
**scrupuleusement** *adj.* scrupulously

**sculpté** *adj.* sculpted
**sculpteur (femme sculpteur)** *m.*, *f.* sculptor (12)
**se (s')** *pron.* oneself; himself; herself; itself; themselves; to oneself, etc.; each other
**sec (sèche)** *adj.* dry; **biscuit** (*m.*) **sec** cookie, wafer
**séché** *adj.* dried
**second** *adj.* second; **seconde classe** second class; **Seconde Guerre** (*f.*) **mondiale** Second World War
**secondaire** *adj.* secondary; **école** (*f.*) **secondaire** secondary school
**secours** *m. s.* help, assistance, aid; *pl.* rescue services; **trousse** (*f.*) **de secours** first-aid kit
**secrétaire** *m.*, *f.* secretary (14)
**section** *f.* section; division
**sécurité** *f.* safety; sense of security; **ceinture** (*f.*) **de sécurité** seat belt; **sécurité routière** highway safety; **sécurité sociale** Social Security
**séducteur/trice** *m.*, *f.* charmer; seducer/seductress
**séduire** (*like* **conduire**) *irreg.* to charm, win over; to seduce
**sein: au sein de** within
**seize** *adj.* sixteen (1)
**seizième** *adj.* sixteenth
**séjour** *m.* living room (5); stay, sojourn
**sel** *m.* salt (6)
**sélectionner** to select
**selon** *prep.* according to (8); **selon moi** according to me, in my opinion
**semaine** *f.* week (1); **la semaine prochaine (passée)** next (last) week (5); **toutes les semaines** every week (10); **une fois par semaine** once a week (5)
**semblable (à)** *adj.* like, similar (to)
**sembler** to seem; to appear; **il semble que** + *subj.* it seems that (16)
**semestre** *m.* semester
**semoule** *f.* semolina
**sénateur** *m.* senator
**Sénégal** *m.* Senegal (2, 8)
**sénégalais** *adj.* Senegalese; **Sénégalais(e)** *m.*, *f.* Senegalese person (2)
**senior** *m.*, *f.* senior citizen
**sens** *m.* meaning; sense; way, direction; **bon sens** common sense; **dans ce sens** to that end (effect)
**sensibiliser (à)** to make (*s.o.*) sensitive (to)
**sensoriel(le)** *adj.* sensory; **perception** (*f.*) **extrasensorielle** extra-sensory perception
**sentiment** *m.* feeling
**sentir** (*like* **dormir**) *irreg.* to feel, sense; to smell (8); **se sentir** to feel; **sentir bon (mauvais)** to smell good (bad)
**séparé** *adj.* separated
**sept** *adj.* seven (1)
**septembre** September (1)
**septième** *adj.* seventh
**sera** (see **être**)
**sereine** *adj.* clear; serene
**série** *f.* series (10); **série télévisée** serial drama (10)
**sérieusement** *adv.* seriously
**sérieux/euse** *adj.* serious (3); **prendre au sérieux** to take seriously
**serpent** *m.* snake
**serré** *adj.* tight, snug
**serrer** to hug, embrace; **se serrer la main** to shake hands

**serveur/euse** *m., f.* bartender; waiter, waitress (7)

**service** *m.* favor; service; military service; serve (*tennis*); **station-service** *f.* gas station (9)

**serviette** *f.* napkin (6); towel; briefcase; **serviette de plage** beach towel (8)

**servir** (*like* **dormir**) *irreg.* to serve (8); **à quoi sert-il?** what is it for?; **servir à** to be of use in, be used for

**ses** *adj. m., f. pl.* his; her; its; one's

**seuil** *m.* threshold; doorstep

**seul** *adj.* alone; single

**seulement** *adv.* only (9)

**sexisme** *m.* sexism (16)

**short** *m.* (*pair of*) shorts (3)

**si** *adv.* so (very); so much; yes (*response to negative question*) (9); **si (s')** *conj.* if; whether (4); **même si** even if; **s'il vous (te) plaît** please (1)

**sida (SIDA)** *m.* AIDS

**siècle** *m.* century (12); **Siècle des lumières** Age of Enlightenment

**siège** *m.* seat (9); place; headquarters

**sien: le/la/les sien(ne)(s)** *pron., m., f.* his/hers

**sieste** *f.* nap; **faire la sieste** to take a nap

**signe** *m.* sign, gesture

**signer** to sign

**signifier** to mean

**significatif/ive** *adj.* significant

**silencieux/euse** *adj.* silent

**simplement** *adv.* simply

**simplicité** *f.* simplicity

**sincère** *adj.* sincere (3)

**sincérité** *f.* sincerity

**se singulariser** to distinguish oneself

**singularité** *f.* peculiarity

**singulier/ière** *adj.* singular; *m., Gram.* singular (*form*)

**sinon** *prep.* if not; otherwise

**site** *m.* site (10)

**situer** to situate, find; **se situer** to be situated; to be located

**six** *adj.* six (1)

**sixième** *adj.* sixth

**ski** *m.* skiing; ski (8); **chaussures** (*f. pl.*) **de ski** ski boots (8); **faire du ski** to ski (5); **lunettes** (*f. pl.*) **de ski** ski goggles (8); **ski alpin** downhill skiing (8); **ski de fond** cross-country skiing (8); **ski nautique** water-skiing (8); **station** (*f.*) **de ski** ski resort

**skier** to ski (2)

**skieur/euse** *m., f.* skier

**smartphone** *m.* smartphone (1)

**SMS** *m.* text message (10)

**SNCF (Société nationale des chemins de fer français)** *f. French national train system*

**snob** *adj. inv.* snobbish (3)

**snowboard: faire du snowboard** to go snowboarding

**sociabilité** *f.* sociability

**sociable** *adj.* sociable (3)

**social** *adj.* social; **logement** (*m.*) **social** housing project; **sécurité** (*f.*) **sociale** Social Security; **siège** (*m.*) **social** head office, headquarters

**société** *f.* society; organization; company (14); **jeux** (*m. pl.*) **de société** board games, group games (15)

**sociologie** (*fam.* **socio**) *f.* sociology (2)

**sœur** *f.* sister (5); **belle-sœur** sister-in-law (5); **demi-sœur** half sister; stepsister

**soi (soi-même)** *pron., neu.* oneself (12); **chez soi** at one's own place, home

**soie** *f.* silk

**soif** *f.* thirst; **avoir soif** to be thirsty (3)

**soigner** to take care of; to treat (14)

**soigneusement** *adv.* carefully

**soin** *m.* care; **avec soin** carefully

**soir** *m.* evening; **ce soir** tonight, this evening (5); **ce soir-là** that evening; **demain soir** tomorrow evening; **du soir** in the evening, at night (6); **hier soir** last night; **le lundi (le vendredi) soir** on Monday (Friday) evenings (5); **tous les soirs** every evening (10)

**soirée** *f.* party (3); evening (7)

**sois gentil!** *interj.* be nice! (6)

**soit: quel(le)(s) que soit (soient)...** whatever may be . . .

**soixante** *adj.* sixty (1)

**sol: sous-sol** *m.* basement, cellar (5)

**solaire** *adj.* solar; **crème** (*f.*) **solaire** suntan lotion (8); **écran** (*m.*) **solaire** sunblock (8); **énergie** (*f.*) **solaire** solar energy (16)

**soldat** *m.* soldier

**solde** *f.* (*soldier's*) pay, wages; **en solde** *m.* on sale

**sole** *f.* sole (*fish*) (7)

**soleil** *m.* sun; **faire du soleil (il fait du soleil)** to be sunny (out) (it's sunny) (5); **le roi Soleil** the Sun King (Louis XIV); **lunettes** (*f. pl.*) **de soleil** sunglasses (8)

**solidaire** *adj.* showing solidarity, loyal

**solidarité** *f.* solidarity; interdependence

**solide** *adj.* solid, sturdy

**solitaire** *adj.* solitary; single; alone (3)

**solitude** *f.* loneliness; solitude (16)

**sombre** *adj.* dark; gloomy

**sommeil** *m.* sleep; **avoir sommeil** to be sleepy (3); **le plein sommeil** deep in sleep

**sommet** *m.* summit, top

**somnambule** *m. f.* sleepwalker

**somptueux/euse** *adj.* sumptuous

**son** *adj., m. s.* his; her; its; one's; *n. m.* sound

**sonate** *f.* sonata

**sondage** *m.* opinion poll, survey (16)

**songer à** to think of (about)

**sonner** to ring (*telephone*)

**sonnette** *f.* bell; doorbell

**sonore** *adj.* sound

**sophistiqué** *adj.* sophisticated

**sorte** *f.* sort, kind; manner

**sortie** *f.* exit; going out; evening out

**sortir** (*like* **dormir**) *irreg.* to leave; to take out; to go out (8)

**sot(te)** *adj.* stupid, foolish

**souci** *m.* care, worry

**se soucier de** to worry about

**soucoupe** (*f.*) **volante** flying saucer

**soudain** *adv.* suddenly (11)

**souffle** *m.* breath of air; puff of wind

**souffrance** *f.* suffering

**souffrir** (*like* **ouvrir**) *irreg.* to suffer (14)

**souhait** *m.* wish, desire

**souhaiter** to wish, desire (16)

**souk** *m. North African market*

**soulagement** *m.* relief

**soulager (nous soulageons)** to relieve

**soulever (je soulève)** to excite; to bring up

**souligner** to underline, emphasize

**soumission** *f.* subservience, submissiveness

**soupe** *f.* soup; **cuillère** (*f.*) **à soupe** tablespoon, soup spoon (6)

**sourcil** *m.* eyebrow

**sourd** *adj.* deaf

**souriant** *adj.* smiling

**sourire** (*like* **rire**) *irreg.* to smile; *m.* smile

**souris** *f.* mouse (1)

**sournois** *adj.* sly, shifty

**sous** *prep.* under, beneath (4); in (*rain, sun*); **sous (la) forme de** in the form of

**sous-marin** *adj.* underwater; *m.* submarine; **plongée** (*f.*) **sous-marine** scuba diving (8)

**sous-sol** *m.* basement, cellar (5)

**soutenir** (*like* **tenir**) *irreg.* to support (16); to assert

**soutien** *m.* support

**souvenir** *m.* memory, recollection; souvenir

**se souvenir** (*like* **venir**) **de** *irreg.* to remember (13)

**souvent** *adv.* often (2)

**spécial** (*pl.* **spéciaux**) *adj.* special

**spécialisé** *adj.* specialized

**spécialiste (en)** *m., f.* specialist (in)

**spécialité** *f.* specialty (*in cooking*)

**spectacle** *m.* show; performance (15)

**spectaculaire** *adj.* spectacular

**spectateur/trice** *m., f.* viewer, spectator

**spirituel(le)** *adj.* spiritual; witty

**splendeur** *f.* splendor

**spontané** *adj.* spontaneous

**sport** *m.* sport(s) (2); **faire du sport** to do (participate in) sports (5); **magasin** (*m.*) **de sports** sporting goods store; **salle** (*f.*) **de sport** gymnasium

**sportif/ive** *adj.* athletic; sports-minded (3); **manifestation** (*f.*) **sportive** sporting event (15); *m., f.* athlete; **retransmission** (*f.*) **sportive** sports broadcast (10)

**squelette** *m.* skeleton

**stable** *adj.* stable; **emploi** (*m.*) **stable** steady job

**stade** *m.* stadium

**stage** *m.* training course; practicum, internship (14)

**standardiste** *m., f.* switchboard operator

**station** *f.* resort (*vacation*); station; **station de métro** subway station (11); **station de ski** ski resort; **station-service** *f.* gas station, garage (9)

**stationnement** *m.* parking

**statut** *m.* status

**steak** *m.* (beef) steak; **steak au poivre** pepper steak; **steak frites** steak with French fries

**stéréotypé** *adj.* stereotyped

**steward** *m.* flight attendant, steward (9)

**stimuler** to stimulate

**stipuler** to stipulate

**stratégie** *f.* strategy

**stricte** *adj.* strict

**studette** *f.* small studio (apartment) with shared bathroom (4)

**studieux/ieuse** *adj.* studious

**studio** *m.* studio (apartment) (4)

**stupide** *adj.* stupid; foolish; **il est stupide que** + *subj.* it's idiotic that (16)

**style** *m.* style; **style de vie** lifestyle

**styliste** *m., f.* fashion designer

**stylo** *m.* pen (1)

**subir** to undergo, be subjected to

**subjonctif** *m., Gram.* subjunctive (*mood*)

**substantif** *m., Gram.* noun, substantive

**substituer** to substitute

**subtil** *adj.* subtle

**subventionner** to support, back (*financially*)

**se succéder (ils se succèdent)** to follow one another

**succès** *m.* success; **à succès** successful

**successeur** *m.* successor

**succession** *f.* series, succession

**sucre** *m.* sugar (6); **canne** (*f.*) **à sucre** sugarcane

**sucré** *adj.* sweetened

**sud** *m.* south; **Amérique** (*f.*) **du Sud** South America; **au sud** to the south (9); **sud-est (-ouest)** southeast (-west)

**Suède** *f.* Sweden

**suffire** (*p.p.* **suffi**) to be enough

**suggérer (je suggère)** to suggest

**se suicider** to commit suicide

**Suisse** *f.* Switzerland (2, 8); **suisse** *adj.* Swiss; **Suisse** *m., f.* Swiss person (2)

**suite: et ainsi de suite** and so on; **tout de suite** immediately (5)

**suivant** *adj.* following

**suivi (de)** *adj.* followed (by)

**suivre** (*p.p.* **suivi**) *irreg.* to follow; to take (*a class, a course*) (12)

**sujet** *m.* subject; topic

**super** *adj. inv., fam.* super, fantastic

**superbe** *adj.* magnificent, superb

**supérieur** *adj.* superior; upper

**supermarché** *m.* supermarket

**supplément** *m.* supplement, addition; supplementary charge

**supplémentaire** *adj.* supplementary, additional

**supportable** *adj.* bearable, tolerable

**supporter** to bear, tolerate; **supporter** *m.* fan (sports)

**supposer** to suppose

**supprimer** to abolish, suppress

**sur** *prep.* on, on top (of) (4); over; out of; about; **donner sur** to overlook

**sûr** *adj.* sure, certain (16); safe; **bien sûr** of course; **il est sûr que** + *indic.* it is certain that (16)

**surchargé** *adj.* overloaded

**surdoué** *adj.* gifted

**sûrement** *adv.* definitely, certainly

**surf** (*m.*) **des neiges** snowboarding

**surface** *f.* surface; **grande surface** shopping mall, superstore

**surfer** to surf; **surfer sur le Web** to surf the web (10)

**surgelé** *adj.* frozen

**surnom** *m.* name, family name

**surnommer** to nickname

**surpopulation** *f.* overpopulation (16)

**surprenant** *adj.* surprising

**surpris** *adj.* surprised (16)

**surtout** *adv.* especially; above all (10)

**survenir** (*like* **venir**) *irreg.* to happen

**survêtement** *m.* track suit, sweat suit

**survivre** (*like* **vivre**) *irreg.* to survive

**survol** *m.* browsing (*Internet*)

**survoler** to fly over

**susceptible (de)** *adj.* capable of, likely to

**suspect(e)** *m., f.* suspect

**symbole** *m.* symbol

**symboliser** to symbolize

**symétrique** *adj.* symmetrical

**sympathique** (*fam., inv.* **sympa**) *adj.* nice, friendly (3)

**symphonie** *f.* symphony

**syndicat** (*m.*) **d'initiative** (local) chamber of commerce, tourist information bureau (11)

**synonyme** *m.* synonym; *adj.* synonymous

**système** *m.* system

**ta** *adj., f. s., fam.* your

**tabac** *m.* tobacco; **bureau** (*m.*) **de tabac** (*licensed*) tobacco store; **café-tabac** *m.* bar-tobacconist (11)

**table** *f.* table (1); **à table** at (to) the table

**tableau** *m.* (chalk)board (1); painting (12); chart

**tablette** *f.* bar (*of chocolate*); a tablet computer, an iPad (1)

**tâche** *f.* task; **tâches ménagères** household tasks

**taille** *f.* waist; build; size; **de taille moyenne** of medium height (3)

**tailleur** *m.* (*woman's*) suit (3)

**tailleuse** *f.* tailoress

**tajine** *m.* tajine (a Moroccan stew)

**talonnade** *f.* heel; back-heel (*rugby, soccer*)

**tambour** *m.* drum

**tandis que** *conj.* while, whereas

**tannage** *m.* tanning (process)

**tant** *adj.* so much; so many; **tant de** so many, so much; **tant mieux** so much the better (15); **tant pis** too bad (15)

**tante** *f.* aunt (5)

**taper** to type; to be scorching; **se taper la cloche** to have a good meal

**tapis** *m.* rug (4)

**tapisserie** *f.* tapestry

**tarbouche** *m.* brimless hat worn by Muslim men

**tard** *adv.* late; **il est tard** it's late; **plus tard** later

**tarif** *m.* tariff; fare, price

**tarifaire** *adj.* tariff

**tarte** *f.* tart; pie (6); **tarte aux pommes** apple tart; **tarte tatin** upside-down apple tart

**tartine** *f.* bread and butter sandwich

**tas: des tas de** lots of, piles of

**tasse** *f.* cup (6)

**tatouage** *m.* tattoo

**tatoueur** *m.* tatooer

**taux** *m.* rate; **taux de change** exchange rate (14); **taux de chômage** unemployment rate (14)

**taxe** *f.* indirect tax

**taxi** *m.* taxi; **chauffeur/euse** (*m., f.*) **de taxi** cab driver

**tchao** *interj.* good-bye

**tchatcher** to talk

**te (t')** *pron., s., fam.* you; to you, for you; **s'il te plaît** *interj.* please (1)

**technicien(ne)** *m., f.* technician

**technique** *f.* technique; *adj.* technical

**techno** *adj.* synthesized (music)

**technologie** *f.* technology

**tee-shirt** (*pl.* **tee-shirts**) *m.* T-shirt (3)

**tel(le)** *adj.* such; **tel père, tel fils** like father, like son; **tel que** such as

**télécarte** *f.* telephone calling card

**télécharger (nous téléchargeons)** to download (10)

**télécommande** *f.* remote control (10)

**télécopieur** *m.* fax machine

**téléphone** *m.* telephone (4); **numéro** (*m.*) **de téléphone** telephone number (10); **téléphone fixe** landline (12); **téléphone portable** cell phone (10)

**téléphoner (à)** to phone, telephone (3); **se téléphoner** to call one another

**téléphonique: répondeur** (*m.*) **téléphonique** (telephone) answering machine

**téléspectateur/trice** *m., f.* television viewer

**télévisé** *adj.* televised; **jeu** (*m.*) **télévisé** game show (10); **journal** (*m.*) **télévisé** television news program (10)

**téléviseur** (*fam.* **télé**) *m.* television set (10)

**télévision** (*fam.* **télé**) *f.* television (1); **télévision numérique terrestre (TNT)** high-definition television (10); **télévision par câble (le câble)** cable television (10); **télévision publique** government-owned television; **télévision satellite** satellite television (10)

**tellement** *adv.* so; so much (11)

**témoin** *m.* witness; **être témoin de** to witness

**tempérament** *m.* temperament, personality

**température** *f.* temperature

**tempête** *f.* storm

**temporaire** *adj.* temporary

**temporel(le)** *adj.* temporal, pertaining to time

**temps** *m.* time; weather (5); *Gram.* tense; **avoir le temps de** to have time to; **de temps en temps** from time to time (2); **depuis combien de temps... ?** since when . . . ?, (for) how long . . . ? (9); **en même temps** at the same time; **en temps de pluie** in rainy weather; **faire un temps pourri** to be rotten weather; **gagner du temps** to save time; **il est temps de** it's time to; **le temps est nuageux** it's cloudy (5); **le temps est orageux** it's stormy (5); **passer du temps** to spend time; **pendant combien de temps... ?** (for) how long . . . ? (9); **perdre du temps** to waste time; **prendre le temps (de)** to take the time (to); **quel temps fait-il?** how's the weather? (5); **temps libre** leisure time (15); **tout le temps** always, the whole time

**tendance** *f.* tendency; trend; **avoir tendance à** to have a tendency to

**tendinite** *f.* tendonitis

**tendre** *adj.* tender, sensitive; soft

**tenir** (*p.p.* **tenu**) *irreg.* to hold; to keep; **tenir à** to be keen about (16); **tenir au courant** to keep up to date; **tenir un journal** to keep a diary

**tennis** *m.* tennis; *pl.* tennis shoes (3); **court** (*m.*) **de tennis** tennis court; **jouer au tennis** to play tennis

**tentant** *adj.* tempting

**tentation** *f.* temptation

**tente** *f.* tent (8)

**tenter (de)** to try, attempt (to)

**terme** *m.* term; expression; **à court (long) terme** in the short (long) run

**terminer (qqch)** to finish (*s.th.*); to end (*s.th.*); **se terminer** to end

**terrain** *m.* field; ground; **terrain** (*m.*) **de camping** campground; **tout-terrain** *adj.* all-terrain (*vehicle*)

**terrasse** *f.* terrace, patio (5)

**terre** *f.* land; earth; **Terre** the planet Earth; **Terre Neuve** *f.* Newfoundland; **par terre** on the ground (4); **pomme** (*f.*) **de terre** potato (6)

**terrine** *f.* (*type of*) pâté, terrine

**territoire** *m.* territory

**terrorisme** *m.* terrorism (16)

**tes** *adj., m., f. pl., fam.* your

**tête** *f.* head (13); **avoir mal à la tête** to have a headache (13); **casse-tête** *m.* puzzle; **tête-à-tête** tête-à-tête, intimate conversation

**texte** *m.* text; passage; **traitement** (*m.*) **de texte** word processing (10)

**texto** *m.* text message (10)

**textoter** to text (*fam.*)

**TGV (Train à grande vitesse)** *m.* (*French high-speed*) bullet train

**thé** *m.* tea (6)

**théâtre** *m.* theater (12); **faire du théâtre** to act, do theater; **pièce** (*f.*) **de théâtre** (*theatrical*) play (12)

**théorie** *f.* theory

**thermes** *m. pl.* thermal baths

**thon** *m.* tuna

**tiède** *adj.* lukewarm, tepid

**tiens** *interj.* well, well (*expresses surprise*); you don't say; **ah, tiens...** oh, there's . . .

**tiers** *m.* one-third; *adj.* third; **Tiers-Monde** *m.* Third World

**tigre** *m.* tiger

**timbre** *m.* stamp; postage stamp (10)

**timide** *adj.* shy; timid

**tiré (de)** *adj.* drawn, adapted (from)

**tirer** to pull, draw (out); **tirer avantage de** to take advantage of

**tissu** *m.* cloth, fabric

**titre** *m.* title; degree

**TNT (télévision numérique terrestre)** *f.* high-definition television (10)

**toi** *pron., s., fam.* you; **et toi?** and you?, how about you? (1); **toi-même** *pron.* yourself (12)

**toilettes** *f. pl.* bathroom, toilet (4); **faire sa toilette** to wash up

**toit** *m.* roof

**tolérance** *f.* tolerance

**tolérer** to tolerate, stand for

**tomate** *f.* tomato (6)

**tombe** *f.* tomb, grave

**tomber** to fall (8); **tomber amoureux/euse (de)** to fall in love (with) (13)

**ton** *adj., m. s., fam.* your; **à ton avis** in your opinion (11)

**tondeuse** *f.* lawn mower

**tondre** to mow (*lawn*)

**tonton** *m., fam.* uncle

**torche: lampe** (*f.*) **torche** flashlight

**tort** *m.* wrong; **avoir tort** to be wrong (3)

**se tortiller** to twist, wriggle

**tortueux/euse** *adj.* twisting

**tôt** *adv.* early; **il est tôt** it's early

**totalement** *adv.* totally, completely

**totalité** *f.* totality, entire amount

**touche** *f.* key (*keyboard*); stroke

**toucher (à)** to touch (14); to concern; to cash (*a check*) (14)

**toujours** *adv.* always (2); still

**tour** *f.* tower (11); *m.* walk, ride; turn; tour; trick; **à tour de rôle** in turn, by turns; **faire le tour de** to go around, take a tour of; **faire un tour (en voiture)** to take a walk (ride) (5)

**tourisme** *m.* tourism; **faire du tourisme** to go sightseeing

**touriste** *m., f.* tourist

**touristique** *adj.* tourist

**tourmenté** *adj.* uneasy; tortured

**tournant: plaque** (*f.*) **tournante** linchpin; hub

**tourné** (*adj.*) **vers** facing

**tourner (à)** to turn (11); to film (a movie)

**tournesol** *m.* sunflower; **huile** (*f.*) **de tournesol** sunflower seed oil

**tournoi** *m.* tournament

**tousser** to cough

**tout(e)** (*pl.* **tous, toutes**) *adj., pron.* all; every (10); everything (9); each; any; **tout** *adv.* wholly, entirely, quite, very, all; **à tout à l'heure** see you soon; **avant tout** *prep.* above all; **en tout** altogether, in all; **en tout cas** in any case, at any rate; **haricots** (*m. pl.*) **mange-tout** green beans; sugar peas; **je n'aime pas du tout...** I don't like . . . at all; **ne... pas du tout** not at all (9); **pas du tout** not at all; **tous ensemble** all together; **tous les après-midi** every afternoon (10); **tous (toutes) les deux** both (of them); **tous les jours** every day (5, 10); **tous les matins** every morning (10); **tous les soirs** every evening (10); **tout à coup** suddenly (11); **tout à fait** completely, entirely; **tout à l'heure** in a while (5); **tout au long de** throughout; **tout de suite** immediately (5); **tout droit** *adv.* straight ahead (11); **tout le monde** everybody, everyone (7); **tout le temps** always, the whole time; **tout va bien** everything is going well; **tout-puissant** *adj.* all-powerful; **tout-terrain** *adj.* all-terrain (*vehicle*); **toute la matinée (la journée, la soirée, la nuit)** all morning (day, evening, night) (7); **toutes les deux heures** every two hours; **toutes les semaines** every week (10)

**toutefois** *adv.* however

**tracasserie** *f.* harassment, hassle

**tracer (nous traçons)** to draw; to trace out; **tracer un itinéraire** to map out an itinerary

**tracteur** *m.* tractor

**traditionnel(le)** *adj.* traditional

**traduction** *f.* translation

**traduire** (*like* **conduire**) *irreg.* to translate (9)

**trafic** *m.* traffic

**train** *m.* train (9); **billet** (*m.*) **de train** train ticket; **en train** by train; **être en train de** to be in the process of (15); **prendre le train** to take the train; **Train à grande vitesse (TGV)** (*French high-speed*) bullet train; **train-train** (*m.*) **quotidien** daily grind, routine

**trait** *m.* feature, trait

**traite** *f.* trade; **traite négrière** slave trade

**traité** *adj.* treated, dealt with

**traitement** *m.* treatment; **traitement de texte** word processing (10)

**traiter** to treat; **traiter de** to deal with

**traiteur** *m.* caterer, deli owner; delicatessen

**trajet** *m.* trip; distance

**tranche** *f.* slice (7); block, slab

**trancher** to slice, cut up

**tranquille** *adj.* quiet, calm

**tranquillité** *f.* tranquility; calm

**transformer** to transform, change; **se transformer** to change

**translucide** *adj.* translucent

**transmettre** (*like* **mettre**) *irreg.* to transmit, convey

**transport(s)** *m.* transportation; **moyen** (*m.*) **de transport** means of transportation (9); **transports en commun** public transportation

**transporter** to carry, transport

**trapéziste** *m., f.* trapeze artist

**travail** (*pl.* **travaux**) *m.* work (2); project; job; employment; **langue** (*f.*) **de travail** working language; **travail d'équipe** teamwork; **travaux** (*pl.*) **pratiques** hands-on (practical) work

**travaillé** *adj.* finely worked; intricate; polished

**travailler** to work (2); **travailler à (pour) son compte** to be self-employed (14)

**travailleur/euse** *m., f.* worker (14); *adj.* hardworking (3); **travailleur/euse indépendant(e)** self-employed worker (14); **travailleur/euse salarié(e)** salaried worker (14)

**travers: à travers** *prep.* through

**traversée** *f.* crossing

**traverser** to cross (9)

**treize** *adj.* thirteen (1)

**treizième** *adj.* thirteenth

**tréma** *m.* dieresis, umlaut (**ë**)

**tremplin** *m.* diving board; springboard

**trentaine** *f.* about thirty

**trente** *adj.* thirty (1)

**très** *adv.* very; most; very much; **très bien** *interj.* very well (good) (1); **très bien, merci** *interj.* very well, thank you; **très (peu) calorique** high (low) in calories

**trésor** *m.* treasure

**trésorier/ière** *m., f.* treasurer

**tricolore** *m.* French flag (*blue, white, red*)

**trimestre** *m.* trimester; quarter (*academic*)

**triomphe** *m.* triumph, success

**triompher** to triumph

**tripes** *f. pl.* tripe

**triste** *adj.* sad (3)

**trois** *adj.* three (1)

**troisième** *adj.* third

**tromper** to deceive; **se tromper (de)** to make a mistake; to be wrong (13)

**trompette** *f.* trumpet

**trop (de)** *adv.* too; too much (of); too many (of) (6)

**trophée** *m.* trophy

**troquet** *m., fam.* bar

**trottoir** *m.* sidewalk

**troubler** to trouble, disturb

**troupeau** *m.* herd

**trousse** *f.* case; kit; **trousse de secours** first-aid kit

**trouver** to find (2); to deem; to like; **se trouver** to be located (situated, found) (13)

**truffe** *f.* truffle

**truite** *f.* trout

**tu** *pron., s., fam.* you

**tube** *m., fam.* hit (song)

**tuer** to kill

**Tunisie** *f.* Tunisia (2, 8)

**tunisien** *adj.* Tunisian; **Tunisien(ne)** *m., f.* Tunisian (*person*) (2)

**turc (turque)** *adj.* Turkish

**Tweet** *m.* tweet

**type** *m.* type, kind; *fam.* guy, fellow

**typique** *adj.* typical

**un(e)** (*pl.* **des**) *art.*, a, an; *adj., pron.* one (1); **un(e) autre** another (15); **un jour** someday (14); **un peu** a little (3); **un peu (de)** a little (of) (6); **une fois** once (11); **une fois par semaine** once a week (5)

**unanime** *adj.* unanimous

**uni** *adj.* united; plain, solid (*color*); **États-Unis** *m. pl.* United States; **Organisation** (*f.*) **des Nations Unies (ONU)** United Nations (UN)

**uniformisateur** *adj.* making s.th. uniform, all the same

**uniformiser** to make uniform

**union** *f.* union; marriage; **Union européenne (UE)** European Union (EU); **union libre** living together, common-law marriage

**unique** *adj.* only, sole; single; singular

**uniquement** *adv.* only

**s'unir** to unite

**unité** *f.* unity; unit; department

**univers** *m. s.* universe

**universel(le)** *adj.* universal

**universitaire** *adj. (of or belonging to the)* university; **cité** (*f.*) **universitaire** (*fam.* **cité-U**) university dormitory; **résidence** (*f.*) **universitaire** dormitory; **restaurant** (*m.*) **universitaire** (*fam.* **resto-U**) university cafeteria (2)

**université** *f.* university (2)

**urbain** *adj.* urban, city

**urgent** *adj.* urgent; **il est urgent que** + *subj.* it's urgent that (16)

**usage** *m.* use; custom

**ustensile** *f.* kitchenware, cookware

**utile** *adj.* useful; **il est utile que** + *subj.* it's useful that (16)

**utilisateur/trice** *m., f.* user

**utilisation** *f.* use

**utiliser** to use, utilize

**utilité** *f.* use; utility, usefulness

**vacances** *f. pl.* vacation (5); **grandes vacances** summer vacation; **partir (aller) en vacances** to leave on vacation; **passer les vacances** to spend one's vacation; **pendant les vacances** during vacation

**vacancier/ère** *m., f.* vacationer

**vache** *f.* cow

**vachement** *adv., fam.* very, tremendously

**vague** *f. (ocean)* wave; **nouvelle vague** new wave *(trend)*

**vaincre** (*p.p.* **vaincu**) *irreg.* to win; to triumph

**vaisselle** *f. s.* dishes; **faire la vaisselle** to wash (do) the dishes (5)

**valable** *adj.* valid

**valeur** *f.* value; worth

**valise** (*fam.* **valoche**) *f.* suitcase (8); **faire sa valise** to pack one's bag

**vallée** *f.* valley

**valoir** (*p.p.* **valu**) *irreg.* to be worth (16); **il vaut mieux que** + *subj.* it is better that (16)

**valorisé** *adj.* valued

**valoriser** to value

**vanille** *f.* vanilla

**vaniteux/euse** *adj.* vain

**variante** *f.* variation

**varier** to vary; to change

**variété** *f.* variety, type; **chanson** (*f.*) **de variété** popular song (15); **spectacle** (*m.*) **de variétés** variety show; floor show (in a restaurant) (15)

**Varsovie** *f.* Warsaw

**vaste** *adj.* vast; wide, broad

**va-t'en!** *interj. fam.* get going!, go away! (13)

**vaut** (see **valoir**)

**veau** *m.* veal (7); calf; **escalope** (*f.*) **de veau** veal scaloppini

**vedette** *f.* star, celebrity *(male or female)*

**végétarien(ne)** *m., f., adj.* vegetarian

**véhicule** *m.* vehicle

**veille** *f.* the day (evening) before; eve

**Veinard!** *interj. fam.* Lucky you!

**vélo** *m., fam.* bike; **à/en vélo** by bike; **faire du vélo** to go cycling (5)

**velours** *m.* velvet

**vendanges** *m. pl.* grape harvest

**vendeur/euse** *m., f.* salesperson

**vendre** to sell (5); **à vendre** for sale

**vendredi** *m.* Friday (1); **le vendredi** on Fridays (5); **le vendredi soir** on Friday evenings (5)

**se venger** (**nous nous vengeons**) to avenge oneself; to take revenge

**venir** (*p.p.* **venu**) *irreg.* to come (8); **venir de** + *inf.* to have just *(done s.th.)* (8)

**vent** *m.* wind; **faire du vent** (**il fait du vent, il y a du vent**) to be windy (it's windy) (5); **vent alizé** trade wind

**vente** *f.* sale; sales; **vente aux enchères** auction

**venter** to be windy; **il vente** it's windy (5)

**ventre** *m.* abdomen, belly; stomach (13)

**verbe** *m.* verb; language

**vérifier** to verify

**véritable** *adj.* true; real

**vérité** *f.* truth

**verlan** *m. French form of slang that reverses syllables* (**l'envers→verlan**)

**verre** *m.* glass (6); **prendre un verre** *fam.* to have a drink *(with s.o.)* (6); **un verre de** a glass of

**verrouillable** *adj.* lockable

**vers** *prep.* around, about *(with time expressions)*; toward, to; about; **tourné** (*adj.*) **vers** facing

**verser** to pour

**version** *f.* version; **en version originale** original version, not dubbed *(movie)*

**vert** *adj.* green (3); *(politically)* "green"; **citron** (*m.*) **vert** lime *(fruit)*; **espace** (*m.*) **vert** open space, greenbelt; **\*haricots** (*m. pl.*) **verts** green beans (6); **poivron** (*m.*) **vert** green (bell) pepper; **tourisme** (*m.*) **vert** ecotourism

**veste** *f.* sports coat, blazer (3); **veste de montagne** hiking (ski) jacket

**veston** *m.* suit jacket (3)

**vêtement** *m.* garment; *pl.* clothes, clothing

**viande** *f.* meat (6)

**vibrer** to vibrate

**victime** *f.* victim *(male or female)*

**victoire** *f.* victory

**vide** *adj.* empty; **vide-grenier** *m.* garage sale

**vidéo** *f., fam.* video(cassette); *adj. inv.* video; **caméra** (*f.*) **vidéo** video camera; **cassette** (*f.*) **vidéo** videocassette; **jeux** (*m. pl.*) **vidéo** video games

**vidéothèque** *f.* video store

**vie** *f.* life (2); **coût** (*m.*) **de la vie** cost of living (14); **niveau** (*m.*) **de vie** standard of living (16)

**Vietnam** *m.* Vietnam (2, 8)

**vietnamien** *adj.* Vietnamese; **Vietnamien(ne)** *m., f.* Vietnamese person (2)

**vieux (vieil, vieille)** *adj.* old (4); **mon vieux (ma vieille)** old friend, buddy

**vif (vive)** *adj.* lively; bright

**vigne** *f.* vine; vineyard

**vignoble** *m.* vineyard

**villa** *f.* bungalow; single-family house; villa

**villageois** *adj.* village style

**ville** *f.* city (1); **centre-ville** *m.* downtown (11); **en ville** in town, downtown

**vin** *m.* wine (6); **coq** (*m.*) **au vin** coq au vin *(chicken prepared with red wine)*; **marchand(e)** (*m., f.*) **de vin** wine merchant (14)

**vingt** *adj.* twenty (1); **vingt et un (vingt-deux . . . )** *adj.* twenty-one (twenty-two . . . ) (1)

**vingtaine** *f.* about twenty

**vingtième** *adj.* twentieth

**violet(te)** *adj.* purple, violet (3); *m.* violet *(color)*

**violon** *m.* violin

**violoncelle** *m.* cello

**virelangue** *m.* tongue twister

**virement** *m.* transfer (money) (14)

**Virginie** *f.* Virginia; **Virginie-Occidentale** West Virginia

**visa** *m.* visa (8); signature

**visage** *m.* face (13)

**vis-à-vis (de)** *adv.* opposite, facing; toward

**viser à** to aim to; to set out to

**visibilité** *f.* visibility

**visionnaire** *m., f.* visionary

**visionner** to watch, view

**visite** *f.* visit (2); **faire une visite** to pay a visit; **rendre visite à** to visit *(s.o.)* (11)

**visiter** to visit *(a place)* (2); **je peux la visiter** I may visit it

**visiteur/euse** *m., f.* visitor

**vitæ: curriculum** (*m.*) **vitæ** résumé (14)

**vite** *adv.* quickly, fast, rapidly; **il faut faire vite** we have to move fast; **venez vite** come quickly

**vitesse** *f.* speed; **limite** (*f.*) **de vitesse** speed limit; **Train** (*m.*) **à grande vitesse (TGV)** *(French high-speed train)* bullet train

**vitres** *f. pl.* windows

**vitrine** *f.* display window, store window

**vivant** *adj.* living; **langues** (*f. pl.*) **vivantes** modern languages

**vive . . .** *interj.* long live . . .

**vivre** (*p.p.* **vécu**) *irreg.* to live (12); **facile (difficile) à vivre** easy (hard) to live with; **vive . . .** *interj.* long live (hurrah for) . . .

**vocabulaire** *m.* vocabulary

**vocal: boîte** (*f.*) **vocale** voice mail (10)

**vœu** (*pl.* **vœux**) *m.* wish

**voici** *prep.* here is/are (2)

**voie** *f.* way, road; course; lane; railroad track; **pays** (*m.*) **en voie de développement** developing nation

**voilà** *prep.* there is/are (2)

**voile** *m.* veil; *f.* sail; **bateau** (*m.*) **à voile** sailboat (8); **faire de la voile** to go sailing (5); **planche** (*f.*) **à voile** windsurfer

**voilier** *m.* sailboat

**voir** (*p.p.* **vu**) *irreg.* to see (10)

**voire** *adv.* indeed

**voisin(e)** *m., f.* neighbor; **voisin(e) de palier** neighbor living on the same landing

**voiture** *f.* car, automobile (4); train car; **faire un tour en voiture** to take a ride (5); **voiture hybride** hybrid car (16)

**voiture-restaurant** *f.* dining car *(train)*

**voix** *f.* voice; **à voix haute** *adv.* in a loud voice; aloud

**vol** *m.* flight (9)

**volaille** *f.* poultry

**volant: objet** (*m.*) **volant non identifié (O.V.N.I.)** unidentified flying object (UFO); **soucoupe** (*f.*) **volante** flying saucer

**volcan** *m.* volcano

**voler** to fly; to steal; **qui vole un œuf vole un bœuf** once a thief always a thief
**volley-ball** (*fam.* **volley**) *m.* volleyball; **jouer au volley** to play volleyball
**volontaire** *m., f., adj.* volunteer
**volontiers** *adv.* gladly
**volonté** *f.* will, willingness
**volupté** *f.* voluptuous pleasure
**vos** *adj., m., f. pl.* your
**voter** to vote
**votre** *adj., m., f.* your; **à votre avis** in your opinion (11)
**vôtre(s): le/la/les vôtre(s)** *pron., m., f.* yours; *pl.* your close friends, relatives
**vouloir** (*p.p.* **voulu**) *irreg.* to wish, want (7); **je voudrais** I would like (6); **que veut dire... ?** what does . . . mean?; **vouloir bien** to be willing; to agree (7); **vouloir dire** to mean (7)
**vous** *pron.* you; yourself; to you; **chez vous** where you live, your place; **et vous?** and you?, how about you? (1); **s'il vous plaît** please (1); **vous-même** *pron.* yourself (12)

**voyage** *m.* trip; **agence** (*f.*) **de voyages** travel agency; **bon voyage** *interj.* have a good trip; **chèque** (*m.*) **de voyage** traveler's check; **faire un voyage** to take a trip (5); **partir (s'en aller) en voyage** to leave on a trip; **projets** (*m. pl.*) **de voyage** travel plans
**voyager (nous voyageons)** to travel (8)
**voyageur/euse** *m., f.* traveler
**voyant(e)** *m., f.* fortune-teller, medium; **voyant** (*m.*) **lumineux** indicator light
**voyelle** *f.* vowel
**voyons,...** let's see, . . . (10)
**vrai** *adj.* true, real (4); **il est vrai que** + *indic.* it's true that (16)
**vue** *f.* view; panorama; sight; **en vue de** with a view toward; **point** (*m.*) **de vue** point of view

**wagon** *m.* train car (9); **wagon-lit** *m.* sleeping car; **wagon-restaurant** *m.* dining car
**Wallonie** *f.* Wallonia (*French-speaking Belgium*)

**W.-C.** *f. pl.* restroom, toilet (4)
**Web** *m.* (World Wide) Web (10)
**week-end** *m.* weekend; **ce week-end** this weekend (5); **le week-end** on weekends (5)
**Wi-Fi** *m.* Wi-Fi (wireless) connection (10)

**xénophobie** *f.* xenophobia

**y** *pron.* there (11); **il n'y a pas de...** there isn't (aren't) . . .; **il y a** there is (are) (1); ago (8); **qu'est-ce qu'il y a dans... ?** what's in . . . ?; **y a-t-il... ?** is (are) there . . . ?
**yeux** (*pl.* of **œil**) *m.* eyes (13)

**zèbre** *m.* zebra
**zéro** *m.* zero
**zone** *f.* zone, area
**zoologique** *adj.* zoological; **jardin** (*m.*) **zoologique** (*fam.* **zoo**) zoological gardens, zoo
**zouk** *m.* zouk music (of Guadeloupe, Martinique, Haiti)

# Lexique anglais-français

This English-French end vocabulary contains the words in the active vocabulary lists of all chapters. See the introduction to the *Lexique français-anglais* for a list of abbreviations used.

**abdomen** ventre *m.* (13)
**able: to be able** pouvoir *irreg.* (7)
**abolish** abolir (16)
**about** (*with time expressions*) vers (6)
**abroad** à l'étranger (9)
**accept** accepter (de) (12)
**accident** accident *m.* (16)
**accomplish** réussir (4)
**according to** selon (8)
**account** compte *m.* (14); **checking account** compte-chèques *m.* (14); **savings account** compte d'épargne (14)
**accountant** comptable *m., f.* (14)
**acquaintance: to make the acquaintance (of)** faire la connaissance (de) (5)
**across from** en face de (4)
**act** *v.* agir (4)
**activities (leisure)** loisirs *m. pl.* (15); **outdoor activities** activités (*f.*) de plein air (15)
**actor** acteur/trice *m., f.* (12)
**address** adresse *f.* (10)
**adore** adorer (2)
**ads (classified)** petites annonces *f. pl.* (10)
**advertisement, advertising** publicité *f.* (10)
**advise** conseiller (à, de) (15)
**aerobics** aérobic *f.* (5); **to do aerobics** faire de l'aérobic (5)
**afraid: to be afraid of** avoir peur de (3)
**after** après (2, 5)
**afternoon** après-midi *m.* (5); **afternoon snack** goûter *m.* (6); **this afternoon** cet après-midi (5)
**afterward** après (5)
**again** de nouveau (11)
**age** âge *n. m.*; **Middle Ages** le Moyen Âge (12)
**ago** il y a (8)
**agree** vouloir (*irreg.*) bien (7)
**agreeable** agréable (3)
**agreed** d'accord (2)
**ahead: straight ahead** tout droit (11)
**airplane** avion *m.* (9)
**airport** aéroport *m.* (9)
**alarm clock** réveil *m.* (4)
**Algeria** Algérie *f.* (2, 8)
**Algerian** (*person*) Algérien(ne) *m., f.* (2)
**all** *adj.*, tout, toute, tous, toutes (9); *pron.* tout(e); **all right** ça peut aller (1); moyen (1); **not at all** ne... pas du tout (9)
**allow (to)** permettre (de) (12)
**almost** presque (6)
**already** déjà (9)
**also** aussi
**always** toujours (2)
**American** (*person*) Américain(e) *m., f.* (2)
**amount** montant *m.* (14)
**amusing** amusant(e) (3)
**and** et (2); **and you?** et vous? (et toi?) (1)
**angry** fâché(e) (16); **to get angry** se fâcher (13)
**another** un(e) autre (15)
**answer** *v.* répondre à (5)
**antique** *adj.* ancien(ne) (4)
**any** en *pron.* (11)
**anyway** quand même (16)

**apartment** appartement *m.* (4); **apartment building** immeuble *m.* (4); **studio apartment** studio *m.* (4)
**apologize** s'excuser (13)
**apparatus** appareil *m.* (10)
**appear** avoir l'air (3); paraitre *irreg.* (16)
**appetizer** *hors-d'œuvre *m. inv.* (7)
**apple** pomme *f.* (7)
**application (job)** demande (*f.*) d'emploi (14)
**apply** (*for a job*) poser sa candidature (14)
**appointment: to have an appointment** avoir (*irreg.*) rendez-vous (3)
**April** avril (1)
**architect** architecte *m., f.* (14)
**arena** arènes *f. pl.* (12)
**argue** se disputer (13)
**arm** bras *m. s., pl.* (13)
**around** (*with time expressions*) vers (6)
**arrival** arrivée *f.* (9)
**arrive** arriver (3)
**art** art (*m.*); **work of art** œuvre (*f.*) d'art (12)
**artisan** artisan(e) *m., f.* (14)
**artist** artiste *m., f.* (14)
**as . . . as** aussi... que (14); **as far as** jusqu'à (11); **as for me** pour ma part (16); **as much (many) . . . as** autant (de)... que (15); **as soon as** dès que (14), aussitôt que (14)
**ashamed: to be ashamed** avoir (*irreg.*) honte (3)
**ask (for)** demander (2); **to ask a question** poser une question (12)
**asleep: to fall asleep** s'endormir *irreg.* (13)
**at** à (2)
**athletic** sportif/ive (3)
**atmosphere** atmosphère *f.* (16)
**attend** assister à (15)
**attendant (flight)** hôtesse (*f.*) de l'air (9), steward *m.* (9)
**attention: to pay attention (to)** faire (*irreg.*) attention (à) (5)
**August** août (1)
**aunt** tante *f.* (5)
**automatic teller (ATM)** guichet (*m.*) automatique (14)
**automobile** voiture *f.* (4)
**autumn** automne *m.* (5); **in autumn** en automne (5)
**awaken** se réveiller (13)

**back** dos *m. s., pl.* (13)
**backpack** sac (*m.*) à dos (3)
**bad** mauvais(e) *adj.* (4); **bad(ly)** mal *adv.*; **it's bad (out)** il fait mauvais (5); **not bad(ly)** pas mal (1); **things are going badly** ça va mal (1); **to feel bad (ill)** aller (*irreg.*) mal (5); **too bad!** dommage! *interj.* (16)
**badly** *adv.* mal (1)
**bag: sleeping bag** sac (*m.*) de couchage (8)
**baguette** baguette (*f.*) (de pain) (6)
**bakery** boulangerie *f.* (7)
**balcony** balcon *m.* (5)
**ball: bocce ball** pétanque *f.* (15)
**bank** banque *f.* (11); **bank (ATM/credit) card** carte (*f.*) bancaire (14); **bank**

**statment** *m.* relevé (14) **the Left Bank** (*in Paris*) Rive (*f.*) gauche (11); **the Right Bank** (*in Paris*) Rive (*f.*) droite (11)
**bar-tobacconist** café-tabac *m.* (11)
**basement** sous-sol *m.* (5)
**bathe** se baigner (13)
**bathroom** salle (*f*) de bains (5); **bathroom sink** lavabo *m.* (4)
**be** être (*irreg.*) (2); **here is/are** voici (2); **how are you?** comment allez-vous? (comment vas-tu?) (1); **it's a . . .** c'est un (une)... (1); **there is/are** il y a; voilà; **to be in the middle (the process) of** être en train de (15)
**beach** plage *f.* (8); **beach towel** serviette (*f.*) de plage (8)
**beans: green beans** *haricots (*m. pl.*) verts (6)
**beautiful** beau, bel, belle (beaux, belles) (3)
**because** parce que (4)
**become** devenir *irreg.* (8)
**bed** lit *m.* (4); **to go to bed** se coucher (13)
**bedroom** chambre *f.* (4)
**beef** bœuf *m.* (6)
**beer** bière *f.* (6)
**begin** commencer (2); **to begin to** (*do s.th.*) se mettre (*irreg.*) à (+ *inf.*) (13)
**behind** derrière (4)
**Belgian** (*person*) Belge *m., f.* (2)
**Belgium** Belgique *f.* (2, 8)
**believe** croire *irreg.* (10); estimer (16); **to believe in (that)** croire à/en (que)
**beret** béret *m.* (3)
**berth** couchette *f.* (9)
**beside** à côté de (4)
**best** le mieux *adv.* (15); le/la/les meilleur(e)(s) *adj.*
**better** meilleur(e) *adj.*; mieux *adv.* (15); **it is better that** il vaut mieux que + *subj.* (16); **so much the better** tant mieux (15)
**between** entre (4)
**bicycle** bicyclette *f.* (8), vélo *m.*; **by bike** à vélo (9); **to go bicycling** faire (*irreg.*) de la bicyclette, du vélo (5)
**big** grand(e) (3)
**bill** (*in a restaurant*) addition *f.* (7); (*currency*) billet *m.*
**biology** biologie *f.* (2)
**black** noir(e) (3)
**blackboard** tableau (noir) *m.* (1)
**blazer** veste *f.* (3)
**blond(e)** blond(e) (3)
**blouse** chemisier *m.* (3)
**blue** bleu(e) (3)
**board games** jeux (*m. pl.*) de société (15)
**boarding pass** carte (*f.*) d'embarquement (9)
**boat** bateau *m.* (8); **sailboat** bateau à voile (8)
**boating: to go boating** faire du bateau (8)
**bocce ball** pétanque *f.* (15)
**body** corps *m.* (13)
**book** livre *m.* (1); **e-book** livre (*m.*) numérique (10); **print book** livre (*m.*) papier (10)
**bookstore** librairie *f.* (2)
**boots** bottes *f. pl.* (3); **hiking boots** chaussures (*f. pl.*) de montagne (8); **ski boots** chaussures (*f. pl.*) de ski (8)
**bore: to be bored** s'ennuyer (13)

**born: to be born** naître *irreg.* (8)
**borrow (from)** emprunter (à) (11)
**boss** chef (*m.*) d'entreprise (14)
**bottle** bouteille *n. f.* (6)
**boulevard** boulevard *m.* (11)
**bowling (lawn)** pétanque *f.* (15)
**boy** garçon *m.* (3)
**boyfriend** copain *m.* (7)
**brave** courageux/euse (3)
**Brazil** Brésil *m.* (8)
**bread** pain *m.* (6); **country-style wheat bread** pain de campagne (7)
**breakfast** petit déjeuner *m.* (6)
**bring** apporter (6); **to bring** (*s.o. somewhere*) amener
**broadcast** émission *n. f.* (10); **sports broadcast** retransmission (*f.*) sportive (10); **to broadcast** émettre (*irreg.*)
**brother** frère *m.* (5); **brother-in-law** beau-frère *m.* (5)
**brown** (*hair*) châtain(e) (3); marron *inv.* (3)
**browse** naviguer (10)
**browser** navigateur *m.* (10)
**brush (one's hair, teeth)** se brosser (les cheveux, les dents) (13); brosse *f.* (13)
**budget** budget *m.* (14)
**build** bâtir (6)
**building** bâtiment *m.* (1); immeuble (*office, apartment*) *m.* (4)
**bus** (*city*) autobus *m.* (5); (*interurban*) autocar *m.* (9)
**business** commerce *m.* (2); **business class** classe (*f.*) affaires (9); **business manager** directeur/trice commercial(e) (14)
**but** mais (2)
**butcher** boucher/ère *m., f.* (14); **butcher shop** boucherie *f.* (7); **pork butcher's shop** charcuterie *f.* (7)
**butter** beurre *m.* (6)
**buy** *v.* acheter (8)
**by** à (2); en (2); par (12); **by (train, plane, bus)** en (9); **by bike** à velo (9)

**cable TV** câble *m.* (10)
**café** café *m.* (2)
**cafeteria (university)** restaurant (*m.*) universitaire (resto-U) (2)
**cake** gâteau *m.* (6)
**call** *v.* appeler (10); **who's calling?** qui est à l'appareil? (10)
**calm** calme (3)
**camcorder (digital)** caméscope *m.* (10)
**camera (digital)** appareil (*m.*) (photo) numérique (10); **digital video camera** caméscope *m.* (10)
**camping** camping *m.* (8); **to go camping** faire (*irreg.*) du camping
**can** (*to be able*) pouvoir *irreg.* (7)
**can (of food)** boîte (*f.*) (de conserve) (7)
**Canada** Canada *m.* (2, 8)
**Canadian** (*person*) Canadien(ne) *m., f.* (2)
**cancel** annuler (11)
**canned goods** conserves *f. pl.* (7)
**cap** casquette *f.* (3)
**car** voiture *f.* (4); **train car** wagon *m.* (9)
**carpooling** covoiturage *m.* (16)
**carafe** carafe *f.* (6)
**card** carte *f.* (3); **bank (ATM/credit) card** carte bancaire (14); **credit card** carte de crédit (14); **debit card** carte de débit (14); **to play cards** jouer aux cartes (3)
**careful: to be careful** faire (*irreg.*) attention (à) (5)

**Caribbean Islands** Antilles *f. pl.* (1)
**carrier (letter)** facteur/trice *m., f.* (14)
**carrot** carotte *f.* (6)
**carry** apporter (7); porter (3)
**cartoon** bande (*f.*) dessinée (15)
**case: in that case** alors (4)
**cash** argent (*m.*) liquide (14); **to cash** (*a check*) toucher (14), encaisser
**castle** château *m.* (11)
**cathedral** cathédrale *f.* (12)
**celebrate** fêter, célébrer (6)
**celebration** fête *f.* (7)
**cell phone** mobile *m.* (10); téléphone portable *m.* (10)
**century** siècle *m.* (12)
**ceremony** cérémonie *f.* (13)
**certain** certain(e) (16); sûr(e) (16)
**chair** chaise *f.* (1)
**chalkboard** tableau (noir) *m.* (1)
**challenge** défi *n. m.* (16)
**chance: games of chance** jeux (*m. pl.*) de hasard (1)
**change** monnaie *n. f.* (10); *v.* changer (14)
**channel** (*television*) chaîne *f.* (10)
**chateau** château *m.* (11)
**check** (*in a restaurant*) addition *f.* (7); (*bank*) chèque *m.* (14); **to cash a check** toucher un chèque (14), encaisser un chèque; **to write a check** faire (*irreg.*) un chèque (14)
**check** *v.* contrôler
**cheese** fromage *m.* (6)
**chemistry** chimie *f.* (2)
**chess** échecs *m. pl.* (3)
**chest (of drawers)** commode *f.* (4)
**chestnut** (*hair color*) châtain (3)
**chicken** poulet *m.* (6)
**child** enfant *m., f.* (5)
**China** Chine *f.* (2, 8)
**Chinese** (*person*) Chinois(e) *m., f.* (2); (*language*) chinois *m.* (2)
**chocolate** chocolat *m.* (6)
**choose** choisir (4)
**chop** (*meat*) côte *n. f.* (7)
**church** (*Catholic*) église *f.* (11)
**citizen** citoyen(ne) *m., f.* (16)
**city** ville *f.* (2)
**civil** civil(e); **civil rights** droits (*m. pl.*) civils (16); **civil servant** fonctionnaire *m., f.* (14)
**class** (*business*) classe (*f.*) affaires (9); **first class** première classe (9); **second class** deuxième classe (9); **tourist class** classe économique (9)
**classical** classique
**classified ads** petites annonces *f. pl.* (10)
**classroom** salle (*f.*) de classe (1)
**clear** *adj.* clair(e) (16)
**clerk (sales)** employé(e) (14)
**click (on)** cliquer (sur) (10)
**climb** *v.* monter (8)
**clock (alarm)** réveil *m.* (4)
**close to** près de (4)
**closet** armoire *f.* (4)
**cloudy: it's cloudy** le temps est nuageux (5)
**clubbing: to go clubbing** aller en boîte (15)
**coat** manteau *m.* (3); **sports coat** veste *f.* (3)
**coffee (cup of)** un café *m.* (2)
**coin locker** consigne *f.* (automatique) (9)
**coins** monnaie *f.* (10)
**cold** froid *m.*; **it's cold** il fait froid (5); **to be cold** avoir (*irreg.*) froid (3)
**collection** collection *f.* (15); recueil *m.* (12)

**comb** peigne *n. m.* (13); **to comb one's hair** se peigner (13)
**come** venir *irreg.* (8); **to come back to** (*someplace*) revenir *irreg.* (8)
**command: to have a command of** maîtriser (14)
**commercial** publicité *n. f.* (10)
**common good** bien (*m.*) commun (16)
**compact disc (CD) player** lecteur (*m.*) de CD (4)
**company** entreprise *f.* (14); société *f.* (14); **company head** chef (*m.*) d'entreprise (14)
**compartment** (*train*) compartiment *m.* (9)
**composer** compositeur/trice *m. f.* (12)
**computer** ordinateur *m.* (1); **computer science** informatique *f.* (2); **desktop computer** ordinateur (*m.*) de bureau (de table) (10), micro-ordinateur (micro) *m.* (10); **laptop computer** ordinateur (*m.*) portable (portable *m.*) (1, 10)
**concern** *v.* toucher (14)
**conflict** conflit *n. m.* (16)
**conformist** conformiste (3)
**Congo (Democratic Republic of)** République (*f.*) Démocratique du Congo (2, 8)
**conservation** conservation *f.* (16)
**conserve** conserver (16)
**consider** estimer (16)
**constantly** constamment (12)
**construct** construire *irreg.* (9)
**consume** consommer (16)
**continue** continuer (11)
**cooking** cuisine *f.* (6); **to cook** faire (*irreg.*) la cuisine (5)
**cool** *adj.* frais (fraîche); **it's cool** il fait frais (5)
**corner** coin *m.* (11)
**cost of living** coût (*m.*) de la vie (14)
**costs** frais *m. pl.* (14)
**Cote d'Ivoire** Côte d'Ivoire *f.* (2, 8)
**country** (*nation*) pays *m.* (2); **country(side)** campagne *f.* (8)
**couple** (*engaged, married*) couple *m.* (13)
**courageous** courageux/euse (3)
**course** (*academic*) cours *m.* (2); **course** (*meal*) plat *m.* (7); **first course** entrée *f.* (7); **main course** plat (*m.*) principal (7)
**cousin** cousin(e) *m., f.* (5)
**cover** *v.* couvrir *irreg.* (14)
**craftsperson** artisan(e) *m., f.* (14)
**crayfish** écrevisse *f.* (7)
**cream** crème *f.* (6); **ice cream** glace *f.* (6)
**credit card** carte (*f.*) de crédit (14)
**croissant** croissant *m.* (6)
**cross** *v.* traverser (9); **cross-country skiing** ski (*m.*) de fond (8)
**crowd** foule *n. f.* (15)
**cup** tasse *f.* (6); **cup of coffee** un café *m.* (2); **wide cup** bol *m.* (6)
**cured** guéri(e) (13)
**current events** actualité *f.* (14)
**curtain** rideau *m.* (4)
**cycling** cyclisme *m.* (15); vélo *m.*; **to go cycling** faire (*irreg.*) du vélo (5)

**daily** quotidien(ne) (13)
**dance** *v.* danser (2)
**date (from)** *v.* dater (de) (12); **to have a date** avoir (*irreg.*) rendez-vous (3); **what is the date?** quelle est la date? (1)
**daughter** fille *f.* (5); **daughter-in-law** bru *f.* (5)

**day** jour *m.* (1); **all day** toute la journée (7); **every day** tous les jours (5); **the day before yesterday** avant-hier (7); **what day is it?** quel jour sommes-nous? (1); **whole day** journée *f.* (7)

**dear** cher/ère (3)

**debit card** carte de débit (14)

**decade: the decade of (the fifties)** les années (cinquante) *f. pl.* (8)

**December** décembre (1)

**decide** décider (de) (12)

**delay** retard *n. m.* (6)

**delicatessen** charcuterie *f.* (7)

**demand** *v.* exiger (16)

**demonstrate (for/against)** manifester (pour/contre) (16)

**dentist** dentiste *m., f.* (14)

**departure** départ *m.* (9)

**deposit (change)** *v.* déposer (14); déposer (la monnaie) (10)

**describe** décrire *irreg.* (10)

**desire** *v.* désirer (15); souhaiter (16)

**desk** bureau *m.* (1)

**desktop computer** micro (-ordinateur) *m.* (10), ordinateur de bureau (de table) (10)

**dessert** dessert *m.* (6)

**destroy** détruire *irreg.* (9)

**detest** détester (2)

**develop** développer (16)

**development** développement *m.* (16)

**dial (the number)** composer (le numéro) (10)

**dice** dés *m. pl.* (4)

**dictionary** dictionnaire *m.* (2)

**die** *v.* mourir *irreg.* (8)

**diet** régime *n. m.* (7)

**different** différent(e) (3)

**difficult** difficile (3)

**digital camera** appareil (*m.*) numérique (10)

**dine** dîner (6)

**dining room** salle (*f.*) à manger (5)

**dinner** dîner *m.* (6); **to have dinner** dîner (6)

**direct** *v.* diriger (14)

**directory (online)** annuaire (*m.*) électronique (10)

**disagreeable** désagréable (3)

**discover** découvrir *irreg.* (14)

**dishes** vaisselle *f. s.*; **to wash (do) the dishes** faire (*irreg.*) la vaisselle (5)

**district** quartier *m.* (2); arrondissement *m.* (11)

**division** (*academic*) faculté *f.* (2)

**divorced** divorcé(e) (5)

**do** faire *irreg.* (5); **do-it-yourself work** bricolage *m.* (15)

**doctor** médecin *m.*, femme médecin *f.* (14); **doctor's office** cabinet (*m.*) medical (13)

**documentary** documentaire *n. m.* (10)

**dog** chien(ne) *m., f.* (4)

**door** porte *f.* (1)

**dormitory** cité (*f.*) universitaire (cité-U) (2)

**doubt** *v.* douter (16); **without a doubt** sans doute (16)

**downhill skiing** ski (*m.*) alpin (8)

**download** *v.* télécharger (10)

**downtown** centre-ville *m.* (11)

**draw** dessiner (10)

**drawers (chest of)** commode *f.* (4)

**dream (of)** *v.* rêver (de) (2)

**dress** robe *f.* (3); **to get dressed** s'habiller (13)

**drink (soft)** boisson (*f.*) (gazeuse) (6); **to drink** boire *irreg.* (6)

**drive** *v.* conduire *irreg.* (9)

**driver** conducteur/trice *m., f.* (9)

**drugstore** pharmacie *f.* (11)

**DSL connection/line** connexion (*f.*) ADSL (10)

**during** pendant (9)

**DVD player** lecteur (*m.*) de DVD (1)

**dynamic** dynamique (3)

**each (one)** chacun(e) *pron.* (15); chaque *adj.* (4)

**ear** oreille *f.* (13)

**early** de bonne heure (6); tôt (6); en avance (6)

**earn** gagner (14)

**east** est *m.* (9); **to the east** à l'est (9)

**easy** facile (3)

**eat** manger (2); **eat a meal** prendre un repas (6)

**e-book** livre (*m.*) numérique (10)

**eccentric** excentrique (3)

**eclair** éclair (*pastry*) *m.* (7)

**economics** économie *f.* (2)

**editor** rédacteur/trice *m., f.* (14)

**egg** œuf *m.* (6)

**eight** *huit (1)

**eighteen** dix-huit (1)

**eighth** le/la *huitième (11)

**elect** élire *irreg.* (16)

**eleven** onze (1)

**eleventh** le/la onzième (11)

**else (s.th.)** autre chose (7)

**e-mail message** mél *m.* (10); courriel *m.* (10)

**employee** employé(e) *m., f.* (14); **s.o. employed (by)** employé(e) (de) (14)

**encounter** rencontre *n. f.* (13); **to encounter** rencontrer (13)

**end by** (*doing s.th.*) finir par (12)

**energy** énergie *f.* (16); **nuclear/solar energy** énergie (*f.*) nucléaire/solaire (16)

**engage: to get engaged** se fiancer (13)

**engagement** fiançailles *f. pl.* (13)

**engineer** ingénieur *m.* (14)

**engineering** génie *m.* (2)

**England** Angleterre *f.* (2, 8)

**English** (*person*) Anglais(e) *m., f.* (2); (*language*) anglais *m.* (2)

**enough (of)** assez de (6)

**enter** entrer (8)

**enthusiastic** enthousiaste (3)

**envelope** enveloppe *f.* (10)

**environment** environnement *m.* (16)

**environmentalist** écologiste *m., f.* (16)

**equal** égal(e) (16)

**era: the era of (the fifties)** les années (cinquante) *f. pl.* (8)

**e-reader** liseuse *f.* (10)

**errands** courses *f. pl.*; **to do errands** faire (*irreg.*) les courses (5)

**especially** surtout (10)

**essential** essentiel(le) (16)

**establish** établir (16)

**establishment: at the establishment of** chez (5)

**estimate** *v.* estimer (16)

**even so** quand même (16)

**evening** soir *m.* (6); **all evening** toute la soirée (7); **entire evening** soirée *f.* (7); **good evening** bonsoir (1); **in the evening** du soir (6); **Monday/Friday evenings** le lundi/le vendredi soir (5); **this evening** ce soir (5)

**event** événement *m.* (12); **sporting event** manifestation (*f.*) sportive (15)

**ever: have you ever . . . ?** avez-vous (as-tu) déjà… ? (9)

**every** tout, toute, tous, toutes (10); **every day (afternoon, morning, evening)** tous les jours (après-midi, matins, soirs) (5); **every week** toutes les semaines (10)

**everybody** tout le monde (7)

**everyday** quotidien(ne) *adj.* (13)

**everyone** tout le monde (9)

**everything** tout (9)

**everywhere** partout (11)

**evidently** évidemment (12)

**exam** examen *m.* (2); **to take an exam** passer un examen (4); **to pass (an exam)** réussir à (4)

**example: for example** par exemple (16)

**exchange** *v.* échanger (10); **exchange rate** cours (*m.*) (14), taux (*m.*) de change (14); **money exchange (office)** bureau (*m.*) de change (14)

**excuse (oneself)** s'excuser (13); **excuse me** excusez-moi (1)

**exhaust** *v.* épuiser (16)

**exhibit** exposition *n. f.* (12)

**expense** dépense *f.* (14); **expenses** frais *m. pl.* (14)

**expensive** cher/ère (3)

**express an opinion** exprimer une opinion (16)

**expression: freedom of expression** liberté (*f.*) d'expression (13)

**extremist ideas** idées (*f.*) extrémistes (16)

**eye** œil *m.* (13) (*pl.* yeux) (3)

**face** visage *n. m.* (13)

**fair** *adj.* juste (16)

**fall** automne *n. m.* (5); **in fall** en automne (5)

**fall** *v.* tomber (8); **to fall in love (with)** tomber amoureux/euse (de) (13)

**false** faux (fausse) (4)

**familiar: to be familiar with** connaître *irreg.* (11)

**family** famille *f.* (5)

**far from** loin de (4)

**farmer** agriculteur/trice *m., f.* (14)

**fat** *adj.* gros(se) (4)

**father** père *m.* (5); **father-in-law** beau-père *m.* (5); **stepfather** beau-père *m.* (5)

**favorite** préféré(e) (5)

**fax** fax *m.* (10)

**February** février (1)

**feel** sentir *irreg.* (8); **to feel bad** aller (*irreg.*) mal (5); **to feel like** avoir (*irreg.*) envie de (3)

**few: a few** *adj.* quelques; quelques-uns/unes *pron.* (9)

**fifteen** quinze (1)

**fifth** le/la cinquième *m., f.* (11)

**fifty** cinquante (1)

**file** fichier *m.* (10)

**fill it up** faire (*irreg.*) le plein (9)

**fillet** (*beef, fish, etc.*) filet *m.* (7)

**film** film *m.* (2)

**filmmaker** cinéaste *m., f.* (12)

**finally** enfin (11)

**find** *v.* trouver (2)

**fine** bien (15); ça va bien (1)

**finger** doigt *m.* (13)

**finish** finir (de + *inf.*) (4); **to finish by** (*doing s.th.*) finir par (+ *inf.*) (4)

**first** d'abord *adv.* (11); premier/ière *adj.* (4); **first of all (at first)** d'abord (11)

**fish** poisson *m.* (6); **fish store** poissonnerie *f.* (7); **fishing** pêche *f.* (15); **to go fishing** aller (*irreg.*) à la pêche (8)

**five** cinq (1)

**fixed-price menu** menu *m.* (7)

**flash of lightning** coup (*m.*) de foudre (13)

**flight** vol *m.* (9); **flight attendant** hôtesse (*f.*) de l'air (9); **steward** *m.* (9)

**floor: ground floor** rez-de-chaussée *m.* (5); **second floor** (*in the U.S.*) premier étage *m.* (5); **third floor** (*in the U.S.*) deuxième étage *m.* (5)

**flower** fleur *f.* (4)

**fluently** couramment (12)

**follow** suivre *irreg.* (12)

**food** nourriture *f.* (6)

**foot** pied *m.* (13); **on foot** à pied (9)

**for** pour (2); (*time*) depuis (9), pendant (9); (*flight*) à destination de (9); **for example** par exemple (16); **for oneself** à son compte (14)

**foreign** étranger/ère (2); **in a foreign country** à l'étranger (9); **foreign language** langue (*f.*) étrangère (2)

**forest** bois *m.* (11); forêt *f.* (8)

**forget (to)** oublier (de) (8)

**fork** fourchette *f.* (6)

**former** ancien(ne) (4)

**formerly** autrefois (11)

**fortunate** heureux/euse (3)

**forty** quarante (1)

**found: to be found** se trouver (13)

**four** quatre (1)

**fourteen** quatorze (1)

**fourth** le/la quatrième (11); **one-fourth** quart *m.* (6)

**France** France *f.* (2, 8)

**free** gratuit(e) (11); **free time** temps (*m.*) libre (15)

**freedom (of expression)** liberté (*f.*) (d'expression) (16)

**French** (*person*) Français(e) *m., f.* (2); (*language*) français *m.*; **French fries** frites *f. pl.* (6); **in French, please** en français, s'il vous plaît (1)

**fresh** frais (fraîche) (5)

**Friday** vendredi *m.* (1)

**friend** ami(e) *m., f.* (2); copain/copine (7)

**friendship** amitié *f.* (13)

**fries** frites *f. pl.* (6)

**from** de (2); **from time to time** de temps en temps (2); **from now on** à l'avenir (14), à partir de maintenant (14)

**front: in front of** devant (4)

**fruit** fruit *m.* (6); **fruit juice** jus (*m.*) de fruit (6)

**fun** *adj.* amusant(e) (3); **to have fun** s'amuser (à) (13)

**fundamentalism** intégrisme *m.* (16)

**funny** drôle (3)

**furious** furieux/euse (16)

**furniture (piece of)** meuble *m.* (5)

**future** avenir *m.* (14); **in the future** à l'avenir (14)

**game** (*sport*) match (15); **games of chance** jeux (*m. pl.*) de *hasard (15); **group, social games** jeux (*m. pl.*) de société (15)

**garden** jardin *n. m.* (5)

**gardening** jardinage *m.* (15)

**garlic** ail *m.* (15)

**garret** chambre (*f.*) de bonne (4)

**gas station** station-service *f.* (9)

**gasoline** essence *f.* (9)

**generally** en général (2)

**geography** géographie *f.* (2)

**geology** géologie *f.* (2)

**German** (*person*) Allemand(e) *m., f.* (2); (*language*) allemand *m.* (2)

**Germany** Allemagne *f.* (2, 8)

**get** obtenir *irreg.* (8); **get going!** va-t'en! (13); **to get along (with)** s'entendre (avec) (13); **to get off, down from** descendre (de) (5); **to get up** se lever (13)

**gift** cadeau *m.* (10)

**girl** fille *f.* (3)

**girlfriend** copine *f.* (7)

**give** donner (2); **to give back** rendre (5)

**glass** verre *m.* (6); **(eye)glasses** lunettes *f. pl.* (8)

**global warming** réchauffement (*m.*) de la planète (16)

**globalization** mondialisation *f.* (16)

**glove** gant *m.* (8)

**go: to go** aller *irreg.* (5); **go away!/get going!** allez-vous-en! (va-t'en!) (13); **how's it going?** ça va? (1); **things are going well** ça va (1); **to be going** (*to do s.th.*) aller + *inf.* (5); **to go back** retourner (8); **to go clubbing** aller en boîte (15); **to go down** (*a street, a river*) descendre (5); **to go fishing** aller à la pêche (8); **to go home** rentrer (8); **to go off, go away** (*to work*) s'en aller *irreg.* (13); **to go out** sortir *irreg.* (de) (8); **to go up** monter (8); **what's going on?** qu'est-ce qui se passe? (15)

**goggles: ski goggles** lunettes (*f. pl.*) de ski (8)

**good** bien *adv.* (15); bon(ne) *adj.* (4); **common good** bien (*m.*) commun (16); **good-bye** au revoir (1); **good day** bonjour (1); **good evening** bonsoir (1); **that's good** tant mieux (15)

**Gothic** gothique (12)

**government** gouvernement *m.* (16)

**grandchild** petit-enfant *m.* (5)

**granddaughter** petite-fille *f.* (5)

**grandfather** grand-père *m.* (5)

**grandmother** grand-mère *f.* (5)

**grandparent** grand-parent *m.* (5)

**grandson** petit-fils *m.* (5)

**gray** gris(e) (3)

**great-grandparent** arrière-grand-parent *m.* (5)

**Greece** Grèce *f.* (8)

**green** vert(e) (3); **green beans** *haricots (*m. pl.*) verts (6)

**grocery store** épicerie *f.* (7)

**ground: on the ground** par terre (4); **ground floor** rez-de-chaussée *m.* (5)

**group games** jeux (*m. pl.*) de société (15)

**guess** *v.* deviner (12)

**guitar** guitare *f.* (4)

**gymnasium** gymnase *m.* (2)

**habitually** d'habitude (5)

**hair** cheveux *m. pl.* (3)

**hairdresser** coiffeur/euse *m., f.* (14)

**Haiti** Haïti *m.* (8)

**half** demi(e) (6); **half brother** demi-frère *m.* (5); **half past (the hour)** et demi(e) (6); **half sister** demi-sœur *f.* (5)

**hall** couloir *m.* (4); **lecture hall** amphithéâtre *m.* (2); **town hall** mairie *f.* (11)

**ham** jambon *m.* (6)

**hand** main *f.* (13); **to hand in** rendre (5)

**handbag** sac (*m.*) à main (3)

**handsome** beau, bel, belle (beaux, belles) (3)

**happen** se passer (15); **what's happening?** qu'est-ce qui se passe? (15)

**happy** heureux/euse (3)

**hardly** peu (3)

**hardworking** travailleur/euse (3)

**hat** chapeau *m.* (3)

**have** avoir *irreg.* (3); **to have** (*to eat; to order*) prendre *irreg.* (6); **to have a drink** (*with s.o.*) prendre un verre (6); **to have breakfast** prendre le petit déjeuner (6); **to have to** devoir *irreg.* (7)

**head** tête *f.* (13); directeur/trice *m., f.* (14); **company head** chef (*m.*) d'entreprise (14)

**healed** guéri(e) (13)

**health** santé *f.* (13)

**hear** entendre (5)

**heart** cœur *m.* (13); **by heart** par cœur (12)

**height: medium height** de taille moyenne (3)

**hello** bonjour (1); (*telephone*) allô (10)

**helmet** casque *m.* (8)

**help** *v.* aider (14)

**here** ici (1); **here is/are** voici (2)

**heritage** patrimoine *m.* (12)

**hi** salut (1)

**high-definition television** TNT *f.*; télévision (*f.*) numérique terrestre

**highway** autoroute *f.* (9)

**hike** randonnée *n. f.* (8); **hiking boots** chaussures (*f. pl.*) de montagne (8); **to go hiking** faire (*irreg.*) une randonnée (pédestre) (8)

**hire** embaucher (16)

**historical** historique *f.* (13)

**history** histoire *f.* (2)

**hobby** passe-temps *m.* (15)

**holiday** fête *f.* (1)

**home** maison *f.* (4); **at the home of** chez (5); **to go home** rentrer (8)

**homeless** sans-abri *m., f. inv.* (16)

**homework** devoirs *m. pl.*; **to do homework** faire (*irreg.*) ses devoirs (5)

**hope** *v.* espérer (6)

**horse** cheval *m.* (8); **to go horseback riding** faire (*irreg.*) du cheval (8)

**hospital** hôpital *m.* (9)

**hostel: youth hostel** auberge (*f.*) de jeunesse (8)

**hot** chaud; **it's hot** il fait chaud (5); **to be hot** avoir (*irreg.*) chaud (3)

**hotel** hôtel *m.* (9)

**hour** heure *f.* (6); **quarter before the hour** moins le quart (6)

**house** maison *f.* (4)

**housework: to do the housework** faire (*irreg.*) le ménage (5)

**how** comment (1); **how are you?** comment allez-vous? (comment vas-tu?) (1); **how much is it?** c'est combien? (1); **how many?** combien (de)? (4); **how much?** combien (de)? (1); **how's it going?** ça va? (1)

**hungry: to be hungry** avoir (*irreg.*) faim (4)

**hurry** *v.* se dépêcher (13); **hurry up!** dépêche-toi! (6)

**hurt** *v.* avoir (*irreg.*) mal (à) (13)

**husband** mari *m.* (5)

**hybrid** voiture (*f.*) hybride (16)

**ice cream** glace *f.* (6)

**ID card** carte (*f.*) d'identité (8)

**idealistic** idéaliste (3)

**if** si; **if I were you** à ta (votre) place (15)

**immediately** tout de suite (5)

**impatient** impatient(e) (3)

**important** important(e) (3)

**impossible: it is impossible that** il est impossible que + *subj.* (16)

**in** à (2); en (2); dans; **in four days (from now)** dans quatre jours (5); **in order to** pour (4); **in the afternoon** de l'après-midi (6)
**include** comprendre *irreg.* (6)
**increase** augmentation *n. f.* (14)
**indispensable** indispensable (16)
**individualistic** individualiste (3)
**industrial** industriel(le) (16)
**inflation** inflation *f.* (16)
**information: tourist information bureau** syndicat *(m.)* d'initiative (11)
**injection** piqûre *f.* (13)
**inspect** contrôler (16)
**instructor** professeur *m., f.* (1)
**intellectual** intellectuel(le) (3)
**intelligent** intelligent(e) (3)
**interest** *v.* intéresser (14)
**interesting** intéressant(e) (3)
**Internet** Internet (10); **on the Internet** sur Internet (10)
**internship** stage *m.* (14)
**intersection** carrefour *m.* (11)
**interview (job)** entretien *m.* (14)
**involve: to get involved (in)** *(a public issue, cause)* s'engager (dans) (16)
**iPad** tablette *f.* (1)
**iPod** iPod *m.* (4)
**island** île *f.* (11)
**isn't it so?** n'est-ce pas? (3)
**it's a/an . . .** c'est un(e)… (1)
**it's me.** c'est moi. (10)
**Italian** *(person)* Italien(ne) *m., f.* (2); *(language)* italien *m.* (2)
**Italy** Italie *f.* (2, 8)
**Ivory Coast** See Cote d'Ivoire

**jacket (ski)** anorak *m.* (8); **suit jacket** veston *m.* (3)
**January** janvier (1)
**Japan** Japon *m.* (2, 8)
**Japanese** *(person)* Japonais(e) *m., f.* (2); *(language)* japonais *m.* (2)
**jeans** jean *m.* (3)
**jewel** bijou *m.* (14)
**job market** marché *(m.)* de l'emploi (14)
**jog** faire *(irreg.)* du jogging (5)
**joke** blague *n. f.* (15)
**juice (orange)** jus *(m.)* (d'orange) (6)
**July** juillet (1)
**June** juin (1)
**just: to have just done s.th.** venir *(irreg.)* de + *inf.* (8)

**keen: to be keen about** tenir à (16)
**key** clé, clef *f.* (5)
**keyboard** clavier *m.* (10)
**kilo** kilo(gramme) *m.* (7)
**kiosk** kiosque *m.* (10)
**kiss** *v.* s'embrasser (13)
**kitchen** cuisine *f.* (5)
**knee** genou *m.* *(pl.* genoux) (13)
**knife** couteau *m.* (6)
**know** connaître *irreg.* (11); **to know (how)** savoir *irreg.* (11)

**lake** lac *m.* (8)
**lamp** lampe *f.* (4)
**language (foreign)** langue *(f.)* (étrangère) (2)
**laptop computer** portable *m.* (1, 10)
**large** gros(se) (4)
**last** dernier/ière (4, 7); passé(e) (7); **last night** hier soir (7)
**late** en retard (6)

**laugh** *v.* rire *irreg.* (15)
**laundry: to do the laundry** faire *(irreg.)* la lessive (5)
**law** droit *m.* (2)
**lawn bowling** pétanque *f.* (15)
**lawyer** avocat(e) *m., f.* (14)
**lazy** paresseux/euse (3)
**lead (clue)** *n.* piste *f.* (14)
**learn** apprendre *irreg.* (à) (6)
**leave (for, from)** partir *irreg.* (à, de) (8); **to leave** *(behind)* laisser (7); **to leave** *(go out)* sortir *irreg.* (8); **to leave** *(s.o. or someplace)* quitter (8)
**Lebanon** *m.* Liban (2, 8)
**Lebanese** *(person)* Libanais(e) *m., f.* (2)
**lecture** conférence *f.* (12); **lecture hall** amphithéâtre *m.* (2)
**left: on the left** à gauche (4); **the Left Bank** *(in Paris)* Rive *(f.)* gauche (11)
**leg** jambe *f.* (13)
**legacy** patrimoine *m.* (12)
**legalization** légalisation *f.* (16)
**leisure activities** loisirs *m. pl.* (15)
**lend (to)** prêter (à) (11)
**less . . . than** moins… que (14)
**let's see, . . .** voyons,… (10)
**letter** lettre *f.* (10); **letter carrier** facteur/trice *m., f.* (10)
**lettuce** laitue *f.* (6), salade *f.* (6)
**library** bibliothèque *f.* (2)
**life** vie *f.* (2)
**lightning: flash of lightning** coup *(m.)* de foudre (13)
**like** aimer (2); **I would like** *(to do s.th.)* je voudrais (+ *inf.*) (6); **to like better** aimer mieux (7)
**likeable** sympa(thique) (13)
**likely** probable (16)
**line: to stand in line** faire *(irreg.)* la queue (5)
**linguistics** linguistique *f.* (2)
**lipstick** rouge *(m.)* à lèvres (13)
**listen** écouter (2)
**literature** littérature *f.* (2)
**little: a little (of)** un peu (de) (3)
**live** habiter (2); vivre *irreg.* (12)
**living: cost of living** coût *(m.)* de la vie (14); **living room** séjour *m.* (5); **standard of living** niveau *(m.)* de vie (16)
**loaf (of bread)** baguette *(f.)* (de pain) (6)
**loan** emprunt *m.* (14)
**locate: to be located** se trouver (13)
**locker (coin)** consigne *(f.)* automatique (9)
**lodging** logement *m.* (4)
**loneliness** solitude *f.* (16)
**long** long(ue) (3)
**longer: no longer** ne… plus (9)
**look (at)** regarder (8); **to look (like)** avoir *(irreg.)* l'air (de) (3); **to look at oneself, look at each other** se regarder (13); **to look for** chercher (2); **to look up** *(a phone number)* consulter l'annuaire (10)
**lose** perdre (5); **to get lost** se perdre (13)
**lot: a lot (of)** beaucoup (de) (1, 6)
**lotion, suntan** crème *(f.)* solaire (8)
**love** *v.* adorer (2); aimer (2); amour *n. m.* (13); **love at first sight** coup *(m.)* de foudre (13); **lover; loving** amoureux/euse (13); **to fall in love (with)** tomber amoureux/euse (de) (13)
**lucky: to be lucky** avoir *(irreg.)* de la chance (8)
**lunch** déjeuner *m.* (6); **to have lunch** déjeuner (6)

**ma'am** Madame (M^me) (1)
**magazine** *(illustrated)* magazine *m.* (4); *(journal)* revue *f.* (10)
**magnificent** magnifique (12)
**maid's room** chambre *(f.)* de bonne (4)
**mail** *v.* poster (10); **mail (a letter)** *v.* mettre (une lettre) à la poste (10); *n.* courrier *m.*; poste *f.*
**mailbox** boîte *(f.)* aux lettres (10)
**main dish** plat *(m.)* principal (7)
**majority: the majority of** la plupart de (12)
**make** faire *irreg.* (5); **make fun of** se moquer de (14); **to make (happen)** réaliser (14)
**makeup: to put on makeup** se maquiller (13)
**man** homme *m.* (2); **young man** jeune homme *m.* (13)
**manage** gérer (14)
**manager** directeur/trice *m., f.* (14); **middle/senior manager** cadre *m.* (14); **top manager** chef *(m.)* d'entreprise (14)
**many: how many?** combien (de)? (4)
**map** plan *(city) m.* (11); carte *(of a region, country) f.* (11)
**March** mars (1)
**market** marché *m.*; **to go to the market** faire *(irreg.)* le marché (5); **job market** marché *(m.)* de l'emploi (14)
**marriage** mariage *m.* (13)
**married** marié(e) (5); **to get married** se marier (avec) (13)
**Martinique** Martinique *f.* (1)
**master** *v.* maîtriser (14)
**masterpiece** chef-d'œuvre *m.* *(pl.* chefs-d'œuvre) (12)
**mathematics (math)** mathématiques (maths) *f. pl.* (2)
**May** mai (1)
**maybe** peut-être (5)
**me: as for me** pour ma part (16); **it's me.** c'est moi. (10); **me neither** moi non plus (3); **me too** moi aussi (3)
**meal** repas *m.* (6)
**mean** *v.* vouloir *(irreg.)* dire (7); **I mean . . .** c'est-à-dire… (10)
**meat** viande *f.* (6)
**media** médias *m. pl.* (16)
**medieval** médiéval(e) (12)
**medium: of medium height** de taille moyenne (3)
**meet** se rencontrer (13); **to meet (for the first time)** faire *(irreg.)* la connaissance (de) (5)
**meeting** rencontre *f.* (13); **to have a meeting** avoir *(irreg.)* rendez-vous (3)
**mention: don't mention it** de rien (1)
**menu** carte *f.* (7); **fixed-price menu** menu *m.* (7)
**merchant (wine)** marchand(e) (de vin) (14)
**messy** en désordre (4)
**metro station** station *(f.)* de métro (11)
**Mexican** *(person)* Mexicain(e) *m., f.* (2)
**Mexico** Mexique *m.* (2, 8)
**middle: Middle Ages** Moyen Âge *m. s.* (12); **to be in the middle of** être *(irreg.)* en train de (15)
**midnight: it is midnight** il est minuit (6)
**military budget** budget *(m.)* militaire (16)
**milk** lait *m.* (6)
**mirror** miroir *m.* (4)
**Miss** Mademoiselle (M^lle) (1)
**mixture** mélange *m.* (7)
**Monday** lundi *m.* (1); **it's Monday** nous sommes lundi

**money** argent *m.* (7); **money exchange (office)** bureau (*m.*) de change (14)
**monitor (computer)** écran *m.* (10); moniteur *m.* (10); *v.* contrôler (14)
**month** mois *m.* (1)
**monument** monument *m.* (11)
**more . . . than** plus... que (14); **no more** ne... plus (9)
**morning** matin *m.* (5); **all morning** matinée toute la matinée (7); **entire morning** matinée *f.* (7); **in the morning** du matin (6); **this morning** ce matin (5)
**Moroccan** (*person*) Marocain(e) *m.*, *f.* (2)
**Morocco** Maroc *m.* (2, 8)
**most (of)** la plupart (de) (12)
**mother** mère *f.* (5)
**mother-in-law** belle-mère *f.* (5)
**motorcycle** motocyclette, moto *f.* (9)
**mountain** montagne *f.* (8); **to go mountain climbing** faire (*irreg.*) de l'alpinisme (8)
**mouse** souris *f.* (1, 10)
**mouth** bouche *f.* (13)
**move in** emménager (4)
**move out** déménager (4)
**movie** film *m.* (2); **movie theater; movies** cinéma *m.* (2)
**mp3 player** mp3 *m.* (10)
**Mr.** Monsieur (M.) (1)
**Mrs.** Madame (M^me) (1)
**much** bien *adv.*; **as much/many . . . as** autant (de)... que (15); **how much?** combien (de)? (1); **so much the better** tant mieux (15); **too much** trop de (6); **very much** beaucoup (1)
**municipal** municipal(e) (11)
**museum** musée *m.* (11)
**mushroom** champignon *m.* (6)
**music** musique *f.* (2)
**musician** musicien(ne) *m.*, *f.* (12)
**must: one must (not)** il (ne) faut (pas) + *inf.* (8)
**myself** moi-même (12)

**naive** naïf/ïve (3)
**name(d): my name is . . .** je m'appelle... (10); **to be named** s'appeler (13); **what's your name?** comment vous appelez-vous? (comment t'appelles-tu?) (10)
**napkin** serviette *f.* (6)
**natural** naturel(le); **natural resources** ressources (*f. pl.*) naturelles (16)
**nature** nature *f.* (16)
**navigate** naviguer (10)
**necessary: it is necessary that** il est nécessaire que + *subj.* (16); **it is necessary to** il faut + *inf.* (8); **to be necessary** falloir *irreg.* (8)
**neck** cou *m.* (13)
**necktie** cravate *f.* (3)
**need** *v.* avoir (*irreg.*) besoin de (3); **one needs** il faut (8); il est nécessaire de (16)
**neighbor** voisin(e) *m.*, *f.* (4)
**neighborhood** quartier *m.* (2)
**nephew** neveu *m.* (5)
**nervous** nerveux/euse (3)
**network** (*television*) chaîne *f.* (10)
**never** ne... jamais (9)
**new** nouveau, nouvel, nouvelle (nouveaux, nouvelles) (3)
**newlyweds** nouveaux mariés *m. pl.* (13)
**news** (*TV program*) informations *f. pl.* (10)
**newspaper (news [on television])** journal *m.* (*pl.* journaux) (2)

**newsstand** kiosque *m.* (10)
**next** ensuite, puis *adv.* (11); prochain(e) *adj.*; **next to** à côté de (4); **next week** la semaine prochaine (5)
**nice** beau (*weather*) (5); gentil(le) (3); agréable (3); sympathique (sympa *inv.*) (3); **be nice!** soyez gentil! (6); **it's nice (out)** il fait beau (5)
**niece** nièce *f.* (5)
**night** nuit *f.* (7); **all night** toute la nuit (7); **at night** du soir (6); **last night** hier soir (7)
**nine** neuf (1)
**nineteen** dix-neuf (1)
**ninth** le/la neuvième (11)
**no** non (1); **no longer, no more** ne... plus (9); **no one, nobody** ne... personne (9)
**noise** bruit *m.* (5)
**noon** midi (6)
**normal** normal(e) (16)
**north** nord *m.* (9); **to the north** au nord (9)
**nose** nez *m.* (13)
**not (at all)** ne... pas (du tout) (9); **not bad(ly)** pas mal (1); **not very** peu (3); **not yet** ne... pas encore (9)
**notebook** cahier *m.* (1)
**nothing** ne... rien (9)
**novel** roman *m.* (10)
**November** novembre (1)
**now** maintenant (2); **from now on** à l'avenir (14), à partir de maintenant (14)
**nuclear: nuclear energy** énergie (*f.*) nucléaire (16); **nuclear power plant** centrale (*f.*) nucléaire (16)
**number (telephone)** numéro *m.* (de téléphone) (10); **to dial the number** composer le numéro (10)

**obliged: to be obliged to** devoir *irreg.* (7)
**obtain** obtenir *irreg.* (8)
**ocean** mer *f.* (8)
**o'clock: it is . . . o'clock** il est... heures (6)
**October** octobre (1)
**odd** drôle (3)
**of** de (2); **of which** dont (14)
**offer** *v.* offrir *irreg.* (14)
**office** bureau *m.* (2); **doctor's office** cabinet (*m.*) medical (13)
**officer (police)** agent (*m.*) de police (14)
**often** souvent (2)
**oil (olive)** huile *f.* (d'olive) (7)
**okay** d'accord (2)
**old** ancien(ne) (4); vieux, vieil, vieille (4)
**on (top of)** sur (4); **on the ground** par terre (4); **on** (*bicycle, horseback, foot*) à (9)
**once** une fois (11); **all at once** tout d'un coup (11); **once a week** une fois par semaine (5)
**one** un(e) (1)
**onion** oignon *m.* (7)
**only** ne . . . que (9); seulement (9)
**open** *v.* ouvrir *irreg.* (14)
**opera** opéra *m.* (15)
**opinion: in my opinion** pour ma part (16); à mon avis (11); **in your opinion** à votre (ton) avis (11); **public opinion** opinion (*f.*) publique (16); **to express an opinion** exprimer une opinion (16); **to have an opinion about** penser de (11)
**optimistic** optimiste (13)
**or** ou (2)
**orange** orange *inv.* (3); (*fruit*) orange *f.* (6); **orange juice** jus (*m.*) d'orange (6)
**order: in order/orderly** en ordre (4); **in order to** pour (2); **to order** commander (6), prendre *irreg.* (*in a restaurant*) (6)

**other** autre (4); **others** d'autres (15); **the other(s)** l'/les autre(s) (15)
**outdoors** de plein air; **outdoor activities** activités (*f.*) de plein air (15)
**over there** là-bas (10)
**overpopulation** surpopulation *f.* (16)
**owe** devoir *irreg.* (7)
**oyster** huître *f.* (7)

**package** colis *m.* (10)
**pain** douleur *f.* (13); **to have pain** avoir (*irreg.*) mal (à) (3)
**paint** *v.* peindre *irreg.* (12)
**painter** artiste peintre *m.*, *f.* (14); peintre *m.*, femme peintre *f.* (12)
**painting** peinture *f.* (12); tableau *m.* (12)
**palace** palais *m.* (12)
**pants** pantalon *m. s.* (3)
**pardon (me)** pardon (1)
**Parisian** *adj.* parisien(ne) (3)
**park** parc *n. m.* (11)
**party** soirée *f.* (3); fête *f.* (7); **political party** parti *m.* (16)
**pass** (*time*) passer (6); **boarding pass** carte (*f.*) d'embarquement (9); **to pass** (*a test*) réussir à (4); **to pass by** passer par (8)
**passenger** passager/ère *m.*, *f.* (9)
**passport** passeport *m.* (8)
**past** passé *n. m.* (8)
**pasta** pâtes *f. pl.* (7)
**pastry, pastry shop** pâtisserie *f.* (7)
**pâté (country-style)** pâté *m.* (de campagne) (7)
**patient** *adj.* patient(e) (3)
**patrimony** patrimoine *m.* (12)
**pay** *v.* payer (10); **to pay attention (to)** faire (*irreg.*) attention (à) (5)
**payment: automatic payment/withdrawal** prélèvement automatique (14)
**pear** poire *f.* (6)
**pen** stylo *m.* (1)
**pencil** crayon *m.* (1)
**pension** retraite *f.* (16)
**pepper** poivre *m.* (6)
**perfectly** parfaitement (14)
**performance** spectacle *m.* (15)
**period** (*of history*) époque *f.* (12)
**permit (to)** *v.* permettre *irreg.* (de) (12)
**person** personne *f.* (3)
**personally** personnellement (16)
**pessimistic** pessimiste (3)
**pharmacist** pharmacien(ne) *m.*, *f.* (14)
**pharmacy** pharmacie *f.* (11)
**philosophy** philosophie *f.* (2)
**phone** See **telephone.**
**photocopy machine** photocopieur *m.* (10)
**physics** physique *f.* (2)
**picnic** pique-nique *m.* (15)
**pie** tarte *f.* (6)
**piece** morceau *m.* (7); **piece of furniture** meuble *m.* (5)
**pilot** pilote *n. m.*, *f.* (9)
**pink** rose (3)
**place** endroit *n. m.* (8); lieu *n. m.* (2); **place of residence** logement *m.* (4); **to place (put)** mettre *irreg.* (10)
**plans** projets *m. pl.* (5)
**plate** assiette *f.* (6)
**platform** (*train station*) quai *m.* (9)
**play** (*theater*) pièce (*f.*) de théâtre (12); *v.* jouer (3); **to play** (*a musical instrument*) jouer de (3); **to play** (*a sport or game*) jouer à (3); faire de (5)

**player (DVD)** lecteur *m.* (de DVD) (4, 10)
**pleasant** gentil(le) (3); agréable (3)
**please** *interj.* s'il vous (te) plaît (1)
**plumber** plombier *m.* (14)
**pocket** poche *f.* (10)
**poem** poème *m.* (12)
**poet** poète *m.*, femme poète *f.* (12)
**poetry** poésie *f.* (12)
**point out** indiquer (15)
**police officer** agent (*m.*) de police (14);
   **police station** commissariat *m.* (11), poste
   (*m.*) de police (11)
**policy** politique *f.* (16)
**polite** poli(e) (12)
**politely** poliment (12)
**political party** parti *m.* (16)
**politician** homme politique *m.*, femme
   politique *f.* (16)
**politics** politique *f.* (16)
**pollute** polluer (16)
**pollution** pollution *f.* (16)
**pool (swimming)** piscine *f.* (11)
**poor** pauvre (3)
**popular song** chanson (*f.*) de
   variété (15)
**pork** porc *m.* (6); **pork butcher's shop
   (delicatessen)** charcuterie *f.* (7)
**Portugal** Portugal *m.* (8)
**possess** *v.* posséder (10)
**possible** possible; **it is possible that** il est
   possible que + *subj.* (16), il se peut que +
   *subj.* (16)
**post office** bureau (*m.*) de poste (10); La
   Poste (11)
**postcard** carte (*f.*) postale (10)
**poster** affiche *f.* (4)
**potato** pomme (*f.*) de terre (6)
**power: purchasing power** pouvoir (*m.*)
   d'achat (16)
**prefer** aimer mieux (2); préférer (6)
**preferable** préférable (16)
**preferred** préféré(e) (5)
**preoccupied** préoccupé(e) (16)
**prepare** préparer (5)
**pretty** joli(e) (4)
**prevent (from)** empêcher (de) (12)
**price** prix *m.* (7); **fixed-price menu**
   menu *m.* (7)
**primary school teacher** professeur (*m.,f.*)
   des écoles (14)
**print book** livre (*m.*) papier (10)
**printer (computer)** imprimante *f.* (10)
**problem** ennui *m.* (9); problème *m.* (16)
**process: to be in the process of** être (*irreg.*)
   en train de (15)
**produce** *v.* produire *irreg.* (9)
**product** produit *m.* (6); **fresh products** les
   produits frais (6)
**professor** professeur *m.*, *f.* (1)
**program** (*TV, radio*) émission *f.* (10);
   **music program (on TV)** émission de
   musique (10)
**proliferation** prolifération *f.* (16)
**propose** *v.* proposer (14)
**protect** protéger (16)
**protection** protection *f.* (16)
**proud** fier/ère (3)
**psychology** psychologie *f.* (2)
**public** public (publique) (11); **public
   opinion** opinion (*f.*) publique (16)
**pun** jeu (*m.*) de mots (15)
**purchasing: purchasing power** pouvoir
   (*m.*) d'achat (16)

**pursue** poursuivre *irreg.* (12)
**put (on)** mettre *irreg.* (8)
**putter (around)** bricoler (15); **puttering
   (around)** bricolage *m.* (15)

**quarter** (*one-fourth*) quart *m.* (6); **quarter**
   (*district*) quartier *m.* (2); **quarter past (the
   hour)** et quart (6); **quarter to (the hour)**
   moins le quart (6)
**Quebec** (*province*) Québec *m.* (2, 8); (*city*)
   Québec *m.*
**queen** reine *f.* (12)
**question: to ask a question** poser une
   question (à) (11)
**quiet** tranquille *adj.* (4)

**radio** radio *f.* (2)
**rain** *v.* pleuvoir *irreg.* (7); **it's raining** il
   pleut (5)
**raincoat** imperméable *m.* (3)
**raise** *v.* augmenter (16); *n.* augmentation (*f.*)
   de salaire (14)
**rarely** rarement (2)
**rate (of exchange)** cours *m.* (14), taux (*m.*)
   de change (14); **(of unemployment)** taux
   de chômage (14)
**razor** rasoir *m.* (13)
**read** lire *irreg.* (10)
**reading** lecture *f.* (15)
**ready** prêt(e) (3); **to get ready** se préparer (13)
**realistic** réaliste (3)
**really** vraiment (12)
**reasonable** raisonnable (3)
**receipt** reçu *m.* (14)
**receive** recevoir *irreg.* (10)
**recognize** reconnaître *irreg.* (16)
**recruit** *v.* recruter (14)
**recycle** recycler (16)
**recycling** recyclage *m.* (16)
**red** rouge (3); **red** (*hair*) roux (rousse) (3)
**redheaded** roux (rousse) (3)
**reform** réforme *f.* (16)
**refuse (to)** refuser (de) (12)
**regret** *v.* regretter (16)
**relate** (*tell*) raconter (1)
**relax** se détendre (13)
**relieved** soulagé(e) (16)
**remain** rester (4)
**remember** se rappeler (13); se souvenir *irreg.*
   (de) (13)
**remote control** télécommande *f.* (10)
**Renaissance** Renaissance *f.* (12)
**rent** *v.* louer (4); location *f.* (3)
**repeat** répéter (1)
**reporter** journaliste *m.*, *f.* (2)
**require** exiger (16)
**rescue** *v.* sauver (16)
**residence: university residence complex**
   cité (*f.*) universitaire (cité-U) (2)
**resource: natural resources** ressources
   (*f. pl.*) naturelles (16)
**rest** *v.* se reposer (13)
**restaurant** restaurant *m.* (2)
**résumé** curriculum (*m.*) vitæ (C.V.) (14)
**return (give back)** rendre (5); (*go home*)
   rentrer (8); (*go back*) retourner (8); (*come
   back to someplace*) revenir *irreg.* (8)
**review** revue *n. f.* (10)
**rhythm** rythme *m.* (16)
**ride: to take a ride** faire (*irreg.*) un tour (en
   voiture) (5)
**right** *n.* droit *m.* (16); **civil rights** droits
   civils (16); **on (to) the right** à droite (4); **the**

**Right Bank** (*in Paris*) Rive (*f.*) droite (11);
   **to be right** avoir (*irreg.*) raison (3)
**river** fleuve *m.* (8)
**road** route *f.* (8)
**roast** rôti *m.* (7)
**roll** *v.* rouler (9)
**Roman** romain(e) (12)
**room** pièce *f.* (5); (*bedroom*) chambre *f.* (4, 5)
**roommate** camarade (*m.*, *f.*) de chambre (4)
**rug** tapis *m.* (4)
**run** courir *irreg.* (13); faire (*irreg.*) du
   jogging (5)
**Russia** Russie *f.* (2, 8)
**Russian** (*person*) Russe *m.*, *f.* (2)

**sad** triste (3)
**sailboat** bateau (*m.*) à voile (8)
**sailing** voile *f.*; **to go sailing** faire (*irreg.*) de
   la voile (5)
**salad** salade *f.* (6)
**salami** saucisson *m.* (7)
**salaried worker** travailleur/euse (*m.*, *f.*)
   salarié(e) (14)
**salary** salaire *m.* (14)
**salmon** saumon *m.* (7)
**salt** sel *m.* (6)
**same** même; **the same one(s)** le/la/les
   même(s) (15)
**sandals** sandales *f. pl.* (3)
**sardines (in oil)** sardines *f. pl.* (à l'huile) (7)
**satellite TV** télévision (*f.*) satellite (10)
**Saturday** samedi *m.* (1)
**sausage** saucisse *f.* (7)
**save** (*rescue*) sauver (16); **savings account**
   compte (*m.*) d'épargne (14); **to save (up)
   money** faire (*irreg.*) des économies (14)
**say** dire *irreg.* (10)
**scanner** scanner *m.* (10)
**schedule** horaire *m.* (12)
**school** école *f.* (10); **primary school teacher**
   professeur des écoles *m.*, *f.* (14)
**screen** écran *m.* (1, 10)
**scuba diving** plongée (*f.*) sous-marine (8); **to
   go scuba driving** faire (*irreg.*) de la
   plongée sous-marine (8)
**sculptor** sculpteur *m.*, femme sculpteur *f.* (14)
**sculpture** sculpture *f.* (14)
**sea** mer *f.* (8)
**season** saison *f.* (5)
**seat** siège *m.* (9); (*theater*) place *f.* (12)
**second** deuxième *m.*, *f.* (11); **second class**
   (*in a train*) deuxième classe (9); **second
   floor** (*in the U.S.*) premier étage *m.* (5)
**secretary** secrétaire *m.*, *f.* (14)
**section** (*of Paris*) arrondissement *m.* (11)
**see** voir *irreg.* (10); **let's see, . . .** voyons…
   (10); **see you soon** à bientôt (5); **to see
   again** revoir *irreg.* (10)
**seems: it seems that** il semble que + *subj.*
   (16); **to seem** avoir (*irreg.*) l'air de (3)
**self-employed: self-employed worker**
   travailleur/euse (*m.*, *f.*) indépendant(e) (14);
   **to be self-employed** travailler à son
   compte (14)
**sell** vendre (5)
**send** envoyer (10)
**Senegal** Sénégal *m.* (2, 8)
**Senegalese** (*person*) Sénégalais(e) *m.*, *f.* (2)
**sense** *v.* sentir *irreg.* (8)
**September** septembre (1)
**series** série *f.* (10); **drama series** (*on TV*)
   série télévisée (10)
**serious** sérieux/euse (3)

**serve** servir *irreg.* (8)

**set the table** mettre le couvert (10)

**settle (down, in)** s'installer (13)

**seven** sept (1)

**seventeen** dix-sept (1)

**several** plusieurs (6)

**sexism** sexisme *m.* (16)

**shave** *v.* se raser (13)

**shelf** étagère *f.* (4)

**shirt** chemise *f.* (3)

**shoes** chaussures *f. pl.* (3); **tennis shoes** tennis *m. pl.* (3)

**shop** (*store*) magasin *m.* (3); **butcher shop** boucherie *f.* (7); **pastry shop** pâtisserie *f.* (7)

**shopkeeper** commerçant(e) *m., f.* (14)

**shopping: to do the shopping** faire (*irreg.*) le marché (5)

**short** court(e) (*hair*) (3); petit(e) (*person*) (3)

**shorts** short *m. s.* (3)

**shot (injection)** piqûre *f.* (13)

**show** spectacle *n. m.* (15); **TV show** émission *f.* (10); **game show** jeu (*m.*) télévisé (10); **reality show** émission (*f.*) de télé réalité (10); **variety/floor show** spectacle de variétés (15); **to show** indiquer (15); montrer (3)

**shower** douche *f.* (4); **to take a shower** prendre une douche, se doucher (13)

**sick** malade (13)

**since** depuis (9); **since when** depuis quand (9)

**sincere** sincère (3)

**sing** chanter

**single** (*person*) *adj.* célibataire (5); *n. m., f.* celibataire (13)

**sir** Monsieur (M.) (1)

**sister** sœur *f.* (5); **sister-in-law** belle-sœur *f.* (5)

**site** site *m.* (10)

**situate: to be situated** se trouver (11)

**six** six (1)

**sixteen** seize (1)

**sixty** soixante (1)

**ski** ski *n. m.* (8); **ski boots** chaussures (*f. pl.*) de ski (8); **ski goggles** lunettes (*f. pl.*) de ski (8); **ski jacket** anorak *m.* (8); **to ski** faire (*irreg.*) du ski (5), skier (2)

**skiing** ski *m.*; **cross-country skiing** ski de fond (8); **downhill skiing** ski alpin (8); **to go skiing** faire (*irreg.*) du ski (5); **waterskiing** ski nautique (8)

**skirt** jupe *f.* (3)

**sleep** *v.* dormir *irreg.* (8)

**sleeping bag** sac (*m.*) de couchage (8)

**sleepy: to be sleepy** avoir (*irreg.*) sommeil (3)

**slice** tranche *f.* (7)

**slipper** pantoufle *f.* (13)

**small** petit(e) (3)

**smartphone** smartphone *m.* (1)

**smell** *v.* sentir *irreg.* (8)

**smoke** *v.* fumer (2)

**smoker** fumeur/euse *m., f.*

**snack: afternoon snack** goûter *m.* (6)

**snobbish** *adj.* snob (3)

**snorkeling** plongée (*f.*) libre (8)

**snow** neige *n. f.*; **to snow** neiger; **it's snowing** il neige (5)

**so** alors (4); *adv.* tellement (11); **so much the better** tant mieux (15); **so-so** comme ci, comme ça (1)

**soap opera** feuilleton *m.* (10)

**sociable** sociable (3)

**sociology** sociologie *f.* (2)

**socks** chaussettes *f. pl.* (3)

**sofa** canapé *m.* (4)

**software program** logiciel *m.* (10)

**solar energy** énergie (*f.*) solaire (16)

**sole** (*fish*) sole *f.* (7)

**solitude** solitude *f.* (16)

**some** en *pron.* (11); quelques-uns/unes *pron.* (15); quelques *adj.* (15)

**someday** un jour (14)

**someone** quelqu'un (de) (15)

**something** quelque chose (de) (9); **something else** autre chose (7)

**sometimes** parfois (9); quelquefois (2)

**somewhat** assez (3)

**son** fils *m.* (5); **son-in-law** gendre *m.* (5)

**song** chanson *f.* (15); **popular song** chanson de variété (15)

**soon** bientôt (5); **as soon as** aussitôt que (14); dès que (14); **see you soon** à bientôt (1)

**sorry** désolé(e) (16); **to be sorry** regretter (16)

**source** source *f.* (16)

**south** sud *m.* (9); **to the south** au sud (9)

**Spain** Espagne *f.* (2, 8)

**Spaniard** Espagnol(e) *m., f.* (2); (*language*) espagnol *m.* (2)

**speak** parler (2)

**spend** (*money*) dépenser (10); (*time*) passer (6)

**spoon (soup)** cuillère *f.* (à soupe) (6)

**sport(s)** sport *m.* (2); **sporting event** manifestation (*f.*) sportive (15); **sports coat** veste *f.* (3); **sports-minded** sportif/ive (3); **to do sports** faire (*irreg.*) du sport (5)

**spring** printemps *m.* (5); **in spring** au printemps (5)

**square** (*in city*) place *f.* (11)

**stairway** escalier *m.* (5)

**stamp** timbre *m.* (10)

**stand: to stand in line** faire (*irreg.*) la queue (5)

**standard: standard of living** niveau (*m.*) de vie (16)

**state** état *m.* (8); **United States** États-Unis *m. pl.* (8)

**station (subway)** station (*f.*) de métro (11); **police station** commissariat *m.* (11); poste (*m.*) de police (11); **service station** station-service *f.* (9); **train station** gare *f.* (9)

**stay** *v.* rester (5)

**steak** bifteck *m.* (6)

**stepbrother** demi-frère *m.* (5)

**stepfather** beau-père *m.* (5)

**stepmother** belle-mère *f.* (5)

**stepsister** demi-sœur *f.* (5)

**steward, stewardess** steward *m.* (9), hôtesse (*f.*) de l'air (9)

**still** encore (9)

**stomach** ventre *m.* (13)

**stop** *v.* arrêter (de) (12); s'arrêter (13)

**store** magasin *m.* (3); **fish store** poissonnerie *f.* (7); **grocery store** épicerie *f.* (7)

**stormy: it's stormy** le temps est orageux (5)

**straight** (*hair*) raide (3); **straight ahead** tout droit (11)

**strange** étrange (16)

**strawberry** fraise *f.* (6)

**street** rue *f.* (4)

**strike** *n.* grève *f.* (16); **to strike** faire (*irreg.*) grève (16)

**stroll** *v.* flâner (12)

**student** étudiant(e) *m., f.* (1)

**studio (apartment)** studio *m.* (4)

**study** étudier (2)

**stylish** chic *inv.* (3)

**suburbs** banlieue *f.* (11)

**subway** métro *m.* (9); **subway station** station (*f.*) de métro (11)

**succeed** réussir (à) (4)

**success** réussite *f.*

**suddenly** soudain (11); tout à coup (11)

**suffer** souffrir *irreg.* (14)

**sugar** sucre *m.* (6)

**suit** (*man's*) costume *m.* (3); (*woman's*) tailleur *m.* (3); **suit jacket** veston *m.* (3)

**suitcase** valise *f.* (8)

**sum** montant *m.* (14)

**summer** été *m.* (5); **in summer** en été (5)

**sun** soleil *m.*; **it's sunny** il fait du soleil (5)

**sunblock** écran (*m.*) solaire (8)

**Sunday** dimanche *m.* (1)

**sunglasses** lunettes (*f. pl.*) de soleil (8)

**suntan: to get a suntan** bronzer (8)

**suntan lotion** crème (*f.*) solaire (8)

**support** *v.* soutenir *irreg.* (16)

**sure** sûr(e) (16)

**surf the web** surfer sur le Web (10)

**surprised** étonné(e) (16); surpris(e) (16)

**survey** sondage *n. m.* (16)

**sweater** pull-over *m.* (3)

**sweetheart** amoureux/euse *m., f.* (13)

**swim** *v.* nager (8); se baigner (13)

**swimming pool** piscine *f.* (11)

**swimsuit** maillot (*m.*) de bain (3)

**Swiss** (*person*) Suisse *m., f.* (2)

**Switzerland** Suisse *f.* (2, 8)

**table** table *f.* (1); **set the table** mettre le couvert (10)

**tablet (computer)** tablette *f.* (1)

**take** prendre *irreg.* (6); **to take** (*a course*) suivre *irreg.* (12); **to take** (*s.o. somewhere*) emmener (12); **to take a ride** faire (*irreg.*) un tour (5); **to take a shower** se doucher (13); **to take a trip** faire (*irreg.*) un voyage (5); **to take a walk** faire (*irreg.*) un tour (5) faire (*irreg.*) une promenade (5); se promener (13); **to take an exam** passer un examen (4); **to take place** se passer (15); **to take one's time** prendre son temps (6); **to take (a long) time** prendre du temps (6)

**tall** grand(e) (3)

**talk: what are you talking about?** qu'est-ce que tu racontes / vous racontez? (15)

**taste** *v.* goûter (7)

**taxes** impôts *m. pl.* (16)

**tea** thé *m.* (6)

**teach** enseigner (à) (12); apprendre (à) (6)

**teacher** professeur *m., f.* (1); **primary school teacher** professeur des écoles *m., f.* (14)

**team** équipe *f.* (15)

**telephone** téléphone *n. m.* (4); (*receiver*) appareil *n. m.* (10); **cell phone** mobile *m.* (10), téléphone (*m.*) portable (4, 10); **telephone number** numéro (*m.*) de téléphone (10); **to telephone** téléphoner (à) (3)

**television** télévision *f.* (1); **cable television** câble *m.* (10); **television channel/network** chaîne *f.* (10); **high-definition television** TNT (télévision numérique terrestre) *f.* (10); **satellite television** télévision satellite (10); **television news program** journal (*m.*) télévisé (10) (See also **broadcast, program, series, show.**)

**tell** dire *irreg.* (10); raconter (10)

**teller: automatic teller machine (ATM)** guichet (*m.*) automatique (14)

**ten** dix (1)

**tennis shoes** tennis *m. pl.* (3)
**tent** tente *f.* (8)
**terrace** terrasse *f.* (5)
**terrorism** terrorisme *m.* (16)
**test** examen *m.* (2); **to pass a test** réussir à un examen (4); **to take a test** passer un examen (4)
**text message** SMS *m.* (10); texto *m.* (10)
**thank you (very much)** merci (beaucoup) (1); **to thank** remercier
**that** cela (ça) *pron.*; que *conj.* (4, 14); qui *rel. pron.* (4, 14); ce, cet, cette, ces *demonstrative adj.* (7); **that is** c'est-à-dire (10)
**theater** théâtre *m.* (12); (*movie*) cinéma *m.* (2)
**then (and)** (et) alors (4); ensuite; puis (11)
**there** là *adv.*; y *pron.* (11); **is/are there . . . ?** il y a… ? (1); **over there** là-bas (10); **there is/are** voilà (2); il y a (1)
**therefore** alors (4); donc (4)
**thick** gros(se) (4)
**think (about)** réfléchir (à) (4); **to think (of, about)** penser (à) (10); **to think (have an opinion) about** penser de (11); **what do you think about . . . ?** que pensez-vous (penses-tu) de… ? (11); **what do you think of that?** qu'en pensez-vous (penses-tu)? (11)
**third floor** (*in the U.S.*) deuxième étage *m.* (5)
**thirsty: to be thirsty** avoir (*irreg.*) soif (3)
**thirteen** treize (1)
**thirty** trente (1)
**this** cela (ça) *pron.*; ce, cet, cette, ces *adj.* (7)
**three** trois (1)
**throat** gorge *f.* (13)
**through** par (12)
**Thursday** jeudi *m.* (1)
**ticket** billet *m.* (6); **ticket window** guichet *m.* (9)
**tidy** en ordre (4)
**tie** (*necktie*) cravate *f.* (3)
**time** fois *f.* (5); heure *f.* (9); temps *m.* (5); **at what time . . . ?** à quelle heure… ? (6); **free time** temps libre (15); **from time to time** de temps en temps (2); **not on time** en retard (6); **on time** à l'heure (9); **the time is . . . o'clock** il est… heures (6); **to pass, spend time** passer du temps (6); **what time is it?** quelle heure est-il? (6)
**tip** pourboire *n. m.* (7)
**tired** fatigué(e) (3)
**to** à (3); (*flight*) à destination de (9)
**tobacconist (bar)** café-tabac *m.* (11)
**tobacco store** bureau (*m.*) de tabac (10)
**today** aujourd'hui (1)
**together** ensemble (8)
**tomato** tomate *f.* (6)
**tomorrow** demain (5)
**too: me too** moi aussi (3); **too bad!** dommage! *interj.* (16); **too much of, too many of** trop de (6)
**tooth** dent *f.* (13)
**top: on top of** sur (4)
**touch** *v.* toucher (14)
**tourist class** classe (*f.*) économique (9); **tourist information bureau** syndicat (*m.*) d'initiative (11)
**towel: beach towel** serviette (*f.*) de plage (8)
**tower** tour *f.* (11)
**town hall** mairie *f.* (11)
**trade** métier *n. m.* (14)
**train** train *m.* (9); **train car** wagon *m.* (9); **train station** gare *f.* (9)
**transfer (money)** virement *m.* (14)

**translate** traduire *irreg.* (9)
**transportation: means of transportation** moyen (*m.*) de transport (9)
**travel** *v.* voyager (8); (*in a car, on a bike*) rouler (9)
**treat** *v.* soigner (14)
**tree** arbre *m.* (5)
**trip: to take a trip** faire (*irreg.*) un voyage (5)
**trouble** ennui *m.* (9)
**truck** camion *m.* (9)
**true** vrai(e) (4); **it's true that . . .** il est vrai que… (16)
**trunk** coffre *m.* (9)
**try (to)** essayer (de) (14); chercher (à) (12)
**T-shirt** tee-shirt *m.* (3)
**Tuesday** mardi *m.* (1)
**Tunisia** Tunisie *f.* (2, 8)
**Tunisian** (*person*) Tunisien(ne) *m., f.* (2)
**turn** *v.* tourner (11)
**TV** télévision *f.* (5)
**twelve** douze (1)
**twenty** vingt (1): **twenty-one** vingt et un (1); **twenty-two** vingt-deux (1)
**two** deux (1)

**ugly** laid(e) (4)
**uhmm . . .** euh… *interj.* (10)
**umbrella** parapluie *m.* (8)
**uncle** oncle *m.* (5)
**under** sous (4)
**understand** comprendre *irreg.* (6); **I don't understand** je ne comprends pas (1)
**unemployment** chômage *m.* (14); **unemployed person** chômeur/euse (14); **unemployment rate** taux (*m.*) de chômage (14)
**unfair: it is unfair that** il est injuste que + *subj.* (16)
**unfortunate** pauvre (3); **it is unfortunate that** il est fâcheux que + *subj.* (16)
**United States** États-Unis *m. pl.* (2, 8)
**university** université *f.* (2); **university cafeteria** restaurant (*m.*) universitaire (resto-U) (2); **university dormitory** cité (*f.*) universitaire (cité-U) (2)
**unjust** injuste (16)
**unlikely** peu probable (16)
**until** jusqu'à (11)
**up to** jusqu'à (11)
**urgent** urgent(e) (16)
**useful** utile (16)
**useless** inutile (16)
**use up** épuiser (16)
**usually** d'habitude (5)

**vacation** vacances *f. pl.* (5)
**variety show** spectacle (*m.*) de variétés (15)
**veal** veau *m.* (7)
**vegetable** légume *m.* (6)
**very** très (1); fort *adv.* (14); **not very** peu (3); **very much** beaucoup (1); **very well, good** très bien (1)
**Vietnam** Vietnam *m.* (2, 8)
**violet** violet(te) (3)
**visa** visa *m.* (8)
**visit** visite *n. f.* (2); **to visit** (*a place*) visiter (2); **to visit** (*s.o.*) rendre visite à (11)
**voice mail** boîte (*f.*) vocale (10)
**voter** électeur/trice *m., f.* (16)

**wait (for)** attendre (5)
**waiter, waitress** serveur/euse *m., f.* (7)
**wake up** se réveiller (13)

**walk** *v.* marcher (13); **to take a walk** se promener (15); faire (*irreg.*) un tour (5); faire (*irreg.*) une promenade (5); **walking** marche *f.* (15)
**wall** mur *m.* (4)
**want** avoir (*irreg.*) envie de (3); désirer (15); vouloir *irreg.* (7)
**war** guerre *f.* (16)
**wardrobe** armoire *f.* (4)
**warm: to be warm** avoir (*irreg.*) chaud (3)
**wash** (*oneself*) se laver (13)
**waste** gaspillage *n. m.* (16); (*material*) déchet *n. m.* (16); **to waste** perdre (5); gaspiller (16)
**watch** *v.* regarder (2); **to watch out (for)** faire (*irreg.*) attention (à) (5)
**water (mineral)** eau (*f.*) (minérale) (6)
**waterskiing** ski (*m.*) nautique (8)
**way** (*road*) chemin *m.* (11)
**wear** porter (3)
**weather** temps *m.* (5); **how's the weather?** quel temps fait-il? (5); **it's bad (nice) weather** il fait mauvais (beau) (5); **weather forecast** météo *f.* (5)
**Web** Web *m.* (10)
**Wednesday** mercredi *m.* (1)
**weary** las(se) (16)
**week** semaine *f.* (1); **every week** toutes les semaines (10); **next week** la semaine prochaine (5); **once a week** une fois par semaine (5)
**weekend: on weekends** le week-end (6); **this weekend** ce week-end (5)
**welcome: you're welcome** de rien (1); il n'y a pas de quoi (7); je vous en prie (7)
**well** bien *adv.* (1); *interj.* eh bien,… (10); **pretty well** ça peut aller (1); **things are going well** ça va bien (1); **very well** très bien (1)
**west** ouest *m.* (9); **to the west** à l'ouest (9)
**what** que (4); qu'est-ce que (1); qu'est-ce qui (15); quel(le) (7); **what?** comment? (1); **what is it?** qu'est-ce que c'est? (4)
**when** quand (4); lorsque; où *relative pron.* (4); **since when** depuis quand (9)
**where** où (4)
**which** lequel, laquelle, lesquels, lesquelles (15); que, qui *relative pron.* (4); quel, quelle, quels, quelles *interr. adj.* (7); **of which** dont (14)
**while: in a while** tout à l'heure (5)
**white** blanc(he) (3); **white-collar worker** employé(e) *m., f.* (14)
**who** qui (4); qui est-ce qui (14); **who is it?** qui est-ce? (1); **who's calling?** qui est à l'appareil? (10)
**whom** qui (4); qui est-ce que; que (14); **of whom** dont (14)
**whose** dont (14)
**why** pourquoi (4)
**wife** femme *f.* (5)
**Wi-Fi (wireless) connection** Wi-Fi *m.* (10)
**willing: to be willing** vouloir (*irreg.*) bien (7)
**win** *v.* gagner (14)
**wind** vent *m.*; **it's windy** il fait du vent, il y a du vent (5)
**windbreaker** blouson *m.* (3)
**window** fenêtre *f.* (1); **(ticket) window** guichet *m.* (9)
**windsurfing** planche (*f.*) à voile (8); **to go windsurfing** faire (*irreg.*) de la planche à voile
**wine** vin *m.* (6); **wine merchant** marchand(e) (*m., f.*) de vin (14)
**winter** hiver *m.* (5); **in winter** en hiver (5)
**wish** *v.* souhaiter (16)

**with** avec (2); par (12)

**withdraw** retirer (14)

**withdrawal: automatic withdrawal/payment** prélèvement automatique (14)

**without: without a doubt** sans doute (16)

**woman** femme *f.* (2); **young woman** jeune femme *f.* (3)

**wonder** se demander (13)

**wood(s)** bois *m.* (11); forêt *f.* (8)

**word** mot *m.* (1); **word processing** traitement (*m.*) de texte (10)

**work** travail *n. m.* (2); **do-it-yourself work** bricolage *m.* (15); **work (of art)** œuvre *f.* (d'art) (12); **to work** travailler (2); (*machine or object*) marcher

**worker** travailleur/euse *m., f.* (14); (*manual*) ouvrier/ière *m., f.* (14); **salaried worker** travailleur/euse *m., f.* salarié(e) (14); **self-employed worker** travailleur/euse (*m., f.*) indépendant(e) (14); **white-collar worker** employé(e) *m., f.* (14)

**world** monde *m.* (8); **World Wide Web** Web *m.* (10)

**worse** pire (14)

**worth: to be worth** valoir *irreg.* (16)

**write (to)** écrire *irreg.* (à) (10)

**writer** écrivain *m.*, femme écrivain *f.* (12)

**wrong: to be wrong** avoir (*irreg.*) tort (3); se tromper (13)

**year** an *m.* (1); **entire year** année *f.*; **to be (vingt) years old** avoir (*irreg.*) (twenty) ans (3)

**yellow** jaune (3)

**yes** oui (1); si (*response to negative question*) (9); **yes, but . . .** oui, mais… (10)

**yesterday** hier (8); **the day before yesterday** avant-hier (8)

**yet: not yet** ne… pas encore (9)

**you: and you** et vous (et toi) (1)

**young** *adj.* jeune (4); **young lady** jeune fille *f.* (3); **young man** jeune homme *m.* (3)

**youth: youth hostel** auberge (*f.*) de jeunesse (9)

# Credits

Image Researcher: Judy Mason
Interior Designer: Preston Thomas
Cover Designer: Preston Thomas

**Photo Credits**

Design Elements
Headphones: © Istockphoto.com/cherkas; Keyboard keys: © Istockphoto.com/malerapaso; Communication icon (couple): © Ariel Skelley/Blend Images/Corbis: Banners for Lea, Hassan, Juliette, and Hector: © McGraw-Hill Education.

**Chapter 1**

Opener (both): © McGraw-Hill Education; **p. 7** (top): © McGraw-Hill Education; **p. 7** (bottom): © Paul Edmondson/Corbis; **p. 12:** © Hemis/Alamy; **p. 16:** Masterfile RF; **p. 18:** © McGraw-Hill Education; **p. 19:** © Paul Edmondson/Corbis; **p. 28:** © McGraw-Hill Education.

**Chapter 2**

Opener (top): © McGraw-Hill Education; Opener (bottom): Universal Images Group/DeAgostini/Alamy; **p. 31** (both): © McGraw-Hill Education; **p. 41:** © Owen Franken; **p. 44:** © Tom Craig/Alamy; **p. 46–47:** © McGraw-Hill Education; **p. 48:** © Comstock Images/Getty Images RF; **p. 48** (inset): © McGraw-Hill Education; **p. 51:** © Owen Franken; **p. 57:** © McGraw-Hill Education.

**Chapter 3**

Opener (top): © McGraw-Hill Education; Opener (bottom): © Hendrik Ballhausen/picture-alliance/dpa/AP Images; **p. 61** (both): © McGraw-Hill Education; **p. 70:** © Corbis/PunchStock RF; **p. 73:** © Owen Franken; **p. 74–76:** © McGraw-Hill Education; **p. 79:** © McGraw-Hill Education; **p. 83:** Courtesy of Les Petites, Paris. © Owen Franken; **p. 85** (top): © Joel Saget/AFP/Getty Images; **p. 85** (bottom): © Owen Franken; **p. 87:** © McGraw-Hill Education.

**Chapter 4**

Opener (top): © McGraw-Hill Education; Opener (bottom): © Mike McQueen/Corbis; **p. 91** (both): © McGraw-Hill Education; **p. 95:** © Journal-Courier/Steve Warmowski/The Image Works; **p. 96:** © Owen Franken; **p. 98:** © McGraw-Hill Education; **p. 102–103:** © McGraw-Hill Education; **p. 104:** © Magwitch/Alamy; **p. 106:** Courtesy of booking.com/© Owen Franken; **p. 110:** PhotoAlto/Alix Minde/Getty Images RF; **p. 112:** © Andy Brilliant; **p. 113:** *Chambre d'Arles*, 1888, Oil on canvas, 56.5 x 74.0 cm. Gogh, Vincent van. Musée d'Orsay Paris. Photo: Alfredo Dagli Orti/The Art Archive/Corbis; **p. 114:** © McGraw-Hill Education; **p. 116** (top): © McGraw-Hill Education; **p. 116** (bottom): Courtesy of FeuFollet/Photo by Blake Bumpus; **p. 117** (top): © McGraw-Hill Education; **p. 117** (bottom): © Corbis.

**Chapter 5**

Opener (top): © McGraw-Hill Education; Opener (bottom): © Camera Lucida/Alamy; **p. 119** (top): © McGraw-Hill Education; **p. 119** (bottom): © Allison Michael Orenstein/Getty Images; **p. 121:** © Owen Franken; **p. 131:** © Oote Boe/Alamy; **p. 132:** © McGraw-Hill Education; **p. 133:** © Allison Michael Orenstein/Getty Images; **p. 134:** © William Ryall RF; **p. 136:** © Sami Sarkis France/Alamy; **p. 140:** © Robert Harding Picture Library Ltd/Alamy; **p. 141:** © The Gallery Collection/Corbis; **p. 143:** © McGraw-Hill Education.

**Chapter 6**

Opener (top): © McGraw-Hill Education; Opener (bottom): © Alex Segre/Alamy Images; **p. 147** (top): © McGraw-Hill Education; **p. 147** (bottom): © MBI/Alamy RF; **p. 152:** © McGraw-Hill Education; **p. 154:** © Imageshop/Alamy RF; **p. 156:** © George Jurasek/Getty Images RF; **p. 160:** © McGraw-Hill Education; **p. 161:** © MBI/Alamy RF; **p. 167:** © Steve Cole/Getty Images RF; **p. 170** (top): © Maggie Janik Photography; **p. 170** (bottom): © Tracy Hebden; **p. 171–172:** © McGraw-Hill Education.

## Chapter 7

Opener (top): © McGraw-Hill Education; Opener (bottom): © Dennis Macdonald/Getty Images; **p. 175** (top): © McGraw-Hill Education; **p. 175** (bottom): © Dave Stamboulis/Getty Images RF; **p. 179** (top): © William Ryall RF; **p. 179** (bottom left): © Walter Pietsch/Alamy; **p. 179** (bottom right): © Foodcollection; **p. 181:** © Ingram Publishing/Superstock RF; **p. 182:** © Jon Hicks/Corbis; **p.184:** © Brett Stevens/cultura/Corbis; **p. 186:** © McGraw-Hill Education; **p. 187:** © Dave Stamboulis/Getty Images RF; **p. 189:** © Owen Franken/Corbis; **p. 191:** © McGraw-Hill Education; **p. 193:** © Mark Harris/Getty Images RF; **p. 194:** © PhotoEdit; **p. 195** (top): © Comstock/Jupiter Images RF; **p. 195** (top middle): Markus Guhl/Getty Images RF; **p. 195** (bottom middle): © FoodCollection RF; **p. 195** (bottom): © Hemera Technologies/JupiterImages RF; **p. 196:** © J.Riou/photocuisine/Corbis; **p. 197:** © Michael Mahovlich/Getty Images RF; **p. 198:** © McGraw-Hill Education.

## Chapter 8

Opener (top): © McGraw-Hill Education; Opener (bottom): © imagebroker/Alamy RF; **p. 201** (top): © Dennie Cody/Getty Images; **p. 201** (bottom): © Jon Arnold/Agency Jon Arnold Images/age fotostock; **p. 203:** © Tom Stewart/Corbis; **p. 206** (top): Courtesy of IBM Archives; **p. 206** (middle): © Roger-Viollet, Paris/The Image Works; **p. 206** (bottom): © Bettmann/Corbis; **p. 208** (top): © Pixtal/age footstock; **p. 208** (bottom): © Purestock/Getty Images; **p. 211** (bottom): © Marco Albonico/age fotostock; **p. 212** (both): © McGraw-Hill Education; **p. 214:** © Owen Franken; **p. 216:** © Dennie Cody/Getty Images; **p. 217:** © Jon Arnold/Agency Jon Arnold Images/age fotostock; **p. 218:** © D. Hurst/Alamy RF; **p. 220:** © Author's Image/PunchStock RF; **p. 222:** © McGraw-Hill Education; **p. 223:** © Corbis/Royalty-Free; **p. 226** (top): © Corbis/Royalty-Free; **p. 226** (bottom): © Jean du Boisberranger/Hemis/Corbis; **p. 228:** © McGraw-Hill Education; **p. 230** (top): © McGraw-Hill Education; **p. 230** (bottom): © Sophie Bassouls/Sygma/Corbis; **p. 231** (top): © McGraw-Hill Education; **p. 231** (bottom): © SEYLLOU/AFP/Getty Images.

## Chapter 9

Opener (top): © McGraw-Hill Education; Opener (bottom): © Bryan F. Peterson/Corbis; **p. 233:** © McGraw-Hill Education; **p. 239:** © Owen Franken/Corbis; **p. 241:** © McGraw-Hill Education; © Owen Franken; **p. 243:** © Owen Franken; **p. 244:** © McGraw-Hill Education; **p. 253:** © Robert Gray/Alamy; **p. 254** (top): © incamerastock/Alamy; **p. 254** (bottom): © Horacio Villalobos/epa/Corbis; **p. 256:** © Gero Breloer/epa/Corbis.

## Chapter 10

Opener (top): © McGraw-Hill Education; Opener (bottom): © Jacques Brinon/AP Images; **p. 259** (top): © McGraw-Hill Education; **p. 259** (bottom): © Owen Franken; **p. 266** (left): © Fabrice Lerouge/Getty Images; **p. 266** (inset): © McGraw-Hill Education; **p. 268:** © Owen Franken; **p. 270:** © claude thibault/Alamy; **p. 273:** © Owen Franken; **p. 274:** © McGraw-Hill Education; **p. 275:** © Owen Franken; **p. 277:** © Mark Dierker/McGraw-Hill RF; **p. 278:** © Glenn Paulina/TRANSTOCK/Corbis; **p. 280:** © OJO Images/Getty Images RF; **p. 281:** © Owen Franken; **p. 282:** © David Hanover/Stone/Getty Images; **p. 285:** © McGraw-Hill Education.

## Chapter 11

Opener (top): © McGraw-Hill Education; Opener (bottom): © Jean-Pierre Lescourret/Corbis; **p. 289** (top): © McGraw-Hill Education; **p. 289** (bottom): © René Mattes/Hemis/Corbis; **p. 294:** © Loïc Venance/AFP/Getty Images; **p. 297:** © Owen Franken/ Corbis; **p. 298:** © Benoit Roland/The Image Works; **p. 299:** © Russell Kord/Alamy; **p. 301:** © Owen Franken; **p. 302:** © McGraw-Hill Education; **p. 303:** © René Mattes/Hemis/Corbis; **p. 304:** © Art Media/Heritage-Images/The Image Works; **p. 305:** © Jacques Guillard/Scope; **p. 306:** © Giraudon/Art Resource; **p. 307:** © Greg Balfour Evans/Alamy; **p. 311:** © Doug Armand/Getty Images; **p. 314:** © Juniors Bildarchiv GmbH/Alamy; **p. 316:** © McGraw-Hill Education.

## Chapter 12

Opener (top): © McGraw-Hill Education; Opener (bottom): © Gala/SuperStock; **p. 319** (top): © McGraw-Hill Education; **p. 319** (bottom): © Christine Osborne/Corbis; **p. 320** (top): © Franz-Marc Frei/Corbis; **p. 320** (bottom): © Jahan/Explorer/Science Source; **p. 321** (left): © Owen Franken; **p. 321** (right): © Vanni Archive/Corbis; **p. 322** (top): © Images de Paris/Alamy; **p. 322** (bottom left): © Keren Su/Corbis; **p. 322** (bottom right): © Steve Vidler/SuperStock; **p. 325:** Gogh, Vincent van (1853–1890) *Self-Portrait*. 1889. Oil on canvas, 65 x 54.5 cm. Location: Musée d'Orsay, Paris, France. Photo: Erich Lessing/Art Resource; **p. 326:** © Erich Lessing/Art Resource, NY; **p. 327:** © Tate Gallery, London/Art Resource, NY; **p. 334:** © McGraw-Hill Education; **p. 335:** © Christine Osborne/Corbis; **p. 336** (top): © Comstock Images/Getty Images; **p. 336** (bottom): © McGraw-Hill Education; **p. 339:** © Paul Seheult/Eye Ubiquitous/Corbis; **p. 341:** © Ingram Publishing RF; **p. 342:** © Corbis/Royalty Free; **p. 343:** © Gauguin, Paul (1848–1903) *Women of Tahiti or On the Beach*. 1891. Oil on canvas, 69.0 x 91.5 cm. Photo: Hervé Lewandowski. Location: Musée d'Orsay, Paris, France. Réunion des Musées Nationaux/Art Resource, NY; **p. 346:** © Globe Photos; **p. 347:** Chagall, Marc (1887–1985) © ARS, NY *The Song of Songs, IV*, 1958. Oil on canvas, 50 x 61 cm. Musée National message biblique Marc Chagall, Nice, France. Gerard Blot/Réunion des Musées Nationaux/Art Resource, NY; **p. 348:**

© McGraw-Hill Education; **p. 350** (top): © Photononstop/SuperStock; **p. 350** (bottom): © Hulton-Deutsch/Corbis; **p. 351** (top): © Demetrio Carrasco/Getty Images; **p. 351** (bottom): © Magritte, René (1898-1967) © ARS, NY. *Le Maître d'école*, 1954. Oil on canvas, 81 x 60 cm. Location: Private Collection. Herscovici/Art Resource, NY.

### Chapter 13

Opener (top): © McGraw-Hill Education; Opener (bottom): © blickwinkel/Alamy Images; **p. 353** (top): © McGraw-Hill Education; **p. 353** (bottom): © Animals/Animals; **p. 356:** © Owen Franken; **p. 358:** © Owen Franken; **p. 360:** © Owen Franken; **p. 361:** © Fototeca Storica Nazionale/Getty Images RF; **p. 364:** © McGraw-Hill Education; **p. 365:** © Animals/Animals; **p. 368** (top): © Nik Wheeler; **p. 368** (bottom): © McGraw-Hill Education; **p. 372:** © Comstock/PunchStock RF; **p. 374:** © McGraw-Hill Education.

### Chapter 14

Opener (top): © McGraw-Hill Education; Opener (bottom): © Christophe Boisvieux/Corbis; **p. 377** (bottom): © Directphoto.org/Alamy RF; **p. 377** (top): © McGraw-Hill Education; **p. 382:** © Owen Franken; **p. 383:** © Christopher Bissell/Getty Images; **p. 384** (top): © McGraw-Hill Education; **p. 386** (top): © Owen Franken; **p. 386** (bottom): Courtesy of Dell; **p. 389:** © Bruce Paton/Panos Pictures; **p. 390** (bottom): © McGraw-Hill Education; **p. 391:** © Directphoto.org/Alamy RF; **p. 392** (left): © Comstock Images/Getty Images; **p. 392** (right): © McGraw-Hill Education; **p. 395:** © DAJ/Getty Images RF; **p. 397:** © Jean-Pierre Lescourret/Corbis; **p. 399:** © William Ryall 2010; **p. 401:** © Purestock/Superstock RF; **p. 403** (top): © Farrell Grehan/Photo Researchers; **p. 403** (bottom): © Hiroko Masuike/AP Images; **p. 404:** © Alfred/SIPA/AP Images; **p. 405:** McGraw-Hill Education.

### Chapter 15

Opener (top): © McGraw-Hill Education; Opener (bottom): © Gail Mooney/Corbis; **p. 409** (top): © Paul Seheult/Eye Ubiquitous/Corbis; **p. 409** (bottom): © Morgan David de Lossy/Corbis; **p. 411:** © Owen Franken; **p. 413:** © Purestock/SuperStock RF; **p. 420:** © McGraw-Hill Education; **p. 421:** © Owen Franken; **p. 422:** © Paul Seheult/Eye Ubiquitous/Corbis; **p. 423:** © Morgan David de Lossy/Corbis; **p. 424:** © Owen Franken; **p. 427:** © Patrick Ward/Alamy; **p. 430:** © Nik Wheeler/Alamy; **p. 432:** © MARCEL MOCHET/AFP/Getty Images; **p. 434:** © McGraw-Hill Education.

### Chapter 16

Opener (top): © McGraw-Hill Education; Opener (bottom): © Roger Ressmeyer/Corbis; **p. 437** (top): © McGraw-Hill Education; **p. 437** (bottom): © Owen Franken/Corbis; **p. 442:** © Richard Wareham Fotografie/Alamy; **p. 443:** © Facelly/Sipa Press; **p. 448** (both): © McGraw-Hill Education; **p. 452:** © McGraw-Hill Education; **p. 453:** © Owen Franken/Corbis; **p. 454:** © Antoine Antoniol/Getty Images; **p. 460:** © William Ryall RF; **p. 462:** © Donald Stampfli/AP Images; **p. 464:** © McGraw-Hill Education; **p. 466** (top): © Jack Fields/Corbis; **p. 466** (bottom): © Dan Christensen; **p. 467** (top): © David Giral/Alamy; **p. 467** (bottom): © Pimental Jean/Kipa Collection/Corbis.

### Text Credits

**Pages 111:** From "Avantages et pièges de la colocation" by Sebastien Thomas, *Quo*. Used by permission of Hachette Filipacchi Associés, Levallois-Perret Cx, France; **170:** Adapted from "Blaff de poissons," http://www.antilles-martinique.com/recettes.html; **314:** «Le chat abandonné» by Paul Degray in *Poésies et jeux de langage CP/CE1*, Christian Lamblin, © Éditions Retz 2003; **346:** "Déjeuner du matin" in *Paroles* by Jacques Prévert, © Éditions GALLIMARD; **372:** "Pour toi mon amour" in *Paroles* by Jacques Prévert, © Éditions GALLIMARD; **432:** Adapted from "Traversée de l'Atlantique à la rame en solitaire" by Nicolas Gonidec, www.antourtan.org. Used by permission; **462:** From *La Réclusion solitaire* by Tahar Ben Jelloun, © by Éditions Denoël, 1976.

### Realia Credits

**Pages 16:** Holidays in Suisse, États-Unis, France: *Air Canada Magazine*; **26:** Ad from the Internet site www.letudiant.fr. Used by permission; **35–36:** Flags © Liber Kartor, Sweden; **55:** Text, logo, and photo used courtesy of Programme spécial de français, École des langues vivantes, Université Laval, Québec; **71:** Magazines Canada 1998: Writer/Art Director, Dennis Bruce; Art, Jerzy Kolacz; **82:** © Yayo/Cartoonists & Writers Syndicate, www.nytsyn.com/cartoons; **124:** *Dernières Nouvelles d'Alsace*; **159:** © *L'Express* 1998; **177:** Restaurant La Guirlande de Julie, Paris, France; **233, 245:** BlaBlaCar website screenshot used by permission; **236:** Text: SNCF; **283:** Book cover *Comment être le meilleur sur Meetic* used by permission of Éditions First; **292:** © MICHELIN Paris Hotel & Restaurants—Permission No. 06-US-006; **380:** Jean-Pierre Adelbert; **426:** Data from Ministère de la Culture et de la Communication in *Francoscopie 1999* by Gérard Mermet (Paris: Larousse); **439:** Parigramme.

# Index

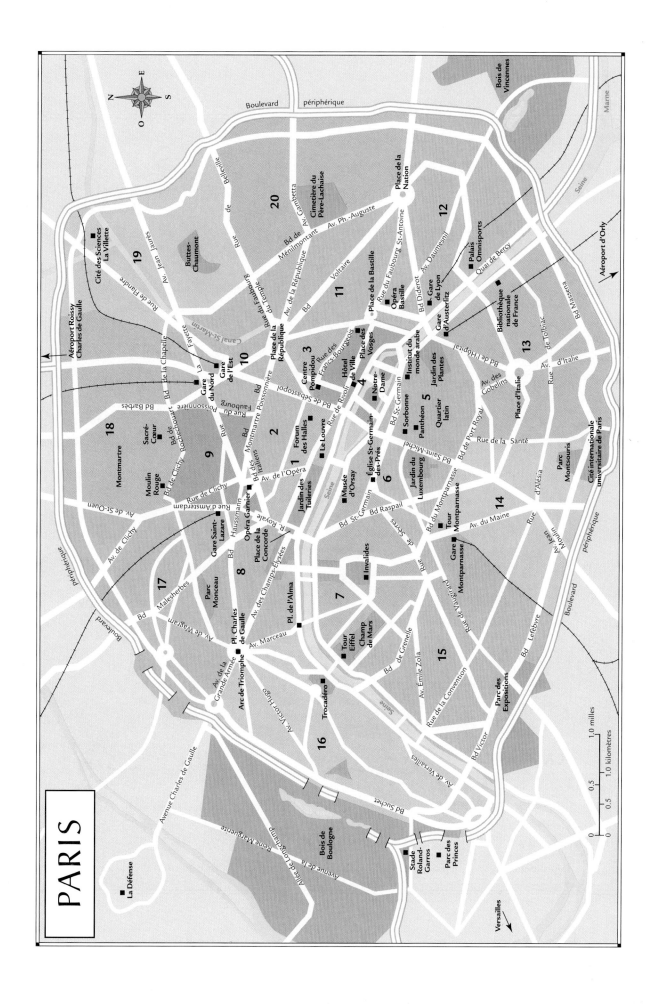

# PARIS

L'ANGLETERRE *f*

Londres

*la Tamise*

LA MER
DU NORD

Amsterdam

LES PAYS-BAS *m*

L'ALLEMAGNE *f*

Dunkerque

Boulogne

Calais

Lille

LA BELGIQUE

Bruxelles

*la Meuse*

LA MANCHE

NORD-PAS-
DE CALAIS

Amiens

LE LUXEMBOURG

Luxembourg

Guernesey

*Les Îles
Anglo-Normandes*

Jersey

Cherbourg

Dieppe

Le Havre

*la Seine*

Rouen

PICARDIE

Reims

Verdun

Brest

Caen

HAUTE-
NORMANDIE

Paris

*la Marne*

LORRAINE

Nancy

ALSACE

Strasbourg

BASSE-
NORMANDIE

Versailles

ÎLE-DE-
FRANCE

*la Seine*

*le Rhin*

BRETAGNE

Rennes

Chartres

CHAMPAGNE-
ARDENNE

*la Moselle*

LES VOSGES *f*

*le Danube*

PAYS DE
LA LOIRE

*la Loire*

Angers

Orléans

BOURGOGNE

FRANCHE-
COMTÉ

Nantes

Blois

CENTRE

Dijon

Besançon

LE JURA

Berne

Tours

Bourges

*la Loire*

LA SUISSE

Poitiers

*la Saône*

Lausanne

*le Lac Léman*

L'OCÉAN *m*
ATLANTIQUE

La Rochelle

POITOU-
CHARENTES

Limoges

Vichy

Genève

MONT BLANC
4808m

LE VAL
D'AOSTE

LIMOUSIN

Clermont-
Ferrand

*le Rhône*

Lyon

Bordeaux

*Gironde*

*la Dordogne*

AUVERGNE

RHÔNE-ALPES

St-Étienne

Grenoble

LES ALPES *f*

*le Pô*

*la Garonne*

LE MASSIF
CENTRAL

*le Rhône*

L'ITALIE *f*

AQUITAINE

MIDI-
PYRÉNÉES

PROVENCE-
ALPES-
CÔTE D'AZUR

Bayonne

Nîmes

Avignon

Arles

Nice

MONACO *m*

Pau

Toulouse

Aix-en-
Provence

Cannes

*l'Ebro*

LES PYRÉNÉES *f*

Montpellier

Carcassonne

Marseille

St-Tropez

L'ESPAGNE *f*

L'ANGUEDOC-
ROUSSILLON

Perpignan

LA MER
MÉDITERRANÉE

LA CORSE

Ajaccio

L'ANDORRE *f*

## LA FRANCE

| 0 | 50 | 100 | 150 MILLES |

| 0 | 50 | 100 | 150 | 200 | 250 KILOMÈTRES |

*m = masculin  f = féminin*

Altitude

| Mètres | | Feet |
|---|---|---|
| 3050 | | 10000 |
| 1525 | | 5000 |
| 610 | | 2000 |
| 305 | | 1000 |
| 152,5 | | 500 |
| 0 | | 0 |

*Le français est
langue officielle ou
administrative*

*Présence importante de
la langue française, sans
statut particulier*

## L'EUROPE<sup>f</sup>

Le français est la langue maternelle majoritaire et/ou officielle.

Le français est langue officielle ou administrative.

Présence importante de la langue française, sans statut particulier

m = masculin    f = féminin

0    250    500 milles
0    250    500 kilomètres

LA SUÈDE
LA FINLANDE
LA NORVÈGE
Oslo
Helsinki
Stockholm
St-Pétersbourg
L'ÉCOSSE<sup>f</sup>
Tallinn
L'ESTONIE<sup>f</sup>
L'IRLANDE<sup>f</sup> DU NORD
Moscou
LA MER
DU NORD
Riga
LE ROYAUME-UNI
LA RUSSIE
L'IRLANDE<sup>f</sup>
LE DANEMARK
LA LETTONIE
Dublin
Copenhague
LA LITUANIE
LA MER BALTIQUE
Vilnius
LES PAYS-BAS<sup>m</sup>
LA RUSSIE
LE PAYS DE GALLES
Kaliningrad
Minsk
L'ANGLETERRE<sup>f</sup>
Berlin
LA BIÉLORUSSIE
Londres
Amsterdam
LA POLOGNE
Varsovie
LA BELGIQUE
L'ALLEMAGNE<sup>f</sup>
Kiev
Bruxelles
Paris
Luxembourg
Prague
L'OCÉAN<sup>m</sup>
LE LUXEMBOURG
LA RÉPUBLIQUE
TCHÈQUE
L'UKRAINE<sup>f</sup>
ATLANTIQUE
LE LIECHTENSTEIN
LA SLOVAQUIE
Vienne
Bratislava
LA MOLDAVIE
Berne
LA FRANCE
Lausanne
L'AUTRICHE<sup>f</sup>
Budapest
Chisinau
Genève
LA SUISSE
LA HONGRIE
LA SLOVÉNIE
LA ROUMANIE
le Val d'Aoste
Ljubljana
Zagreb
LE PORTUGAL
Andorre-la-Vieille
LA CROATIE
Bucarest
Madrid
MONACO<sup>m</sup>
LA BOSNIE-
HERZÉGOVINE
LA
Belgrade
SERBIE
Lisbonne
L'ANDORRE<sup>f</sup>
L'ITALIE<sup>f</sup>
Sarajevo
LE MONTÉNÉGRO
LA MER
NOIRE
La Corse
Podgorica
Sofia
LA BULGARIE
L'ESPAGNE<sup>f</sup>
Ajaccio
Rome
Skopje
Istanbul
LA MER ADRIATIQUE
Tirana
LA MACÉDOINE
L'ALBANIE<sup>f</sup>
LA GRÈCE
LA TURQUIE
LA MER ÉGÉE
LA MER MÉDITERRANÉE
Athènes
L'AFRIQUE<sup>f</sup>
LE MAROC
L'ALGÉRIE<sup>f</sup>
LA
TUNISIE
La Crète

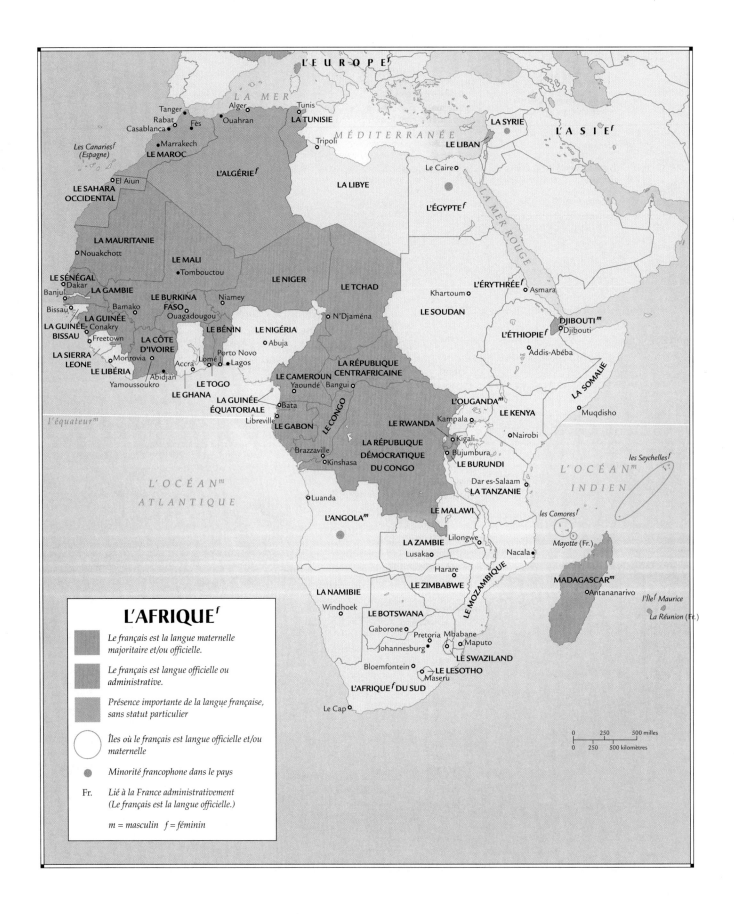

# L'AFRIQUE*f*

L'EUROPE*f*

LA MER
MÉDITERRANÉE

L'ASIE*f*

Tanger
Rabat
Casablanca
Fès
Marrakech

Alger
Ouahran

Tunis
LA TUNISIE

Tripoli

LA SYRIE

LE LIBAN

Le Caire

Les Canaries*f*
(Espagne)

LE MAROC

El Aiun

L'ALGÉRIE*f*

LA LIBYE

L'ÉGYPTE*f*

LE SAHARA
OCCIDENTAL

LA MAURITANIE
Nouakchott

LE MALI
Tombouctou

LE NIGER

LE TCHAD

Khartoum

L'ÉRYTHRÉE*f*
Asmara

LE SÉNÉGAL
Dakar
Banjul
LA GAMBIE
Bissau
LA GUINÉE
BISSAU
Conakry
LA GUINÉE
Freetown
LA SIERRA
LEONE
Monrovia
LE LIBÉRIA
Yamoussoukro

Bamako
LE BURKINA
FASO
Ouagadougou

Niamey

LE SOUDAN

DJIBOUTI*m*
Djibouti

LA CÔTE
D'IVOIRE
Abidjan

Accra
LE GHANA

Lomé
LE TOGO

LE BÉNIN

Porto Novo
Lagos

N'Djaména

L'ÉTHIOPIE*f*
Addis-Abéba

LE NIGÉRIA
Abuja

LE CAMEROUN
Yaoundé
Bangui

LA RÉPUBLIQUE
CENTRAFRICAINE

LA SOMALIE

Muqdisho

LA GUINÉE
ÉQUATORIALE
Bata
Libreville
LE GABON
LE CONGO
Brazzaville
Kinshasa

l'équateur*m*

LA RÉPUBLIQUE
DÉMOCRATIQUE
DU CONGO

L'OUGANDA*m*
Kampala
LE RWANDA
Kigali
Bujumbura
LE BURUNDI

LE KENYA
Nairobi

les Seychelles*f*

L'OCÉAN*m*
INDIEN

L'OCÉAN*m*
ATLANTIQUE

Luanda

L'ANGOLA*m*

Dar es-Salaam
LA TANZANIE

LE MALAWI

les Comores*f*

Mayotte (Fr.)

MADAGASCAR*m*

Lilongwe
LA ZAMBIE
Lusaka

Nacala

Antananarivo

l'Île*f* Maurice

La Réunion (Fr.)

Harare
LE ZIMBABWE

LE MOZAMBIQUE

LA NAMIBIE
Windhoek

LE BOTSWANA
Gaborone

Johannesburg

Pretoria Mbabane
Maputo

LE SWAZILAND

Bloemfontein

LE LESOTHO
Maseru

L'AFRIQUE*f* DU SUD

Le Cap

Le français est la langue maternelle
majoritaire et/ou officielle.

Le français est langue officielle ou
administrative.

Présence importante de la langue française,
sans statut particulier

Îles où le français est langue officielle et/ou
maternelle

Minorité francophone dans le pays

Fr.    Lié à la France administrativement
       (Le français est la langue officielle.)

m = masculin   f = féminin

0        250       500 milles
0     250    500 kilomètres

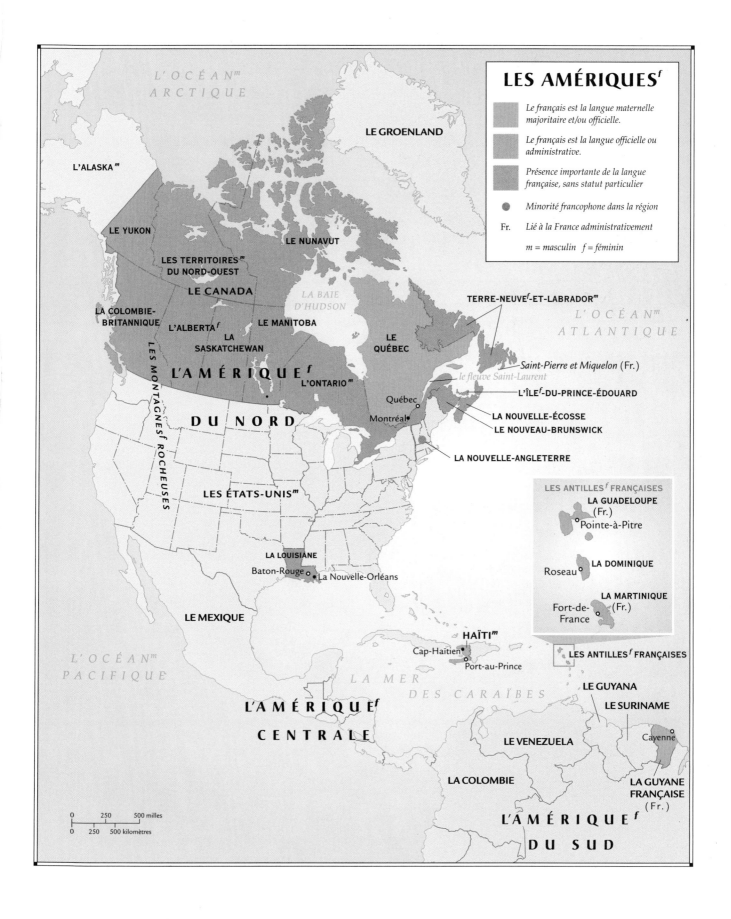

# LES AMÉRIQUES<sup>f</sup>

LES AMÉRIQUES<sup>f</sup>

Le français est la langue maternelle majoritaire et/ou officielle.

Le français est la langue officielle ou administrative.

Présence importante de la langue française, sans statut particulier

● Minorité francophone dans la région

Fr. Lié à la France administrativement

m = masculin  f = féminin

L'OCÉAN<sup>m</sup> ARCTIQUE

LE GROENLAND

L'ALASKA<sup>m</sup>

LE YUKON

LE NUNAVUT

LES TERRITOIRES<sup>m</sup> DU NORD-OUEST

LE CANADA

LA BAIE D'HUDSON

TERRE-NEUVE<sup>f</sup>-ET-LABRADOR<sup>m</sup>

L'OCÉAN<sup>m</sup> ATLANTIQUE

LA COLOMBIE-BRITANNIQUE

L'ALBERTA<sup>f</sup>

LE MANITOBA

LA SASKATCHEWAN

LE QUÉBEC

Saint-Pierre et Miquelon (Fr.)

le fleuve Saint-Laurent

L'AMÉRIQUE<sup>f</sup>

L'ONTARIO<sup>m</sup>

L'ÎLE<sup>f</sup>-DU-PRINCE-ÉDOUARD

Québec

LA NOUVELLE-ÉCOSSE

DU NORD

Montréal

LE NOUVEAU-BRUNSWICK

LES MONTAGNES<sup>f</sup> ROCHEUSES

LA NOUVELLE-ANGLETERRE

LES ÉTATS-UNIS<sup>m</sup>

LA LOUISIANE

Baton-Rouge  La Nouvelle-Orléans

LE MEXIQUE

L'OCÉAN<sup>m</sup> PACIFIQUE

HAÏTI<sup>m</sup>

Cap-Haïtien

Port-au-Prince

LA MER DES CARAÏBES

L'AMÉRIQUE<sup>f</sup> CENTRALE

LE VENEZUELA

LA COLOMBIE

## LES ANTILLES<sup>f</sup> FRANÇAISES

LA GUADELOUPE (Fr.)

Pointe-à-Pitre

Roseau  LA DOMINIQUE

LA MARTINIQUE (Fr.)

Fort-de-France

□ LES ANTILLES<sup>f</sup> FRANÇAISES

LE GUYANA

LE SURINAME

Cayenne

LA GUYANE FRANÇAISE (Fr.)

L'AMÉRIQUE<sup>f</sup> DU SUD

0    250    500 milles

0    250    500 kilomètres

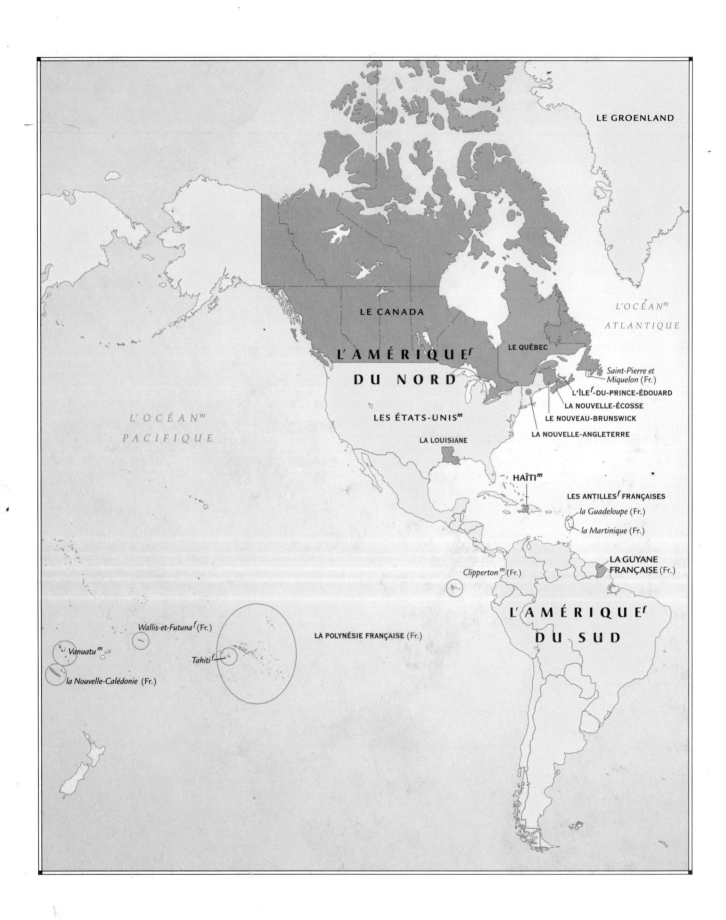

LE GROENLAND

LE CANADA

L'OCÉAN<sup>m</sup> ATLANTIQUE

L'AMÉRIQUE<sup>f</sup> DU NORD

LE QUÉBEC

Saint-Pierre et Miquelon (Fr.)

L'ÎLE<sup>f</sup>-DU-PRINCE-ÉDOUARD

LA NOUVELLE-ÉCOSSE

LE NOUVEAU-BRUNSWICK

LA NOUVELLE-ANGLETERRE

L'OCÉAN<sup>m</sup> PACIFIQUE

LES ÉTATS-UNIS<sup>m</sup>

LA LOUISIANE

HAÏTI<sup>m</sup>

LES ANTILLES<sup>f</sup> FRANÇAISES

la Guadeloupe (Fr.)

la Martinique (Fr.)

LA GUYANE FRANÇAISE (Fr.)

Clipperton<sup>m</sup> (Fr.)

L'AMÉRIQUE<sup>f</sup> DU SUD

Wallis-et-Futuna<sup>f</sup> (Fr.)

LA POLYNÉSIE FRANÇAISE (Fr.)

Vanuatu<sup>m</sup>

Tahiti<sup>f</sup>

la Nouvelle-Calédonie (Fr.)